This Book
Belongs To

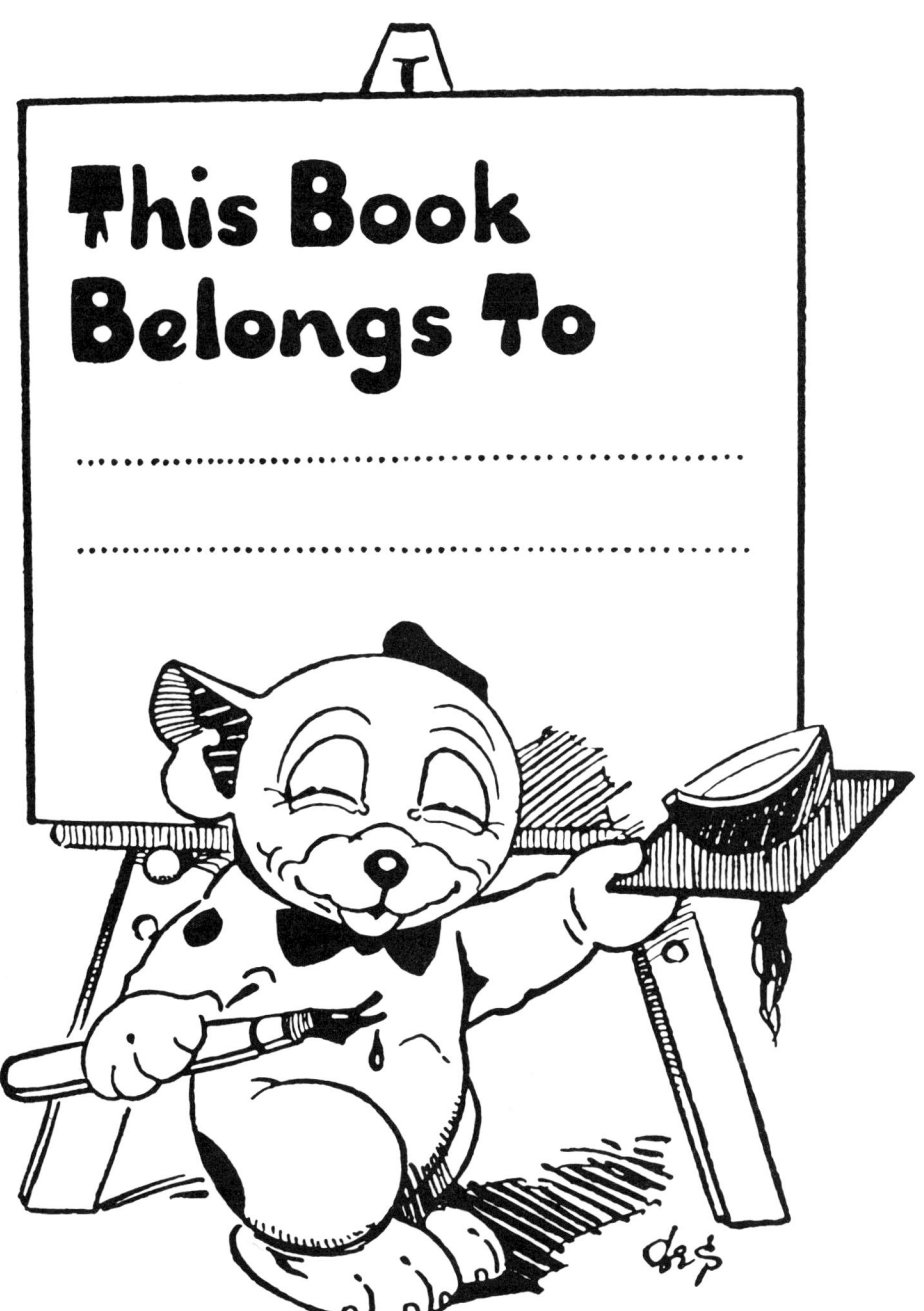

For
Wanda, Grace, William and Jane
and especially Vivienne
with our love

Acknowledgements

No book can come to fruition without the help and encouragement of many people along the way. Ours is no exception and the following have all given advice and support more valuable than they probably realise: Jane Allport, Anne Babb, Celia Bailey, Laurie Bamford, Edward Broad, Richard Brown, Tim Burnham, Len and Bodil Cowling, Richard Dennis, Kaveh Dideban, Brian and Moira Farnham, Denis Gifford, Doreen Greene, Nicholas Haywood, Michael Heseltine, June and Georgina Keates, Vivienne Kynaston, Keith and Julie Lessiter, Margaret McLean, Roy and Jan Mance, Yvonne Mole, Judy Morgan-Anstee, Steve Nicholas, John Nicol, Nigel Oram, Gordon Osborne, Francis Owen, Terry Parker, Walter Rigdon, Lorraine Shepherd, Freda Simmons, the late Hubert Studdy, Melvin Studdy, Christine Whittaker and Wendy Wort.

Paul Babb and Gay Owen
8-8-88

Print, Design and Reproduction by Flaydemouse, Yeovil, England
Photography by Mike Bruce at Gate Studios
Published and distributed by Richard Dennis,
Shepton House, Shepton Beauchamp, Ilminster, Somerset TA19 OJT

ISBN 0 903685 23 X

© Text Paul Babb and Gay Owen, photographs Richard Dennis
The character 'Bonzo' is the copyright of the estate of George Studdy

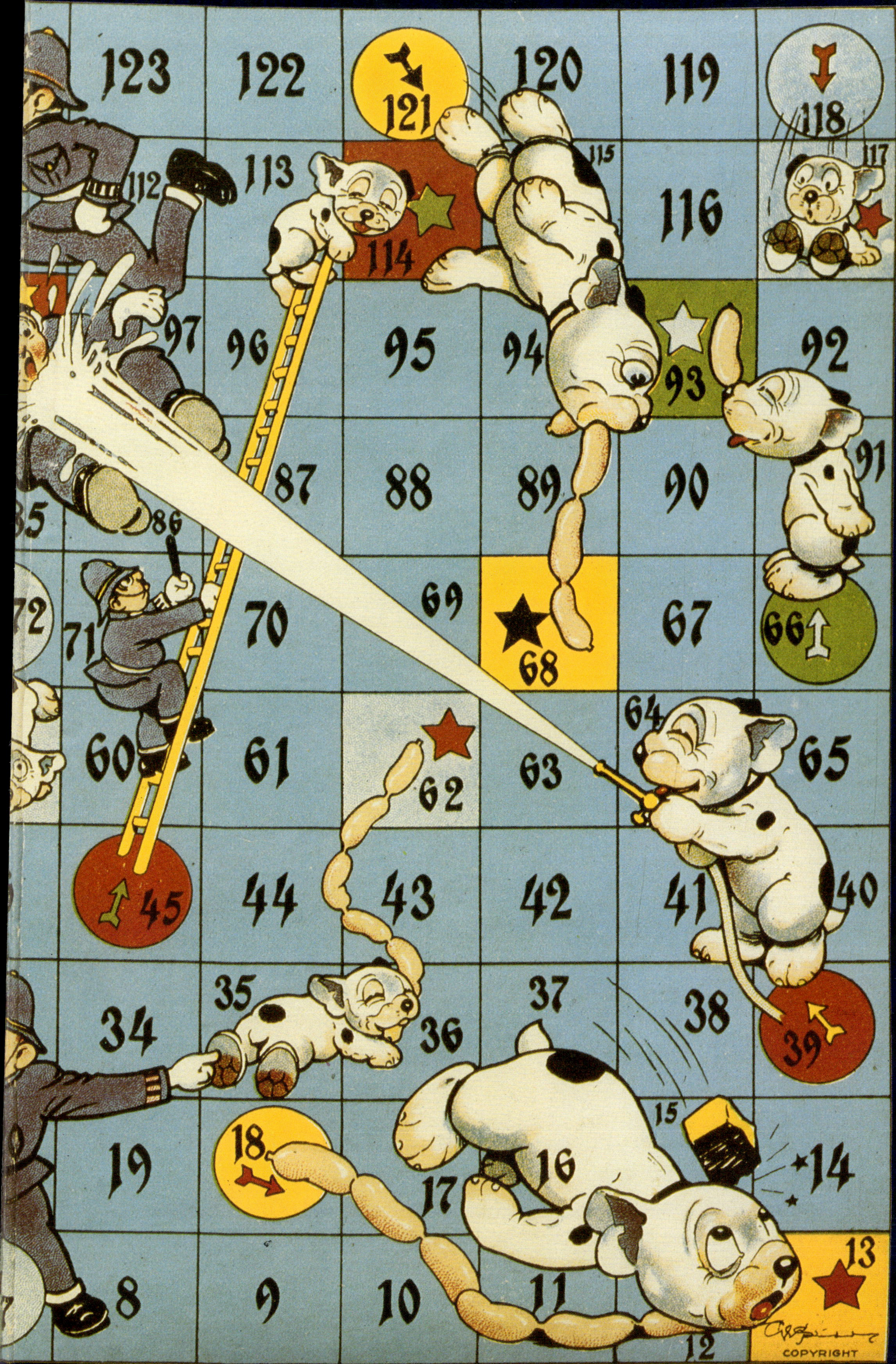
123 122 121 120 119 118
112 113 114 115 116 117
97 96 95 94 93 92
85 86 87 88 89 90 91
72 71 70 69 68 67 66
60 61 62 63 64 65
45 44 43 42 41 40
34 35 36 37 38 39
19 18 17 16 15 14
8 9 10 11 12 13
COPYRIGHT

The thrilling new Game of The Bonzo Chase

by *[signature]*

The antics of this sly mischievous little pup make the Kiddies shriek with laughter and Grown-ups enjoy the fun just as much.

"BONZO CHASE" consists of a folding board, lithographed in most brilliant colours and the necessary accessories packed in a bright attractive box.

The "Bonzo" Chase
by George E. Studdy.

Hallo' kiddies, I do love sausages, don't you? Whenever I get a few, somebody interferes and I have never eaten one in comfort yet. Have you ever tried to climb on to a pile of plates? – if not – see what happens in square 57. I love policemen because I can run faster than they can, but I hate boys who throw stones at innocent puppies, see square 13 – I'm sure its an unlucky number! – If you get into square 39, you really must go up to square 98 and give my love to the wet policeman. From square 45 you will have a lovely ladder to climb, but don't fall down again as I did from square 121. Then do try and dodge square 127 because if not, you'll probably lose the game and never be able to end up with me on square 130 all bright and smiling,

With love from "Bonzo".

Rules of the Game.

1. Two, three or four players can compete.
2. Each player in turn throws the die or spins the indicator and travels the number of spaces shown on die or indicator starting of course from No. 1 in left-hand corner.
3. The first to reach or pass 130 is the winner.
4. Should a player land on any square with a coloured arrow on it, he must follow the picture starting from that space until he reaches a square with a star of the same colour; for instance, a player arriving on 39 will go up to 98 or – 121 goes back to 68.

Published by J. W. SPEAR & SONS.

The above descriptions are taken from the inside of box lids from two versions of the game.

BONZO

THE LIFE and WORK of GEORGE STUDDY

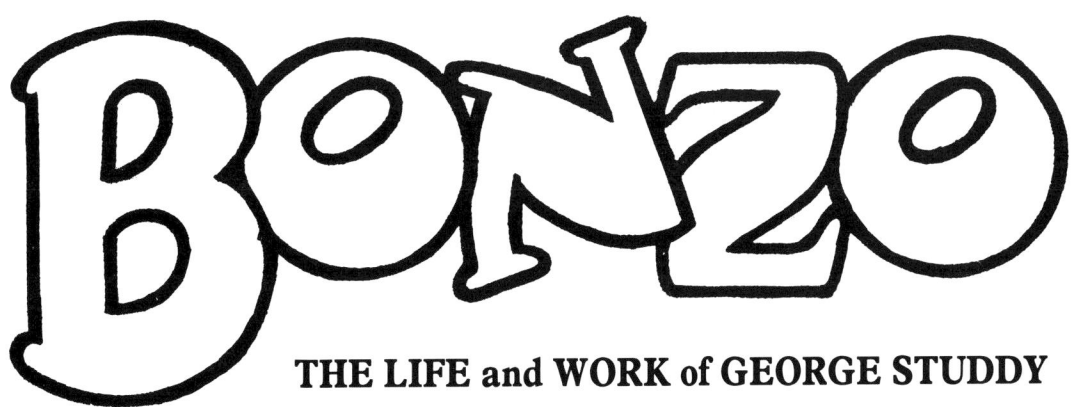

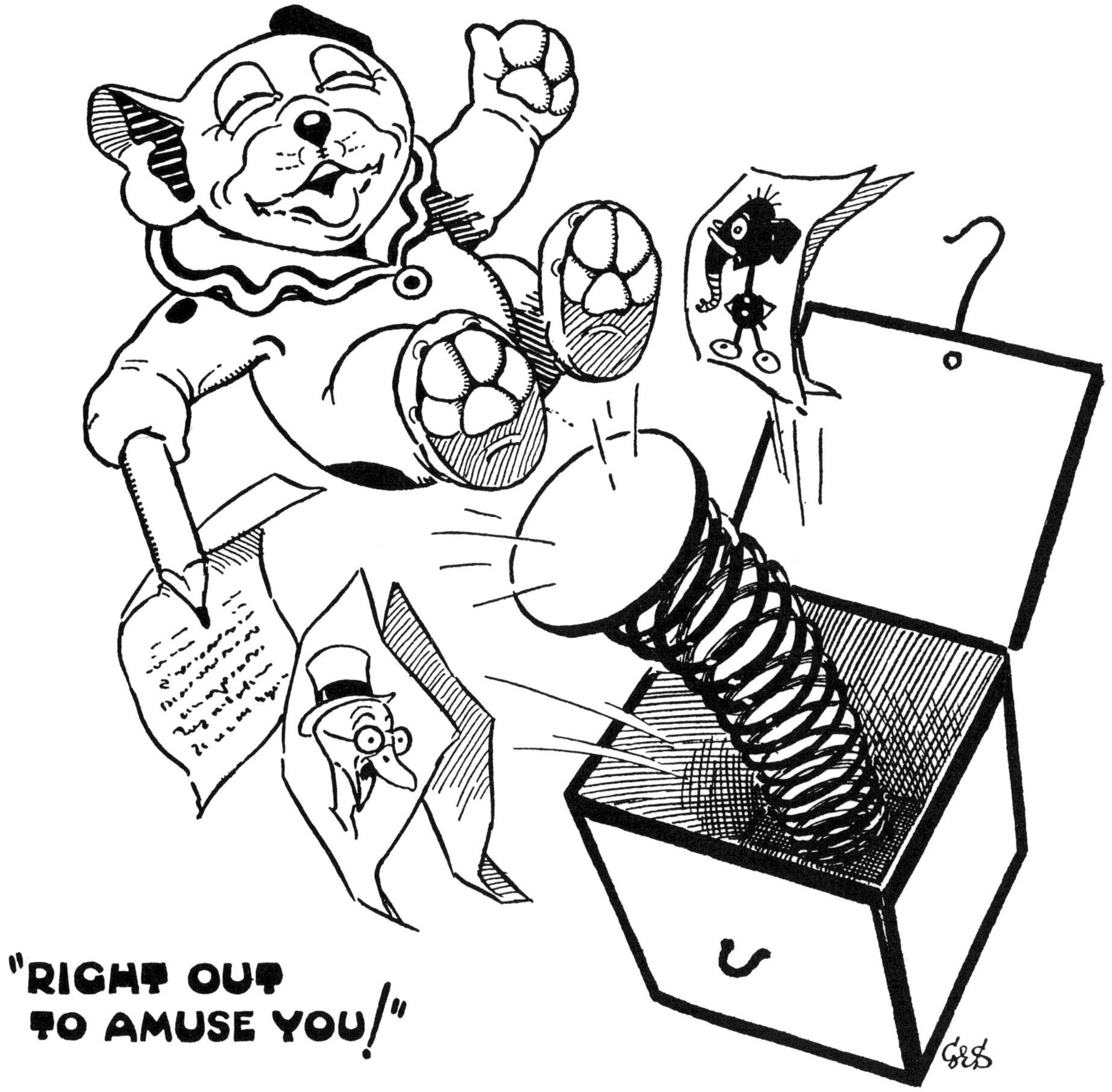

"RIGHT OUT TO AMUSE YOU!"

Paul Babb and Gay Owen

Foreword by Beryl Cook

RICHARD DENNIS
Shepton Beauchamp, Somerset, England. 1988

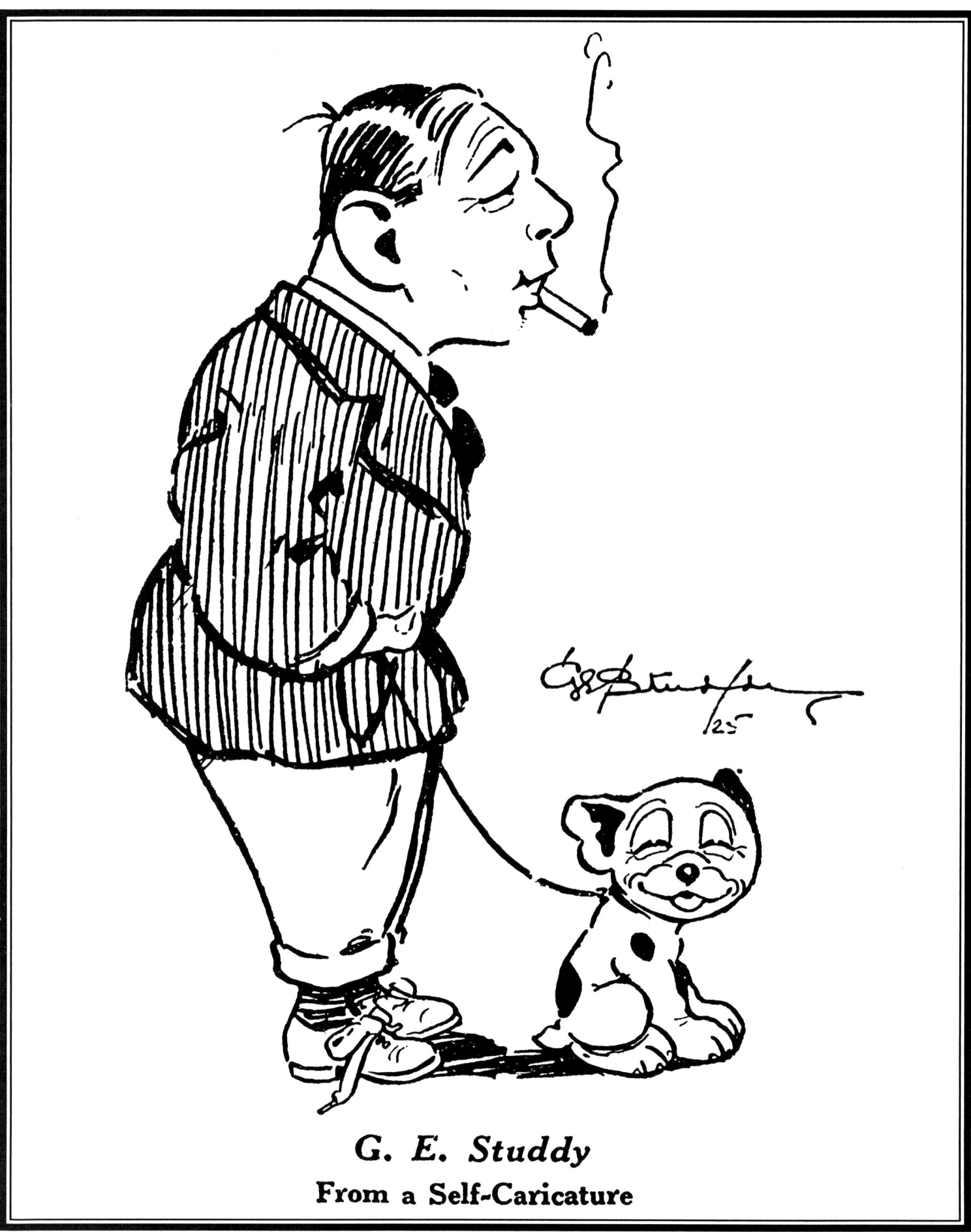

G. E. Studdy

From a Self-Caricature

FOREWORD

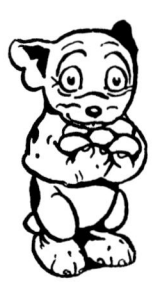 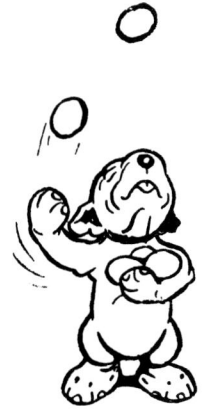 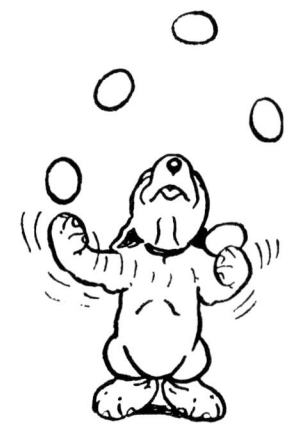

When I first started collecting Bonzos it was because of the sheer pleasure his books had given me when I was a child. I can remember being helpless with laughter as I read them, quite uncontrollable. Of all the things I have collected Bonzo has been the most difficult to find, especially the small, fat, books that I so enjoyed. Difficult to find also has been information about his author, George Studdy, whom I've grown to admire as an artist, his prints and cards giving me inspiration when I'm having problems in drawing our dogs. I became curious to know whether he had a dog like Bonzo to use as a model, how he had started and what other things did he draw and paint? At last I'm going to find out.

Beryl Cook

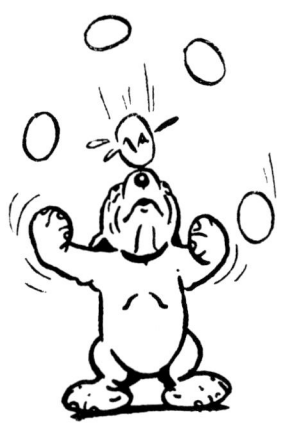 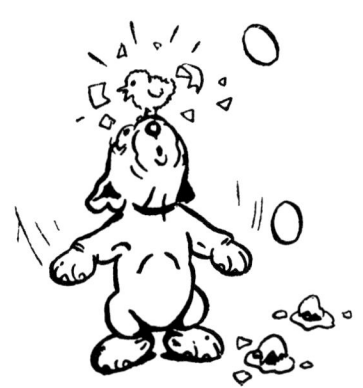 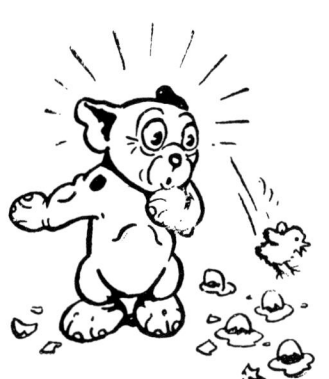

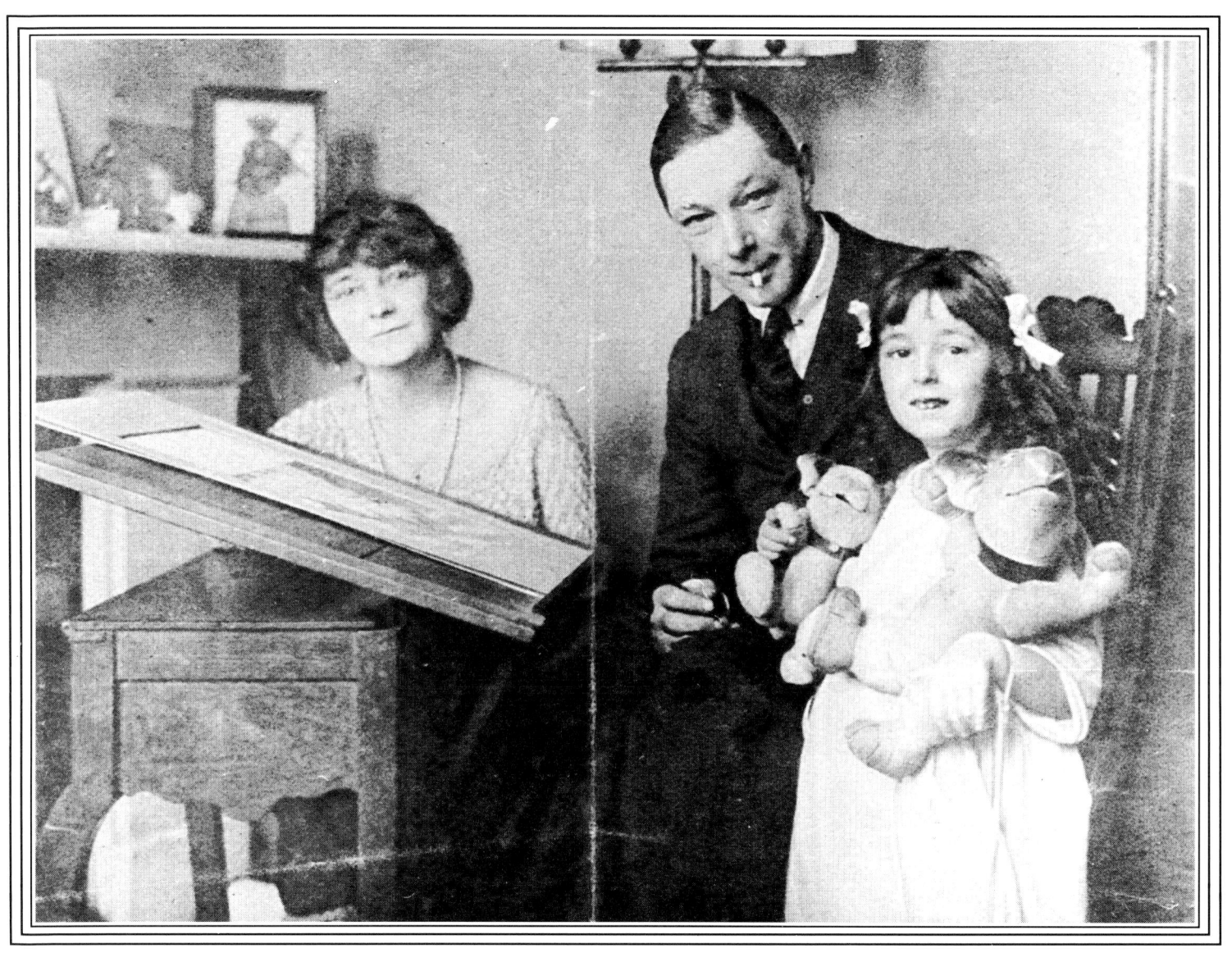

A STUDDY FAMILY : BONZO WITH HIS MASTER. MRS. STUDDY, MISS STUDDY, AND ONE OF THE BONZOLINES.

BEGINNINGS

It is often said that every dog has his day, and conversely it could be argued that every day has its dog. For adults and children alike in the nineteen twenties and thirties there was only one contender for that title – Bonzo. During those decades between the wars he was unrivalled in Britain as the most popular cartoon character of his time. Across the Atlantic Felix the cat was running a parallel course under the guidance of Pat Sullivan, an Australian, who had emigrated to The United States in 1914. Mickey Mouse, probably the most famous character of all time, was not conceived by Walt Disney until 1927 by which time Bonzo was already a firm favourite in America.

His attraction to all age groups was, perhaps, one of the main secrets of his success. In the eyes of a child he was a charming and cuddly pup, yet he could be more than a little risqué in his appeal to parents. He was the eternal scamp, forever getting in and out of every scrape imaginable and always bouncing back for more.

His arrival on the scene was a gradual one spanning several years. For a long time he appeared anonymously as 'The Studdy Dog' in both periodicals and postcards, named after his creator George Ernest Studdy. During these formative years his physical form and character became more and more developed until he became the one and only Bonzo.

George Studdy was born on 23rd June 1878, the first son of Ernest Holdsworth and Constance Julia Hayter Studdy, at 2, St. Jean D'Acre Terrace, Devonport, Plymouth. His father was a lieutenant in the 32nd Regiment, Argyll and Sutherland Highlanders. The Studdys had three children, the eldest being Ernestine, then George and lastly Hubert. The discipline of the children's upbringing was very strict, not, as one might imagine, owing to their father's military

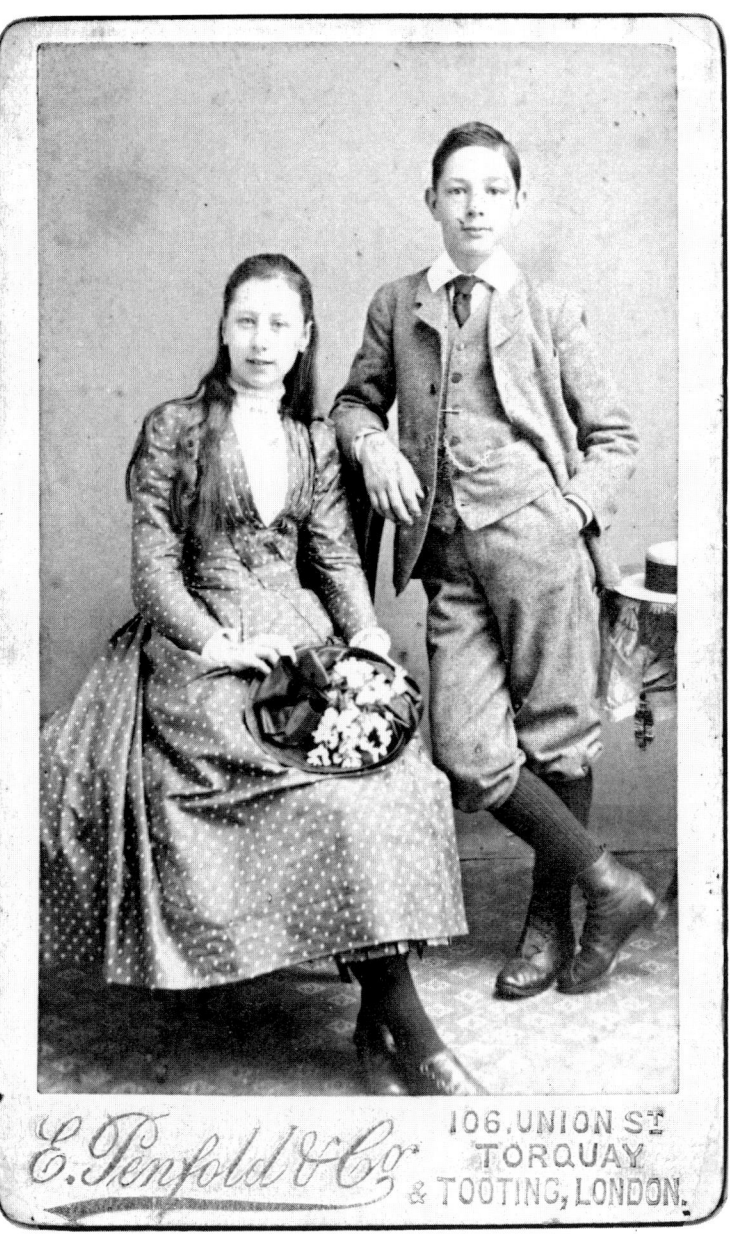

George Studdy with his sister Ernestine, c. 1890.

background, but because their mother was a religious woman who imposed a harshly repressive regime on her entire family. Each Sunday church had to be attended three times without fail, and the only permitted reading matter was the Bible. Both boys' 'Sunday best' clothes included stiff white collars that were restricting and uncomfortable. All in all, George regarded it as the most hateful day of the week. He felt increasingly stifled by the repressive and sombre atmosphere. As an adult, he would become estranged from all religion and never set foot inside a church if he could possibly help it.

Ernestine, on the other hand, readily accepted her mother's puritan ways, and throughout her long life, showed exemplary piety. Like her mother she practised strict temperance; detesting alcohol in any form. Hubert, the youngest of the three children, enjoyed the liturgy of the High Church with it's rituals and fine vestments, and eventually took up the ministry as a career. His chosen calling suited him admirably, for he was both witty and eloquent, his sermons attracting large congregations. Unlike his mother and sister he saw the more joyous side of religion. Not for him their strict abstinence; he was always glad of a glass of good sherry.

George's father was temperamentally suited to discipline of a different kind. He loved army life and the fellowship of his brother officers. In his leisure time he was fond of hunting and shooting and all manner of outdoor activities. Nor was he averse to a good drink from time to time. A combination of these factors landed him in hot water many years later. On a visit to George and his wife in Chiswick, having perhaps taken a little more alcohol than was good for him, he was apprehended shooting at the ducks in a local park. Constance disapproved of his hedonistic attitude to life, and she regularly made her feelings felt forcefully. Her preaching finally drove him to leave her but she would never agree to a divorce which would have betrayed her principles.

In his formative years George identified very much with his father and shared his love of the outdoors. They would often go off together on fishing trips, a sport that was to become a passion for the rest of his life. He had ample opportunities to develop his skill with the rod when he lived for a while with his maternal uncle, C. Hayter Hames, a country squire of the old school, and master of the Mid-Devon foxhounds. He did not show the same aptitude for hunting, however, since he was unable to stay on a horse for

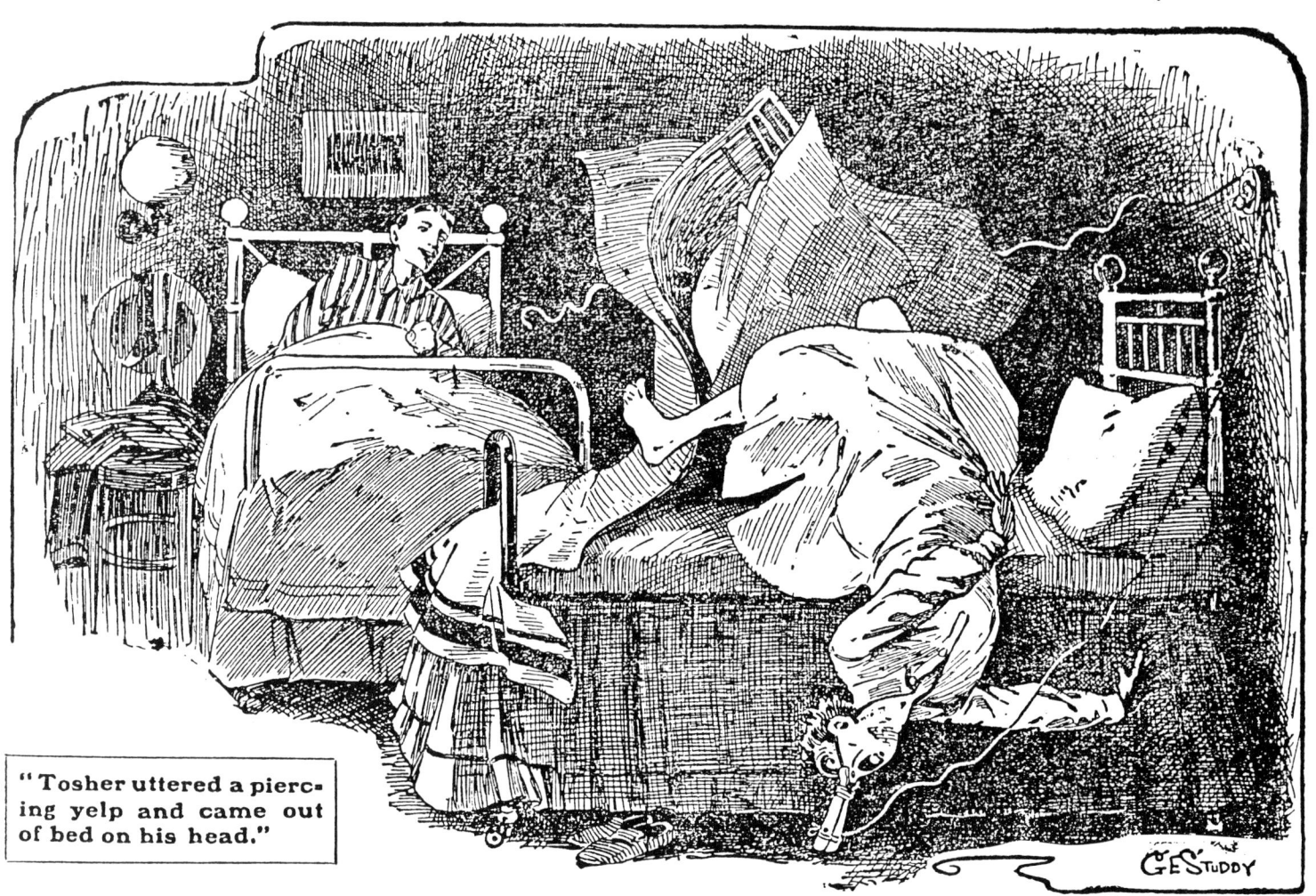

"Tosher uttered a piercing yelp and came out of bed on his head."

An illustration for *The Merry Medicos*, a series in *The Big Budget Comic* of 1904. The stories were similar in style to those in *The Boy's Own Paper*, mainly text with accompanying line drawings.

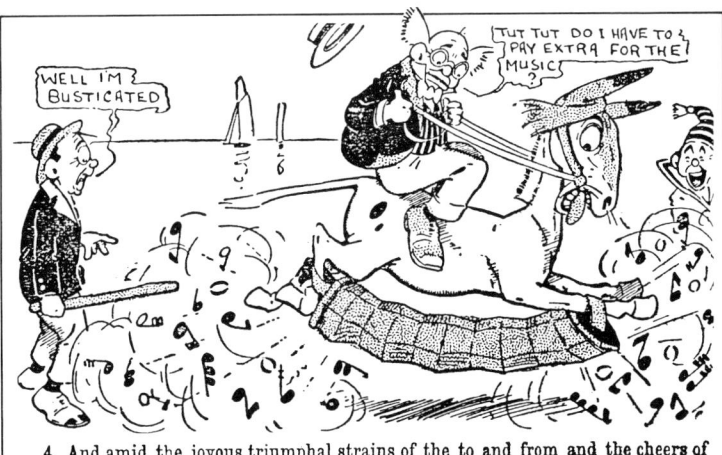

4. And amid the joyous triumphal strains of the to and from and the cheers of the bystanders, the Professor started his handicap across the golden sands of time —er, rather, Margate, at an express rate.

A Professor Helpemon cartoon from *The Big Budget Comic* in 1903

longer than a few minutes. He became quite famous in the neighbourhood; for his activities in the hunting field, but as a pedestrian rather than as a horseman. Often he would trudge back home through the fields covered with mud, his horse nowhere to be seen, to be greeted by a loud chorus from the locals, "Master Garge have varled arf agin!" While in Devon he tried his hand at shooting, but he was so upset after killing his first animal that he decided the sport was not for him.

Ernest Studdy hoped that one of his sons would follow him into a military career, and with this in mind George was sent to start his preparatory education at his father's old school, Clifton College in Bristol, which had connections with Sandhurst. His time there was unfortunately cut short a year early because of an accident that he suffered in a hayfield. A pitchfork went through his foot which had to be splinted for several months. The injury required fourteen operations and at that time the treatment was only available in London. It meant regular attendance at the hospital, so for convenience George stayed with his aunt in south east London. During his time there he gained admission to Dulwich College in order to continue his education. Because of his injury he was unable to take part in most of the sporting activities, much to his dismay, but made up for it in the gymnasium where he excelled on the rings and parallel bars and was to win many prizes. His enthusiasm for the sport persisted into adulthood, and he won a gold medal at Marylebone when he was in his thirties.

He left Dulwich College in the summer of 1896 but was still not fit enough to be considered for the army. He had few definite alternatives in his mind and although he was fond of sketching it was not considered a proper profession. He used to spend so much time drawing engines and making cardboard models that his family thought his future might lie in engineering, so he was sent to serve an apprenticeship at the Thames Iron Works. His working hours were from 7.30 am until 6.00 pm for which he was paid the princely sum of eight shillings (40p) a week. The company operated a system of fines to encourage their employees' punctuality. George had to travel ten miles to work and was frequently late. He became so frustrated at having to pay back the bulk of his wages in fines that he gave up the job after only a few months.

His next attempt at employment was to last much longer. He took a job with a firm of stockbrokers and was paid half the commission on all the orders he introduced. He lasted three years there. Friends made up the bulk of his clients and he subsequently maintained that the barrel began to run dry when none of them had any money left to invest, and he had to look actively for new contacts.

The aunt in Dulwich proved to be the most important person in his early career. She took him under her wing and made him a gift of £100. She had always been aware of his love of art and she hoped he would use the money to strike out in that direction. He attended evening classes at Heatherley's (previously Leigh's) in Newman Street, just north of Oxford Street, the oldest school of its kind in London, and he revelled in his new found freedom. He was proud of the traditions of the school which counted Dante Gabriel Rossetti, Edward Burne-Jones, Leighton, Millais and George du Maurier among its illustrious former pupils. He went for one term to Calderon's Animal School in South Kensington where, as well as drawing and painting, he learnt animal anatomy for the first time. This was to prove his most valuable training, for he carried the skills learnt there throughout his entire career.

Although his aunt's sponsorship was very generous for those days, it eventually ran out and he had to think about earning a living. He was sharing a studio with friends from art school, and used to work hard for a week or so until he had amassed enough drawings to fill a portfolio. Then he

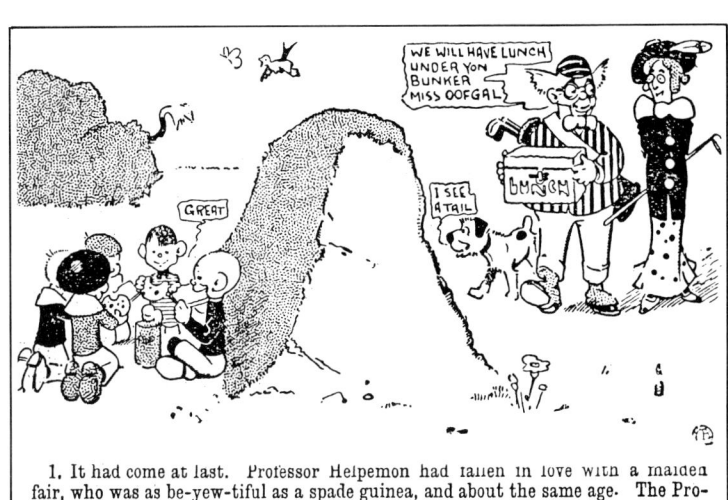

1. It had come at last. Professor Helpemon had fallen in love with a maiden fair, who was as be-yew-tiful as a spade guinea, and about the same age. The Professor had arranged a little luncheon party in the country——

A frame from one of Studdy's earliest strip cartoons, Professor Helpemon, published in *The Big Budget Comic* in 1903.

took it to Fleet Street and elsewhere offering the contents for sale. Sometimes he sold a few, ensuring that his rent money was safely in hand; other times he returned home dejectedly with the complete collection.

He regarded the sale of his first picture as a major triumph and was delighted to receive the full asking price of eighteen pence (7½p). For a while he kept to this price and made enough money to maintain his modest lifestyle. When, a little later, he managed to sell a batch of comic drawings for the magnificent sum of of five shillings each, he was overjoyed. He was sensible enough to realise that this had been a windfall, but gradually increased the price to half a crown (12½p) and eventually five shillings on a regular basis. When he had reached the point of being paid ten shillings a drawing, he knew he was on his way.

During the Boer War, the training received at Calderon's proved most useful when he was commissioned by various newspapers and magazines to draw Royal Artillery horses galloping into action. Comic Cuts was the first publication to buy his work regularly and he gradually built up a clientele among the Fleet Street publishers. Punch published only one of his cartoons, on 24th December 1902, but he befriended many of the famous artists and illustrators who regularly contributed to the magazine.

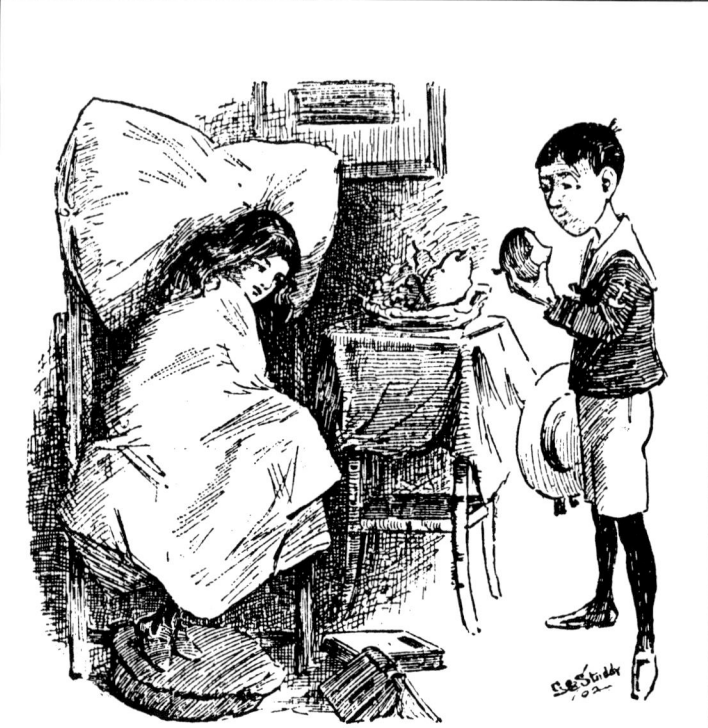

Tommy. "I SAY, ELSIE, IF YOU LIKE, I'LL COME AND SEE YOU EVERY DAY WHILST YOU ARE ILL."

Studdy's only published contribution to *Punch*.

In 1903 he was producing sketches regularly for 'Professor Helpemon', a cartoon strip featured in the comic, The Big Budget Boys Weekly. He had also entered the field of postcards producing a comic science-fiction series called 'The Last Man' which was published by Academy Picture Postcards. He had already started a relationship with Valentine's Postcards of Dundee that was to last for over 46 years. They published a series of six cards under the title of "The Evolution of the Motor Car" depicting cars as they might have been from prehistoric times right through to the future. At this time, of course, Bonzo was still a long way off but George asked his brother Hubert, a great storyteller, to write a tale involving a comic dog, which he could illustrate. He was quite impressed with the end result and unknown to Hubert submitted his drawings together with the unedited manuscript to The Tatler. It was accepted for publication and the brothers were well rewarded. Unfortunately, however, Hubert had lampooned several of the villagers that he and George had known as boys; they narrowly escaped a libel suit by grovelling apologies all round.

From the start of his career as an artist a large part of George's income came from producing drawings for advertisements. Early in his career, he drew a series for the Sandeman Stanley Cotton Belting Co. Ltd., which featured cavemen demonstrating a series of Heath-Robinsonesque machines driven by Stanley belts. During this period the caveman was a popular source of imagery and was used extensively by artists such as Lawson Wood and E. T. Reed, as well as Studdy.

In the early 1900's there were many more gentleman's clubs than exist today. Several catered specially for artists and designers, and in general the camaraderie was such that deep friendships were formed between members of like interests. George was, naturally, a member of several arts clubs, joining the London Sketch Club in 1905 and later the Savage Club. The former was then situated at 79 Wells Street, near Oxford Street, in London. The membership boasted virtually every major illustrator of the day, including John Hassall, William and Charles Heath Robinson, Phil May, H. M. Bateman, Lawson Wood, Tom Browne, Cecil Aldin, Bert Thomas, Harry Rountree, Edmund Dulac and, surprisingly, Lord Baden-Powell, the founder of the Boy Scout movement, who, in his early years in the army, had supplemented his meagre pay by sending drawings to illustrated journals.

On Fridays, the principal night at the club, a drawing class was always held from seven to nine, after which the work was put on display for criticism by the assembled members and their guests. There was a meal to follow with copious quantities of wine and beer and, needless to say, lively conversation. The tradition is still upheld today at

IF SCIENCE COULD CREATE BEASTS:
SUGGESTIONS FOR LABOUR-SAVING ANIMALS.

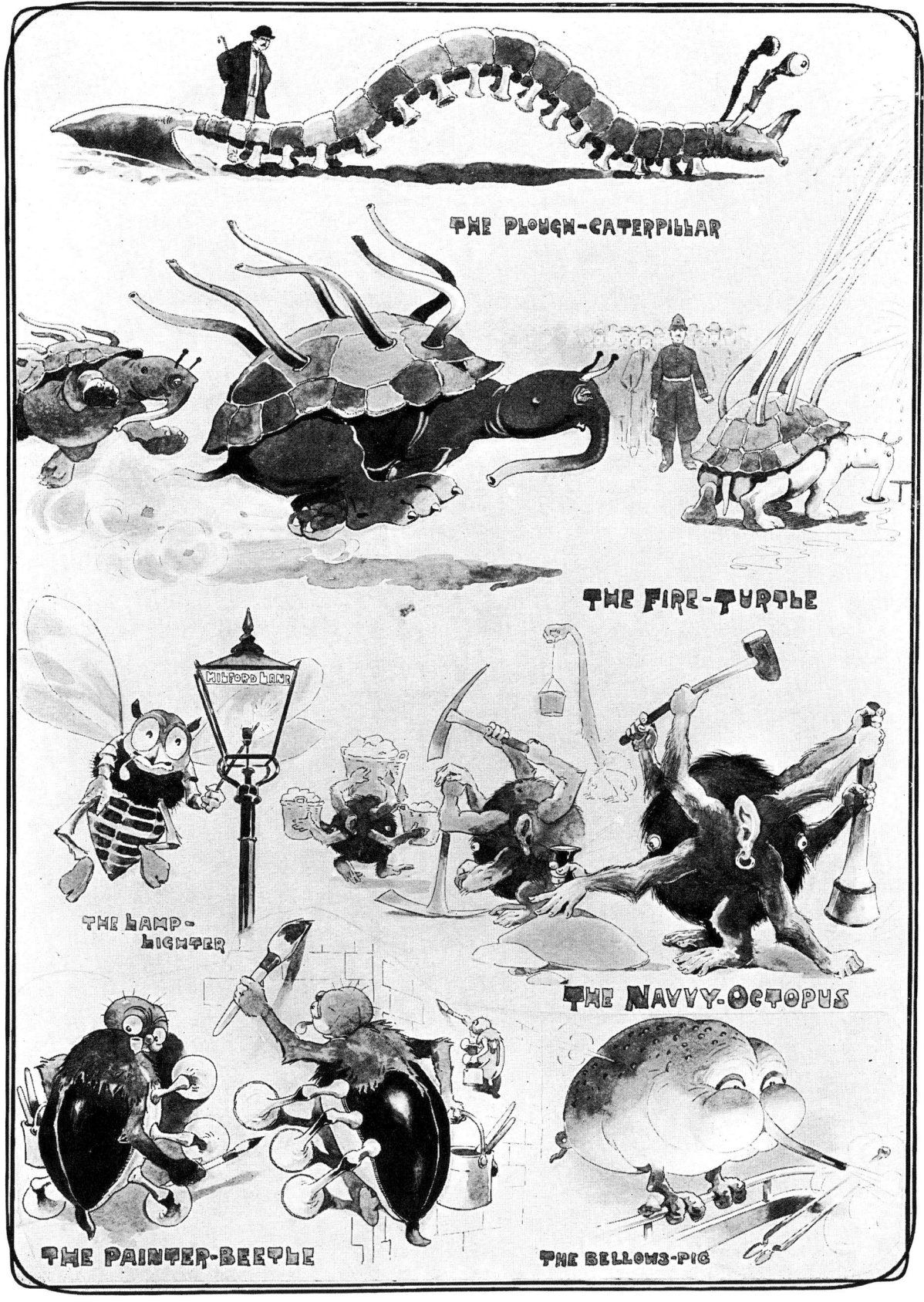

Professor Ostwald, of Leipzig University, is of opinion that before very many years have passed science will be in a position to create a form of life as advanced as that of our domestic animals. "Why not, then," he asks, "create forms of animal life capable of doing many of the things which only human beings can do to-day? By specialising, it may be possible, for instance, to create a type of animal capable of doing the heavy work of the world—creatures of vast physical strength coupled with a higher form of intelligence than has been evolved as yet in any animal excepting man."

Drawn by G. E. Studdy.

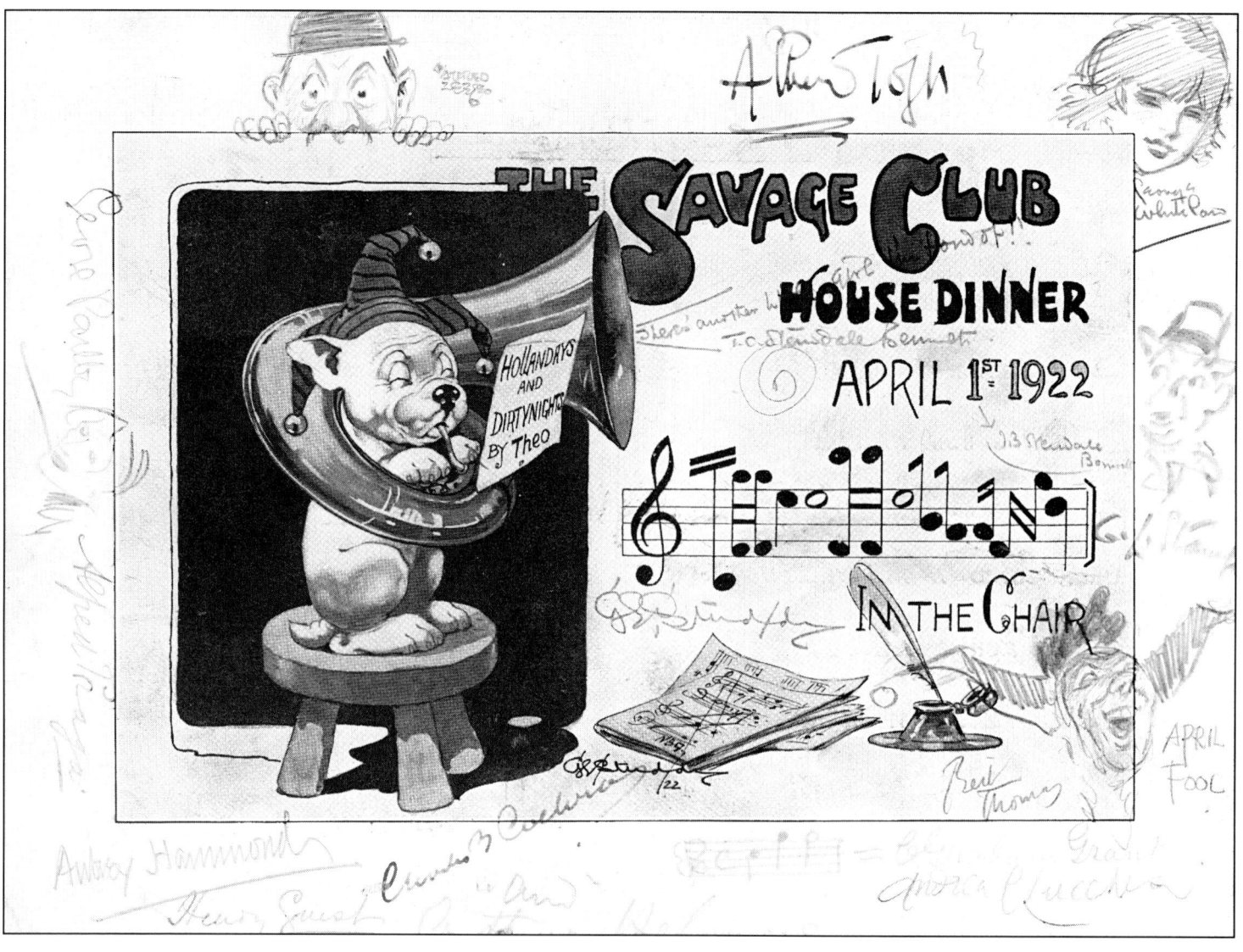

A Savage Club dinner menu featuring Bonzo and autographed by fellow guests including Bert Thomas, Alfred Leete and George Whitelaw.

their premises in Dilke Street, Chelsea. The Savage Club also still exists, sharing premises with the Lansdowne Club in Berkeley Square, although memberhsip has never been limited to artists, and includes entertainers, musicians, writers, scientists and lawyers. As at the London Sketch Club, there were many formal dinners where the members could enjoy the company of their fellow artists. The Savage had a traditional advantage in that they included among their members Royal princes and even heirs to the throne. The future George VI took the chair at the 77th annual dinner in 1934 when he was the Duke of York and second in succession. It was customary for a prince to resign from the club when he ascended the throne, so the club never counted a monarch among its members.

By 1912 Studdy had a formidable reputation as an illustrator and cartoonist, his work appearing in many periodicals, including The Tatler, The Bystander, The Graphic, The Sketch and the Illustrated London News. It was at roughly this time that he established one of his most important business relationships when he was asked by The Sketch to produce a weekly full-page drawing. He had worked for them spasmodically for a few years, but this was a real breakthrough. He drew a series entitled 'The End of the World' but it was, unfortunately, never published as the drawings were destroyed in a fire at the magazine's offices. Nevertheless it was this liason that was to launch Bonzo on his spectacular career some ten years later.

1912 was an important year for George Studdy in more ways than one. On June 15th he married Blanche Ernestine Landrin at the church of Our Lady of the Rosary, Marylebone, London. He was 33 years old and she six months younger. They made a very attractive couple, Blanche, a dark eyed Parisian beauty with marvellous bone structure and George, slim and dark haired with strikingly green eyes. They had met when Blanche was living in London with her sister Gabrielle who was married to Hunter Crawford of the Crawfords Biscuit family. George had asked her to model for him at his studio, and they soon discovered that they had much in common. They were both artistic, musical and of a generous disposition; a strong affection soon developed between them. Nevertheless when it came to their respective personalities it was a case of opposites attracting each other. He was shy and unassuming, she was extrovert, theatrical and flamboyant. He loved the calm of the countryside whereas she loved the hustle and bustle of city life. He smoked heavily, she not at all. He was a typical Englishman, she as French as the Eiffel Tower.

While he was courting Blanche, George made a great effort to talk to her in her native tongue, but as their relationship grew and her command of English became more assured, he gradually dropped French and eventually spoke to her only in English. Although he was more or less an atheist, George had promised Blanche's parents that any offspring would be brought up in the Catholic faith, and they gladly gave the match their blessing.

The couple honeymooned in Paris and Blanche was able to show George her home city. Once when they were in a restaurant, George's national pride asserted itself. A waiter asked him politely, "Vous êtes étranger, monsieur?"; the reply came indignantly, "Non, je ne suis pas étranger, je suis Anglais!"

On their return George took Blanche to stay with his Uncle at Chagford House in Devon. In the back of his mind he hoped that she would become captivated by the raw beauty of the area and they could settle down nearby. Unfortunately her first impressions of Dartmoor had the opposite effect and when she loudly exclaimed "Mon Dieu!" he knew he had failed and they returned to live in London.

An odd comic dog had been creeping into George's pictures over the years along with several other animal characters, but the first dog which, as he put it, "could run by itself", appeared in Pearson's Magazine. The drawing depicted a running hound with a wasp sitting on its tail and was captioned, "When you're on to a good thing stick to it". It was also produced as a framed print together with a companion picture entitled "When you see a good thing go for it". The pair had a very wide sale, and the publishers asked for more pictures of the dog, but these were not, alas, such a success.

George had faith in the character, however, and several of the early Studdy dogs appeared in advertisments. Among the products they were used to promote were Sphere Supenders, Woollvena Quilts, Swan Ink, Pan Yan Pickle and Eclipse Razors.

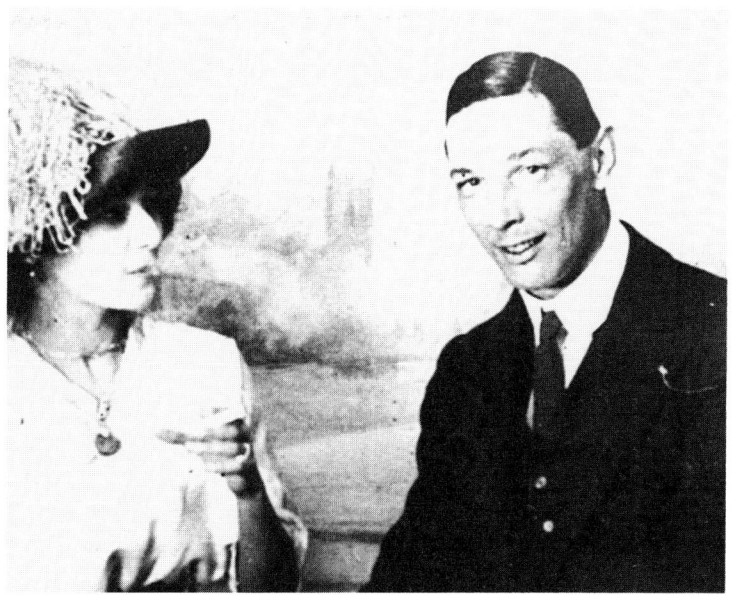

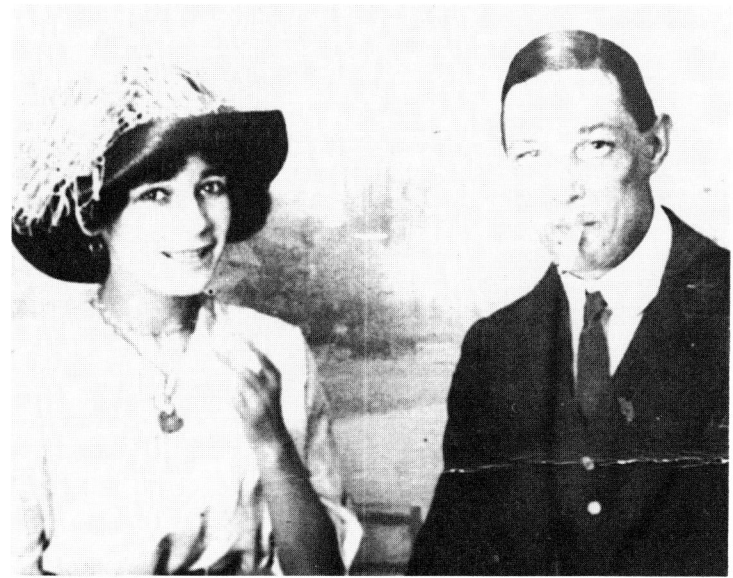

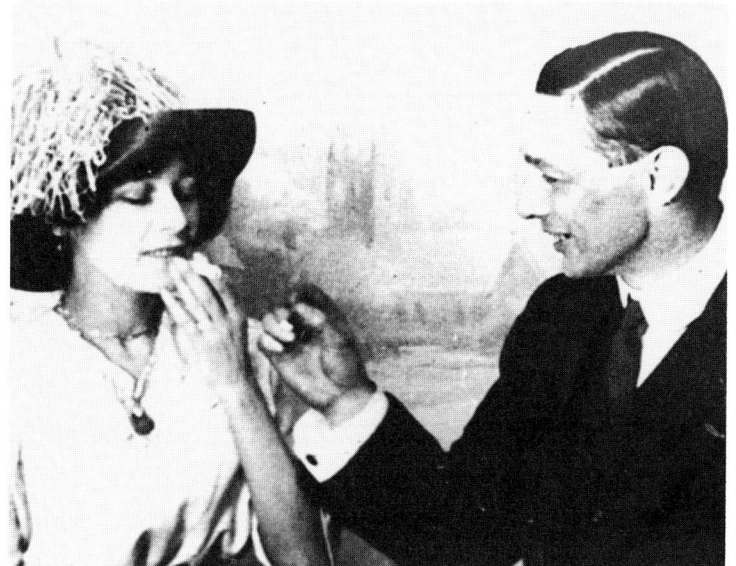

Three frames from a flicker book, made by Biofix of 56, The Strand, London. Although Blanche was a non-smoker George persuaded her to pretend for the benefit of the camera.

"O Moments Big as Years!"

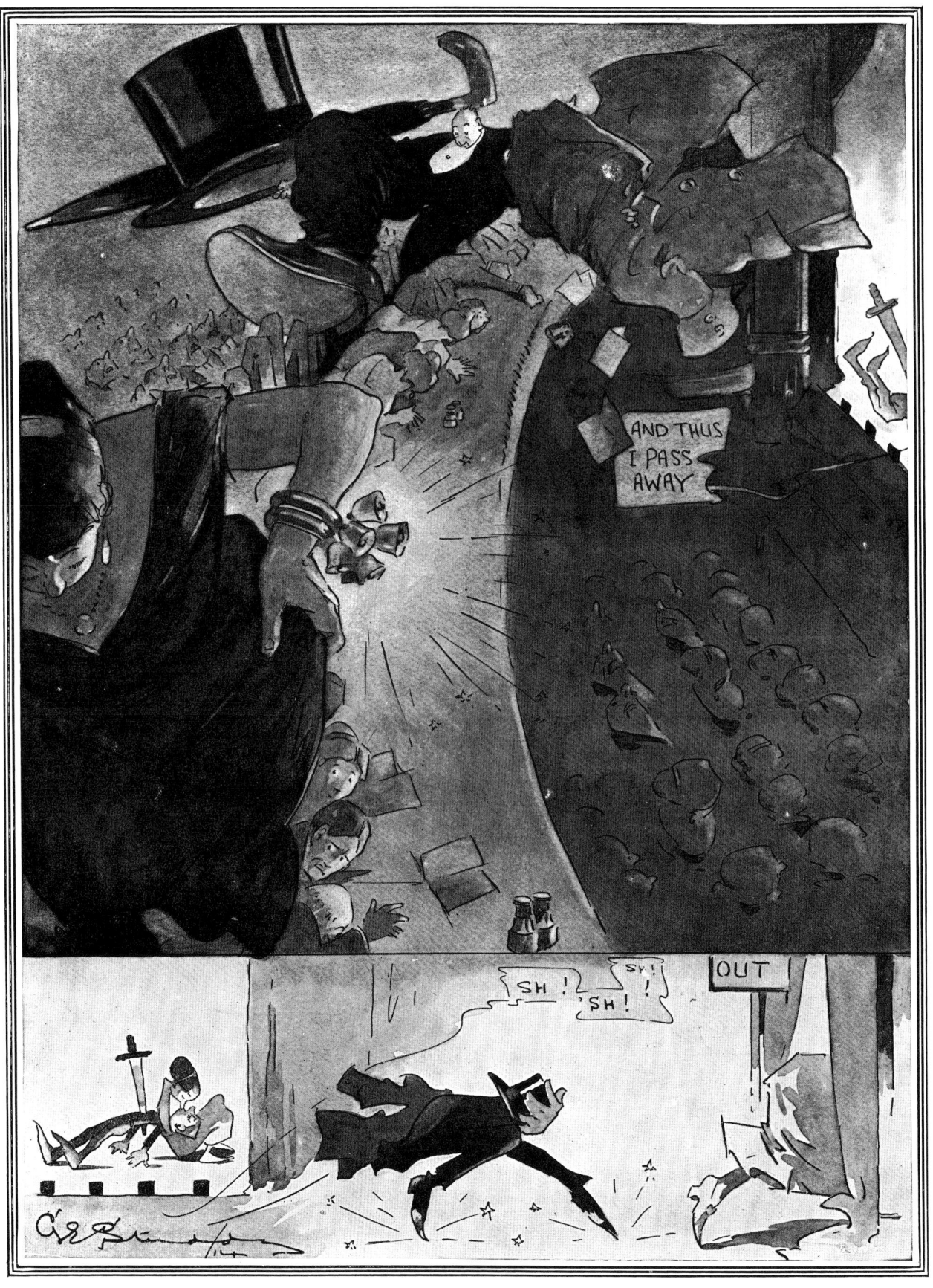

No. XI.—WHEN WE HAVE TO LEAVE THE THEATRE IN THE DEATH SCENE IN ORDER TO CATCH OUR LAST TRAIN.

Drawn by G. E. Studdy.

In June 1913 an exhibition opened at Holland Park Hall, Kensington entitled 'The Laughter Show'. Included were works by most of the famous artists and illustrators of the day, John Hassall, Tony Sarg, Fred Buchanan, Bert Thomas and George Studdy amongst them. All proceeds were donated to charity and attendances were encouragingly high. In addition to the normal exhibition format the artists took turns to draw 'pavement sketches while you wait', although they did not, of course, use real flagstones and all the work was sold to swell the funds.

Shortly afterwards The Society of Humorous Art had their second exhibition at Goupil and Company's gallery in Bedford Street, London. Once again the list of contributors read like an artistic Who's Who and included Dudley Hardy, H. M. Bateman, George Belcher, Bert Thomas, John Hassall, Arthur Watts, George Morrow and Tony Sarg. Even in this illustrious company George was not to be

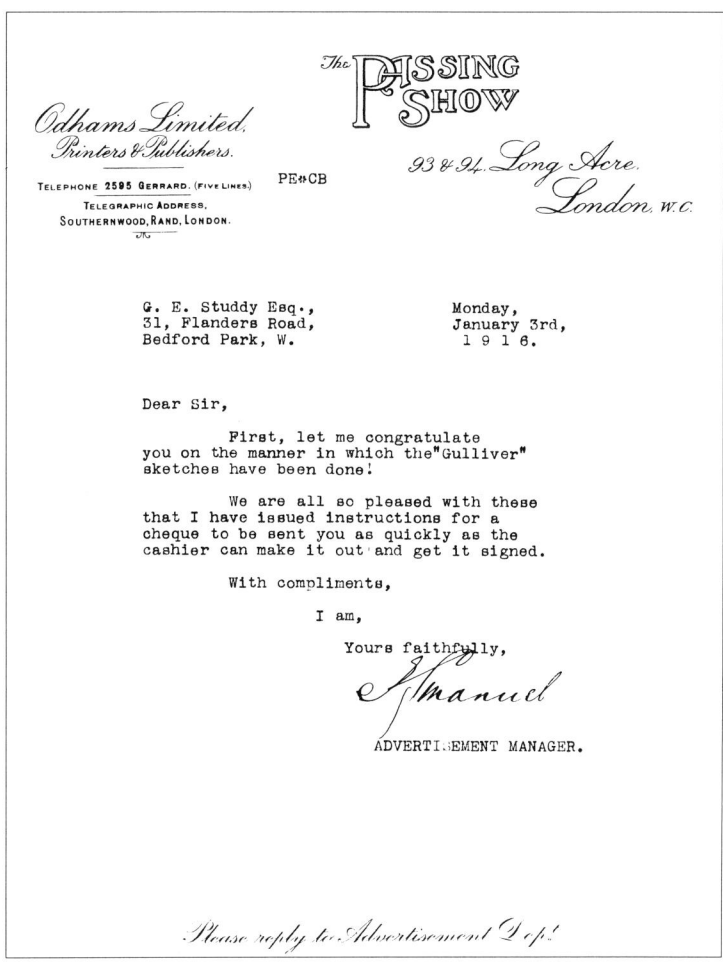

A letter from a satisfied customer.

overshadowed. A review of the exhibition in 'What's On' magazine stated that "Quite the best piece of work pictorially is 'The Sea Serpent' by G. E. Studdy and the success of the exhibition is largely due to this young artist who exhibits several excellent drawings".

Later that year The Brook Street Gallery held an exhibition of his work which included many of his 'Studdy Dog' originals and a series entitled 'Etiquette of angling'. These reflected his continuing passion for his favourite sport.

He was a regular contributor to The Field magazine where his drawings and paintings illustrated the humorous side of fishing as well as the other country sports. Many were issued separately as prints at a later date. The success of this relationship led to The Field eventually publishing a book on the subject in 1914. Written by Studdy's good friend Hugh Tempest Sheringham, another avid fisherman, it was entitled 'Fishing – A Diagnosis', superbly illustrated by George. Eleven years later they collaborated on a rather belated sequel, 'Fishing, its Cause, Treatment and Cure'.

Meanwhile, after the office fire at The Sketch, which had destroyed 'The End of the World' drawings, Studdy had submitted to the paper a new series entitled 'O Moments

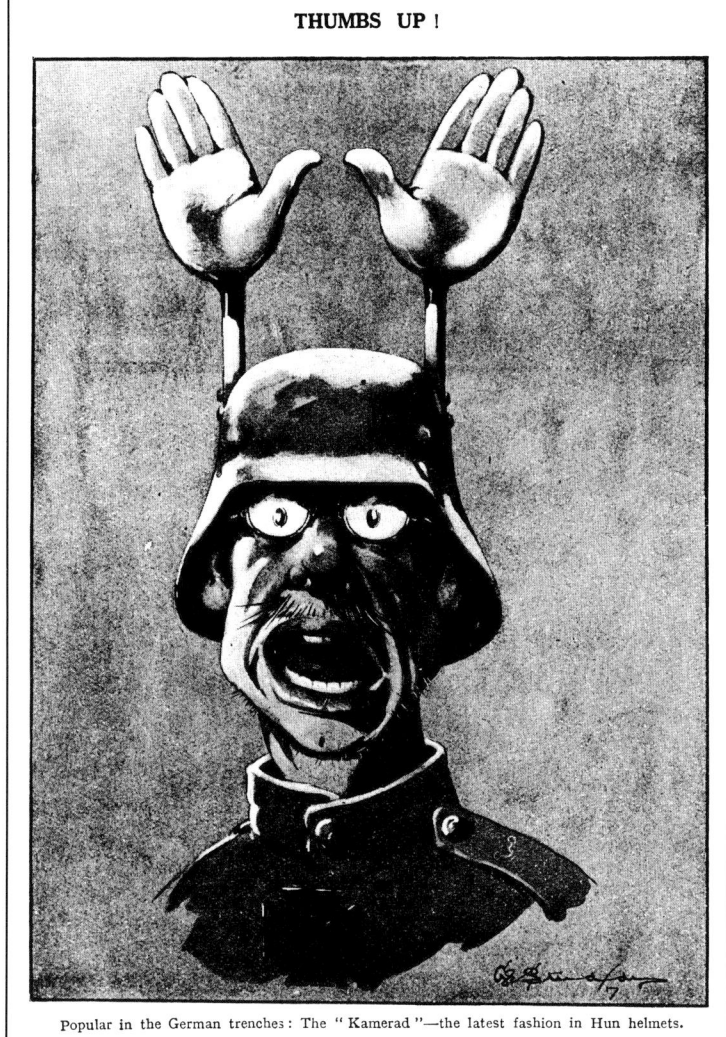

THUMBS UP !

Popular in the German trenches: The "Kamerad"—the latest fashion in Hun helmets.

A contribution by Studdy to the 1914-18 propaganda war in which cartoonists were able to play a major part.

Big as Years', which was readily accepted. These illustrated many of the embarassing situations in which everyone finds themselves at one time or another.

This was soon to be followed by another series of humorous drawings which looked weekly at the First World War and lasted until its end.

It was a great sadness to George that the army rejected him when he tried to enlist. His medical record revealed that the childhood injury to his foot would have prevented him marching the long distances necessary on active service. Furthermore, he was by then in his mid-thirties which was also not in his favour. Fortunately he had his work to occupy him and distract him from the disappointment. Artists' agents Francis & Mills represented him at this time and provided him with a great deal of work, removing the drudgery of looking for clients and commissions himself. The firm represented many top class artists and illustrators, including Mable Lucy Attwell.

They presented George with his first opportunity to work in film animation, when Gaumont commissioned him to make a series of three short cartoons entitled 'Studdy's War Studies', released monthly from December 1915. Together with his graphic work, the films gave him the

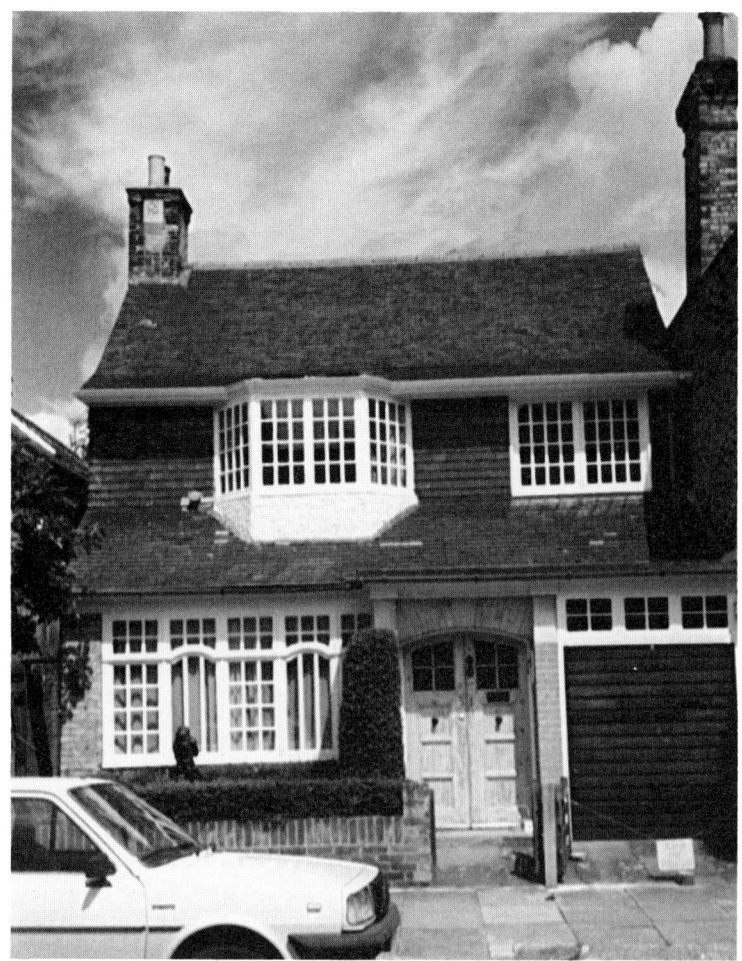

The house at 31 Flanders Road, Chiswick as it is today.

opportunity to contribute to the war effort in a way that helped to keep up the morale of the nation.

During the war George and Blanche had set up home at 31 Flanders Road in Bedford Park, West London, which had been an area popular with artists for nearly half a century. It was convenient for central London, which suited Blanche, and boasted some fine parks and lovely river walks. They lived close to several of his professional colleagues including Cecil Aldin, the other great canine artist, and Lawson Wood of 'Granpop' fame. It was at their home in Flanders Road that their first child, a son, was born in 1916. He was given the name of Holdsworth, an old family name, but tragically died when only a few weeks old. Both parents were devastated at the loss of their baby and George, in his grief, drew a sensitive portrait of his dead son as if he were sleeping peacefully. He was buried in the Catholic Cemetery in Chiswick.

After the Armistice in 1918, George was still supplying The Sketch with weekly full-page illustrations, much as he had done before. It was felt that the subject-matter should be somewhat lighter now that the nation was not engulfed in the gloomy business of war. The editor expressed an interest in 'The Studdy Dog', which George had developed during the preceding few years, and suggested that they give it a six month trial in the magazine. It proved such an

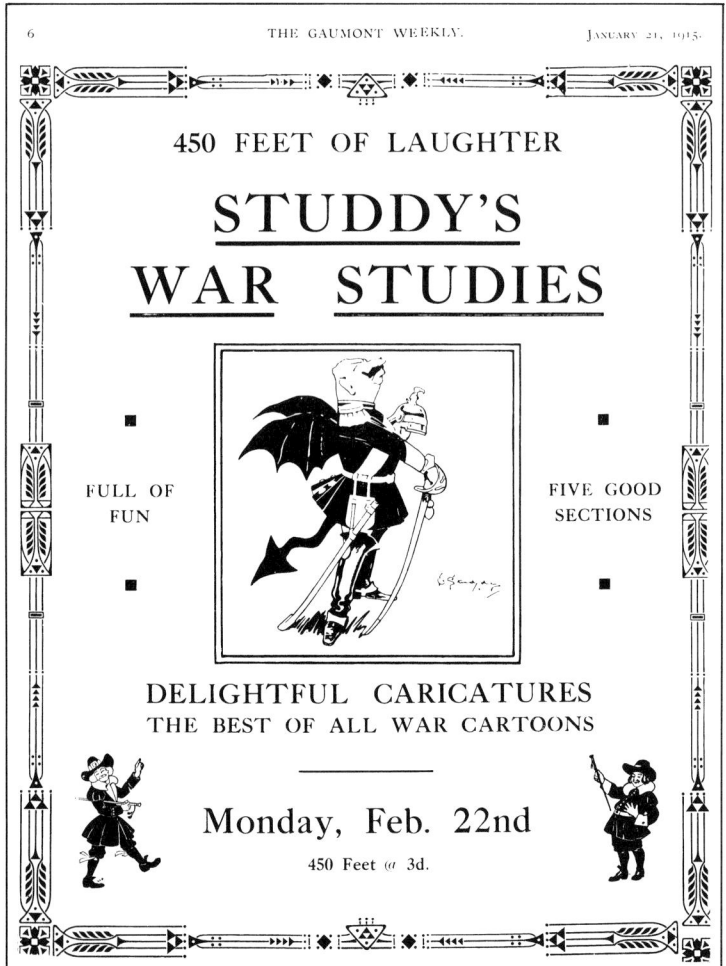

A trade advertisement for Studdy's First World War films. The Kaiser received little sympathy.

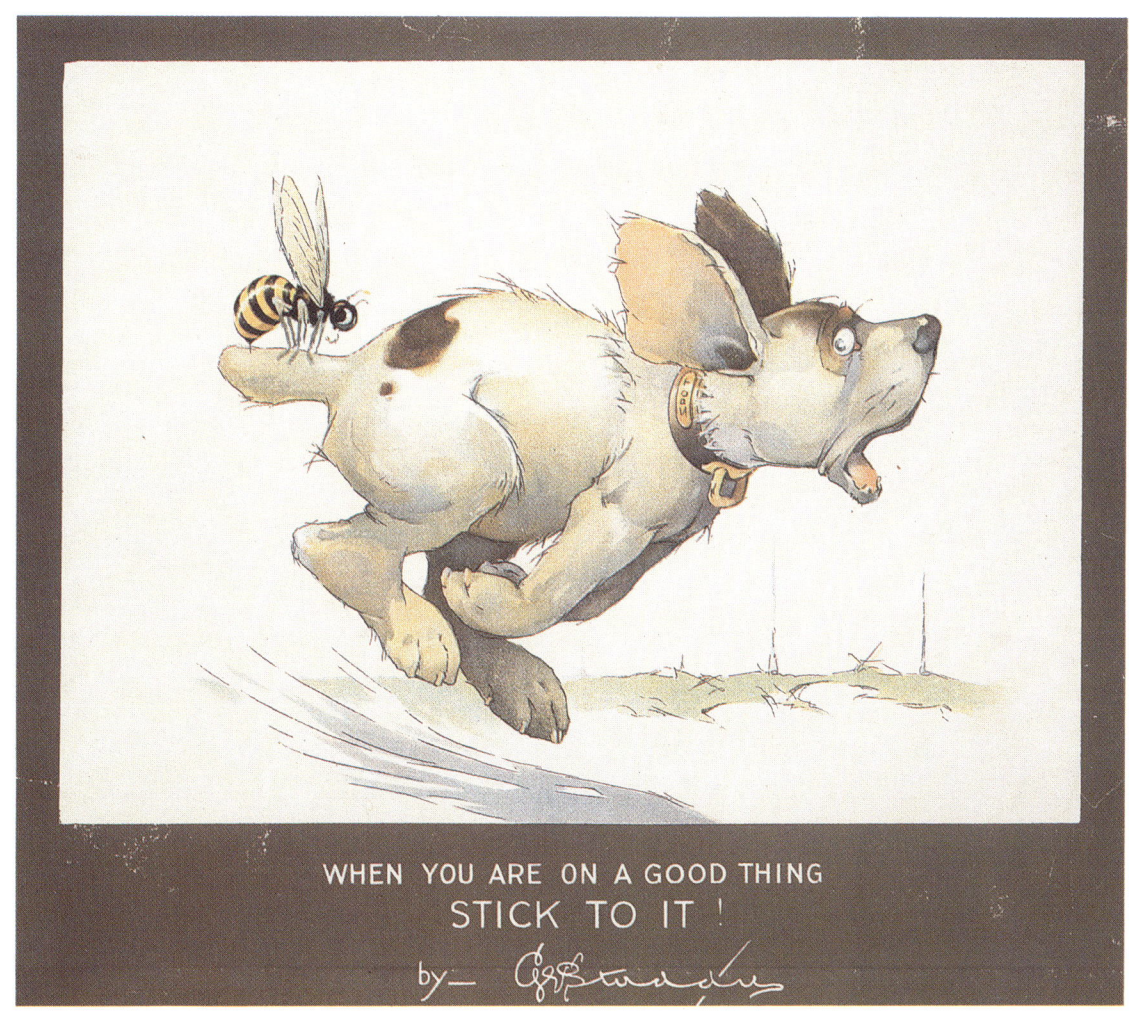

The first dogs 'That ran by themselves'.

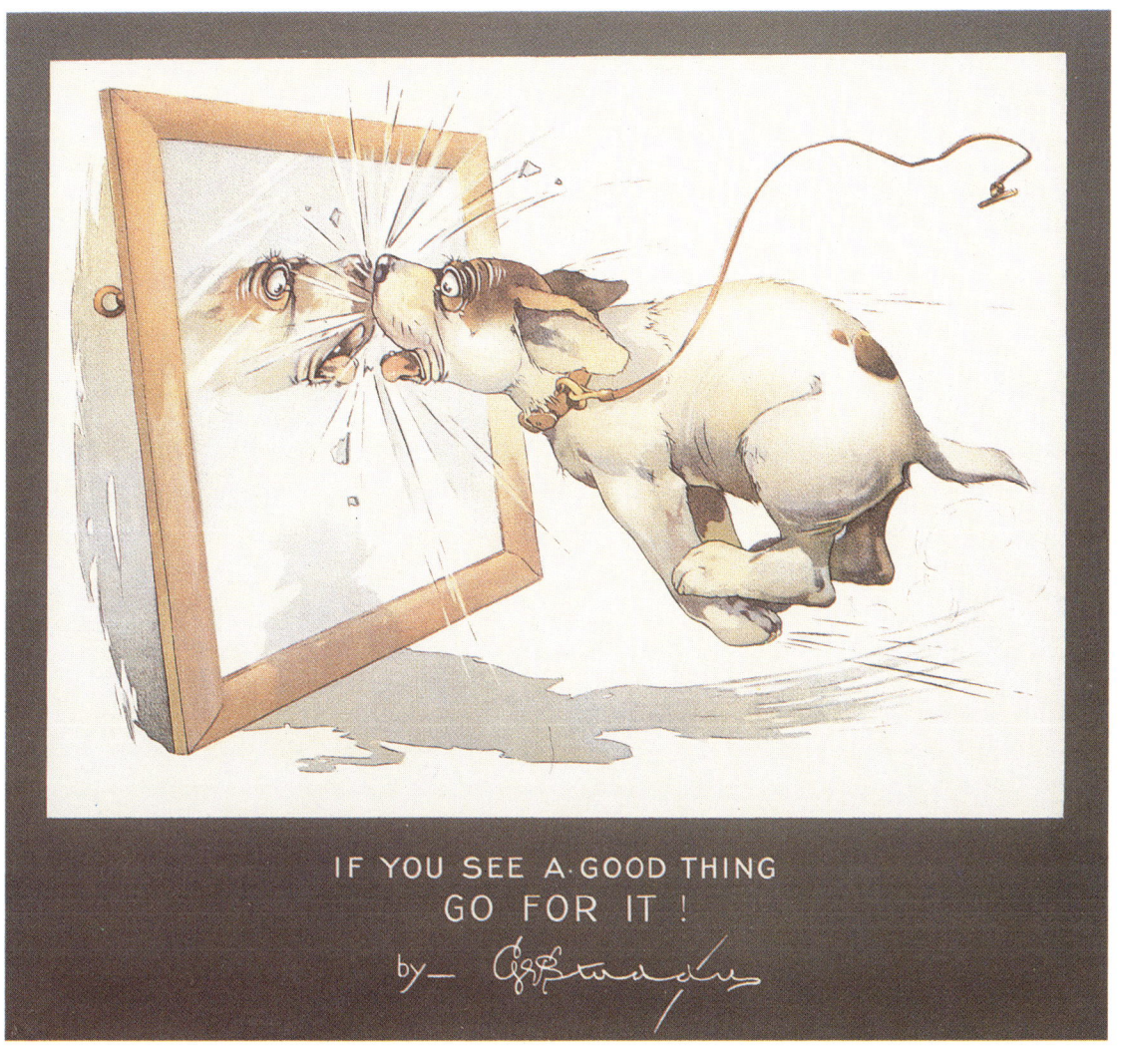

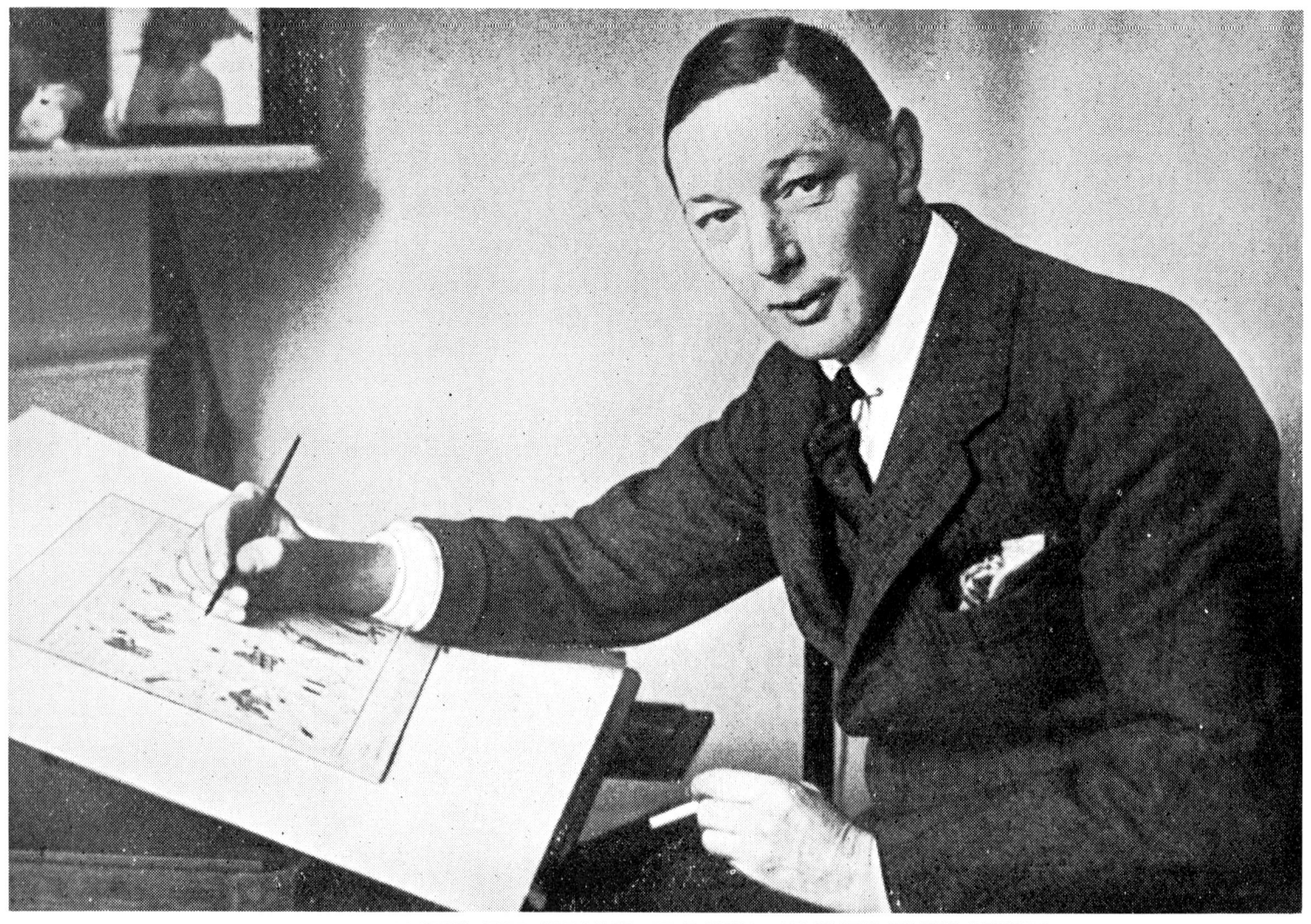

MR. G. E. STUDDY, THE CREATOR OF BONZO, AT WORK IN HIS STUDIO.

enormous success that the theme was continued without a break for many years. The character was being developed all the time and became more definite in form, moving away from recognised breeds and turning more into a cartoon version of a dog. The cheeky antics of the pup struck a chord in the hearts of Sketch readers young and old, but the animal was only known as the Studdy Dog, a very anonymous title indeed. The editor, Bruce Ingram, had several letters complaining about the fact that, since the dog was regarded as the Nation's pet, his name, if he had one, should be divulged. The ommission was rectified in the issue of 8th November 1922 when 'This Week's Studdy' became 'This Week's Bonzo'. The illustration shows the dog having just swatted a large wasp after what had apparently been quite a battle. The wasp, before meeting it's end, had managed to sting Bonzo in the eye which was swollen enormously. Beside them on the floor lay a book entitled 'Famous Fights'. The caption reads 'Taking the Count', to which is appended a note announcing the official naming of Bonzo. It is interesting that it was Bruce Ingram who suggested the name, and not Studdy, who did not care for it much.

One of the penalties of fame was that George was forever being interviewed by the press, who always seemed to ask the same questions, albeit dressed up in different guises. "How did you think up Bonzo, and exactly what sort of dog is he?" George tired of this incessant interrogation that seemed to keep being repeated even after he had explained himself scores of times. He tried hard to think up new and witty answers. In the Royal Magazine he gave the following version:

"Scientists take a few fossil bones of an extinct animal and design therefrom the complete common ancestor of various living types. At least they say so. Now Bonzo seems to me to have arrived in the same manner, only reversed. Either the terrier, sealyam, bull dog or bull terrier meets the eye during the course of a half mile walk. From the semblance of various traits or features of these four breeds, Bonzo has been evolved into the complete imaginary design of their common ancestor. The young of all existing types show stronger resemblance to their ancient progenator than the adults, so the grown-up puppy-like Bonzo strictly observes this law of nature. Formula: 4 pups/post bellum x 1,000,000 BC^2/Bonzo Saurus = Bonzo".

Another of his versions appeared in Tit-Bits in 1926 where he gives a slightly different explanation. "Some years ago a certain professor declared that in time to come we should all make use of mechanical contrivances, something like robots, to do our housework, to carry us to our offices on our shopping and sports trips – in fact to do everything and take us everywhere. This idea appealed to me and I made a cartoon of it for the editor of The Sketch. My robot took the form of a queer animal with the hind legs and tail of a dog but without a head to it. You will see from the illustration below what I mean. From that robot dog developed Bonzo. I knew at once that I had found in those hind legs and stubby tail the germ of a really funny idea, and I went on experimenting with it until Bonzo as he is today finally emerged".

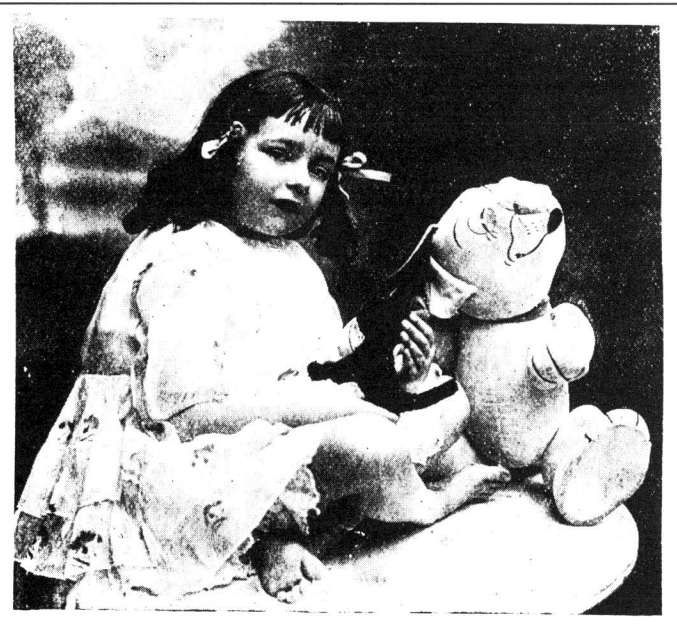

BONZO'S NOSE IS PUT OUT OF JOINT : MISS VIVIAN STUDDY PAYS TOO MUCH ATTENTION TO PUSSY.
Our photograph shows Miss Vivian Studdy, the little daughter of Mr. G. E. Studdy, the creator of the famous Bonzo, with a pussy cat, to which she is paying far too much attention to please our hero, the well-known Bonzo.—[*Photograph by Mabel Robey.*]

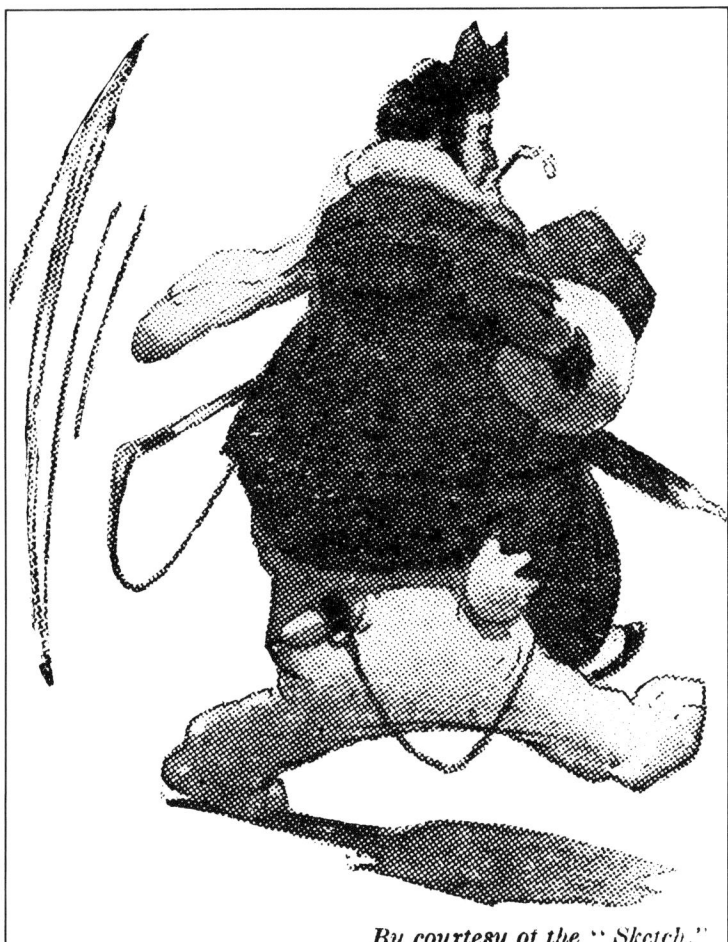

By courtesy of the "Sketch."
The Dog-Robot from which Mr. Studdy first got the idea for Bonzo.

The process of evolution that George has outlined was, of course, tongue in cheek, but Bonzo had by this time become such a popular character that some people took it rather too seriously. Major J. E. Power, a well known dog breeder, asked for George's advice in order to produce a new variety to be called the Bonzo Terrier. His attempts involved the cross breeding of several strains in order to achieve his aim, but thankfully he failed dismally.

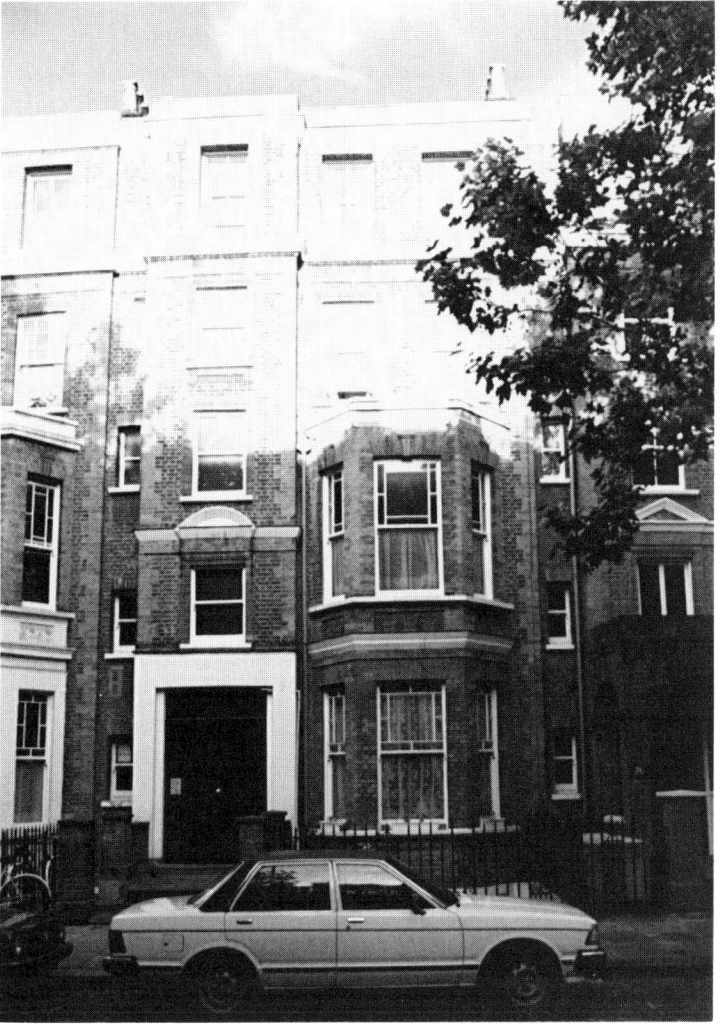

75 Philbeach Gardens, Earls Court.

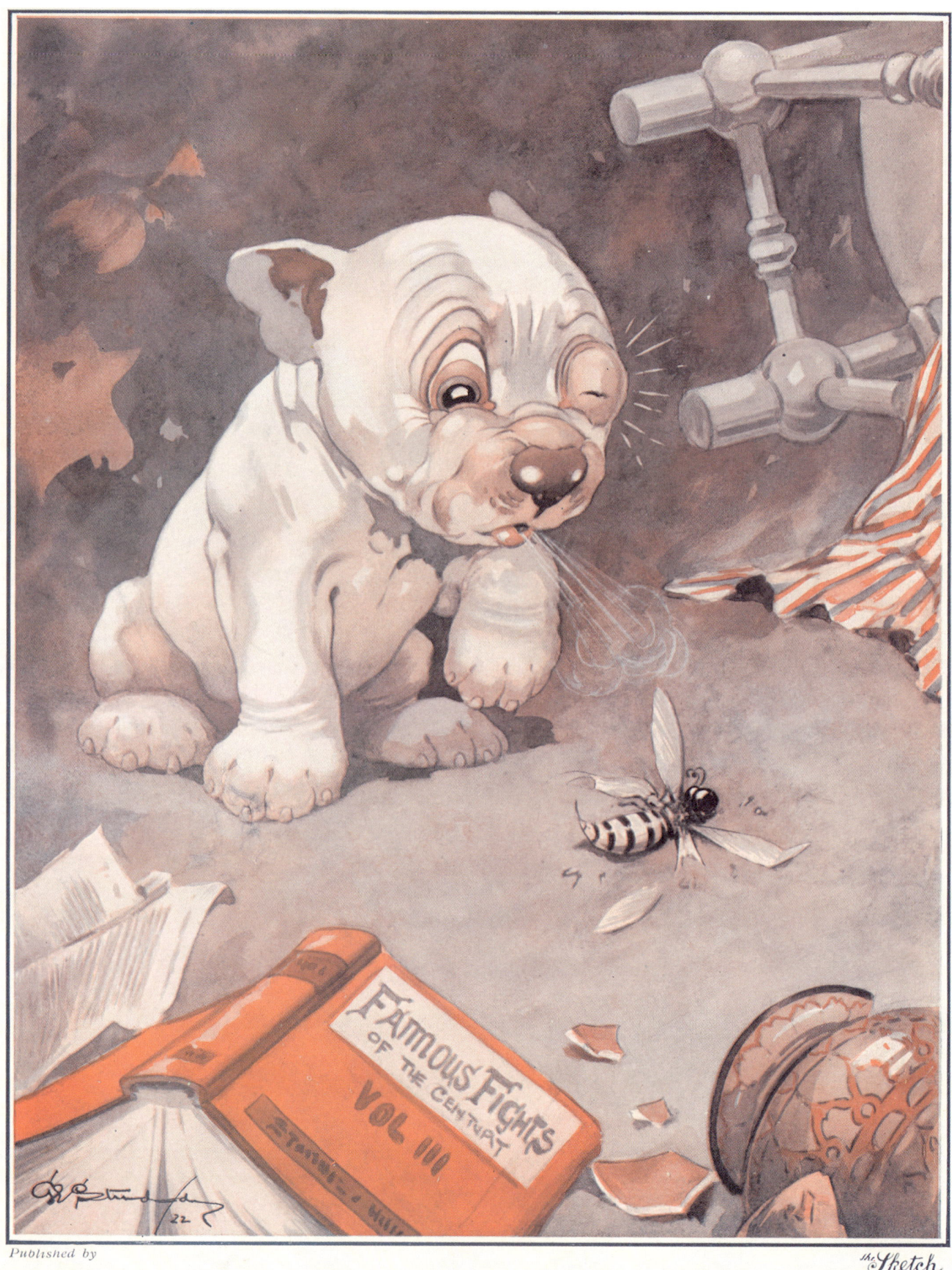

TAKING THE COUNT.

Bonzo has a few rounds with a wasp.

The first 'official' portrait of Bonzo. He had previously appeared in *The Sketch* as *The Studdy Dog*. The magazine announced his name as follows: "A large number of readers have shown themselves curious as to the name of the famous Studdy dog. To satisfy them we announce that his name is "Bonzo"."

Bonzo in Search of His Forefathers.

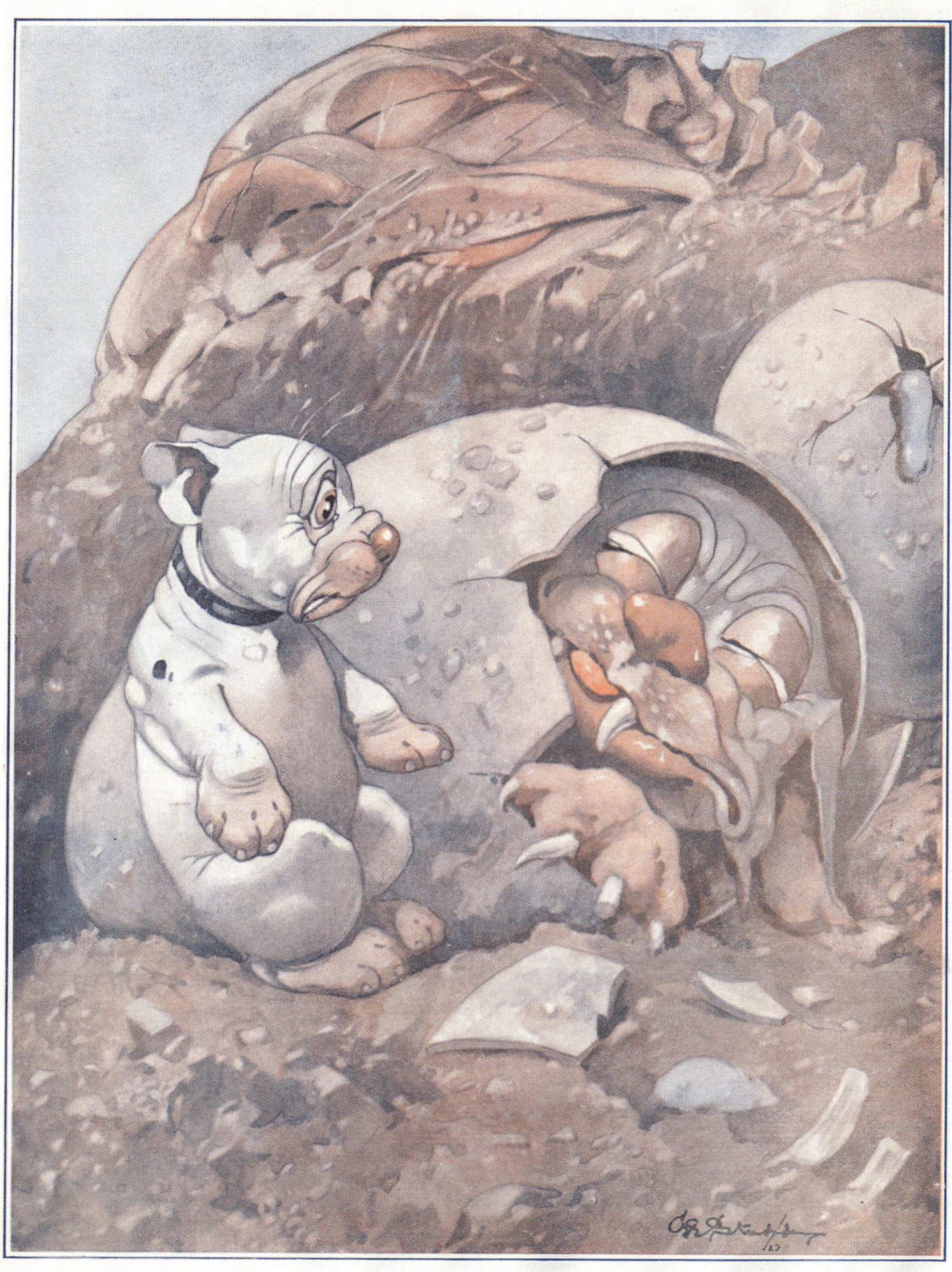

BONZO DISCOVERS THE BONZOSAURUS EGG.

The Sketch, January 9th, 1924.

The fame of Bonzo brought the Studdys a comfortable life. They had by 1922 moved to a large first floor flat at 88 Philbeach Gardens in Kensington together with a maid and a nanny called Nurse Gibbons. Philbeach Gardens, was slightly nearer to town than Chiswick but close to the greenery of both Holland Park and Kensington Gardens. Four years later they purchased the freehold of number 75. The house was bought with sitting tenants and the Studdys lived on the three bottom floors. They needed all the extra space as they employed a cook, a cleaner and house parlourmaid, as well as a governess and nanny to attend to their little daughter Vivienne Georgette. She was a particularly special child to them as they nearly lost her with typhoid fever when she was only eighteen months old. After the death of Holdsworth they took no chances and sat up with her night after night until she recovered. The many sleepless nights were well rewarded, and she has continued to enjoy splendid health to this day.

There were always dogs in the Studdy household, but none remotely resembling Bonzo. Blanche always had a

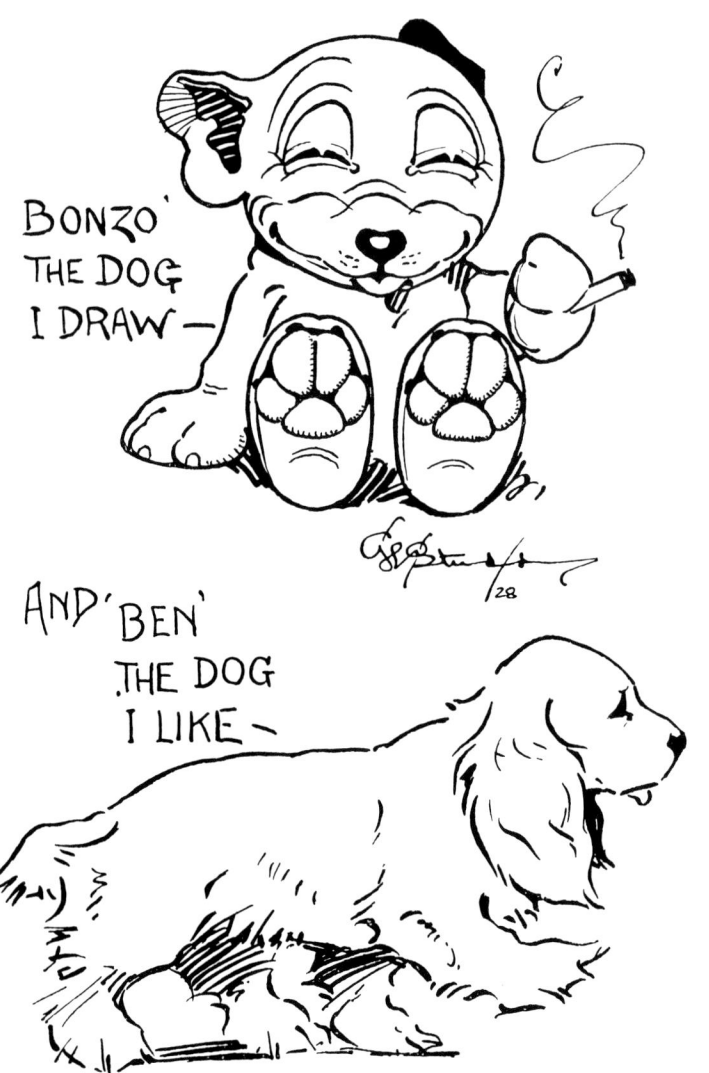

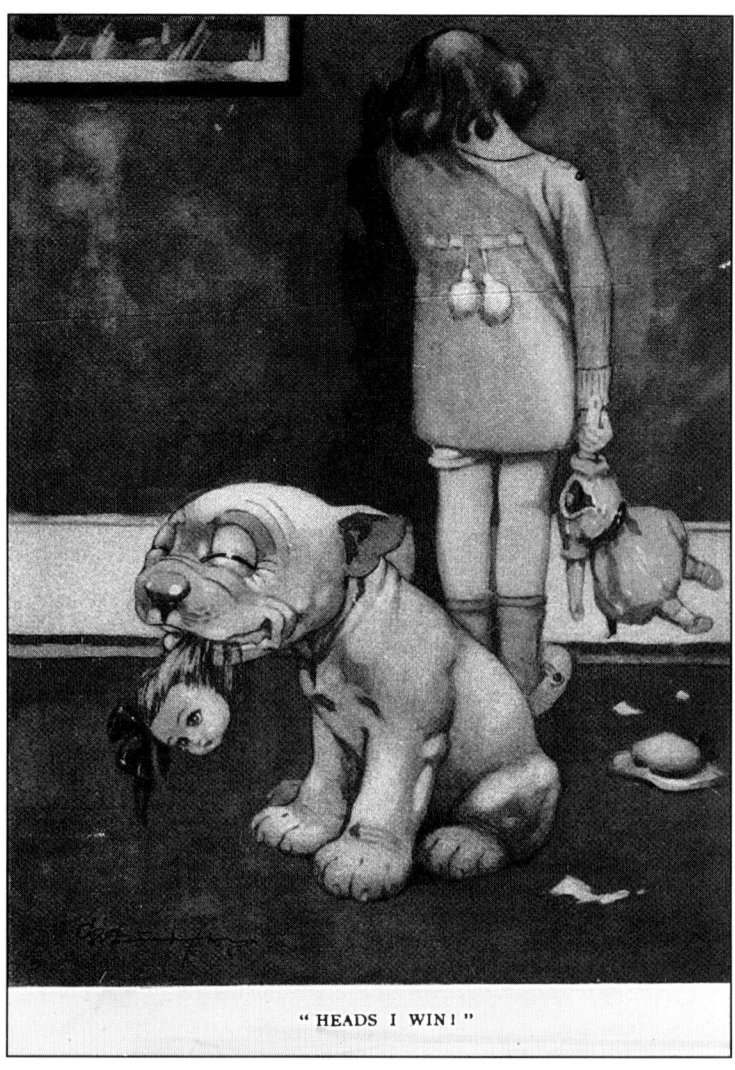

"HEADS I WIN!"

Although Vivienne Studdy was happy to model for this painting she was very unhappy with the result.

Pekinese as her personal pet, each named Chee Kee. It is no coincidence that Bonzo's girl friend was also a Pekinese of the same name. George had no inclination to own a dog called Bonzo, having a succession of cocker spaniels which he always called Ben.

He was true to his motto – 'Work whilst others play' – and often worked seven days a week, either in his studio in Hornton Street or in the basement of Philbeach Gardens. Francis & Mills were able to provide more than enough work for him, and his only problem was to keep his output up to their input. He enjoyed a strict daily routine, always rising early and breakfasting with his young daughter. Each morning throughout her childhood he drew a picture on her boiled egg to amuse her, a habit he was to revive when Vivienne presented him with a grand-daughter, Zelda. Blanche on the other hand preferred to take breakfast in bed and face the world gradually.

After leaving Vivienne in the capable hands of her nanny, George would make his way to his studio, light his first cigarette of the day and start work. He found 'Gold

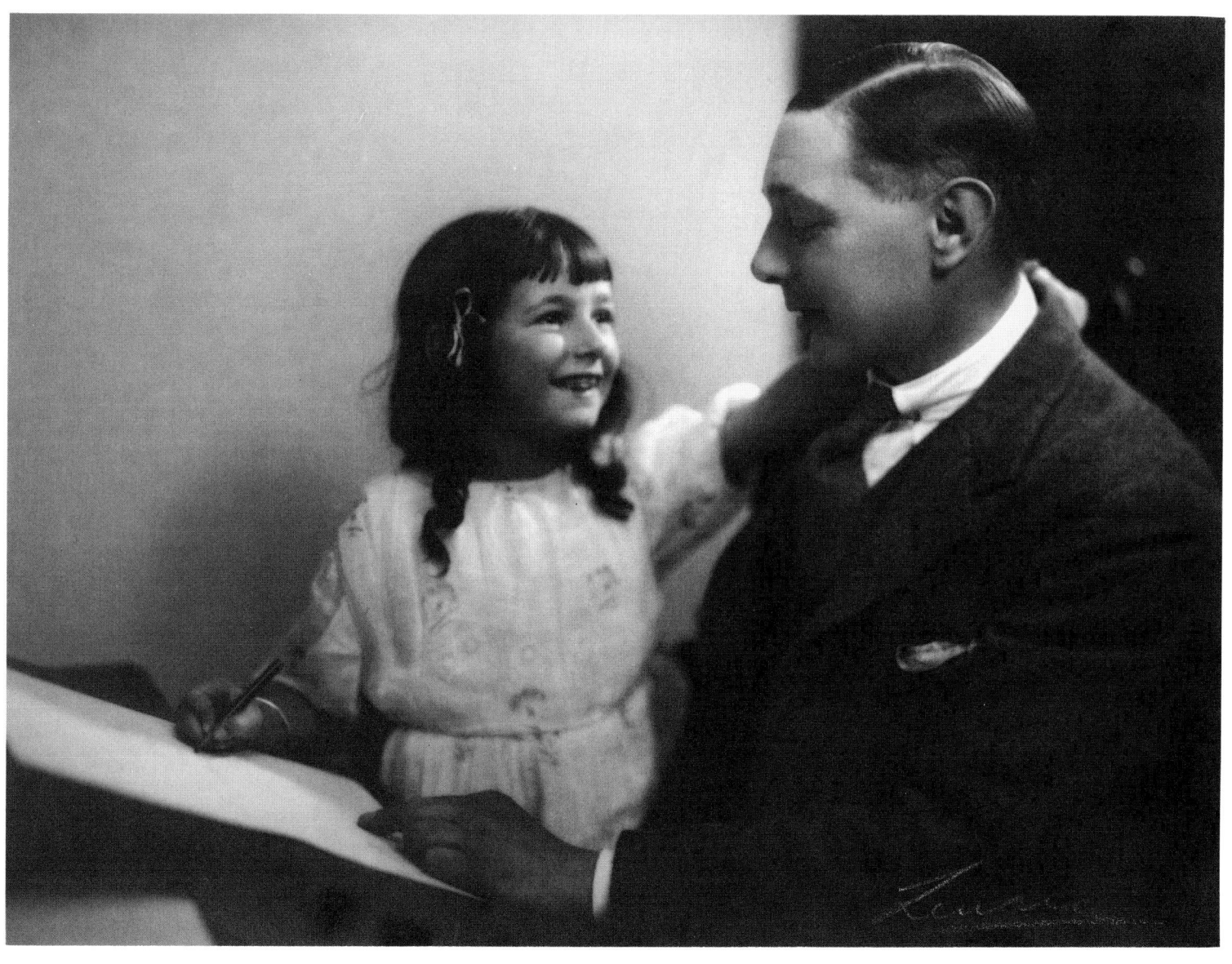

A publicity photograph of George Studdy with his daughter Vivienne.

Flake' tobacco a great aid to concentration and smoked almost continuously throughout the day, using a long cigarette holder to keep the smoke from his eyes whilst drawing. Usually only the first half of each cigarette was smoked; he would discard the rest to smoulder in an ashtray. Around 12.15 he used to adjourn to the local pub for a couple of half pints then return home for lunch and back to work just after 1.00. Occasionally during the day Vivienne might pop in to see him and pass judgement. He always found this a real pleasure and took time out to chat with her, often taking the opportunity to use her as a model for one of his illustrations. She was extremely cross with him when one of these pictures was published in The Sketch. It showed a little girl crying with her face to the wall sobbing and holding a headless doll. In the foreground was a grinning Bonzo with the poor doll's head hanging from his mouth. Vivienne was not too upset about the subject matter, as she knew what a scoundrel Bonzo was supposed to be, but George had drawn her with socks half way down her legs and a glimpse of white knicker peeping from below her dress. She still remembers it and insists she would never have been so dishevelled.

Until she was fifteen years old, Vivienne took her meals in her room, with her governess. George and Blanche dined each evening at about 8.00 after which, if he was busy, he would sometimes carry on working for another hour or two. When they spent the evening at home, he loved to listen to music on his gramophone, or perhaps play the piano. He was not as adept as Blanche and could only play by ear as he had never had any formal musical training and could not read music. Blanche was able to put her talents to good use as she was an active member of a local dramatic and operatic society in Earls Court. She also often sang to raise money for charity. Although it was usual in those days to 'dress' for dinner, George preferred to remain in his normal day clothes whenever possible.

No. I.—The Knave of Spades

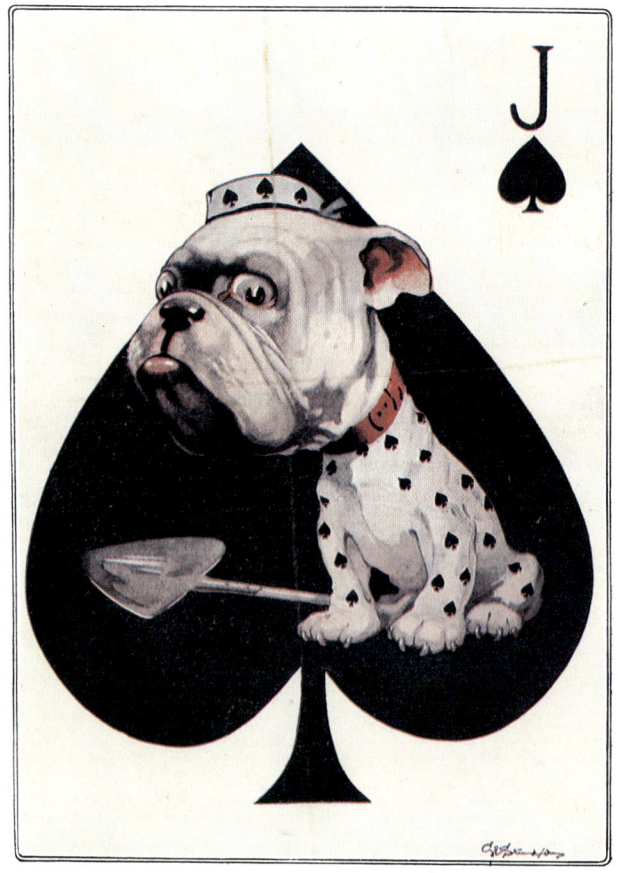

BY G. E. STUDDY

Very bold and bad is this ugly lad (his condition, you see's distressing);
To get tricks with this hound, it is always found, takes a deal of acute "finessing"

No. II.—The Queen of Hearts

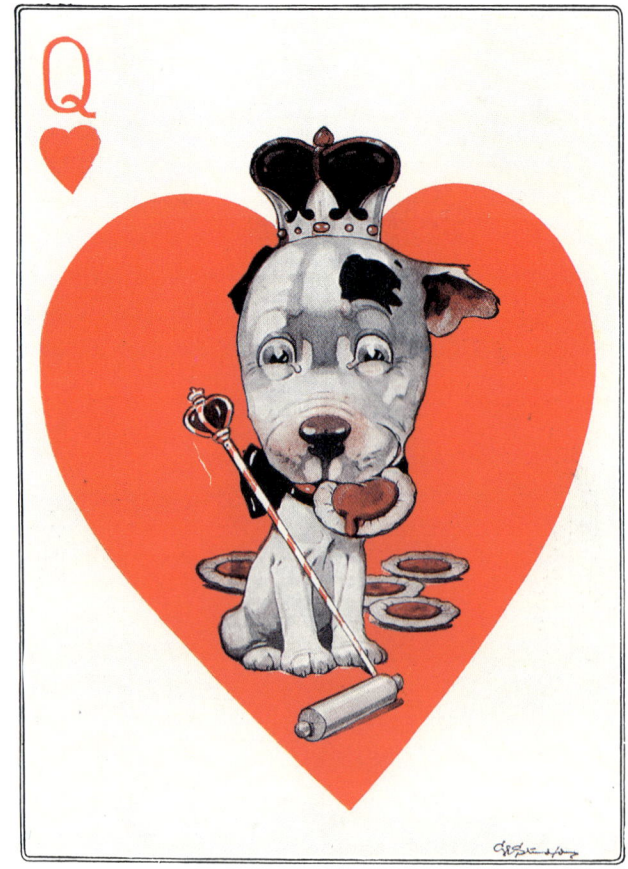

BY G. E. STUDDY

Here's the Queen of Hearts with the usual tarts, a girl we're unable to save
From certain disgrace (against King and Ace) when alone with a rascally knave
(Continued on page 58)

No. III.—The King of Diamonds

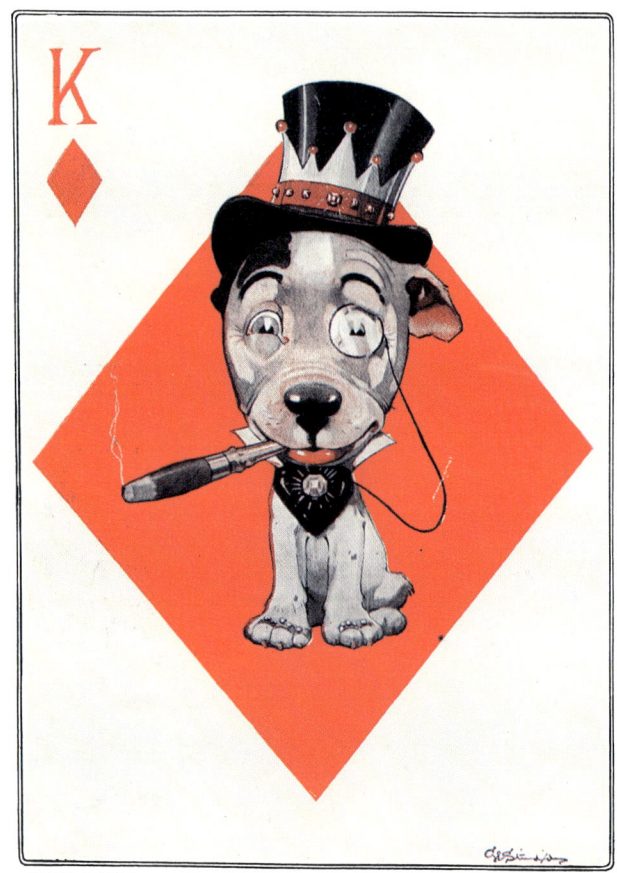

BY G. E. STUDDY

(Continued from page 51)
This Diamond King is having his fling away in a hotel at Brighton;
When allied with the Joker (and others) at Poker, he causes your courage to heighten

No. IV.—The Knave of Clubs

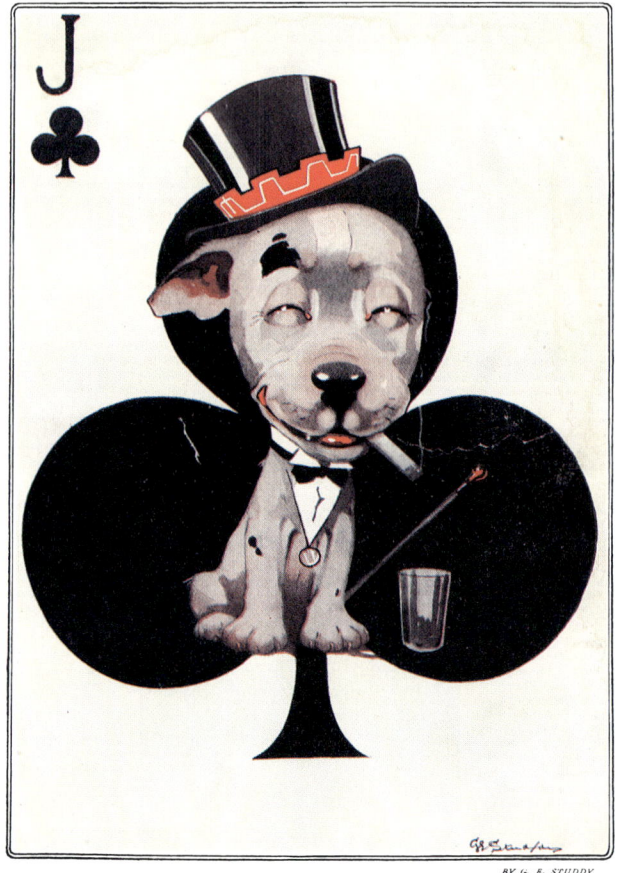

BY G. E. STUDDY

A Clubman gay is this Knave in play; he is mostly at home in Mayfair,
And with whiskey and "splash" he is cutting a dash, which he drinks without turning a hair!

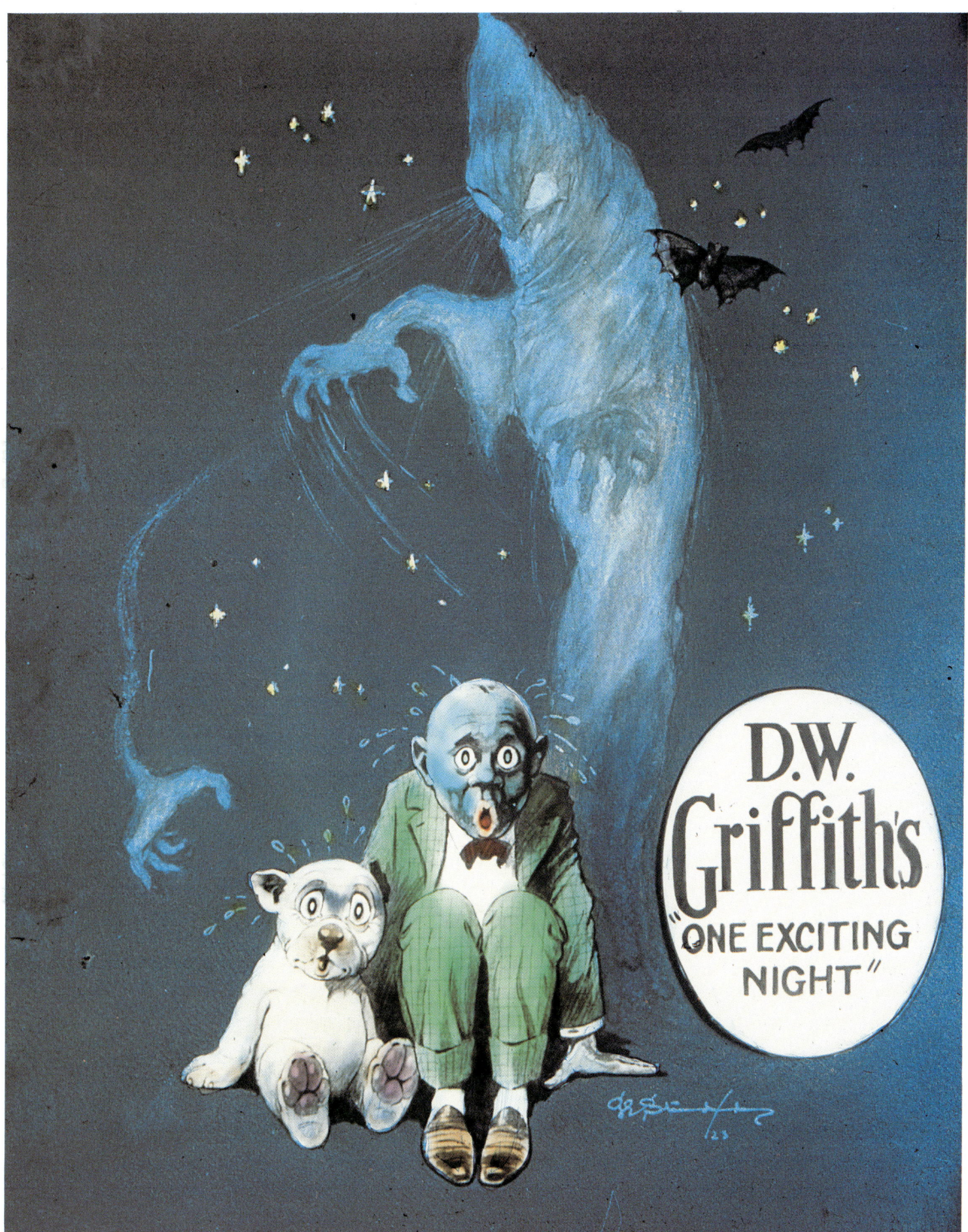

Bonzo was included in advertisements for this silent film. The illustration is taken from a glass magic lantern slide, used in cinemas as a forerunner of the modern 'trailer'.

Sunday evenings were open house at Philbeach Gardens and friends from all branches of the arts would pop in and take advantage of the standing invitation. Blanche used to provide a good cold buffet supper. Regular visitors included the artists Edgar Downes, John Hassall, Charles Heath-Robinson, Arthur Ferrier, David Ghilchick, H. M. Bateman and Alfred Leete. After supper and a few drinks had been consumed they would gather round the piano for some music. Blanche, a trained mezzo-contralto and violinist, would often get proceedings under way and encouraged Vivienne to accompany her on the piano. George was content to sit in the background, enjoying the music from a distance with his whisky and the hushed conversation of a friend or two.

In keeping with their status the Studdys were able to enjoy many of the comforts that George's hard work provided. In the 1920's the average family did not own a motor car but in 1922 the Studdys took delivery of their first car, a brand new Ruston and Hornsby with a soft hood that could be taken down in warm weather. Amid much excitement, George and the driver climbed into the front and with Blanche, Vivienne and her nurse occupying the rear seats, they set off for their first ride. Although Bonzo's widespread fame had brought many such material benefits, George refused to be carried away by his success and kept his feet firmly on the ground. Whenever possible he avoided personal publicity and preferred to use Bonzo as his mouthpiece. Despite this he was constantly barraged with requests from the media for interviews and although he often found them tiresome he accepted that they were a necessary evil in promoting his work. The public were always hungry for details of his working methods, lifestyle and, of course, there was the perpetual question of Bonzo's origins.

All the Studdy pets traditionally possessed four legs and a thick coat of fur. This changed when they inherited an African grey parrot said to be 100 years old. It had outlived most of their relatives in Devon and came to occupy the hallway of the Kensington house as a slightly less than welcome guest. Often, when the door bell rang, George would sigh "Not another bloody visitor" which was soon picked up by the parrot. Blanche became very skilled at quickly throwing a blanket over the cage to keep the bird quiet whenever anyone came to the door. Although Vivienne had always been surrounded by Bonzos she was also a fan of Pip, Squeak and Wilfred who appeared regularly in The Daily Mirror. They ran a club for their young readers with the grand name of 'The Wilfredian League of Gugnuncs'. Not only was Vivienne a Gugnunc but she also enrolled the parrot whose photograph appeared in the paper as the oldest living member. Eventually, after some two years had passed, Blanche tired

Bonzo Baffled

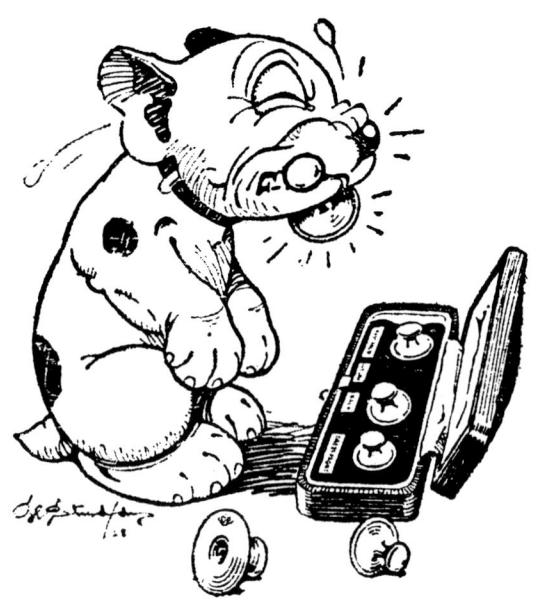

A Study by Studdy.

Emphasizing the supreme strength and rigidity of O.P. Studs; which features are attained by their one-piece, lighthouse-shaped construction and, further, are backed by a guarantee of FREE replacement if O.P. Studs should EVER break.

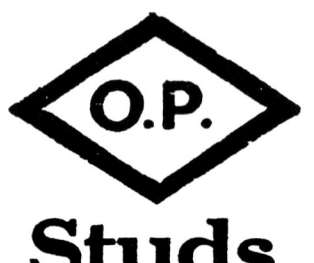

Studs

Handy doeskin Wallet or case of Six—one for each purpose—in 9-ct. Gold, 25/-; Wallet or case of Four, 15/6. Also sold separately.

From leading Jewellers.

See the O.P. mark on every stud. In case of difficulty apply direct.

G. H. Johnstone & Co. Ltd.,
Northampton Street, Birmingham.

STUDY YOUR STUDS

Advertisement from *Punch* 1929.

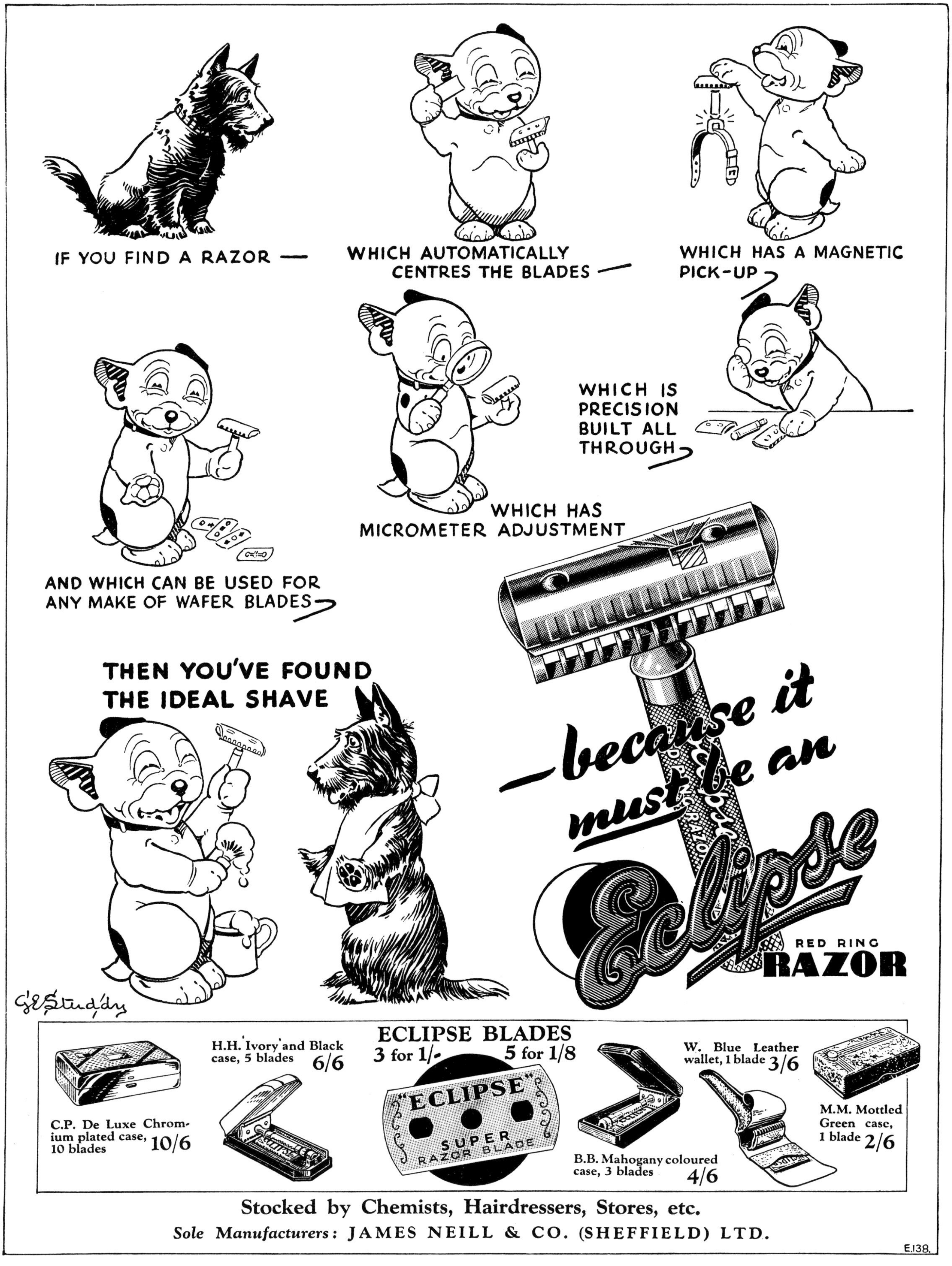
IF YOU FIND A RAZOR —
WHICH AUTOMATICALLY CENTRES THE BLADES —
WHICH HAS A MAGNETIC PICK-UP
AND WHICH CAN BE USED FOR ANY MAKE OF WAFER BLADES
WHICH HAS MICROMETER ADJUSTMENT
WHICH IS PRECISION BUILT ALL THROUGH
THEN YOU'VE FOUND THE IDEAL SHAVE
—because it must be an
Eclipse
RED RING RAZOR
G.E. Studdy
ECLIPSE BLADES
3 for 1/- 5 for 1/8
"ECLIPSE" SUPER RAZOR BLADE
C.P. De Luxe Chromium plated case, 10 blades 10/6
H.H. 'Ivory' and Black case, 5 blades 6/6
B.B. Mahogany coloured case, 3 blades 4/6
W. Blue Leather wallet, 1 blade 3/6
M.M. Mottled Green case, 1 blade 2/6
Stocked by Chemists, Hairdressers, Stores, etc.
Sole Manufacturers: JAMES NEILL & CO. (SHEFFIELD) LTD.
E.138.

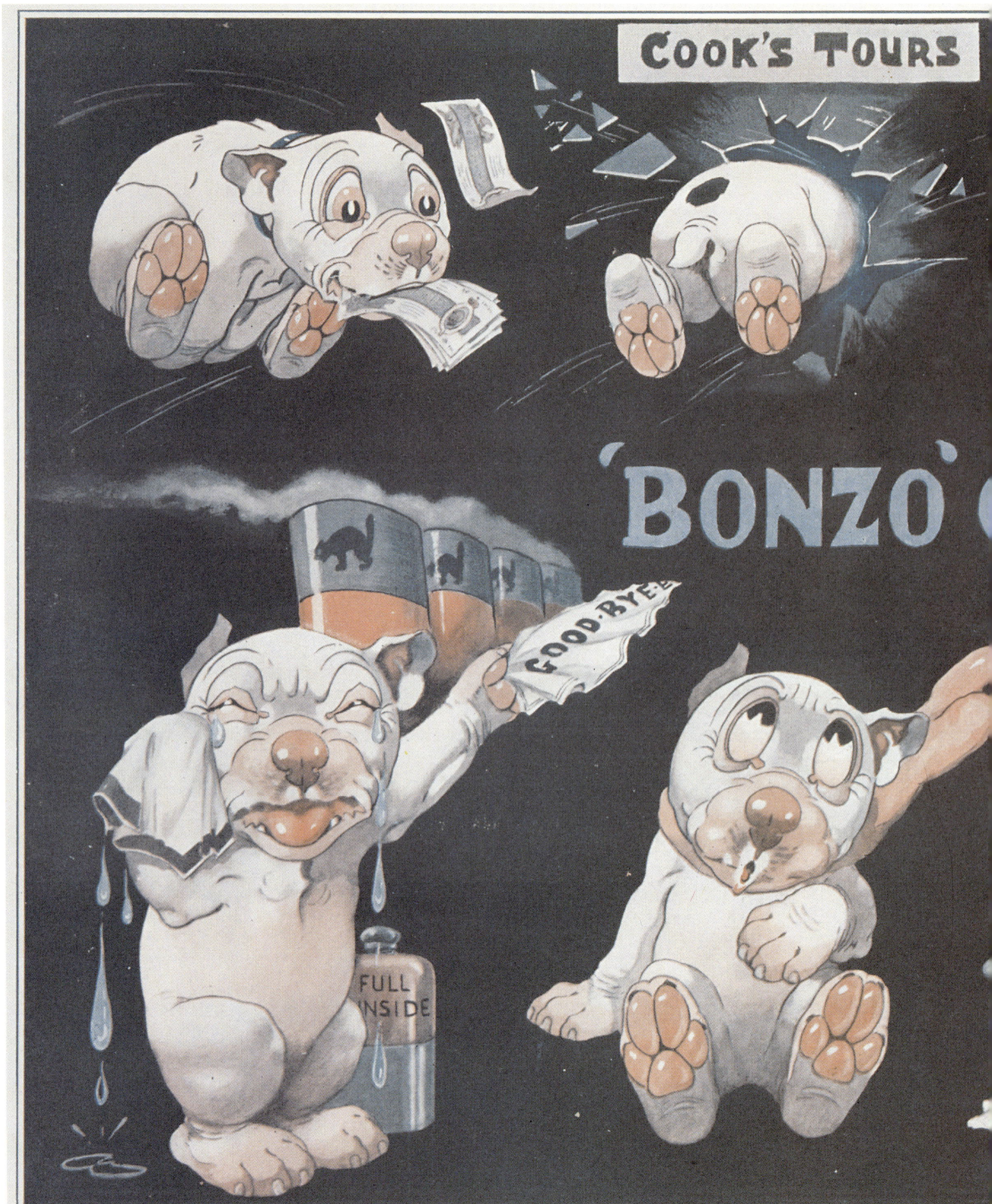

BONZO A STAR TURN AGAIN—IN "FROM DOVER STREET

Bonzo, "The Sketch" favourite, is one of the stars who are seen in the latest Cochran revue, "From Dover Street to Dixie," produced last week at the London Pavilion. He appears on a curtain illustrating his journey (unaccompanied by the Bonzolines) from England to America. The first part of the revue is set in England; but in the latter half, the company is transported to America, so the Studdy Curtain illustrates the

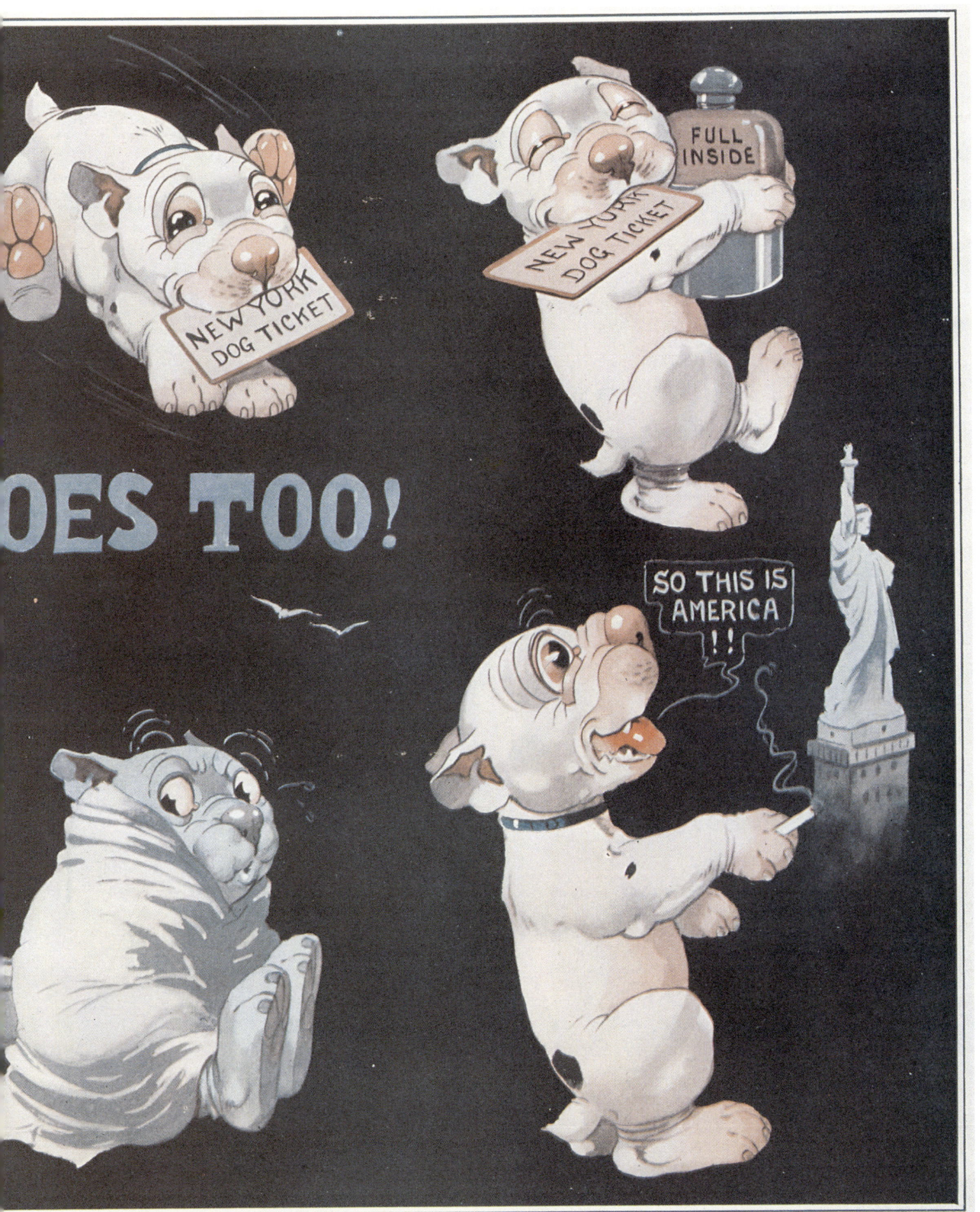

"DIXIE": THE STUDDY CURTAIN AT THE LONDON PAVILION.

of the bird and it was passed on to yet another unsuspecting distant relative.

Bonzo's name was adopted by a large proportion of the nation's canine population, but he also started appearing in slightly more unusual guises. The winners of the relay contest in the Air Forces Annual Pageant at Hendon were a team from Halton, flying three planes called Bonzo, Bonzolean and Bonzolets.

In the early nineteen twenties The Sketch brought out a series of six portfolios of Bonzo cartoons, cleverly re-using the printing plates that had been made for the weekly illustrations. The first of these, 'The Studdy Dogs Portfolio', appeared in 1922 and contained fifteen colour plates and a specially designed title page and cover. It cost two shillings (10p). Further portfolios were brought out periodically until 1925 when 'Bonzo's Star Turns' completed the set. This had only eight plates but they were loosely mounted on brown art paper and were eminently suitable for framing. By this time the cost had risen to three shillings and sixpence (17½p).

1923 marked Bonzo's stage debut in Jack Buchanan's production of 'Battling Butler' at the Adelphi Theatre, soon to be followed by 'From Dover Street to Dixie' at the London Pavillion. George designed the stage curtain for the latter, depicting Bonzo's journey from England to the

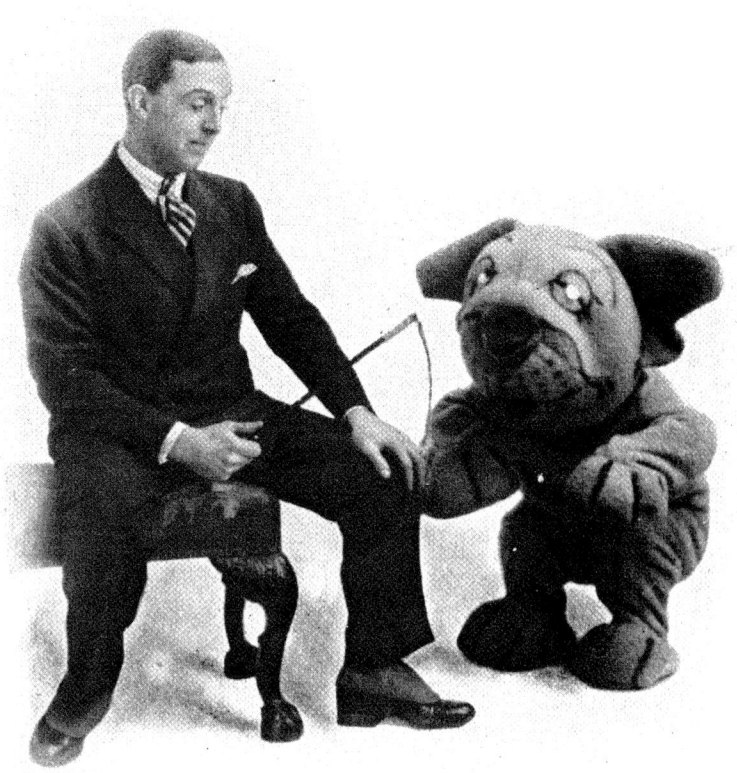

MR. LUPINO LANE TREATS HIS BONZO FIRMLY! THE PEKOE OF THE BIRMINGHAM "ALADDIN," AND MR. GEORGE ATTERBURY AS HIS STUDDY DOG.

United States accompanied by 'The Bonzolines'. George Atterbury, dressed in a velvet dog costume, played the part of Bonzo in both productions. He also appeared in the part in a Christmas pantomime at Birmingham alongside Lupino Lane as Pekoe. The following spring, Atterbury as Bonzo joined Lee White at the Queen's Theatre, London, in a revue entitled 'Come In'. The show was unfortunately very badly received by critics and public alike and was greeted with almost as much booing as applause. Bonzo appeared in only one number in the show and this was the only item which escaped a universal panning. One reviewer wrote: "If more of the show had been up to the standard of Miss Lee White's Bonzo song, it could have been saved." This was no setback to Bonzo who went on stage again that Christmas in 'The Sleeping Beauty', a pantomime at the Lyceum Theatre. The show was a great success with Eric Bock playing the part of Bonzo.

George's work still appeared regularly on the London art gallery circuit in the company of his illustrious circle of friends and contemporaries. In March 1923 he exhibited several works at The Walker Gallery, including a painting of three rather drunken rodents propped against an upturned and empty glass. It was appropriately captioned "Three Blind Mice" and was well received by the public. When, at the private view, Blanche was asked from where he found his models, she smiled wickedly and replied "Ah! Ask the cat".

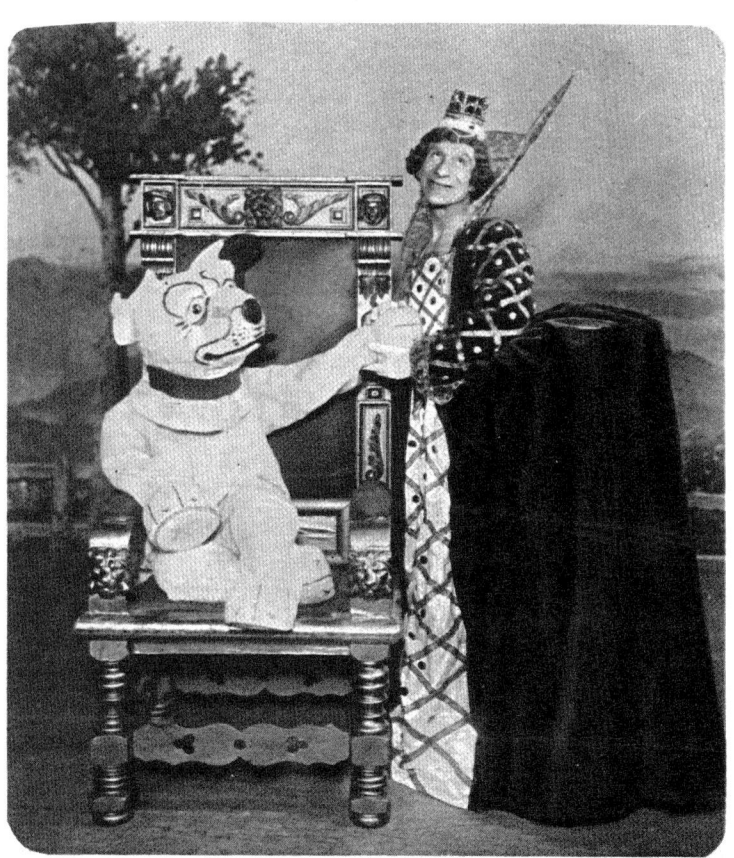

BONZO, THE DOG (ERIC BOCK), IN "THE SLEEPING BEAUTY," THE PANTOMIME AT THE LYCEUM: A WORLD-FAMOUS "SKETCH" FRIEND BEING CARESSED BY QUEEN GUINEVERE

PLAYS OF THE MOMENT · 1923

No. XXX. "Battling Butler" (Plus Bonzo).

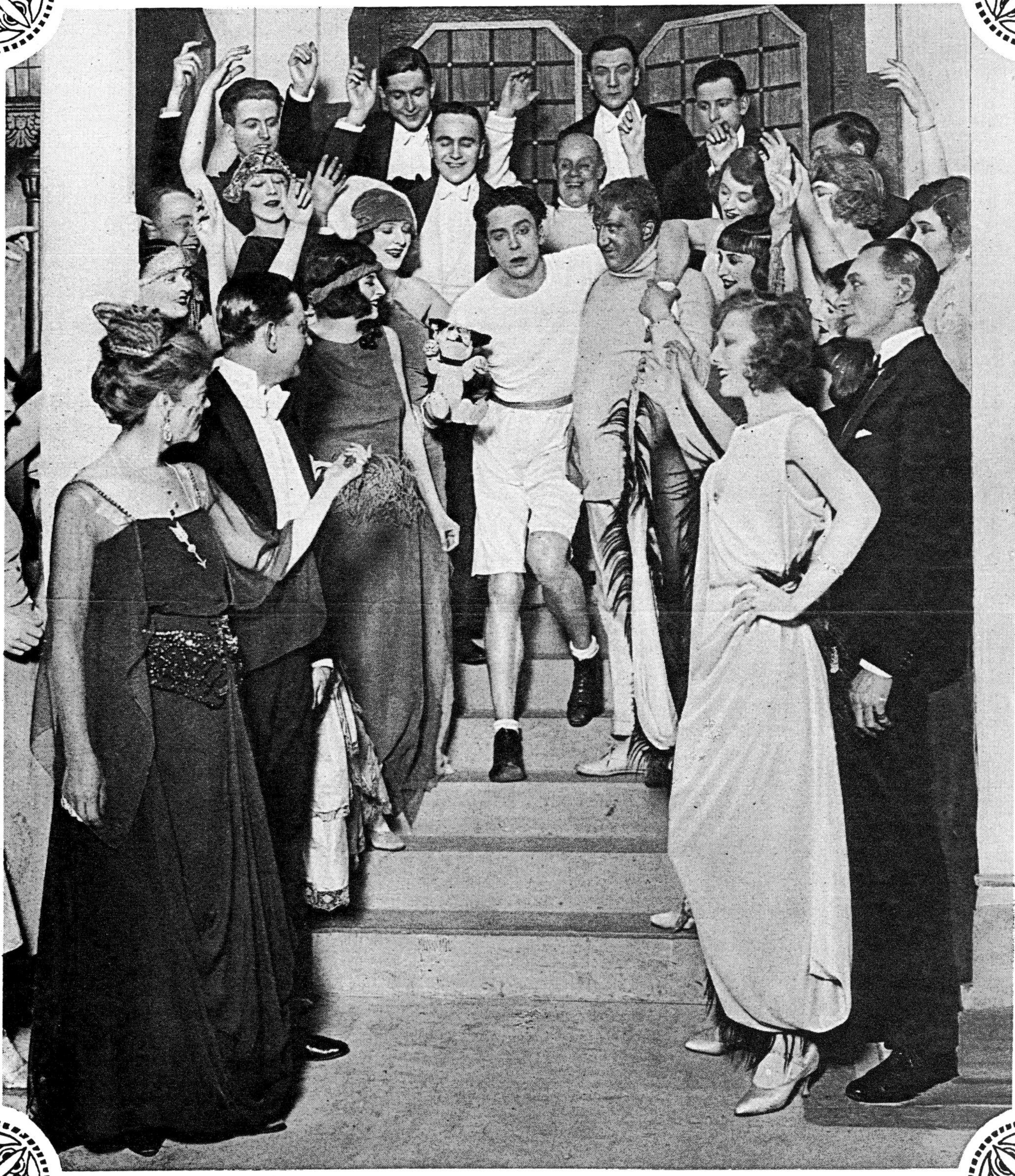

BATTLING BUTLER FINDS THAT BONZO BRINGS HIM GOOD LUCK: MR. JACK BUCHANAN (CENTRE) WITH MISS SYDNEY FAIRBROTHER (LEFT), AND MISS PHYLLIS TITMUSS (RIGHT).

"Battling Butler," which has now moved to the Adelphi, is one of the most entertaining productions imaginable. Alfred Butler has an elderly wife—played to perfection by Miss Sydney Fairbrother—and in order to win himself a little freedom from home ties, he pretends to be Battling Butler, the professional boxer. He keeps up the deception even when he has to face the prospect of a real entry into the ring; but all is well in the end, for with the help of lucky Bonzo, of "The Sketch," he gets the credit of winning the fight without having to knock out an opponent.

Photograph by Stage Photo. Co.

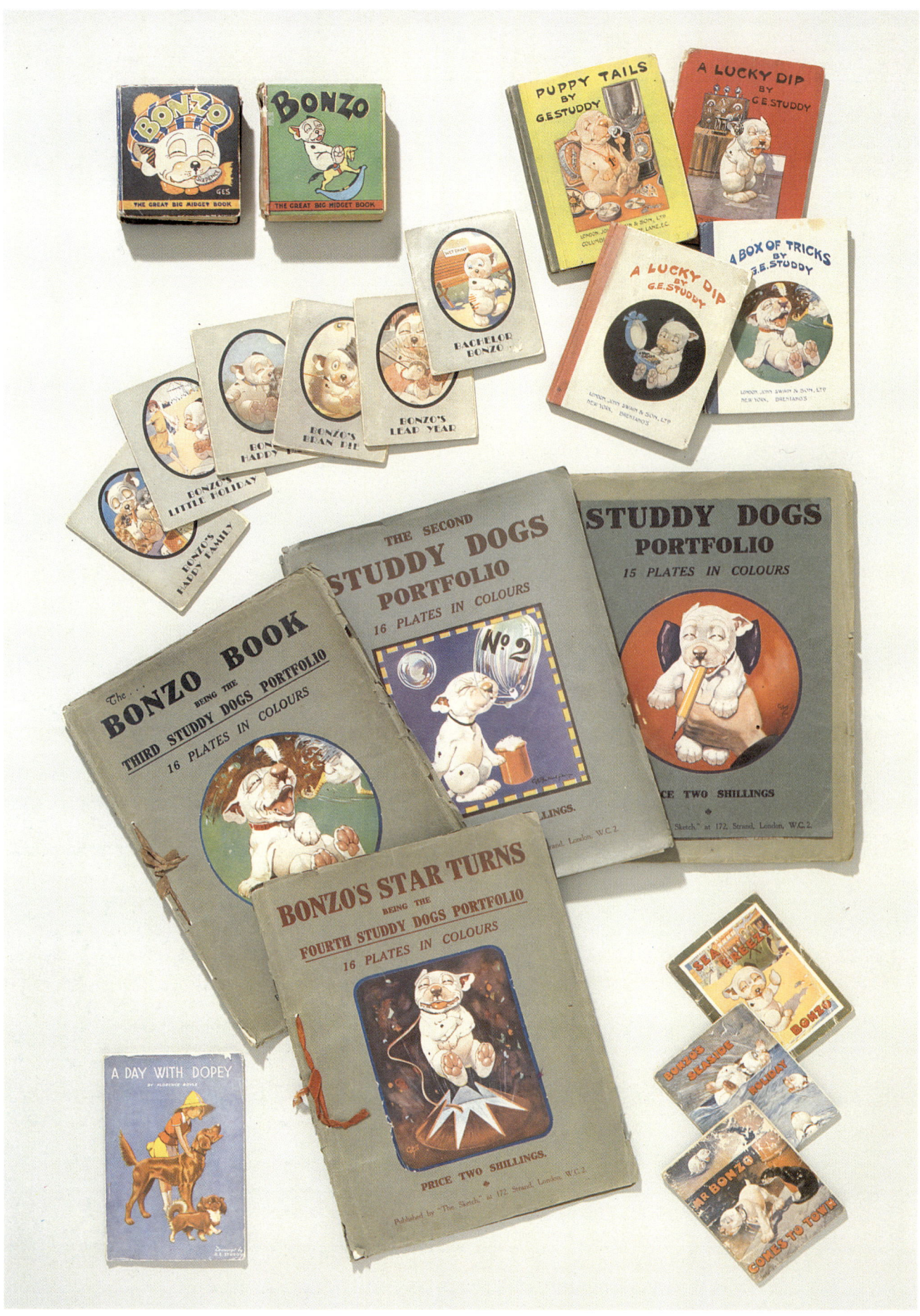

Some of the small Bonzo pocket books including two aptly named *Great Big Midget Books*. In most cases the illustrations were taken from previously published post cards or book plates. Four of the six *Sketch* portfolios are shown each with up to fifteen colour prints re-using the plates made for the weekly Bonzo cartoon in the magazine. Only the title page was specially drawn for each issue.

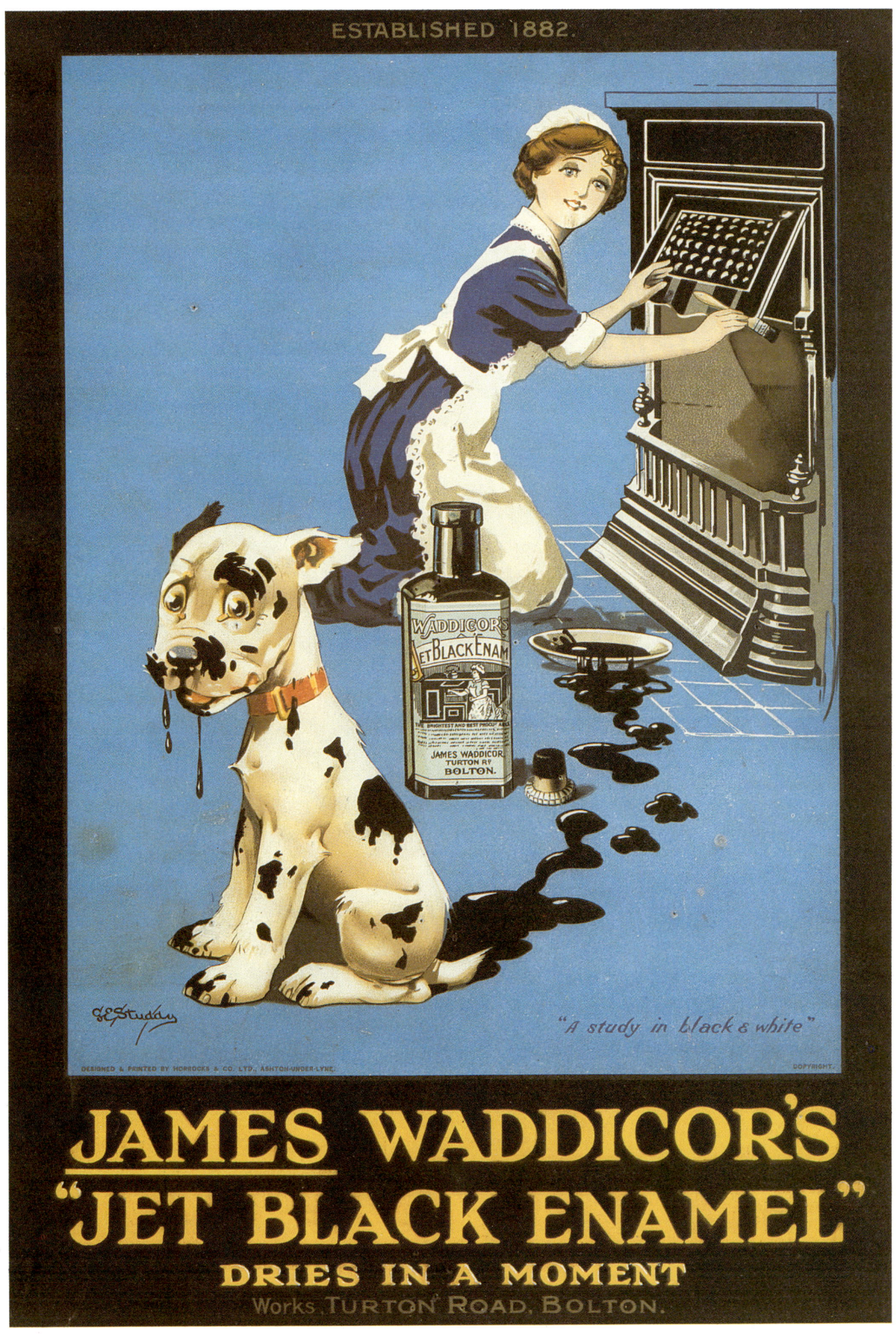

A shop display card c. 1920 with an early Studdy dog getting into the kind of mess that so often typified Bonzo's behaviour.

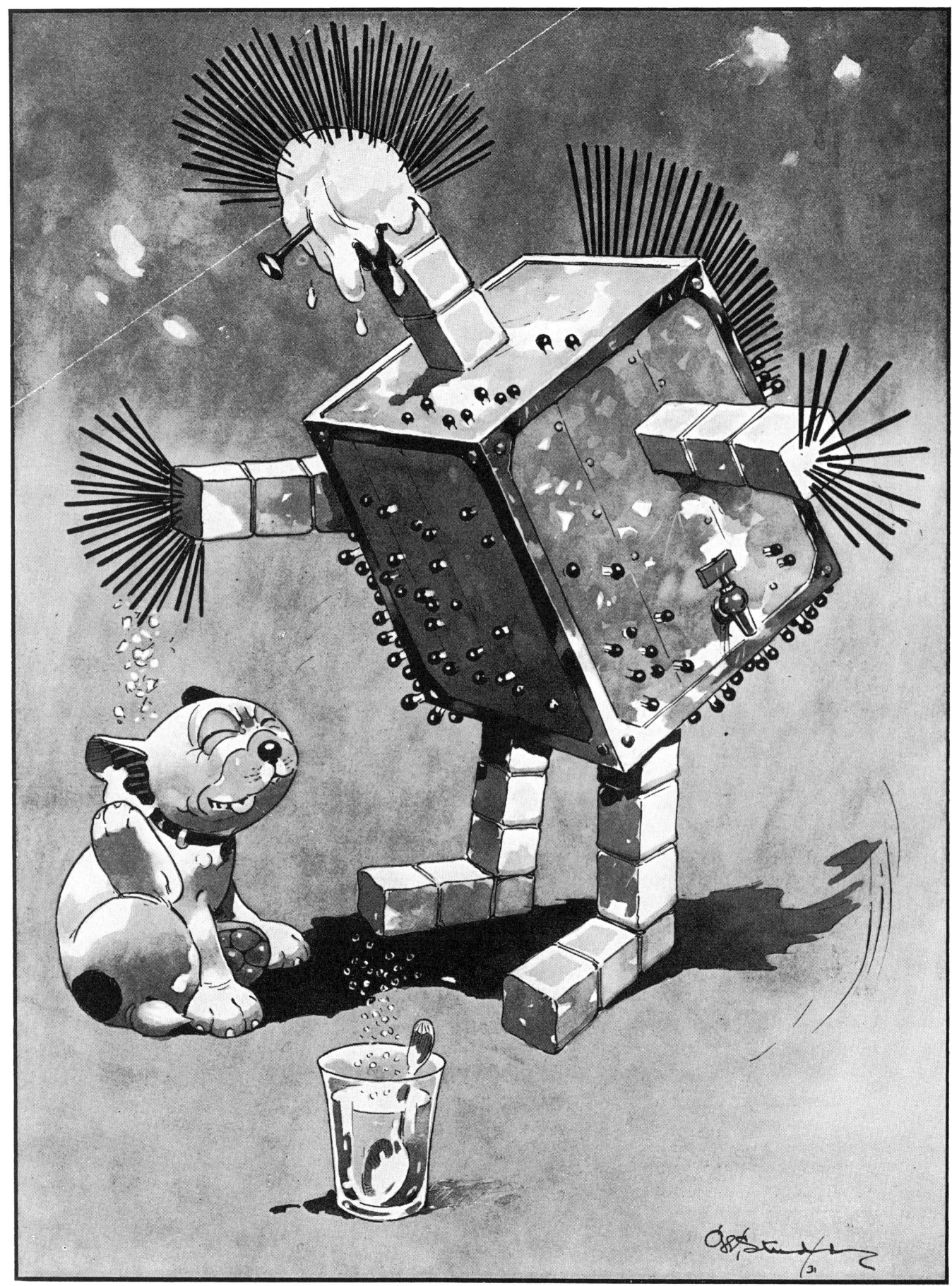

THE "FIVE-SHILLING MAN" AS VISUALISED BY G. E. STUDDY

The following, according to Dr. Thomas Lawson, are all the ingredients of the body of an average man of 10 stone:— Ten gallons of water; enough fat for seven bars of soap; carbon for 9,000 lead pencils; phosphorus for 2,200 match heads; magnesium for one dose of salts; iron for one medium-sized nail; lime enough to whitewash a chicken coop; and enough sulphur to rid a dog of fleas. And the lot can be bought for five shillings!

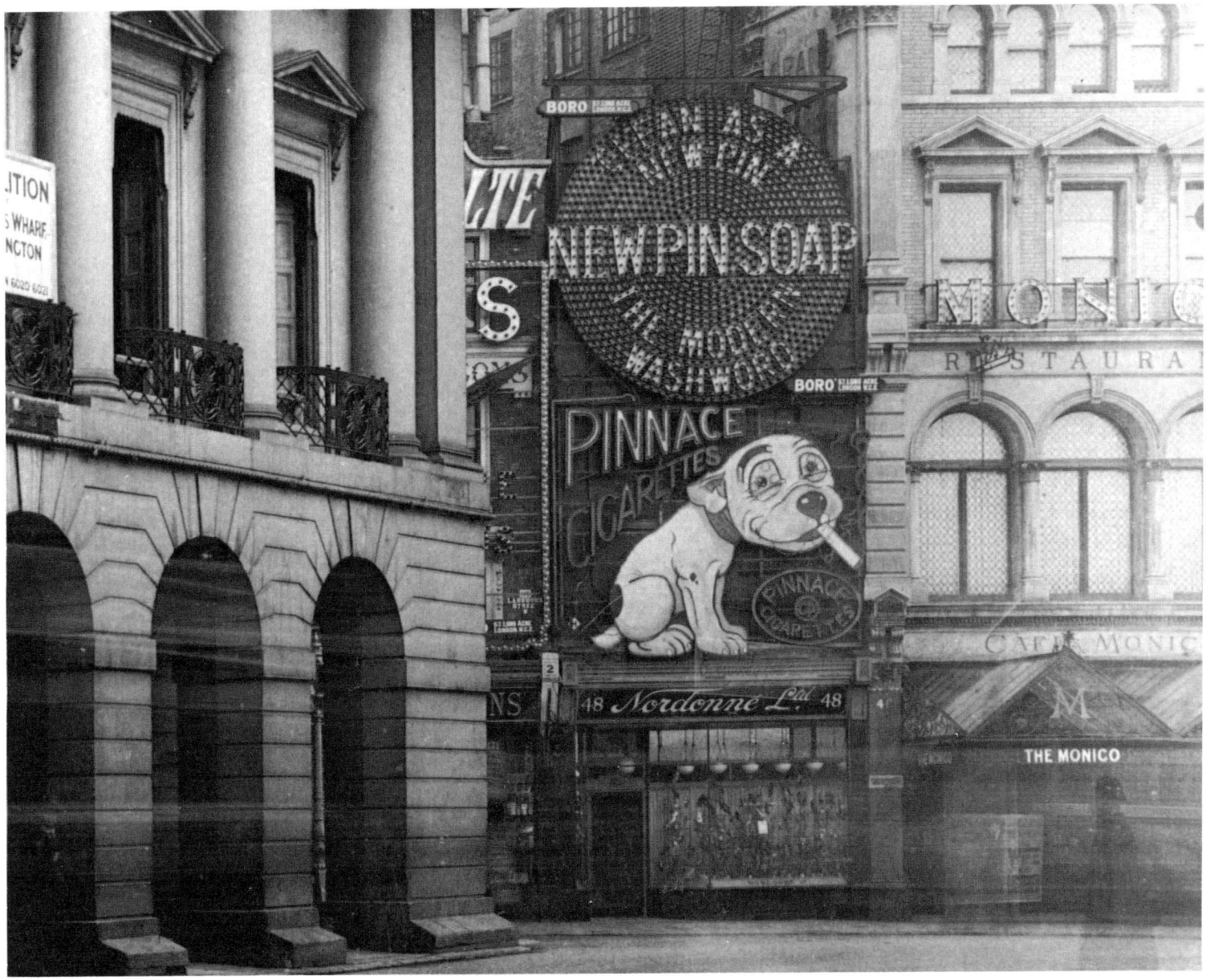

Bonzo as he appeared in Piccadilly Circus c. 1925. He looked down from the junction of Regent Street and Glasshouse Street on the north side of the Circus.

Bonzo was featured among the first neon signs put up in Piccadilly Circus. When the area was developed in 1924, the press were not slow to boast that London now had an answer to New York's Times Square. Bonzo was very much in the thick of it: a gigantic neon likeness twitched its ears, and rolled its eyes, while smoke curled slowly upwards as the dog puffed on his 'Pinnace' cigarette. Images of Bonzo were to be found everywhere; in addition to the postcards and books, new areas of merchandising had opened up. There were glass perfume bottles and inkwells, china egg cups, jugs, pots, ashtray and condiment sets. At the top end of the market there were porcelain Bonzos from both the Royal Doulton and Royal Worcester factories. Spears of Enfield produced several games based on Bonzo. Their catalogue for 1930 included 'Ring Bonzo', 'Bobby Bonzo', 'Bonnie McBonzo' and 'Bonzo's Bone', all of which involved throwing a set of rings at a model cut-out of Bonzo or over metal hooks. There was also 'The Bonzo Chase' which was based on the old game of snakes and ladders. They were priced from 3/7½p right up to 18/- for the de-luxe version of 'The Bonzo Chase'. Jig-saws were another way of reproducing The Sketch illustrations and many different designs on plywood were produced. There were also several velvet toys brought on to the market, mostly by Chad Valley but also by Deans Rag Book Company. At Christmas they lined the shelves of nearly every toy shop in the land. Harrods put on a particularly fine display and the Bonzo toys were only rivalled by those of the other main animal character of the time, Felix the Cat.

Having achieved fame on the stage, Bonzo moved to the cinema screen with a series of twenty six animated cartoon

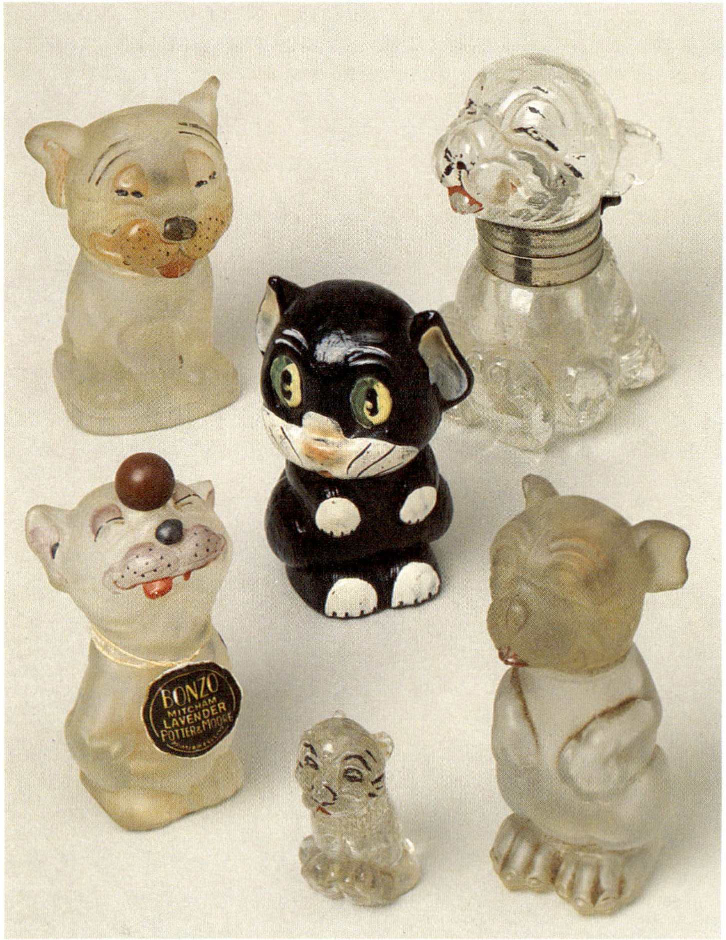
BONZO
MITCHAM
LAVENDER
POTTER & MOORE

Four scent bottles, three of Bonzo and one of Ooloo. The bottom left still has it's original label from Potter and Moore and cost 1/6d. Top right is an ink well, the hinged head forming the cover. In the foreground is a small solid glass version.

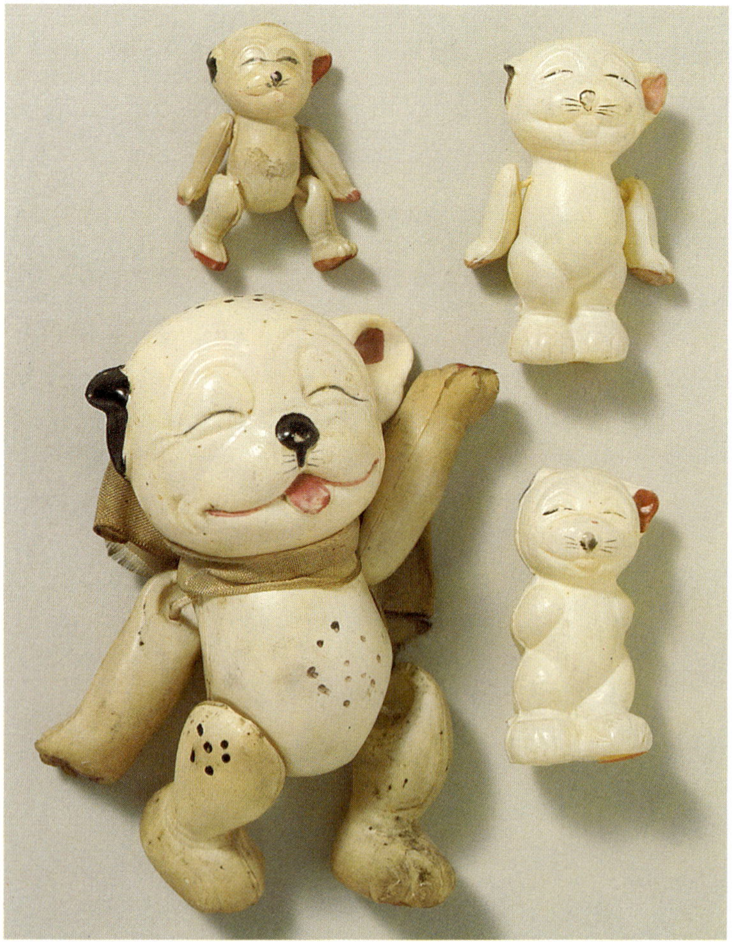

Celluloid Bonzos of Japanese origin. They are very light and fragile and were possibly used as novelties in Christmas crackers, the smallest 1 inch high.

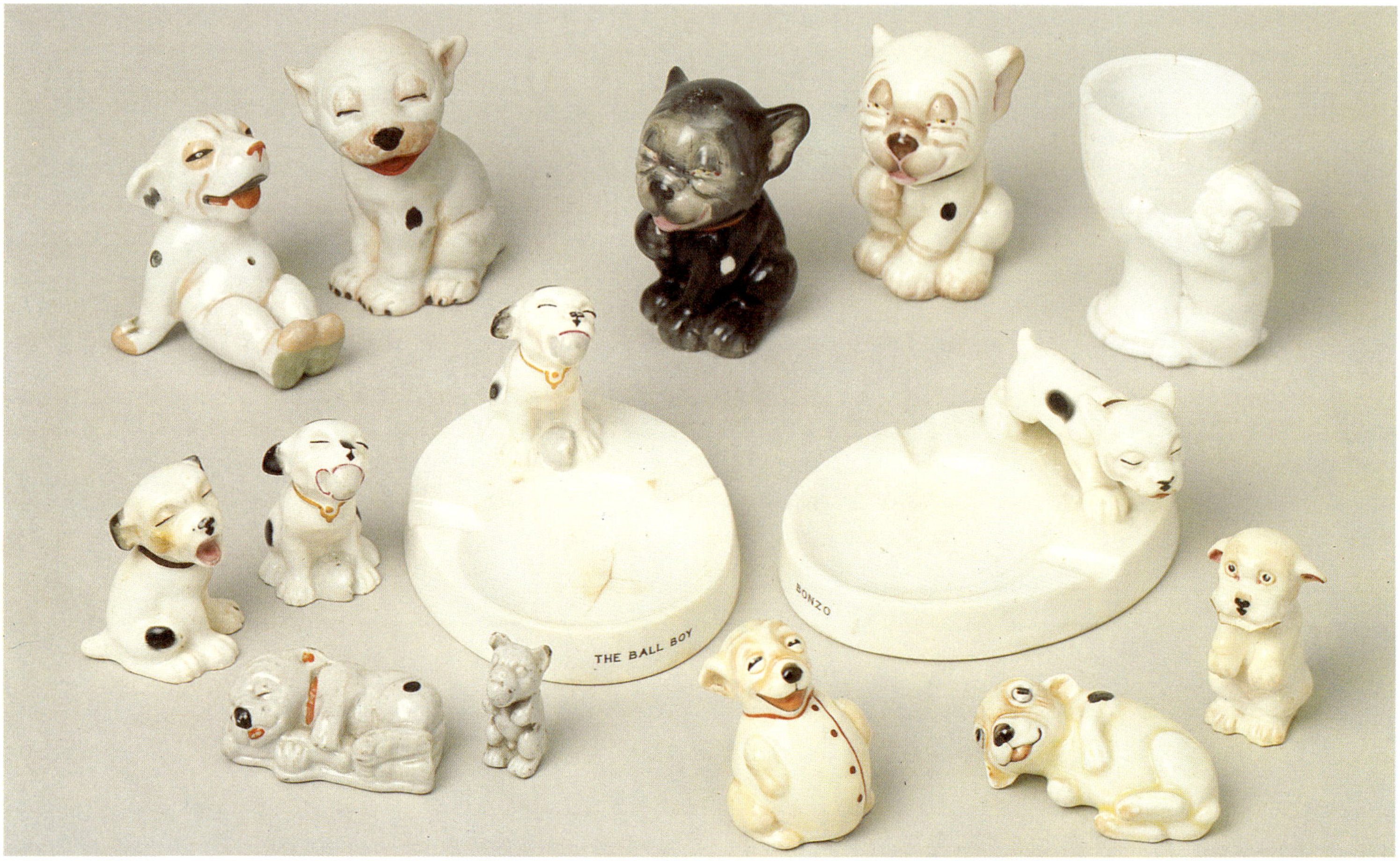
THE BALL BOY
BONZO

A collection of china Bonzos. Although many were sold cheaply these were of high quality. The black and white pair at the top are Royal Worcester who also made a similar version for use as a pepper pot. The central group, including the two ashtrays, were produced by Grafton China and marked *Swains Studdy Series*, based on three of the R.P.S. Series post card illustrations. In the right foreground the laughing dog and the one lying down are by Royal Doulton. The egg cup at the back is of opaque white glass.

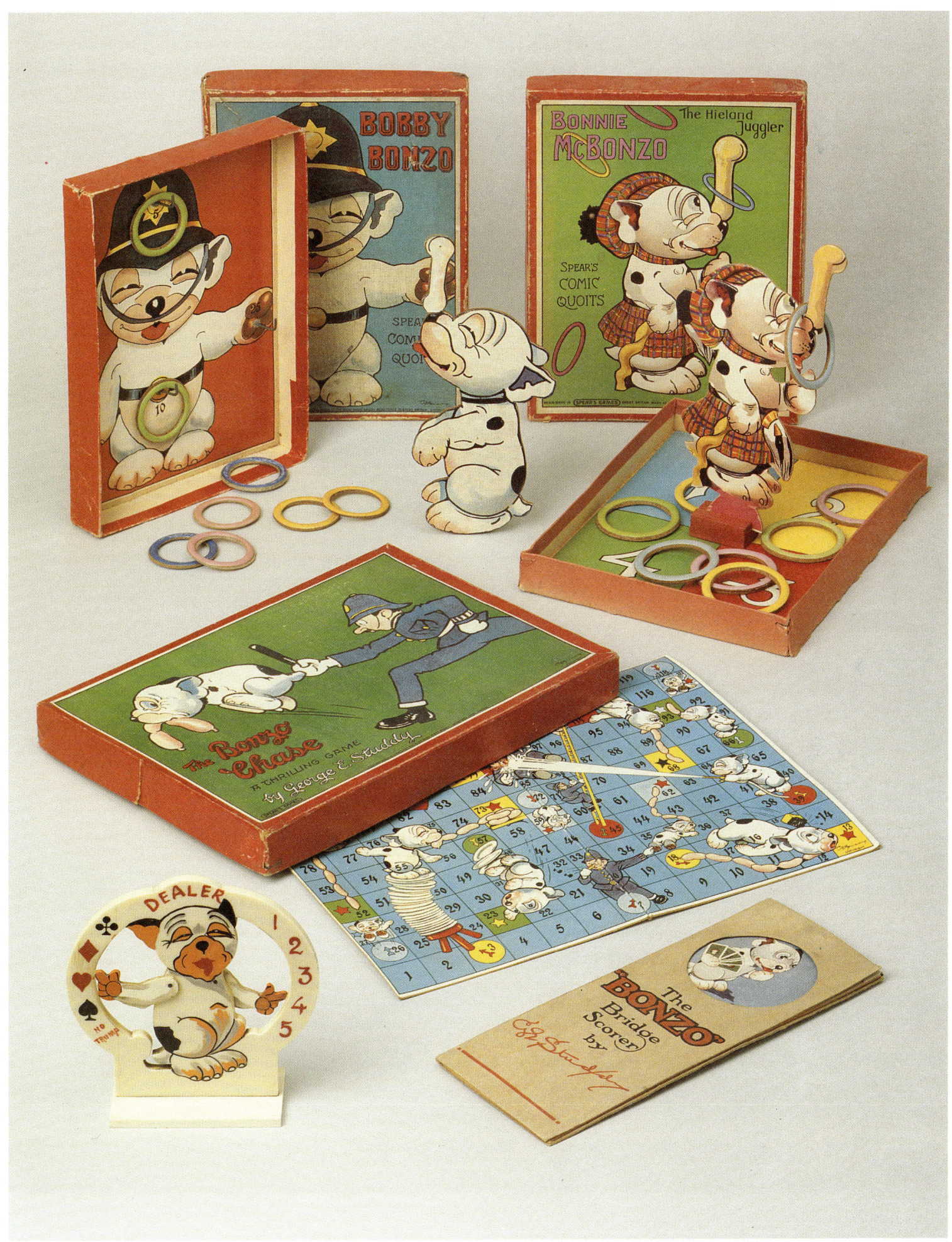

These games were licensed during the late 1920's and early 1930's. Those at the top were made by *Spears Games* including *The Bonzo Chase* board game based on *Snakes and Ladders* which is reproduced as the end papers of this book. In the foreground are a Bridge scoring pad and a Trump indicator.

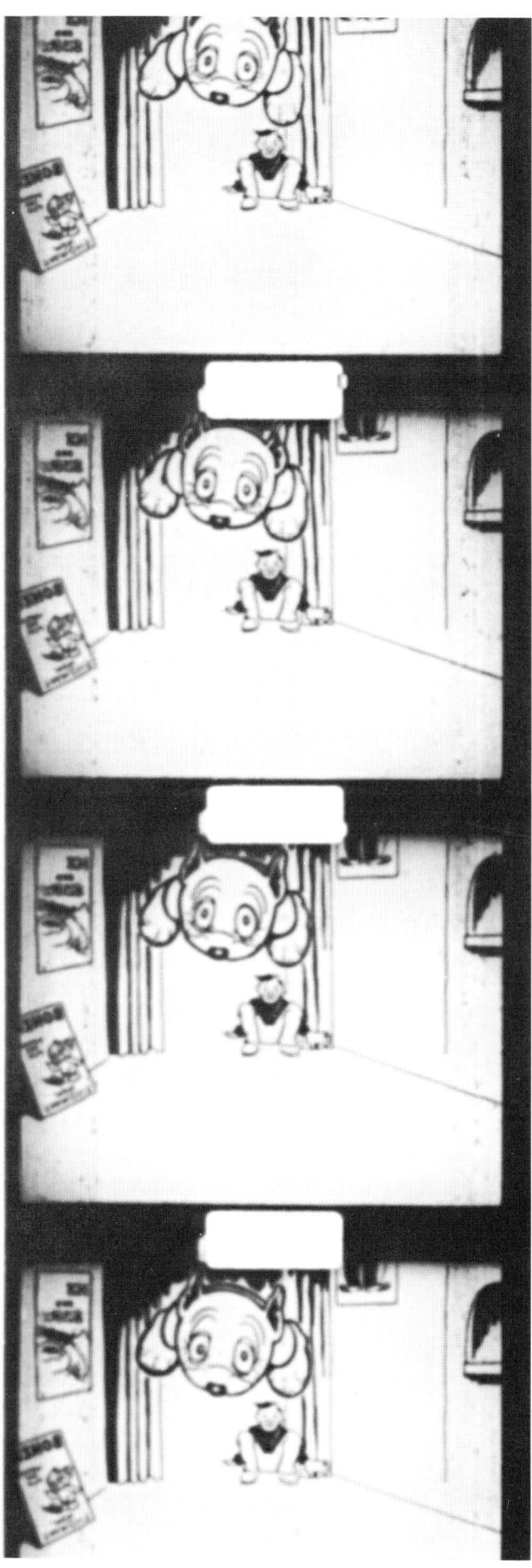

Frames from the 9.5mm silent home movie version of *Tally Ho Bonzo*. It ran for 8 minutes and was released by *Pathescope*.

films issued under the general title of 'Bonzoland'. George, with ten other artists under his direction, worked hard to create the thousands of drawings that were needed to make up each film. Produced by William Ward for New Era Films the cartoons were between eight and twelve minutes long. At roughly the same time Pathe Freres Cinema Ltd. were about to release films about a character called 'Pongo the Pup'. George was afraid that the public might mistake Pongo for Bonzo, so he filed an application in the High Court for an injunction restraining Pathe from advertising or exhibiting the films. After a lengthy, legal battle, Mr. Justice Talbot threw out the application on the grounds that he could not understand why people reading an advertisment for Pongo should expect to see Bonzo. He added, perhaps with some irritation, that he thought that Bonzo had received more publicity from the case than could possibly have been otherwise expected, and should be grateful

The earliest film starring Bonzo, entitled 'A Sausage Snatching Sensation', was first shown at the premiere of 'Zeebrugge' on Tuesday 14th October, 1924, at the Marble Arch Pavilion. It was an historic occasion in more ways than one. The premiere was attended by King George V and Queen Mary, the first time that a reigning sovereign had watched a film performance in a public cinema. The press gave the cartoon as many rave reviews as the main feature and the public could hardly wait for the film to be distributed. America led the world in animated films at that time, particularly with Felix the Cat. European animation was comparatively crude, and very few films were exported due to their rather primitive techniques. With the arrival of Bonzo the situation changed almost overnight.

After the first screening, George had reluctantly agreed to give a talk to the assembled audience. He still felt awkward in such situations but realised that it was necessary for the sake of publicity for the films. A reporter from the Daily Sketch interviewed him at home on the Sunday prior to the premiere, when his anxiety and dread of publicity were beginning to overwhelm him.

'The author of Bonzo appeared to be in the depths of despondency when I called at his flat late on Sunday night to find out the latest stop press development regarding his prodigy. "Oh, Bonzo's alright bless his baby heart" he said with a twisted smile. "He'll face the public without a tremor as you will see. It's myself I'm thinking of." "Yourself? But why to goodness....." "Can't you understand? Can't you put yourself in my place? How slow you journalists are on the uptake." And he handed me a fat corona. "All these years Bonzo has just been Bonzo – a silly, portly puppy, behaving or misbehaving himself in some perfectly idiotic manner just for the moment, but leaving it at that, if you can follow what I mean, whereas on

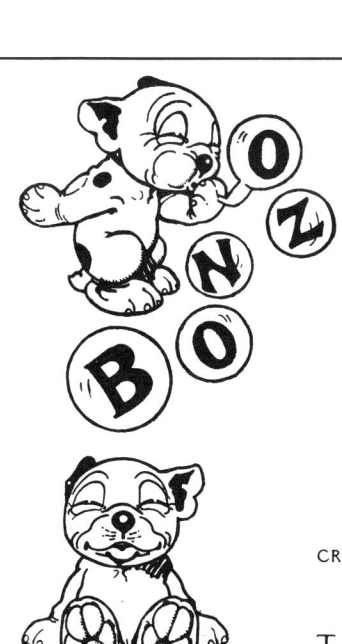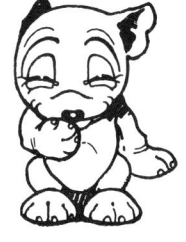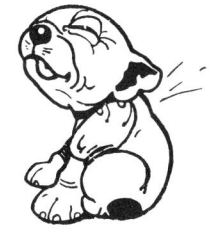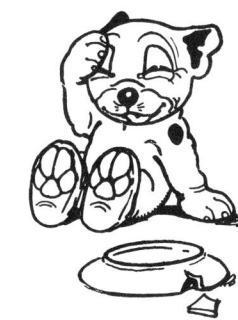

BONZO

CREATED, DRAWN, AND PERSONALLY SUPERVISED

BY

THE WORLD-FAMOUS ARTIST

G. E. STUDDY

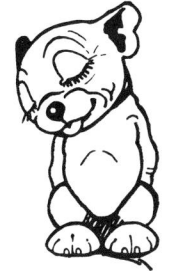 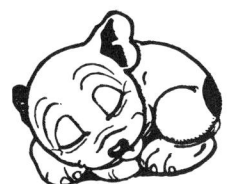

Produced by

W. A. WARD

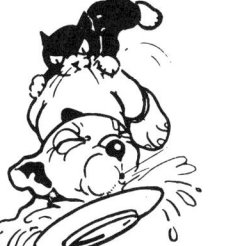 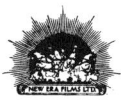

Controlled throughout the World by

NEW ERA FILMS, LTD.

26/27, Darblay Street
Wardour Street
London, W.1

Telephone: REGENT 5319.   Telegrams: NURAFILIM, WESDO, LONDON.

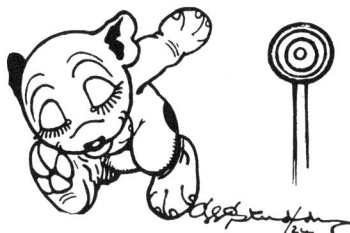 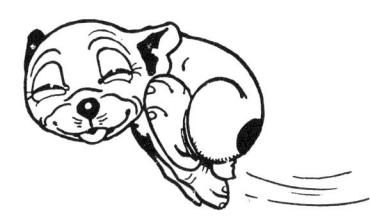 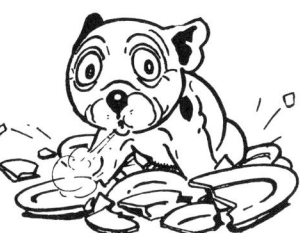

NEW ERA FILMS LTD., take great pride in presenting BONZO to the trade. An introduction to this screamingly funny little chap and his creator, Mr. G. E. Studdy, would be superfluous, as their names are world-famous, but in their screen partnership it will be recognised at once that they have achieved a great deal more than the important fact that they have added very considerably to the gaiety of the world.

To date it has not been found possible to produce animated cartoons in this country on a technical level with those emanating from the United States, but in BONZO it will be found that a completely new standard in this highly technical work has been established, which will be accepted as the world's pattern.

The drawings in themselves are a work of art, and animation never before attempted has been produced to perfection. The scenarios, too, which are the work of Mr. Studdy, are the essence of comedy, and the character is, without doubt, the most humorous and lovable little fellow the screen has ever known.

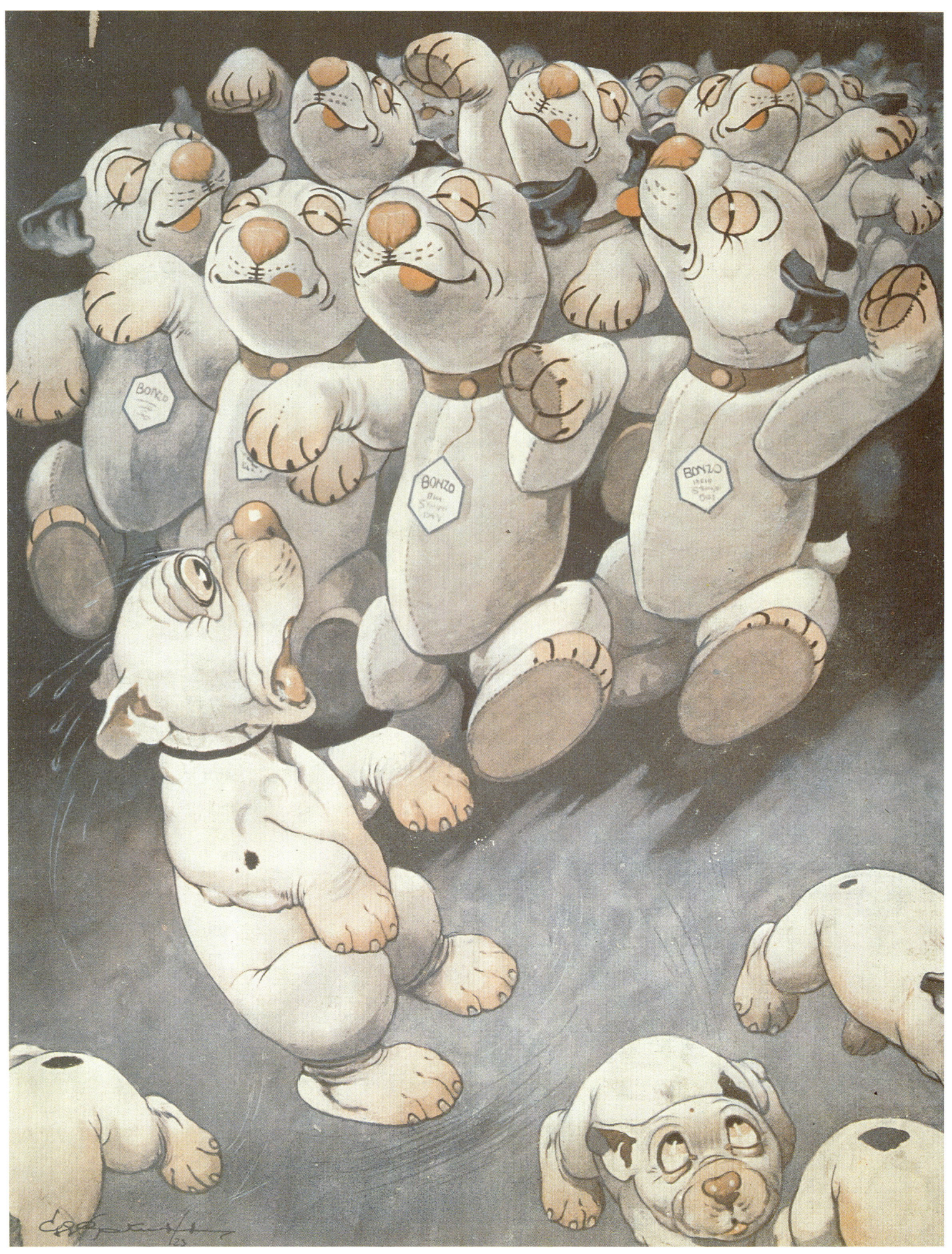

WHO SAID "ROBOTS"?
(Bonzo is obsessed by this season's toy.)

Bonzo soft toys are subtly promoted in this cartoon from *The Sketch* 20th June 1923.

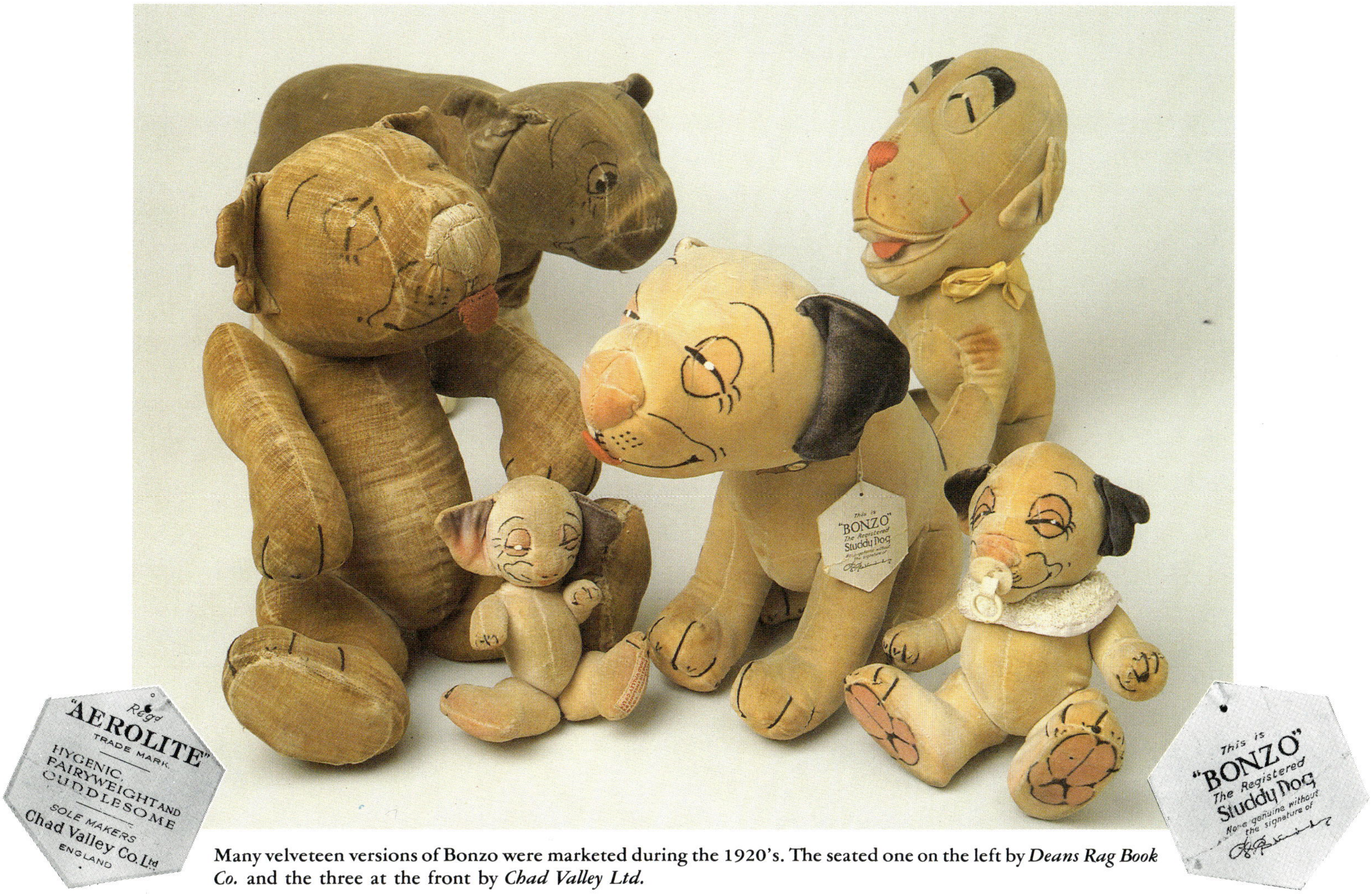

Many velveteen versions of Bonzo were marketed during the 1920's. The seated one on the left by *Deans Rag Book Co.* and the three at the front by *Chad Valley Ltd.*

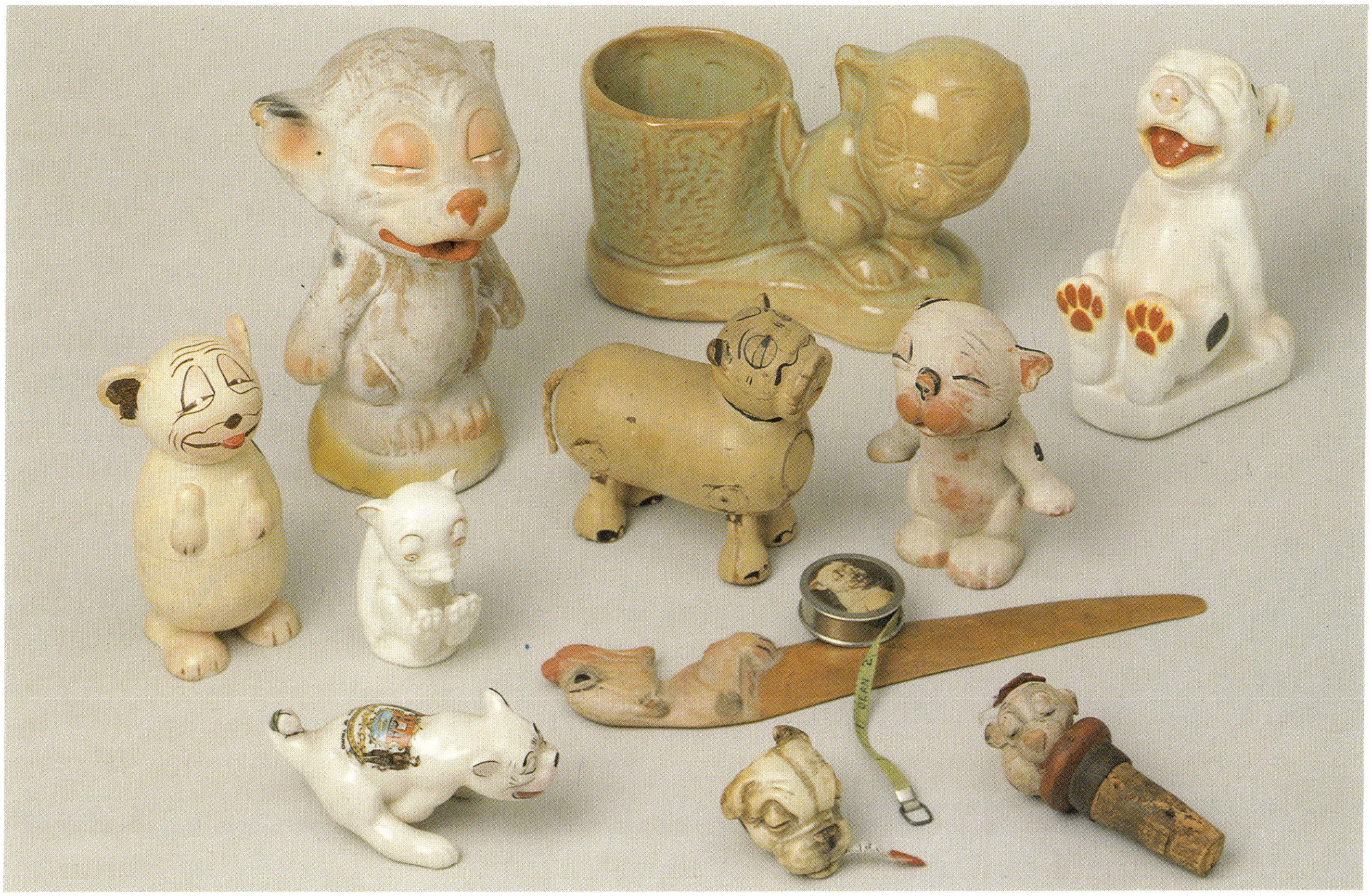

A mixed selection of Bonzo collectables including a bottle stopper, two tape measures and a paper knife. The two crested china dogs are based on Studdy dogs, the running one with the inscription 'When you're on to a good thing stick to it' and a painted bee on its tail. The strange dog in the centre is made of wood and walks when placed on a slope. To his right the Bonzo is made of rubber and squeaked when pressed.

41

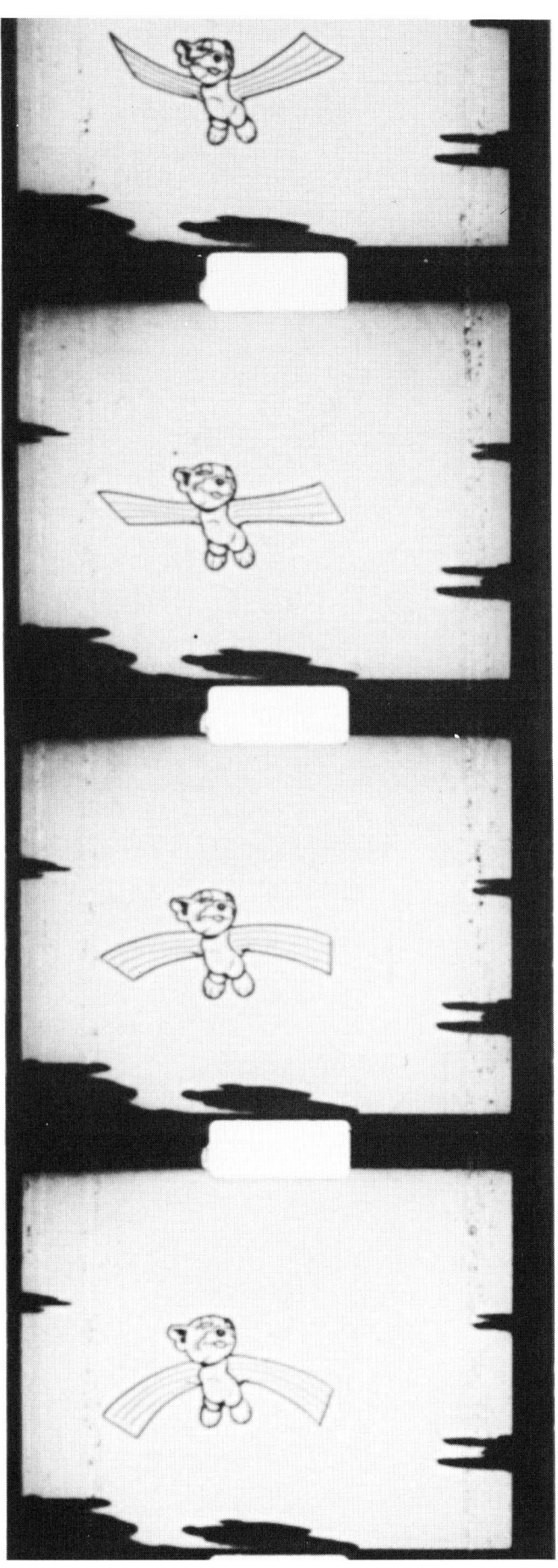

A strip from the 9.5mm film *Bonzo the Traveller*. It ran for 8 minutes in the cinema, but for the home movie market another 4 minutes from *Polar Bonzo* were added.

Tuesday . . . . . ." "Yes? On Tuesday?" "Well on Tuesday he won't leave it at that at all. He's got to carry on for one thousand feet of film . . . . . ". "One thousand Bonzo feet?" "Oh for heavens sake don't perpetrate that hoary joke again – it's been loosed off in this room a dozen times at least," he exclaimed. "Also for the same sake don't ask me what first made me think of Bonzo, or what breed of dog he is supposed to be, or whether he just came into or out of my head, because I'm going to hit the man who puts those questions to me again. As I was saying – one thousand feet of film he's got to carry on for, and not only that, he's got to keep you laughing during those thousand feet, which are the equivalent of a quarter of an hour, for if he doesn't I am a ruined man and I shall have to give up sketching and sidetrack my wife, and retire into a monastery, and . . . . ." "Come, come" I said, "it can't be so bad as all that: seeing that he is descended from . . . . ." "Don't!" he cut in tragically. "As you love me – if you love me – don't say that he is descended from the Bonzosaurus, or that he is Trés Bonzo, because that is more than my jangled nerves can stand tonight".

"Do you know that I have had no holiday this summer, and that I've been working on the film version of that canine atrocity from ten in the morning until seven at night for weeks? If I am carried out struggling on Tuesday night . . . . ." He paused, then went on: "Yes, that is what has been harassing me, though I haven't told you so, it's this hateful speech I've got to make. Bonzo and me facing the audience, hand in hand, so to speak. Think of it! And I shall be expected to make a "funny" speech, I know I shall," and he groaned. "I've created Bonzo and I am told he has made some people laugh – though he has only made me shiver; you've no idea the anxiety he has caused me at times when I have had to produce him again and again, and each time with some alleged funny tag attached to him. I'm no good at public speaking. No good at all. Directly I face a crowd of faces all staring up at me I 'come over queer', as they say in my native county Devon, and every thought my head had in it flies right out".

"Pas Bonzo", I murmured. "I beg your pardon?" He had risen slowly and his eyes glittered down upon me. I fancied I heard him snarl. "Pas what? Just say that again, will you? My bulldog is in the next room. Didn't you hear him growl?" "I was going to ask," I said hurriedly, "if you think of evolving any more comic turns out of the animal world." "Comic turns be bothered. No. But – well, I've got a fish up my sleeve". I glanced quickly at his cuff. "A fish?" "You'll hear about it later. There's a world of humour in a fish if you look at it the right way". I was about to make some fatuous allusion to a dog-fish, when the bulldog growled again and I deemed it prudent to depart'.

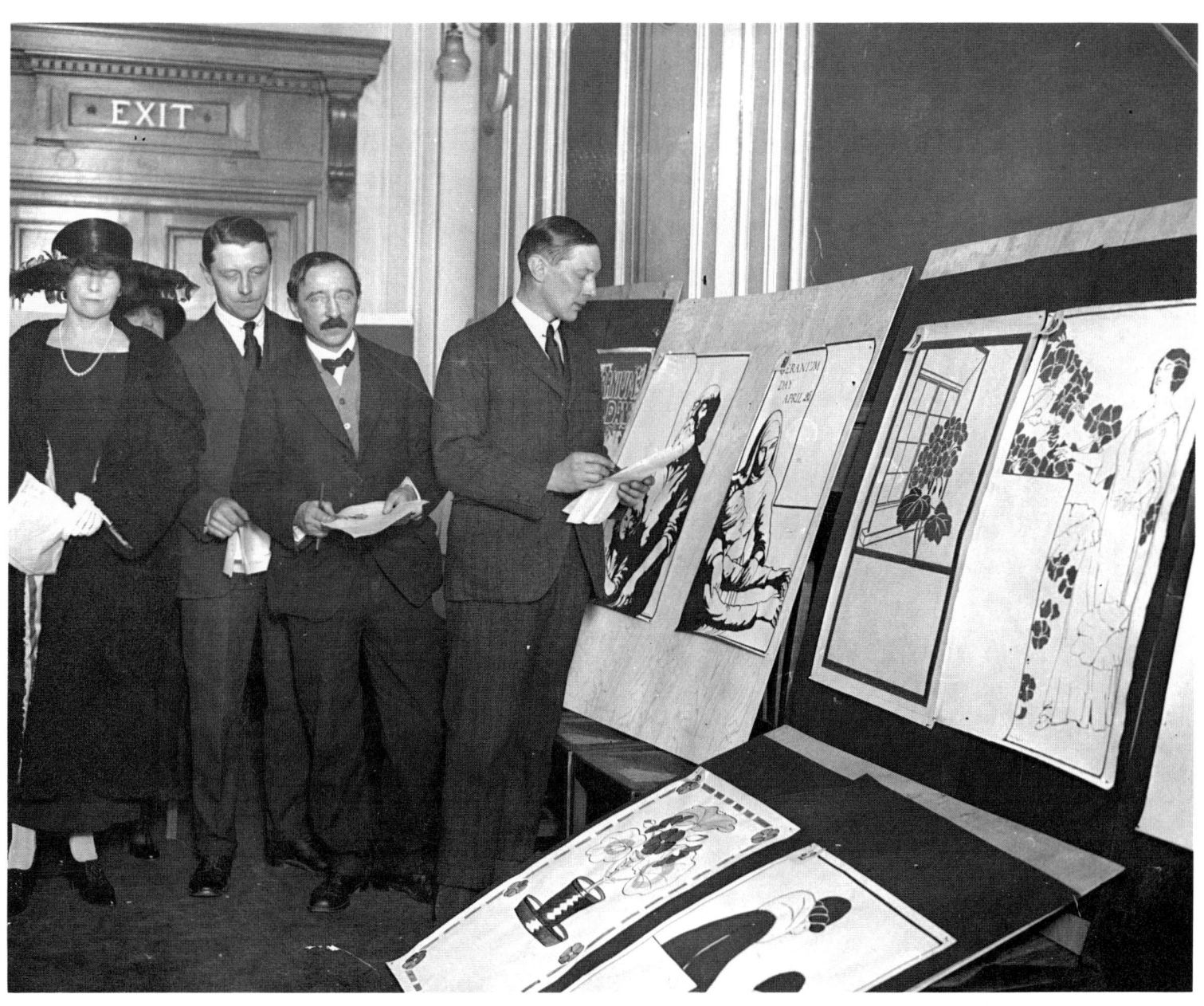

George Studdy judging an art competition in the early 1920's.

Of course, Bonzo did indeed keep the audiences laughing and George was elated, relaxed and relieved when he got up to make his speech. It gave him the confidence to continue with his team of animators to make the remaining 25 films. They were released fortnightly throughout the country, a remarkable feat since he estimated at one time that they would take three weeks each to produce.

Amongst the titles were "Playing the Dickens in an Old Curiosity Shop", "Bonzolino", "Detective Bonzo and the Black Hand Gang", "Bonzo The Bullfighter", "Tally Ho Bonzo" and "Bonzo the Traveller".

Bonzo's fame was now truly international. He made his mark in the United States where he was syndicated in several newspapers, and also in India, South Africa and South America. In Europe his books, advertisements and postcards were translated in many languages, and of course the Japanese were not slow to latch on to the commercial possibilities he presented.

Royal patronage continued. When Princess Marie Louise was organising the magnificent dolls' house for Queen Mary, she decided that the workmanship and detail were to be second to none, commissioning the best craftsmen and designers in the land to work on the construction and furnishings. George was amongst the artists who were asked to submit miniature paintings to hang on the walls. He produced a tiny portrait of Bonzo to match the scale of the model which may still be seen displayed alongside Queen Mary's Dolls' House at Windsor Castle. The Queen sent him a letter of thanks, and expressed the hope that the House would raise a great deal of money for charity when it was exhibited at the British Empire Exhibition of 1924.

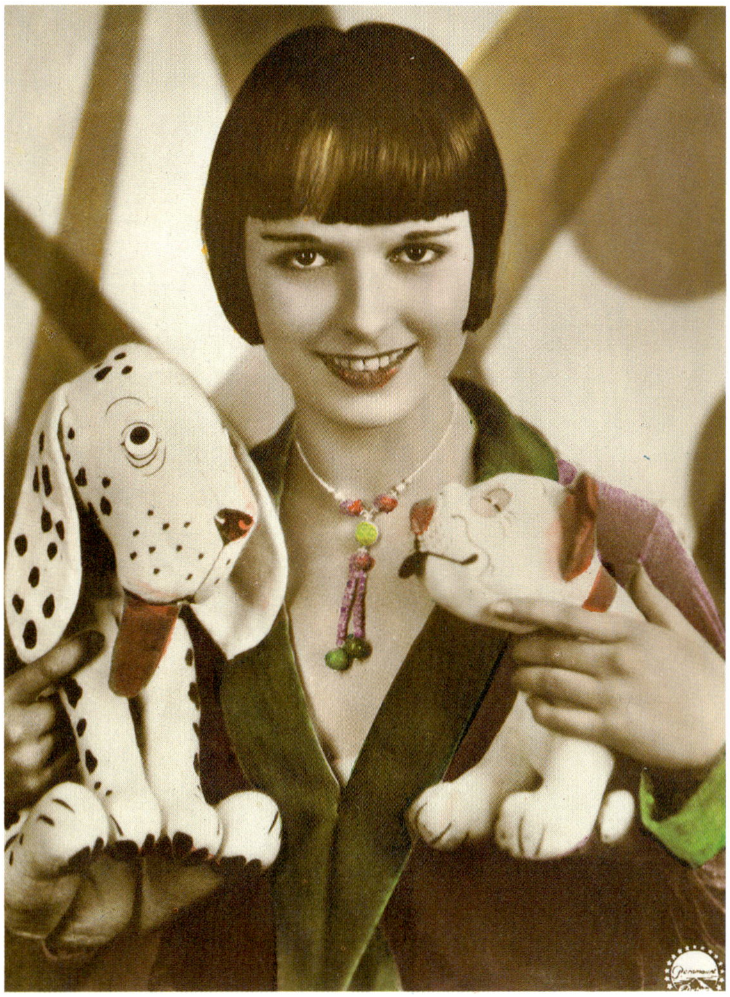

A publicity photograph of the film star Louise Brooks with her Bonzo soft toy. The other dog was named *Dismal Desmond*.

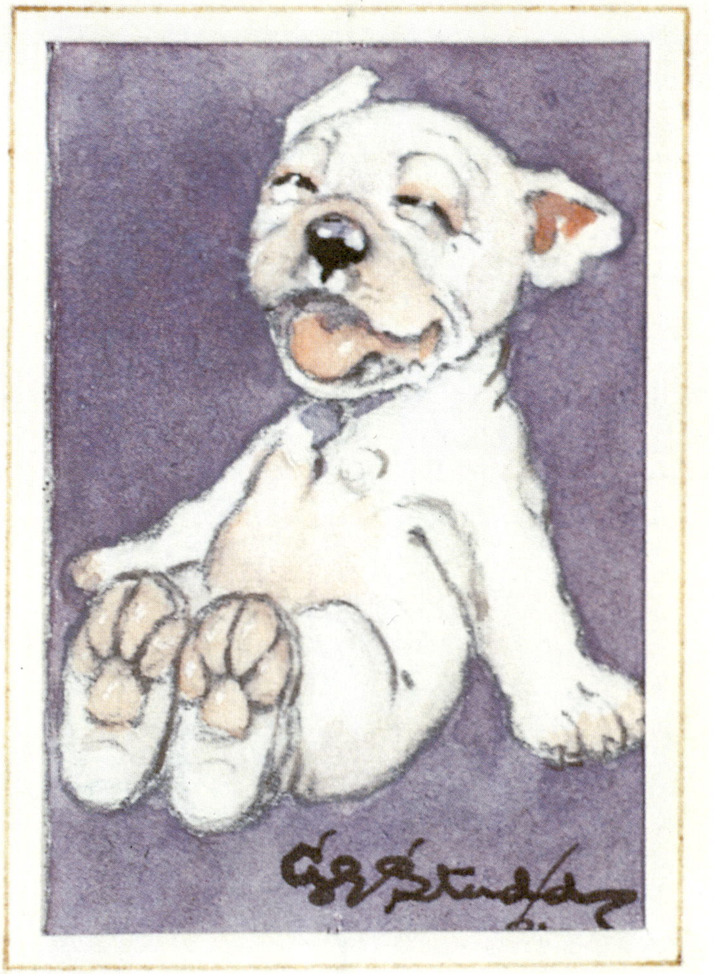

The miniature painting commissioned for Queen Mary's Dolls House which can be seen in Windsor Castle.

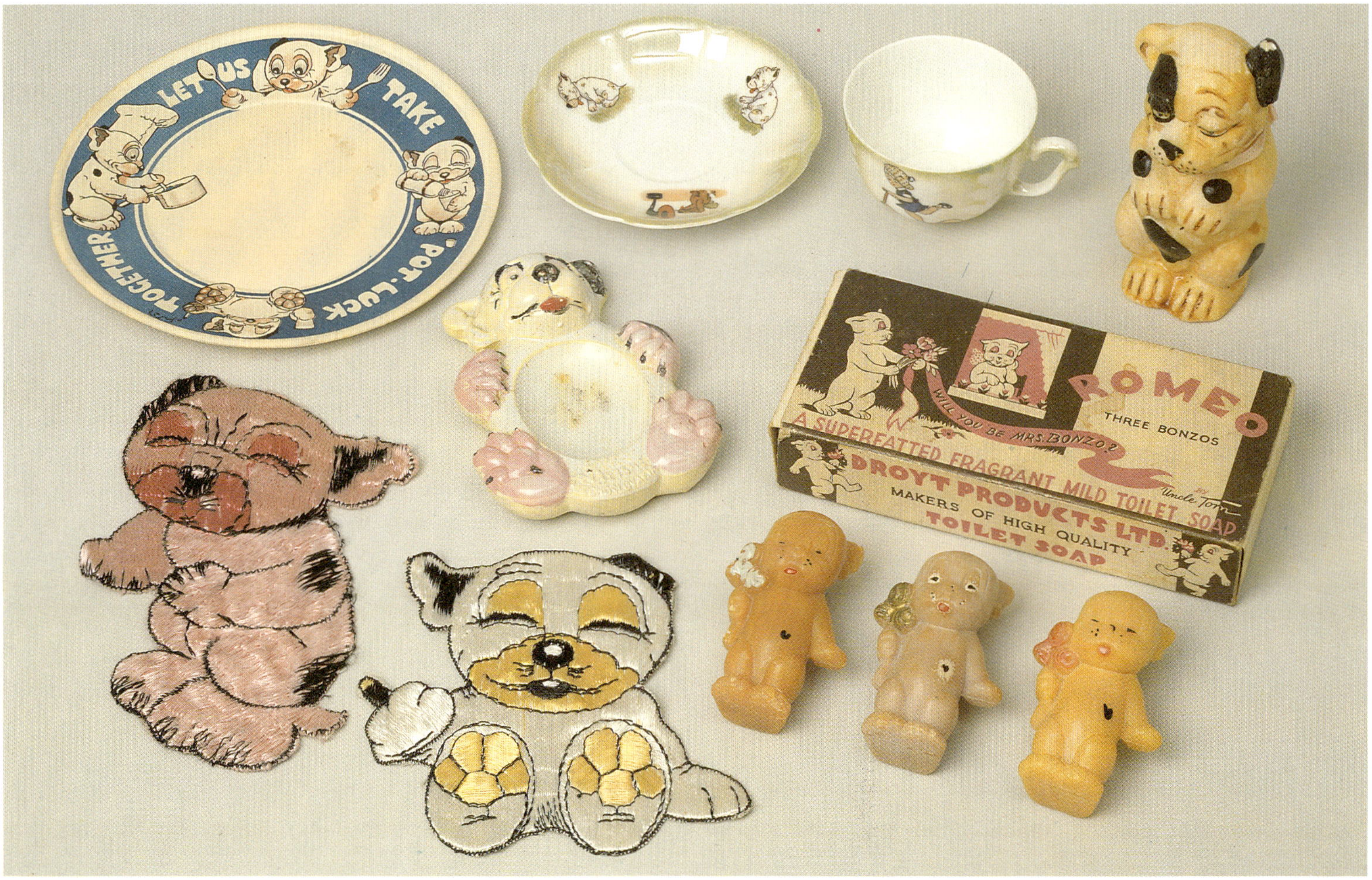
LET US TAKE POT-LUCK TOGETHER
ROMEO
THREE BONZOS
WILL YOU BE MRS. BONZO?
A SUPERFATTED FRAGRANT MILD TOILET SOAP
DROYT PRODUCTS LTD.
MAKERS OF HIGH QUALITY
TOILET SOAP

A large amount of merchandise was produced for children. Clockwise from top left: a disposable paper plate, a child's cup and saucer, Bonzo soap, three soaps with their original box, two rayon woven patches and in the centre a plaster soap dish.

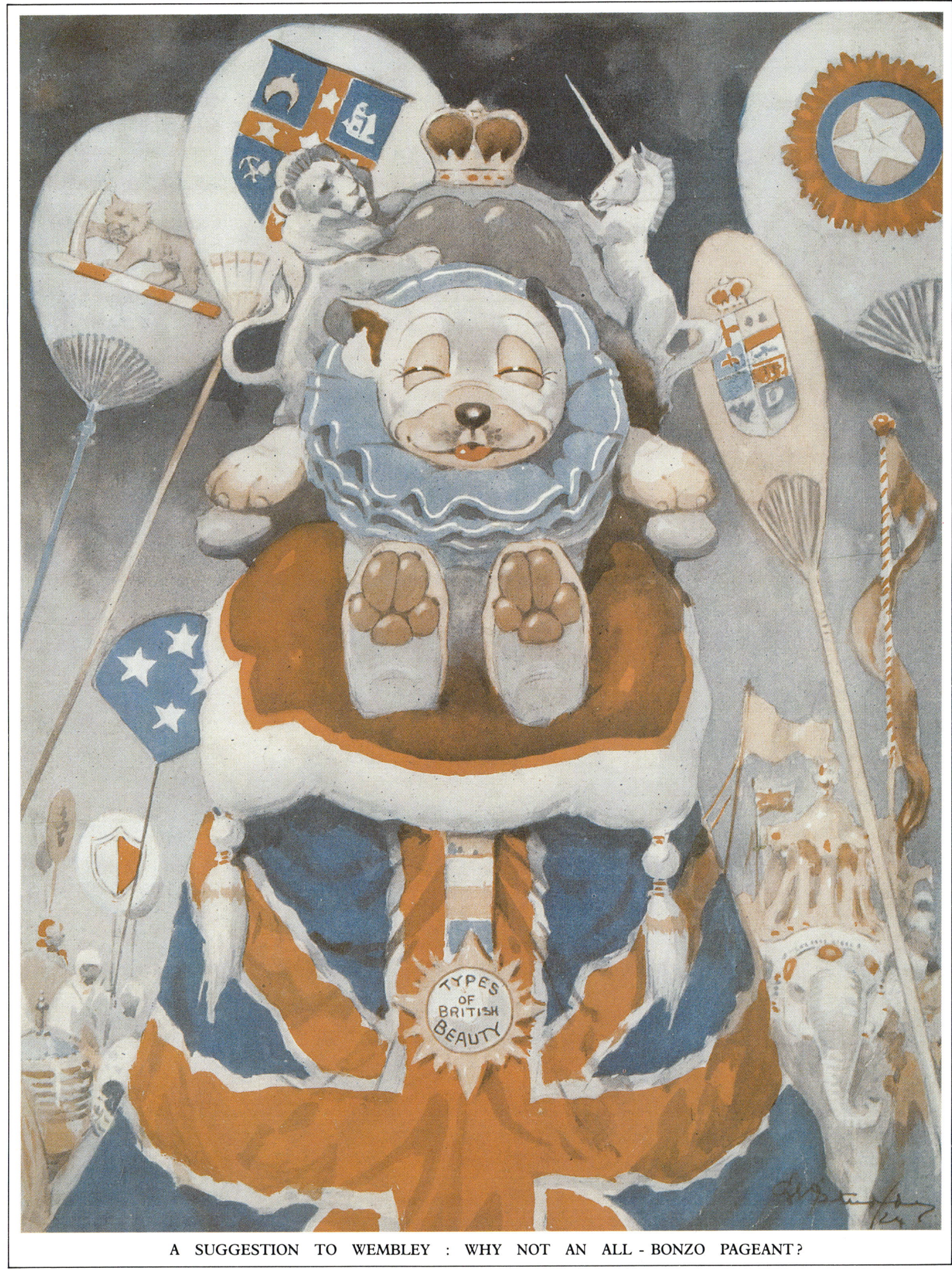

Bonzo celebrating the 1924 British Empire Exhibition at Wembley. *The Sketch* 23rd July 1924.

Blot out Rats and Mice

WASTE caused by rats and mice is a dead loss. Through the ravages of the rodents, the collective sum of individual losses amounts to millions of pounds.

Why allow this enormous waste to go on? The Ratin Scientific System will free you of the presence of rats and mice at a very small cost.

Write or 'Phone:—

RATIN
109 KINGSWAY, LONDON, W.C.2
Telephone: Holborn 227.

The pun in this advertisement is doubly effective in that it is printed on a blotter.

Bonzo's huge popularity resulted in a stream of fan letters from the dog's many admirers. Queries from the public, like the press, were often repetitive and George quickly grew weary of replying with the same stock answers time after time. A woman who wanted to know how he drew his dogs, and from where he found his inspiration, proved to be the last straw. He wrote a purposely flippant reply to the effect that he knew she was not really interested in Bonzo, but in him! He said that he assumed that she had fallen in love with his photograph in The Sketch, and perhaps she would like to know if he was married, and even if he had any particular vices. He did, however, include a signed sketch of Bonzo. The joke totally backfired when she took his letter as a gross insult, returning the sketch accompanied by a less than polite letter. For a while he was more careful when replying to his fan mail.

Some letters proved useful however. A small girl wrote that she thought Bonzo was a "Cinderella sort of dog", giving George the idea for a Sketch picture in which a dejected and miserable Bonzo is seen sitting all alone by the fire – the caption was, of course, 'Cinderella'. With the necessity to produce such a vast amount of work at a constant rate, any ideas which supplemented those in his own overworked mind were gratefully received.

George, like Blanche, was keenly interested in charity work, and his kind and generous nature was often prevailed upon to assist all manner of worthy causes. He sold sketches in 1923 on behalf of St. Dunstan's Hospital to help soldiers who had been blinded in the First World War. In 1924 he travelled down to Devon to help his brother, Hubert, raise money towards a new organ for his church in Cockington and spent the whole day at a local fete drawing pictures and signing autographs for the assembled masses. He often donated a drawing or painting to a particular charity in order that they could reproduce them to raise funds. Two wonderful examples he did, without payment, were for Doctor Barnardo's Homes and The Princess Beatrice Hospital in Earls Court.

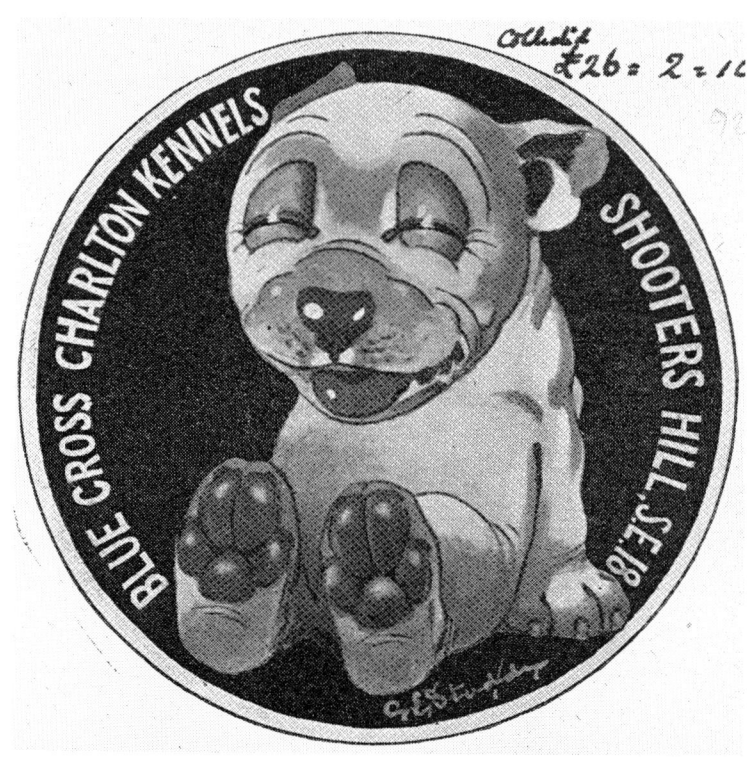

The amusing "Studdy" Picture specially drawn by that famous artist to aid a worthy cause.

One of Studdy's many contributions to charity. The *Blue Cross Kennels* operated a quarantine station for the dogs of soldiers and sailors returning home from abroad who could not afford the fees. Replicas of this sketch were sold to raise funds, £26.2.10d. (£26.14p.) as noted.

The World's Famous
BONZO JIG-SAW PUZZLES

Thirty-one of the latest and best drawings by the famous artist Mr. G. E. STUDDY, reproduced in colour and made into Jig-saw Puzzles on the interlocking system in Satin Walnut. There are about 100 pieces in each puzzle.

Causes endless interest and amusement to both young and old. When completed the puzzle makes a beautifully printed picture, size 10 inches by 7 inches.

Price **3/6** each.   Post Free **3/10**

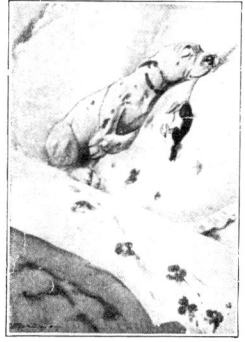 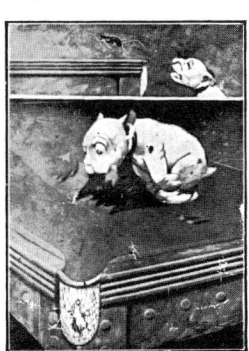 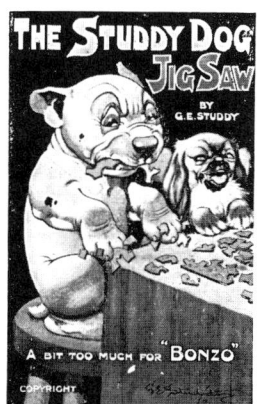 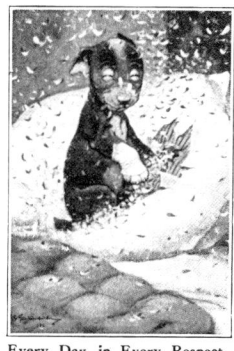 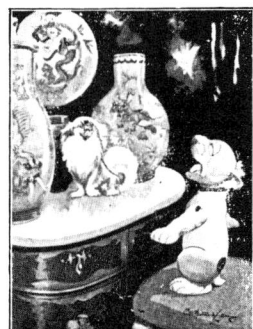

THE END OF A PERFECT DAY.   BONZO RUNS THROUGH.   Every Day, in Every Respect, I am Getting Better and Better.   BONZO CONGRATULATES CHEE-KEE.

List of Subjects Now Ready.

1. The End of a Perfect Day.
2. Also Ran.
3. Far from de Old Folks at Home.
4. Every Day, in Every Respect, I am Getting Better and Better.
5. A-tish-oo !
6. Missed.
7. Oh, Help !
8. The Orgy.
9. That's What I Think of You.
10. As Master Sees Me.
11. That Coal-Black Mammy o' Mine.
12. Grand Guignol.
13. Such Stuff as Dreams are Made On.
14. The Beggar's Opera.
15. Why the Dickens did You Cut Me Off ?
16. Bonzo's Spirit is Willing.
17. His Mistress's Vice.
18. Bonzo Tries to Swim the Channel.
19. Bonzo Congratulates Chee-kee on Finding *Her* Ancestors.
20. Bonzo the Peace-maker.
21. Bonzo Runs Through.
22. Bonzo's Dud Show.
23. Bonzo Meets a Road Hog.
24. Battling Bonzo Wins in the 1st Round.
25. Bonzo Suffers from Overwork.
26. Bonzo to the Rescue.
27. Bonzo Listens In.
28. Bonzo Lets Polly Out for a Bit.
29. Bonzo Removes an Infernal Machine from the Bed.
30. Bonzo, Chee-kee, and Jock Remember Their New Year's Resolutions.
31. Bonzo Adopts Chee-kee's Pup.

BONZO ASH-TRAYS & PIN-TRAYS
MADE IN ROYAL SEMI-PORCELAIN WARE IN BROWN ART SHADES WITH GILT EDGES.

A series of 6 of the Most Famous Studdy Dog Pictures as Ash-trays and Pin-trays.

The List of Subjects :
His Master's Vice.   The Faithful Heart.   Coal Black Mammy.   Why the Dickens did You Cut Me Off ?   Missed.   Fair Exchange.

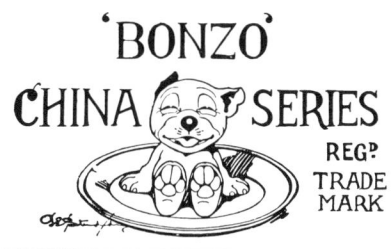

Price of Ash-trays, **3/-** per pair ; Set of Six, **10/6** post free.

Price of Pin-trays, **2/-** per pair ; Set of Six, **7/6** post free.

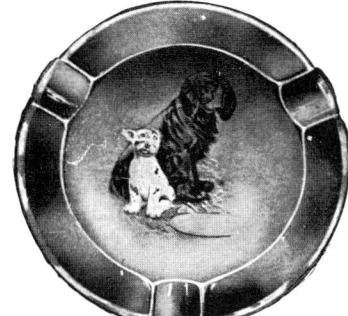 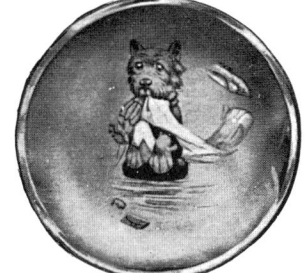 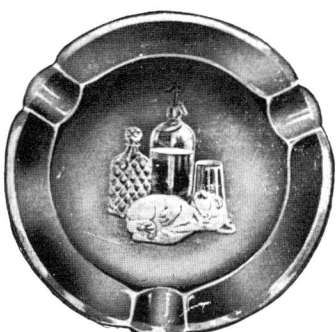

COAL BLACK MAMMY.   THE FAITHFUL HEART.   HIS MASTER'S VICE.

Other Bonzo Novelties such as Cups, Saucers, Plates, etc., will be ready shortly.

Bonzo Jig-saw Puzzles and all China-ware and Novelties obtainable from all Stationers, Booksellers, and Stores in the United Kingdom, or direct from the Makers,

A. V. N. JONES & CO., 64, Fore Street, LONDON, E.C.2.

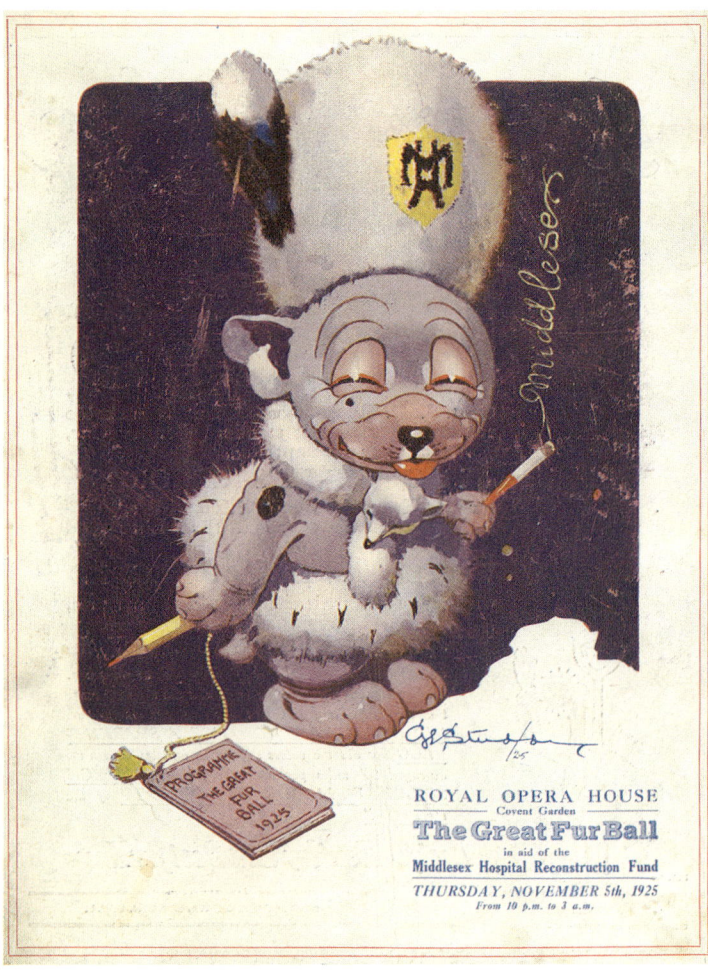

Programme for *The Great Fur Ball* held at The Royal Opera House, Covent Garden, to raise funds for the Middlesex Hospital.

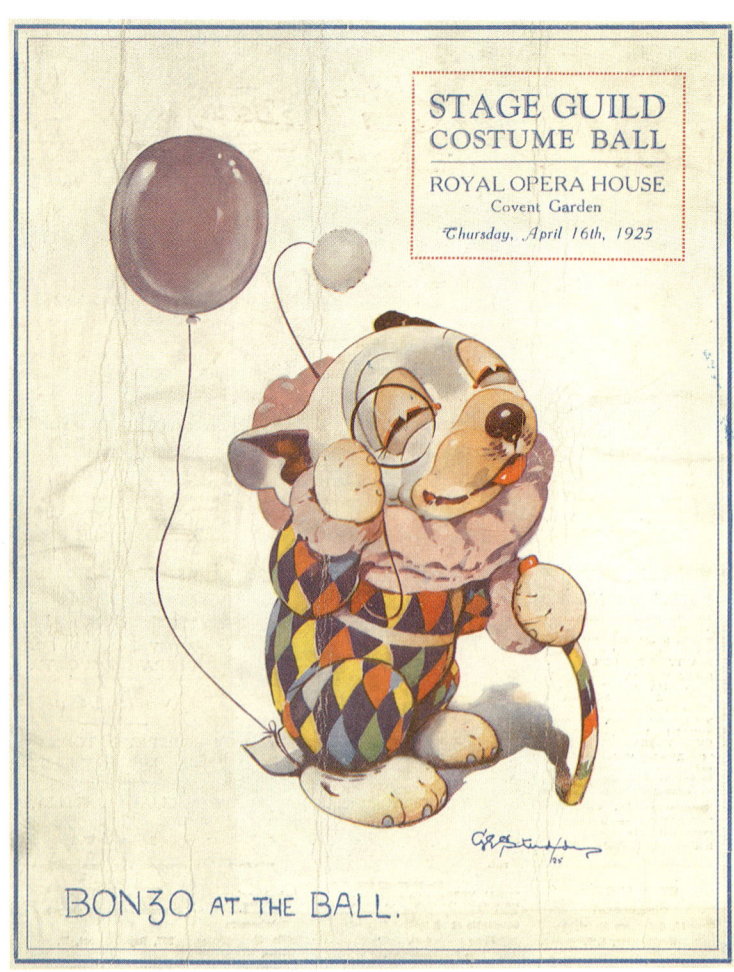

A Covent Garden programme for the *Stage Guild Costume Ball*.

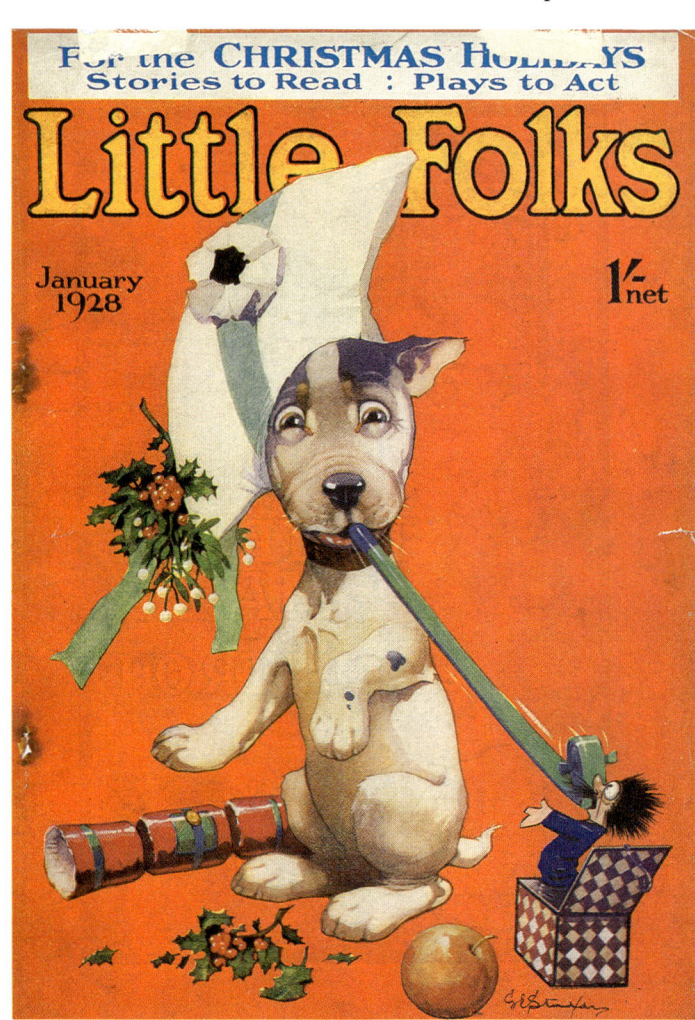

The January 1928 cover of *Little Folks Magazine* featuring a non-Bonzo type dog.

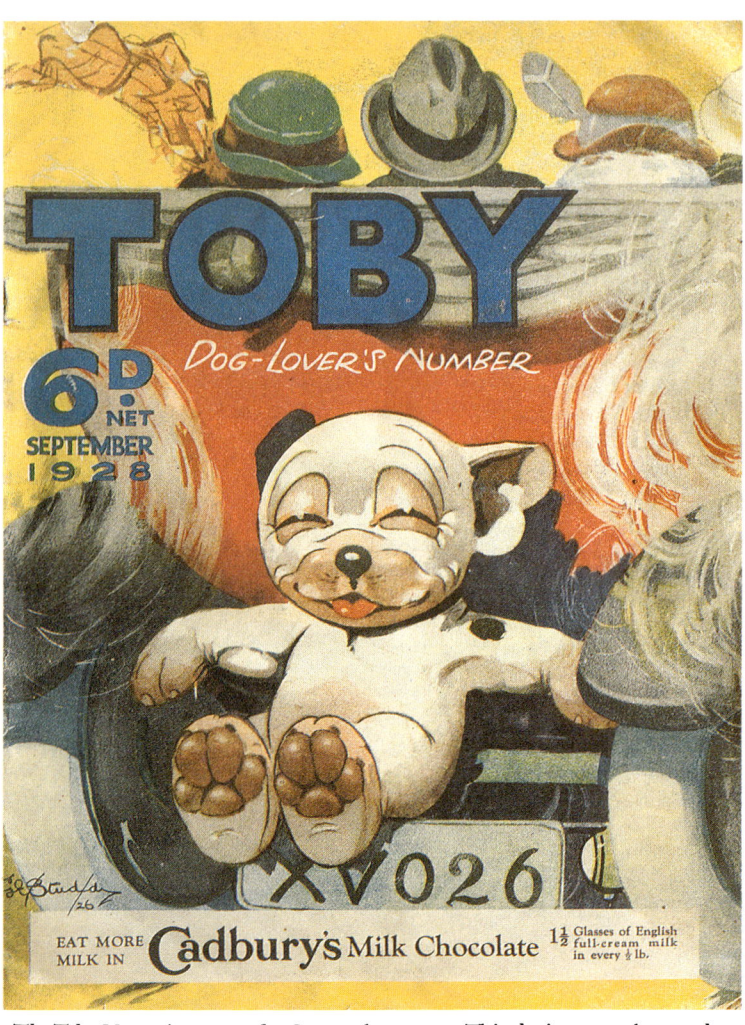

The Toby Magazine cover for September 1928. This design was also used as a post card.

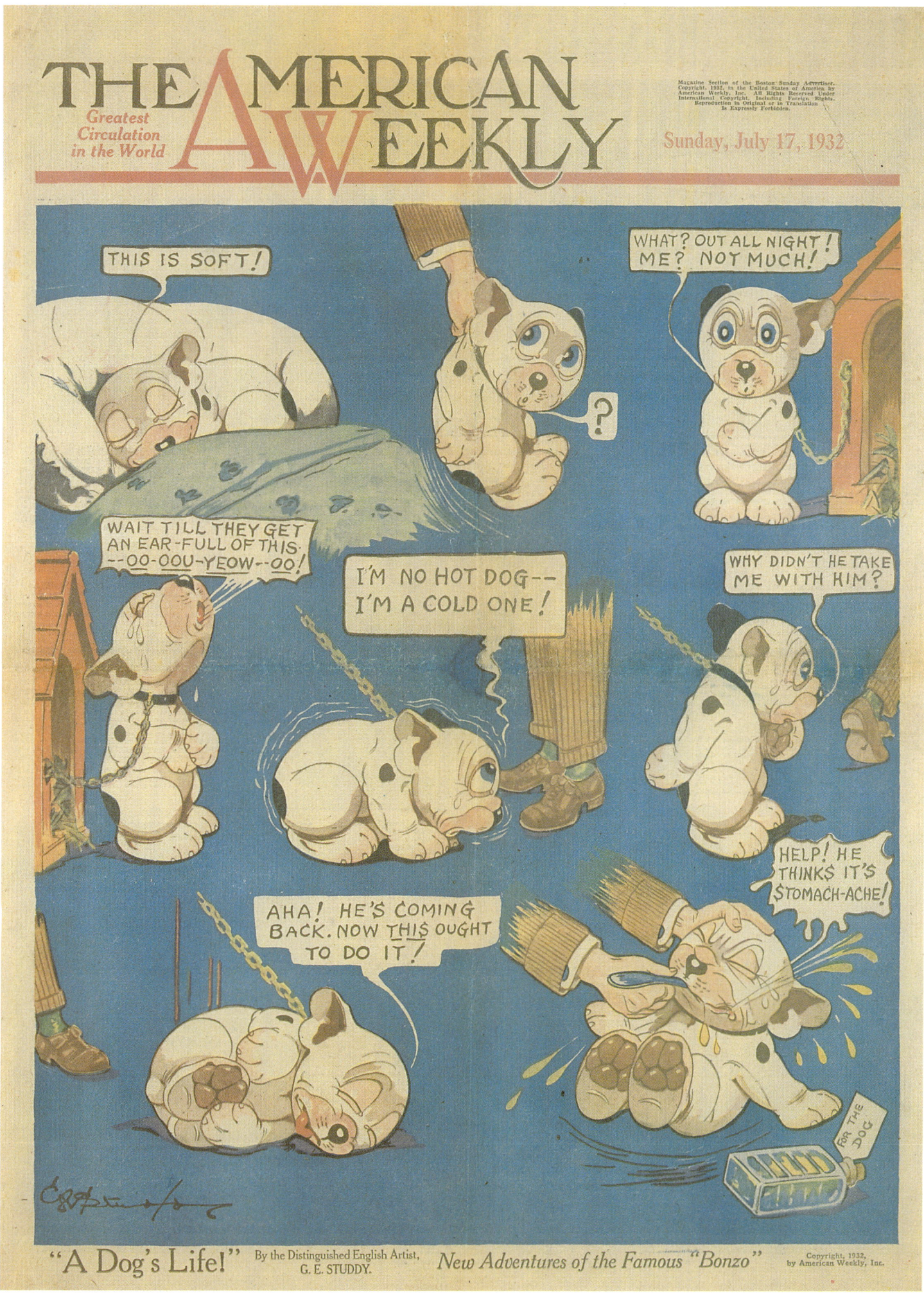

Studdy's work was widely syndicated in the United States and the importance given to this strip illustrates Bonzo's popularity.

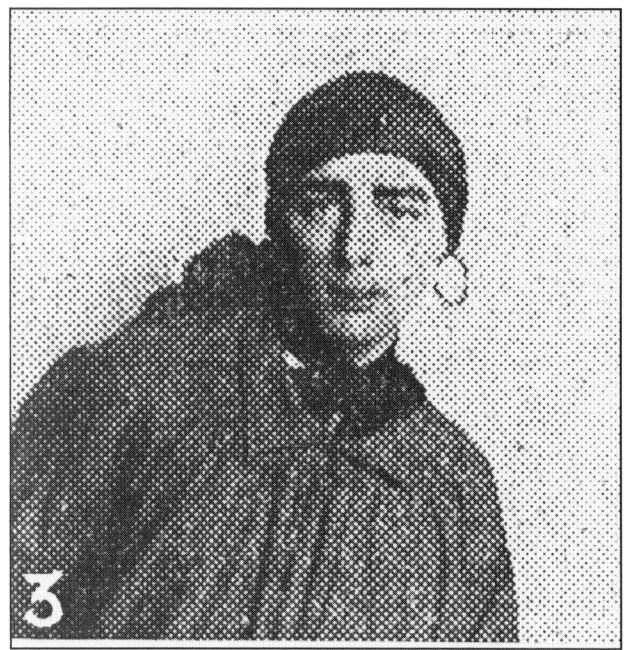

A press cutting of Studdy at a costume ball wearing his favourite pirate costume.

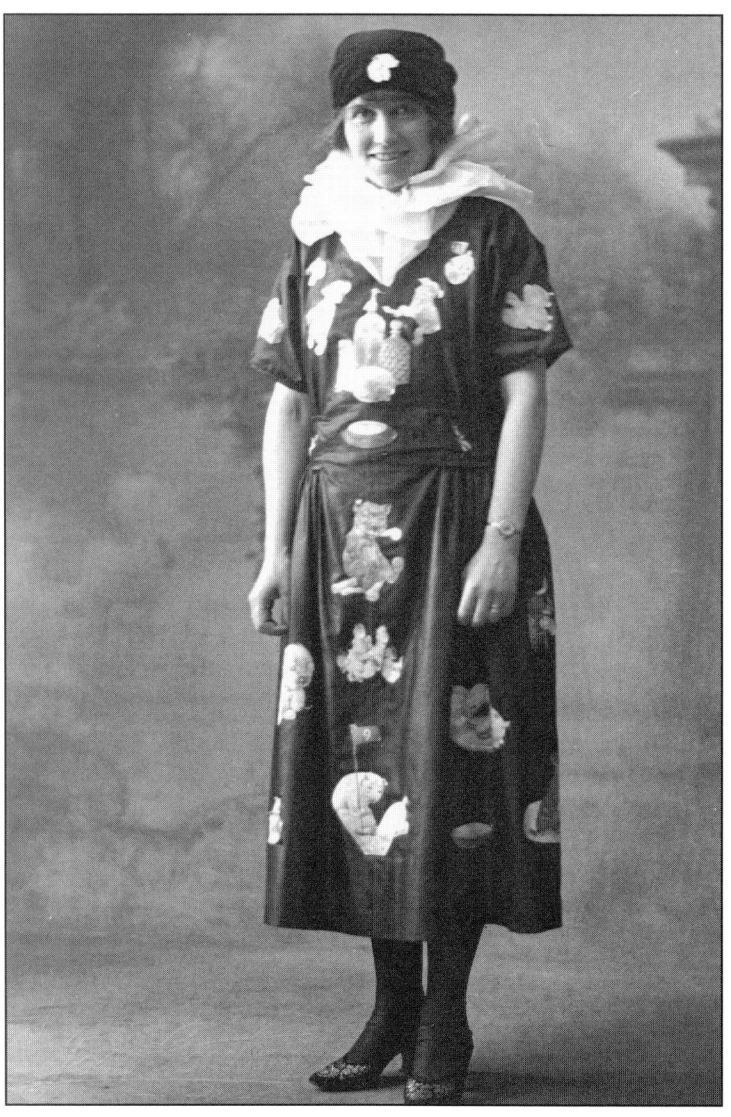

An ingenious fancy dress costume made by cutting out *Sketch* Bonzo plates and fixing them on a plain dress and hat. The studio portrait was taken by Jose Goulart of Horta, Açôres, (Portugal), c.1925.

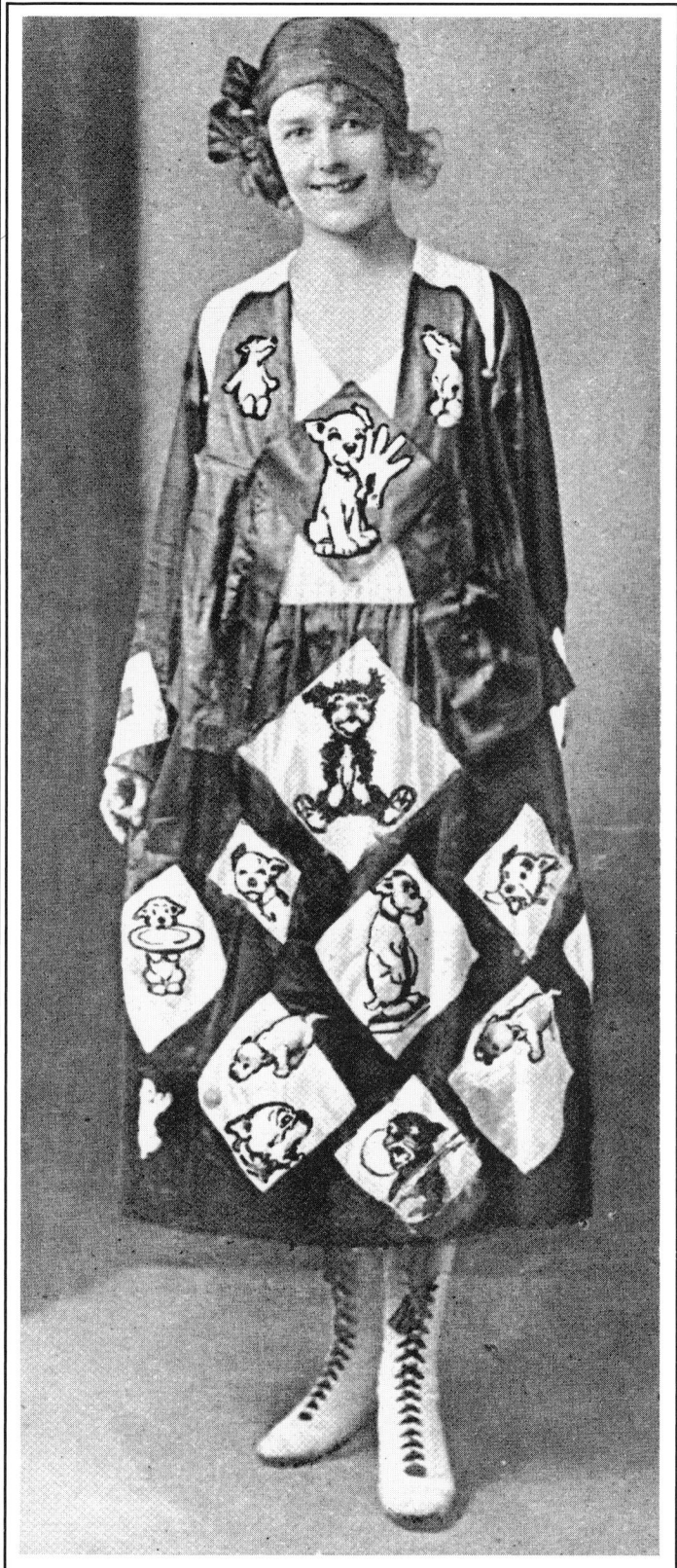

AS "MISS STUDDY" AT THE SKETCH CLUB BALL: MISS ARNOLD IN A DOGGY FANCY DRESS.

Miss Arnold wore this original fancy dress at the Sketch Club Ball. "Sketch" readers will recognise the creations of that clever canine artist Mr. G. E. Studdy on her dress.—[*Photograph by Oxford Studios.*]

Through his membership of both the London Sketch Club and the Savage Club he produced occasional designs for invitations and menus for their regular dinners and 'smokers' which took place throughout the year. A Bonzo graced the programme cover for the Stage Guild's first costume Ball which was held at the Royal Opera House, Covent Garden. Personal appearances were in great demand and George preferred this way of meeting his public to the strained atmosphere of standing up and delivering a speech to a silent audience. To publicise the arrival of the cartoon films New Era set up a 'Bonzo Booth' which demonstrated the processes involved in the making of an animated film. It appeared at the Film Trades Summer Show to raise money for their benevolent fund and was regularly manned by the staff of draughtsmen, and often by George himself.

Later in 1925 he joined forces with, amongst others, John Hassall, John Galsworthy, Sybil Thorndike and H. G. Wells to raise funds to help the cat artist Louis Wain, who had lost all his money and was suffering so badly from schizophrenia that he had had to be committed to a mental asylum. Another drawing of Bonzo was to be found gracing the cover of the programme for The Great Fur Ball which was held at Covent Garden in aid of the Middlesex Hospital Restoration Fund.

On a personal level George's generosity was almost boundless. He always found it difficult to refuse anybody who came to him with a hard luck story and once gave the massive sum of £200 to a destitute stranger who came to his door pleading for help. He even arrived home one freezing winter night without his rather expensive overcoat, and when questioned by Blanche, casually explained that he had given it to a street musician whom he felt had needed it much more than he did, and anyway he could easily go out and buy another. He never worried about his own financial security, being quite sure that his drawings would continue to earn him a good living far into the future. Although he and his family lived in some style and comfort, George spent little on himself. He dressed simply but comfortably and, rather than dressing up smartly and going out on the town, he preferred to carry on with his work, go fishing or stay at home with his family. One of the few exceptions to this rule, however, was the London Sketch Club Annual Ball, which was attended by all his artist friends, and to which he always looked forward with pleasant anticipation. Everyone took an enormous amount of trouble to design and make extremely lavish and exotic fancy dress costumes. Blanche enjoyed the evenings thoroughly and was always superbly turned out. George, on the other hand, thought the effort all rather too much and wore the same costume year after year. He was an eternal pirate in a costume he had first worn during the war at a

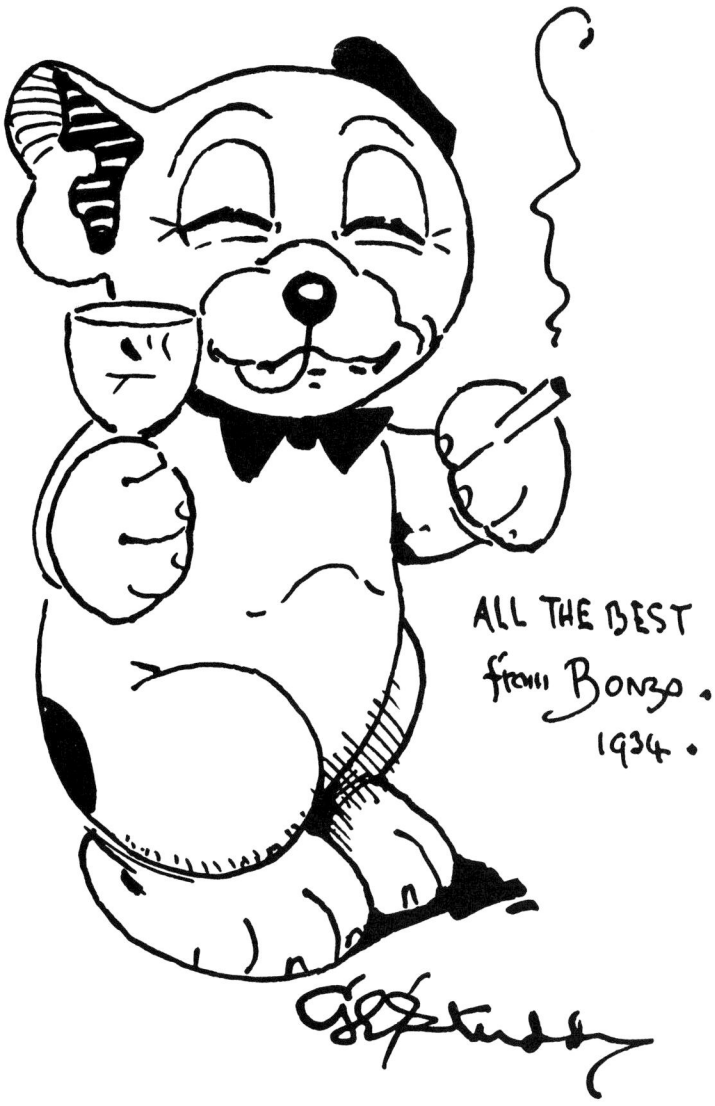

A typical 'lightning sketch' that Studdy was always happy to give as an autograph. Although drawn in a few moments the quality of his draughtsmanship is evident.

'Printer's Pie' Dinner where many of the artist guests were asked to come as 'Pie-rates'.

It was of dark blue material accompanied by a headband, earrings and blackened face. Blanche, unlike George, loved to dance. In their own different ways, they both entered into the spirit of the Ball.

Vivienne attended school at The Assumption Convent in Kensington Square, London. Her classmates were well aware that her father was a celebrity of some note, and frequently she arrived home with a batch of autograph albums for his attention. She would return them to their owners the following day complete with a Bonzo sketch. For a time he seemed to be illustrating their books almost every night but he was too kind to refuse.

George, in his heart, would have liked to leave London and move to the peace of his beloved English countryside, but it was important for his work that he stay in town. Blanche was a town dweller through and through. For six

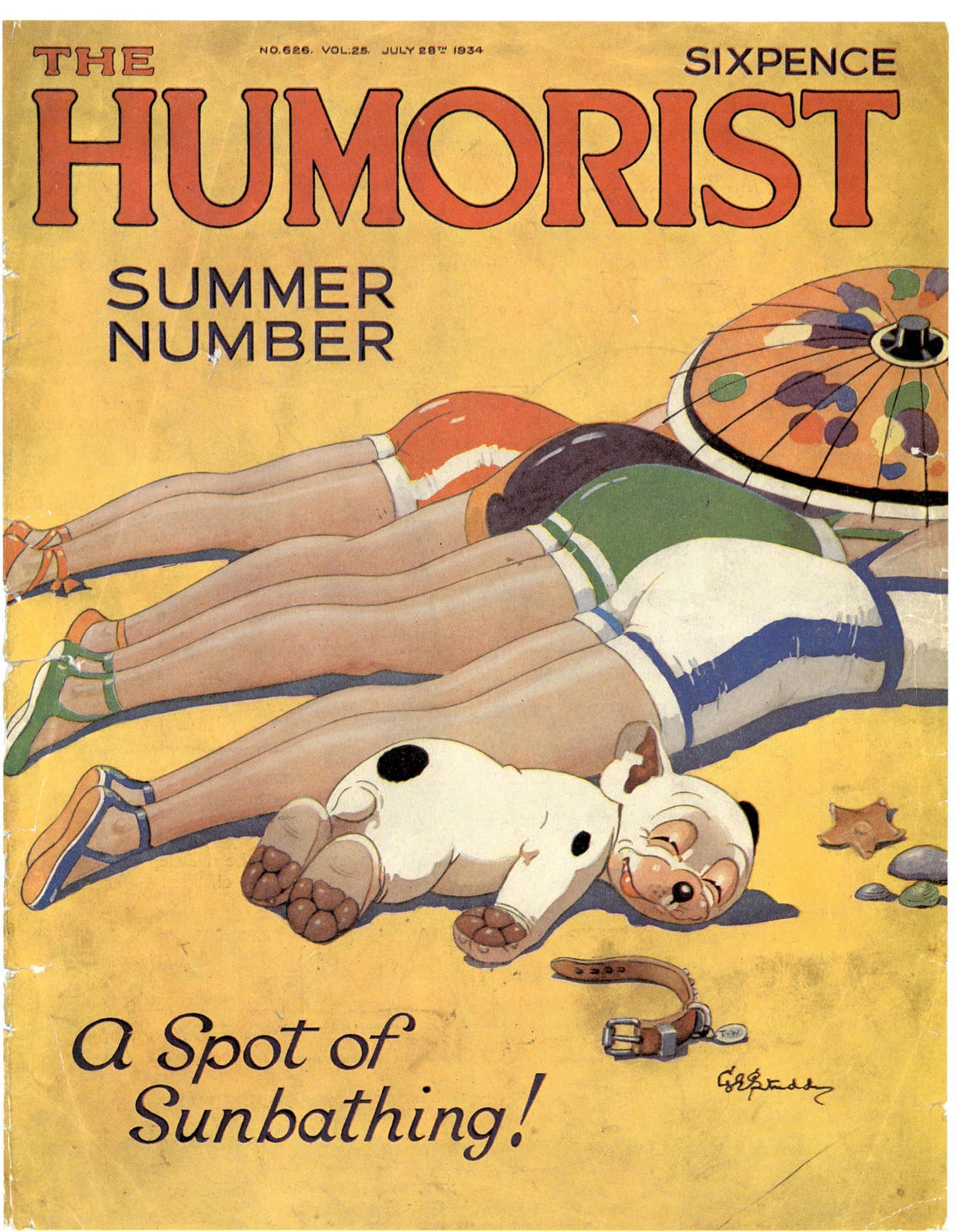

One of many covers Studdy designed for magazines. The image was also used on a postcard.

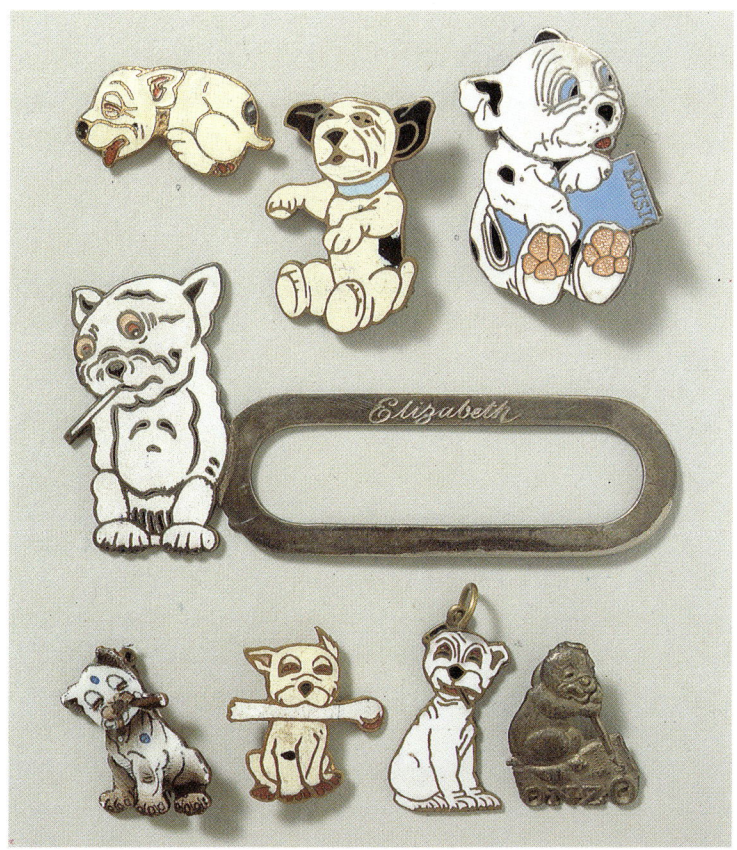

Enamel Bonzos. The badge top left and the one holding the bone were made by Stratton for Christmas 1924. Top right is the only modern badge made c.1980. The napkin holder in the centre is silver plated and engraved *Elizabeth*.

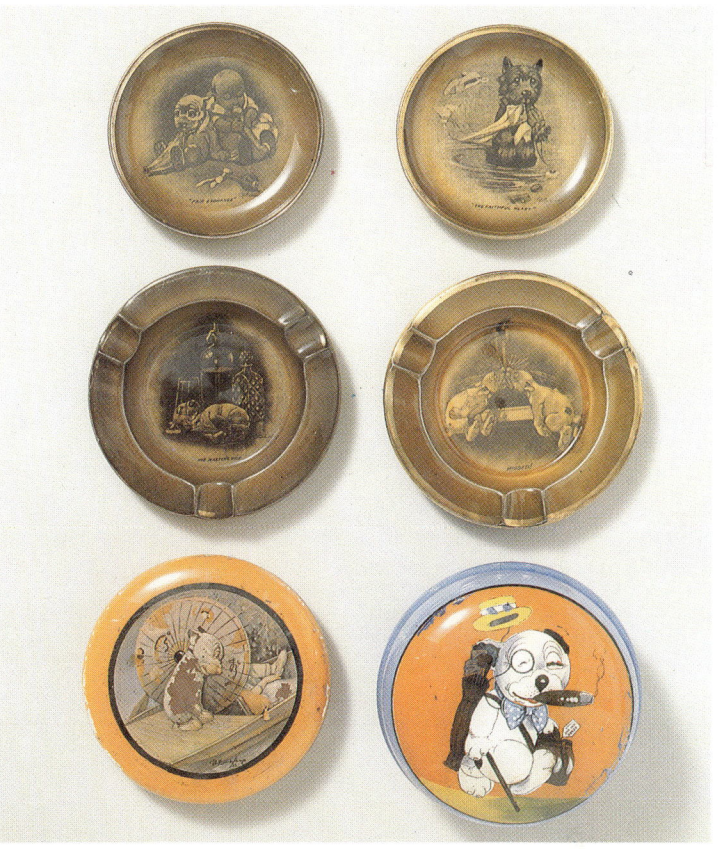

Two pin trays and two ash trays from the *Bonzo China Series*. The illustrations were taken from the R.P.S. Series of post cards. At the bottom are two lids from glass powder bowls. The pictures were fixed to the back of the glass and then lacquered.

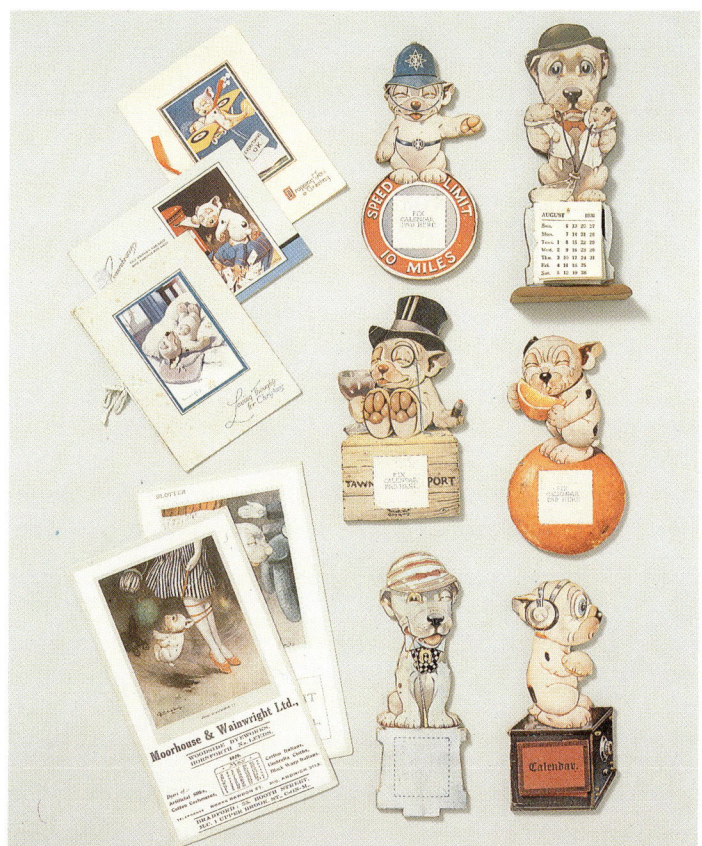

Top left, images previously used by Valentines for their post cards were reduced and placed on Birthday and Greeting cards. They were also used on the promotional blotters below overprinted with the advertiser's name. To the right are six cut-out Bonzo calendars. They were sold in paper form for 3d. plus 1d. postage and another 1d. for the calendar pad. They were then to be stuck to plywood and cut out with the fret-saw that every young boy possessed.

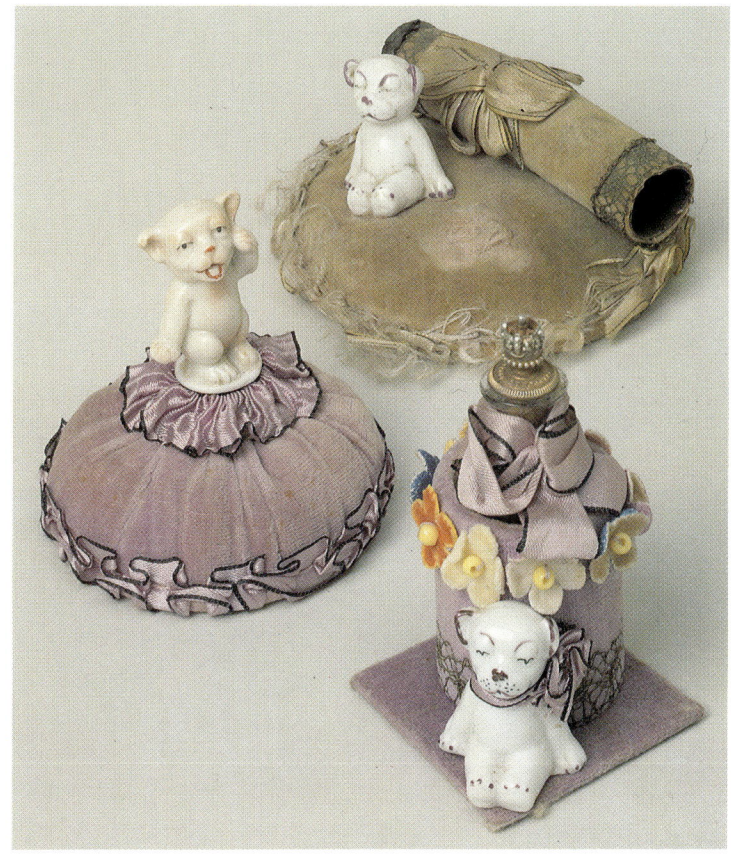

Although many Bonzo ornaments were made for the younger market these were intended for the dressing table of a young lady. The top one has lost a dog leaving the outline on the base. The central one would have taken the hat pins and brooches whilst the other houses an ornate scent bottle.

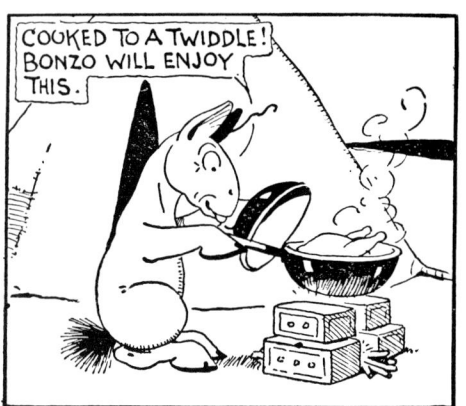
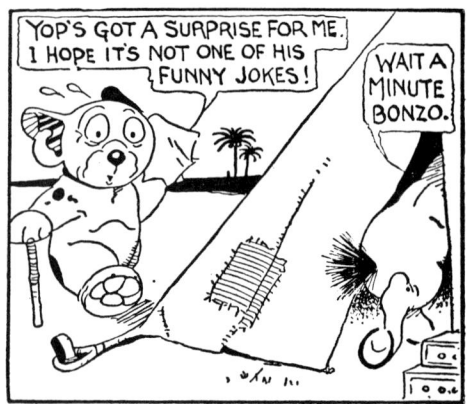
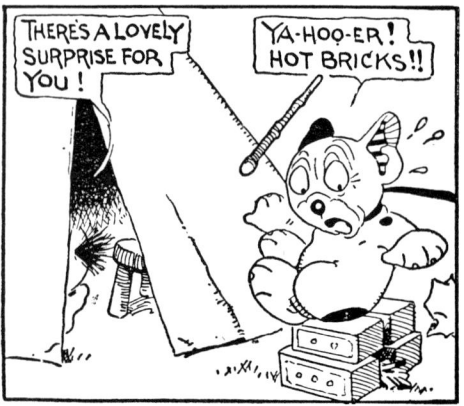
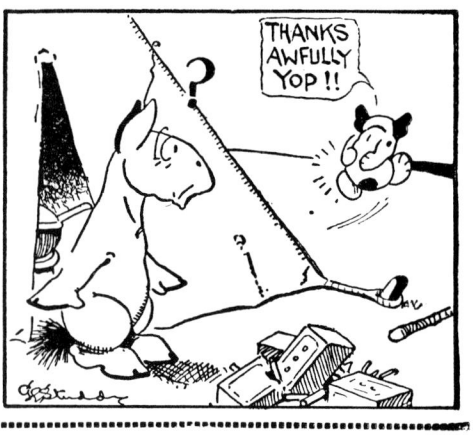

Yop appeared in his own strip in *The Sunday Graphic* c.1933, although Bonzo appeared regularly as a 'guest'.

weeks each year she would leave their Kensington house and take Vivienne to France to visit her family and spend the summer holiday with them. George could not afford to take that amount of time away from his work and rarely joined them. He would, however, sometimes slip away to the country and spend time on the bank of one of his favourite rivers with his rod and his thoughts. He could not imagine a more peaceful way of occupying his time, and revelled in the camaraderie of other anglers. Occasionally the whole family took an Easter holiday together in Devon where many of his relatives and friends lived.

George had worked for The Sketch on a regular basis since before 1912 and from January 1920 until July 1927 Bonzo had been a weekly fixture, almost without fail. During this time a variety of additional characters had been tried out in other magazines and books, not to replace Bonzo, but in the hope that they might have the same success he enjoyed. Apart from Chee-Kee the Pekinese, there was Yop the donkey, Bill, a small terrier, and a mouse called Tony. They were joined by a fluffy black cat named Ooloo, as wicked and as crafty as Bonzo. She developed from being the victim of many of Bonzo's practical jokes to finally becoming his best ally, and sharing in many of his pranks.

It was decided in July 1927 to give Bonzo a holiday in case the readers were becoming tired of him every seven days. George thought that a change might be as good as a rest, and substituted Bonzo with a wonderful series of cartoons, so totally different that they did not feature a single animal. They ran for three months under the heading 'Studdy's Motor Emotion Series' and illustrated in a humorously exaggerated way the pitfalls of motoring in those days.

After this there was a gap of fifteen months when Sketch readers were deprived of any Studdy cartoons. He returned at the beginning of 1929, but not with Bonzo. His new offering was headed 'Exit Bonzo – Enter Ooloo! The new load of mischief!' and Bonzo never appeared in The Sketch again.

When George originally conceived a dog character to be the medium for his humour it was more or less based on a recognizable breed, or mixture of breeds. Throughout the mid 1920's Bonzo had gradually developed into a much more stylised character and moved away from any sort of real dog. Although the change had been made as a natural progression of George's style, it became clear that some people liked the old dog while others preferred the new. Hubert Studdy was among the latter, and, to explain his opinion, he used to tell a story of an event in his brother's childhood. At the age of eleven, George drew a picture of a gnome sitting on a toadstool and sent it to a postal art course for advice and criticism. "He may do well," came the reply, "if, in the future, he avoids the ugly and the grotesque." His recollection of this many years later moved Hubert to observe: "It was on this that he made his reputation, didn't he?" However, devotees of the earlier cartoon, featuring the more realistic dogs, would surely have been outraged.

Although animals had dominated George's work for most of his career, he often branched out into other subjects. On many occasions he drew caricatures of actors to accompany first night reviews of plays and musicals in London's theatre-land. He would sit in the half light of the auditorium and draw his rough sketches on a small pad balanced on his knee. These he would later work up to their finished state in the calm of his studio.

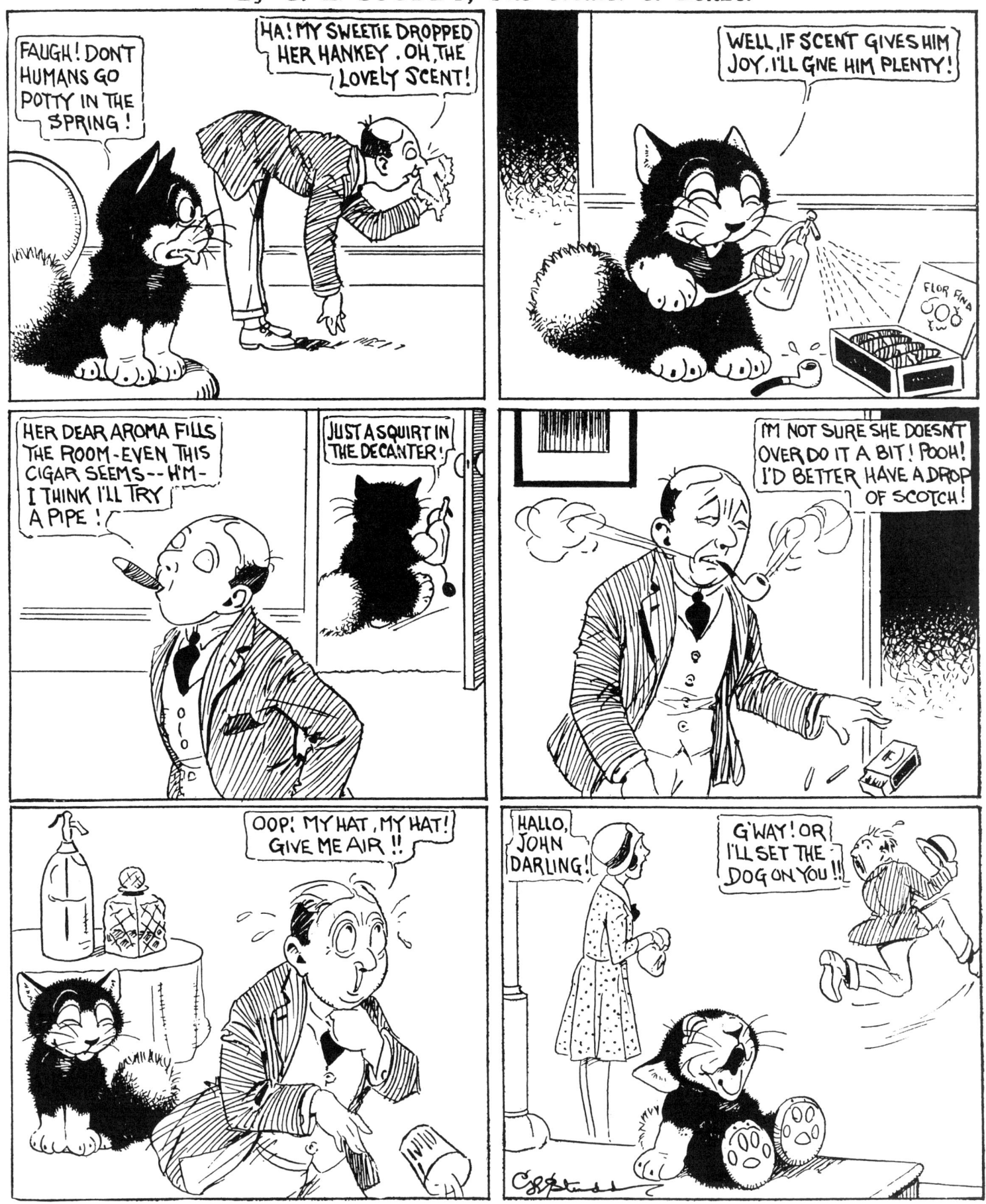

OOLOO AND THE SCENT-SPRAY.

Ooloo cartoons ran for a while in *The Humorist* magazine. Although a cat she got up to the same antics as Bonzo.

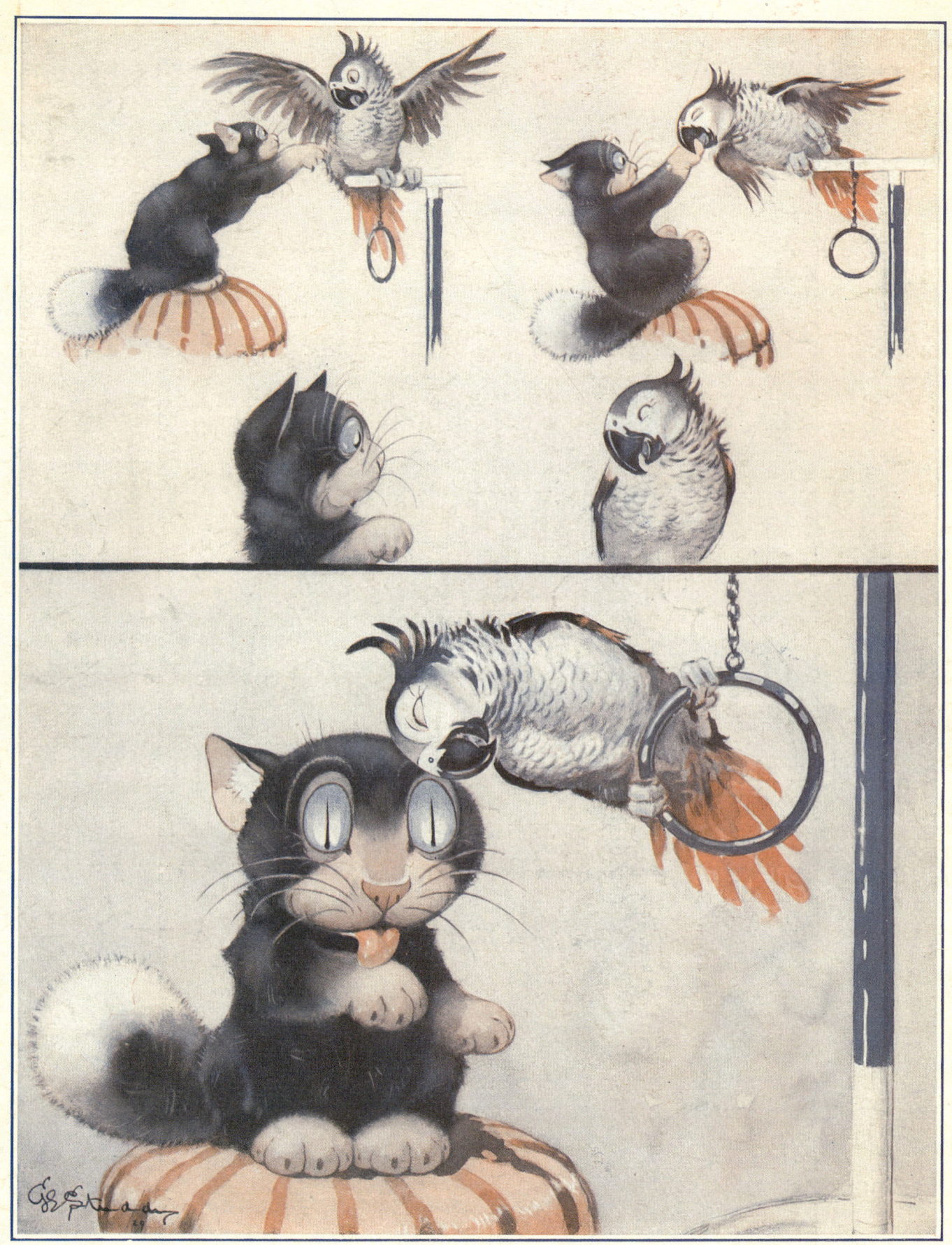

OOLOO UP AGAINST THE BEAK: A BLOOD=BROTHERHOOD.

Ooloo, the "Sketch" and Studdy cat, imagined that he was a match for any mortal bird; but when he found himself up against the beak of the family parrot, he revised his opinion. The inauspicious opening of the friendship, however, was soon overcome, and Ooloo and the parrot are now blood-brothers.

SPECIALLY DRAWN FOR "THE SKETCH" BY G. E. STUDDY.

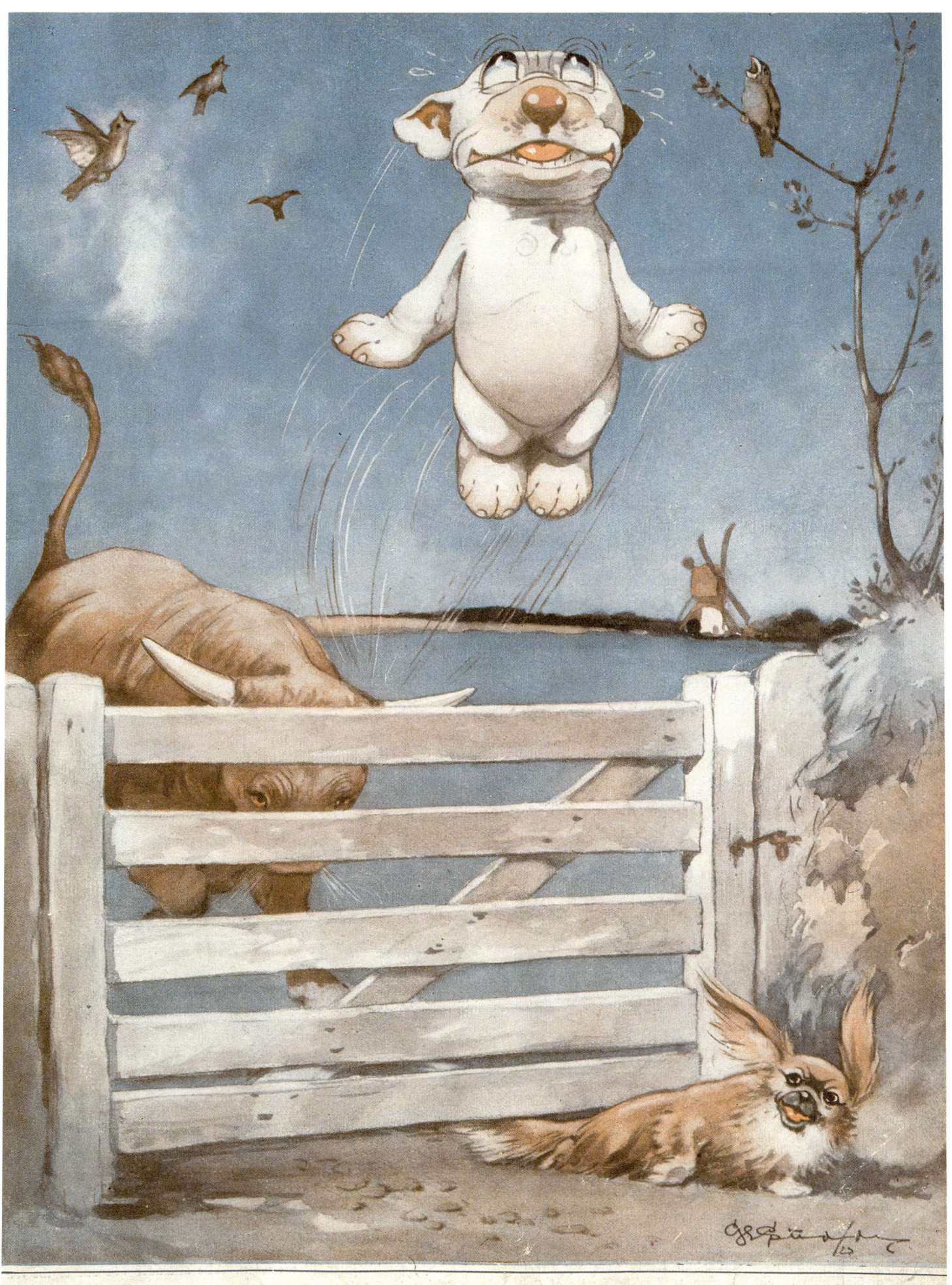

BONZO GETS THAT SPRING FEELING. [DRAWN BY G. E. STUDDY

The reason for Bonzo's Spring feeling is obvious. Chee-Kee takes the easy way.

The Sketch 14th March 1923.

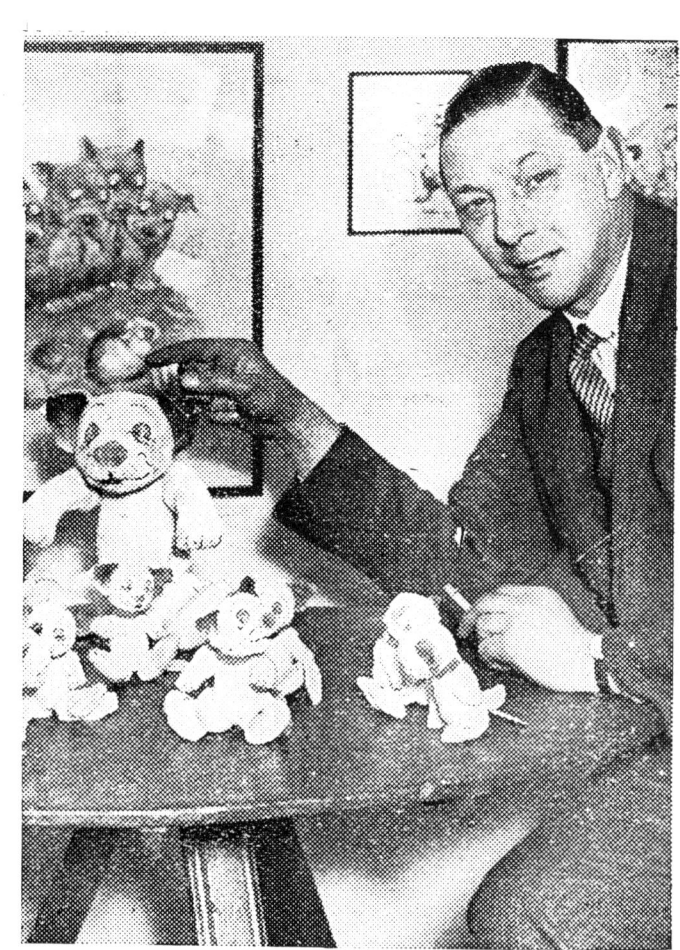

A press cutting from *The Daily Sketch*, 8th December, 1926.

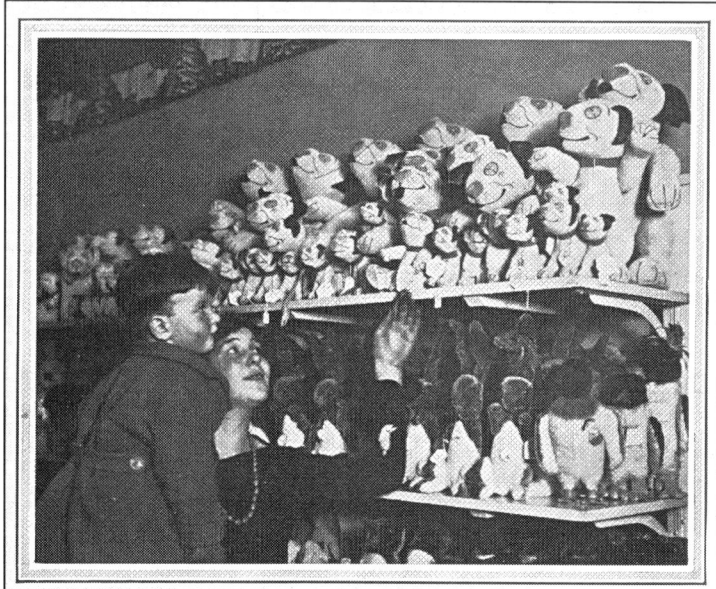

The toy department at Harrods ready for Christmas 1924.

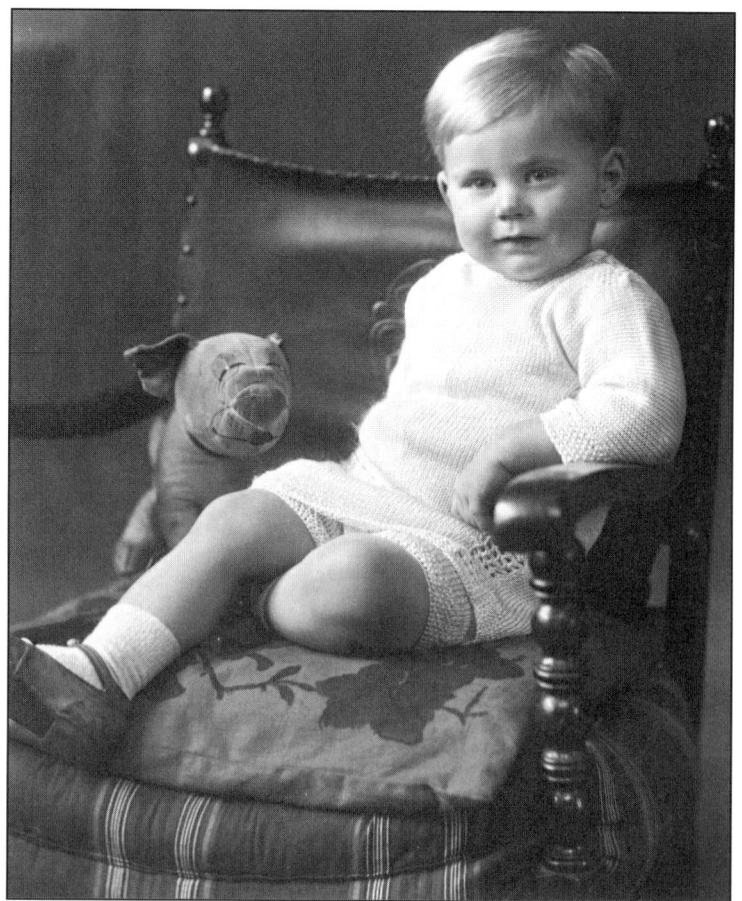

A studio portrait of a young boy with his favourite dog.

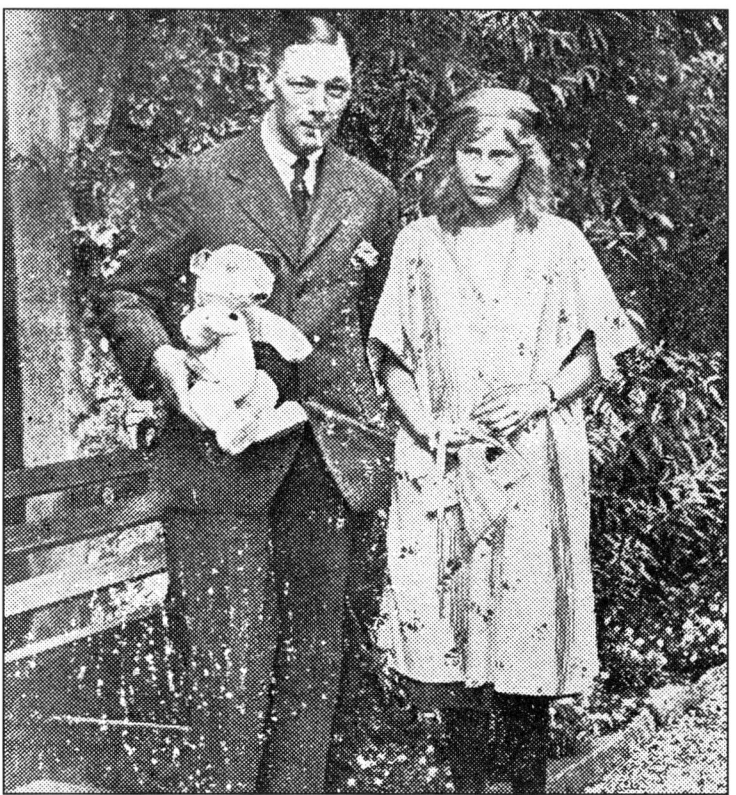

Studdy with a young admirer and a toy Bonzo. Taken from a Torquay newspaper, possibly whilst in Devon helping brother Hubert raise funds for his church.

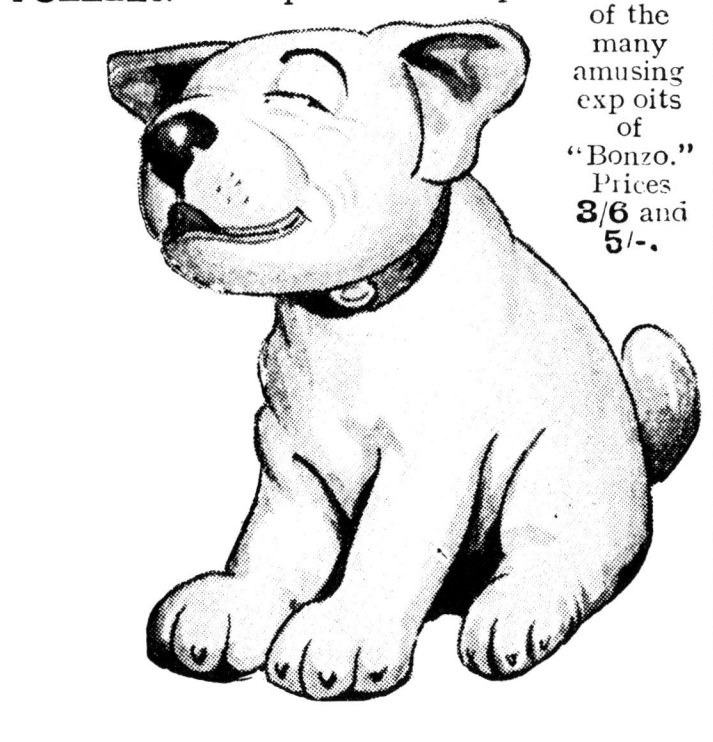

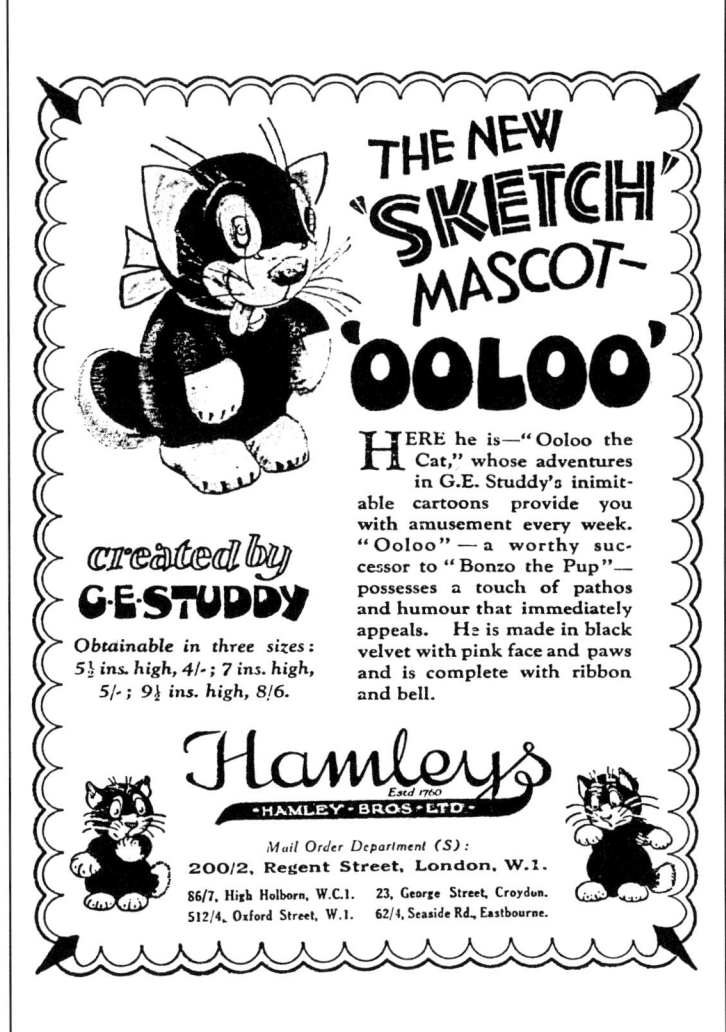

Part of Hamleys toy shop advertising for Christmas 1923, taken from *Good Housekeeping* magazine.

Although Bonzo toys were still selling well, by 1929 Hamleys were promoting Ooloo in their advertisements.

On one occasion he was afforded the luxury and peace of a box in which to sketch but made the mistake of arriving a short time after the curtain had been raised. In the dim light he bore a striking resemblance to King George VI and within a moment the whole audience was standing to attention in respectful silence and gazing up at their 'king'. The actors on the stage were totally ignored, and the play ground slowly to a halt. The management knew who was really sitting in the box and an announcement was made that it was not His Majesty the King up there but the famous Bonzo artist, Mr. George Studdy. This completely changed the atmosphere, and the audience's reverent silence was broken by loud and spontaneous applause for their much admired hero.

At this time George was constantly producing more and more Bonzo material. His main postcard publisher, Valentines of Dundee, kept him busy working on well over five hundred different card designs. They had bought drawings from him since before the First World War, and the firm's patronage continued until his death in 1948.

Dean's published many Bonzo books, including the Bonzo Annuals which they introduced in 1935. After the first four of these had been released, Europe was plunged into the Second World War and no more were produced until 1947. Although George died a year later, annuals were published until 1952, when they finally came to an end. Both Valentine's and Dean's decided to use another artist to illustrate their cards and books, but the graphic quality was, by comparison, extremely poor, contributing to Bonzo's final decline.

Although the demand for Bonzo never diminished during George's lifetime, the financial slump in the United States affected him badly. Poor investments and his renowned generosity removed much of his financial cushion. He was forced to cash some of his insurance policies to redress the balance. His accountant was also affected by the crash, to the extent that he was driven to suicide. His distraught widow came to George for help and, despite his own problems, he gave her £2,000 which, in those days, was a small fortune.

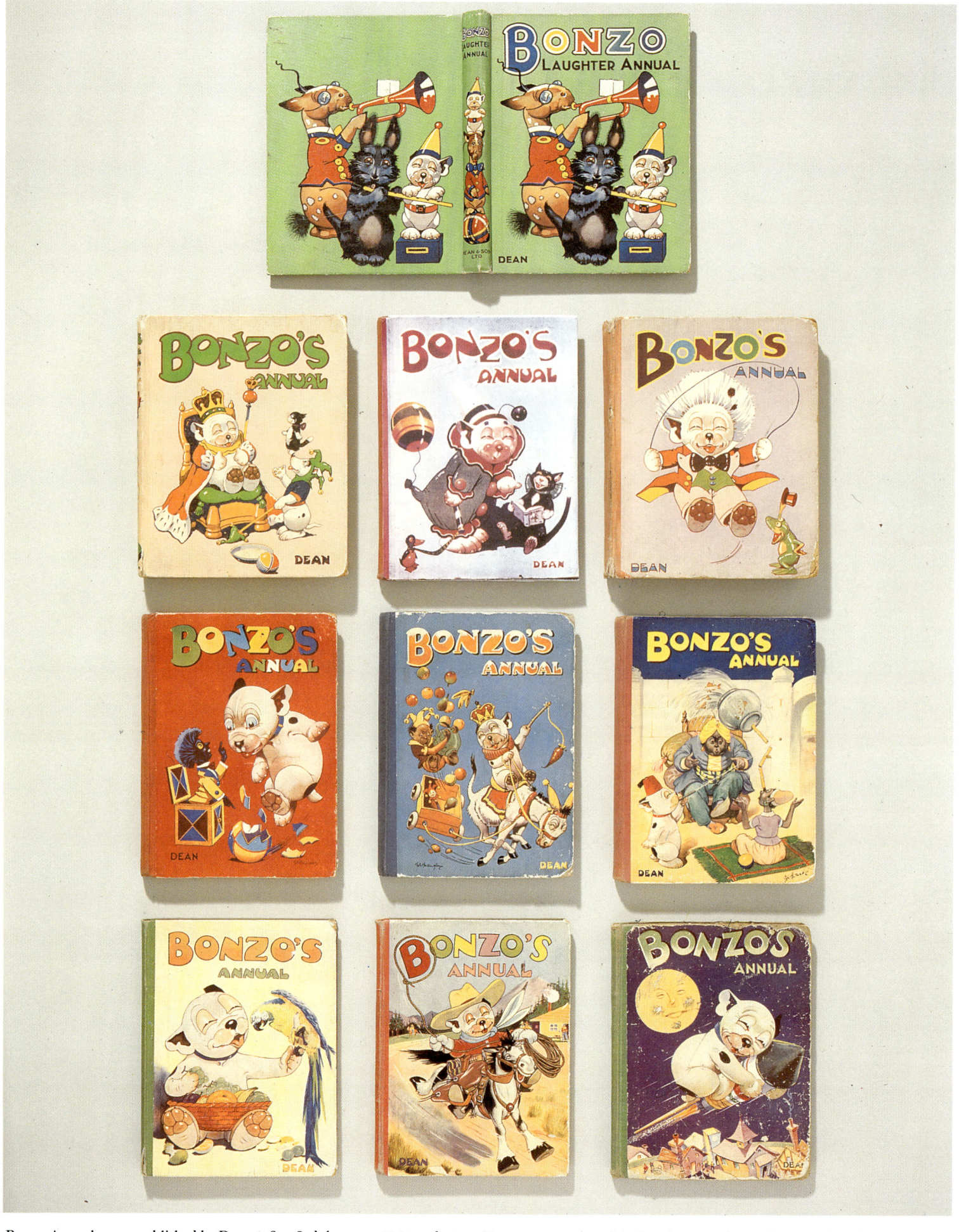

Bonzo Annuals were published by Dean & Son Ltd. between 1935 and 1952. None were produced during the second World War and Studdy was able to complete only two more before his death. The 1949 issue, although having a cover drawn by Studdy, is the work of a less talented artist. The poor quality of artwork continued in the remaining three Annuals, certainly affecting their sales. *Valentines of Dundee* were the only other publisher to employ another artist to draw Bonzo, their attempts can be seen in the post card section at the end of this book. None of the Annuals bear their year of publication but in the above illustration they are arranged in sequence. From the top: 1935, 1936, 1937, 1938, 1947, 1948, 1949, 1950, 1951 and 1952.

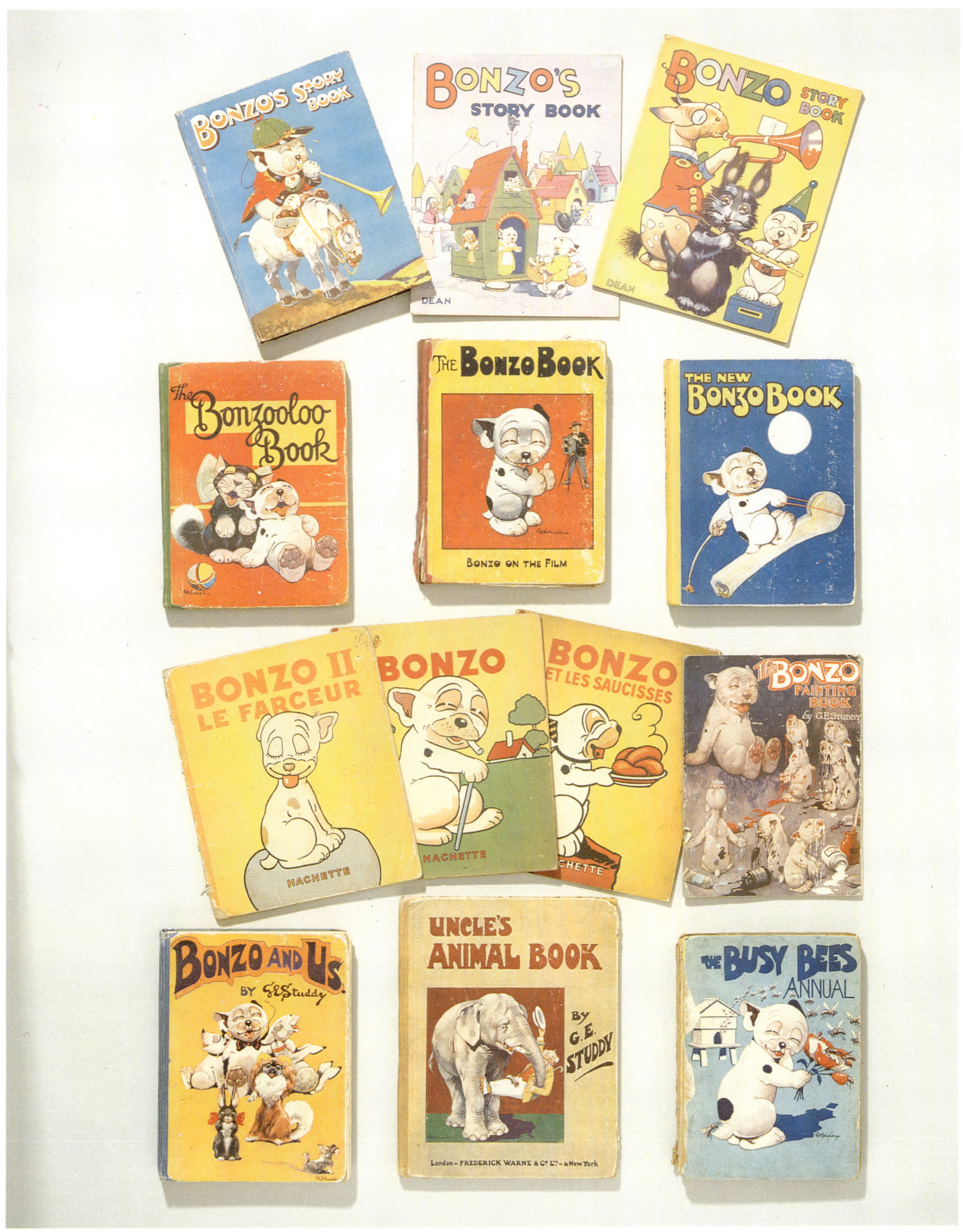

A selection of Bonzo books published in tandem with the Annuals, and often to a similar formula – the *Bonzo Story Book* top left, *The Bonzo Book* and *The New Bonzo Book* in the second row. The other two *Bonzo Story Books* are soft backed and sold for less. The *Bonzooloo Book* and *Bonzo and Us* involved other Studdy characters in Bonzo stories. In the third row are three of the strip cartoon books published by Hachette in France, the covers were probably done by a French artist and are rather crude but the strips inside have a great charm – beside is one of several painting books that were published. *Uncle's Animal Book* has no link with Bonzo other than it was written and drawn by Studdy. It tells of a boy's journey to a strange land and of the weird animals he meets there – possibly influenced by Edward Lear. The *Busy Bees Annual* is one of many for which Studdy provided only the cover.

AN ATTRACTIVE SEASIDE LINE

COWAN'S "BONZO" PAILS
(Regd.)

Size 8½ ins. x 7½ ins.

Filled with

"Bonzo" Toffee - - - 4 lbs.
"Bonzo" Assorted Candies 4 lbs.
"Bonzo" Assorted Caramels 7 lbs.

Empty pails can be retailed at 1/- each, and will be in great demand at the Seaside this Season.

Order early to secure prompt delivery.

COWAN & McKAY, Manufacturing Confectioners, **Oxford Street, Glasgow.**

A 1925 trade advertisement for Bonzo Toffee in *The Confectioners Union* magazine. The sweets were also sold in smaller tins decorated with Bonzo and are illustrated on page 65.

At the outbreak of World War II the Studdys were still living in Philbeach Gardens and George was determined to help his country in whatever way he could. He went down to Portsmouth and worked as a draughtsman in the Royal Naval Dockyards. It was important to him that he should contribute to the war, but he was already sixty and too old to take an active part in any fighting. Everybody in Portsmouth was so involved in the war effort that they did not connect George Studdy the draughtsman with George Studdy the artist. One day his identity was discovered when an officer came up to his desk and asked sheepishly if he was in fact the creator of Bonzo, as it had been nagging at his mind for a few days since he had recognised his name. The news spread around the Dockyard like wildfire and he was often asked for sketches and autographs by both colleagues and Naval officers alike.

The rest of the Studdy family moved out of London for most of the war but Blanche and Vivienne did not join George. Portsmouth, unfortunately, would have been a case of 'out of the frying pan and into the fire'. He almost lost count of the number of times he returned to his various lodgings after work only to find a pile of rubble where the house had been. Vivienne, accompanied by her mother, went in the opposite direction to the Lake District,

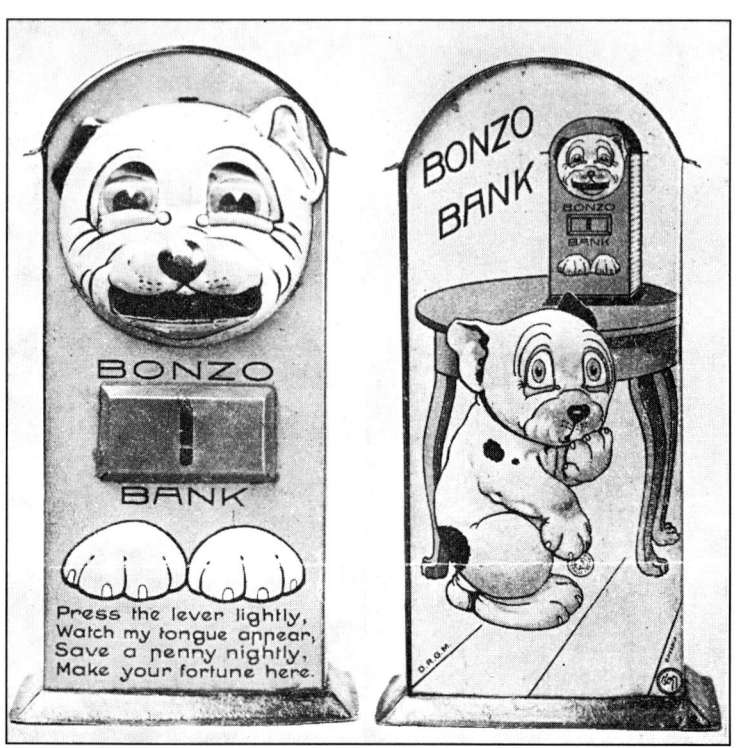

A rare Bonzo money box of German origin with D.G.R.M. printed on the back and a trade mark consisting of a double S within a circle and the word *Bavaria*. The front and sides are mainly red, the back yellow and the top and base are black. When the lever was pressed Bonzo's tongue popped out to receive a coin accompanied by the lowering of his eyes. When released the coin was swallowed and the eyes returned to normal. There is a similar bank featuring Mickey Mouse.

"SPHERE" SUSPENDERS

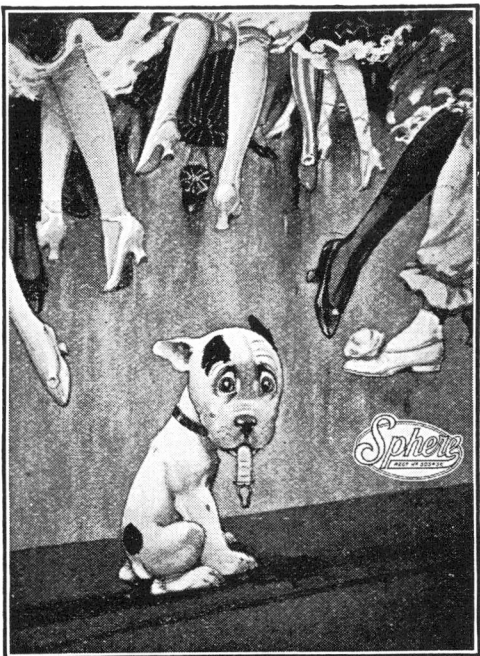

**Hi! Stop the Band!
A Lady has dropped her Suspender.**

LADIES — Ask your Draper for "Sphere" Suspenders with the Oval-Octo Button. The "Sphere Oval-Octo" will not tear your finest hose.

GENTLEMEN — Ask your Outfitter for "Sphere" Braces and the "Sphere Broadway" Garter. The "Sphere Broadway" Garter for men is a new "Sphere" speciality, made of 1¾" wide "spring-easy" elastic. It is most comfortable in wear, and will not cause varicose veins.

"Sphere" goods are noted for Quality—Finish—and—Reliability.

"SPHERE" SUSPENDERS—BRACES—GARTERS.

Manufactured by Faire Bro's. & Co. Ltd., Leicester.

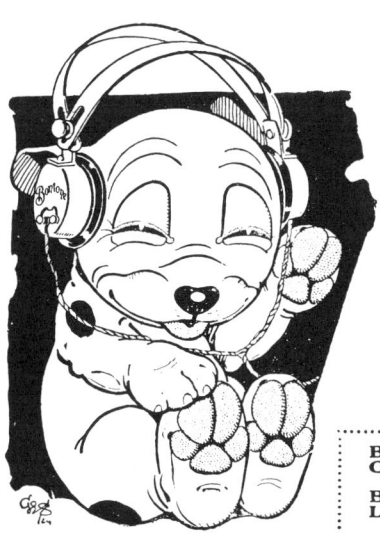

Hello! Hello!! Hello!!!

Let it be known that a progressive English firm now offer their

ALL BRITISH HEADPHONES

at prices and quality that will compete with any other 'phones on the world's market, be they of British or foreign manufacture.

BONTONE ORIGINALS — 11/6
BONTONE LIGHTWEIGHTS — 12/6
Post Free.

We guarantee to forward by return of post. We guarantee to replace if phones do not give entire satisfaction and same are returned to us within 10 days of purchase undamaged.

SPECIFICATION:—Simply adjusted, comfortable and highly polished "Featherweight" Headbands. Specially designed permanent magnets. Perfectly matched coils, wound to a total resistance of 4,000 Ohms. Best quality 5 ft. 6 in. cords, serrated Swedish Iron Pole Pieces, beautifully polished Trolite Earcaps.

Remember that behind this offer is the name of BONTONE, with a sale exceeding 100,000 phones. Better value than the above cannot be obtained at double their purchase price.

BONTONE PHONES may be obtained from all Radio Stores, or direct from the actual manufacturers:

B. D. & Co. (Ed. A. BOYNTON).
Admiralty and War Office Contractors,
167-173, GOSWELL ROAD, LONDON, E.C.1.

THE WORLD FAMOUS "Woollvena" PURE DOWN QUILTS

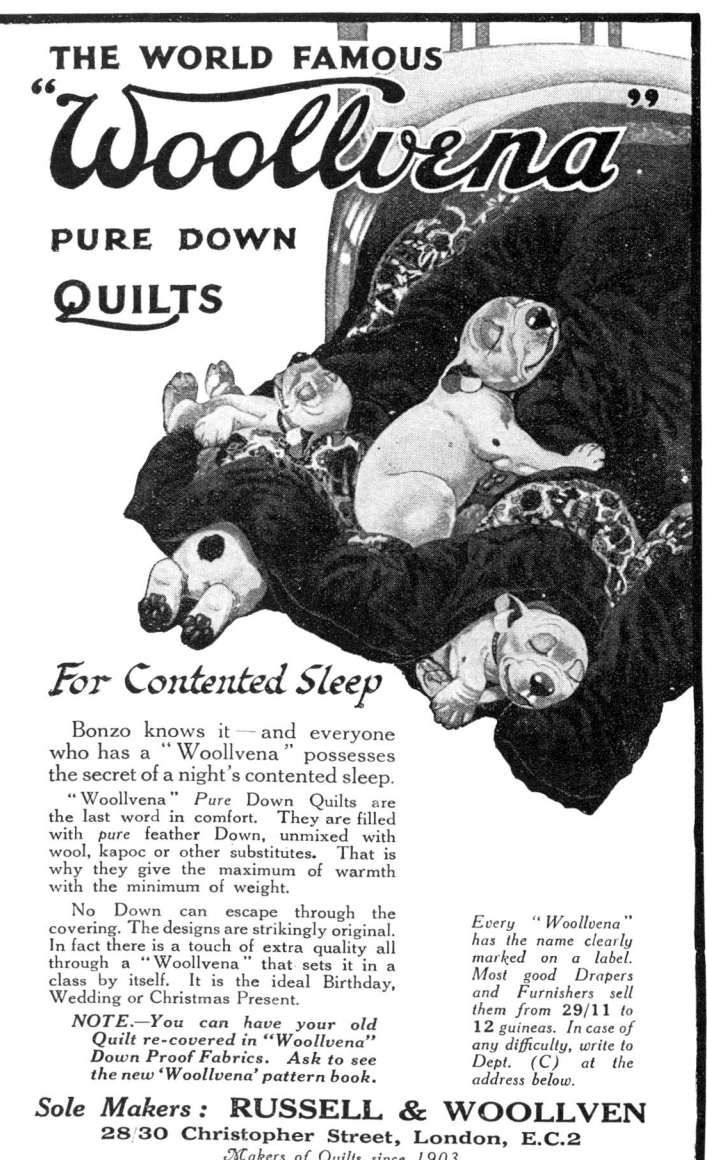

For Contented Sleep

Bonzo knows it—and everyone who has a "Woollvena" possesses the secret of a night's contented sleep.

"Woollvena" Pure Down Quilts are the last word in comfort. They are filled with pure feather Down, unmixed with wool, kapoc or other substitutes. That is why they give the maximum of warmth with the minimum of weight.

No Down can escape through the covering. The designs are strikingly original. In fact there is a touch of extra quality all through a "Woollvena" that sets it in a class by itself. It is the ideal Birthday, Wedding or Christmas Present.

NOTE.—You can have your old Quilt re-covered in "Woollvena" Down Proof Fabrics. Ask to see the new 'Woollvena' pattern book.

Every "Woollvena" has the name clearly marked on a label. Most good Drapers and Furnishers sell them from 29/11 to 12 guineas. In case of any difficulty, write to Dept. (C) at the address below.

Sole Makers: RUSSELL & WOOLLVEN
28/30 Christopher Street, London, E.C.2
Makers of Quilts since 1903

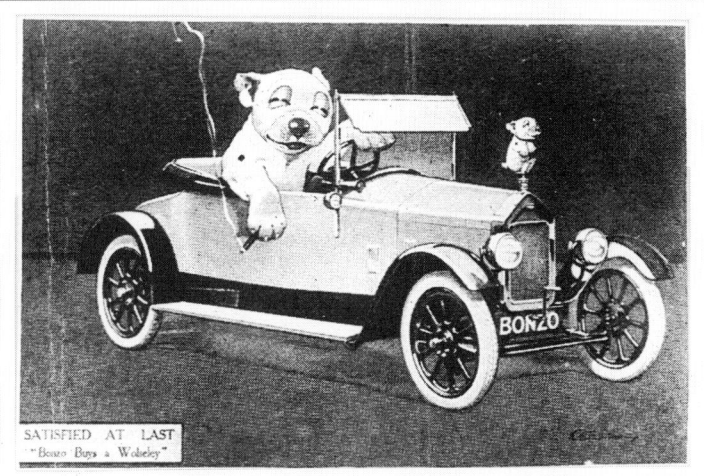

BONZO IS SATISFIED AT LAST! THE FAMOUS STUDDY DOG IN HIS WOLSELEY "TEN."

Everyone who is acquainted with Bonzo realises that he knows a good thing when he sees one, and so will not be surprised to see from the above that he has bought a Wolseley "Ten."—[*From the Drawing by G. E. Studdy.*]

Bonzo's potential to promote and advertise products was enormous and covered a wide range of goods from suspenders to cars.

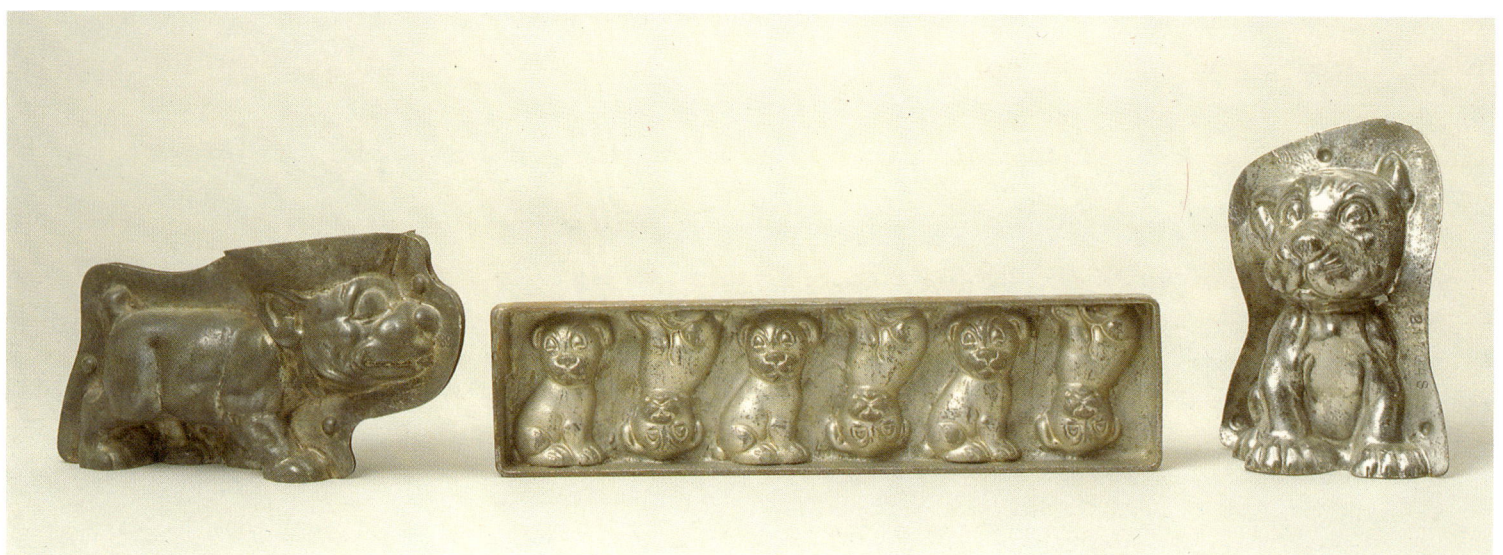

Three Bonzo chocolate moulds. The central one produced small solid dogs whilst the others made hollow three-dimensional ones. The mould on the left is in three parts and that on the right two.

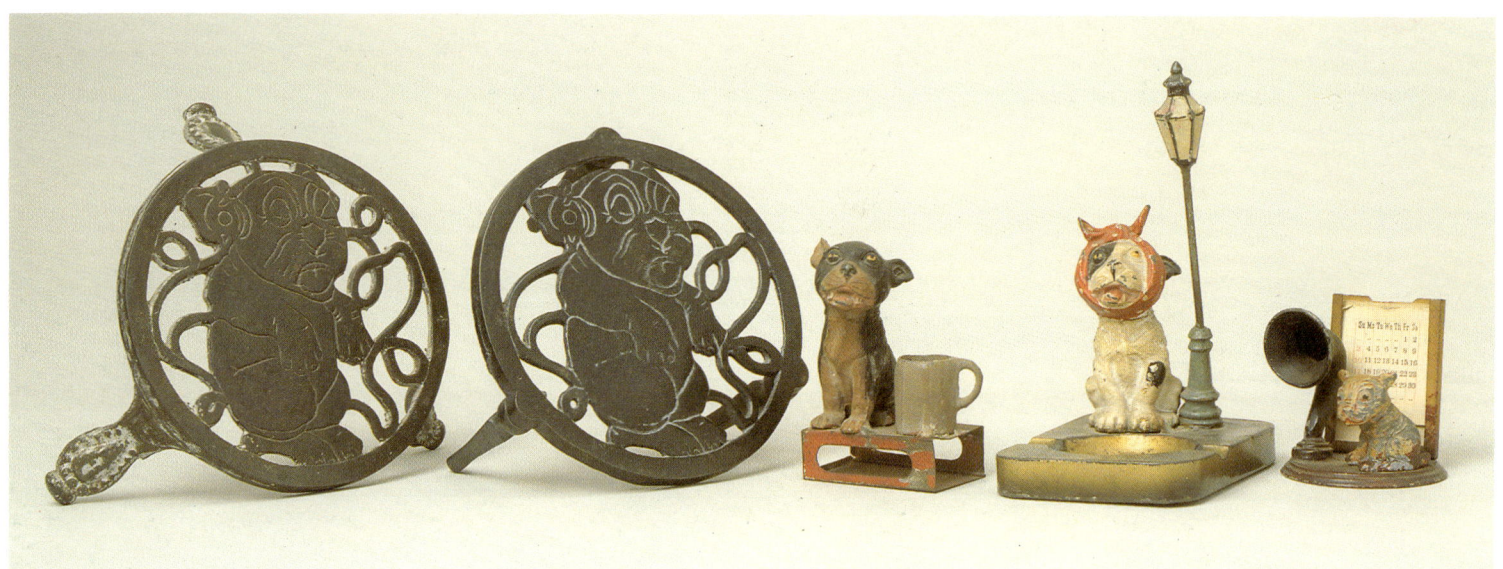

Cast metal trivets of basically the same design but with different feet. A matchbox holder, ashtray and calendar all featuring cast metal Studdy dogs.

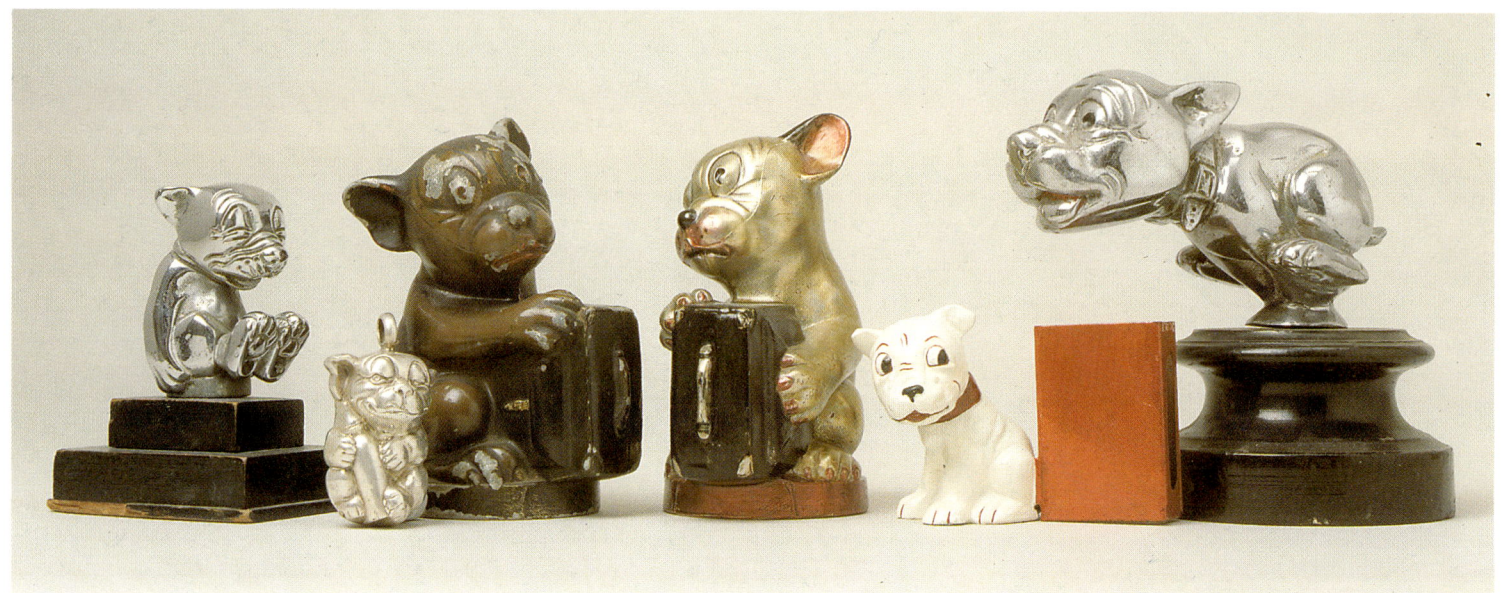

Left to right: A chrome plated car mascot inscribed *Bonzo* on the back of the collar. A silver plated child's rattle featuring Bonzo holding a baby's bottle. Two cast metal money boxes. An early cast metal match box holder and a large car mascot known as *The Telcote Pup* (after the manufacturer) – in 1922 it sold for 3 guineas.

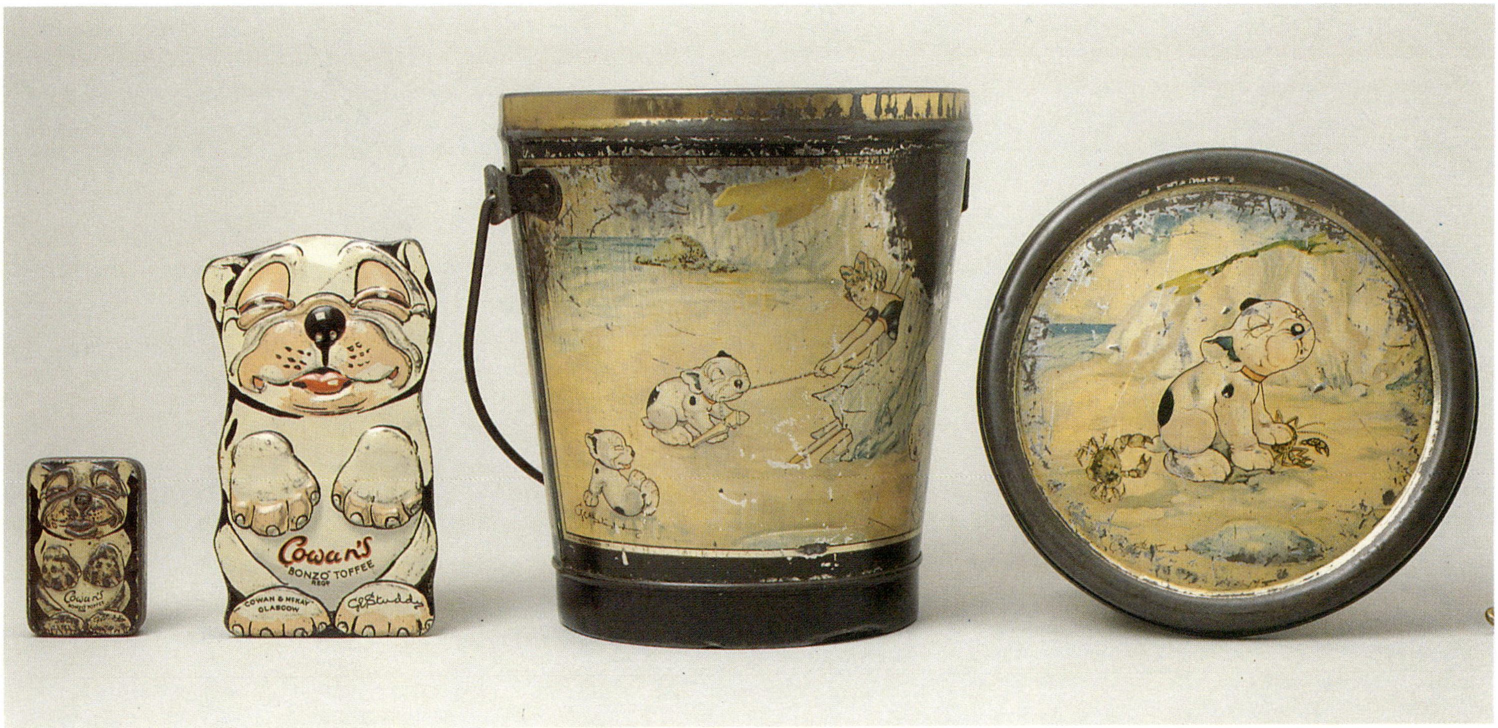
Cowan's
BONZO TOFFEE
COWAN & McKAY
GLASGOW

Tins used to package Bonzo toffees, manufactured by Cowan and McKay of Glasgow. The lithographic printing was of high standard for such everyday objects. The small tin on the left has *Bonzo* in slight relief on a simple rectangular shape. The larger one in the centre is also stamped in relief but the shape of the lid follows the outline of the drawing. The bucket is shown alongside its lid and can also be seen in the advertisement on page 62.

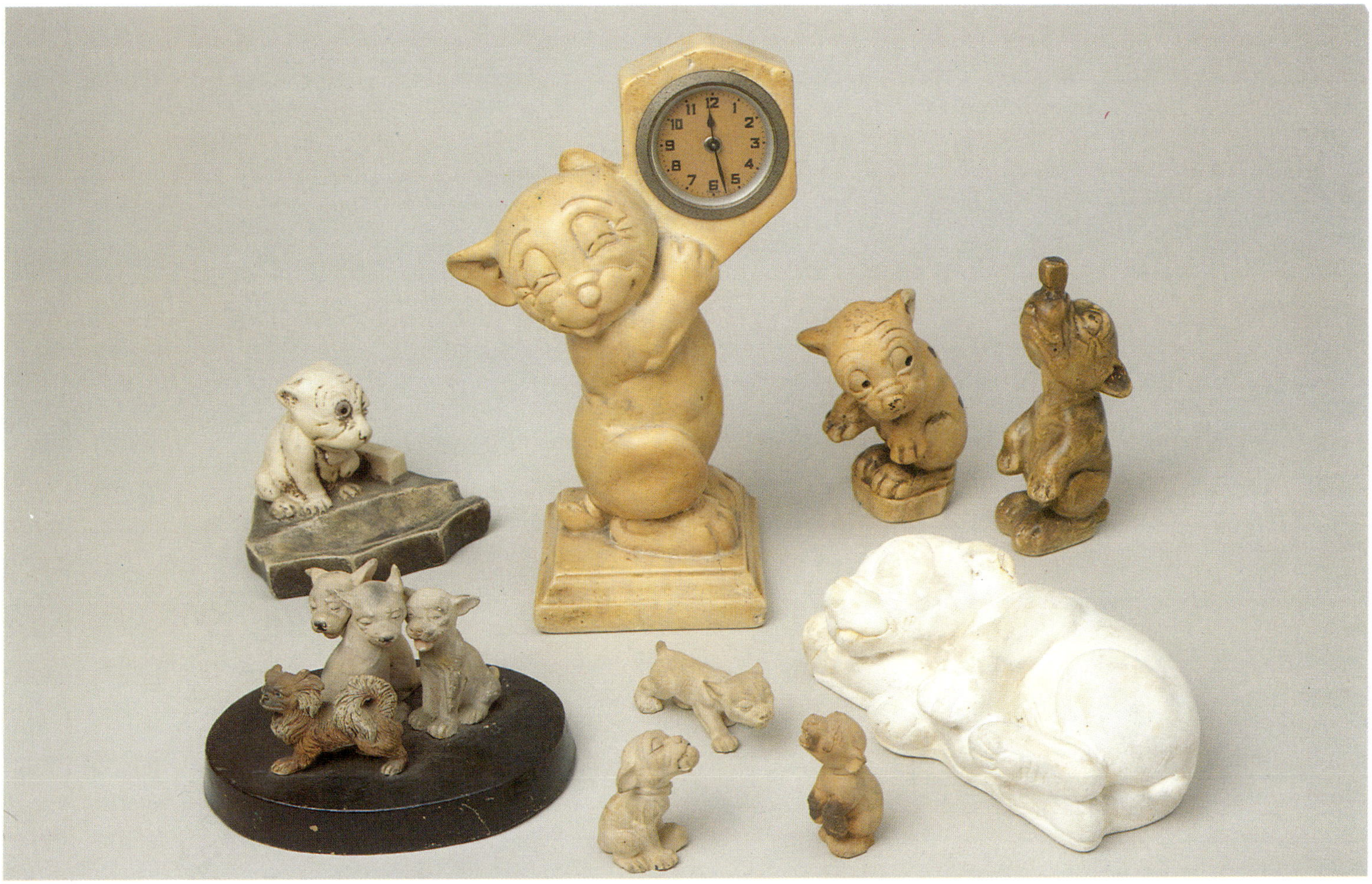

A group of plaster and pottery Bonzos. The ashtray top left is based on the *Taking the count* illustration for *The Sketch* shown on page 20. The plaster clock and the large sleeping Bonzo were made in Britain by *Artisco*. The two smaller figures at the back are also taken from the pages of *The Sketch*. Bottom left is a three dimensional version of R.P.S. post card No.1033 *Carry Your Tail, My Lord*. Two of the small figures at the front are identical to the Grafton China ash trays on page 36.

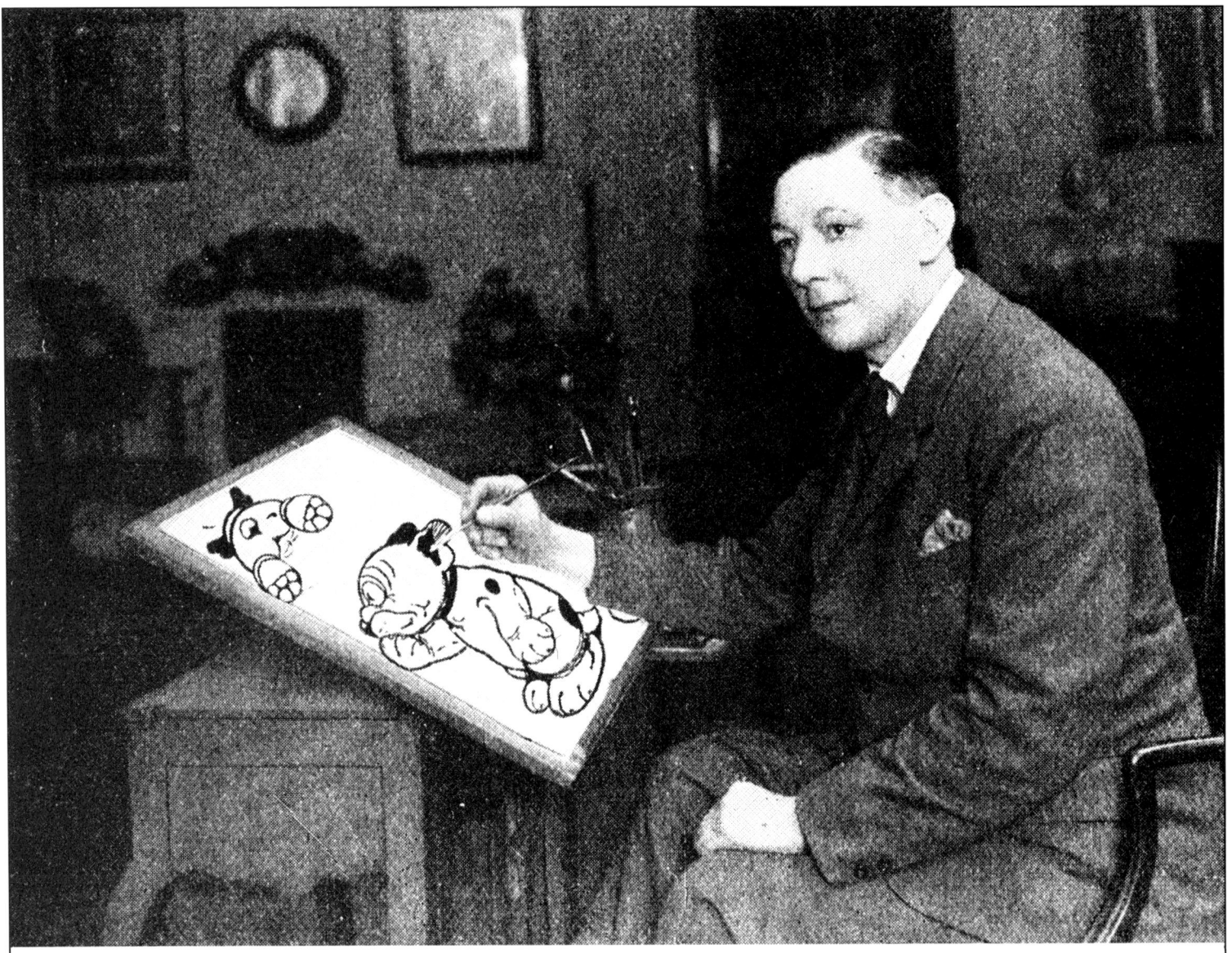

G. E. STUDDY is the father of Bonzo. When "DAS MAGAZIN" first introduced the ingenious cartoonists humorous white dogs to it's German readers it was impossible to imagine just how popular they would become. Today BONZO is known to every child. Each issue of "DAS MAGAZIN" carries a new adventure. Through the sale of soft toys, pins, brooches, car-mascots, flags and picture post-cards the popularity has been increased even further. Our readers will therefore be even more interested in meeting the father of BONZO face to face.

This tribute appeared in the German *Das Magazin* in the 1930's under the heading *Men who make us laugh*. It illustrates perfectly the popularity Bonzo enjoyed on the continent.

where in 1940 she married a young naval officer at Windermere. The following March she returned to London and applied to enlist in the WRNS. The attempt was thwarted when she discovered she was pregnant and promptly rejoined Blanche in Cumbria. By 1943 she had moved with her husband and baby daughter to Largs in Ayrshire where the news reached them that a German V1 rocket had landed on Philbeach Gardens.

Although it did not fall directly onto number 75, it was close enough to cause the inside of the house to collapse. Luckily nobody was inside at the time and there were no casualties. The house was in the care of Mr and Mrs Simmons who had arrived on the doorstep a few years earlier looking for work and accommodation.

The couple were from Totnes in Devon, and Mrs Simmons had worked for the Studdy family on and off for several years in the West Country, and had known George since she started work as a kitchen maid. On their arrival in London the couple offered to act as caretakers in return for a roof over their heads. Fortunately on the night of the bombing they were sheltering across the road in the crypt of St. Cuthberts church. Vivienne came down from

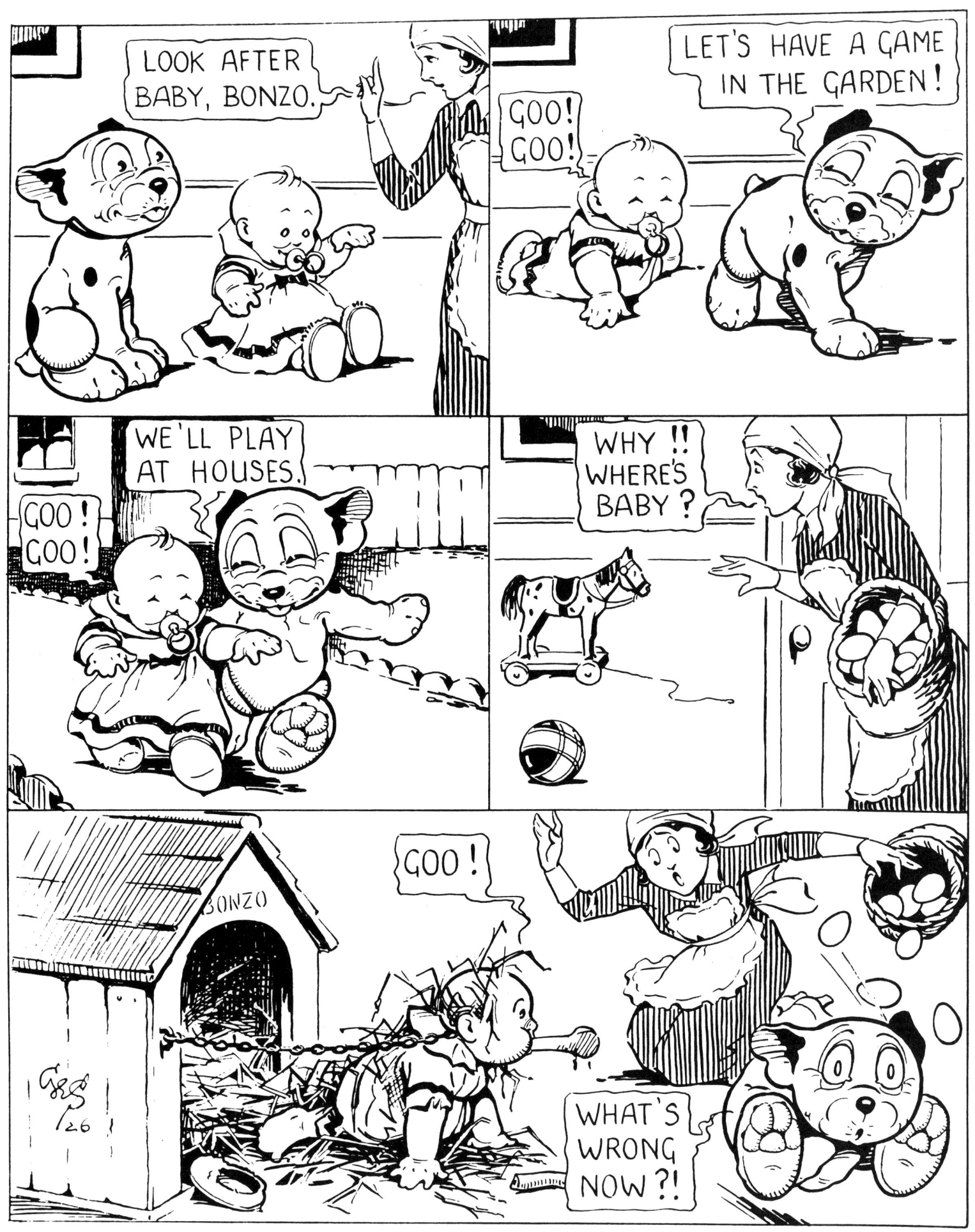

A typical black and white cartoon strip from *The New Bonzo Book*.

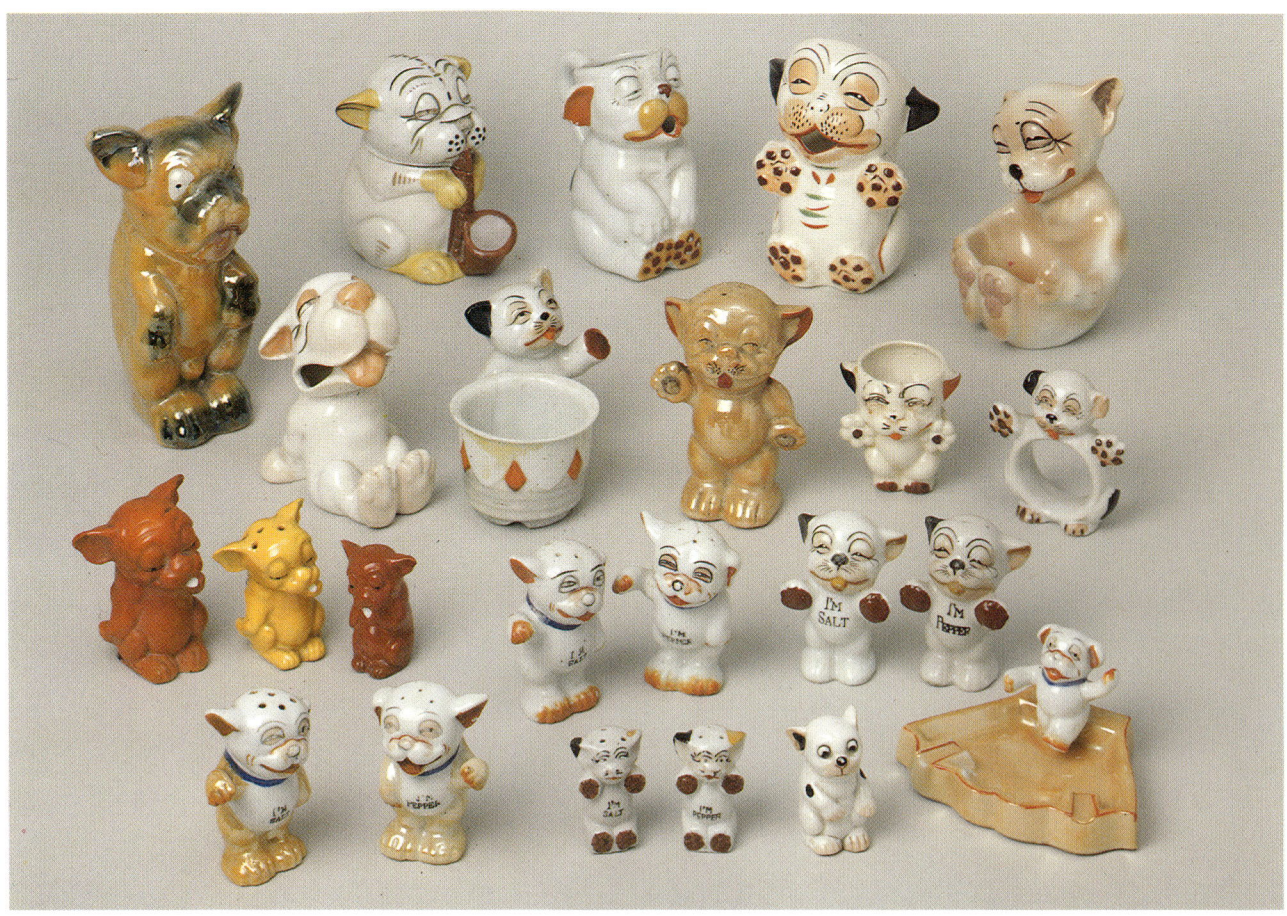

The Japanese produced large quantities of very cheap china Bonzos. The quality of the painting ranged from fine to crude. Many of them were intended to be useful as well as decorative. Amongst the objects illustrated are pepper and salt pots, jugs, ashtrays, a napkin ring and an egg cup.

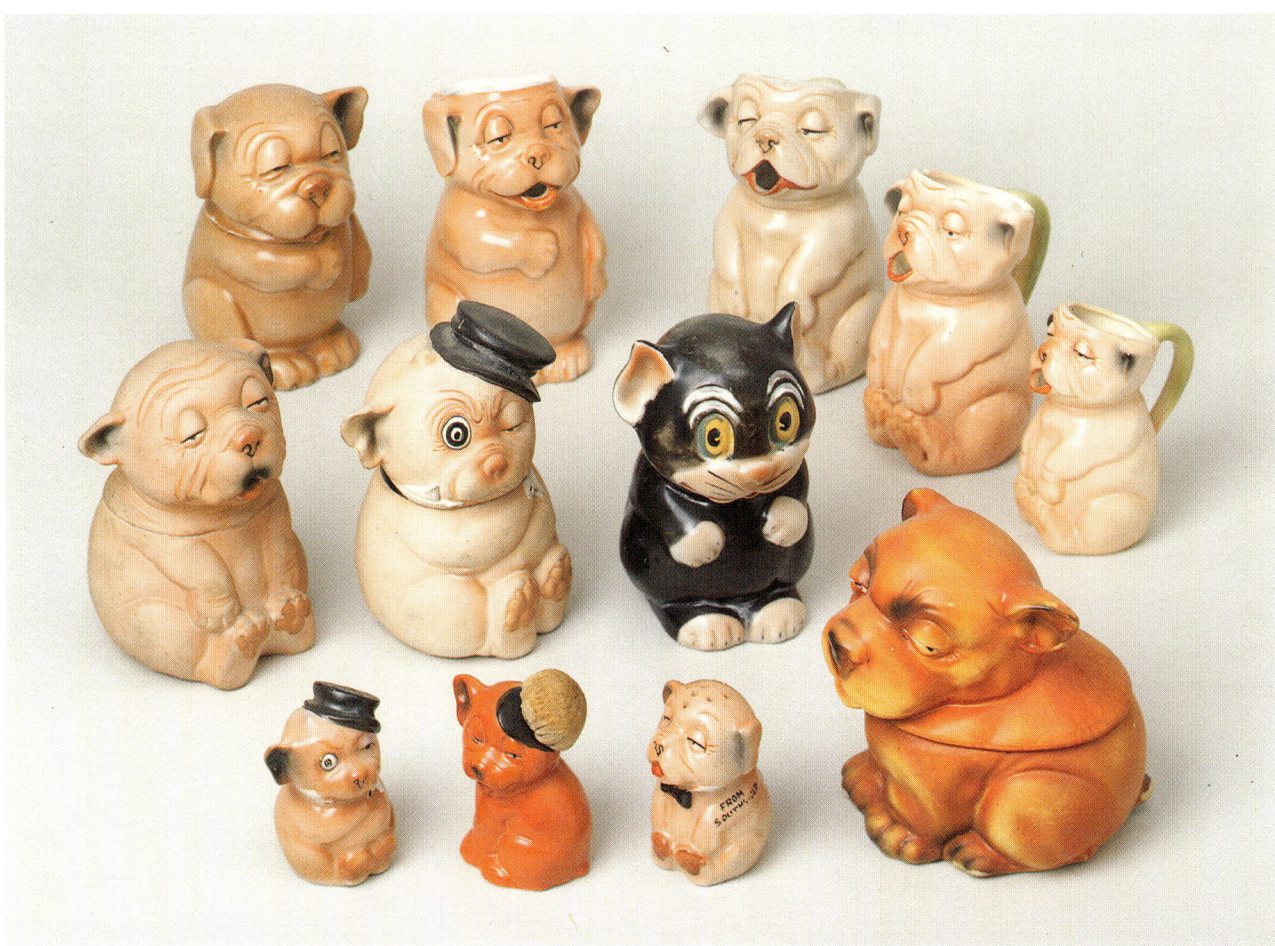

A much higher standard of modelling and finish was achieved with this group. The back row shows four jugs including a set of three. All the other large pieces have removable heads. The exception is on the left of the centre row which also has an opening at the mouth and was used as a string holder. The small figures in the front row comprise a pin cushion flanked by two pepper pots.

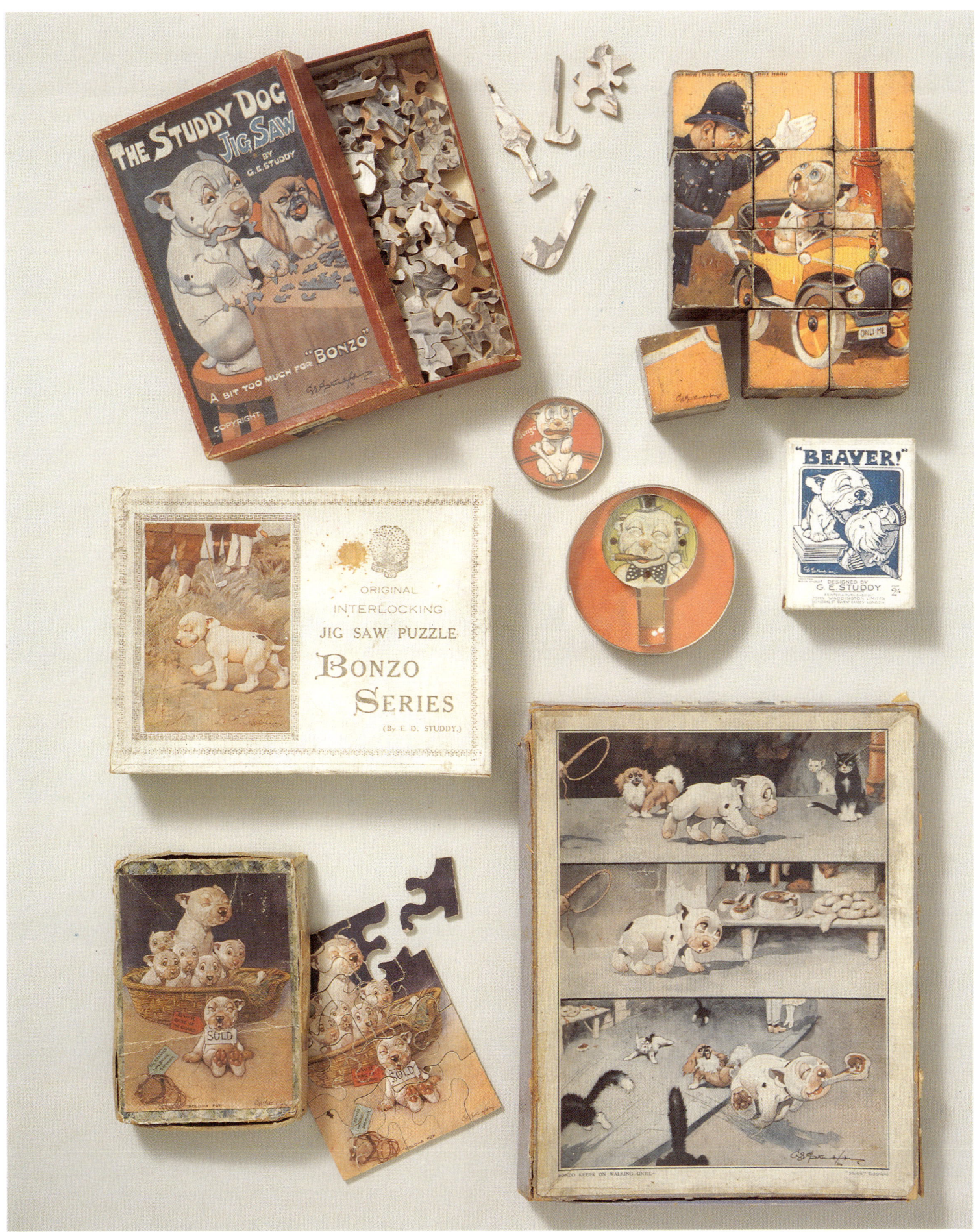

Many jigsaws were produced, often re-using printing blocks already made for other purposes. The top left is novel in that many of the pieces are shaped as everyday objects including an umbrella, a pipe and a walking stick. Top right is a set of wooden building blocks probably re-using a book plate. Bonzo appears on only one of the six sides. Below is a card game designed by Studdy for Waddington's. Although Bonzo appears on the cover he has no part in the game and the drawing on the cards is rather untypical. At the centre are two glass covered puzzles, one where balls must be rolled into Bonzo's eyes and the other where a bone fits into his mouth.

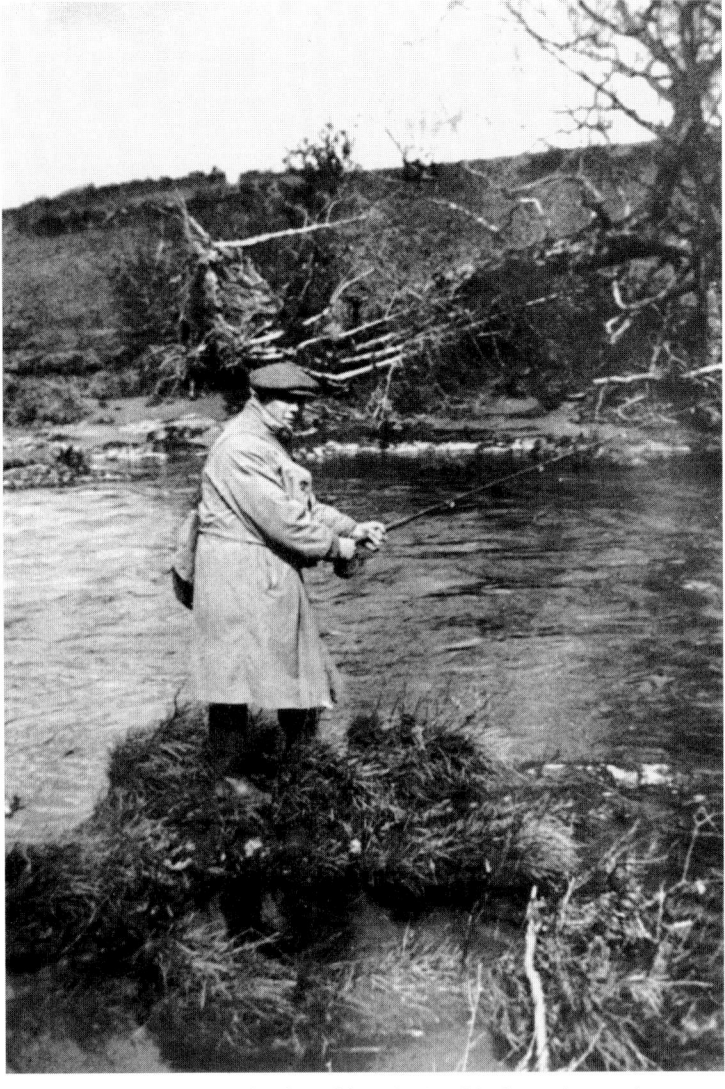

A family photograph of Studdy enjoying his favourite pastime.

Scotland to inspect the damage and see what she could salvage from the wreckage. Sadly, much of George's original artwork was stored in the basement and that which was not destroyed by the bomb was looted.

She then went with her daughter Zelda to stay with George in Portsmouth. At the end of the war the house was rebuilt and the family was reunited once more in Philbeach Gardens.

George might have been a wealthy man but his natural generosity coupled with a much lower income during the war years, meant that life was not quite as easy as it had been. He decided to diversify and produced a series of postcards for Humouresque in a style similar to the one developed by Donald McGill whose risqué seaside postcards had been popular for many years. He did not think it fitting to sign these with his own name and he became 'Cheero' for a short while.

By 1947 the crisis had abated and work was returning to normal. In September, George started to suffer very severe chest pains and eventually consulted his doctor who was a long-time angling friend and would be straight-forward and honest. Dr. Pinches recognised exactly what the symptoms indicated, and George too had strong suspicions. When the unpleasant truth had to be faced, the doctor told his friend that it was almost certainly cancer. The fact that George was a constant smoker was certainly the main cause, but it was aggravated by the dusty atmosphere of wartime Portsmouth.

Having just moved into their rebuilt house, Blanche became busy furnishing the interior in the up-to-date style. It was very popular then to decorate with bright colours, probably as a direct reaction to the drab austerity of the 'utility' furnishings of the war years. She decided that their sofas and armchairs should be starkly covered in black, with bright scatter cushions to provide a stunning contrast. When George returned from his depressing visit to Dr. Pinches, the suite had been delivered but Blanche had not had time to arrange the cushions and he was greeted by vast expanses of black. Even in this situation, his dry sense of humour came to the fore, and as he walked into the sitting room he said to Blanche, "You're a little bit previous aren't you?" His joke was not shared by his wife who, totally devastated, burst into tears.

Vivienne and her husband had been stationed in Malta for two years with the navy when a letter came from George breaking the news. She returned to London in October 1947 to visit him, and the family celebrated with an outing to The Victoria Palace Theatre to see The Crazy Gang. This was to be the last time George was able to leave the house socially.

By November he was beginning to lose the use of his left arm and within a few months was confined to his bed. Mrs Simmons helped Blanche nurse him and they all tried to make things as normal as possible.

For some time George had been writing a book of his own about fishing, based on his memories of trips with Doctor Pinches. They had enjoyed companionship in the sport roughly twice a year for a very long time. It was to be called either 'The Doc and I' or 'Let's go fishing'. He wrote with his right hand for as long as he was able, and when he lost the use of it by dictation to Vivienne.

He died on July 25th 1948 and was cremated at Golders Green Cemetery. He did not leave much money or many possessions. His legacy to the world was his work which is still with us and still makes people of all ages laugh and smile. Although Bonzo made his last appearance more than thirty years ago he remains in the hearts and memories of countless people who will never forget him.

He Made The World Laugh

ARTIST OF IMMORTAL BONZO DIES IN KENSINGTON

A man who made the whole world laugh with his immortal Bonzo dog, which crossed all barriers of language and came on postcards, in magazines, chocolate shapes, car mascots, and a hundred and one other forms into homes of every land, died quietly, away from the glare of publicity, in Philbeach Gardens, Kensington, last week. He was George Ernest Studdy, aged seventy, an artist who started as an illustrator in "Comic Cuts", and became one of the best known illustrators of the day.

He began his career as an engineer's draftsman, but soon turned to humorous drawing. When the Bonzo era began, the immortal dog was reproduced in every possible form, from stuffed toys to chocolate figures. Full-plate Bonzo illustrations were a regular feature in the "Sketch".

There were other characters, including Ooloo the Cat, but none achieved the popularity of Bonzo, and George Studdy must have drawn as many Bonzos as there are dogs in London. He did other work, all of it excellent, but he will go down in history as the creator of Bonzo.

When he was not working (he only gave up at the beginning of his eleven months' illness), his hobby was fly-fishing, and he wrote many articles for the fishing journals. He was one of the

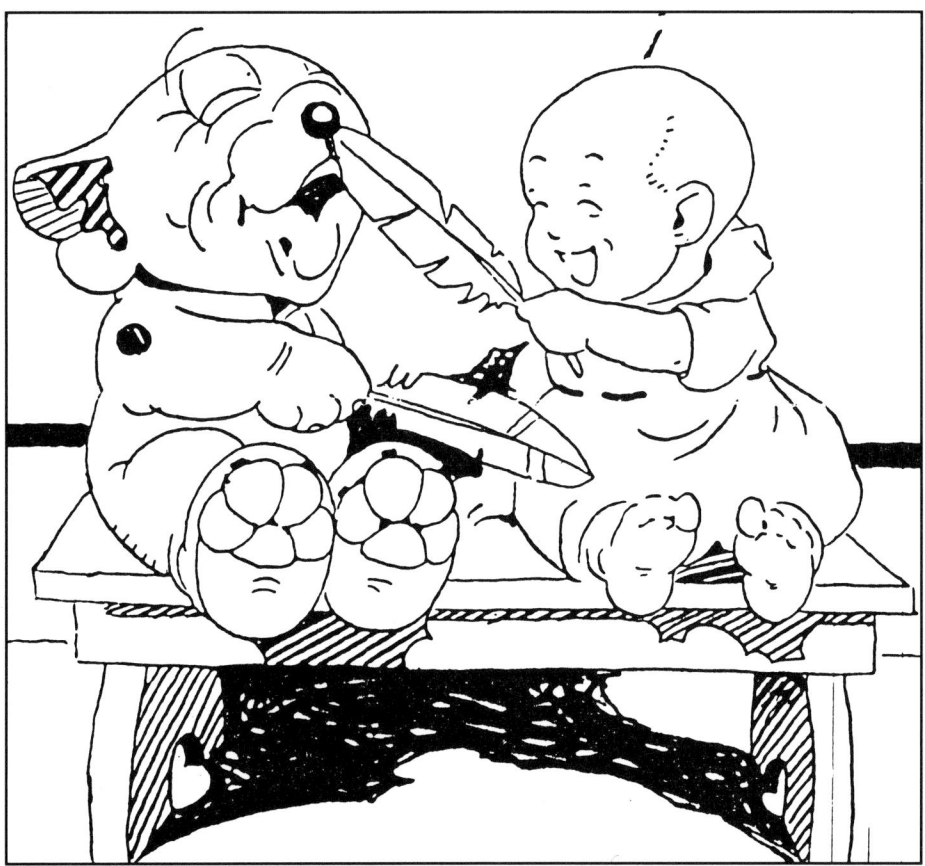

was a dog in every anatomical respect, a white supple-bodied bull terrier, with a broad grin and sleepy eyes. As the years progressed, the terrier became a caricature of a terrier, until the button-nosed, elephant-eared, pudge-footed creature that was Bonzo was evolved. In one infringement case it was stated in evidence that Bonzo had twenty features which were definitely not canine, making him a creature apart.

For many years George Studdy did a weekly comic strip for an American syndicate. Bonzo was registered as a trade mark and registered as a design in nearly every country in the world, and

oldest members of the London Sketch Club, and used to be a regular attendant at their Balls.

On the whole, he led a secluded life, he had a dry wit, but was a kindly and generous man, making friends easily and keeping them throughout his lifetime. He was known to many people in the neighbourhood of his home, for he had been a resident in Philbeach Gardens for about thirty years. Not all who knew him realised that he was the genius behind the millions of gaily coloured Bonzos that capered on postcards in cities and towns and villages all over the country.

He leaves a widow and one daughter.

The Feather Ticklers – a section of one of George Studdy's comic strips of the immortal "Bonzo"

Studdy's obituary notice from *The Kensington News* and *West London Times*, Friday, August 13th 1948.

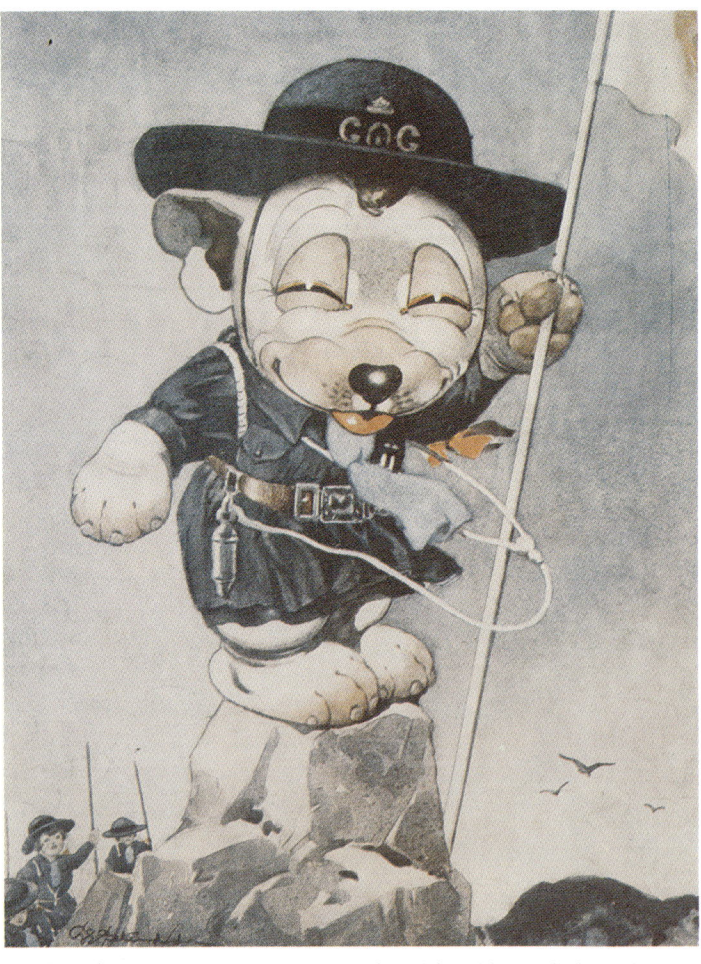
11th February 1925. Bonzo gives the girl guides a little assistance.

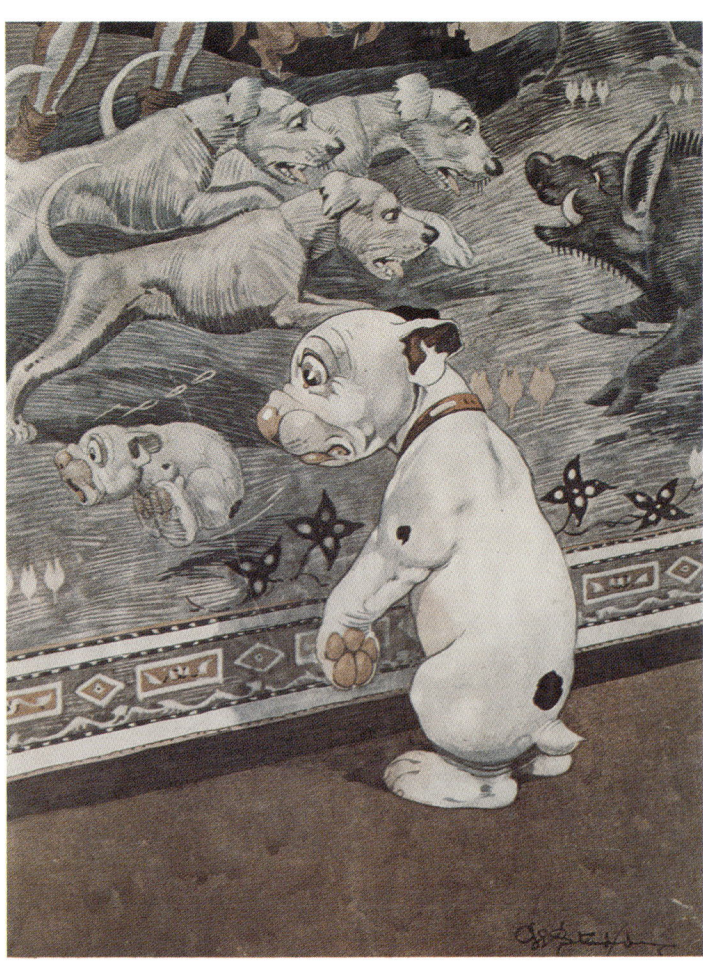
23rd January 1924. Bonzo finds a trace of his ancestral courage in an old tapestry!

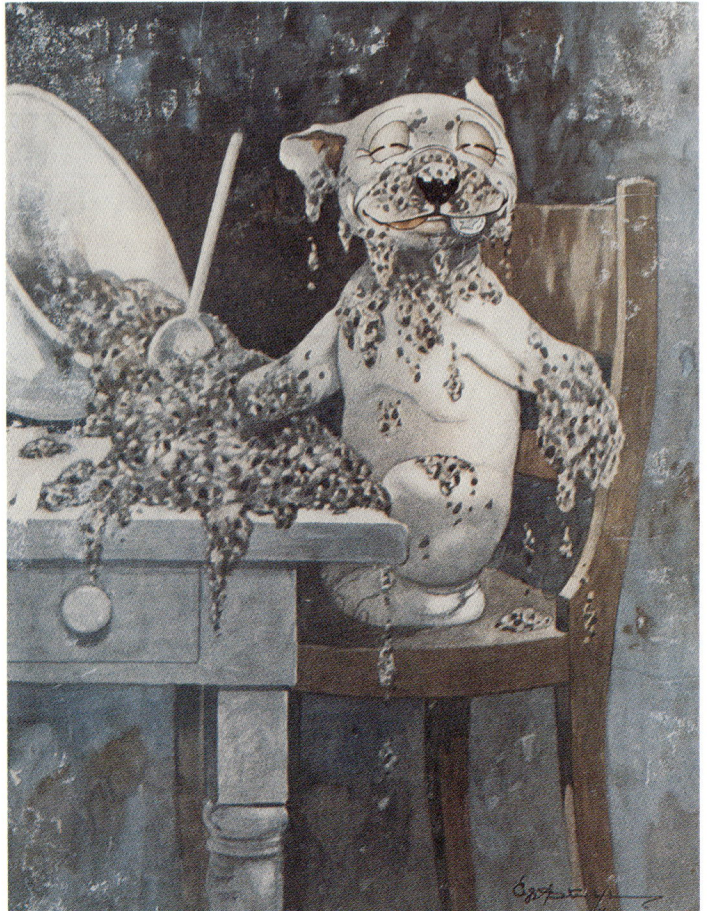
5th December 1923 Bonzo saves the sixpence, but spoils the pudding. (IV Thursday's good deed:)

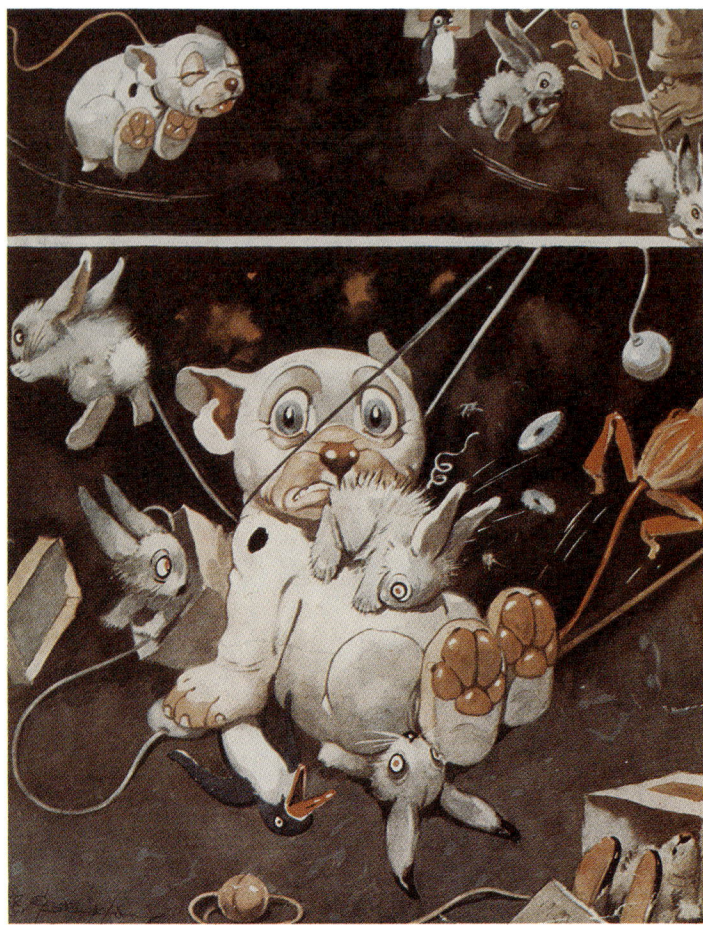
24th September 1924. "YOICKS!"

Above and opposite. Some of the weekly contributions to *The Sketch* that made Bonzo a popular institution.

Bonzo in Search of His Forefathers.

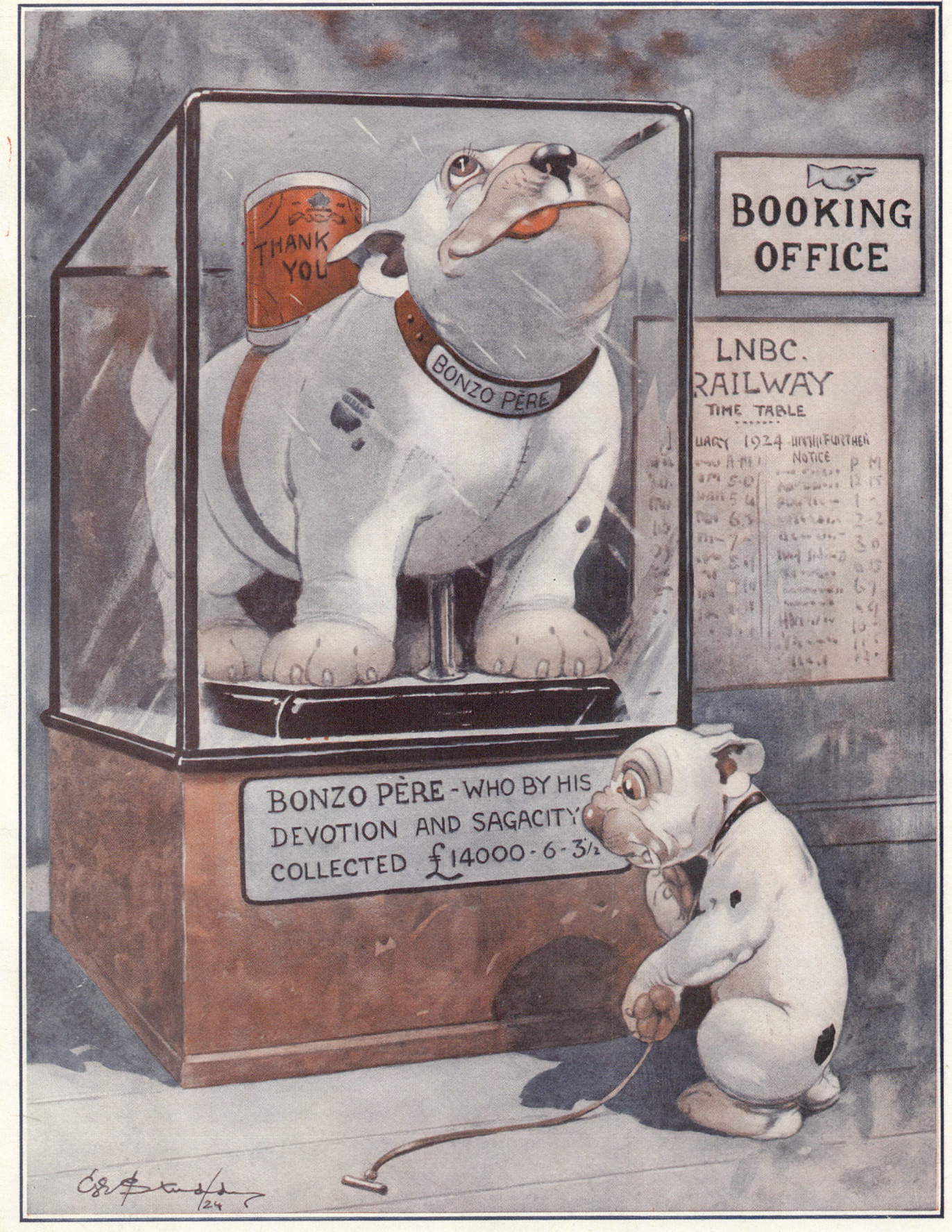

BONZO FINDS HIS FATHER — AND WONDERS WHERE THE CASH WENT!

SPECIALLY DRAWN FOR "THE SKETCH" BY G. E. STUDDY.

NOTE.—*The Best of all the Bonzo Books—"BONZO'S STAR TURNS"—is now on sale, and should be secured without delay, before it is sold out.*

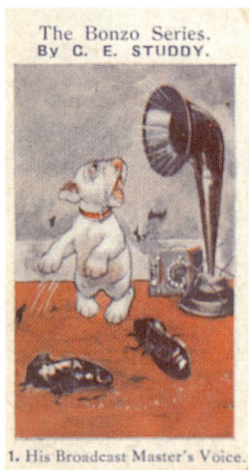
1. His Broadcast Master's Voice.

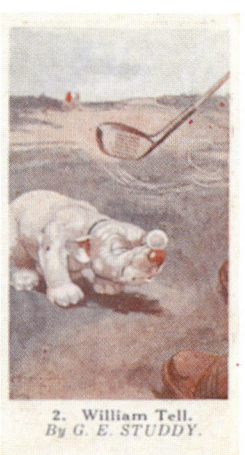
2. William Tell. By G. E. STUDDY.

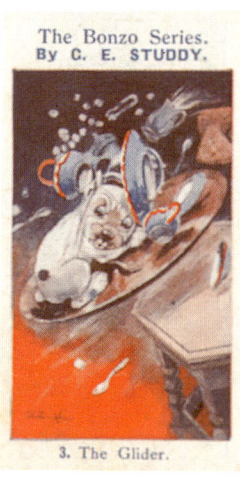
3. The Glider.

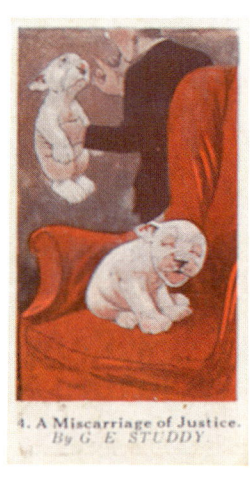
4. A Miscarriage of Justice. By G. E. STUDDY.

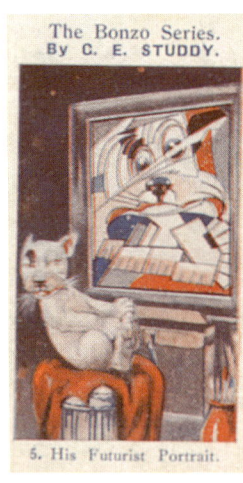
5. His Futurist Portrait.

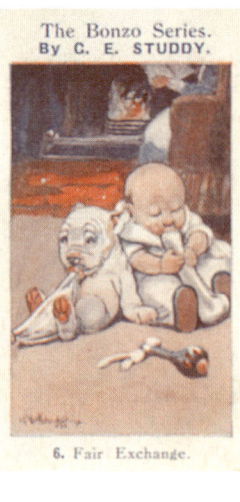
6. Fair Exchange.

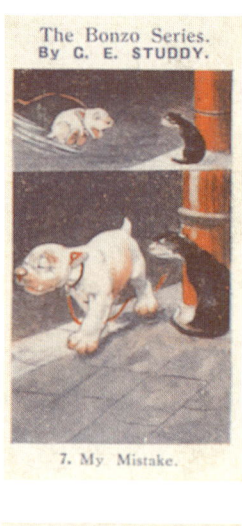
7. My Mistake.

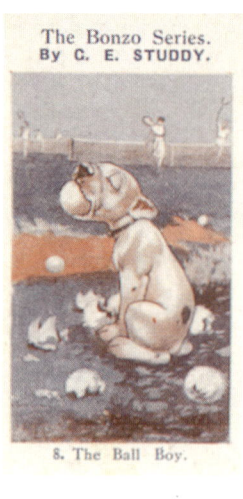
8. The Ball Boy.

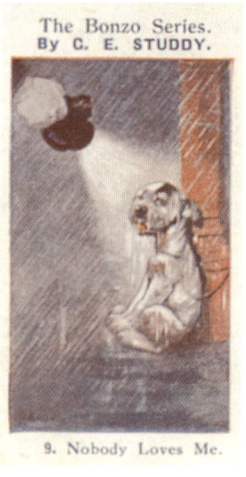
9. Nobody Loves Me.

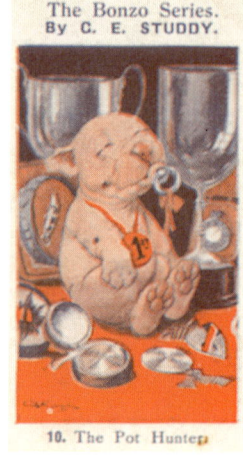
10. The Pot Hunter.

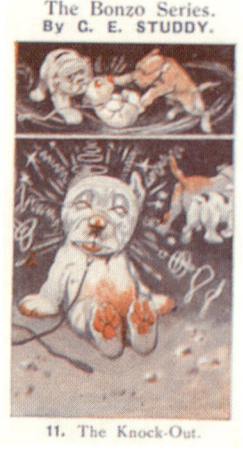
11. The Knock-Out.

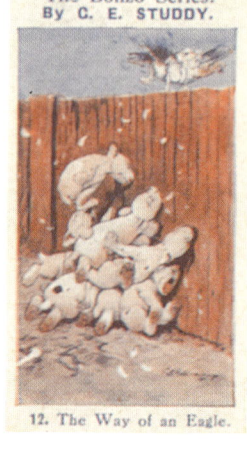
12. The Way of an Eagle.

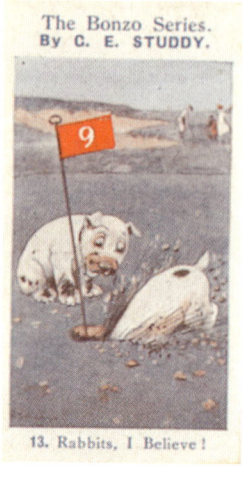
13. Rabbits, I Believe!

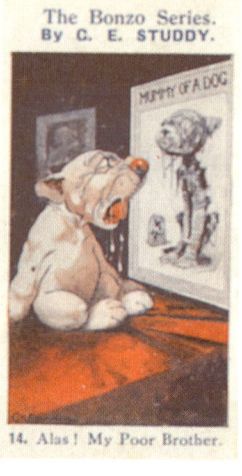
14. Alas! My Poor Brother.

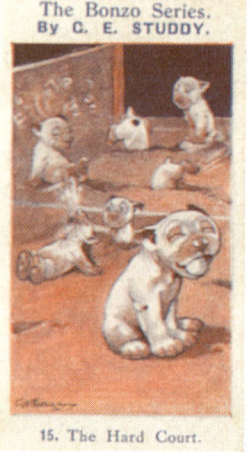
15. The Hard Court.

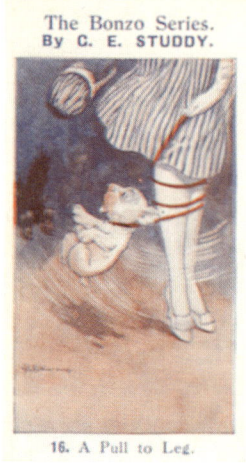
16. A Pull to Leg.

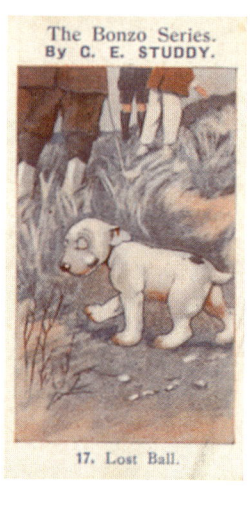
17. Lost Ball.

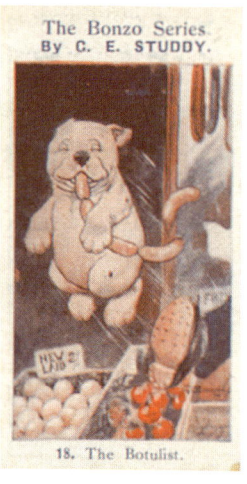
18. The Botulist.

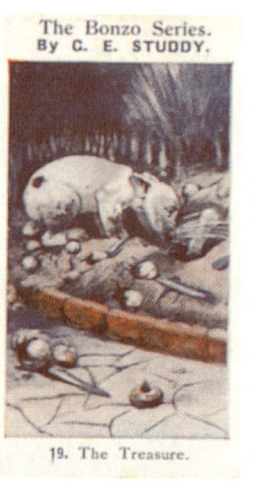
19. The Treasure.

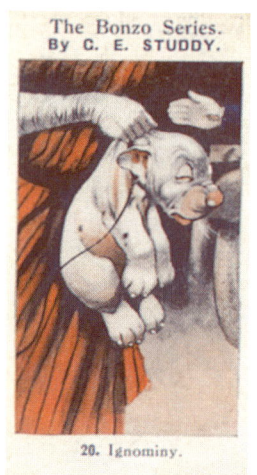
20. Ignominy.

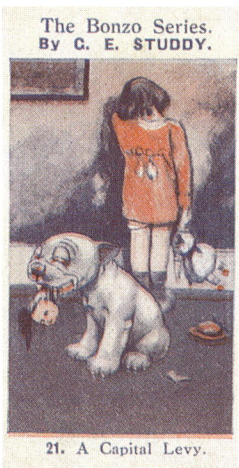 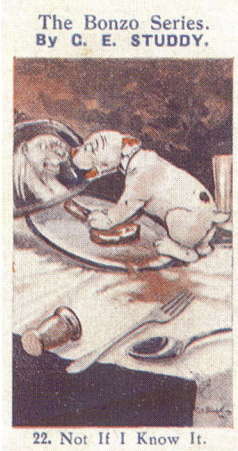 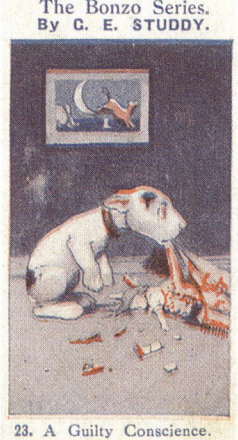 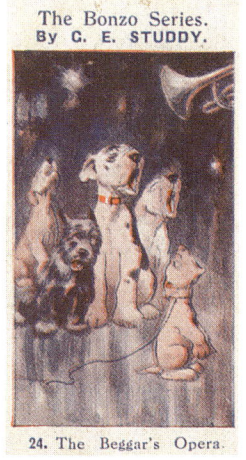 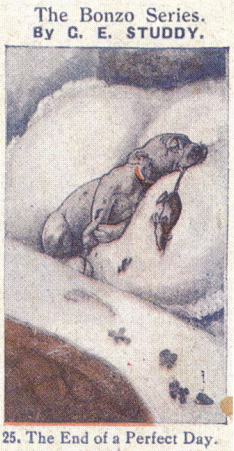

Opposite and above: Singleton and Coles, John Player & Son Ltd., and Spratt's Dog Food each issued a set of 25 cigarette cards with these illustrations but with different backs. *Below:* A selection from a rare issue of Norwegian cigarette cards. There are in excess of 190 in the set and were issued by Sossidi Cigaretter who used images from a variety of sources. The reverse of the cards is shown bottom right.

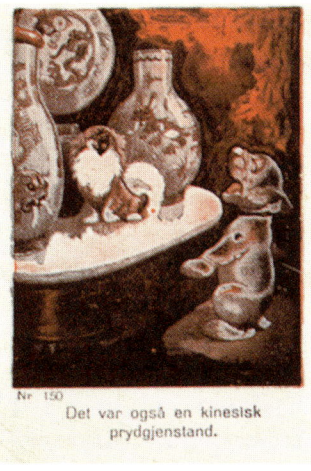 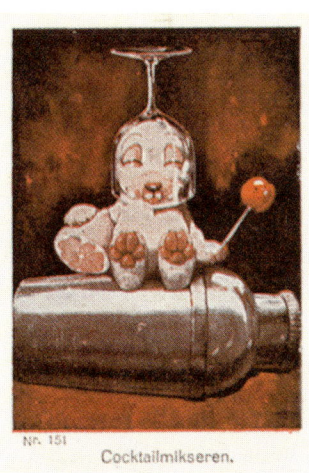 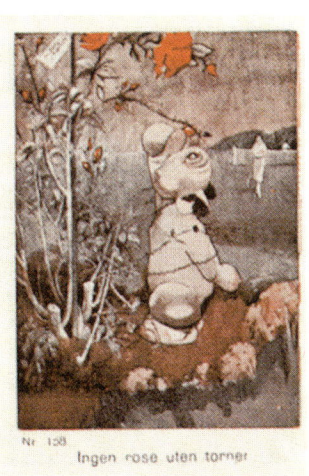 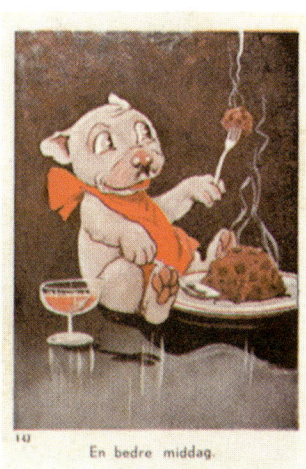

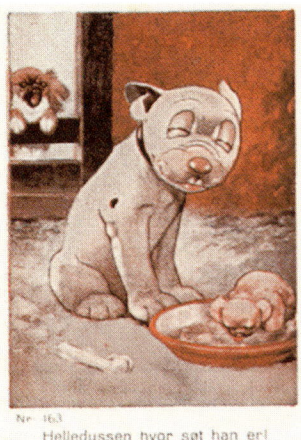 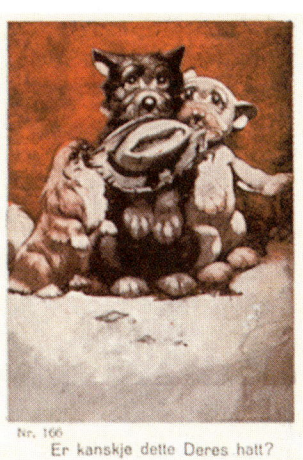 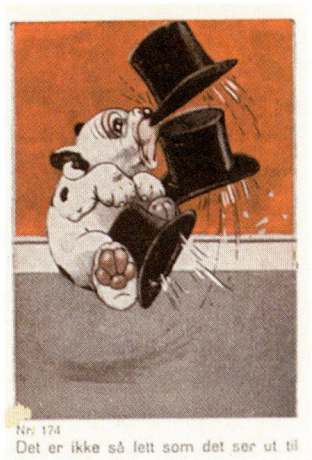 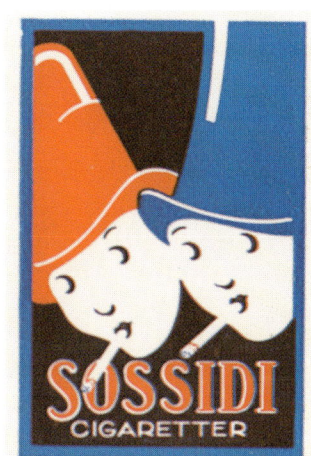

CATALOGUE OF POSTCARDS (Please refer to explanatory notes on page 121)
VALENTINE & SONS LTD. DUNDEE AND LONDON.

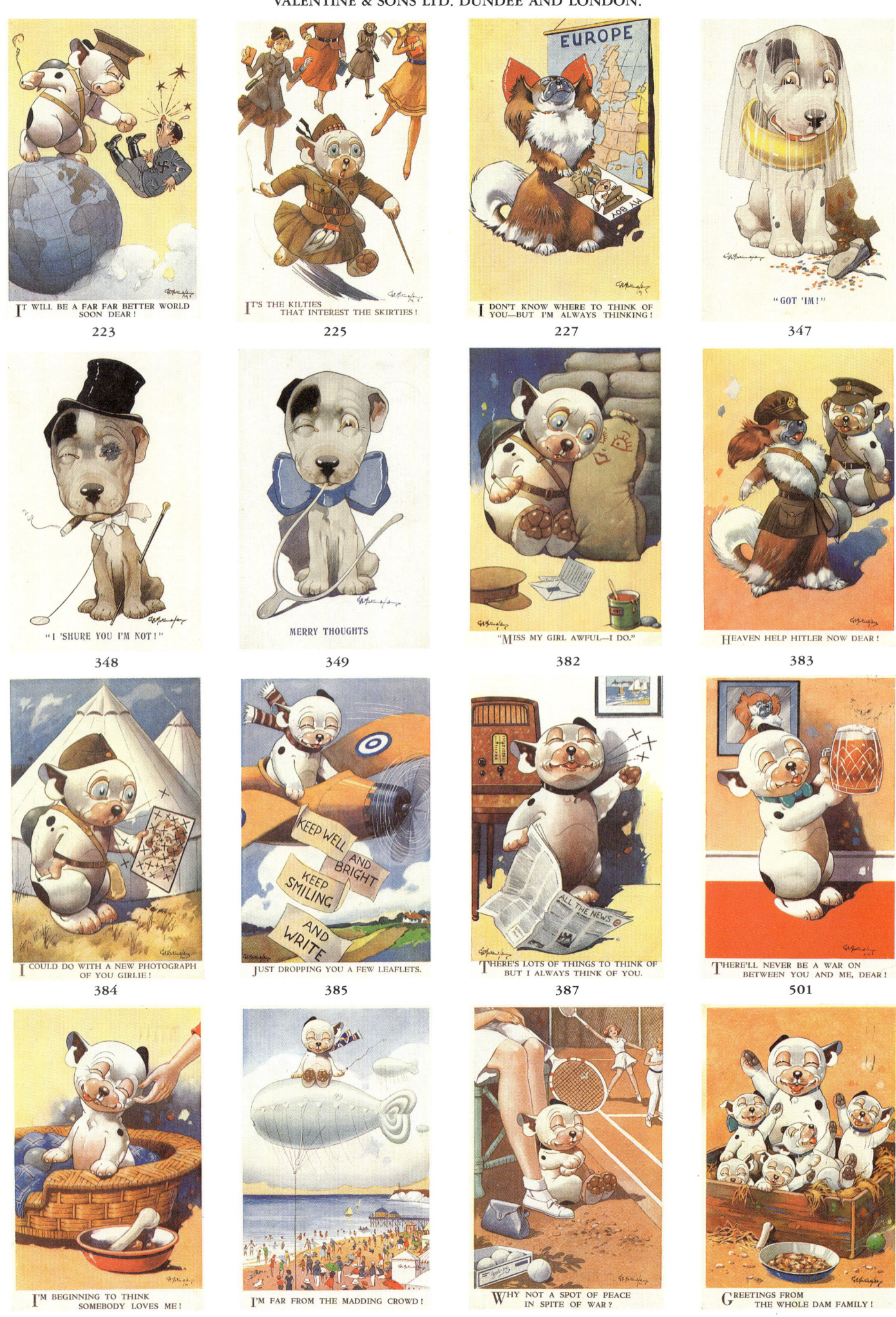

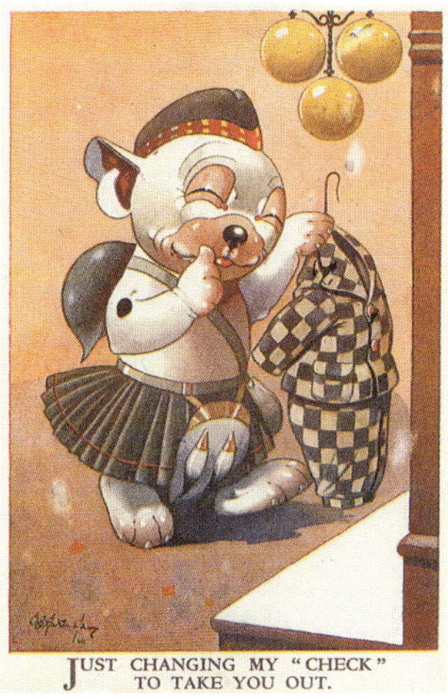
JUST CHANGING MY "CHECK" TO TAKE YOU OUT.
506

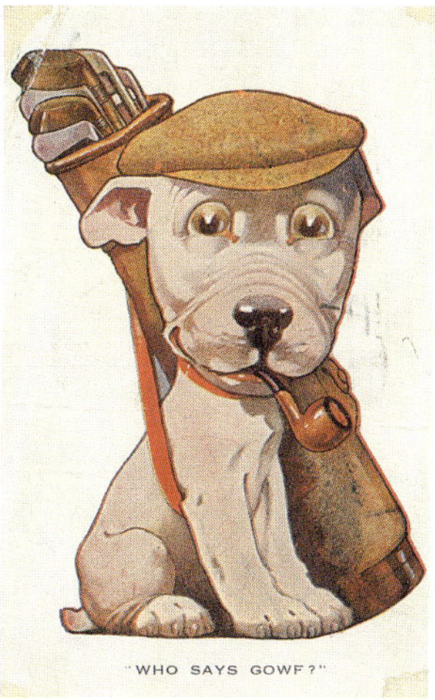
"WHO SAYS GOWF?"
638

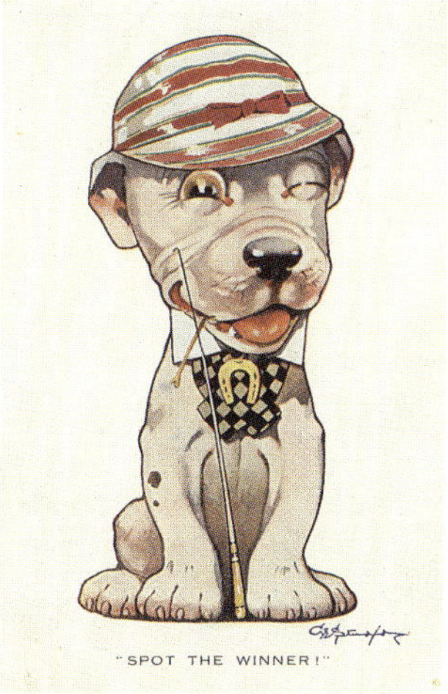
"SPOT THE WINNER!"
639

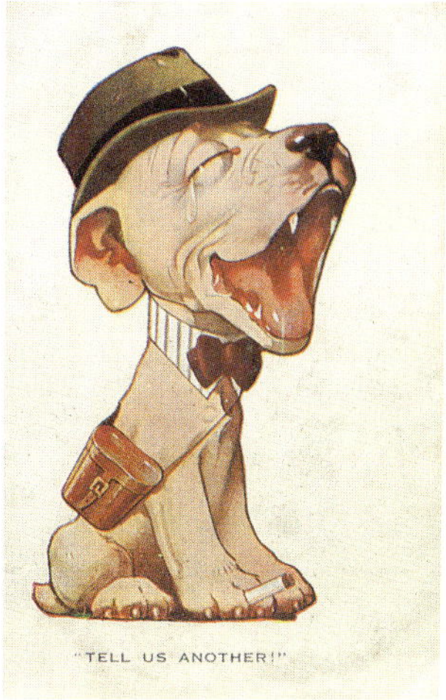
"TELL US ANOTHER!"
640

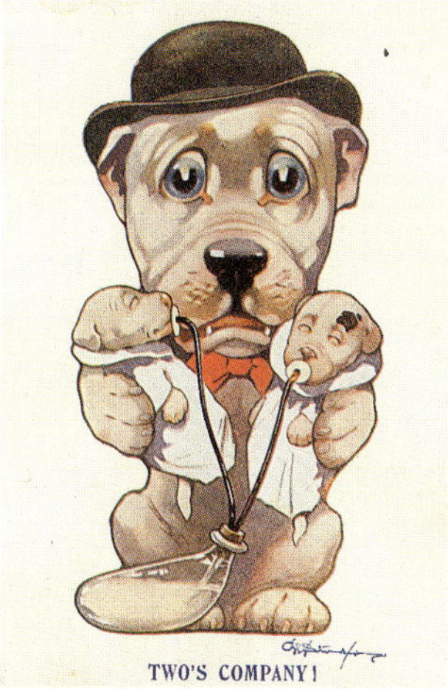
TWO'S COMPANY!
641

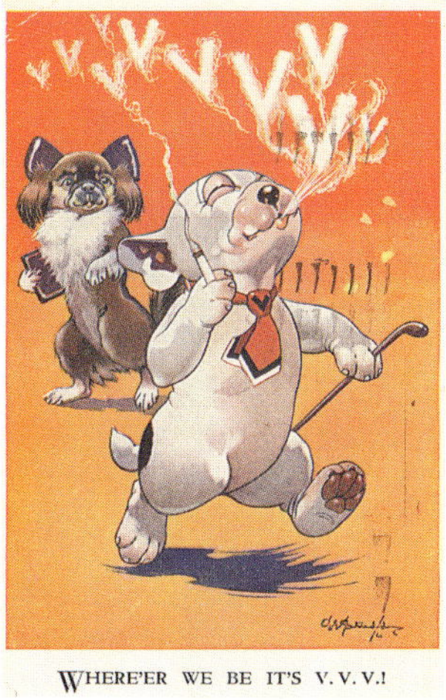
WHERE'ER WE BE IT'S V. V. V.!
709

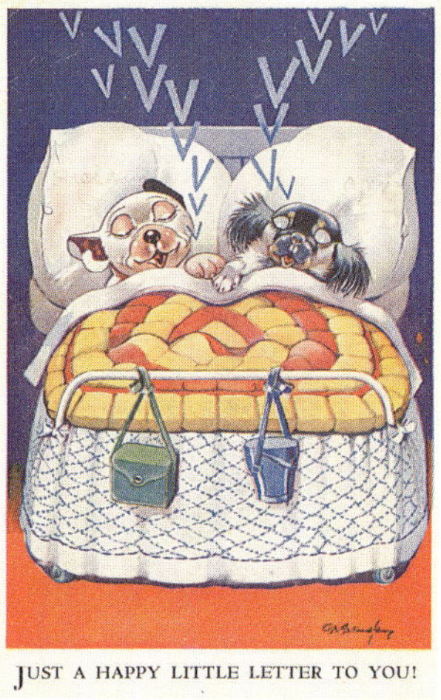
JUST A HAPPY LITTLE LETTER TO YOU!
710

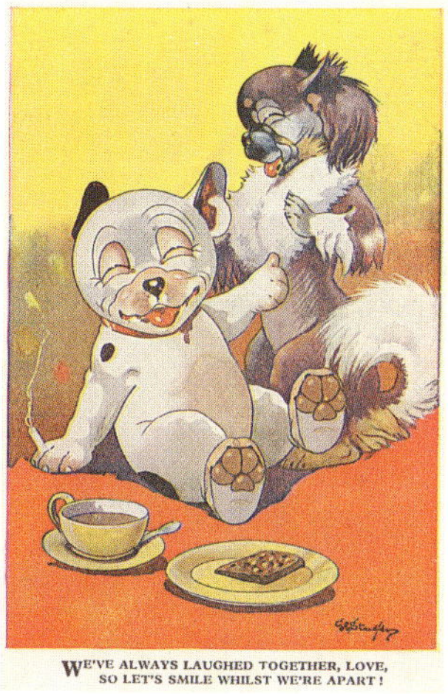
WE'VE ALWAYS LAUGHED TOGETHER, LOVE, SO LET'S SMILE WHILST WE'RE APART!
711

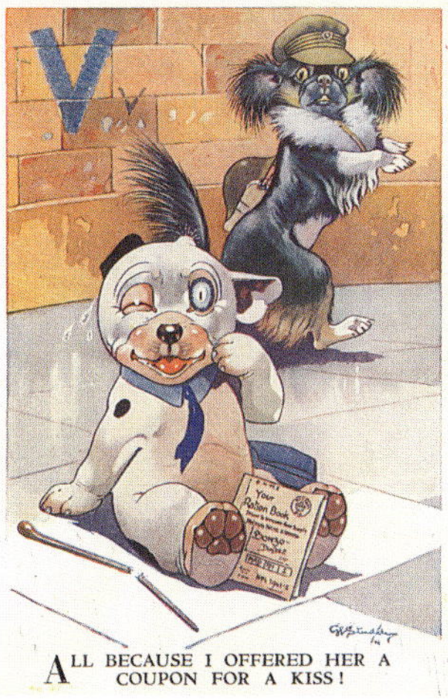
ALL BECAUSE I OFFERED HER A COUPON FOR A KISS!
712

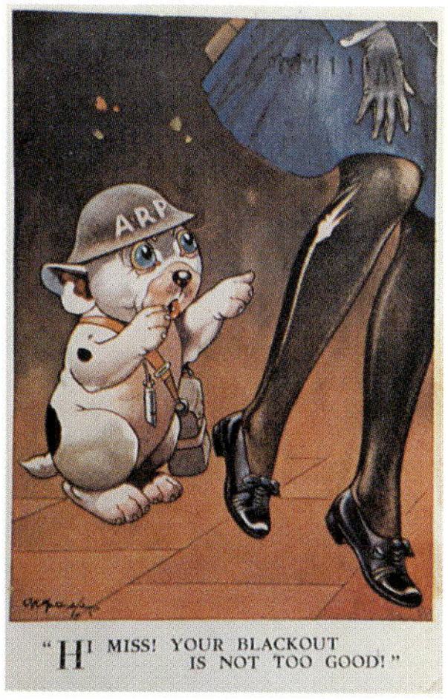
ARP
"HI MISS! YOUR BLACKOUT IS NOT TOO GOOD!"
713

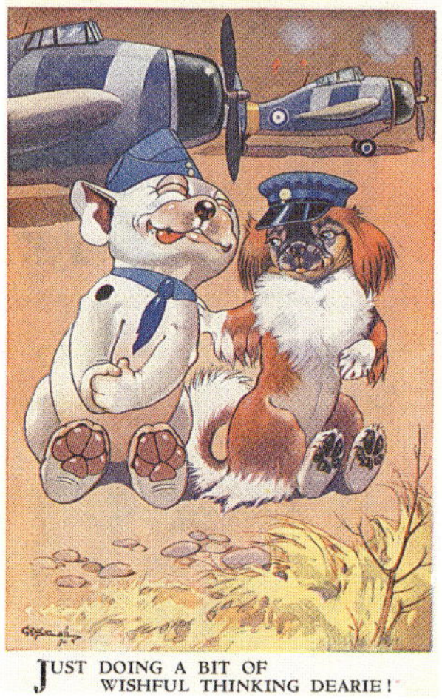
JUST DOING A BIT OF WISHFUL THINKING DEARIE!
714

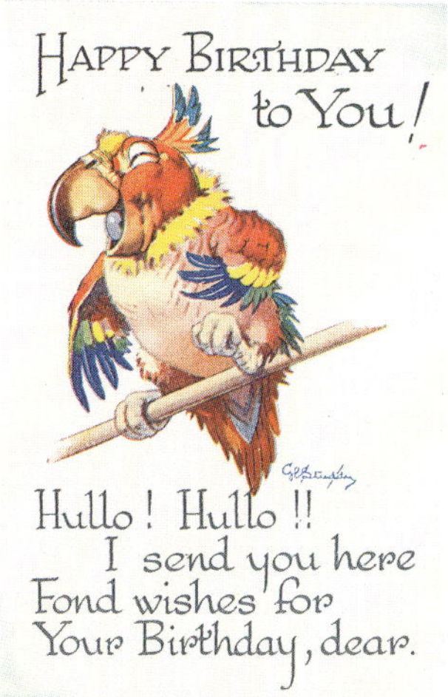
HAPPY BIRTHDAY to You!
Hullo! Hullo!!
I send you here
Fond wishes for
Your Birthday, dear.
843

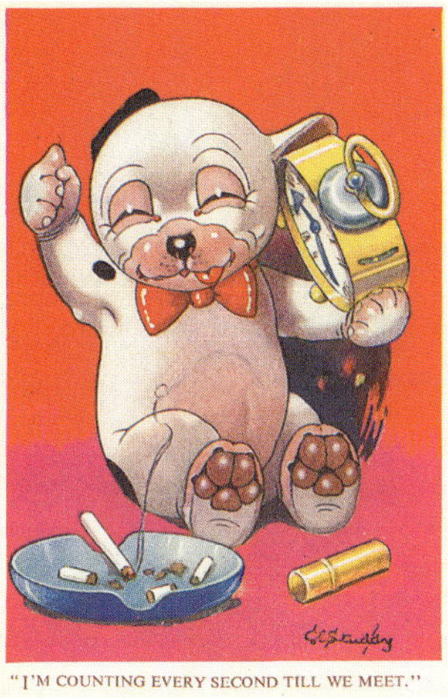
"I'M COUNTING EVERY SECOND TILL WE MEET."
888

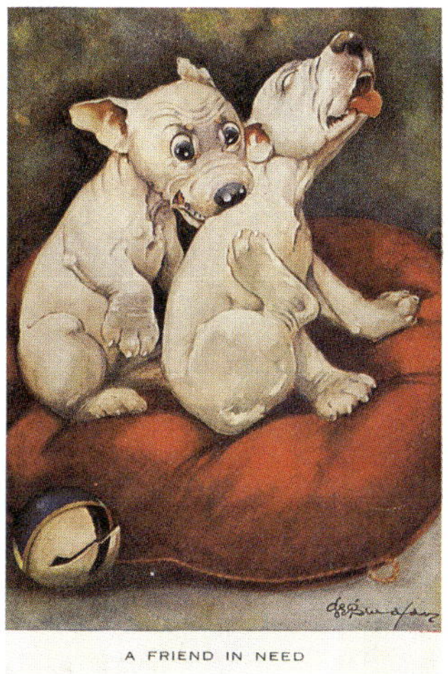
A FRIEND IN NEED
912

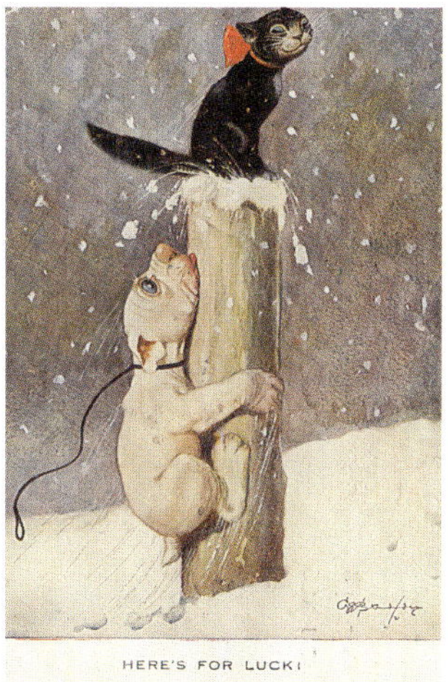
HERE'S FOR LUCK!
914

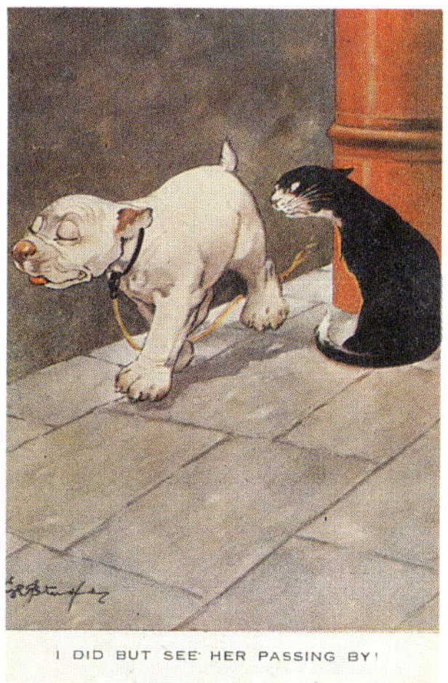
I DID BUT SEE HER PASSING BY!
915

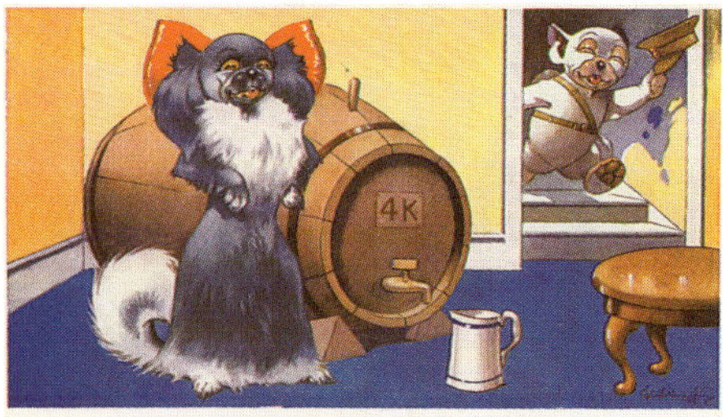
"I'M EXPECTING YOU ANY TIME DEAR!"

222

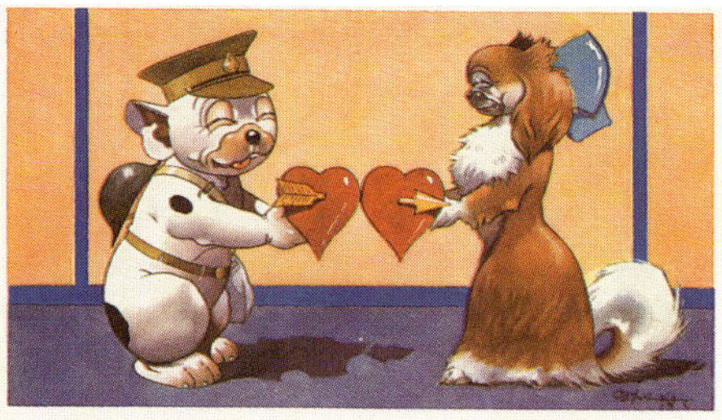
"FOR THE DURATION AND EVER AFTER!"

224

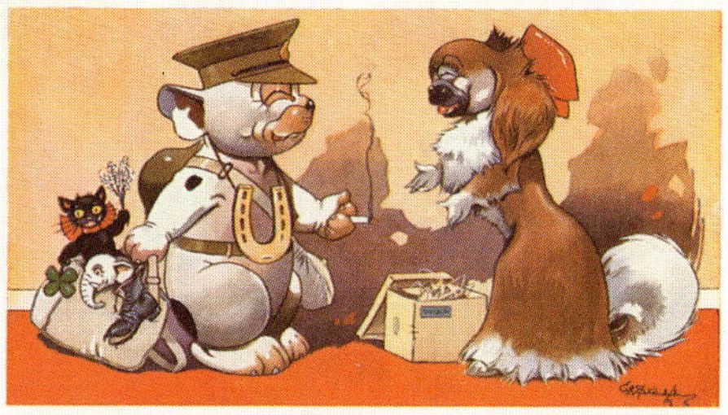
YOU CAN SEE I WISH YOU GOOD LUCK!

226

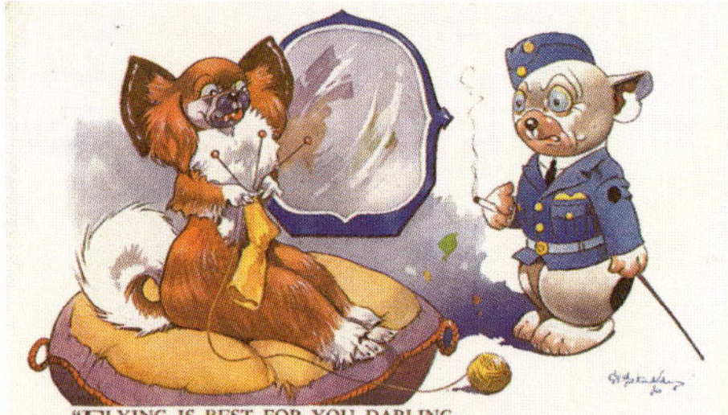
"FLYING IS BEST FOR YOU DARLING—
IT KEEPS YOU AWAY FROM THE GIRLS."

379

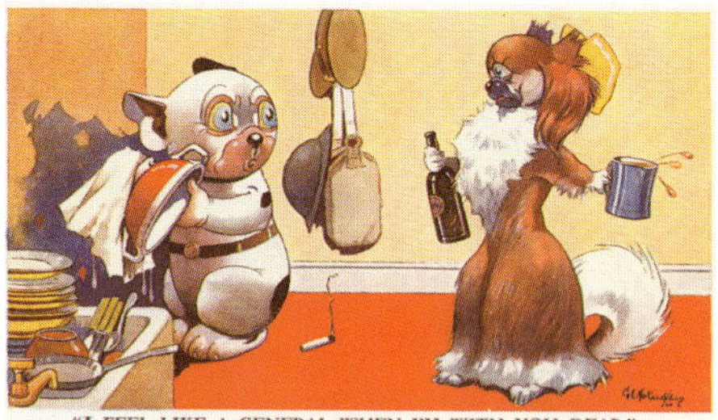
"I FEEL LIKE A GENERAL WHEN I'M WITH YOU DEAR."

380

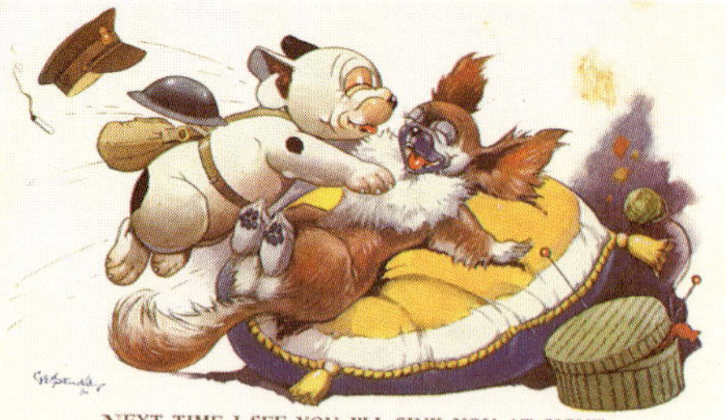
NEXT TIME I SEE YOU I'LL SINK YOU AT SIGHT.

381

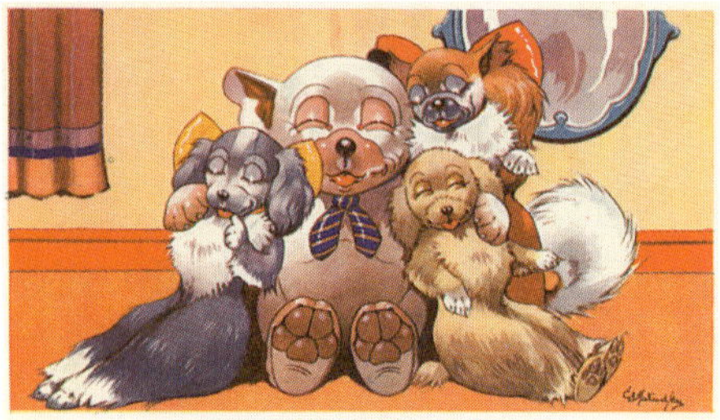
THEY CAN'T RATION LOVE.

386

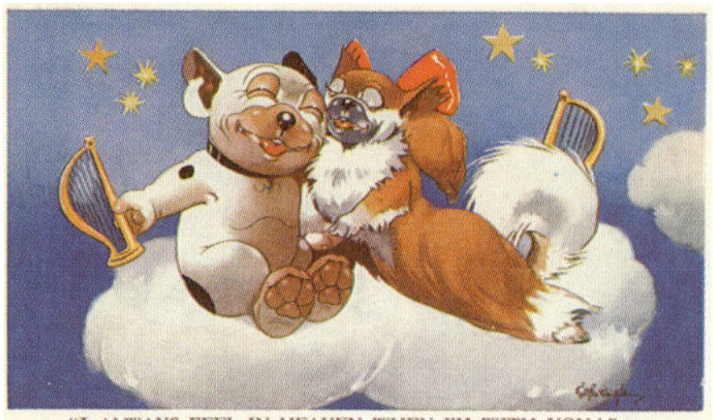
"I ALWAYS FEEL IN HEAVEN WHEN I'M WITH YOU!"

389

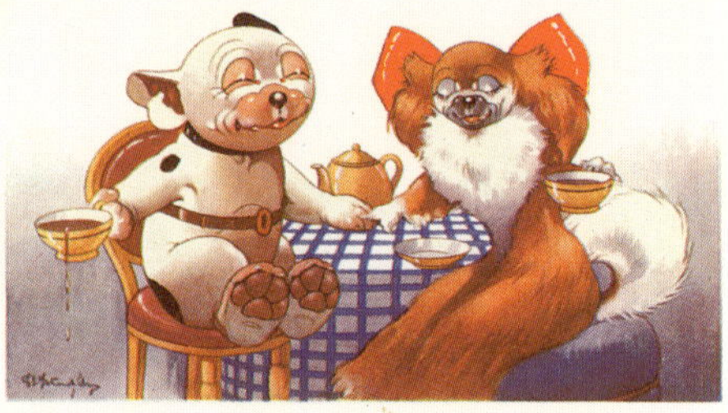
"I'M NEVER SHORT OF SUGAR, 'COS YOU'RE SO VERY SWEET!"

390

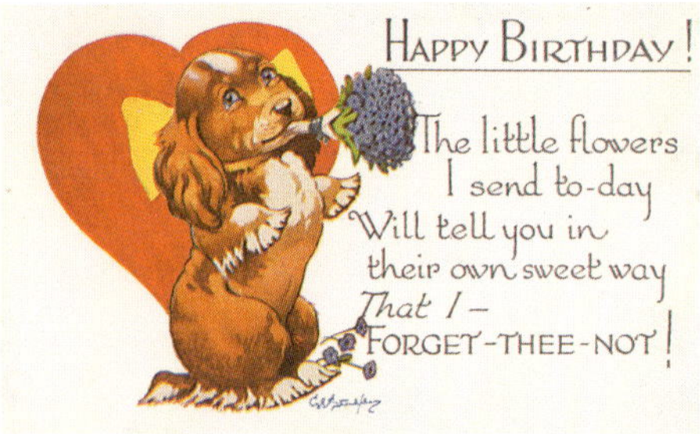
HAPPY BIRTHDAY!
The little flowers
I send to-day
Will tell you in
their own sweet way
That I –
FORGET-THEE-NOT!

840

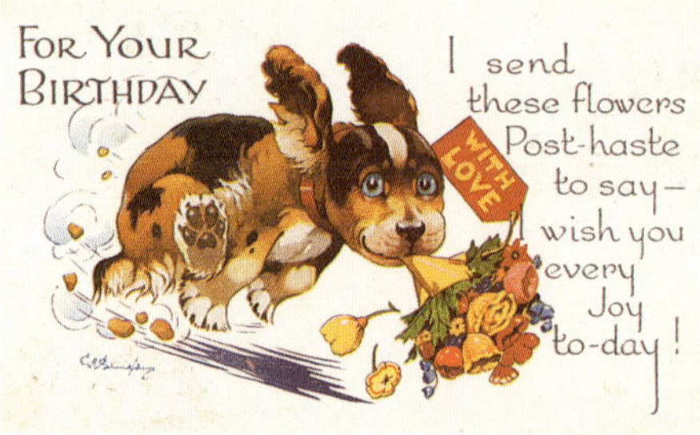
FOR YOUR BIRTHDAY
WITH LOVE
I send
these flowers
Post-haste
to say–
wish you
every
Joy
to-day!

841

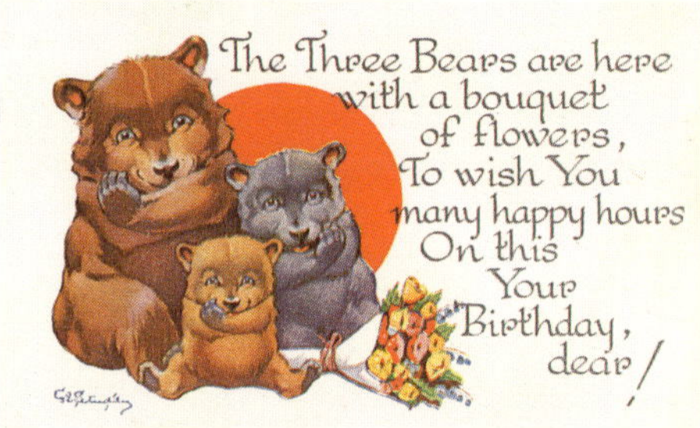
The Three Bears are here
with a bouquet
of flowers,
To wish You
many happy hours
On this
Your
Birthday,
dear!

842

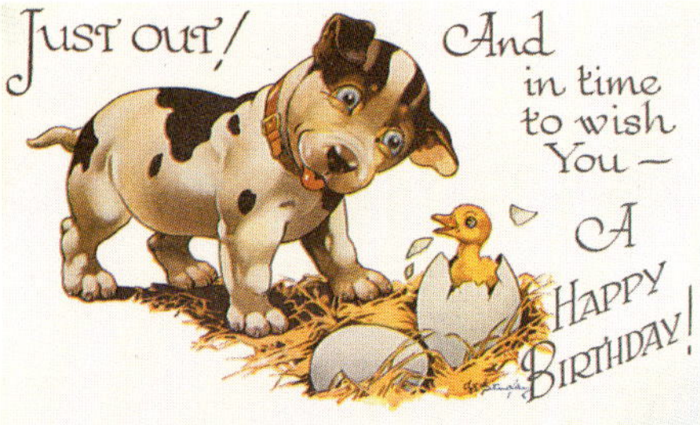
JUST OUT!
And
in time
to wish
You –
A
HAPPY
BIRTHDAY!

844

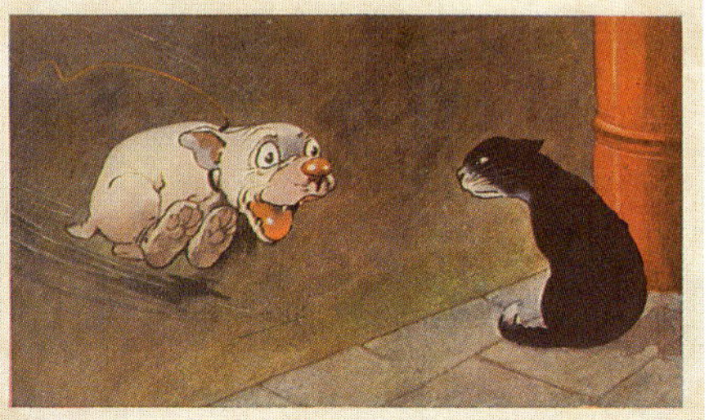
YOURS IN HASTE.

913

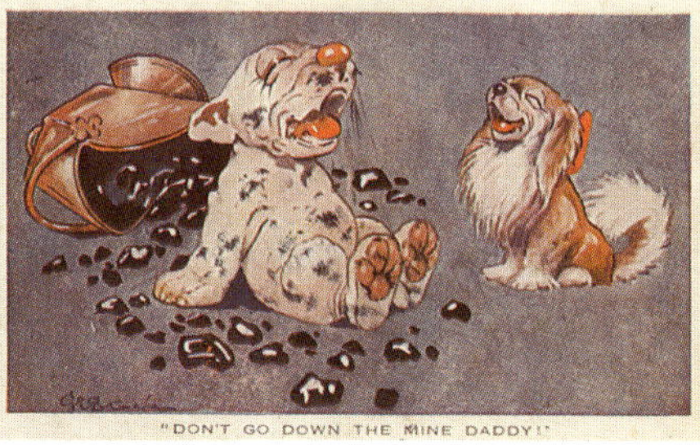
"DON'T GO DOWN THE MINE DADDY!"

916

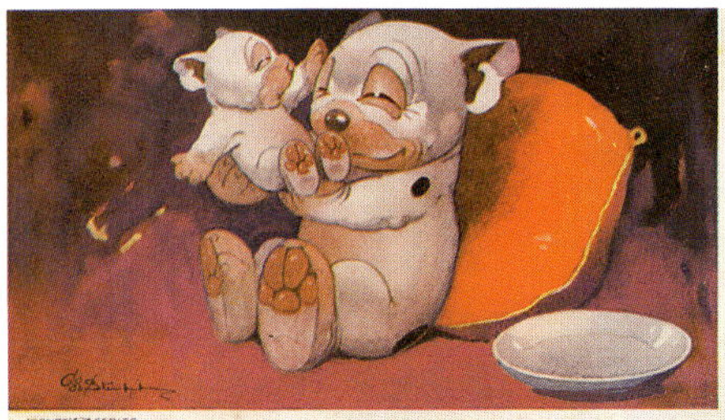
"MY WONDERFUL ONE!"

931

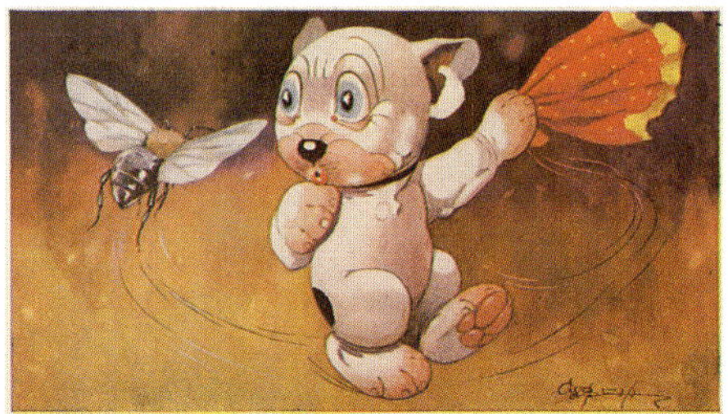
STILL BUZZING AROUND!

932

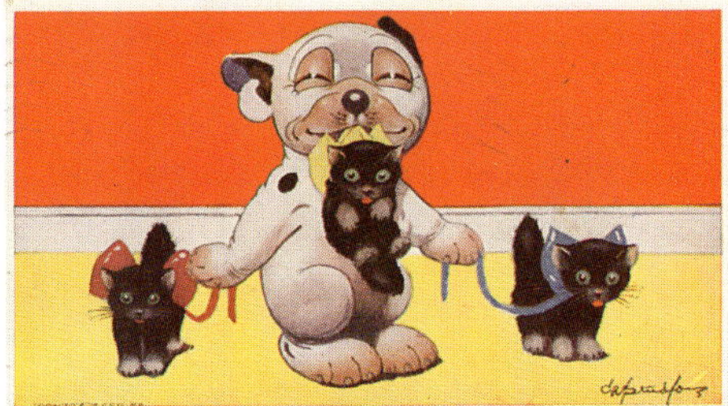
"BONZO" BRINGS YOU GOOD LUCK

933

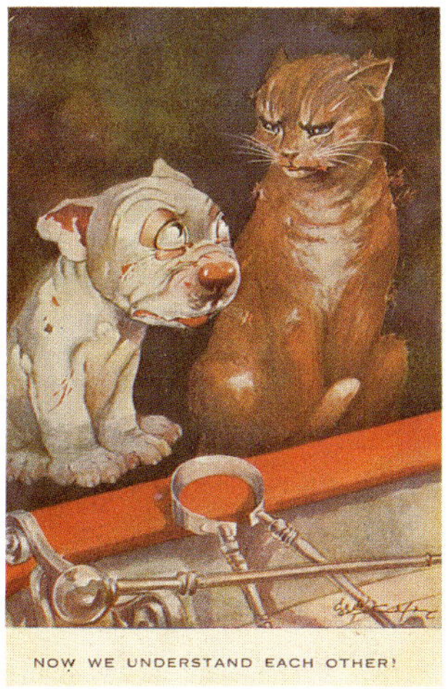

VALENTINE & SONS LTD.

917	918	918	918
918	918	918	967
968	990	991	992
993	994	995	996

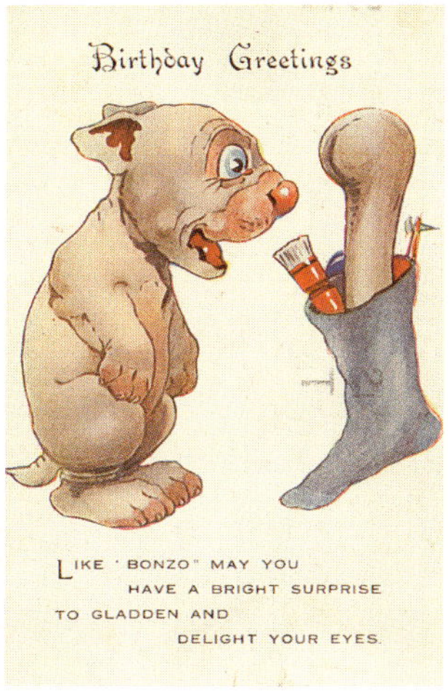

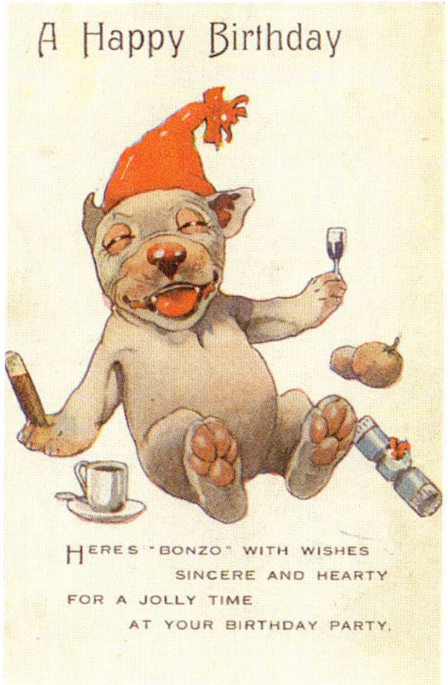

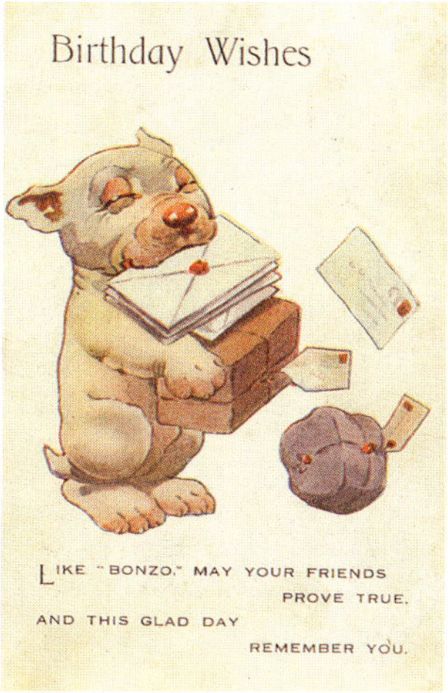

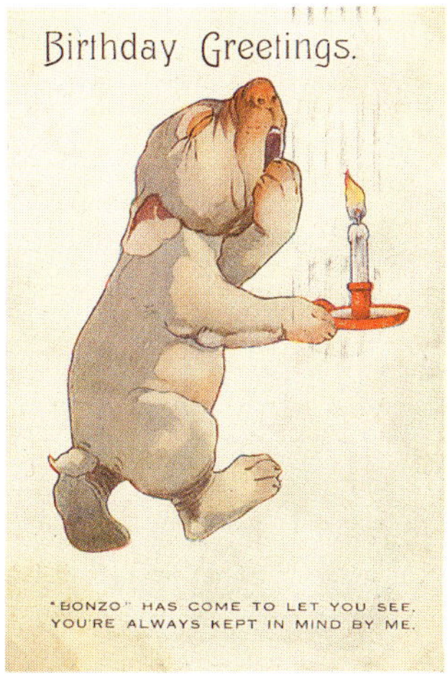

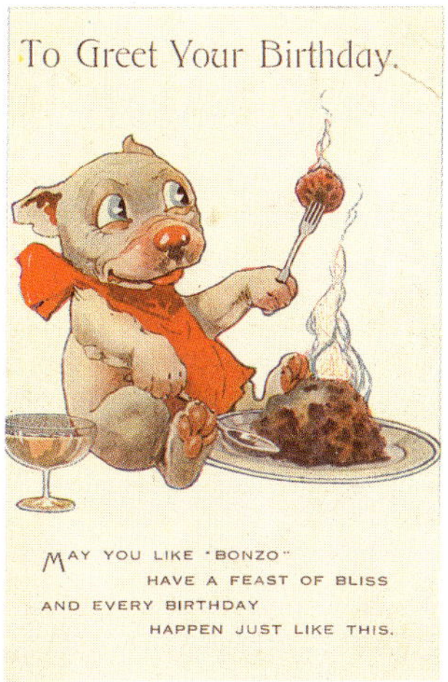

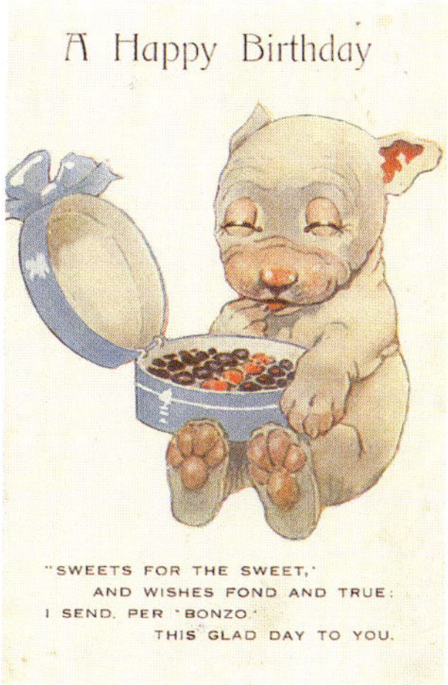

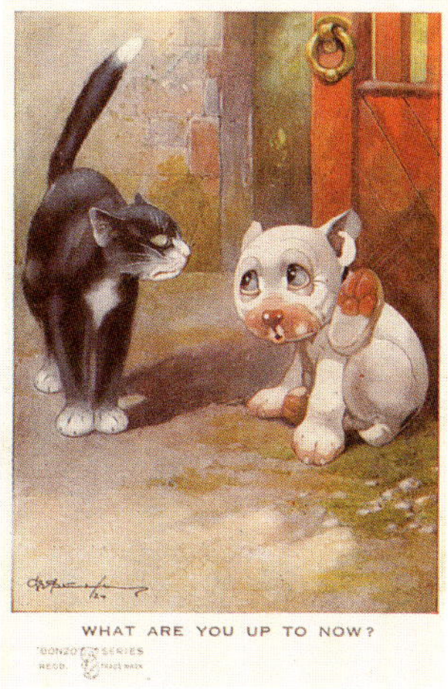

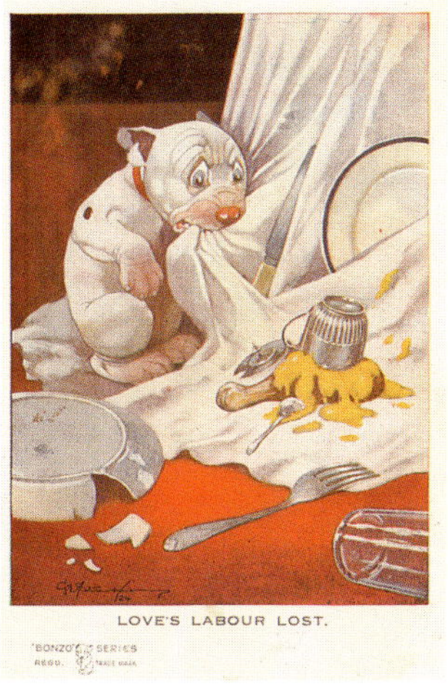

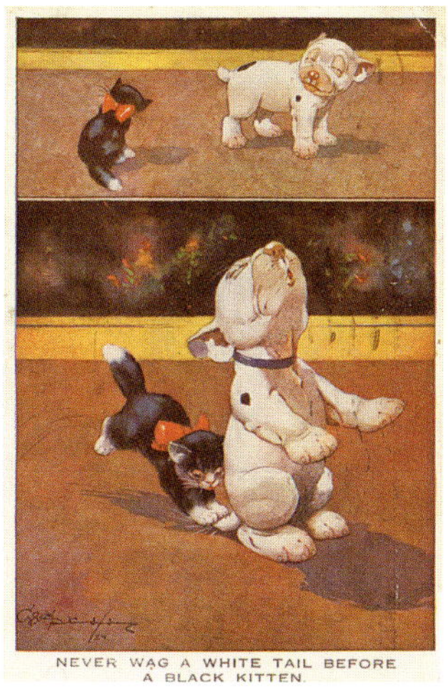

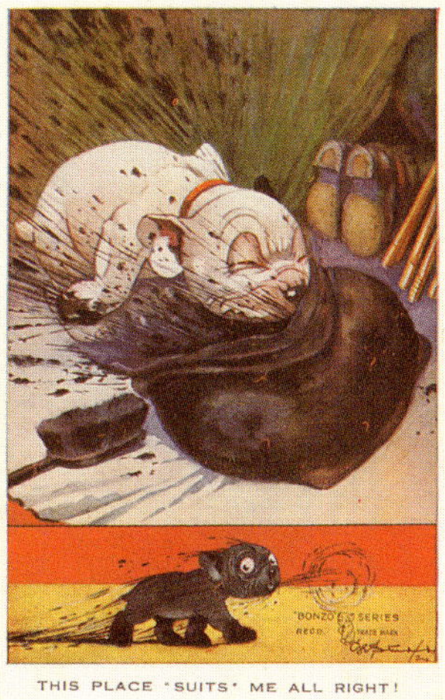

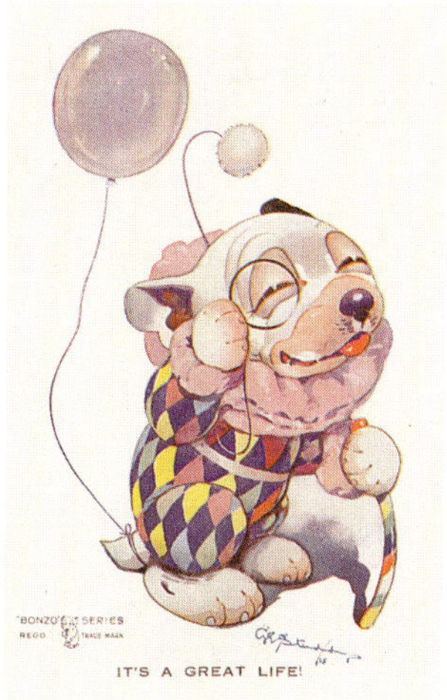

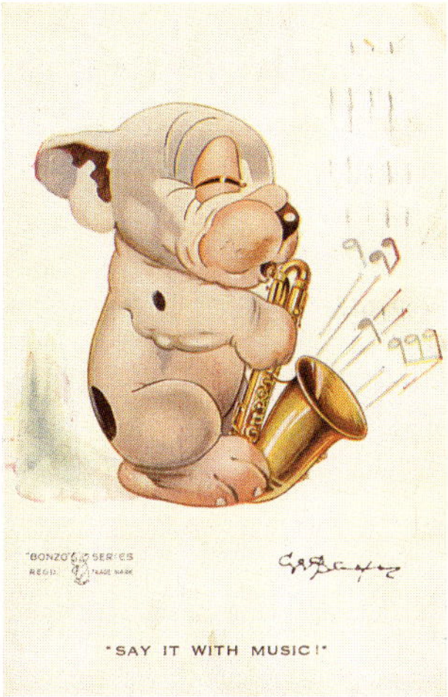

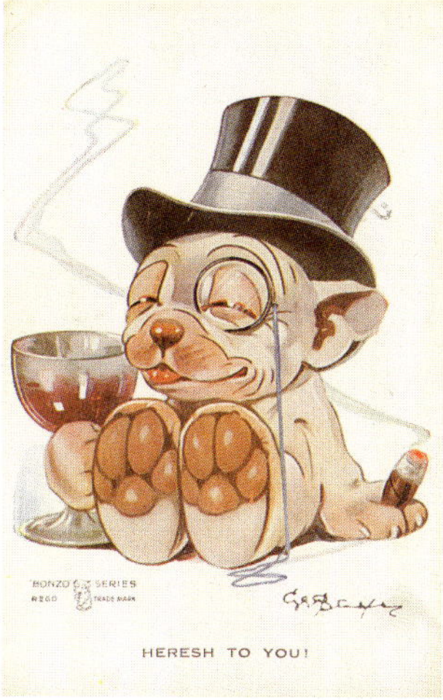

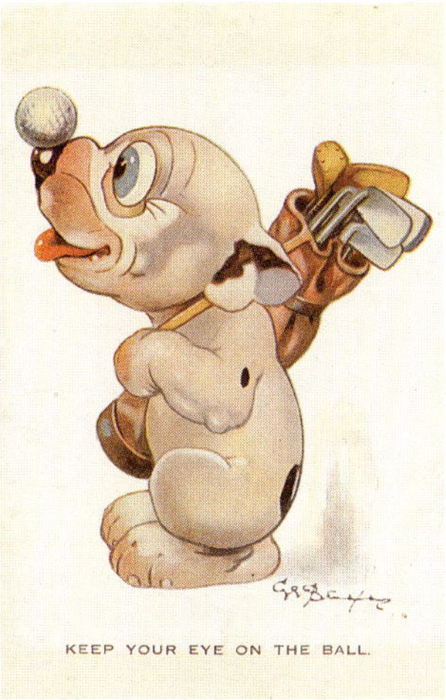

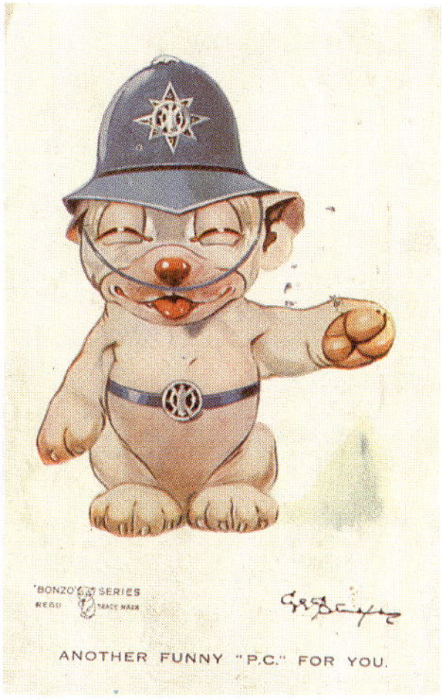

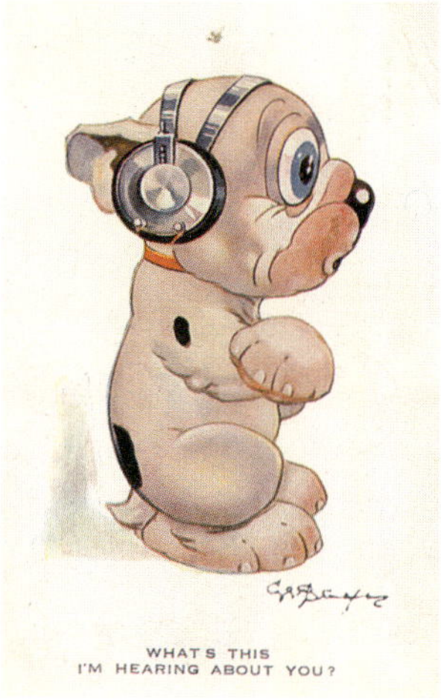
WHAT'S THIS
I'M HEARING ABOUT YOU?

998

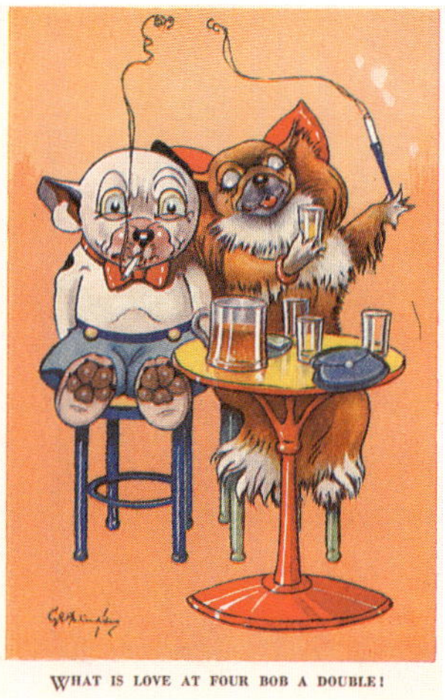
WHAT IS LOVE AT FOUR BOB A DOUBLE!

1016

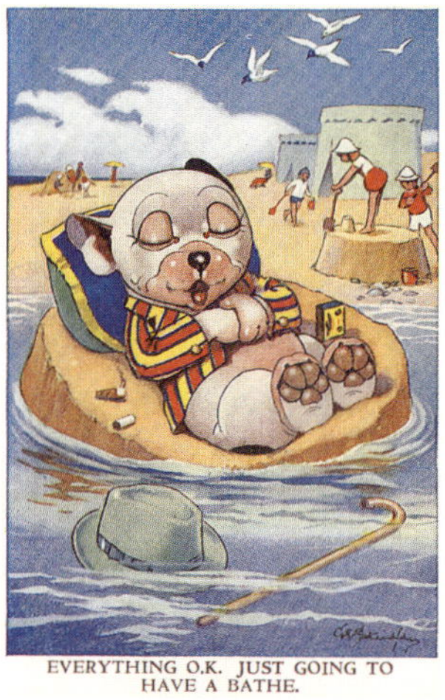
EVERYTHING O.K. JUST GOING TO
HAVE A BATHE.

1017

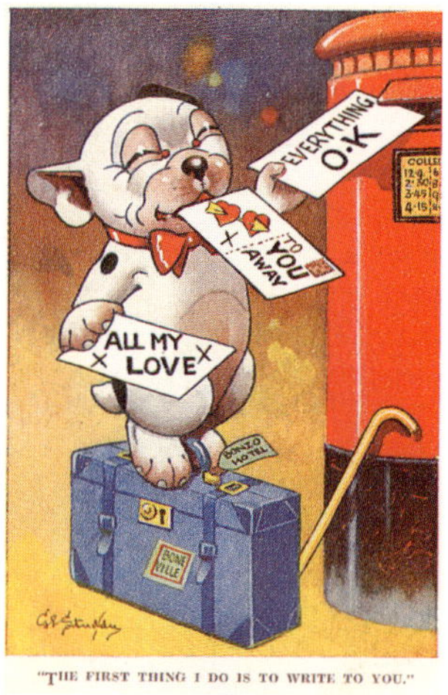
EVERYTHING O.K
TO YOU AWAY
ALL MY LOVE
"THE FIRST THING I DO IS TO WRITE TO YOU."

1018

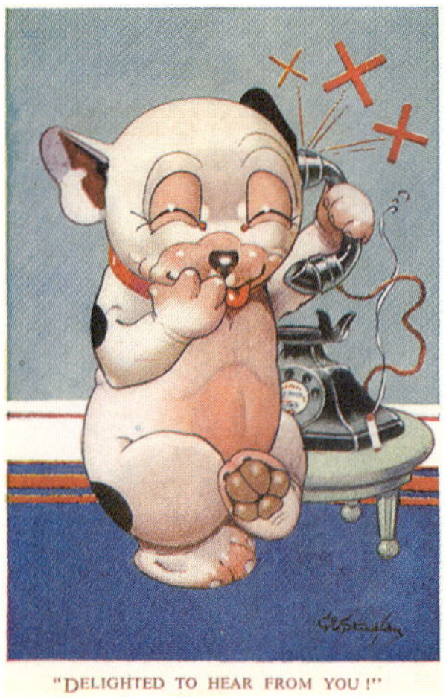
"DELIGHTED TO HEAR FROM YOU!"

1019

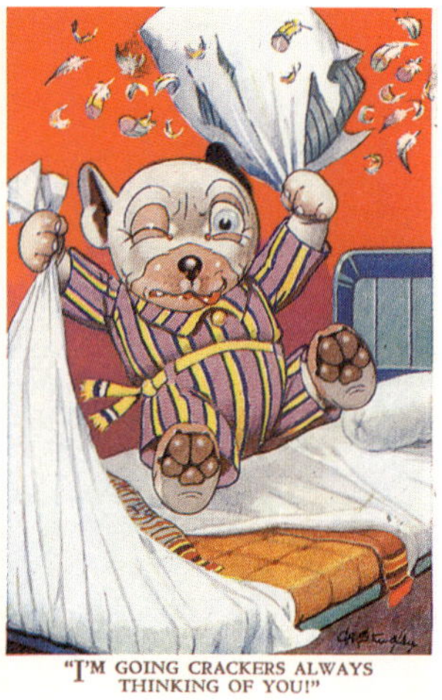
"I'M GOING CRACKERS ALWAYS
THINKING OF YOU!"

1020

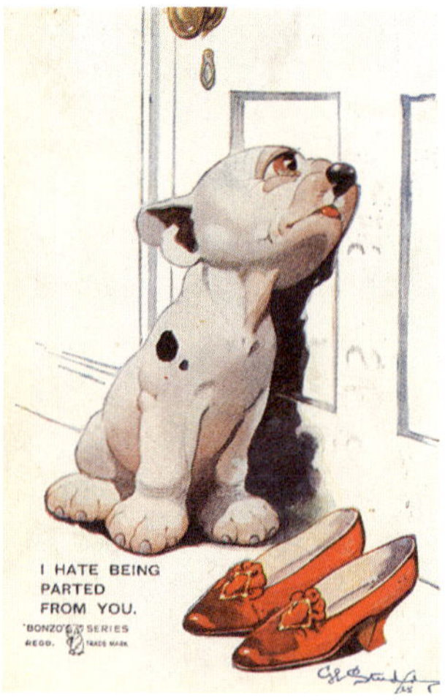
I HATE BEING
PARTED
FROM YOU.
"BONZO" SERIES

1053

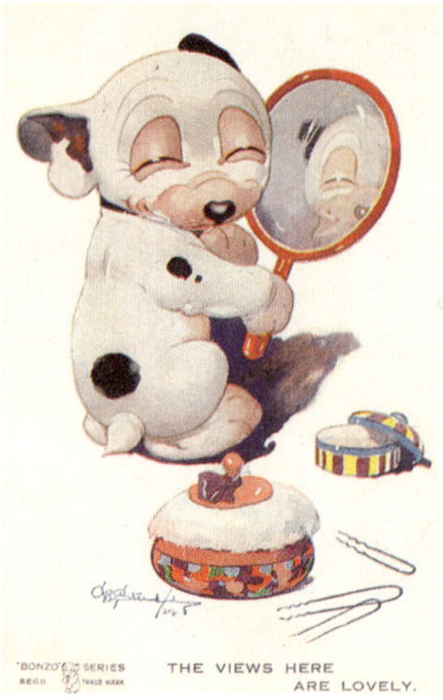
"BONZO" SERIES
THE VIEWS HERE
ARE LOVELY.

1054

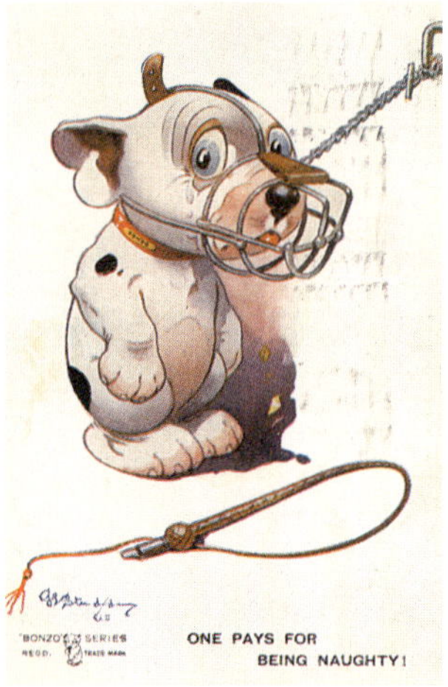
"BONZO" SERIES
ONE PAYS FOR
BEING NAUGHTY!

1055

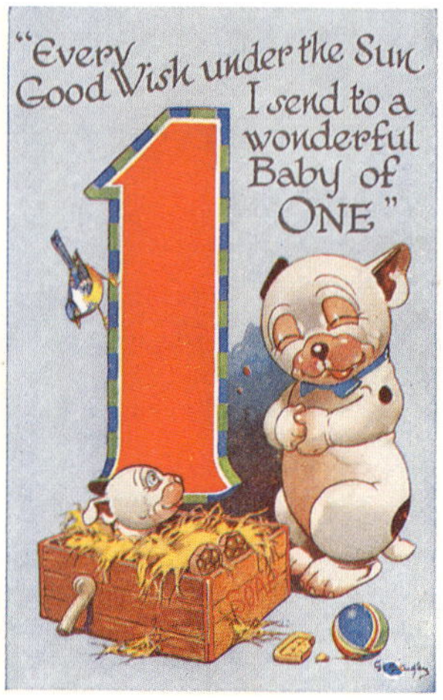
"Every Wish under the Sun
I send to a
wonderful
Baby of
ONE"

1053B

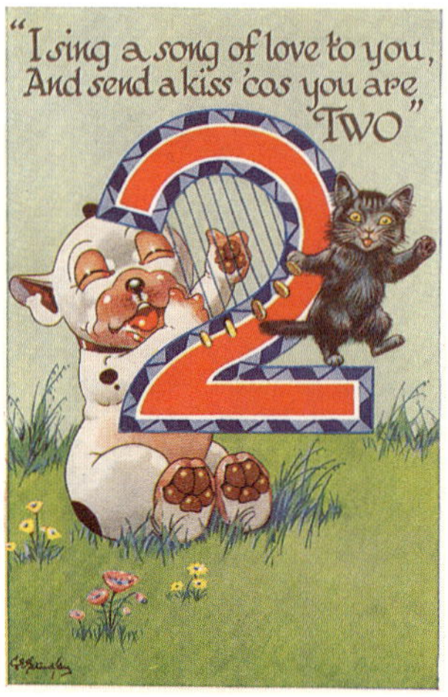
"I sing a song of love to you,
And send a kiss 'cos you are
TWO"

1054B

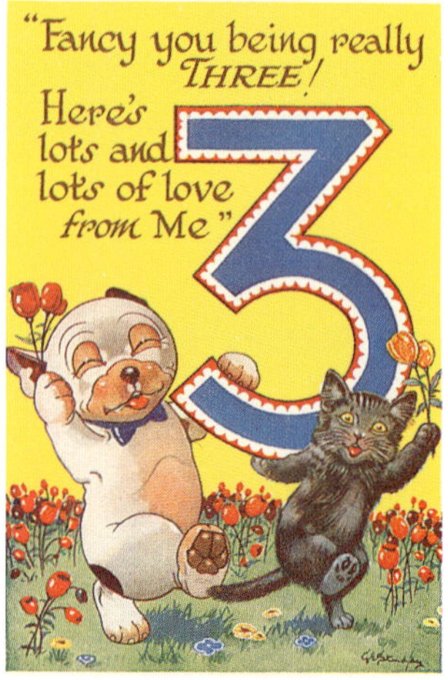
"Fancy you being really
THREE!
Here's
lots and
lots of love
from Me"

1055B

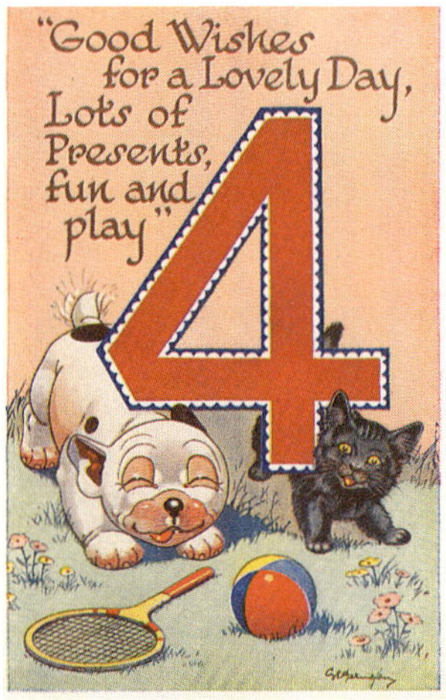
"Good Wishes
for a Lovely Day,
Lots of
Presents,
fun and
play"

1056B

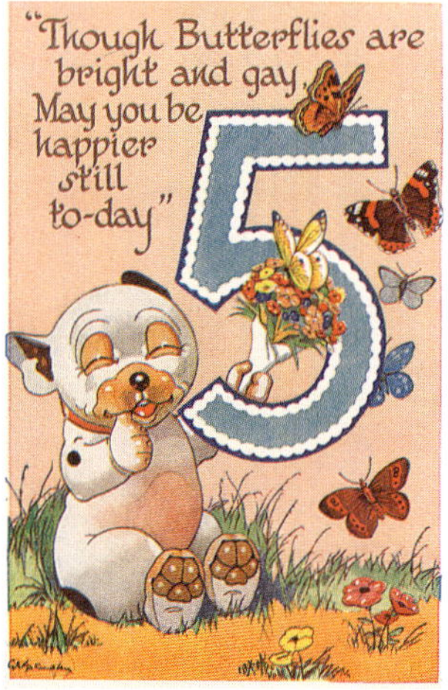
"Though Butterflies are
bright and gay
May you be
happier
still
to-day"

1057B

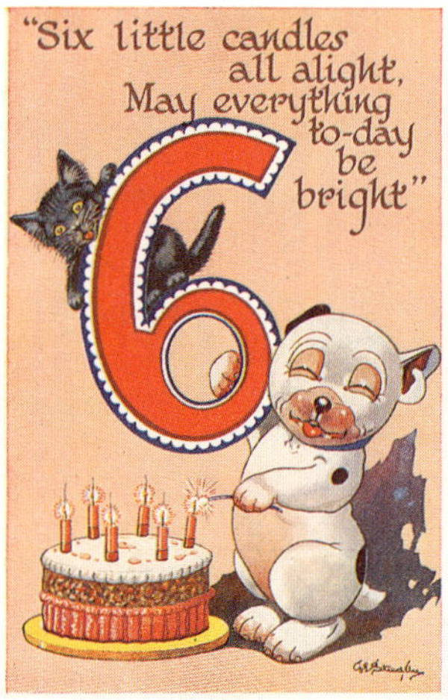
"Six little candles
all alight,
May everything
to-day
be
bright"

1058B

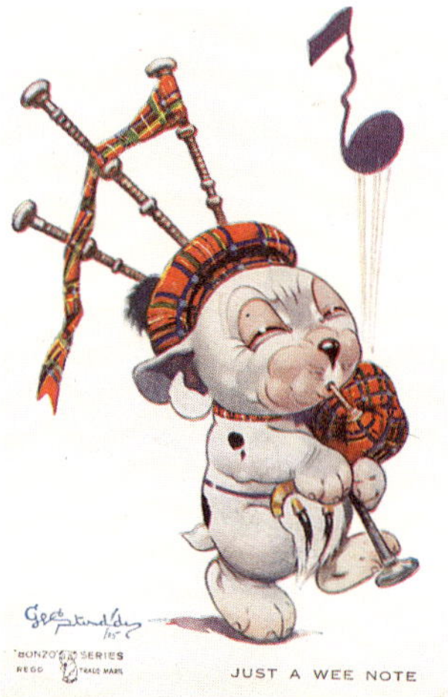
"BONZO" SERIES
JUST A WEE NOTE

1060

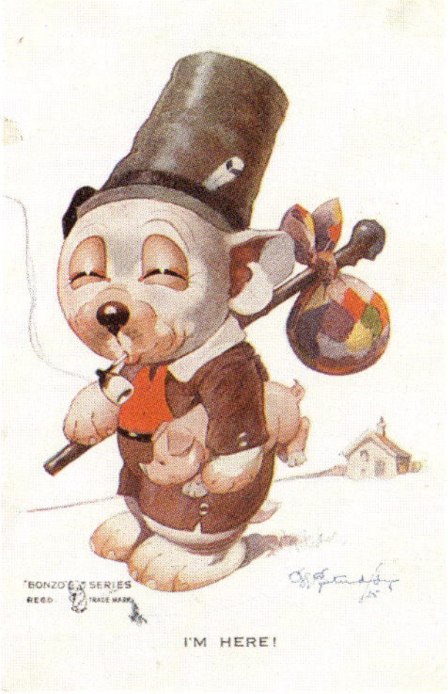
I'M HERE!

1073

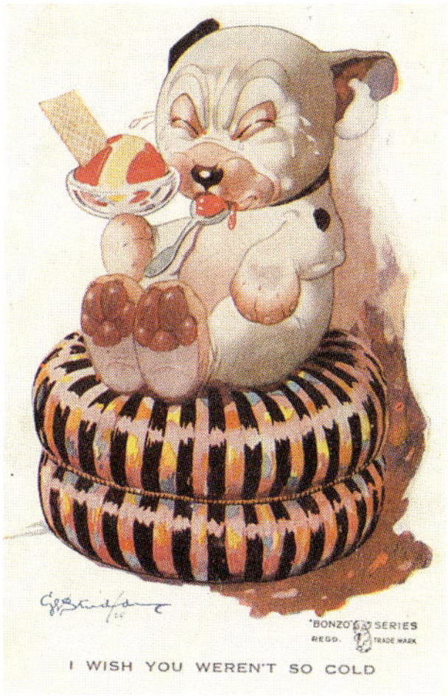
I WISH YOU WEREN'T SO COLD

1074

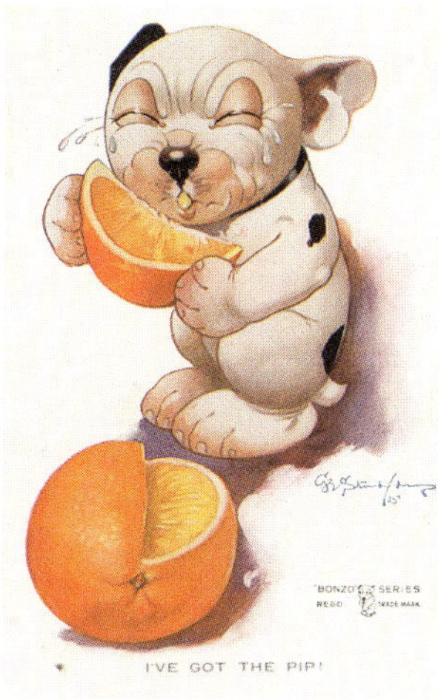
I'VE GOT THE PIP!

1075

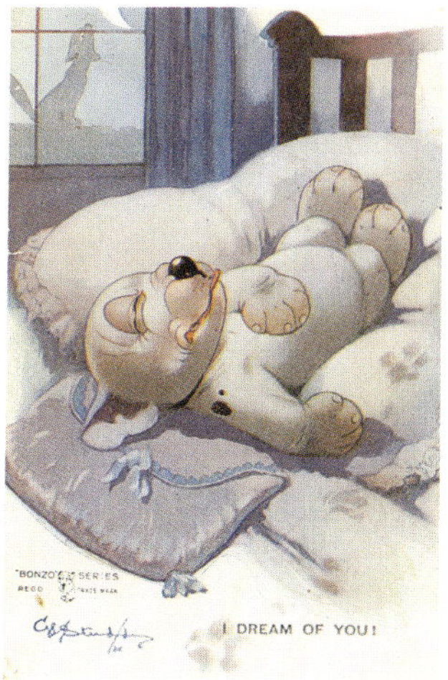
I DREAM OF YOU!

1076

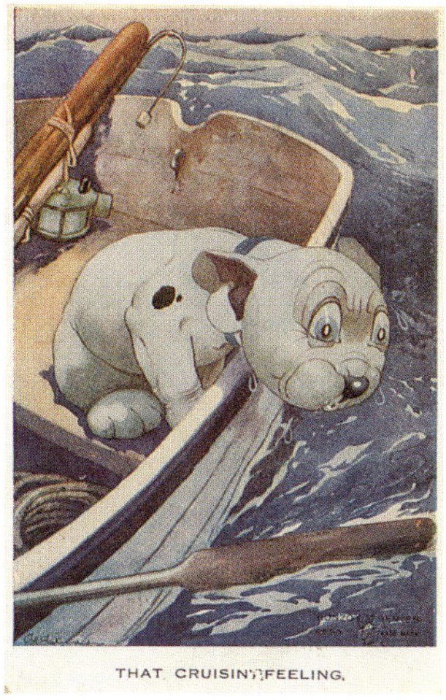
THAT CRUISING FEELING.

1077

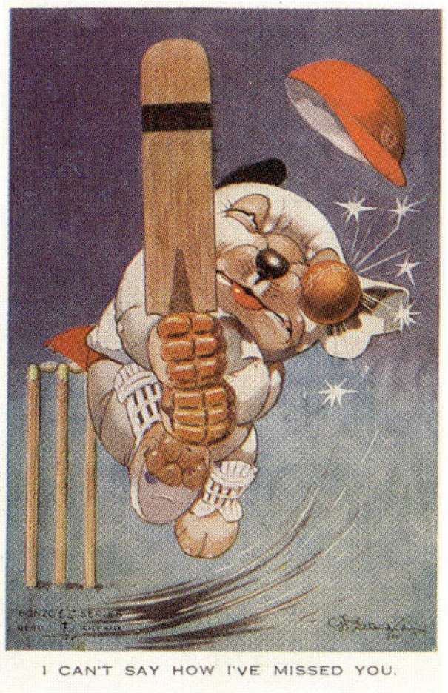
I CAN'T SAY HOW I'VE MISSED YOU.

1078

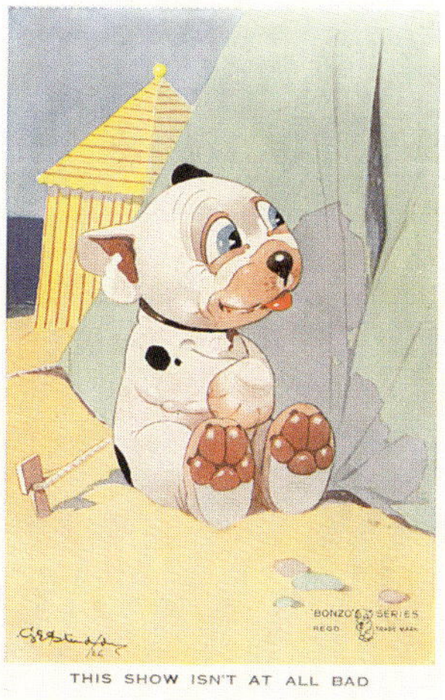
THIS SHOW ISN'T AT ALL BAD

1079

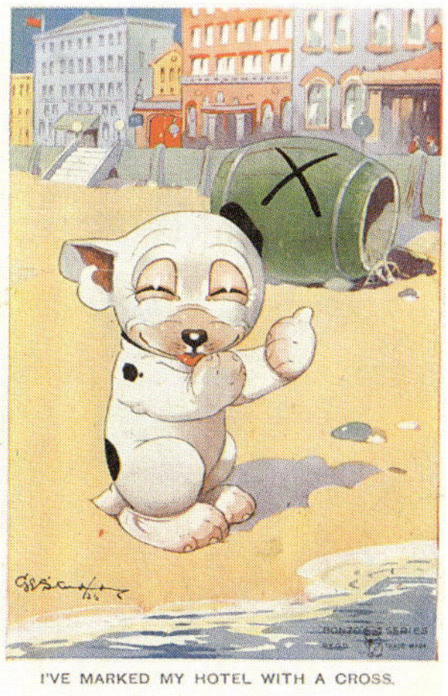
I'VE MARKED MY HOTEL WITH A CROSS.

1120

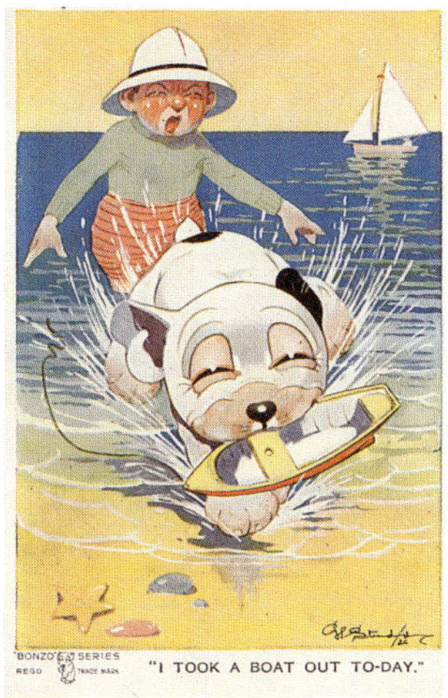
"I TOOK A BOAT OUT TO-DAY."

1121

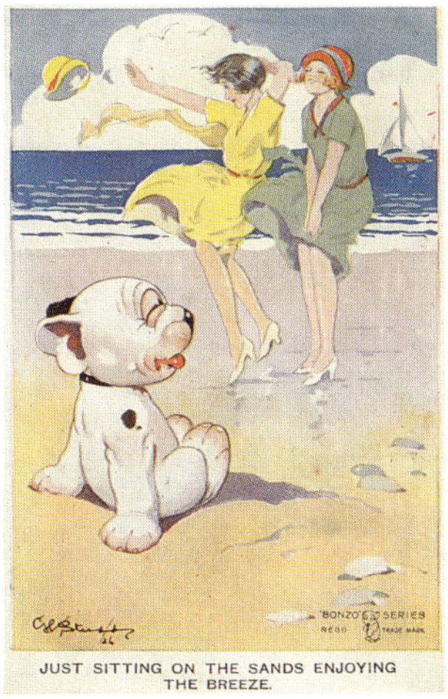
JUST SITTING ON THE SANDS ENJOYING THE BREEZE.

1122

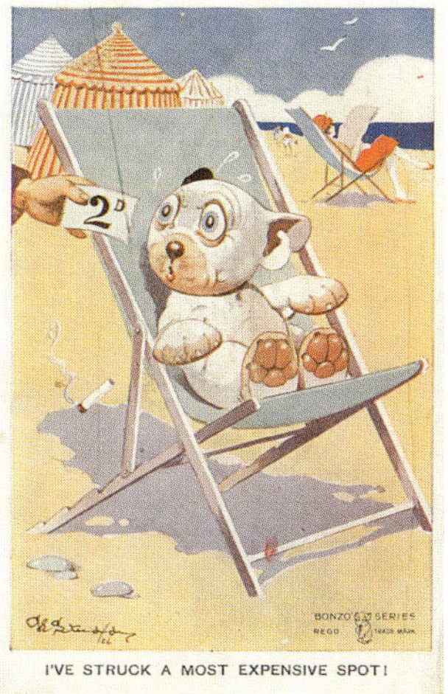
2D
I'VE STRUCK A MOST EXPENSIVE SPOT!

1123

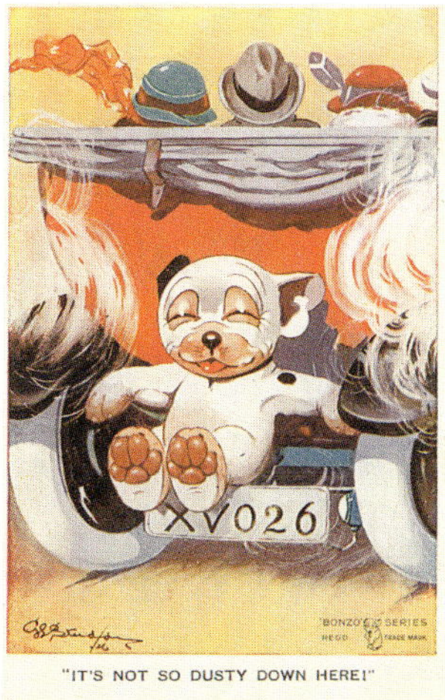
XV026
"IT'S NOT SO DUSTY DOWN HERE!"

1124

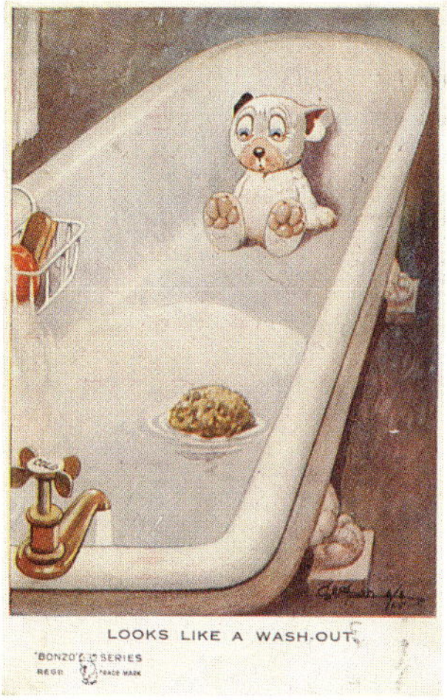
LOOKS LIKE A WASH-OUT.

1125

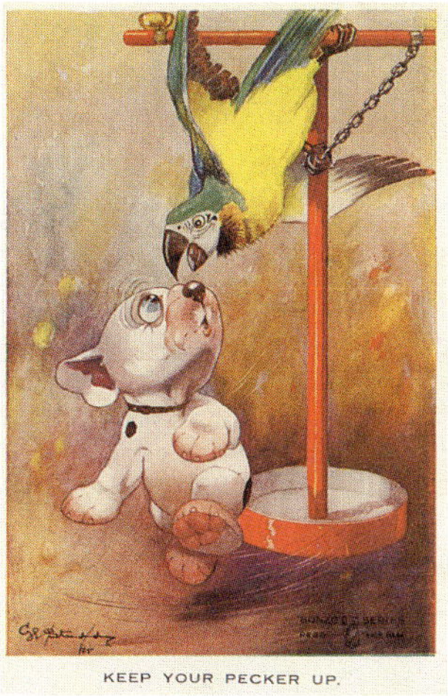
KEEP YOUR PECKER UP.

1126

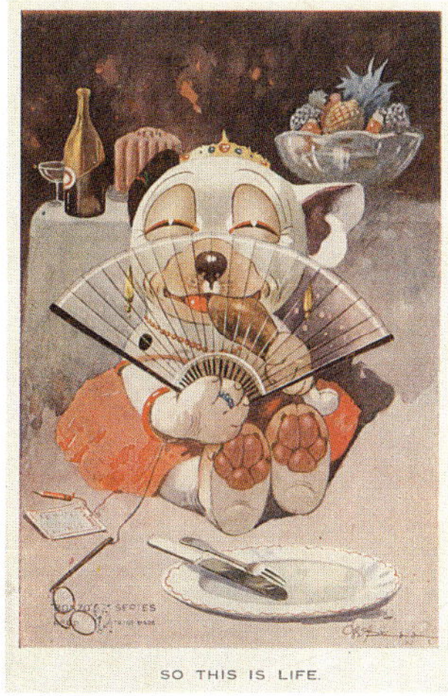
SO THIS IS LIFE.

1127

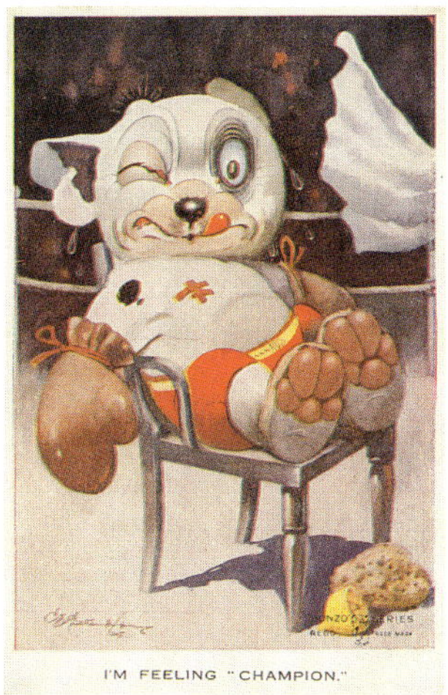
I'M FEELING "CHAMPION."

1128

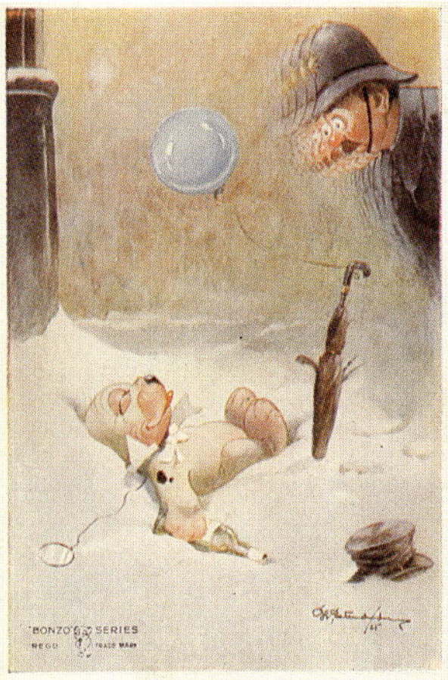

HULLO! EVERYBODY!

1129

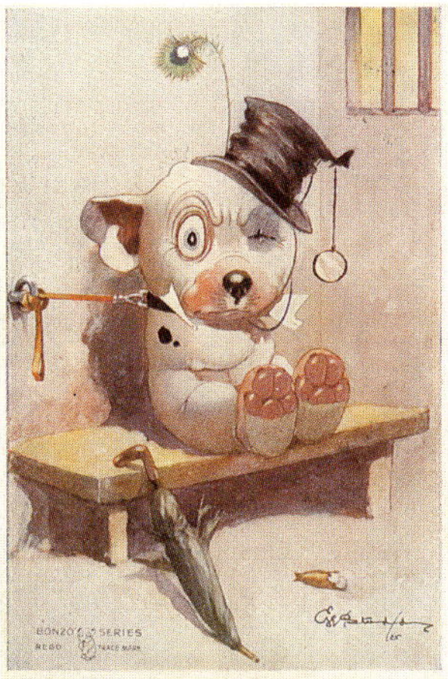

I SHALL BE HERE FOR SOME TIME!

1130

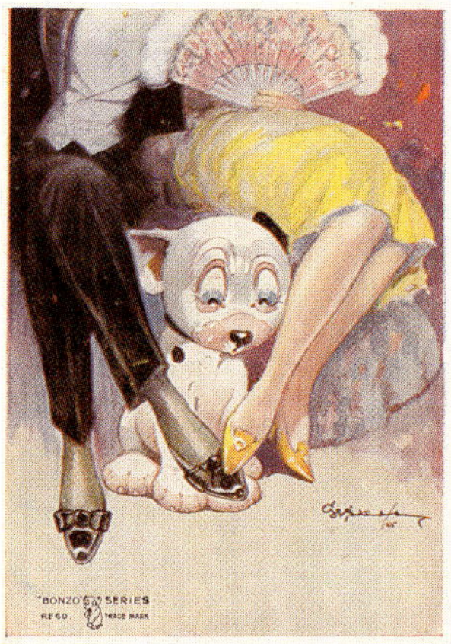

"THE FIRST MOVE IN THE GAME."

1132

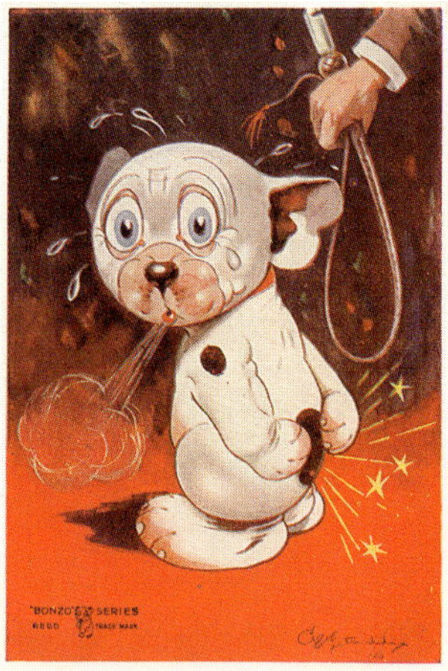

I'M STRUCK ON THIS PLACE!

1133

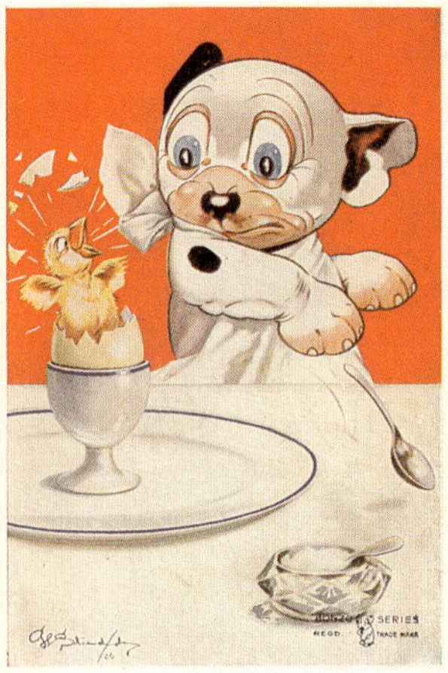

I WAS SURPRISED TO HEAR FROM YOU!

1134

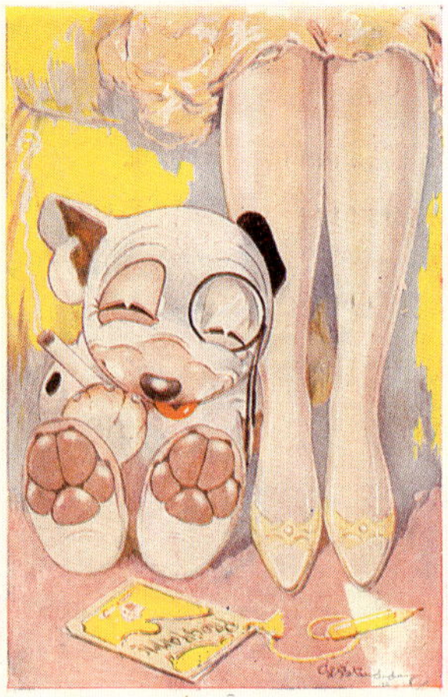

GENTLEMEN PREFER SITTING OUT!

1135

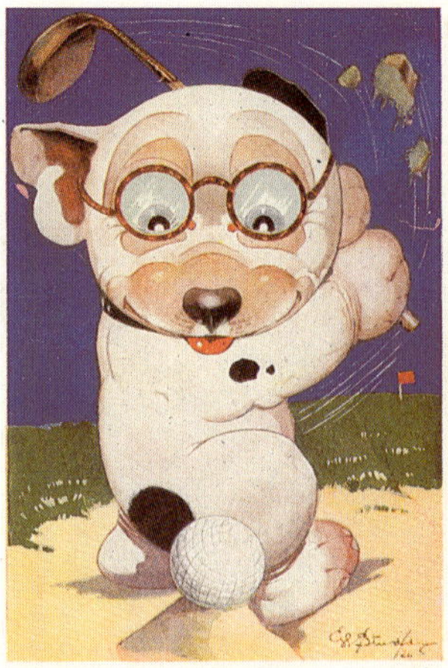

I'M MISSING YOU DREADFULLY

1200

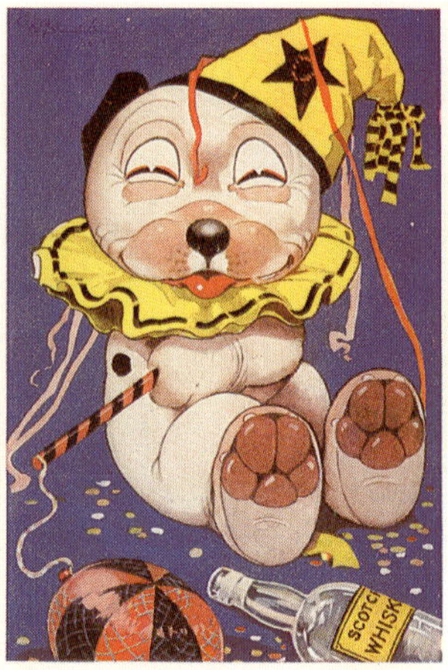

I'M IN GREAT SPIRITS HERE!

1201

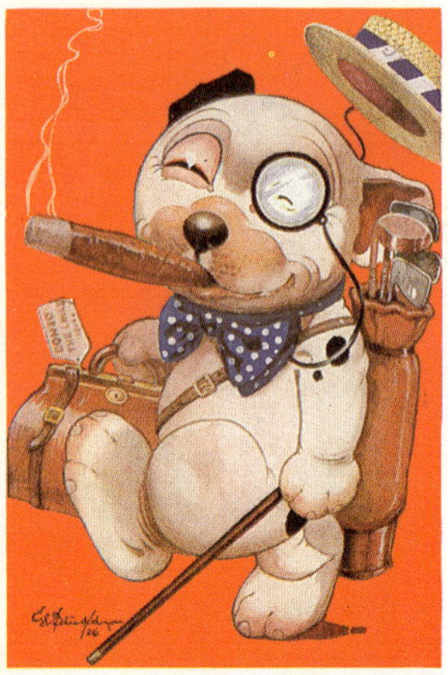

EVERY DOG HAS HIS DAY!

1202

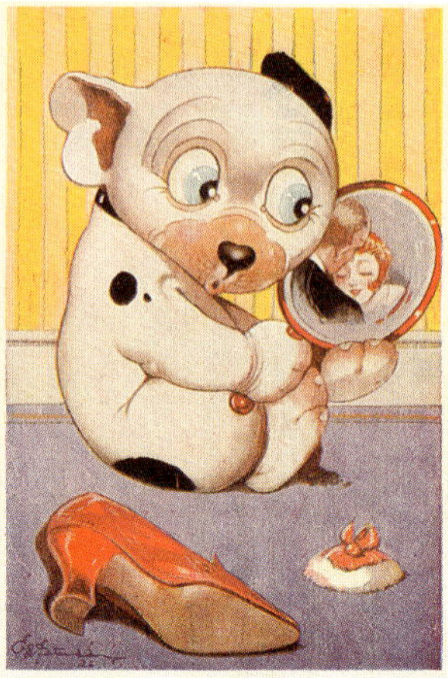

I'VE GOT MY EYE ON YOU!

1203

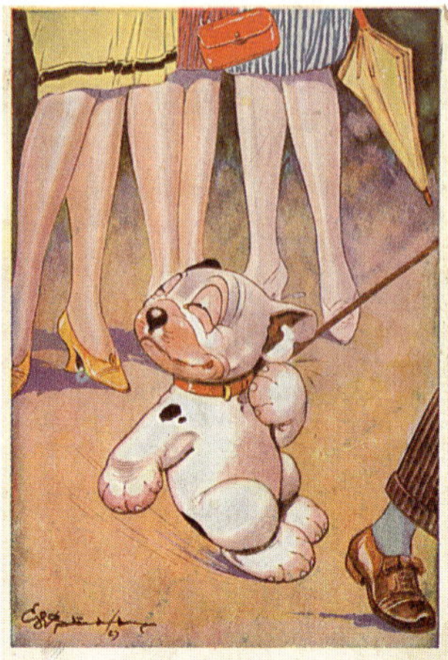

I WISH I COULD HANG ON HERE!

1205

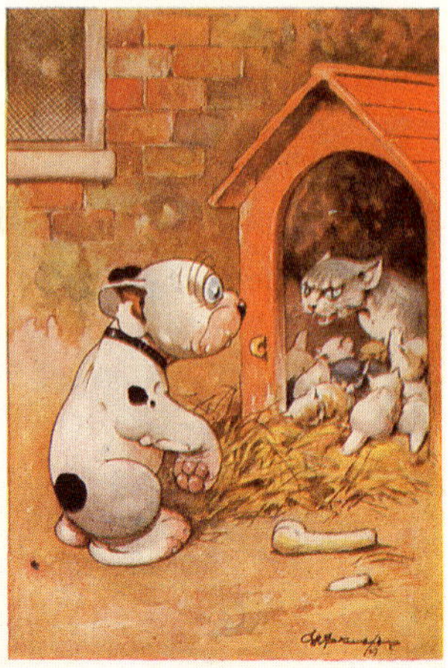

I DON'T LOOK LIKE GETTING HOME YET!

1206

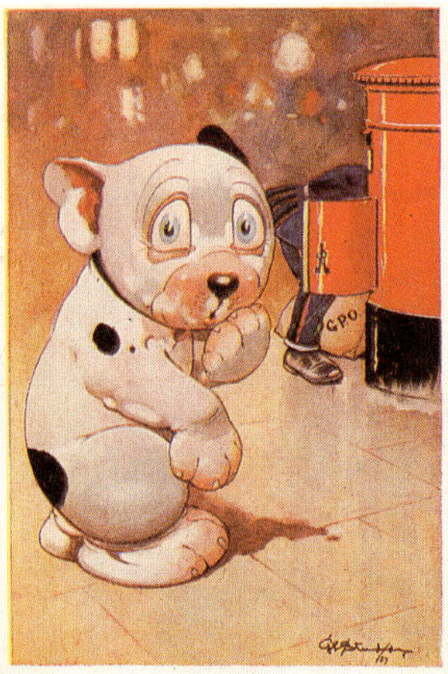

I'VE JUST REMEMBERED I FORGOT TO WRITE YOU!

1207

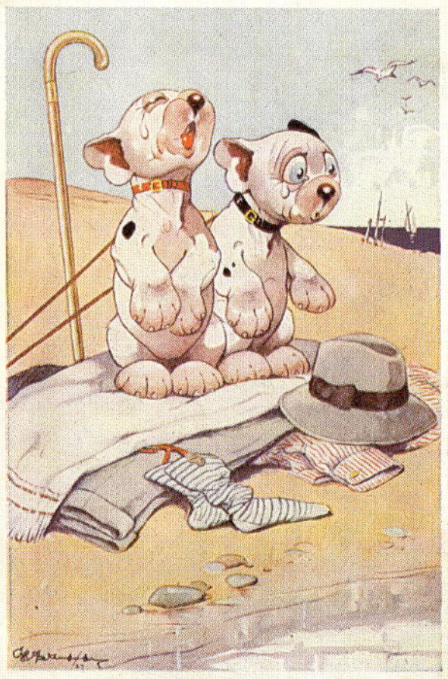

IT'S PERFECTLY AWFUL WITHOUT YOU

1208

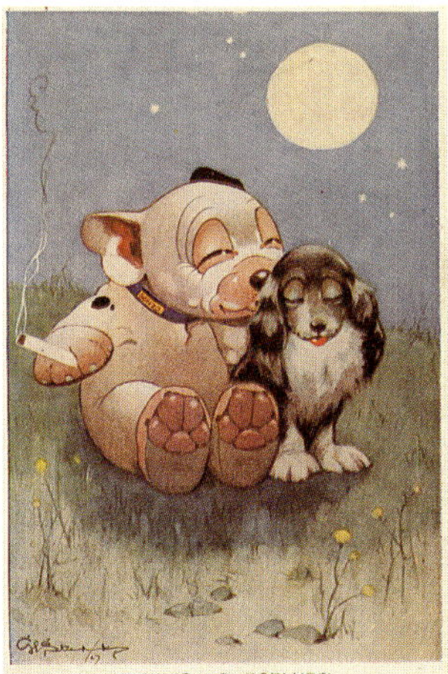

BETWEEN OURSELVES

1209

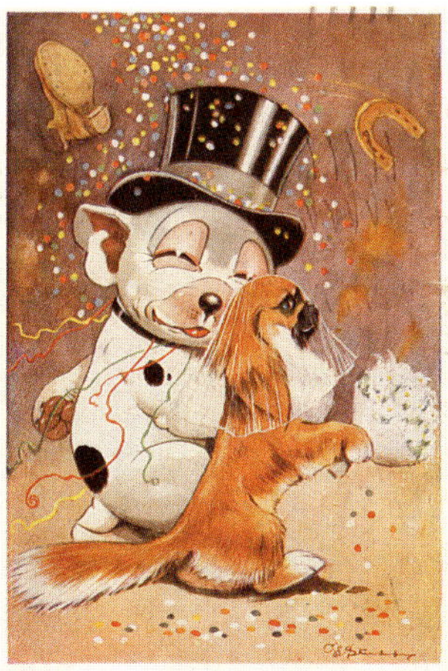

WHEN'S YOURS COMING OFF?

1210

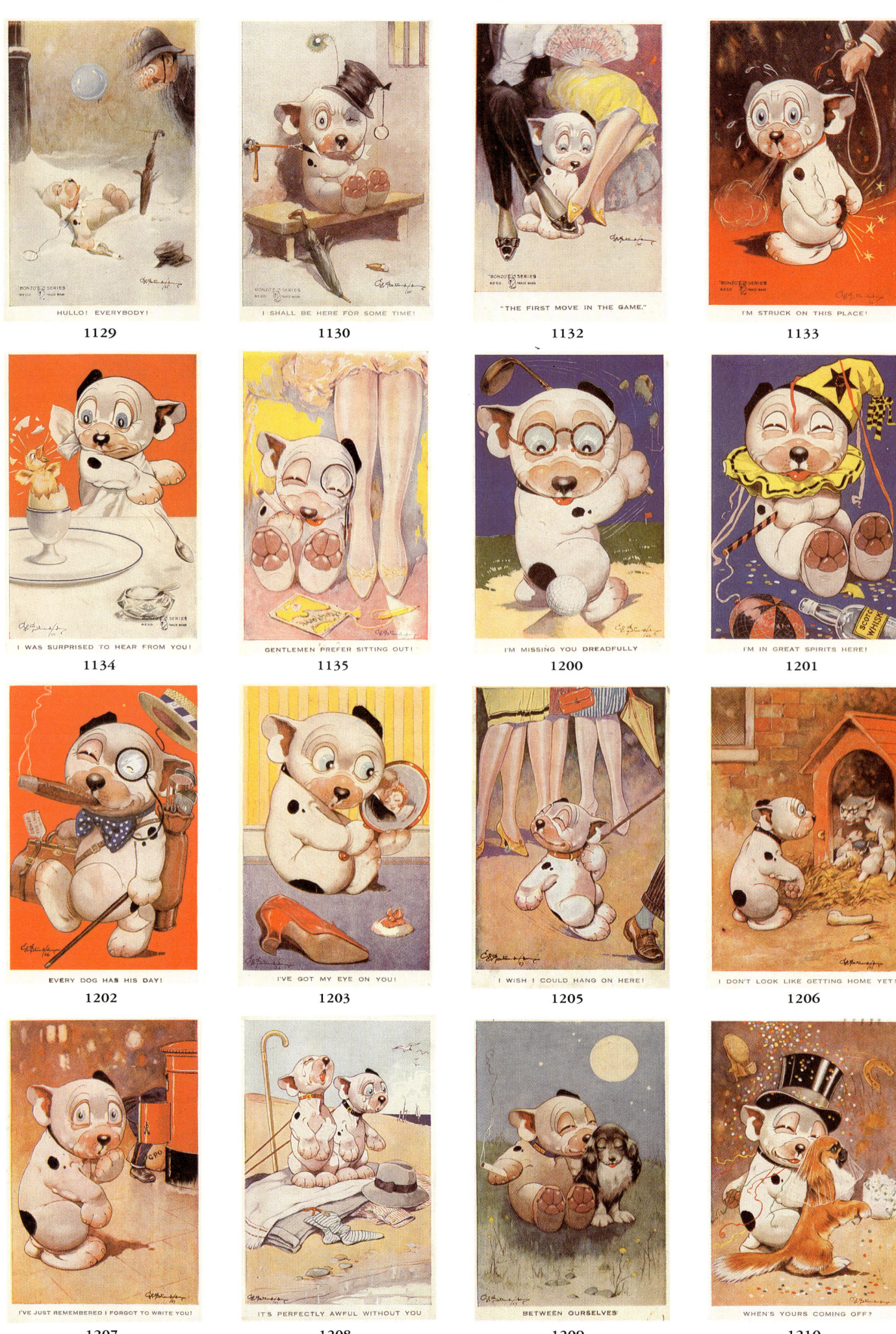

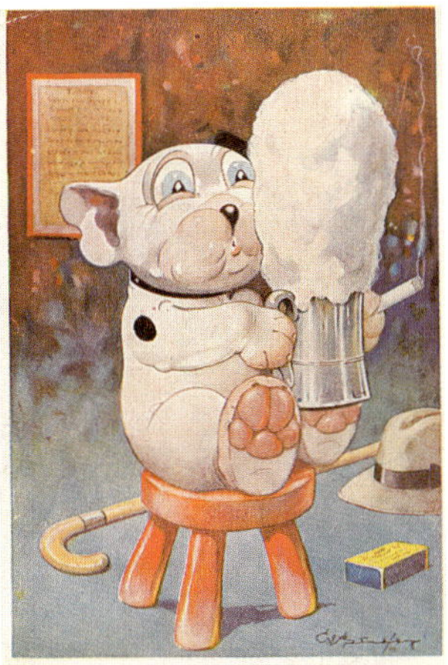
THE MORE WE HAVE TOGETHER THE MERRIER WE WILL BE

1211

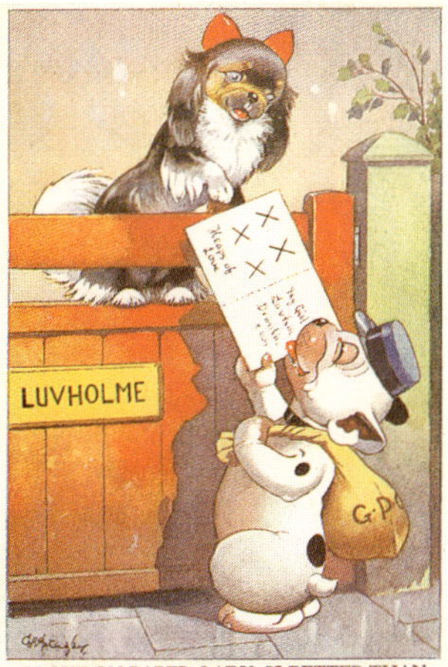
LUVHOLME
"LOVE ON PAPER, LADY, IS BETTER THAN NO LOVE AT ALL."

1237

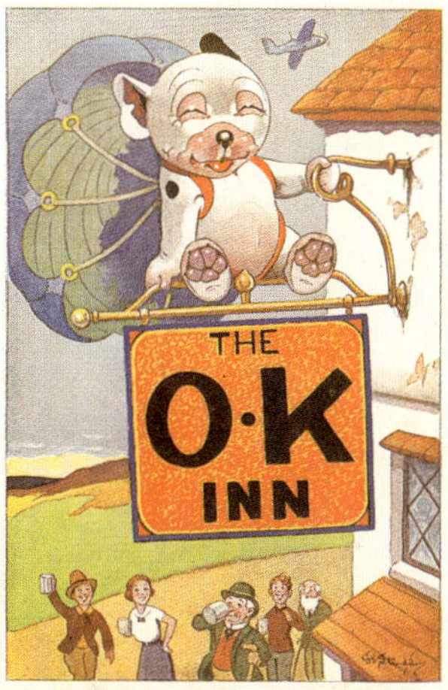
THE
O·K
INN
"I'VE DROPPED IN ON AN IDEAL SPOT."

1238

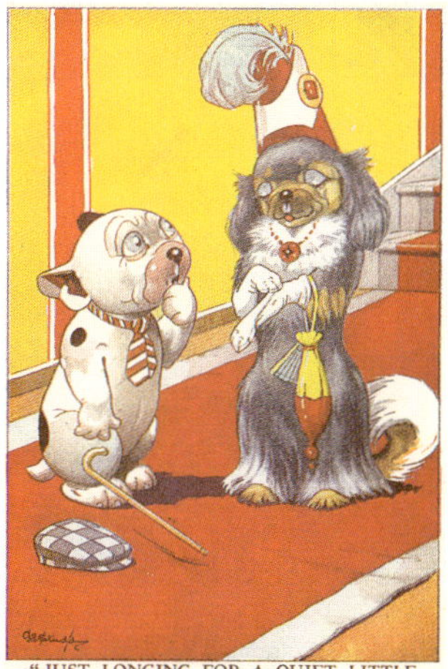
"JUST LONGING FOR A QUIET LITTLE EVENING WITH YOU."

1239

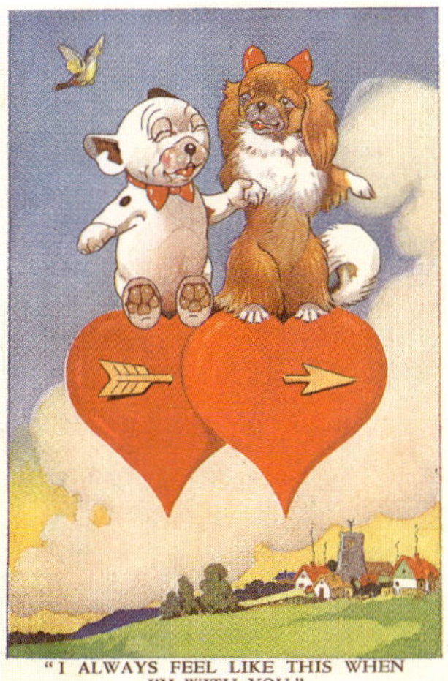
"I ALWAYS FEEL LIKE THIS WHEN I'M WITH YOU."

1240

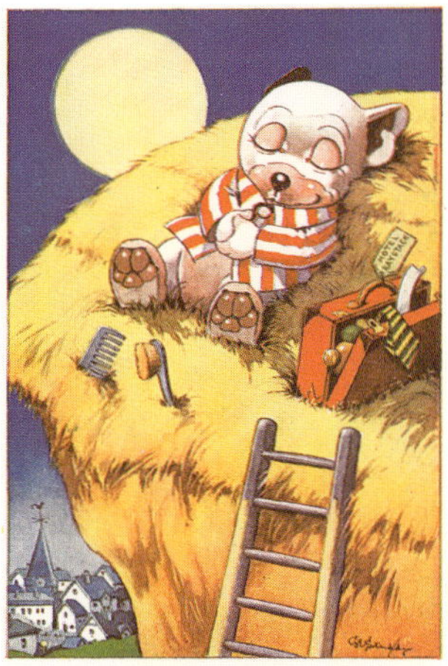
EVERYTHING O.K. HOTEL GRAND.

1241

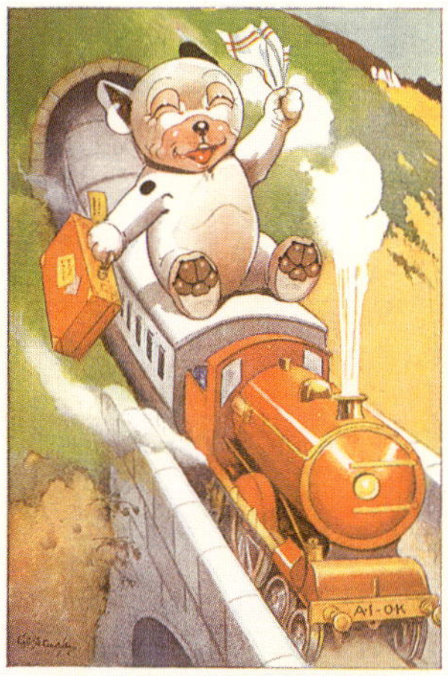
A1-OK
I'LL SOON BE SEEING YOU AGAIN.

1242

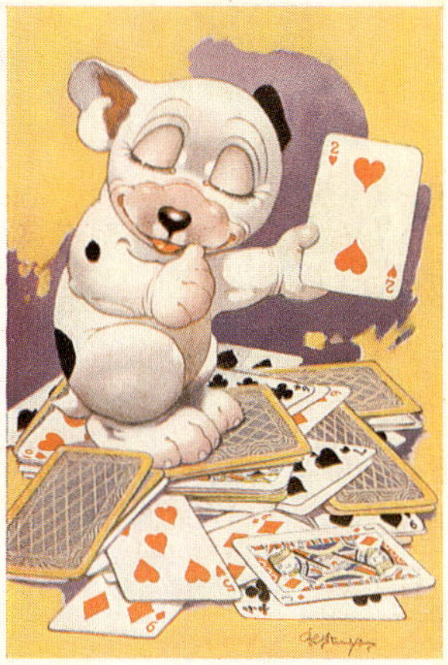
THIS MAKES ME THINK OF YOU!

1254

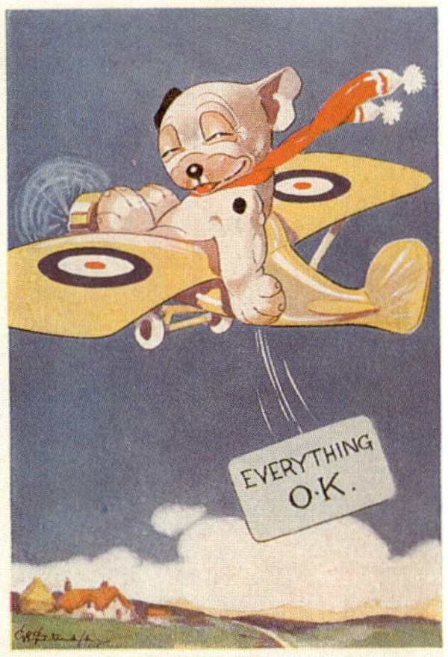
EVERYTHING
O·K.
JUST DROPPING YOU A CARD!

1255

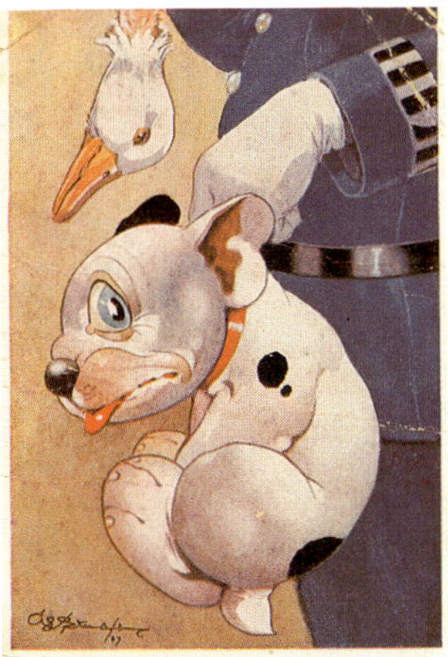
CAN'T SAY WHEN I'M COMING BACK.

1256

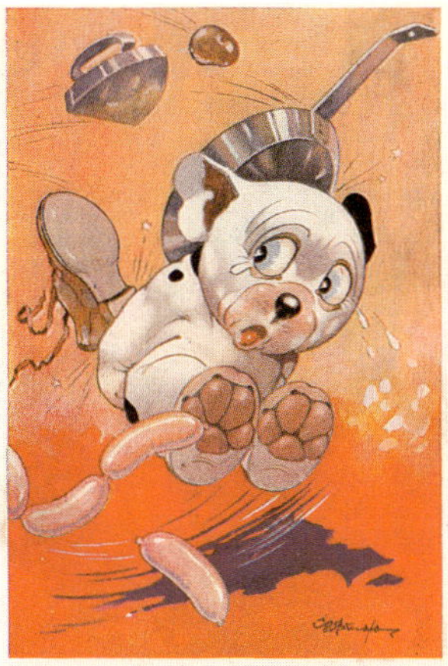
IF I ONLY THOUGHT YOU'D MISS ME— BUT YOU DON'T!

1257

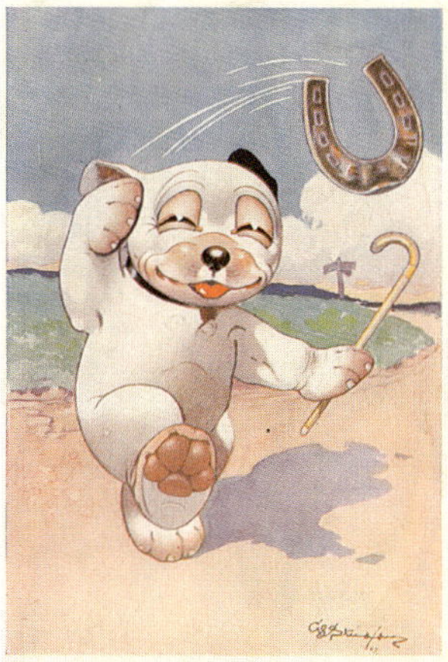
I'M SENDING YOU THIS FOR LUCK!

1258

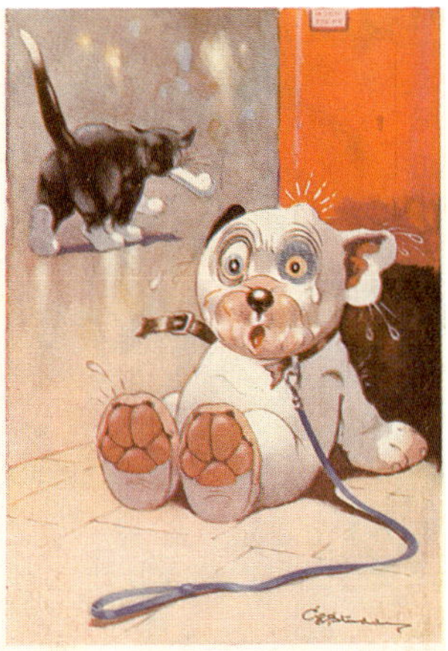
CHEERIO! I'M STILL ALIVE!

1259

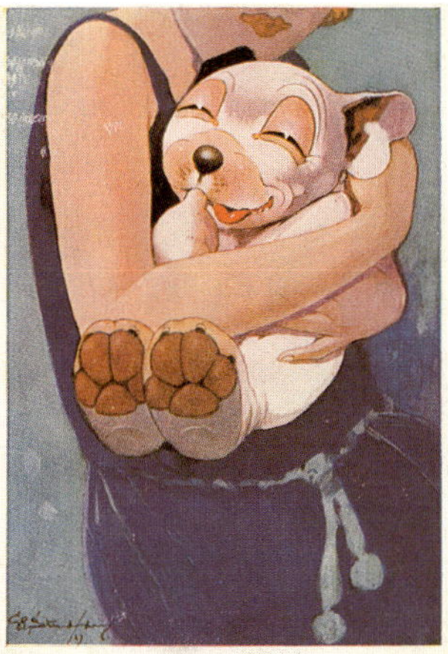
DON'T WORRY ABOUT ME!

1260

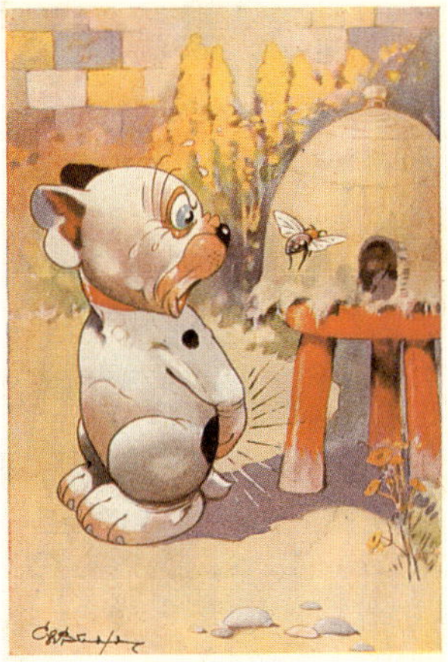
GIVE MY LOVE TO ALL AT HOME

1261

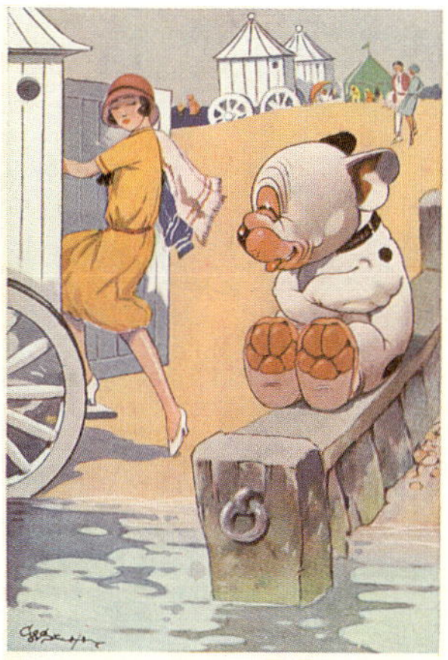
LOOKING FORWARD TO SEEING YOU AGAIN!

1262

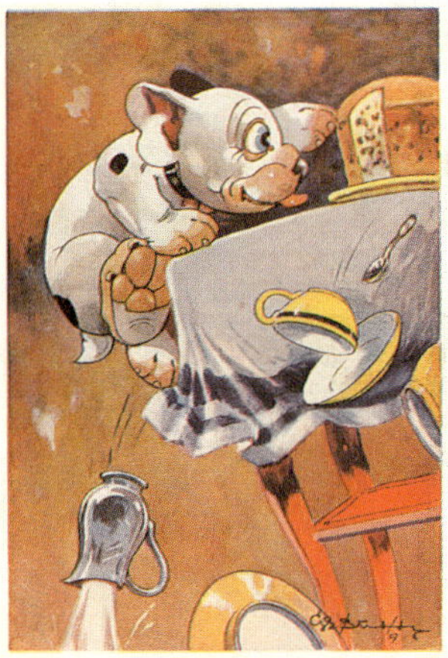
I'M GETTING ON FINE HERE!

1263

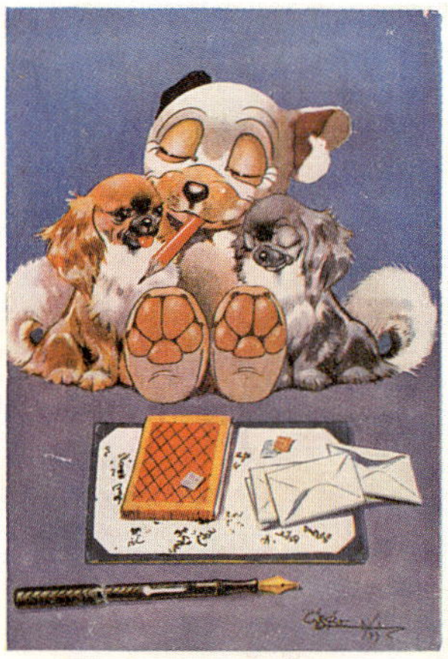
I REALLY HAVEN'T TIME TO WRITE!

1264

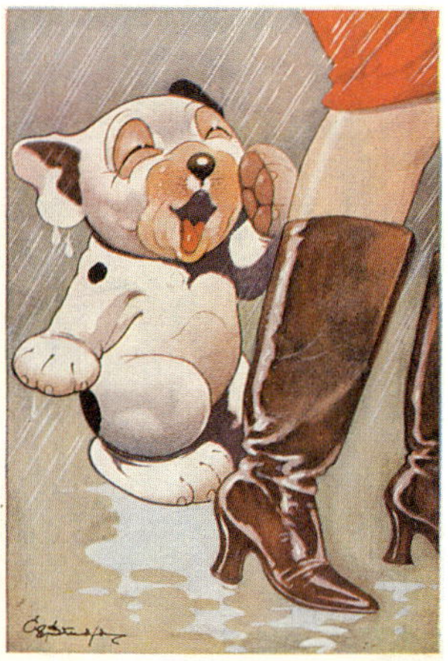
I DIDN'T DO IT!

1265

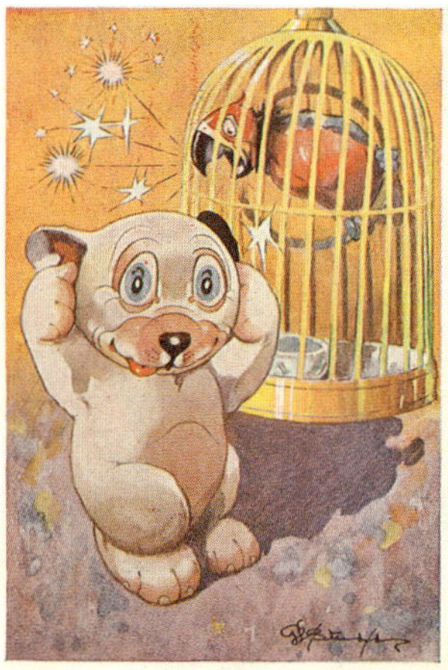
I LOVE HAVING SOMEONE TO TALK TO

1288

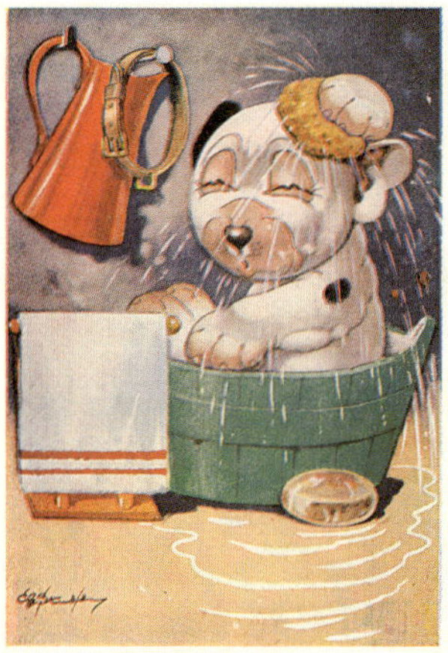
"WHILE THERE'S LIFE, THERE'S SOAP!"

1289

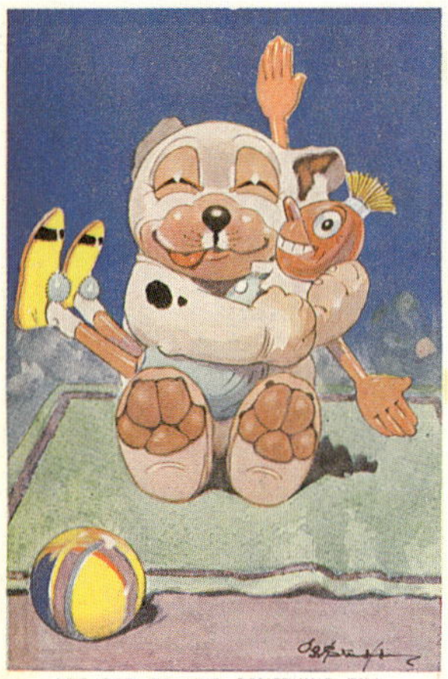
I'VE GOT TO HUG SOMETHING TILL WE MEET AGAIN.

1290

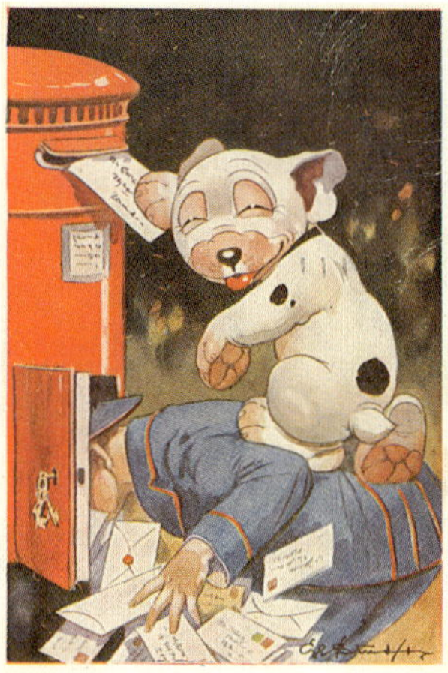
JUST A LINE FOR AULD LANG SYNE.

1292

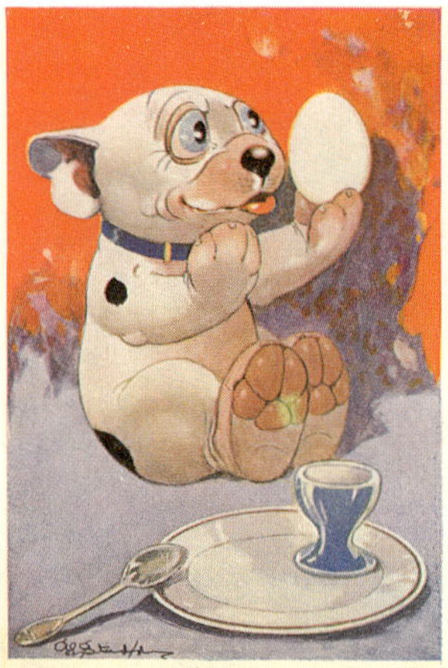
I'M JUST WONDERING IF YOU'RE AS GOOD AS YOU LOOK.

1293

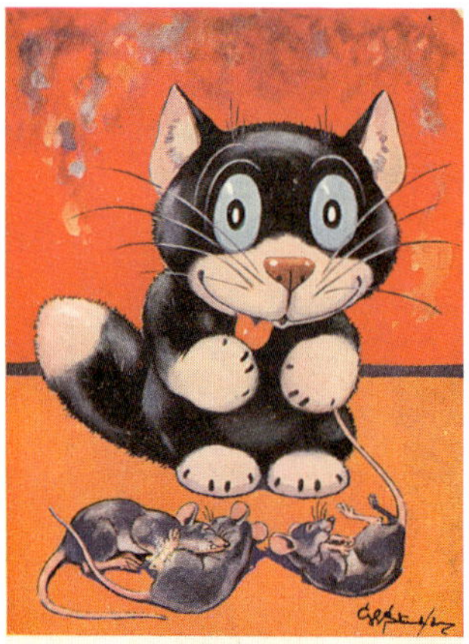
HAD A KILLING TIME LATELY.

1294

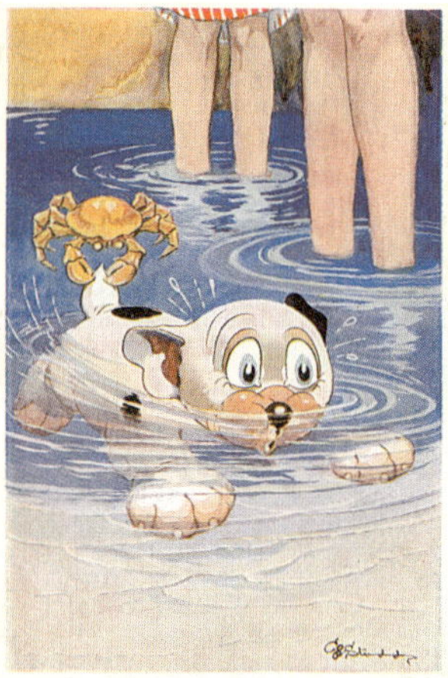
UP TO MY EYES JUST NOW!

1307

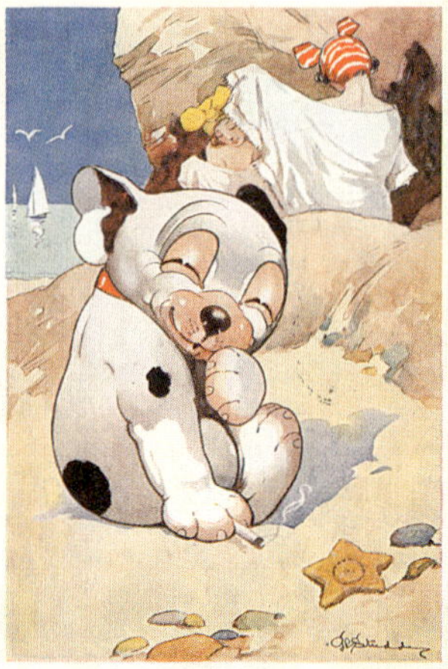
NOTHING TO WRITE HOME ABOUT.

1308

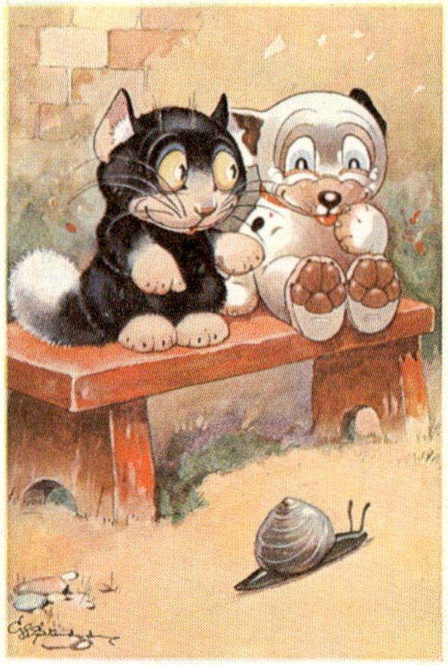
THAT REMINDS ME— SOME FOLKS ARE A BIT SLOW.

1309

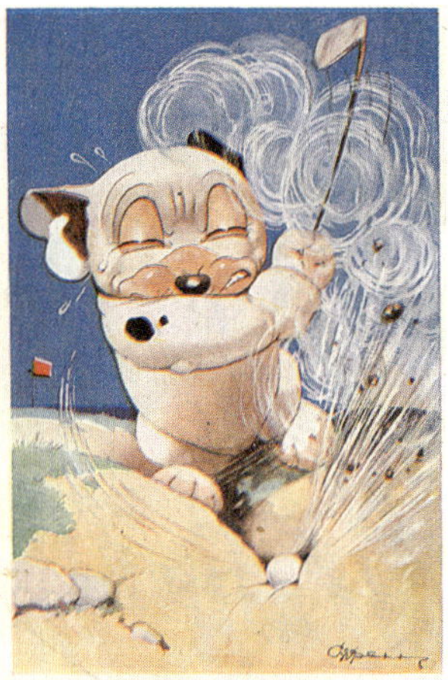
I'M RAISING QUITE A DUST HERE.

1310

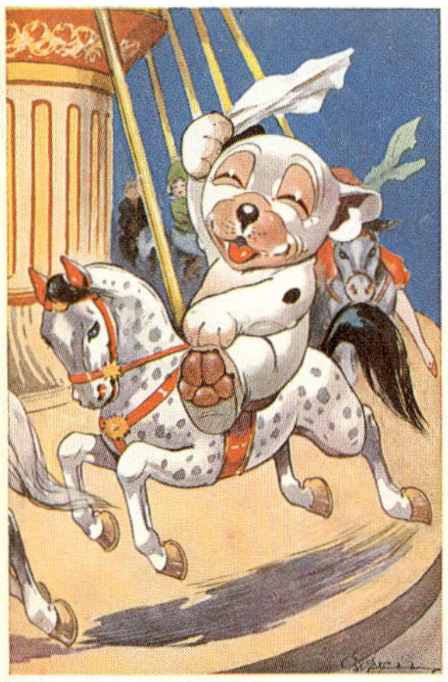
"I'LL BE ROUND AGAIN SOON!"

1311

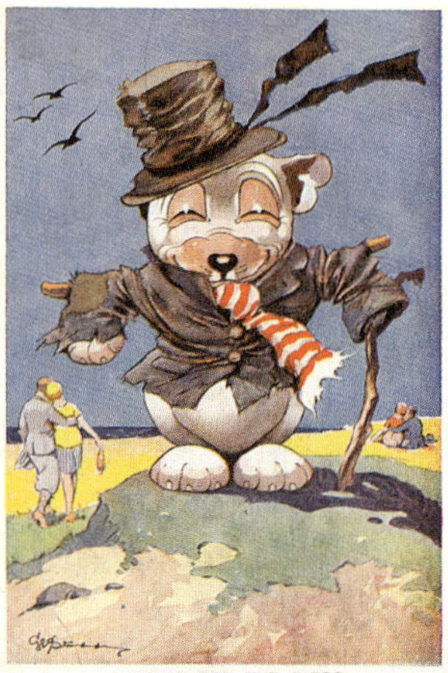
KEEPING OFF THE BIRDS.

1312

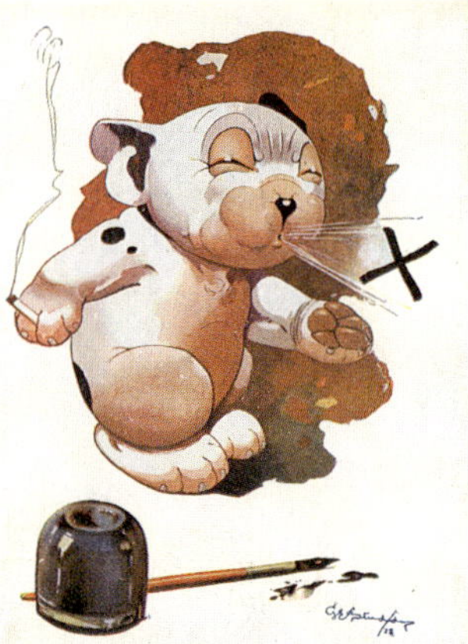
JUST TIME TO BLOW YOU A KISS

1368

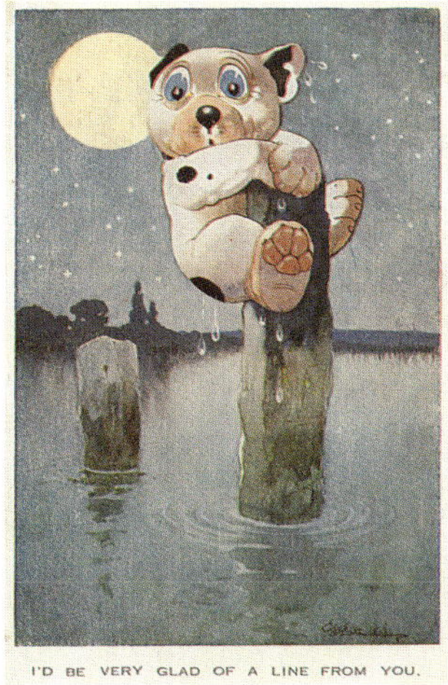
I'D BE VERY GLAD OF A LINE FROM YOU.
1369

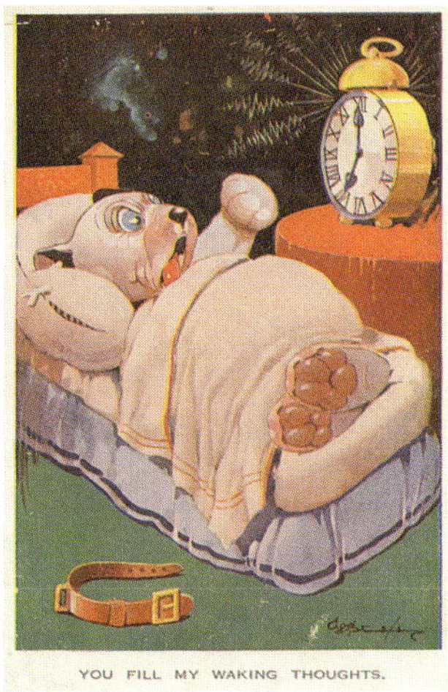
YOU FILL MY WAKING THOUGHTS.
1370

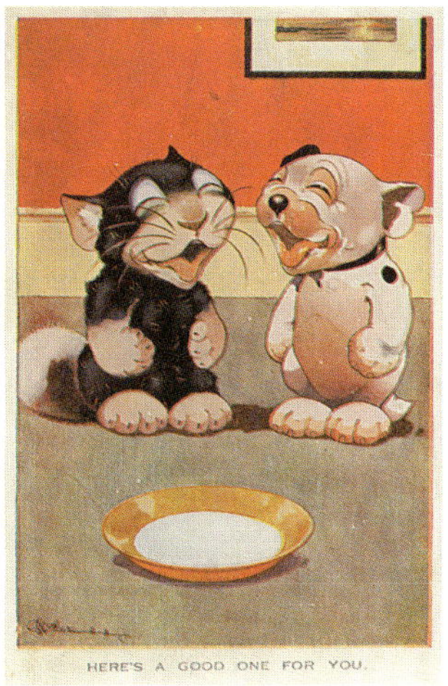
HERE'S A GOOD ONE FOR YOU.
1371

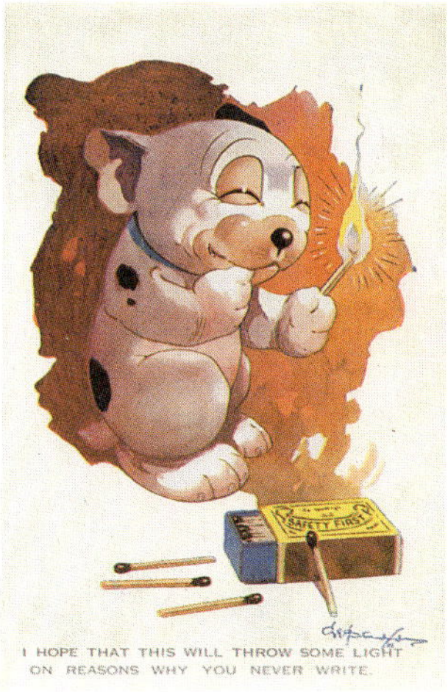
I HOPE THAT THIS WILL THROW SOME LIGHT
ON REASONS WHY YOU NEVER WRITE.
1372

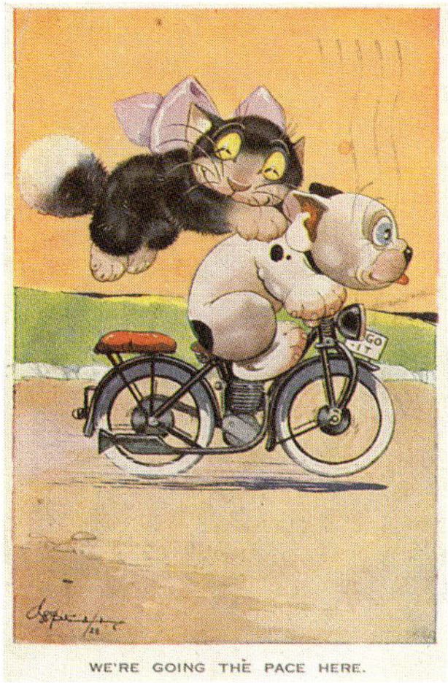
WE'RE GOING THE PACE HERE.
1373

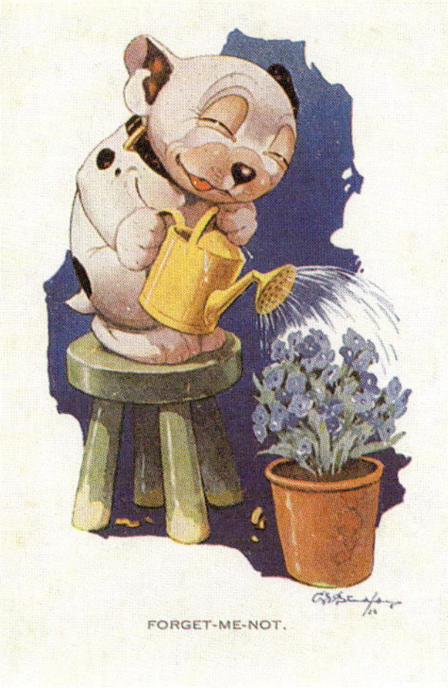
FORGET-ME-NOT.
1374

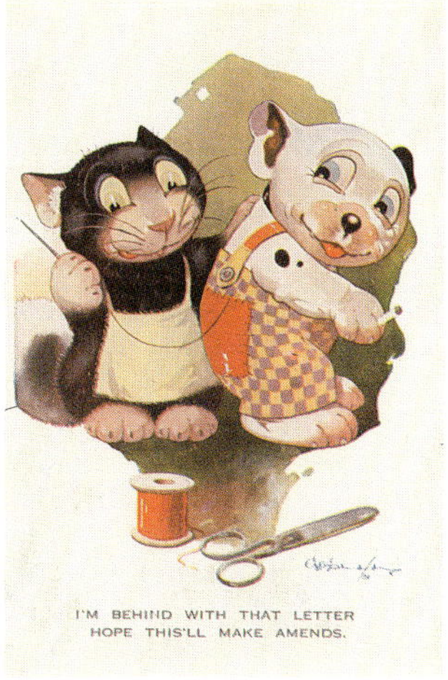
I'M BEHIND WITH THAT LETTER
HOPE THIS'LL MAKE AMENDS.
1375

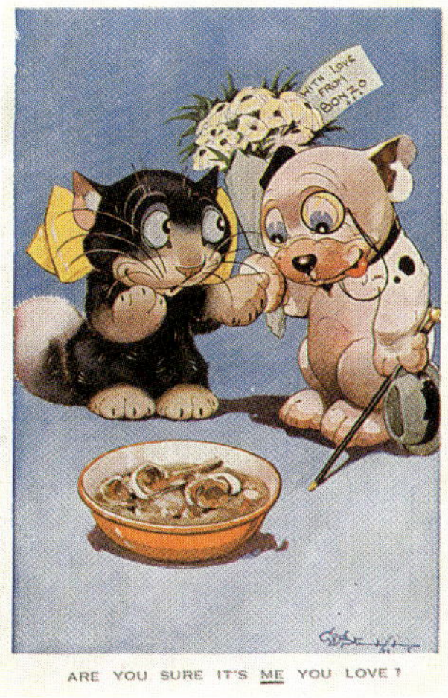
ARE YOU SURE IT'S ME YOU LOVE?
1376

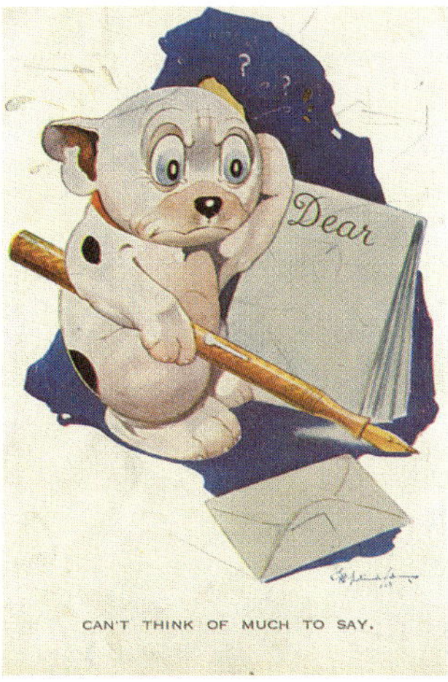
Dear
CAN'T THINK OF MUCH TO SAY.
1377

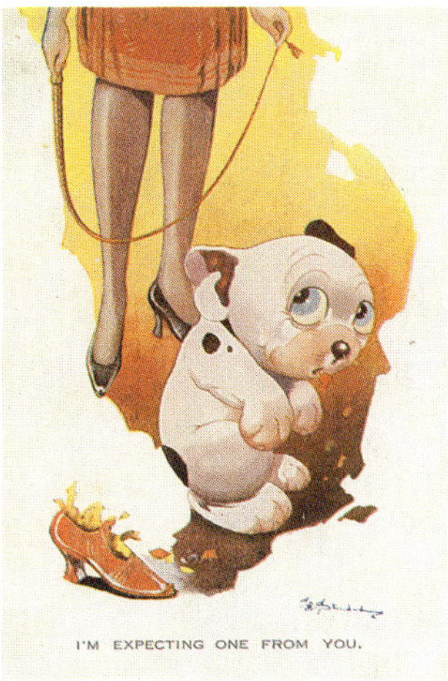
I'M EXPECTING ONE FROM YOU.
1378

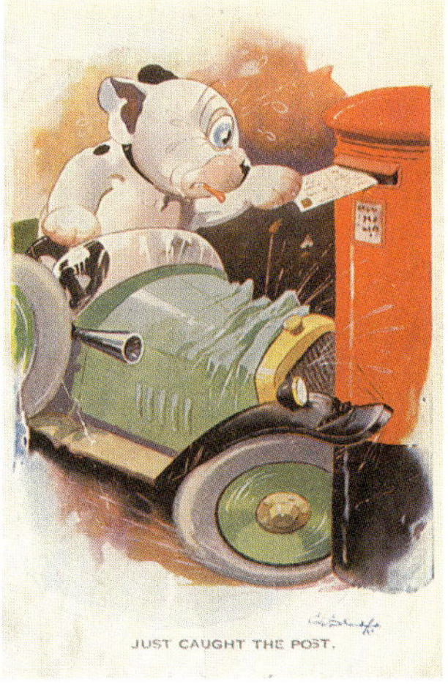
JUST CAUGHT THE POST.
1379

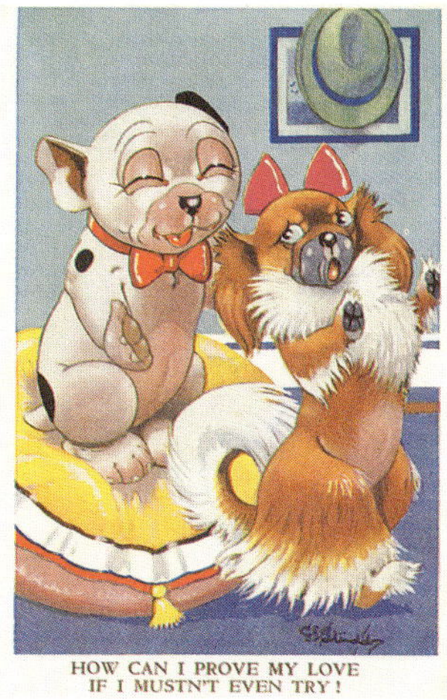
HOW CAN I PROVE MY LOVE
IF I MUSTN'T EVEN TRY!
1408

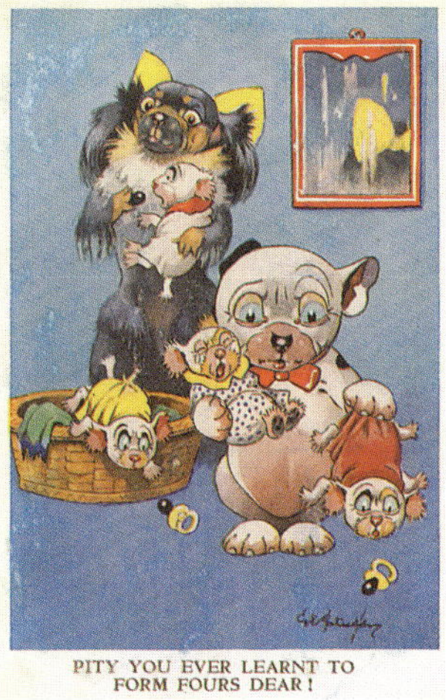
PITY YOU EVER LEARNT TO
FORM FOURS DEAR!
1409

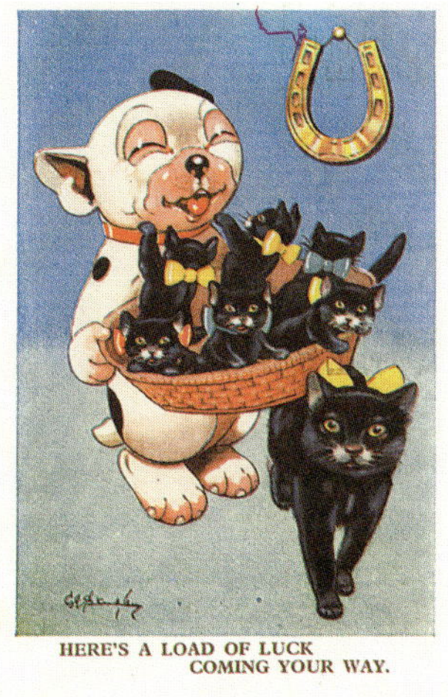
HERE'S A LOAD OF LUCK
COMING YOUR WAY.
1410

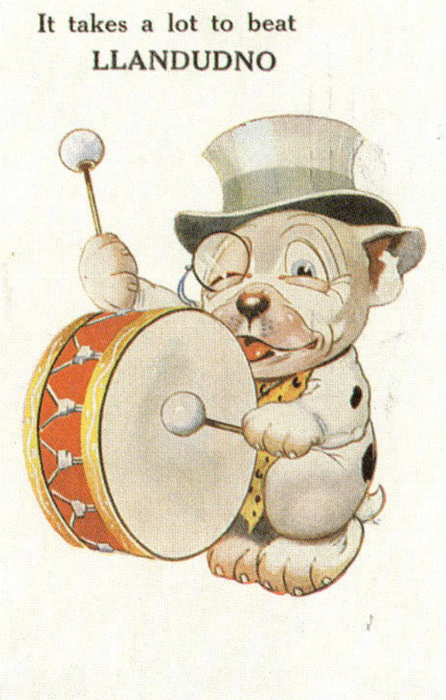
It takes a lot to beat
LLANDUDNO
L1435

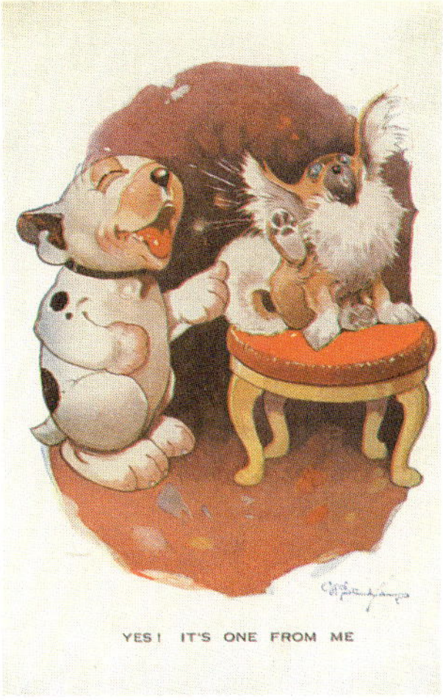
YES! IT'S ONE FROM ME
1514

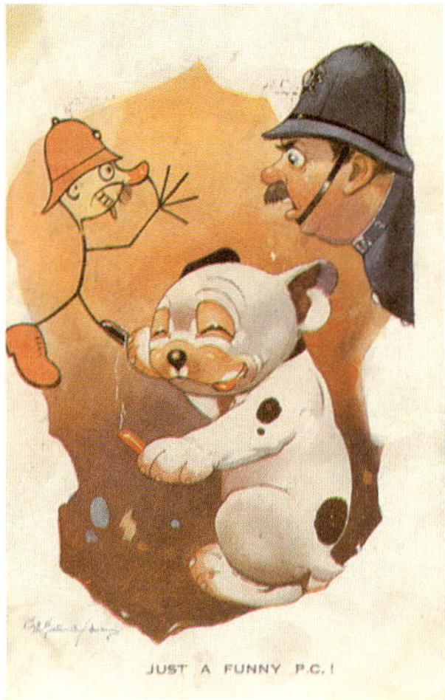
JUST A FUNNY P.C.!
1515

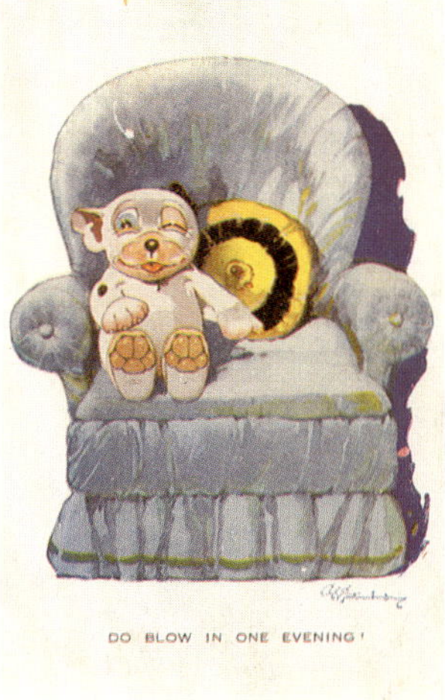
DO BLOW IN ONE EVENING!
1516

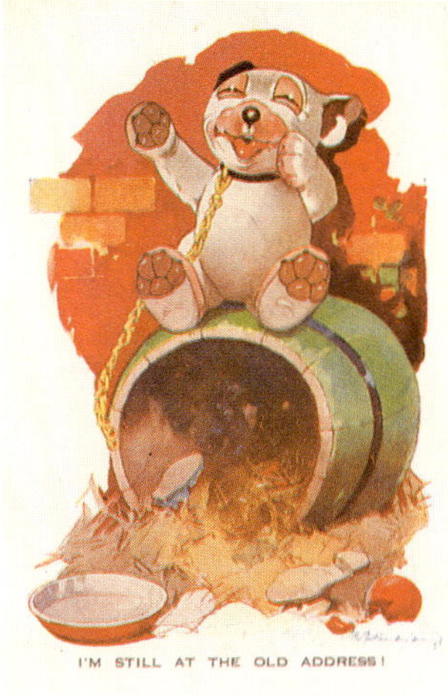
I'M STILL AT THE OLD ADDRESS!
1517

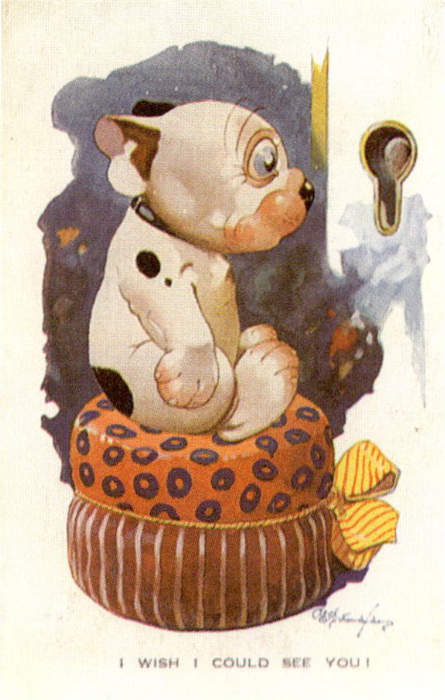
I WISH I COULD SEE YOU!
1518

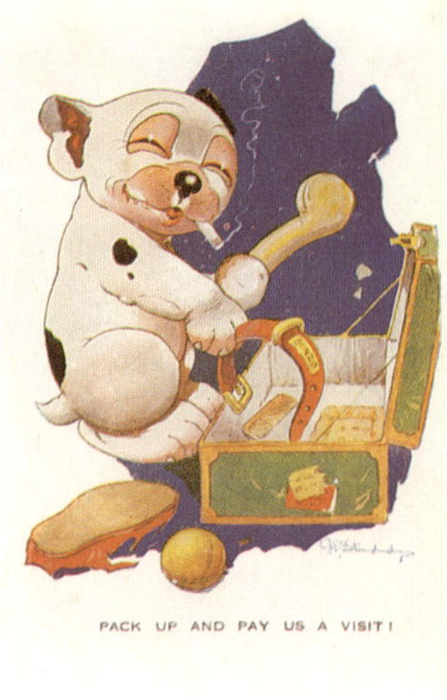
PACK UP AND PAY US A VISIT!
1519

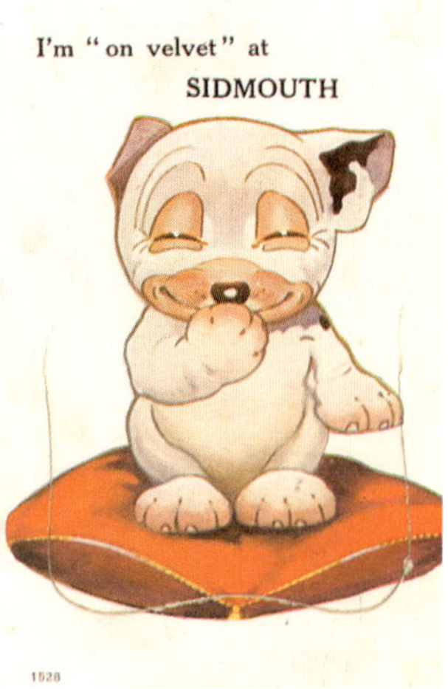
I'm "on velvet" at
SIDMOUTH
1528
1528

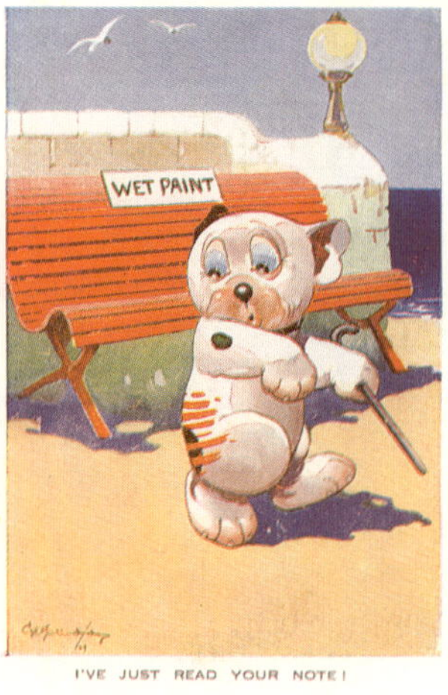
WET PAINT
I'VE JUST READ YOUR NOTE!
1562

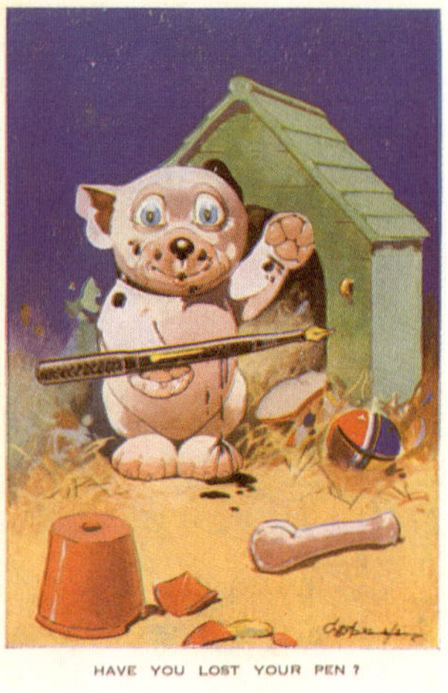
HAVE YOU LOST YOUR PEN?
1563

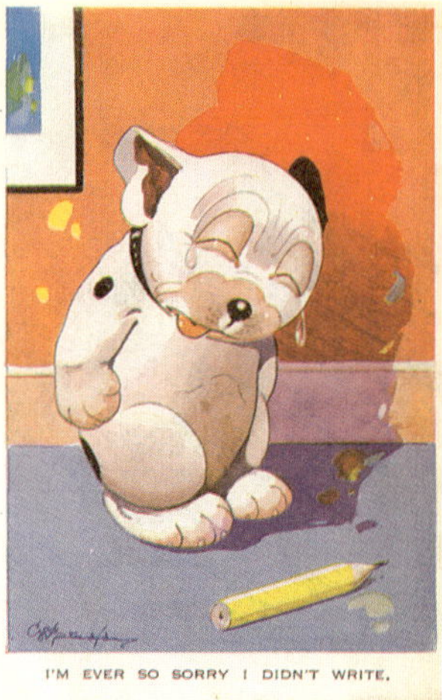
I'M EVER SO SORRY I DIDN'T WRITE.
1564

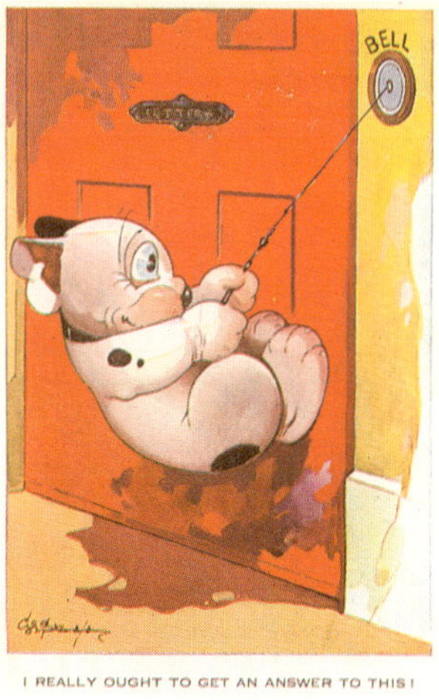
BELL
I REALLY OUGHT TO GET AN ANSWER TO THIS!
1565

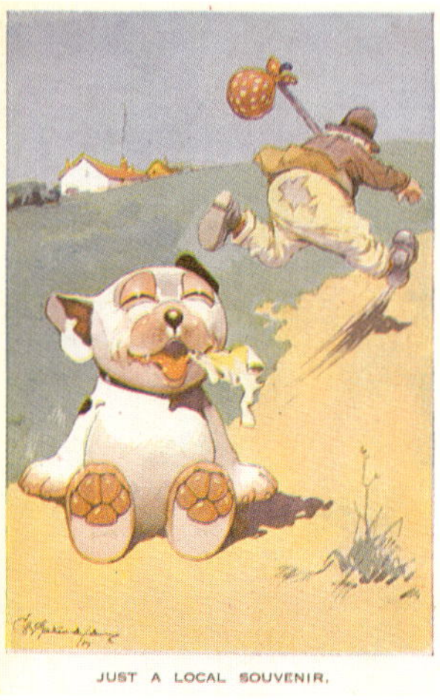
JUST A LOCAL SOUVENIR.
1566

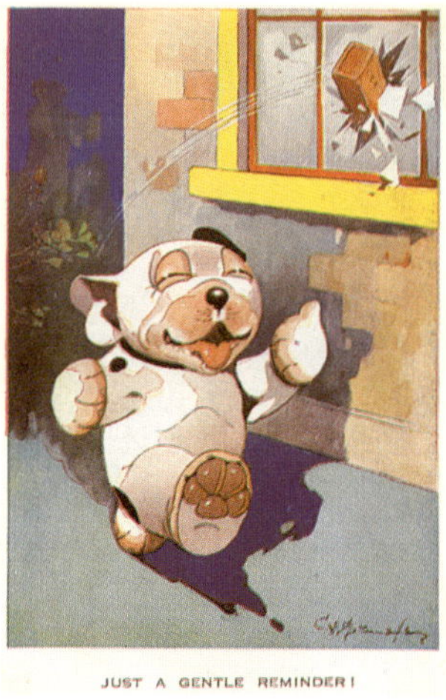
JUST A GENTLE REMINDER!
1567

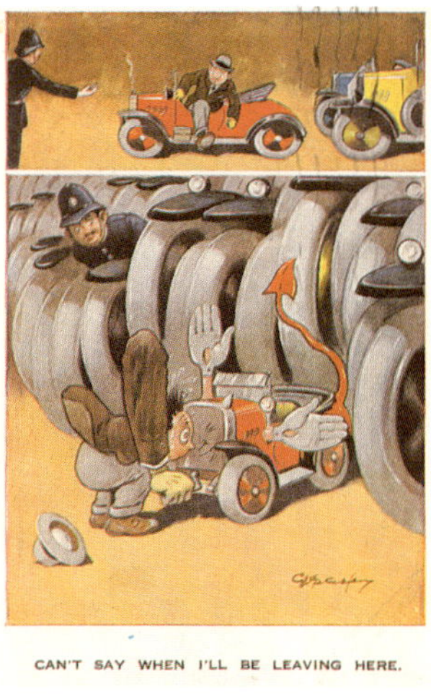
CAN'T SAY WHEN I'LL BE LEAVING HERE.
1568

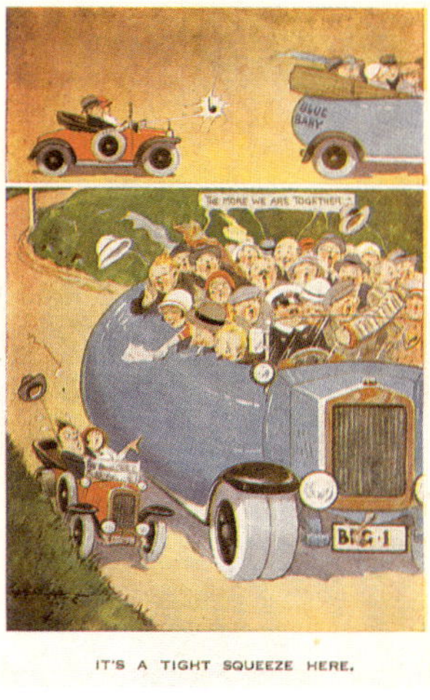
IT'S A TIGHT SQUEEZE HERE.
1569

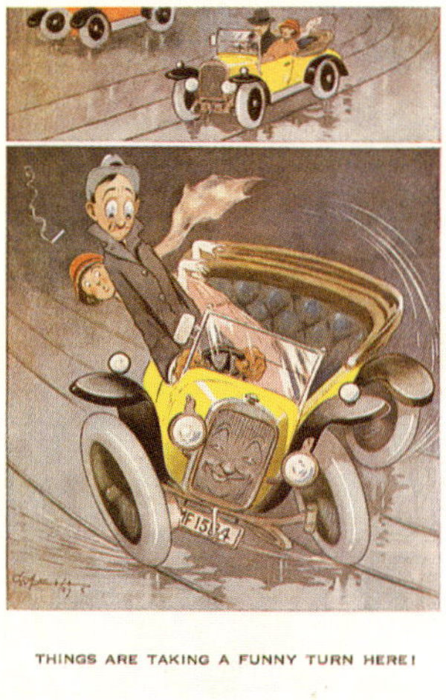
THINGS ARE TAKING A FUNNY TURN HERE!
1570

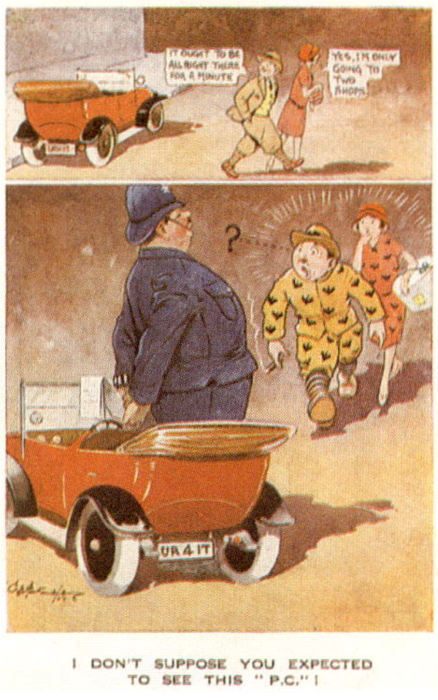
I DON'T SUPPOSE YOU EXPECTED
TO SEE THIS "P.C."!
1571

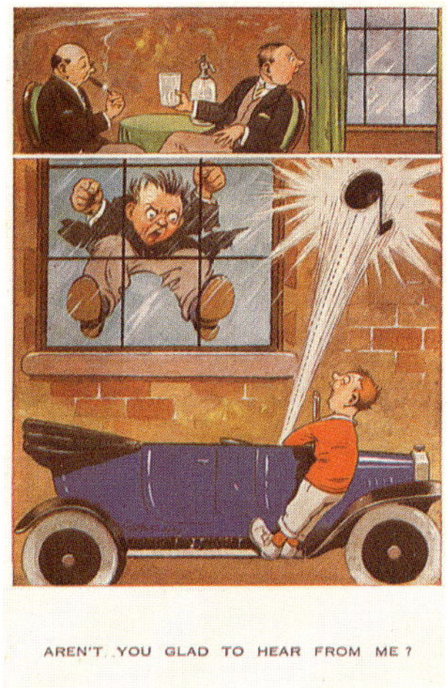
AREN'T YOU GLAD TO HEAR FROM ME?
1572

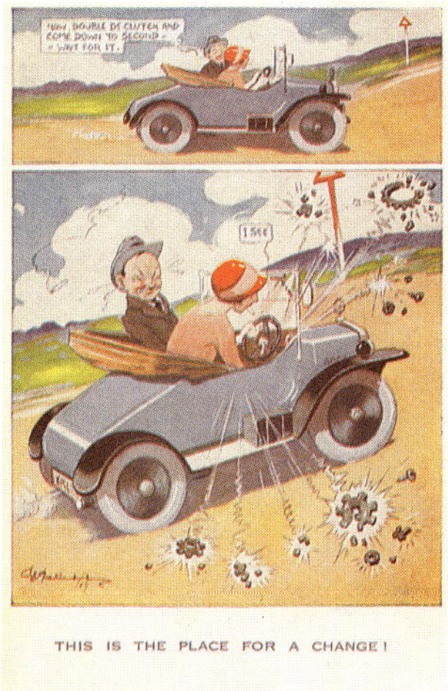
THIS IS THE PLACE FOR A CHANGE!
1573

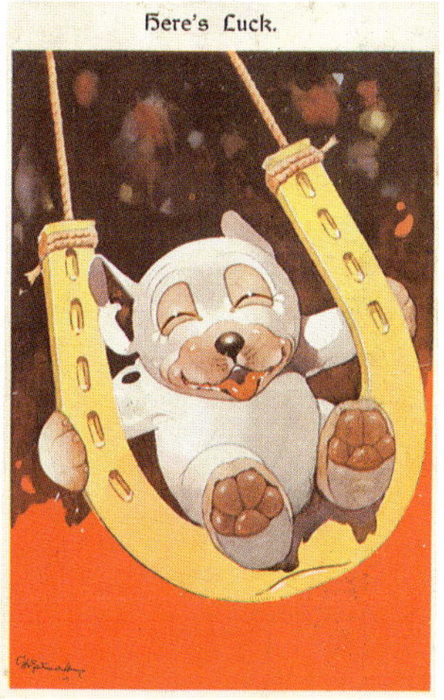
Here's Luck.
1636

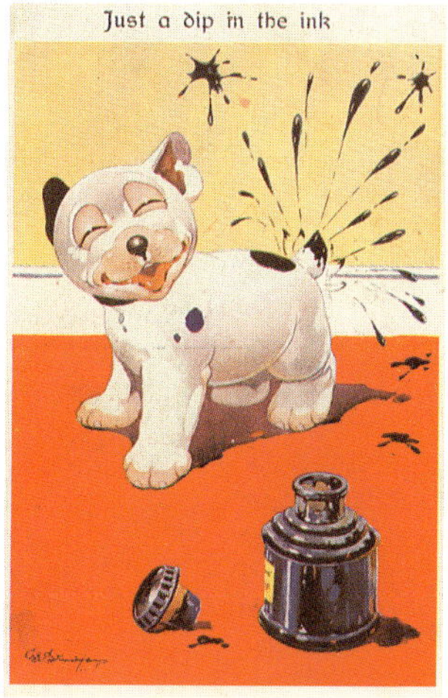
Just a dip in the ink
1638

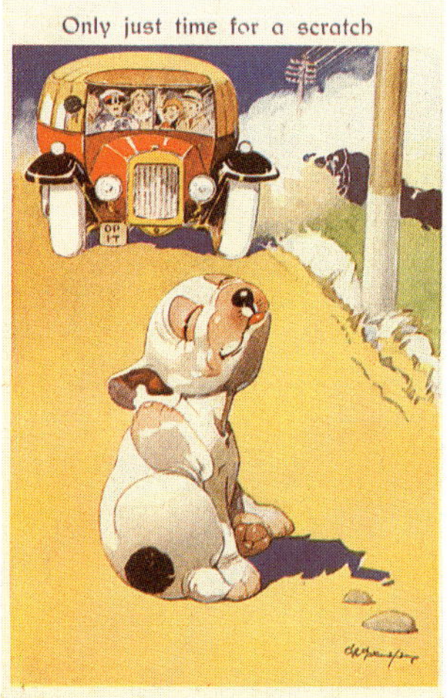
Only just time for a scratch
1640

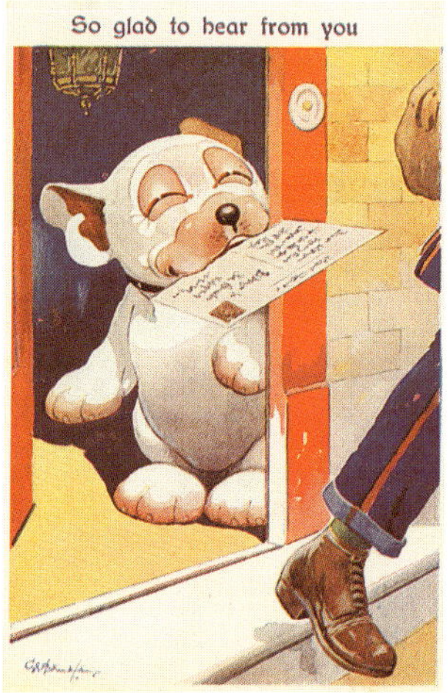
So glad to hear from you
1641

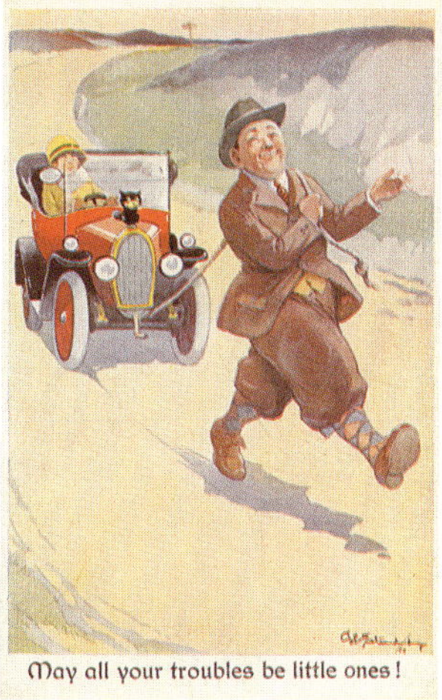
May all your troubles be little ones!
1642

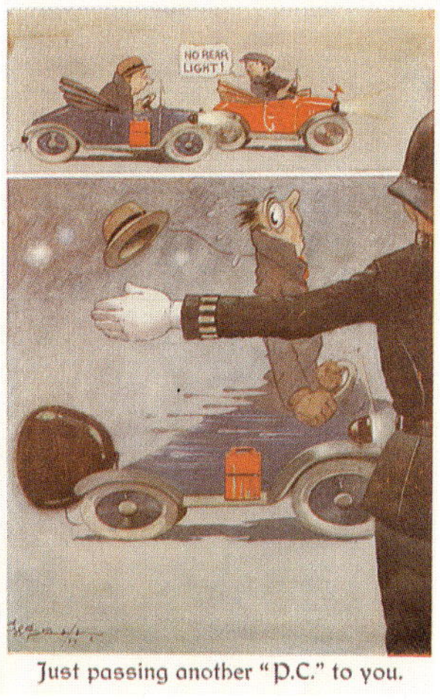
NO REAR LIGHT!
Just passing another "P.C." to you.
1643

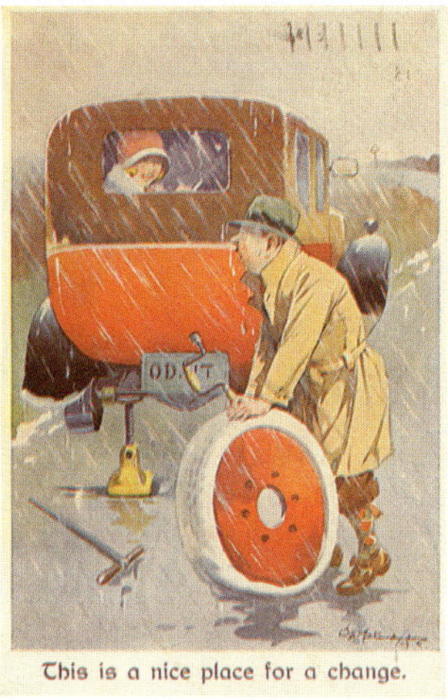
This is a nice place for a change.
1644

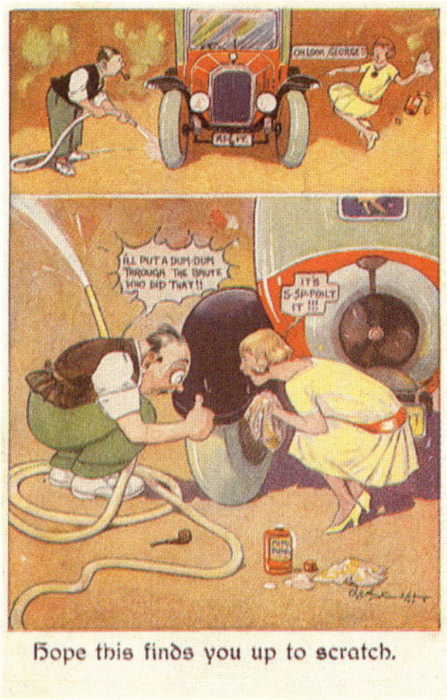
Hope this finds you up to scratch.
1645

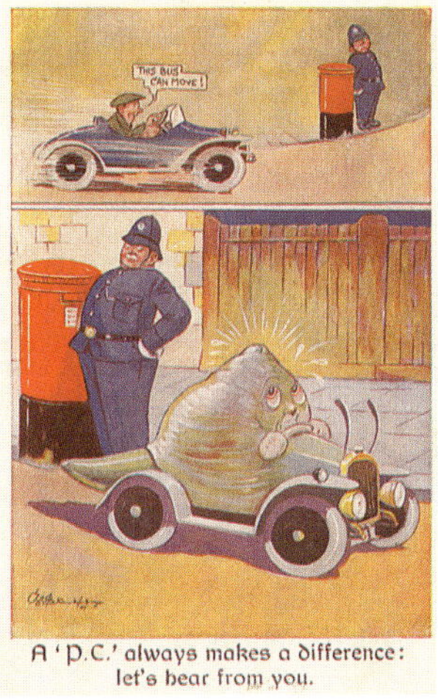
A 'P.C.' always makes a difference:
let's hear from you.
1646

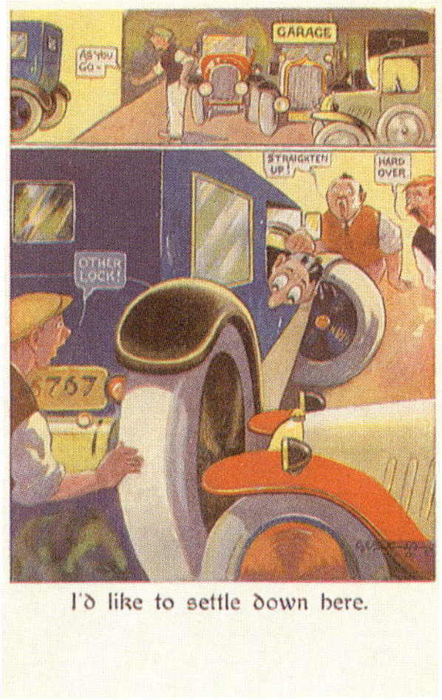
GARAGE
I'd like to settle down here.
1647

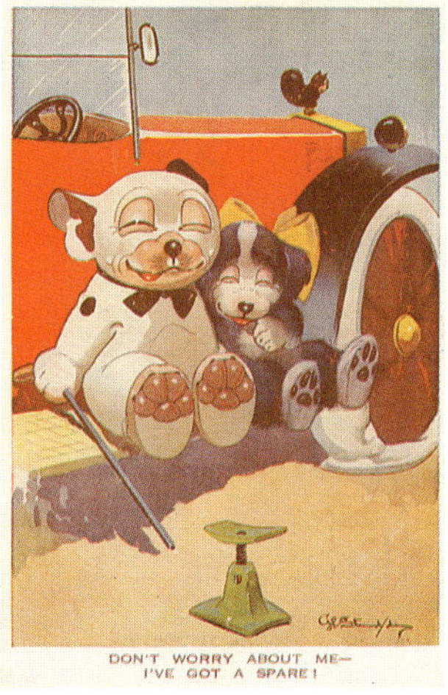
DON'T WORRY ABOUT ME—
I'VE GOT A SPARE!
1688

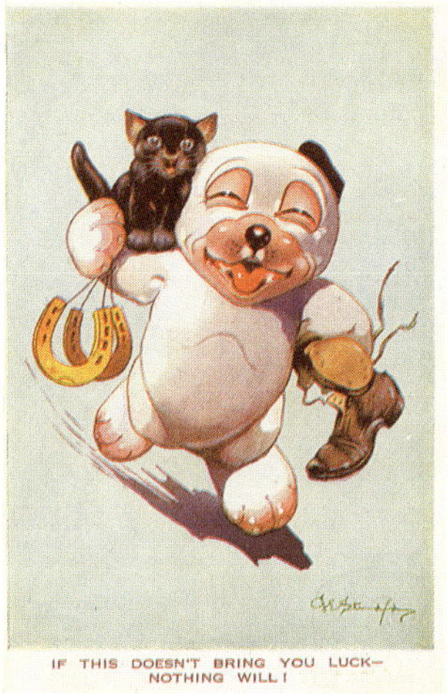
IF THIS DOESN'T BRING YOU LUCK—
NOTHING WILL!
1689

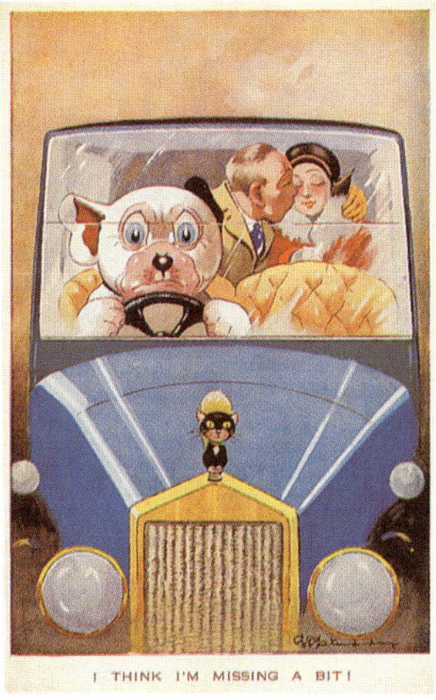
I THINK I'M MISSING A BIT!
1690

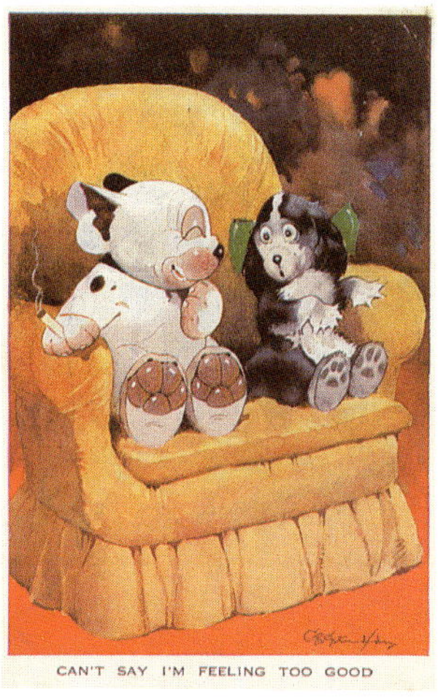
CAN'T SAY I'M FEELING TOO GOOD
1691

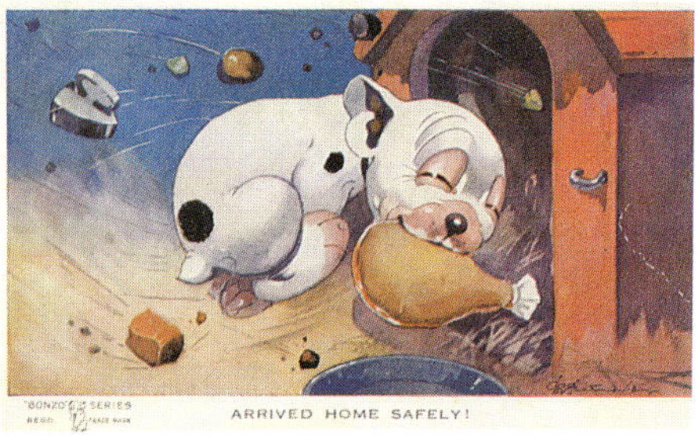
'BONZO' SERIES
ARRIVED HOME SAFELY!

934

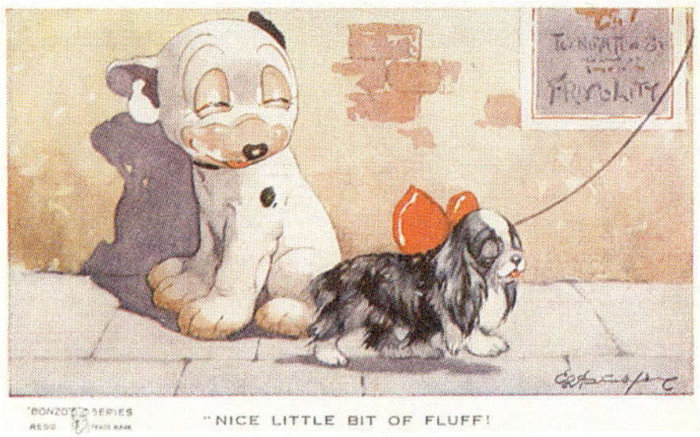
'BONZO' SERIES
"NICE LITTLE BIT OF FLUFF!"

935

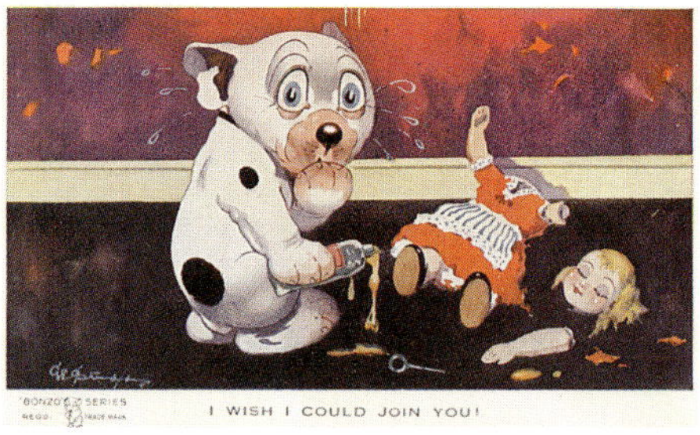
'BONZO' SERIES
I WISH I COULD JOIN YOU!

936

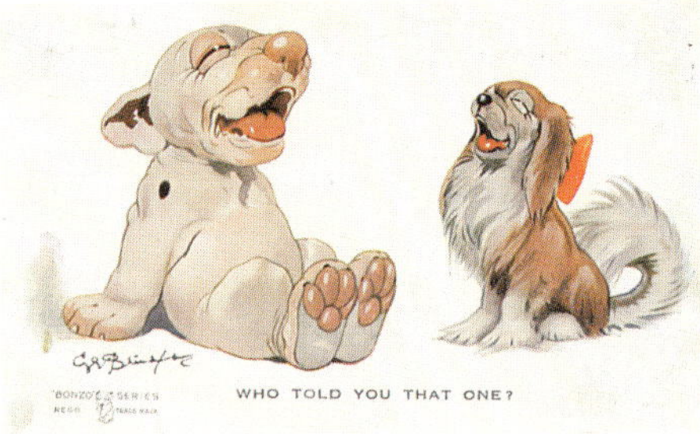
'BONZO' SERIES
WHO TOLD YOU THAT ONE?

997

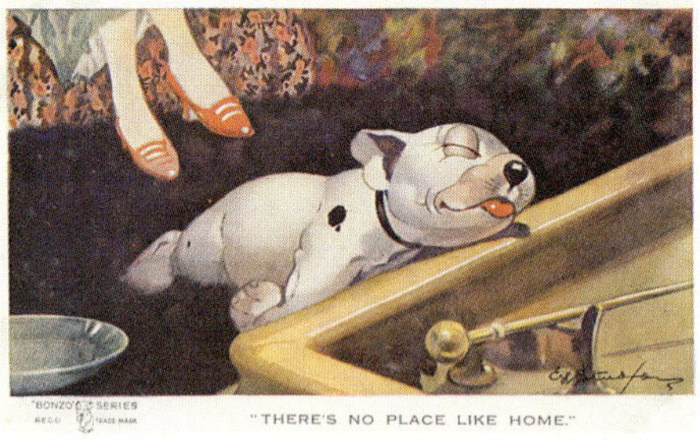
'BONZO' SERIES
"THERE'S NO PLACE LIKE HOME."

1051

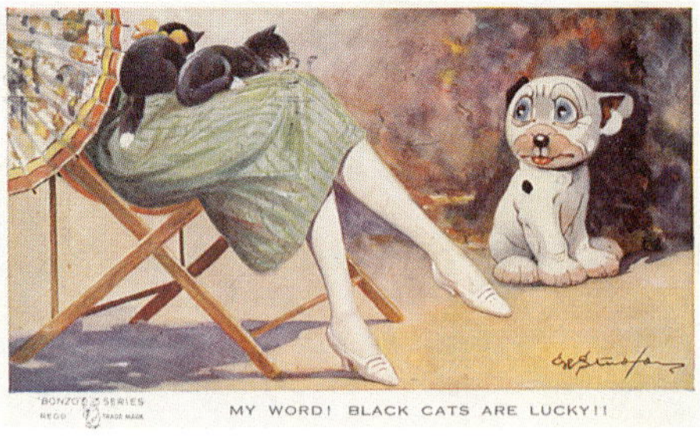
'BONZO' SERIES
MY WORD! BLACK CATS ARE LUCKY!!

1052

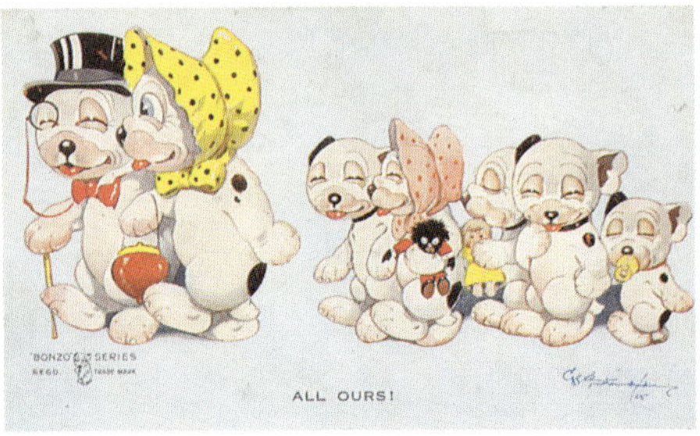
'BONZO' SERIES
ALL OURS!

1131

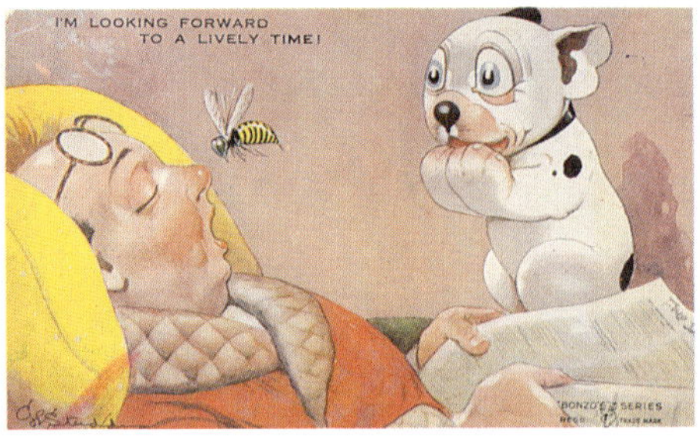
I'M LOOKING FORWARD TO A LIVELY TIME!
'BONZO' SERIES

1136

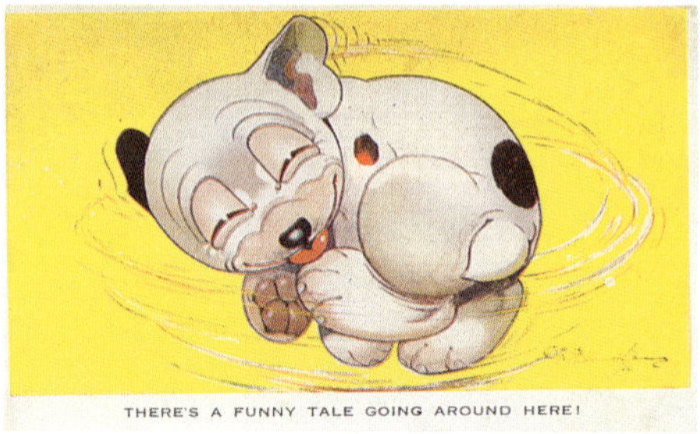
THERE'S A FUNNY TALE GOING AROUND HERE!

1204

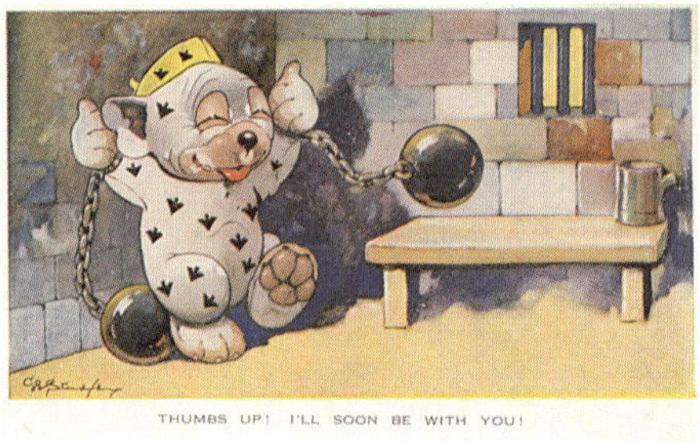
THUMBS UP! I'LL SOON BE WITH YOU!

1291

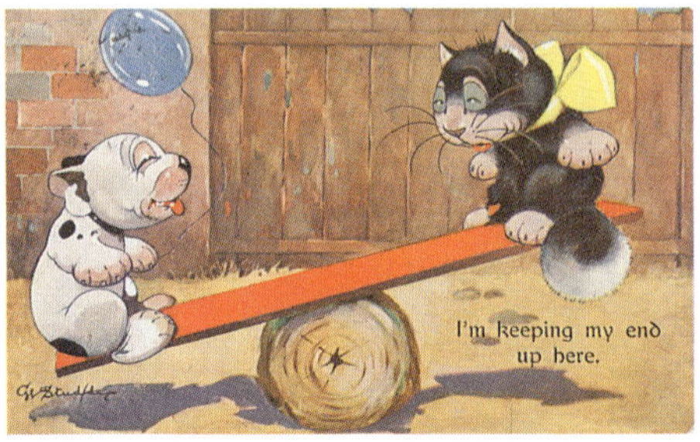
I'm keeping my end up here.

1637

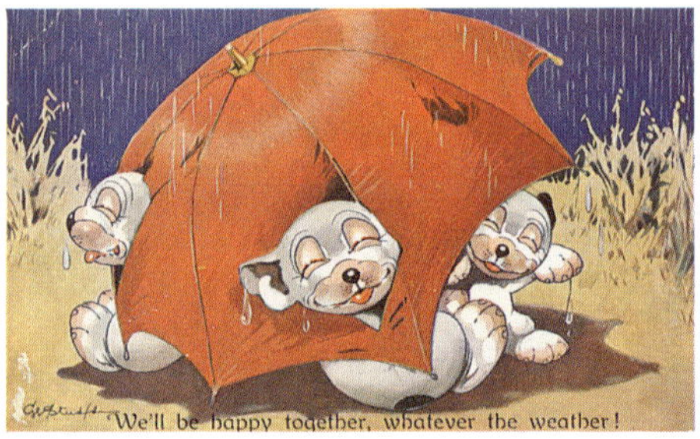
We'll be happy together, whatever the weather!

1639

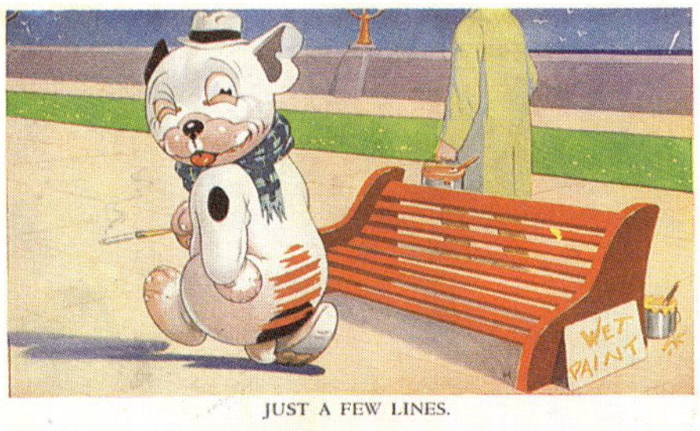
WET PAINT
JUST A FEW LINES.

*1734

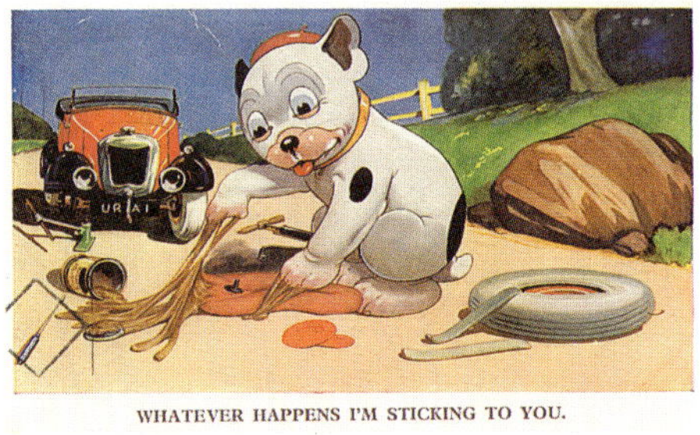
WHATEVER HAPPENS I'M STICKING TO YOU.

*1735

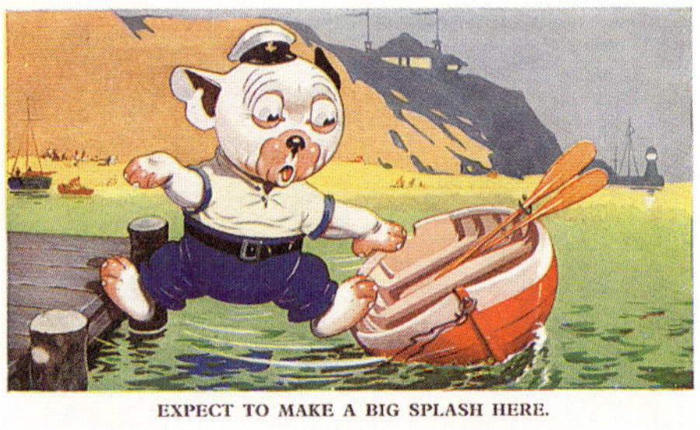
EXPECT TO MAKE A BIG SPLASH HERE.

*1736

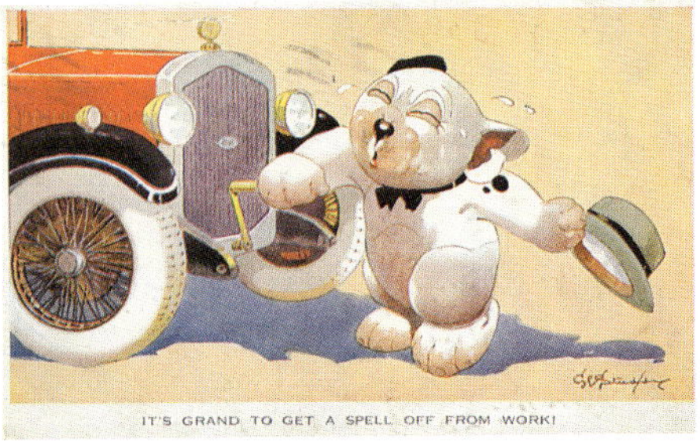
IT'S GRAND TO GET A SPELL OFF FROM WORK!

1767

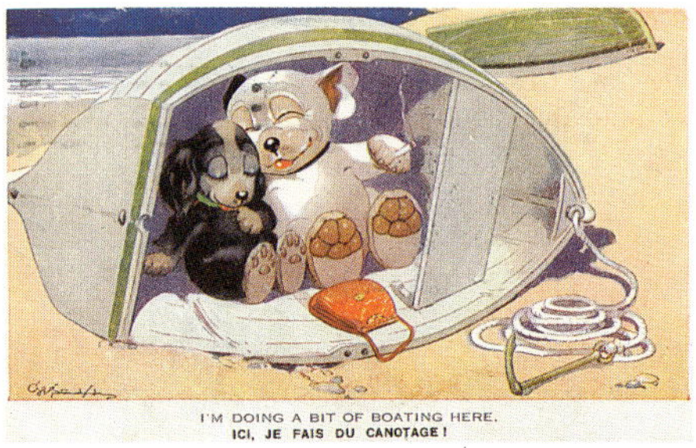
I'M DOING A BIT OF BOATING HERE.
ICI, JE FAIS DU CANOTAGE!

1770

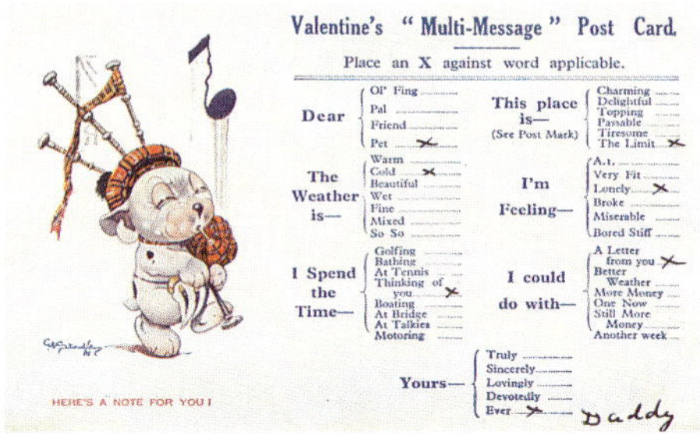
Valentine's "Multi-Message" Post Card.
Place an X against word applicable.
Dear — Ol' Fing, Pal, Friend, Pet
This place is— (See Post Mark) — Charming, Delightful, Topping, Passable, Tiresome, The Limit
The Weather is— Warm, Cold, Beautiful, Wet, Fine, Mixed, So So
I'm Feeling— A.1., Very Fit, Lonely, Broke, Miserable, Bored Stiff
I Spend the Time— Golfing, Bathing, At Tennis, Thinking of you, Boating, At Bridge, At Talkies, Motoring
I could do with— A Letter from you, Better Weather, More Money, One Now, Still More Money, Another week
Yours— Truly, Sincerely, Lovingly, Devotedly, Ever
Daddy
HERE'S A NOTE FOR YOU!

1777

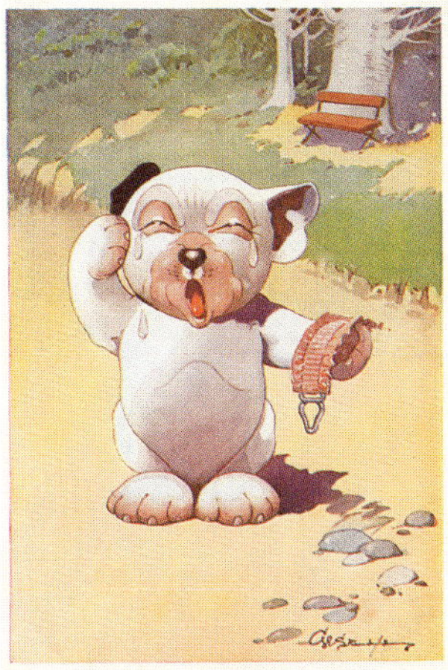

DON'T SAY IT'S BROKEN OFF!

1692

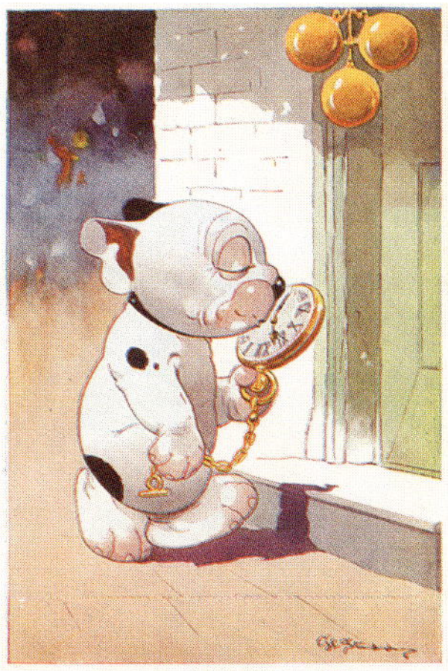

KEEP NICE AND BRIGHT, DEAR, TILL WE MEET AGAIN!

1693

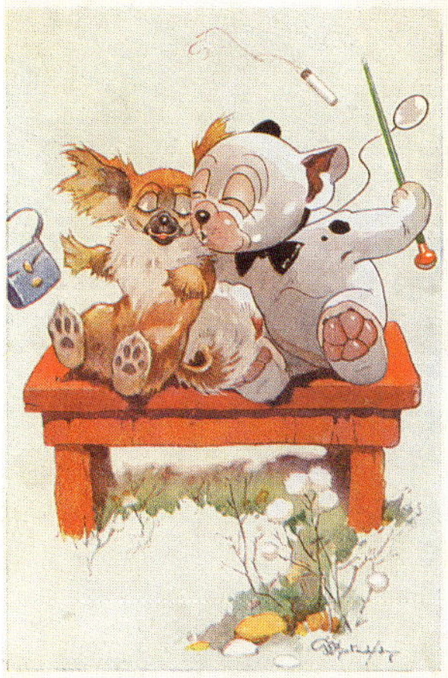

MOVIES ARE BETTER THAN TALKIES!

1694

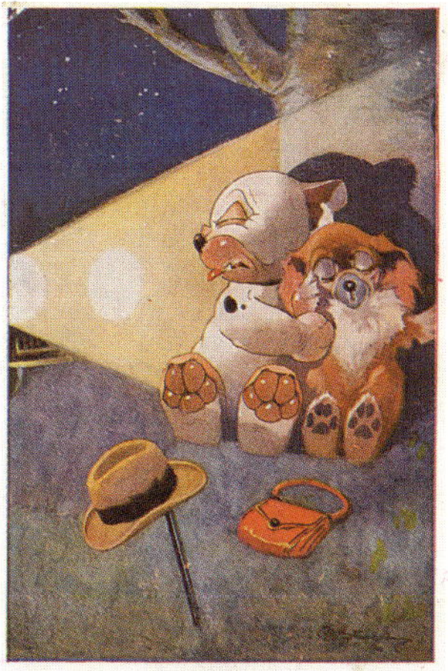

PLEASE DON'T MAKE LIGHT OF THIS!

1695

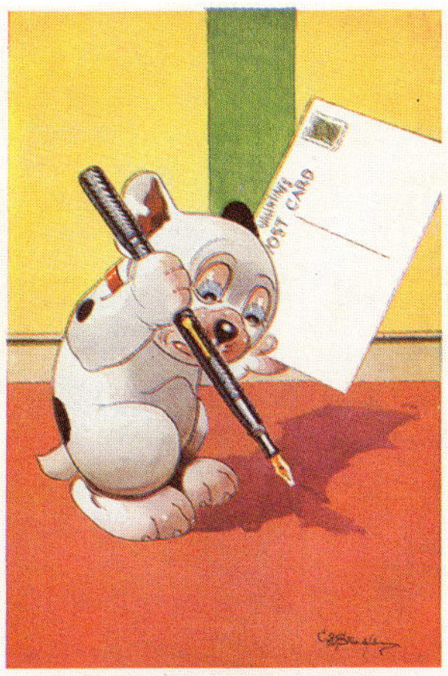

GO ON! SAY YOU'VE RUN OUT OF JUICE AGAIN!

1696

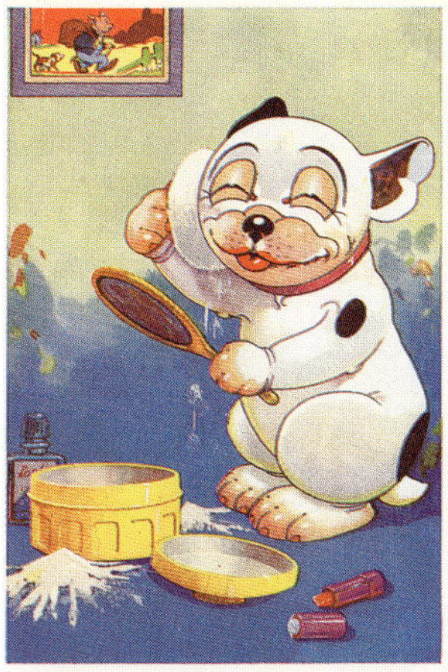

LET'S MAKE UP AND BE FRIENDLY.

*1696

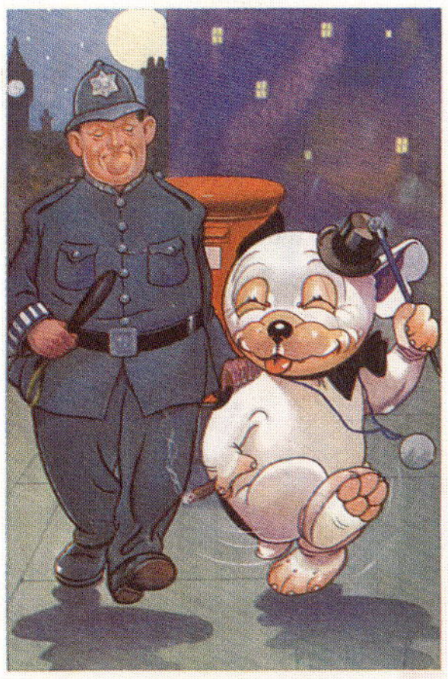

SORRY—UNAVOIDABLY DETAINED.

*1697

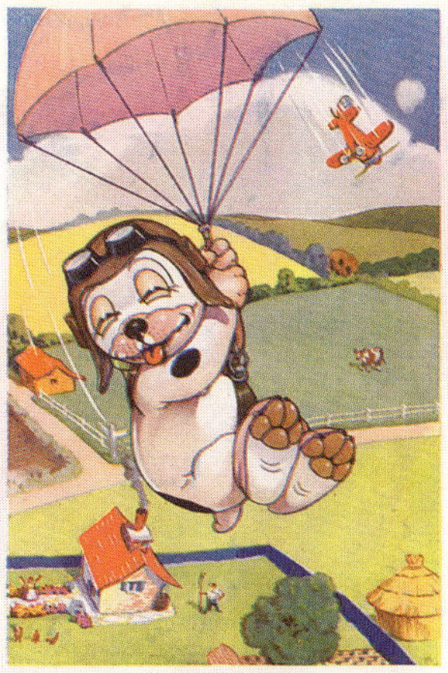

I'M DROPPING IN SOON.

*1698

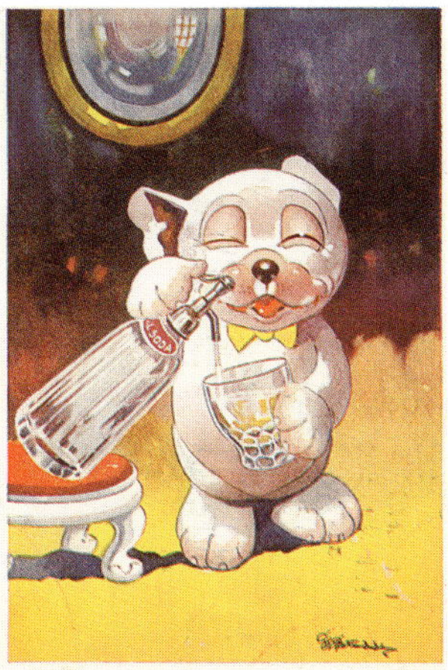

I'M SURE I SHALL LIKE THIS SPOT.

1768

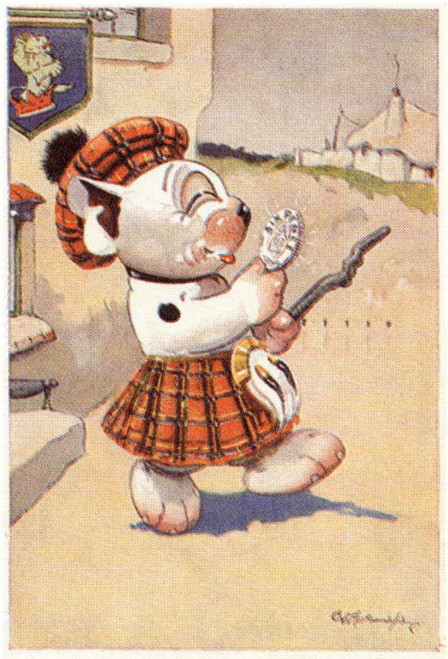

YOU AND I WERE NEVER MEANT TO PART DEAR!

1769

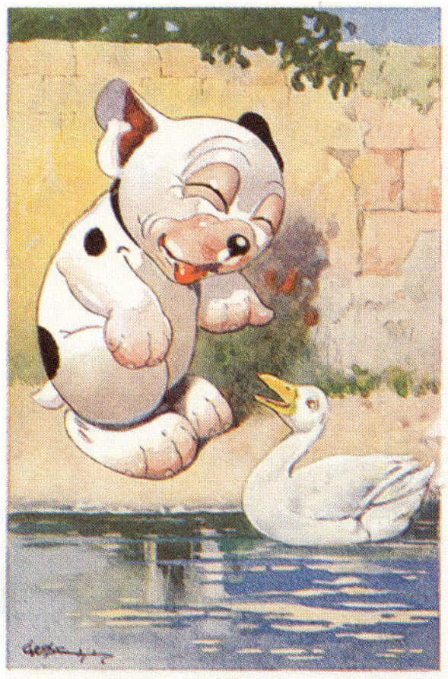

THIS IS JUST TO SAY YOU REALLY ARE A DUCK!

1771

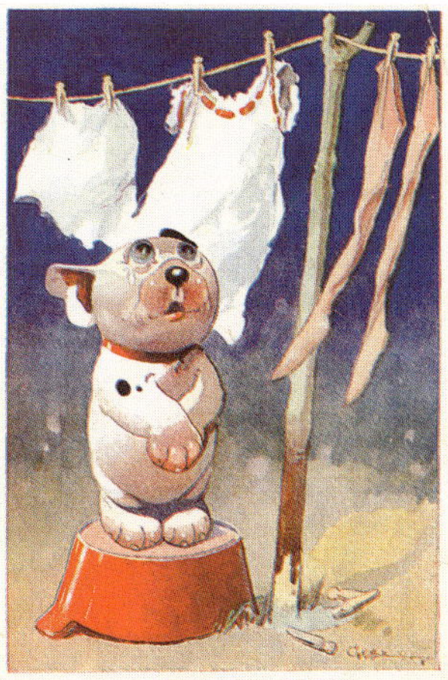

A LINE TO REMIND YOU OF ME!

1772

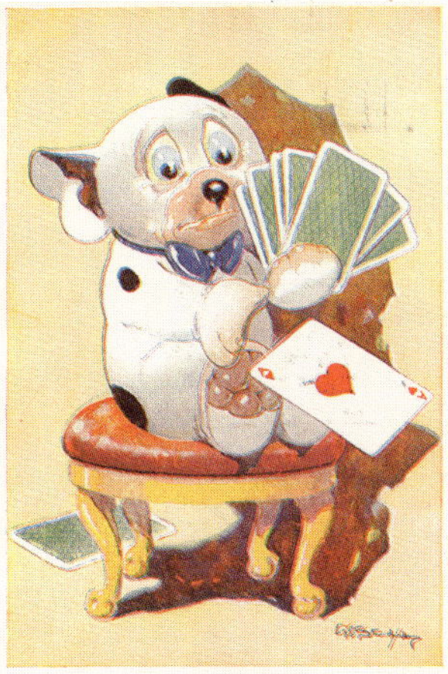

I'VE LOST MY HEART PROPERLY THIS TIME!

1816

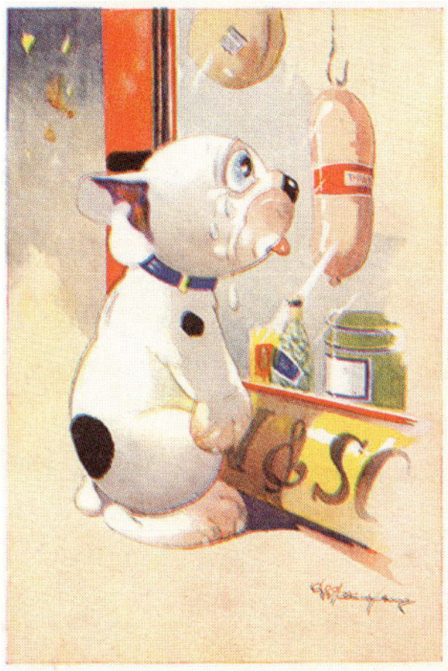

I HATE BEING AWAY FROM YOU!

1817

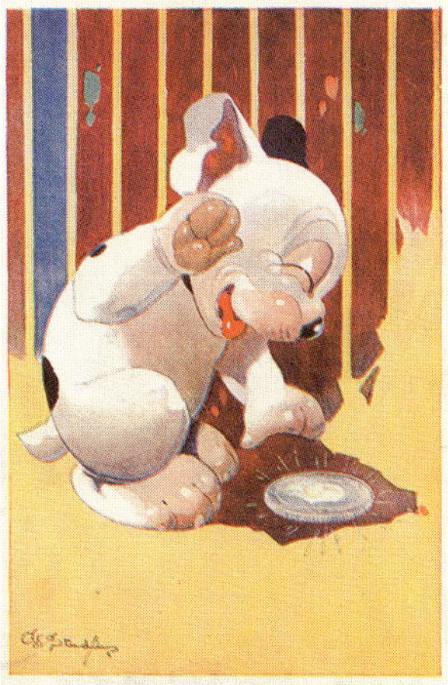

I'M LUCKY TO HAVE FOUND YOU!

1818

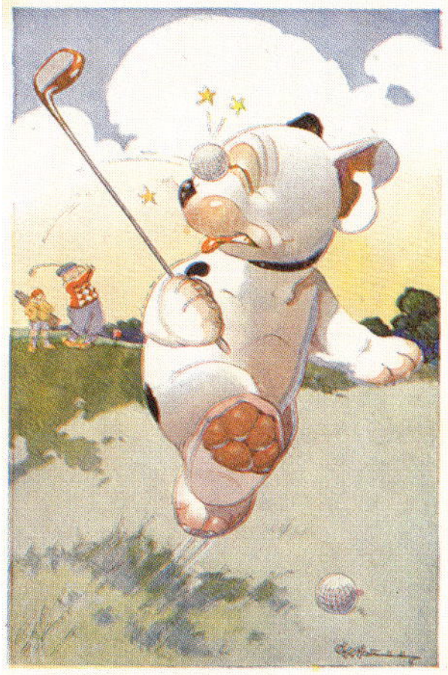

YOU'VE FAIRLY CAUGHT MY EYE!

1819

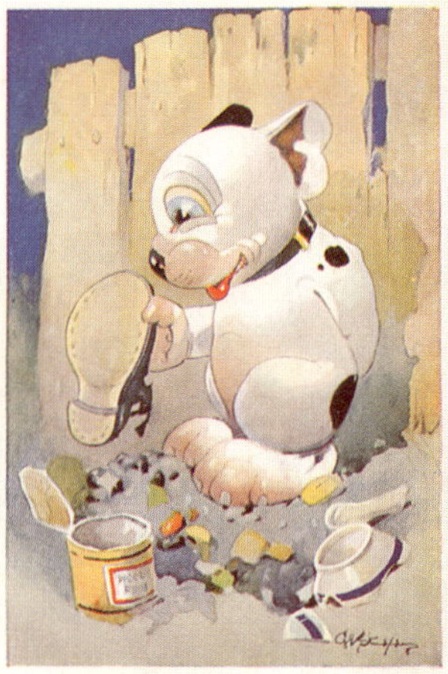
I NEVER FORGET AN OLD ACQUAINTANCE.

1820

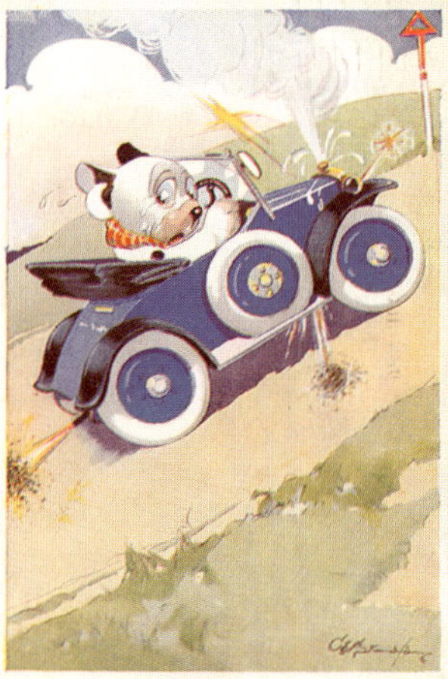
I HOPE YOU ARE GOING ON ALL RIGHT!

1821

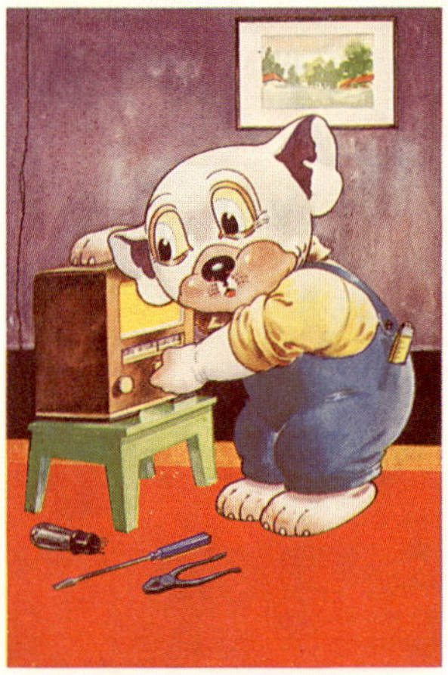
I HAVEN'T HEARD FROM YOU.

***1894**

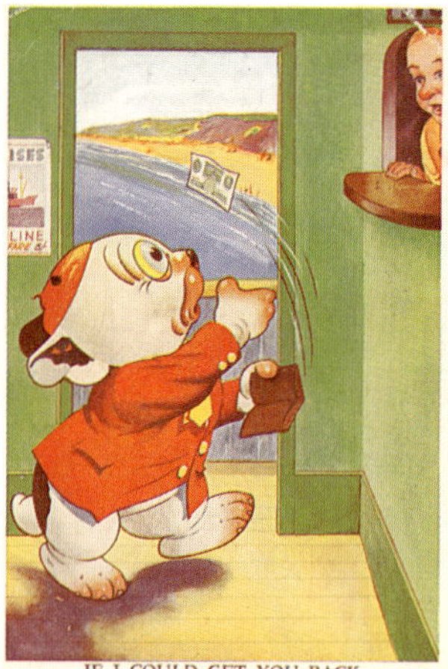
IF I COULD GET YOU BACK
I'D NEVER LET YOU GO.

***1895**

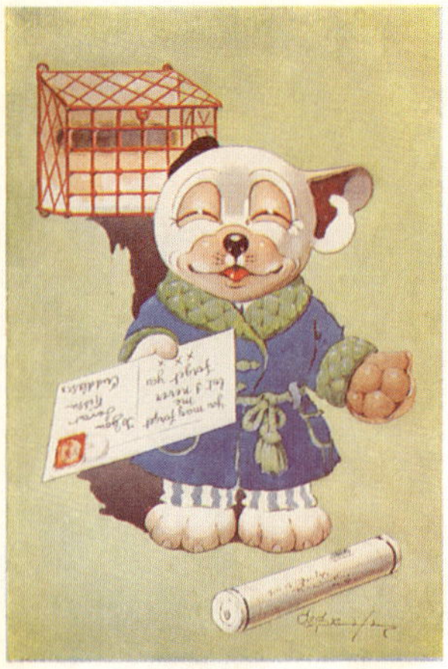
"HERE'S ONE FOR YOU—WHERE'S MINE?"

1902

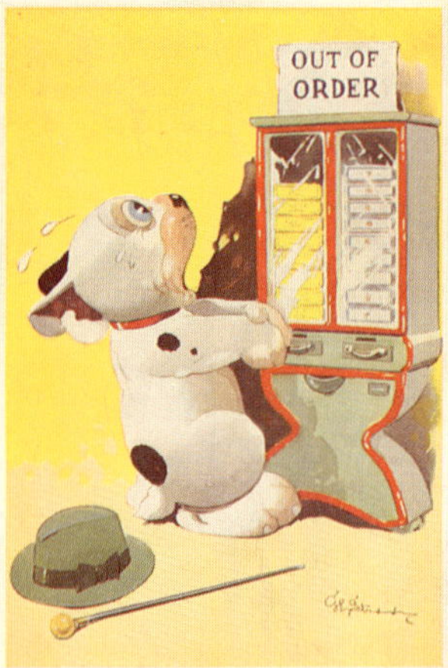
OUT OF
ORDER
I WISH I'D SEEN YOU BEFORE!

1903

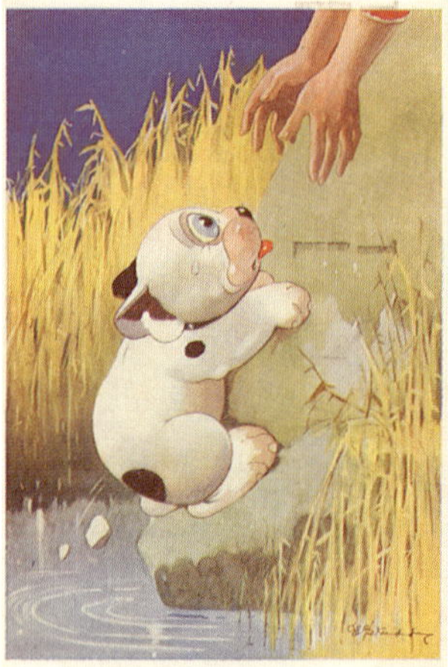
I WISH I WAS GRIPPING YOUR HAND.

1904

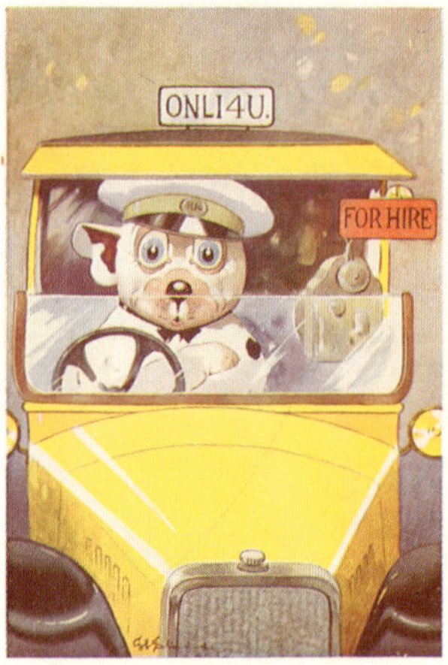
ONLI4U
FOR HIRE
WATCHING AND WAITING FOR SOMEONE!

1905

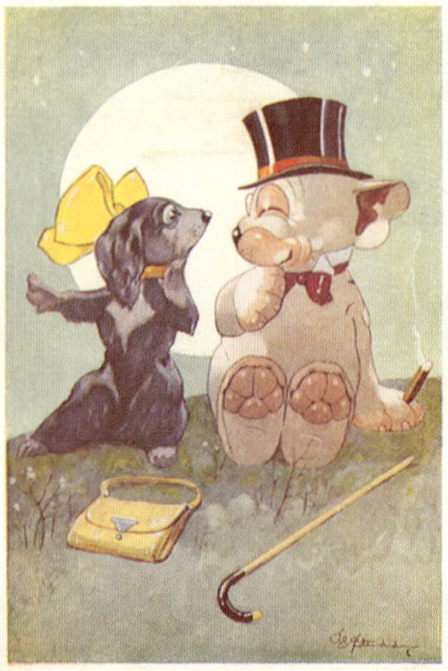
"AREN'T YOU GLAD THE SPEED LIMIT'S GONE?"

1906

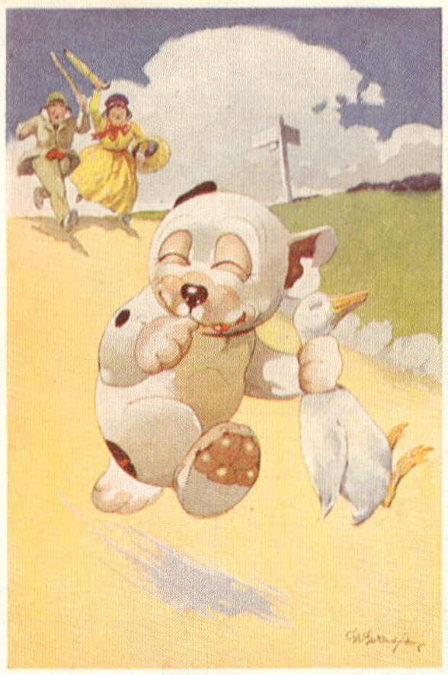
I'M TOO FAR AWAY TO BE KISSED.

1907

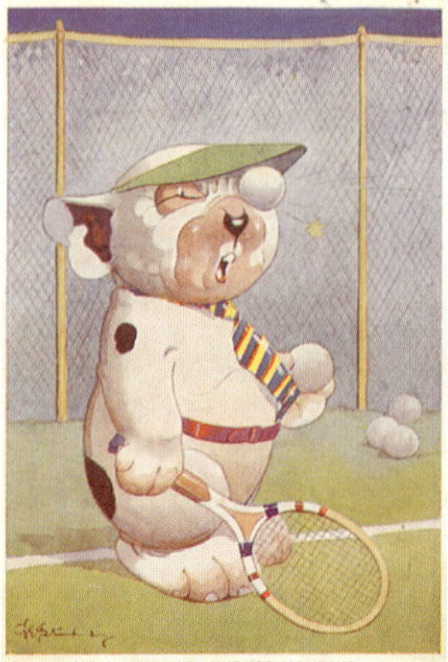
YOU WEREN'T EXPECTING THIS.

1949

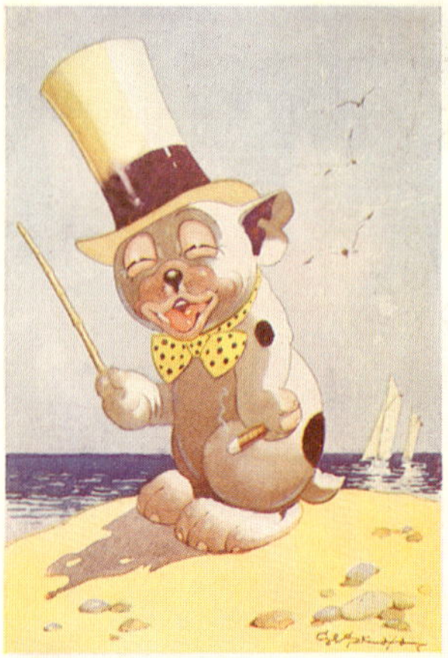
AHM GITTIN' AS BROWN AS A NIGGER

1950

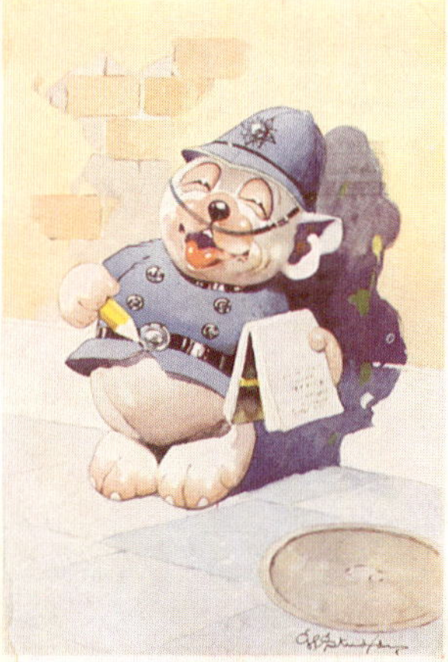
O! BABY—AIN'T YOU BIN NAUGHTY!

1951

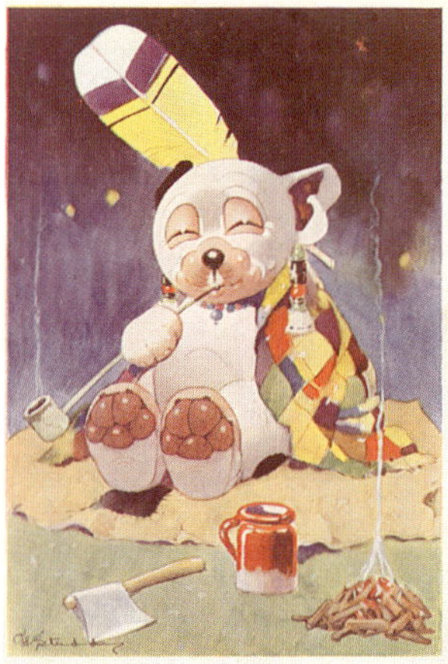
O.K. CHIEF!

1953

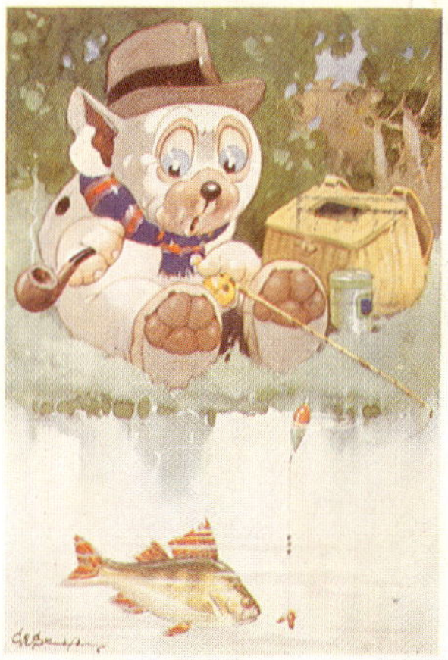
I'M THINKING OF YOU AND YOU ALONE OLD THING

1954

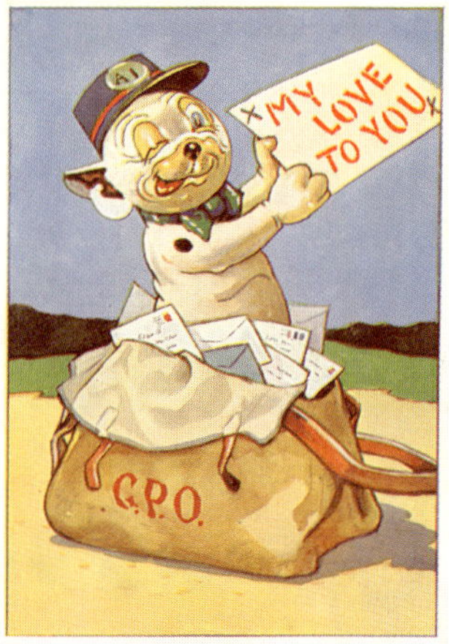
MY LOVE TO YOU
G.P.O.
YOUR ONE OUT OF THE BAG!

***1981**

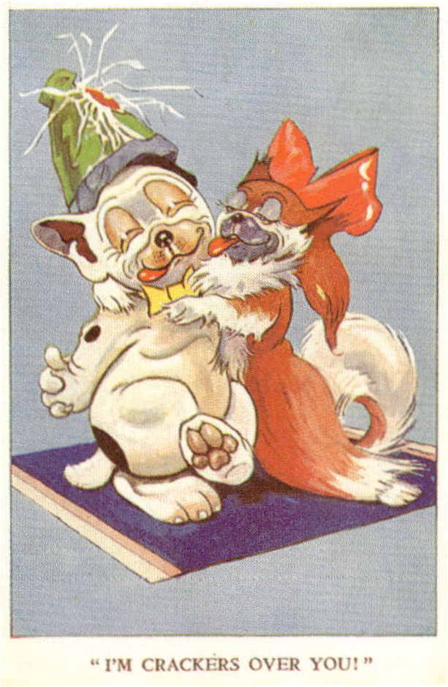
"I'M CRACKERS OVER YOU!"

*1982

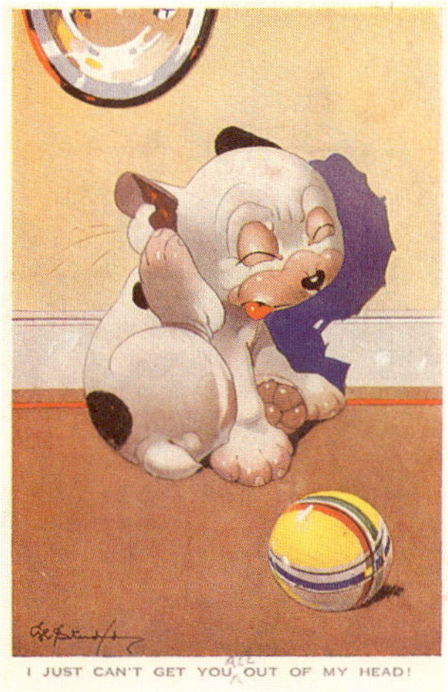
I JUST CAN'T GET YOU OUT OF MY HEAD!

2021

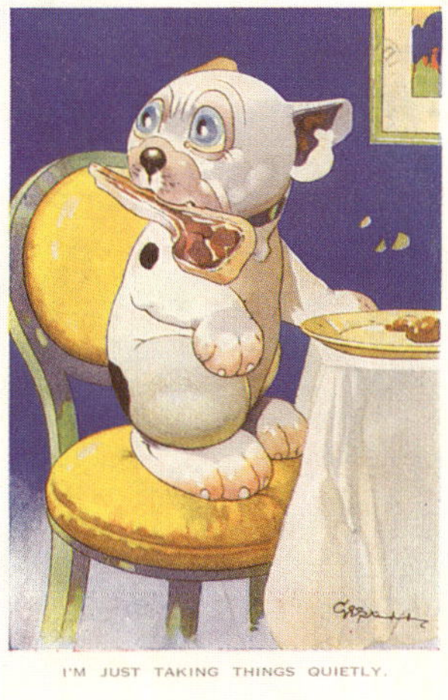
I'M JUST TAKING THINGS QUIETLY.

2022

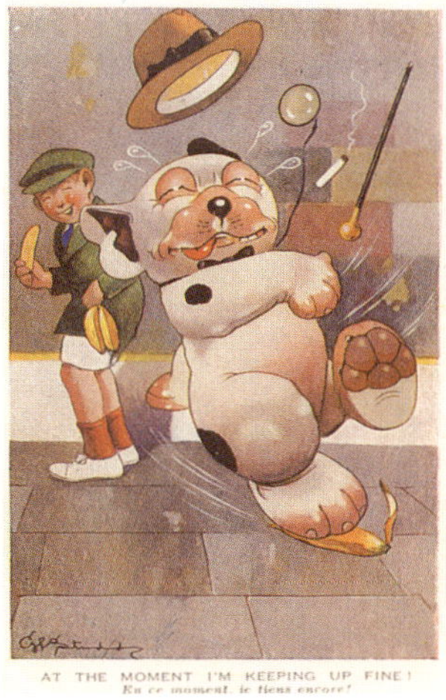
AT THE MOMENT I'M KEEPING UP FINE!
En ce moment, je tiens encore!

2023

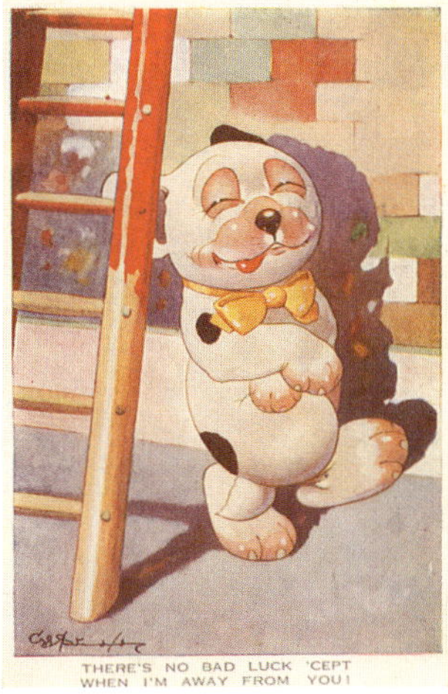
THERE'S NO BAD LUCK 'CEPT WHEN I'M AWAY FROM YOU!

2024

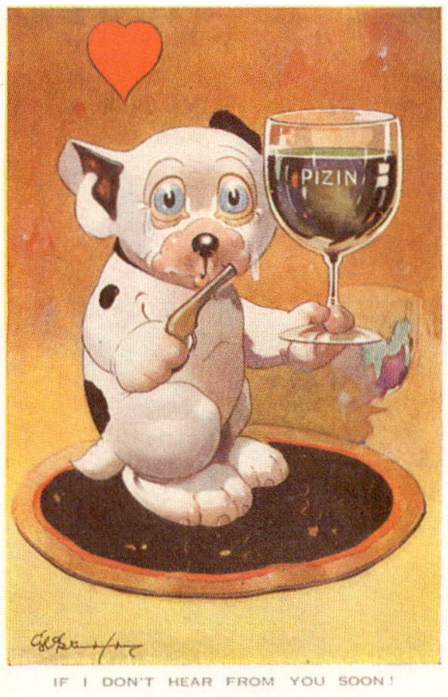
PIZIN
IF I DON'T HEAR FROM YOU SOON!

2025

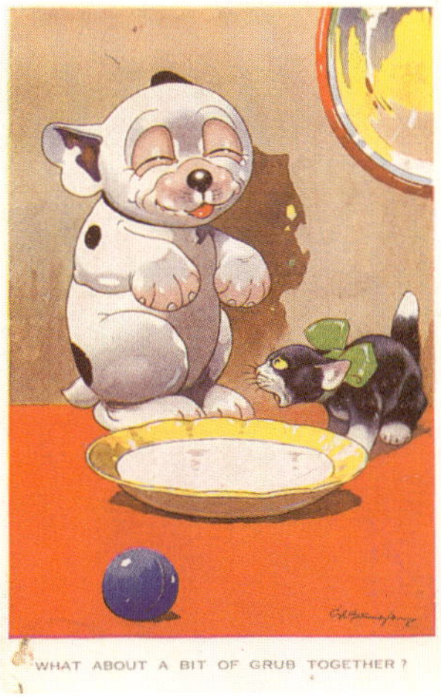
WHAT ABOUT A BIT OF GRUB TOGETHER?

2026

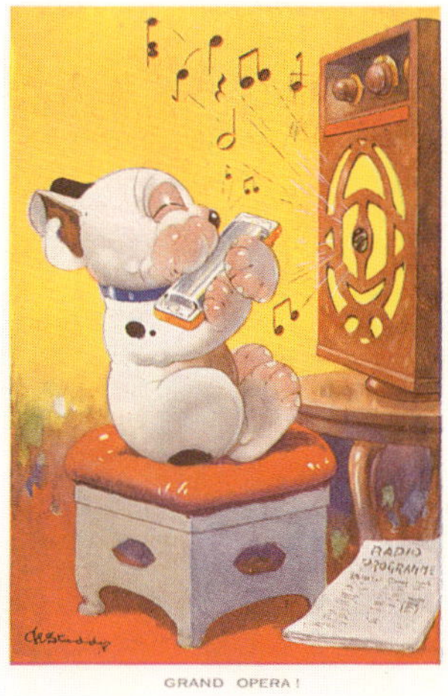
GRAND OPERA!

2143

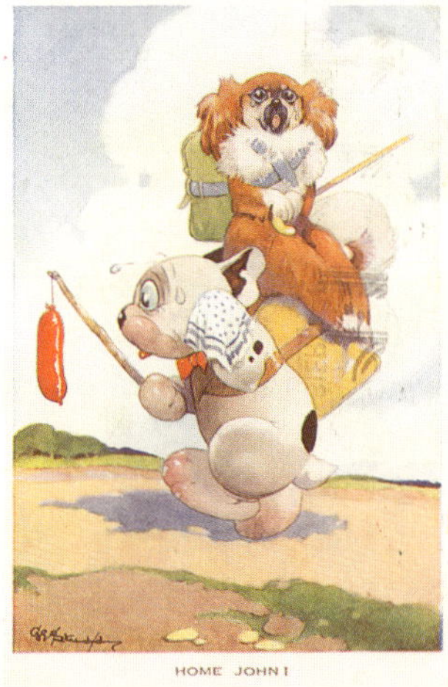
HOME JOHN!

2144

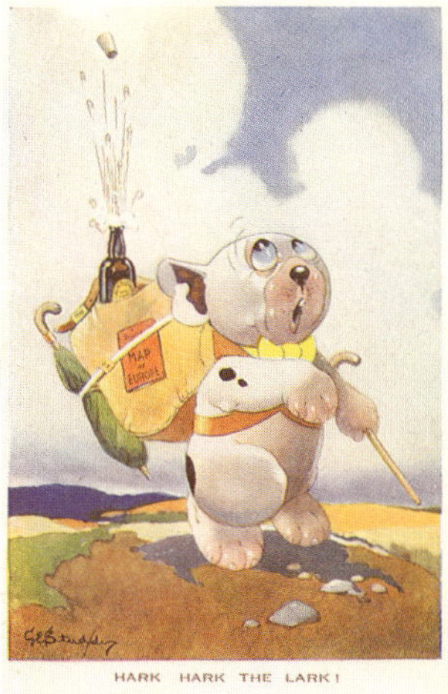
HARK HARK THE LARK!

2145

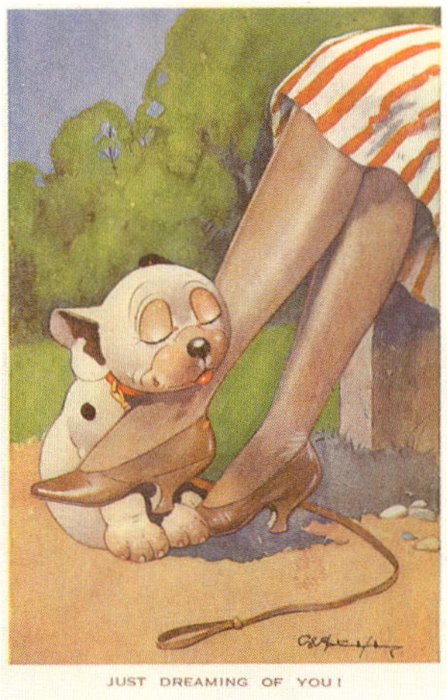
JUST DREAMING OF YOU!

2146

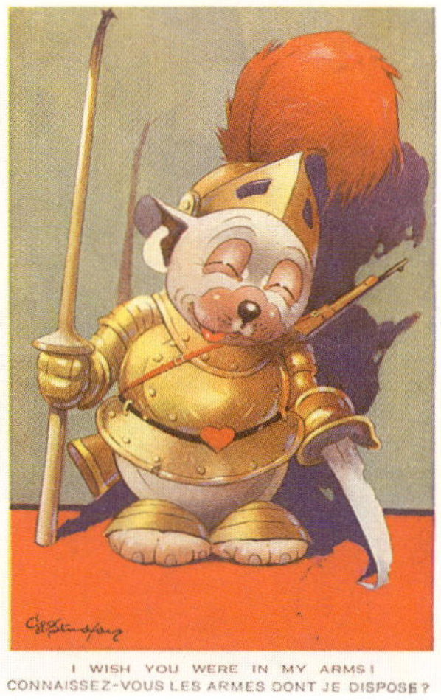
I WISH YOU WERE IN MY ARMS!
CONNAISSEZ-VOUS LES ARMES DONT JE DISPOSE?

2147

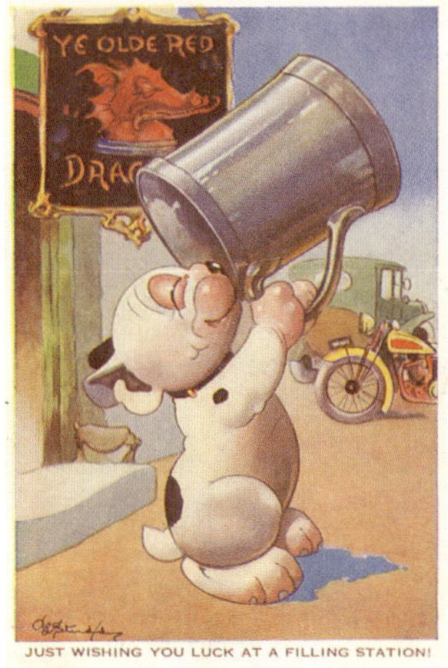
YE OLDE RED
DRAG
JUST WISHING YOU LUCK AT A FILLING STATION!

2148

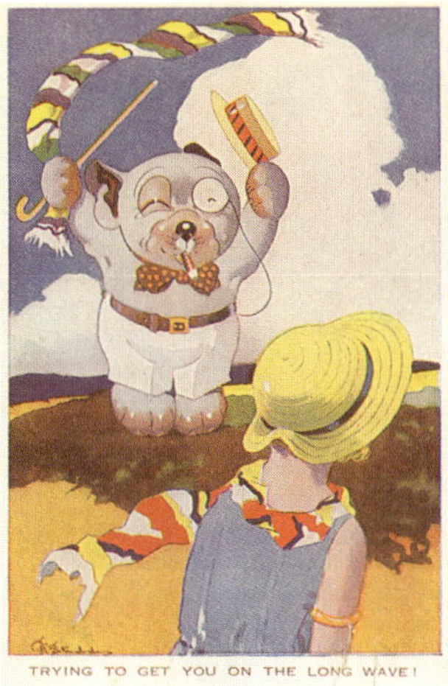
TRYING TO GET YOU ON THE LONG WAVE!

2193

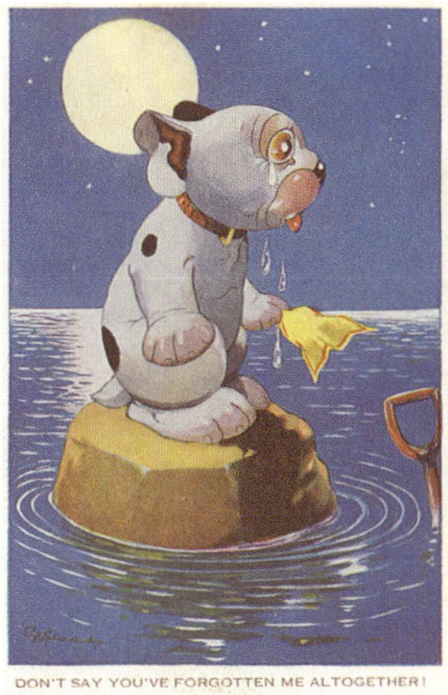
DON'T SAY YOU'VE FORGOTTEN ME ALTOGETHER!

2194

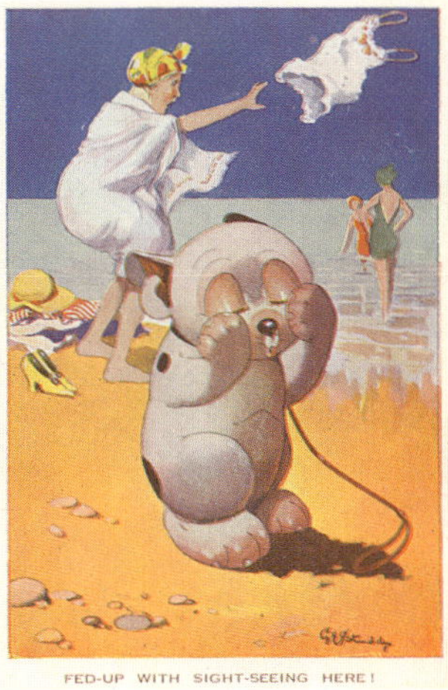
FED-UP WITH SIGHT-SEEING HERE!

2195

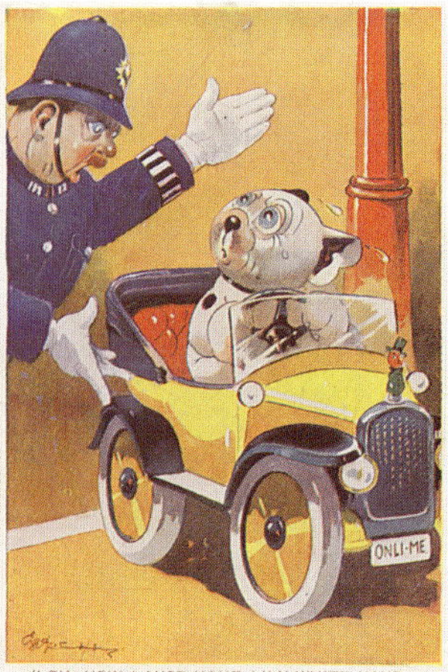
ONLI-ME
" OH, HOW I MISS YOUR LILY-WHITE HAND AND LONG TO SEE YOU SMILE ! "

2196

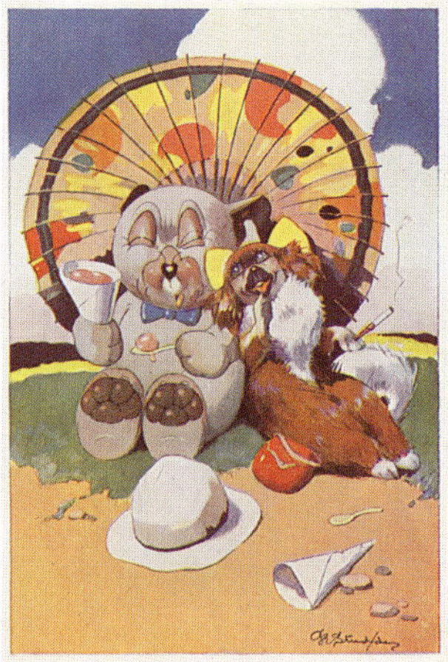
HAVING A JOB TO KEEP COOL.

2197

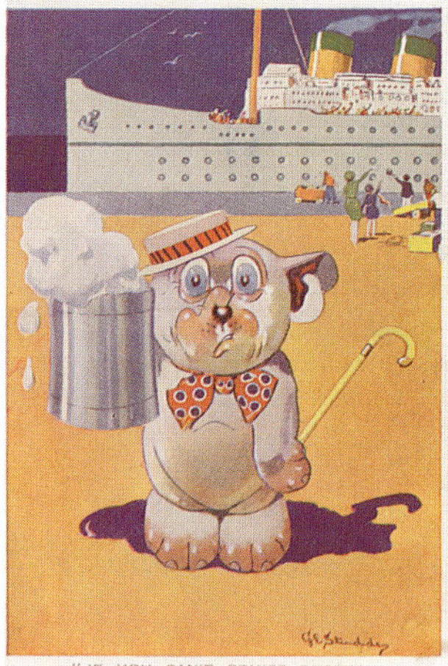
" IF YOU CAN'T CRUISE—BOOZE ! "

2198

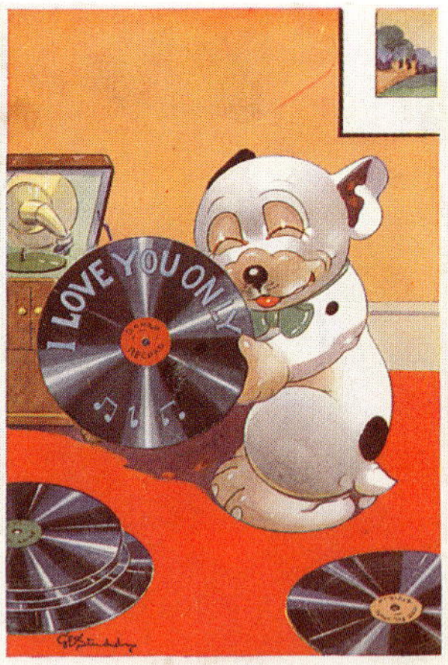
I LOVE YOU ONLY
MY FAVOURITE !

2279

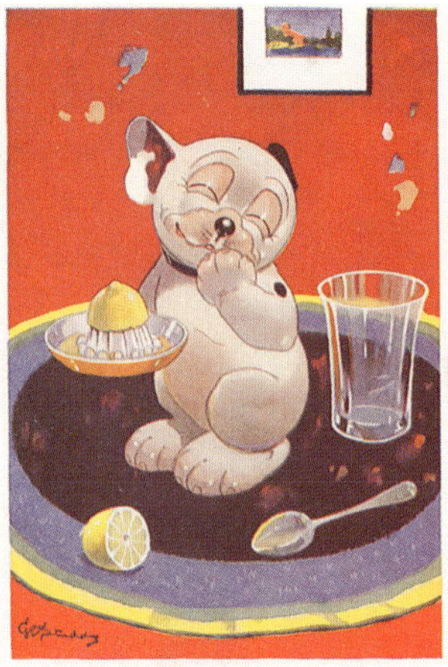
WISH I COULD SQUEEZE YOU TOO !

2280

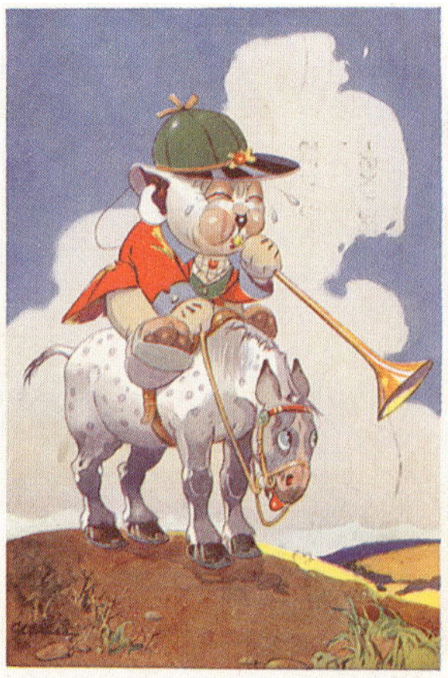
I'LL GET A NOTE OUT OF YOU OR BUST.

2281

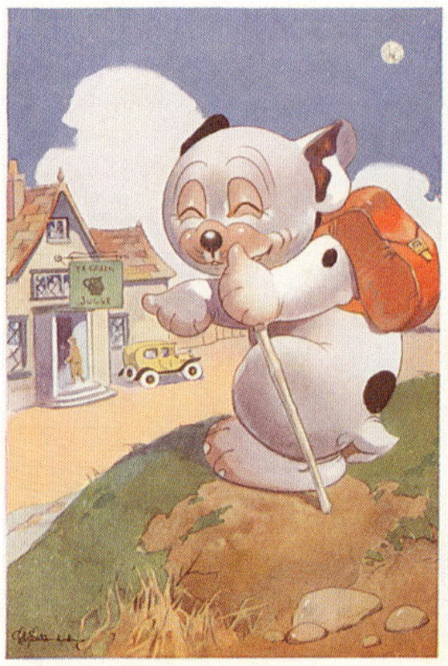
WISH YOU COULD JOIN ME.

2282

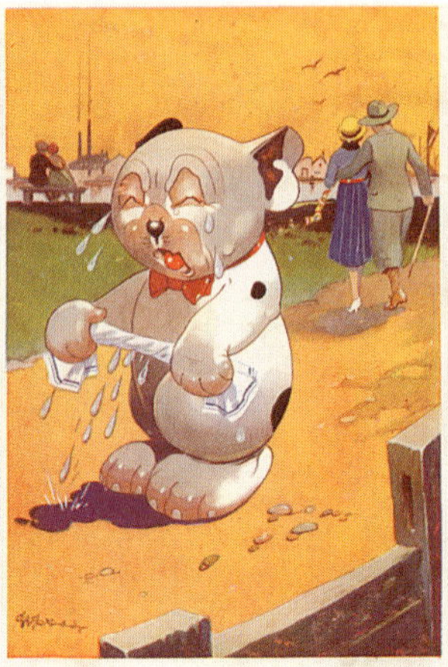
" NO ! I AIN'T LONELY, NO ! "

2283

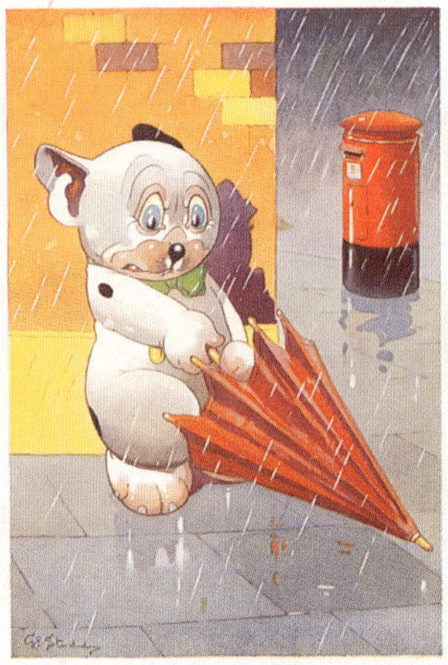
I CAN'T DO WITHOUT YOU FOR LONG.

2284

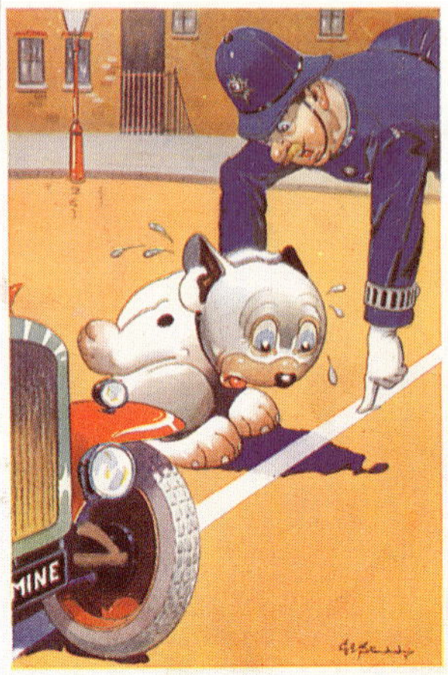
MINE
ONLY ONE LITTLE LINE.

2285

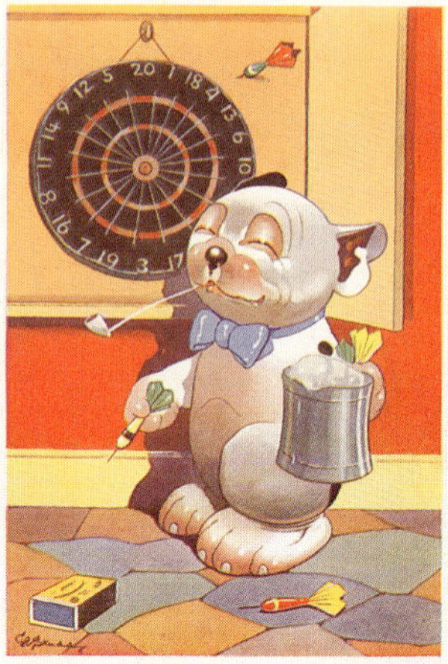
I'M FEELING CHAMPION.

2286

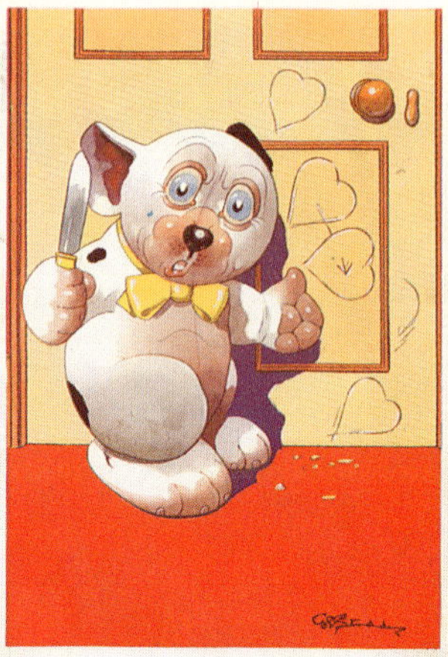
HANG IT, I MUST BE IN LOVE !

2287

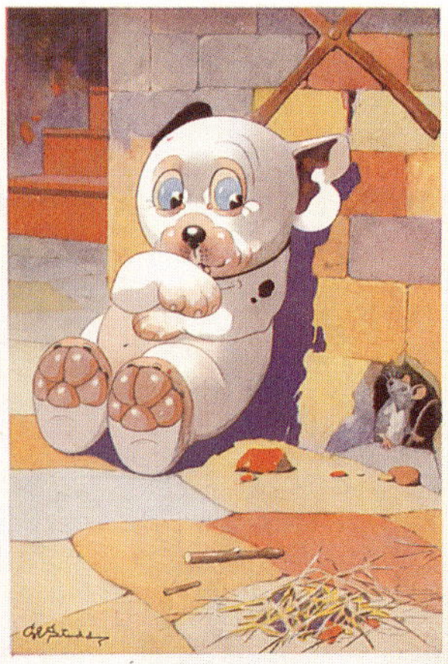
NOT A CHEEP FROM YOU, YET.

2288

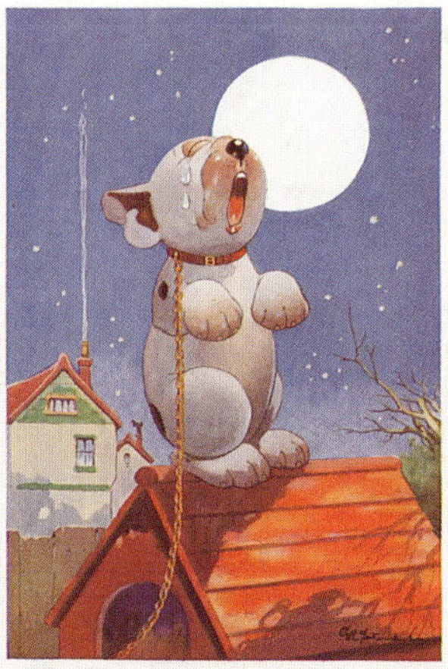
HAPPY DAYS AND LONELY NIGHTS.

2289

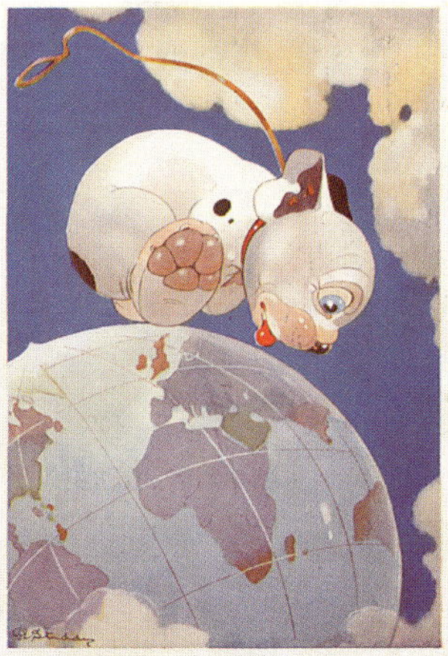
WHERE ON EARTH HAVE YOU GOT TO ?
Où diable, pouvez-vous vous trouver?

2290

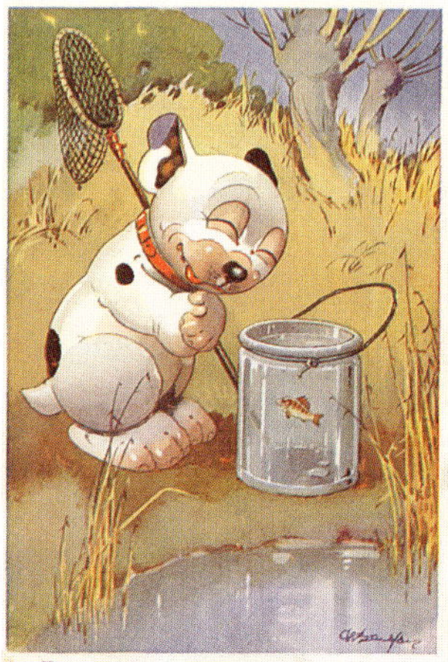
I LUV YOU MORE THAN YOU LUV ME.
Je crois que je vous aime plus que vous ne m'aimez.

2387

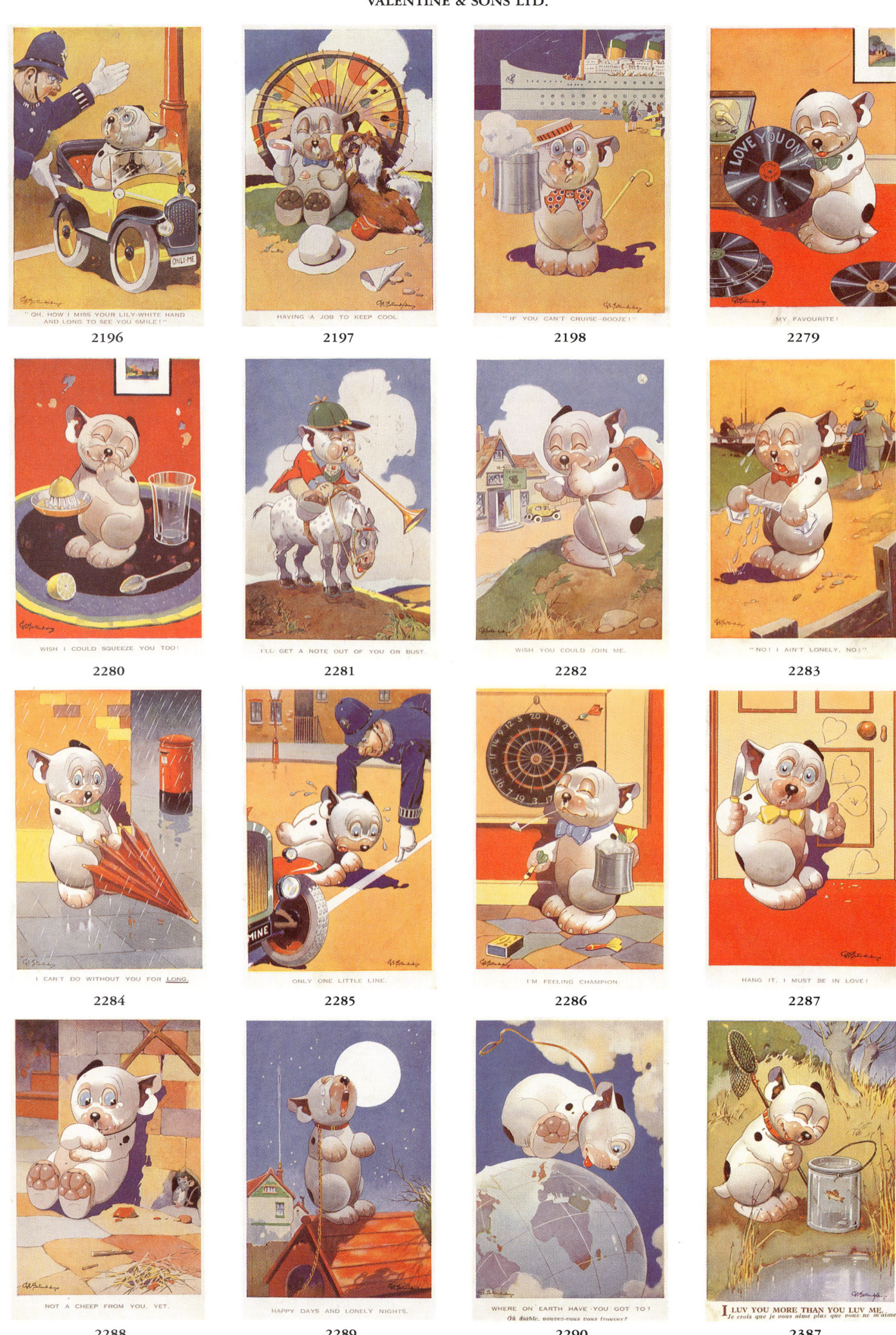

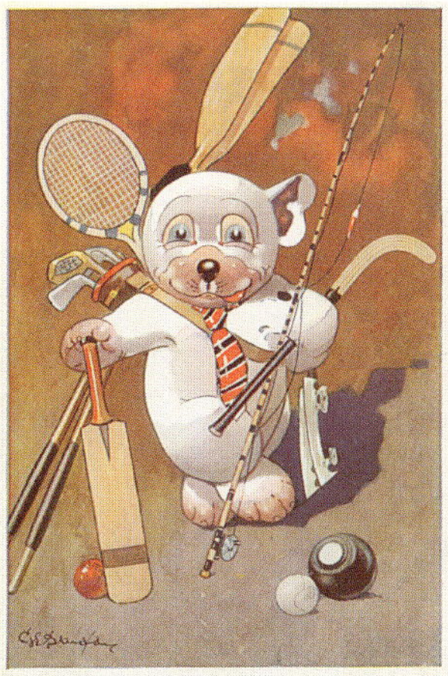

I CAN PLAY OTHER GAMES AS WELL.

2388

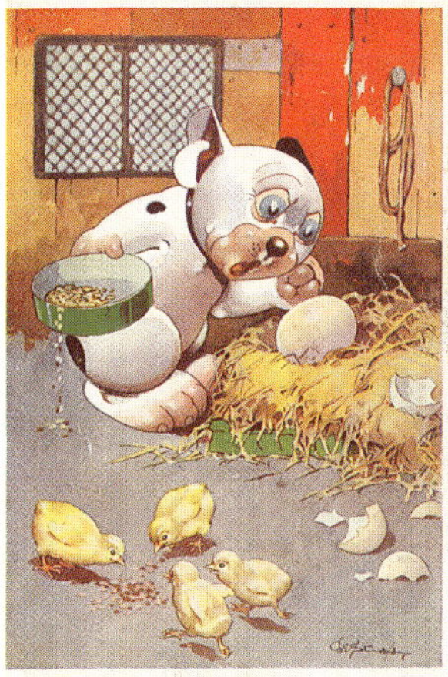

"COME OUT AND HAVE SOME GRUB."

2389

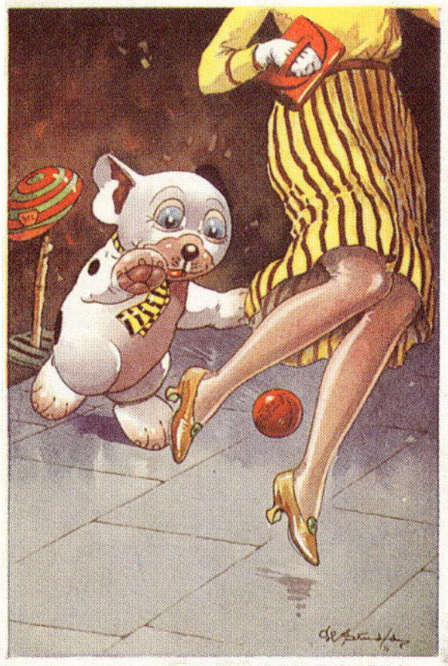

BONZO TESTS THE LEG THEORY!
"THIS ONE'S FOR YOU!"

2390

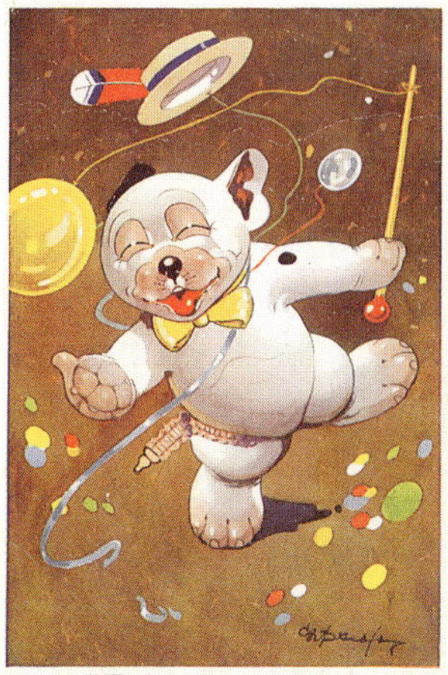

"BALLYHOO OLD BEAN!"

2391

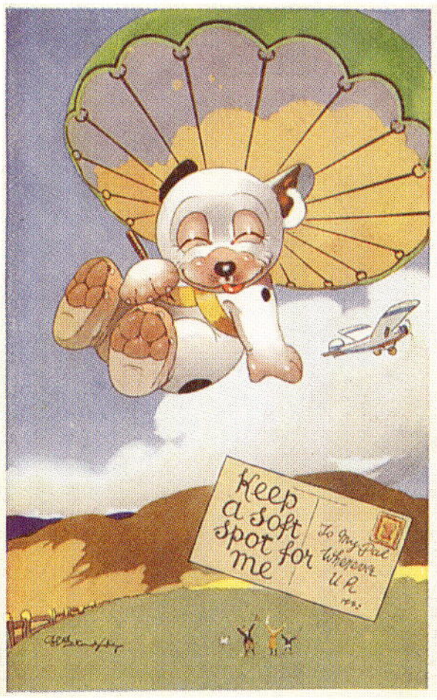
Keep a soft spot for me

2392

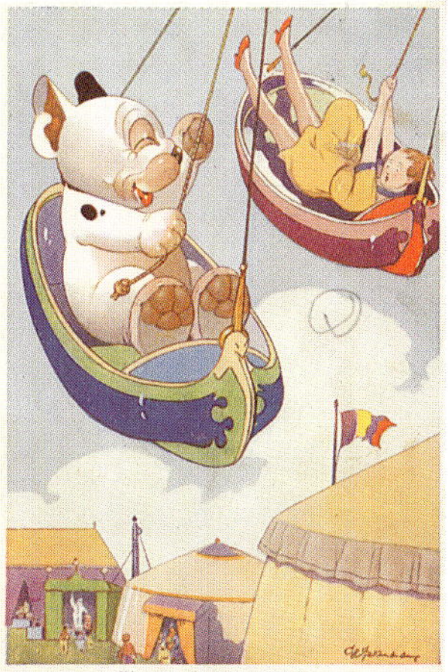

Vite, que je vous revoie!
BOB UP AGAIN SOON DEAR!

2426

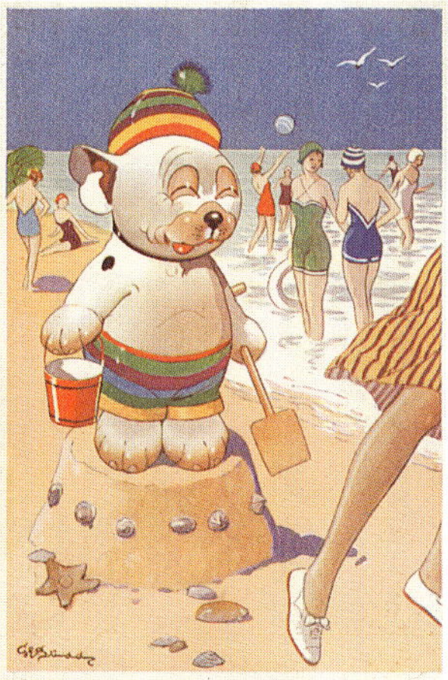

FEELING TEN YEARS YOUNGER ALREADY!

2427

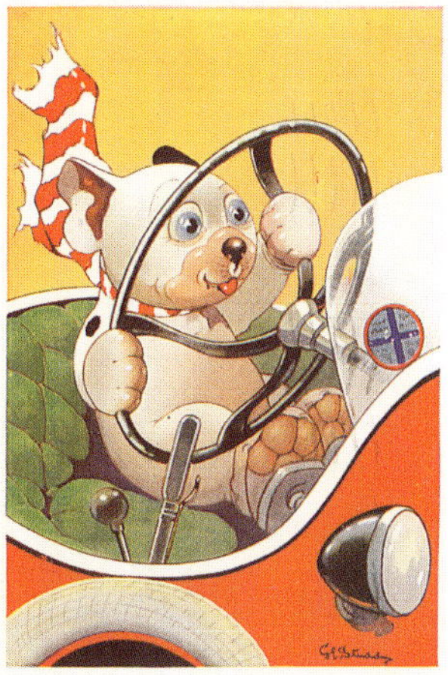

JUST MANAGING TO KEEP THINGS GOING!

2428

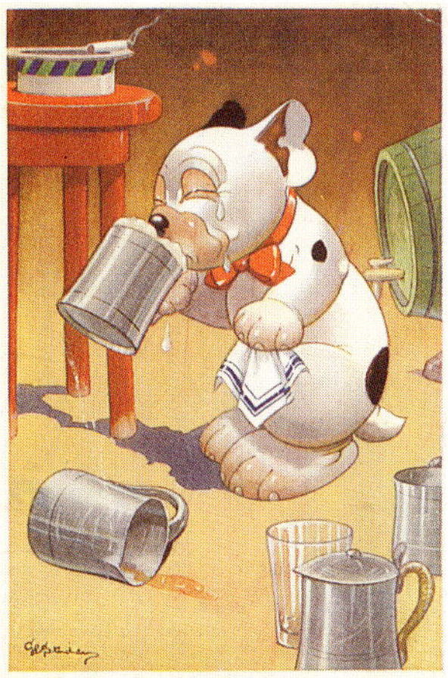

TRYING TO BEER UP WITHOUT YOU!

2429

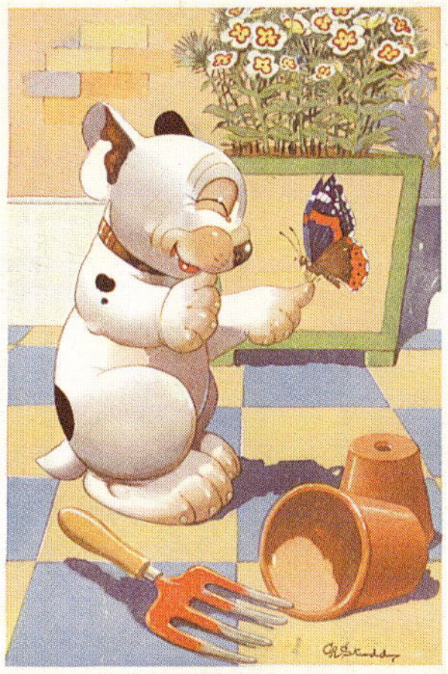

FANCY YOU FALLING FOR ME!

2430

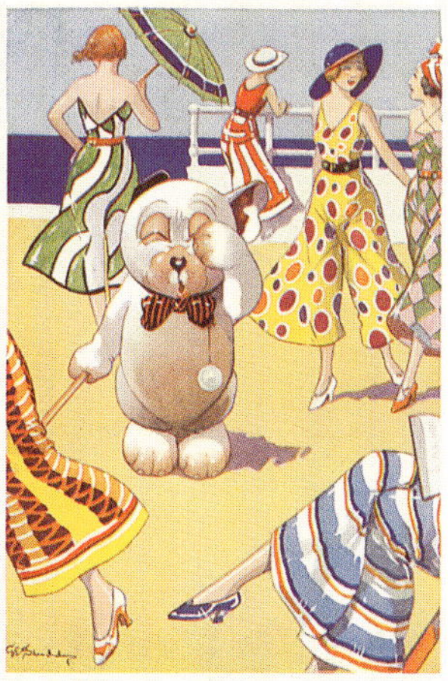

HAVING A DAZZLING TIME!

2431

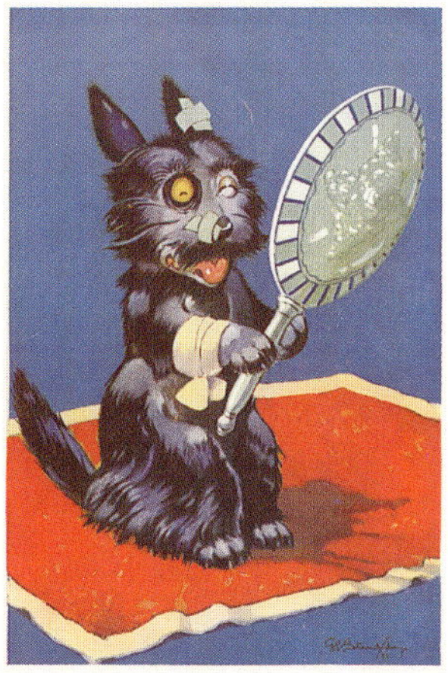

ALL FOR THE LOVE OF A LADY.

2505

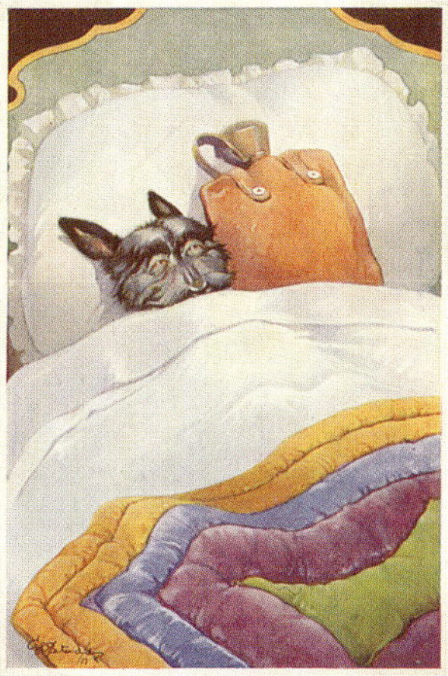

TWO'S COMPANY.

2506

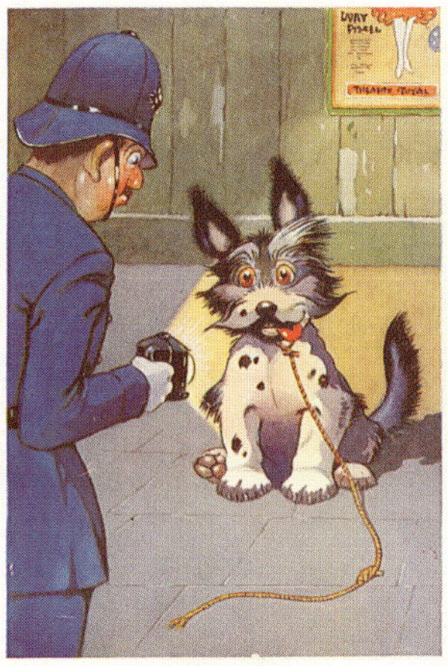

YOU'LL NEVER FIND ANOTHER LIKE ME.

2507

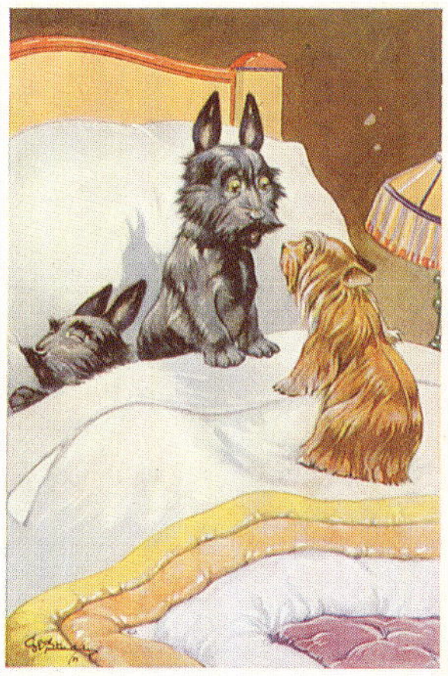

THREE'S A CROWD.

2508

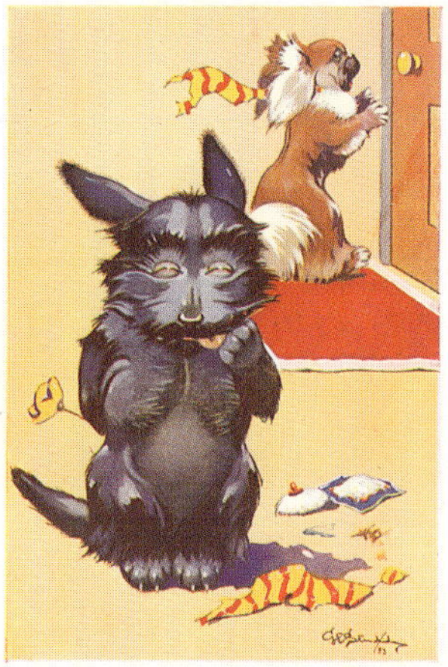

NICE GIRLS NEVER TELL.

2509

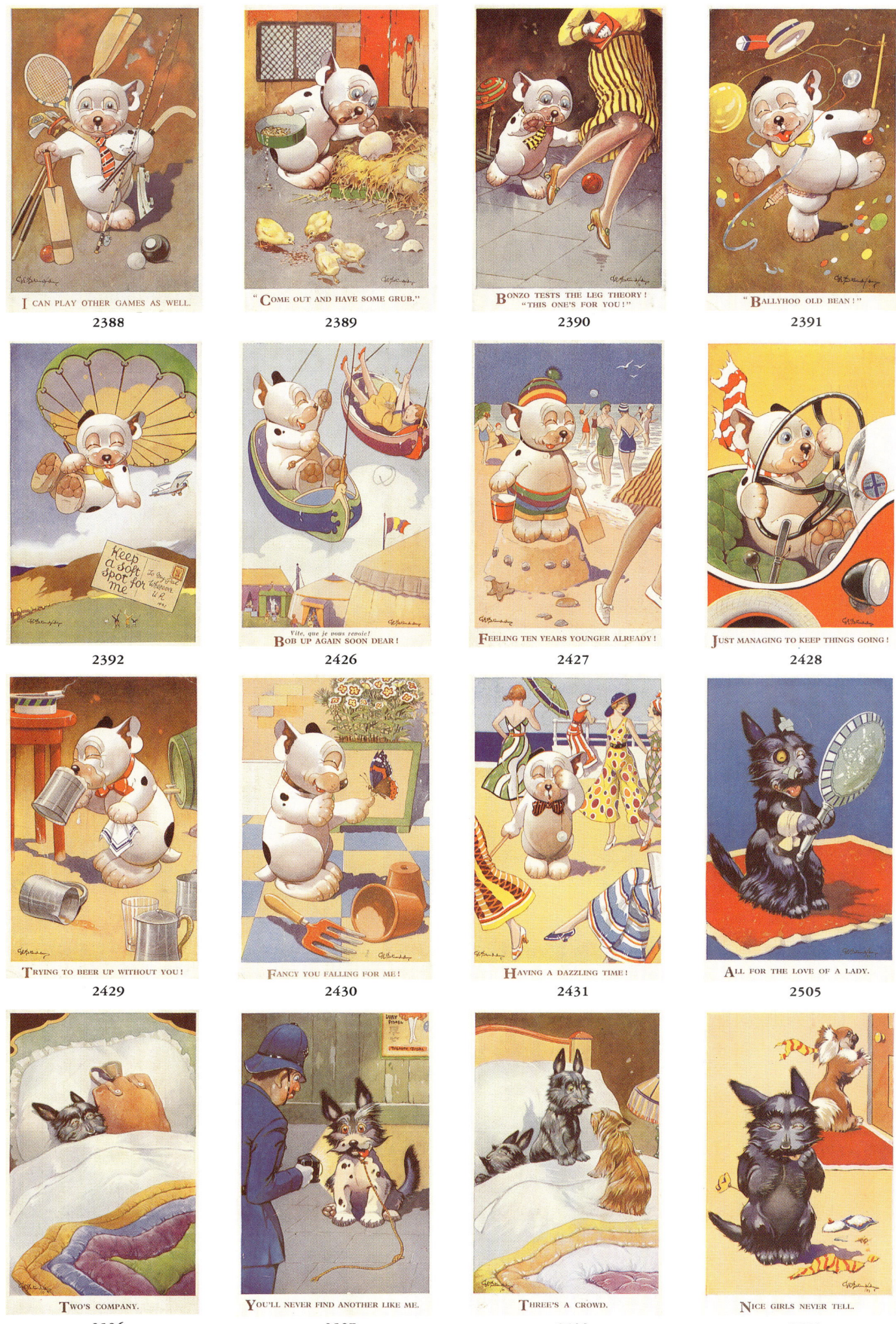

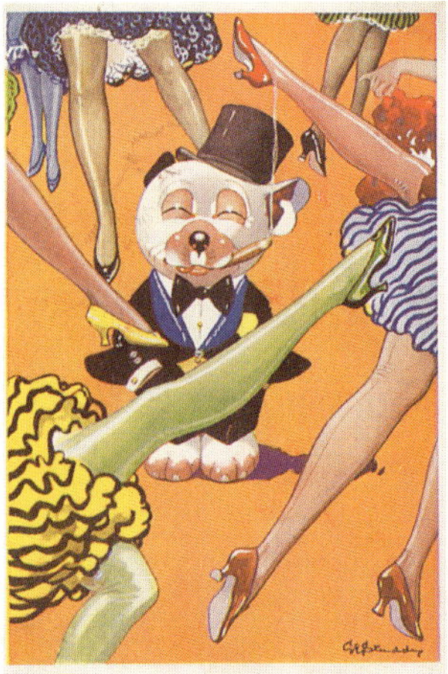

Not having too bad a time!

2510

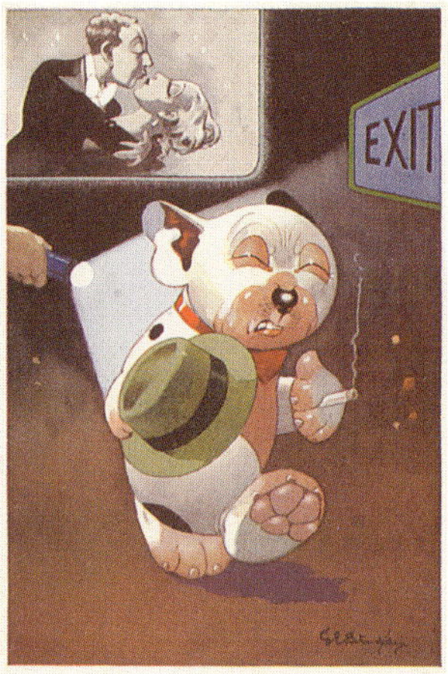
EXIT

Seeing it ain't like doing it!

2511

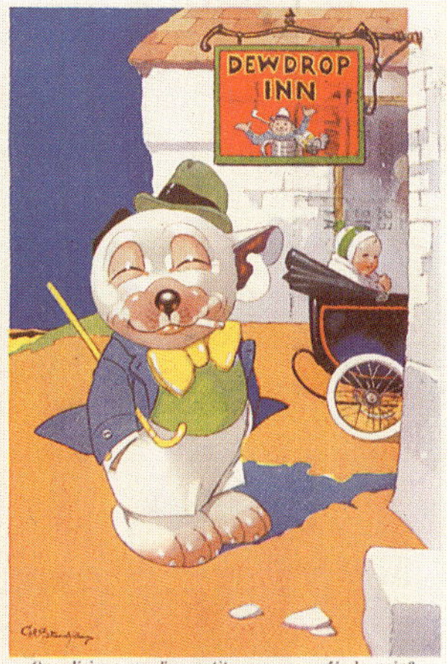
DEWDROP
INN

Que diriez-vous d'un petit verre au café du coin?
What about a wee one?

2512

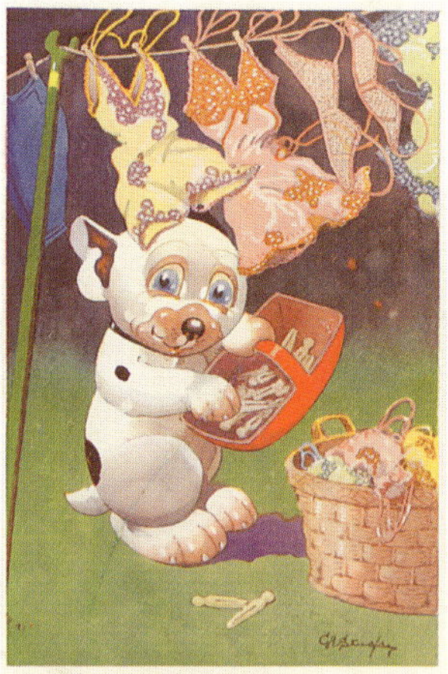

Things aren't what they used to be.

2513

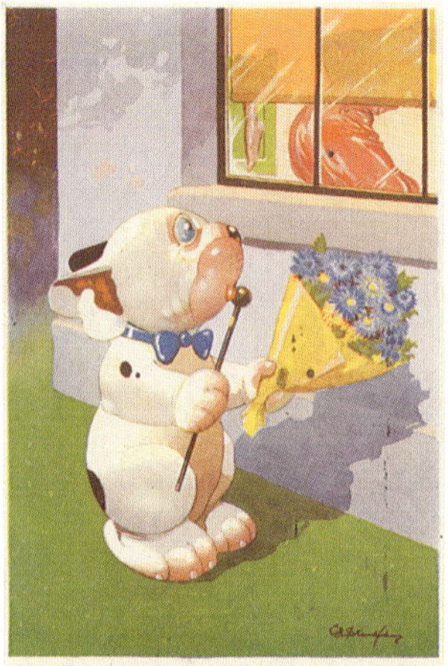

I wish I could see your face.

2514

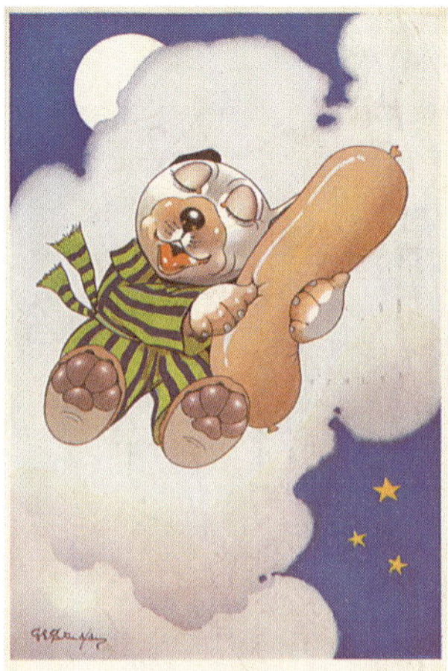

I often dream of you.

2515

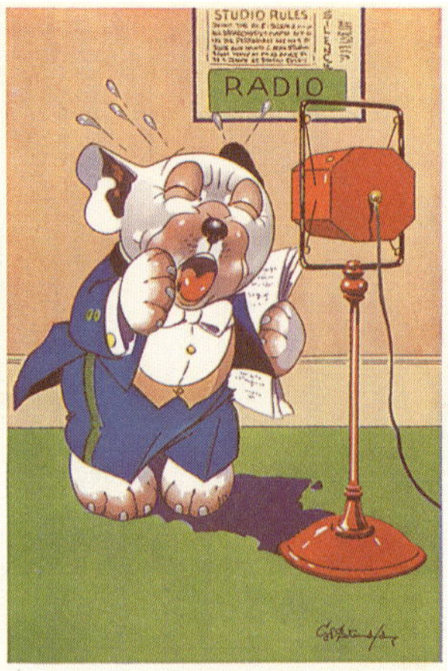
STUDIO RULES
RADIO

"Good-night, everybody, go - o - d-night!"

2516

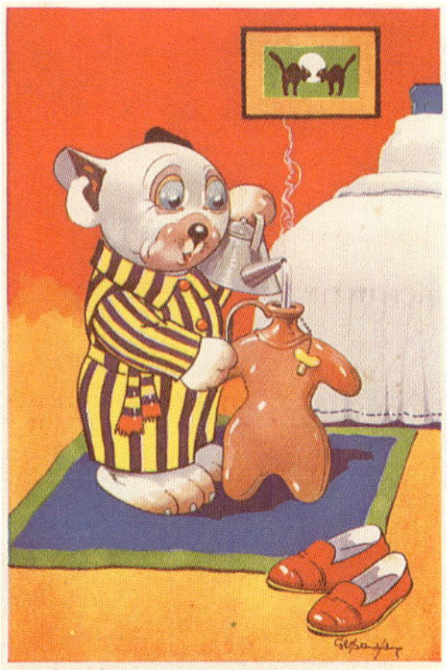

"Nighty-night, old thing."

2517

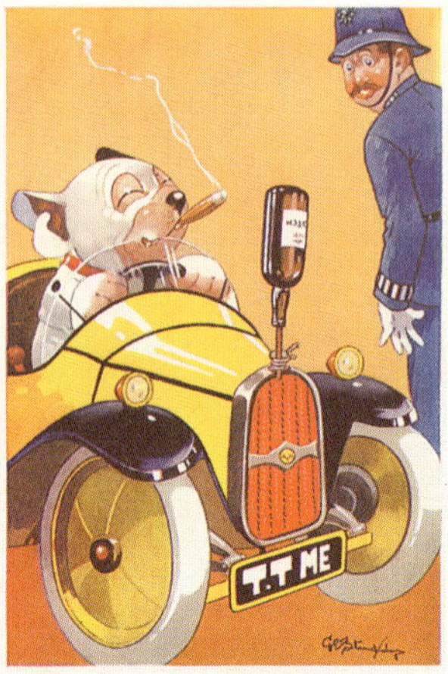
T.T ME

Just to amuse you.

2518

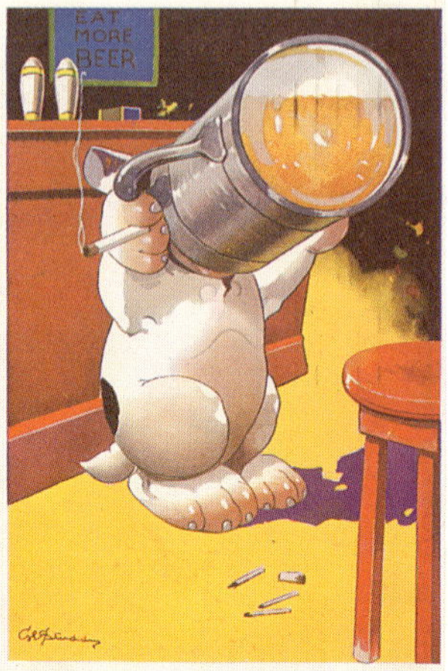
EAT
MORE
BEER

"Hope to see you again soon!"

2519

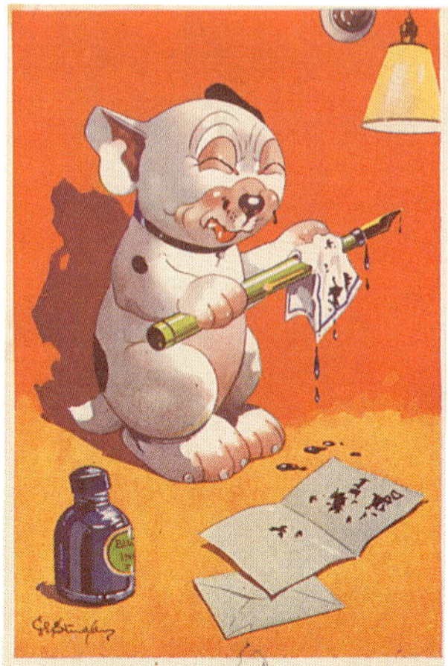

"My pen is too full for words!"

2520

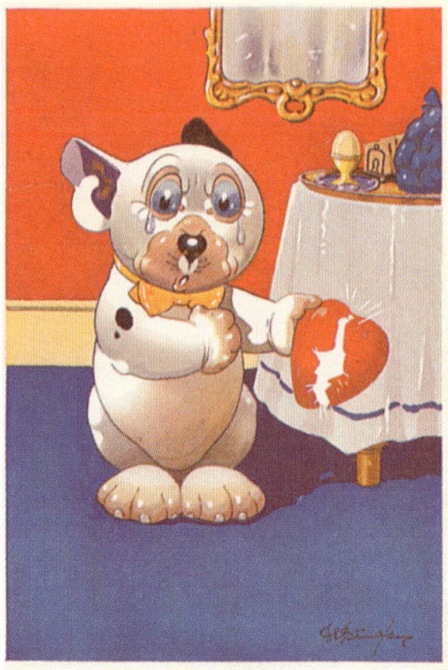

"Just 'cos I haven't heard from you."

2521

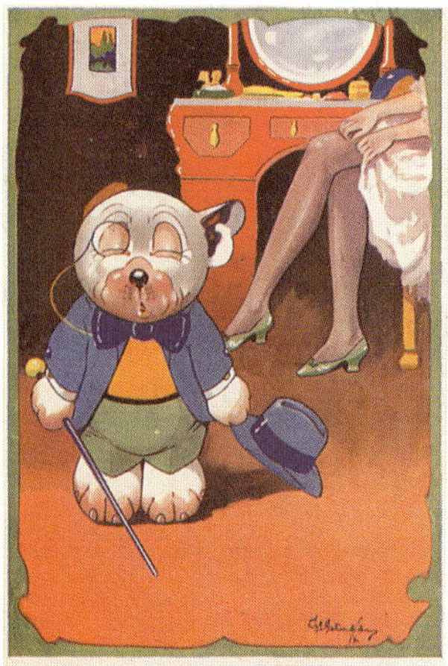

I'll be looking your way soon.

2661

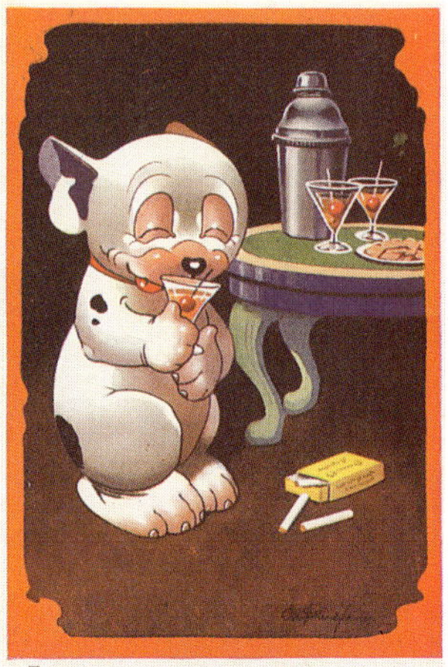

I'm getting much too fond of you.

2662

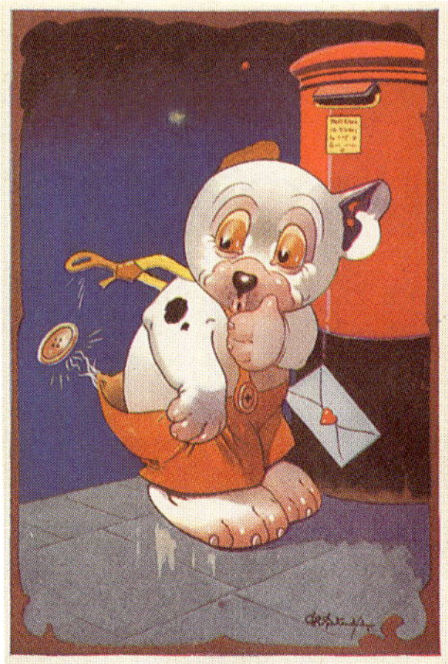

Directly we part I miss you!

2663

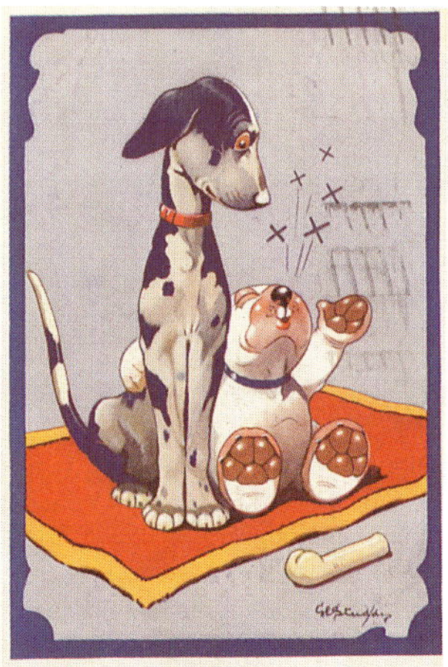

I think you are simply great.

2664

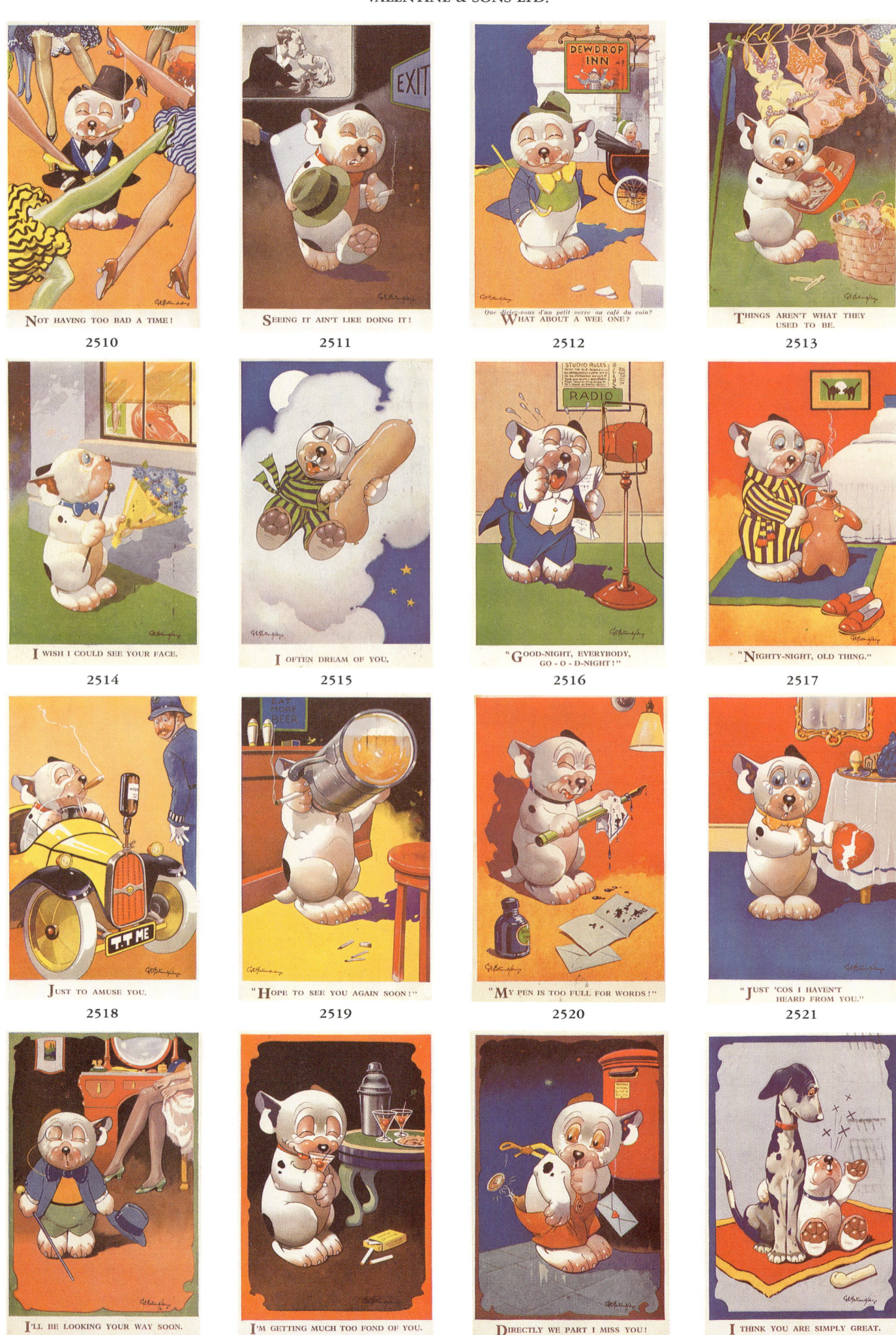

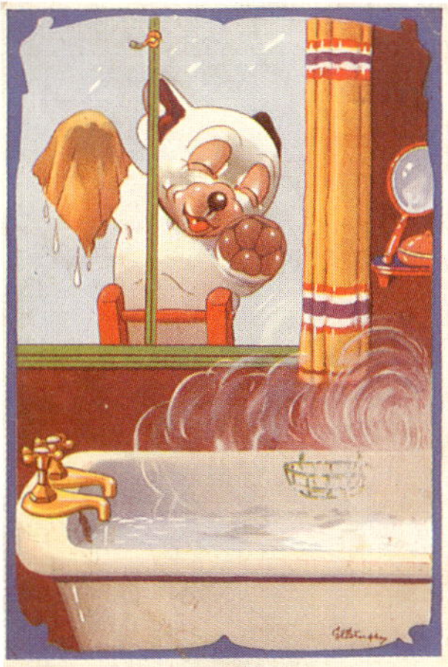

I'M NEVER TOO BUSY TO SEE YOU.

2665

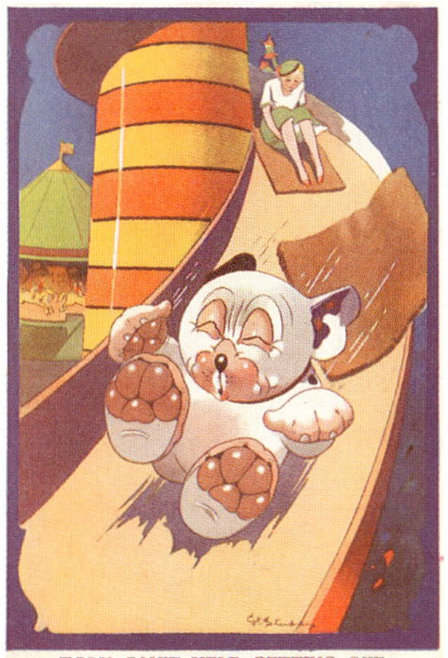

YOU CAN'T HELP GETTING OFF DOWN HERE.

2666

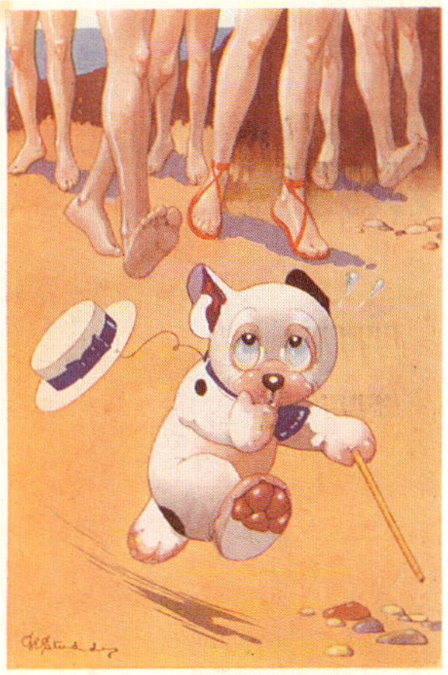

"I'M NO ANGEL, BUT I'M NOT A NUDIST!"

2691

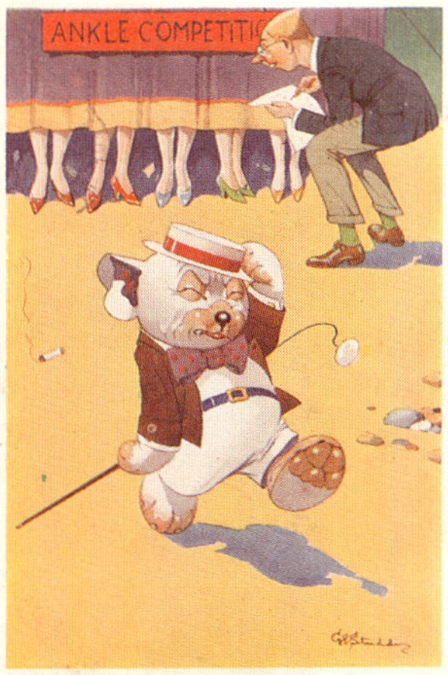
ANKLE COMPETITI

"HAVING A HECK OF A NAUGHTY TIME!"

2692

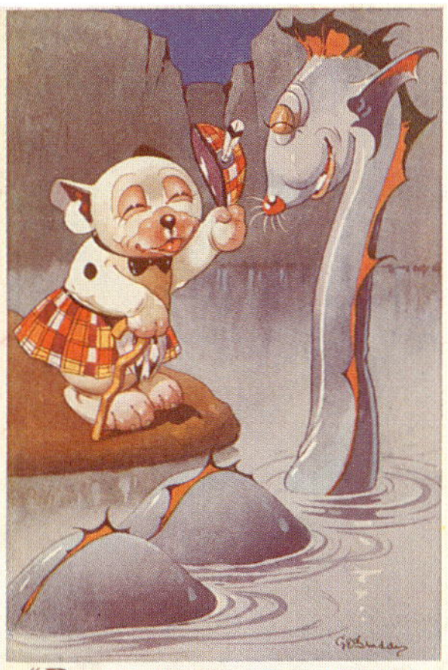

"BOB UP AND SEE ME SOMETIME!"

2693

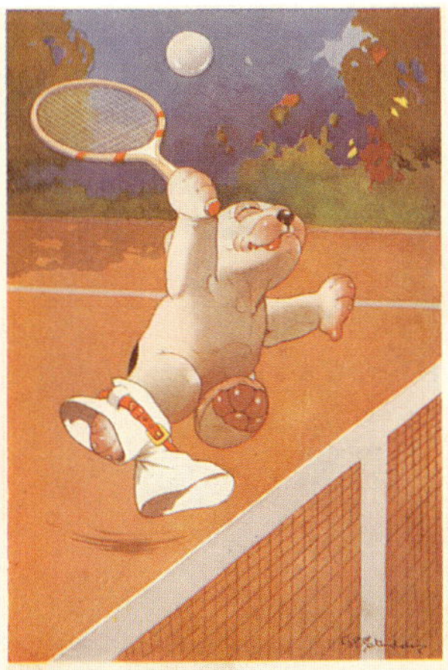

"GIVE ME SHORTS FOR FREEDOM!"

2694

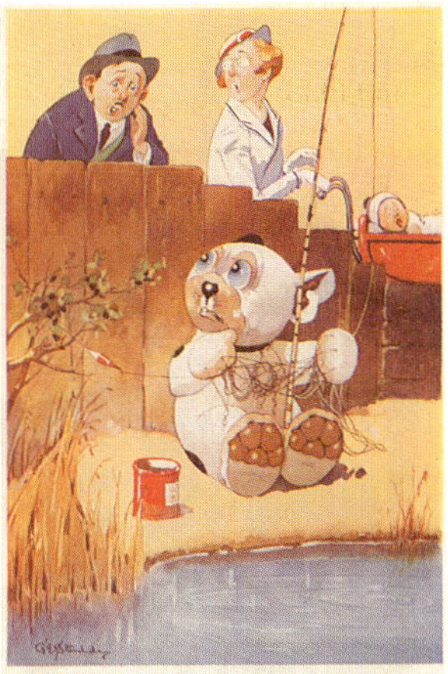

"CHEER UP, OLD SPORT! THAT'S NOTHING TO THE MARRIAGE KNOT!"

2695

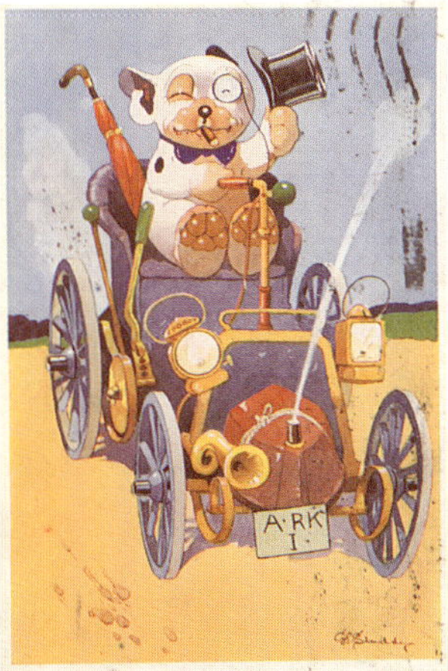
A·RK
I

"I'LL BE SEEIN' YE YET!"

2696

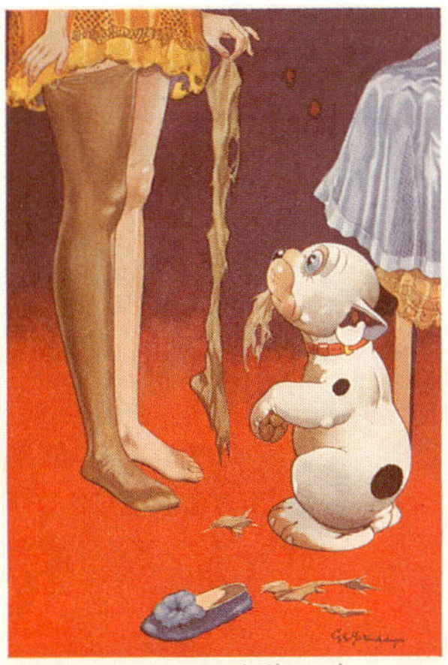

Je ne le ferai plus, mais dites-moi que vous m'aimez encore!

2846

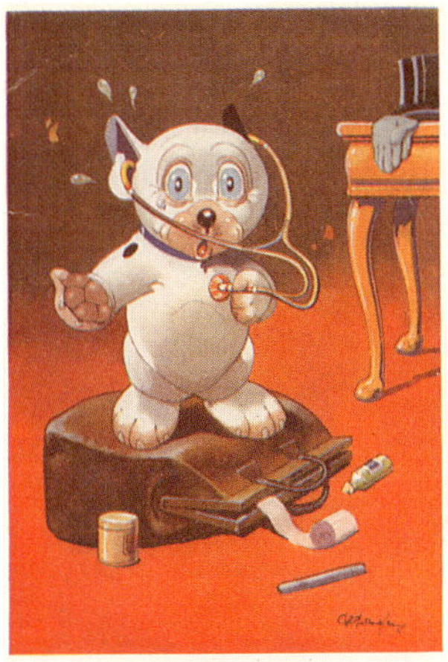

"GOLLY! WHERE'S MY HEART?"

2847

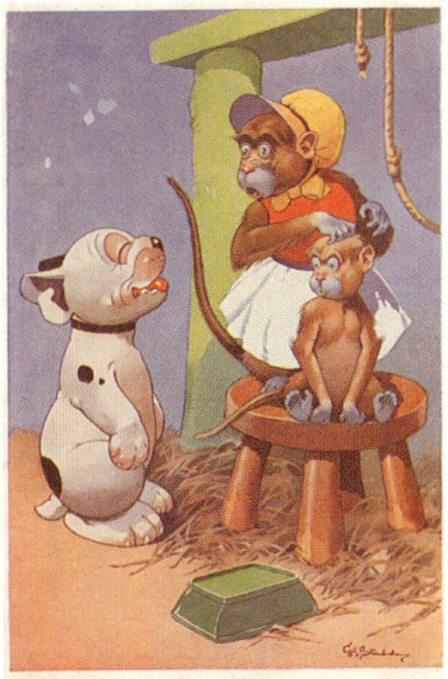

"HOW'S LIFE?"

2848

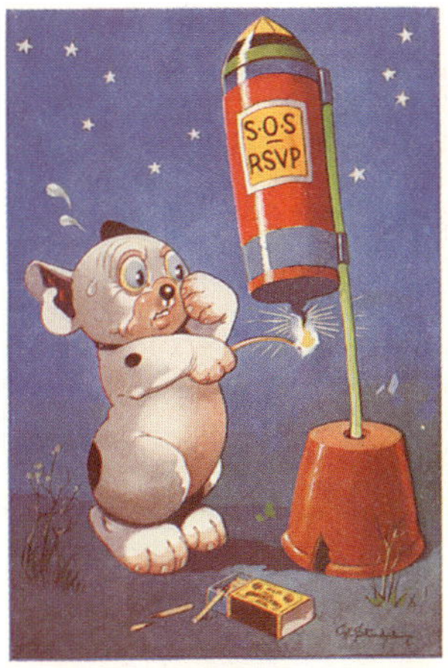
S·O·S
RSVP

"THIS OUGHT TO WAKE YOU UP!"

2849

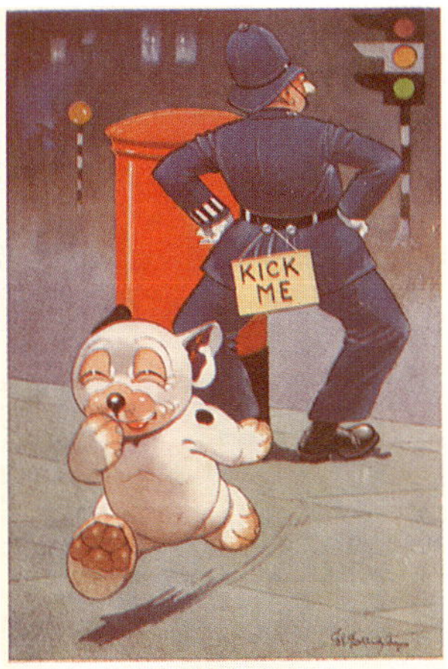
KICK
ME

"PUT A WORD ON A P.C."

2850

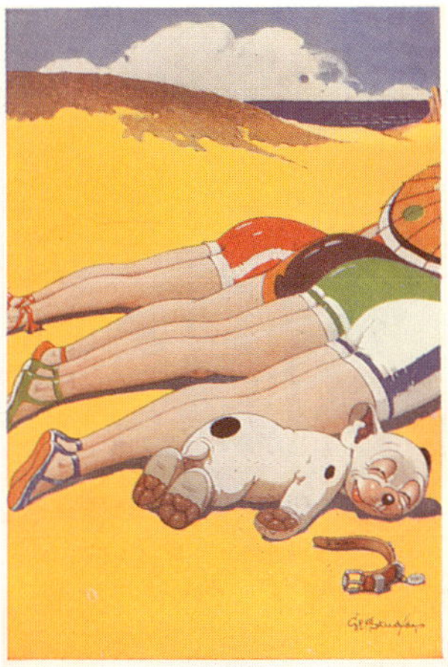

"DOING A SPOT OF SUN-BATHING."

2851

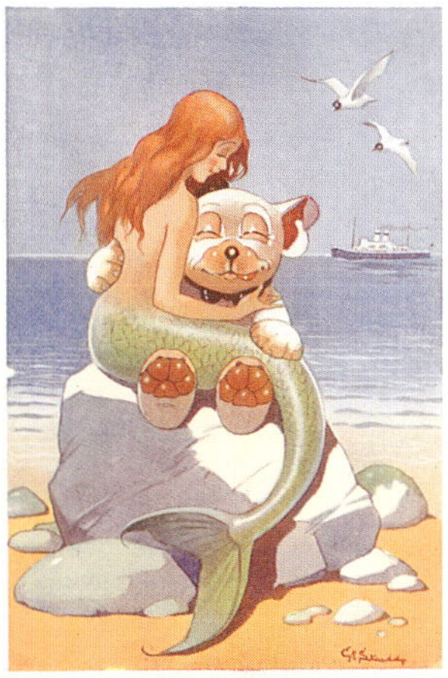

I'M A POOR FISH, BUT I LOVE YOU

2982

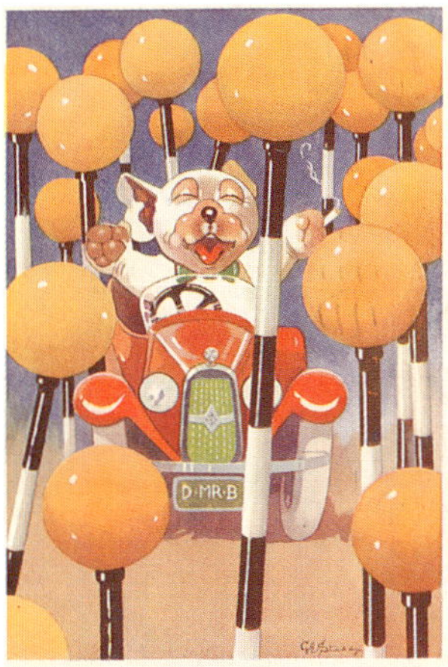
D·MR·B

LIFE IS SO DIFFERENT SINCE I MET YOU

2983

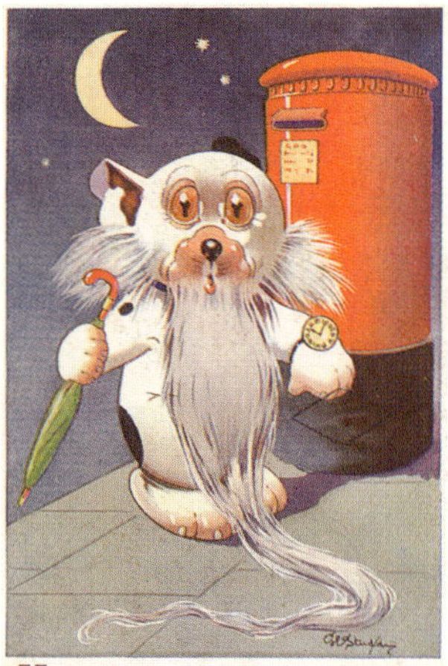

How much longer before I see you

2984

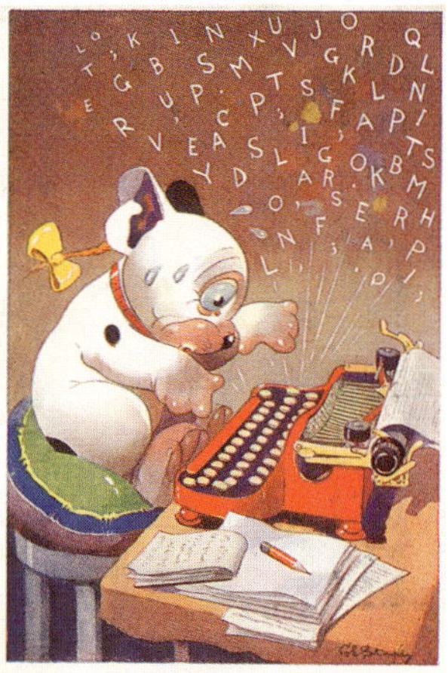

Just a few words

2985

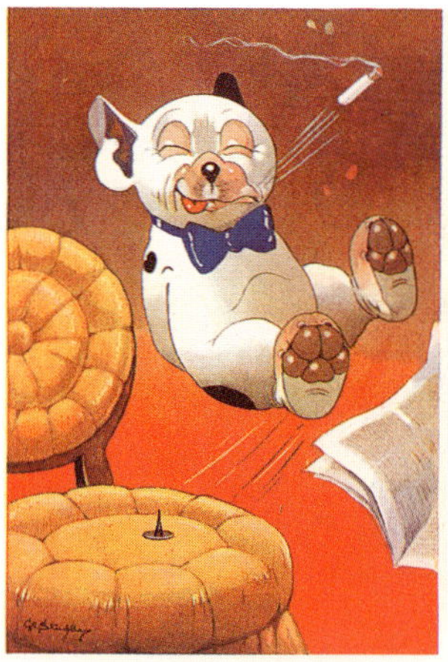

And how's things at your end?
Comment la trouvez-vous?

2986

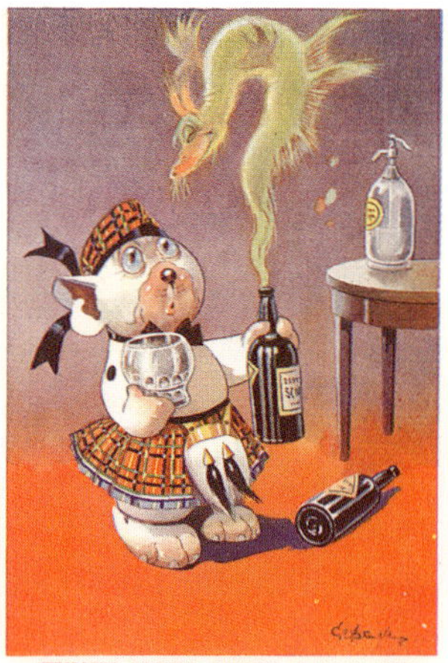

That's queer, there wasn't one in the other bottle

2987

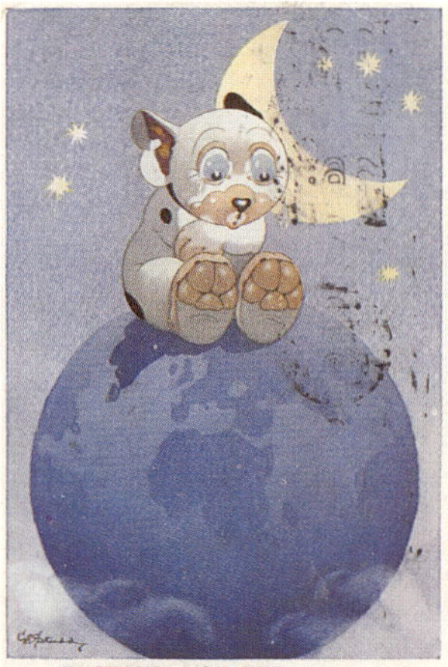

Without you, the whole world's blue!

3027

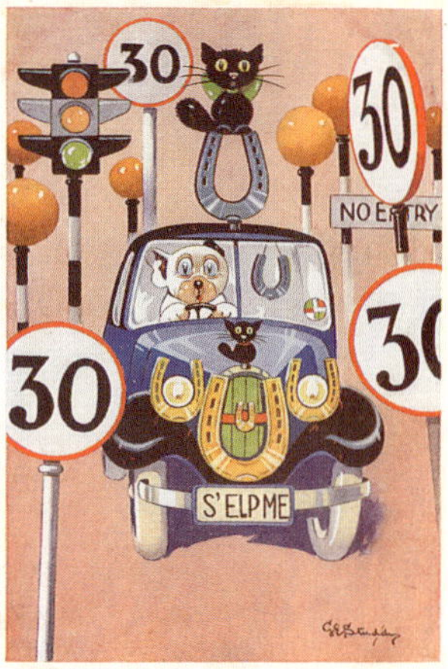
30
30
30
30
S'ELPME

Here's luck in the dirty thirties!

3028

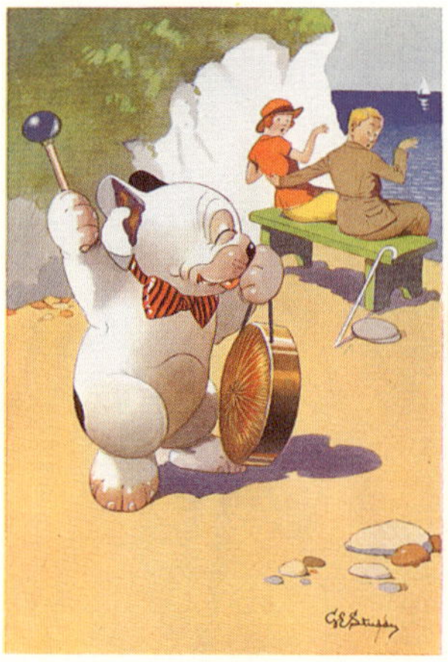

I think it's time you heard from me!

3029

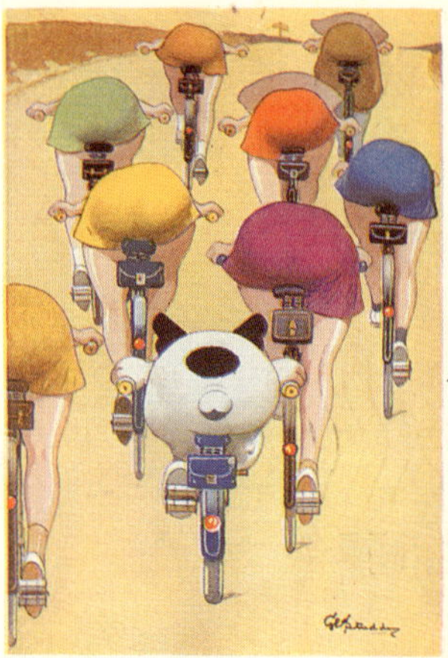

Shall I never see your face again?

3030

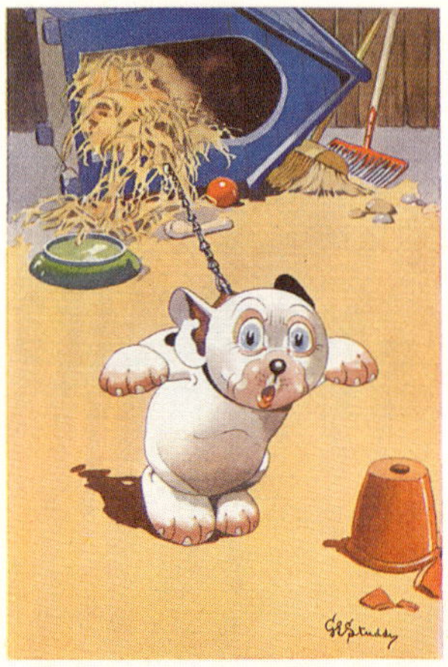

Been frightfully tied up lately.

3031

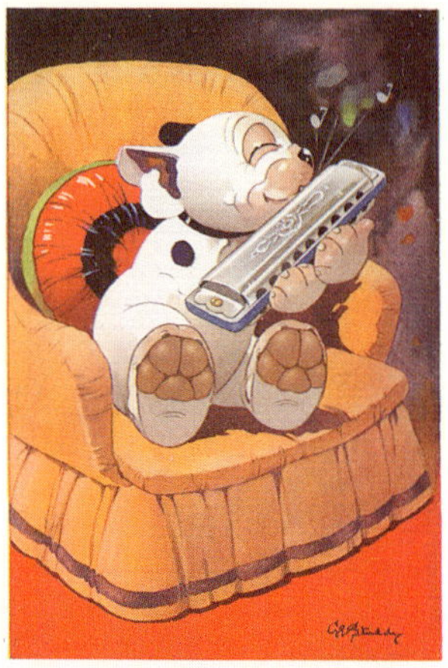

Oh! how I wish this were you!

3032

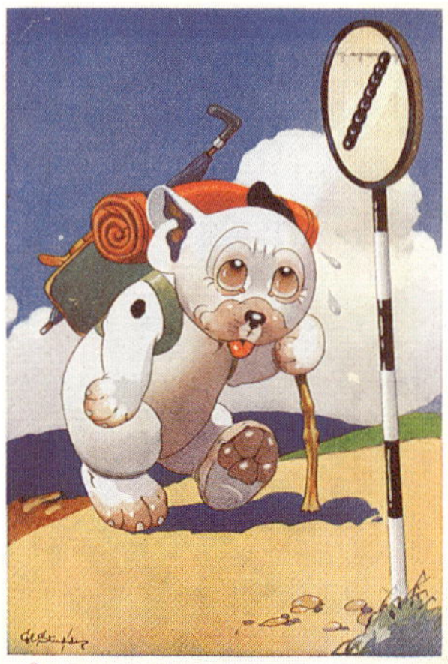

Alas, you were not made for me!

3110

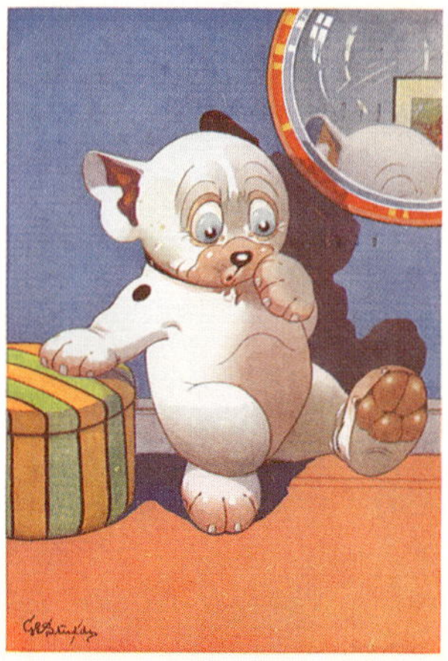

Don't say I've got no leg appeal.

3111

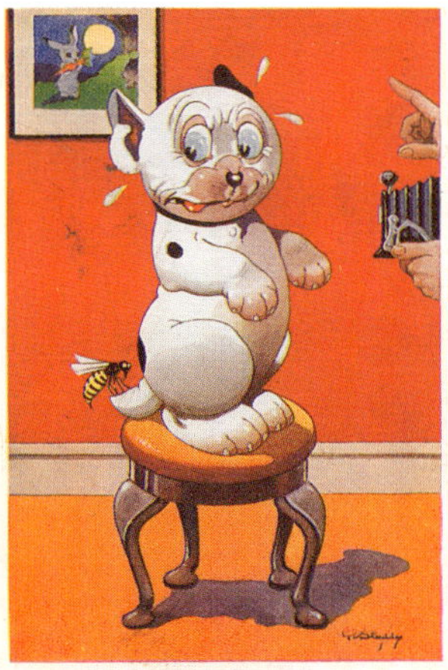

Try to keep smiling.

3112

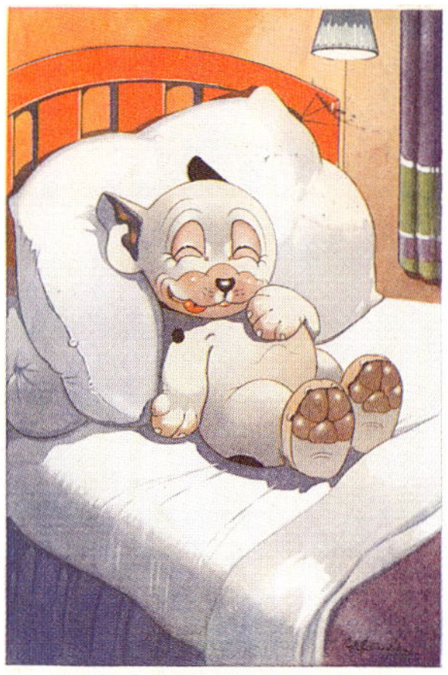

How I wish you were here to kiss me good-night!

3113

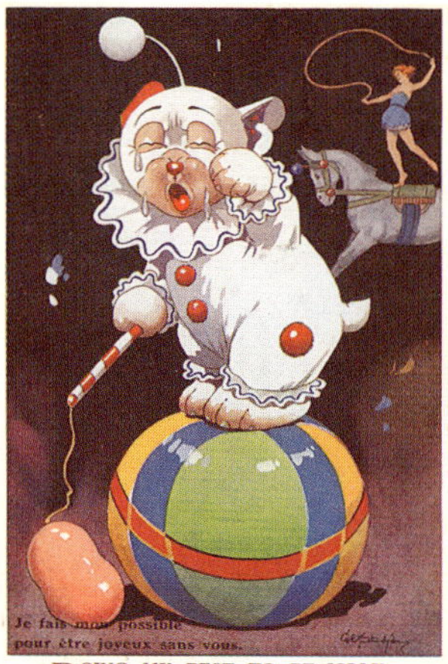

Doing my best to be jolly without you.

3114

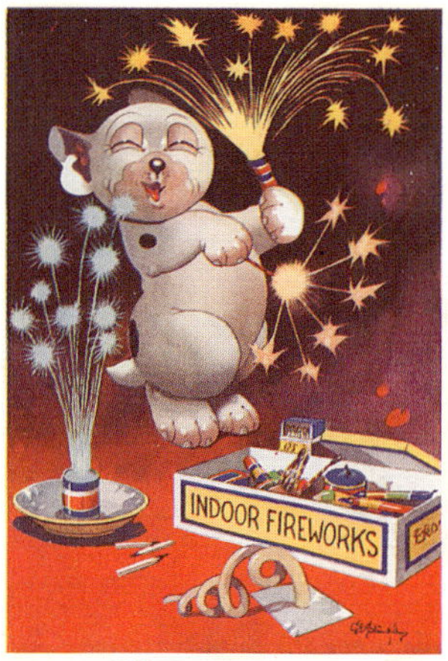
INDOOR FIREWORKS

Why be married?

3115

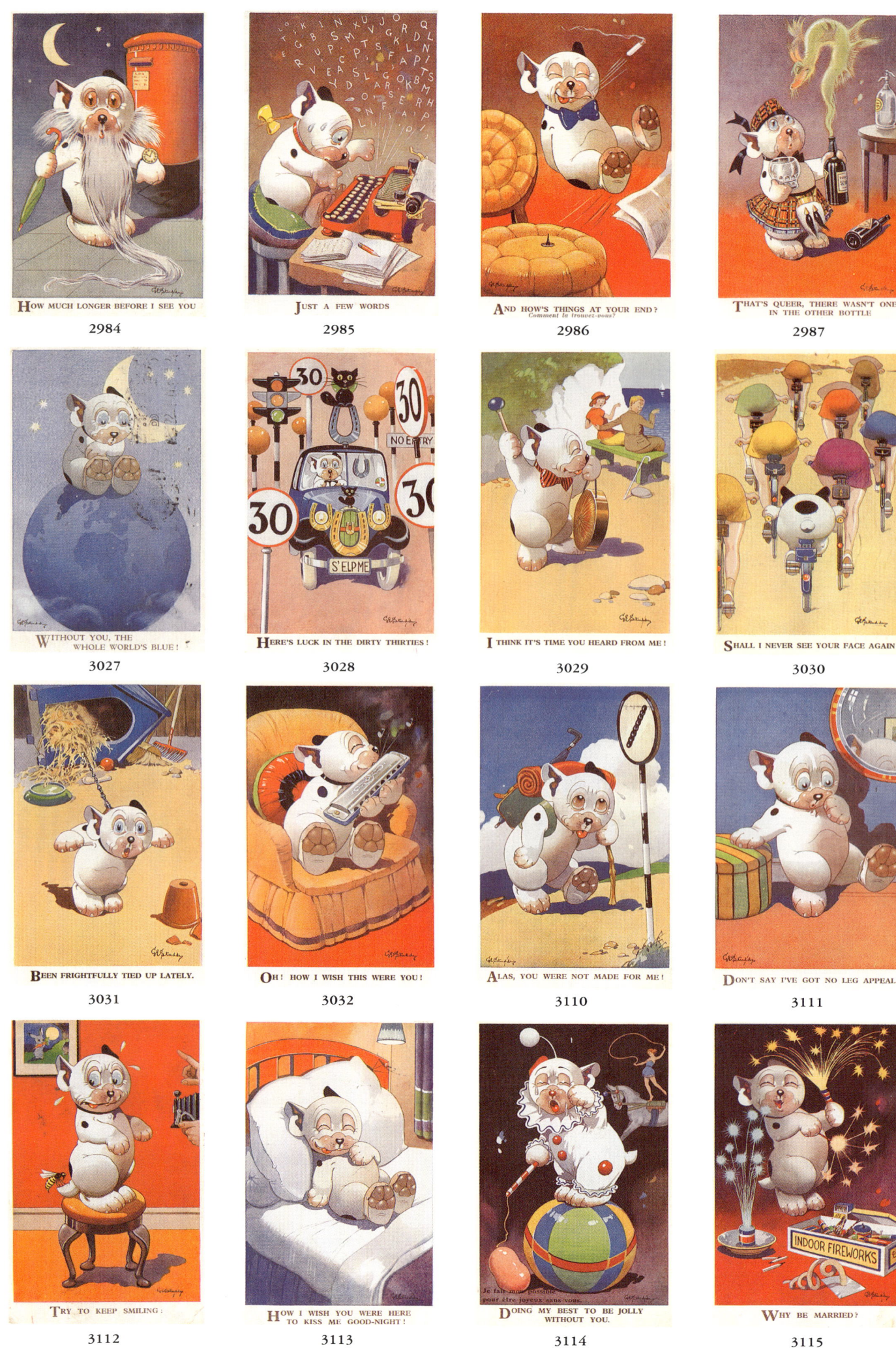

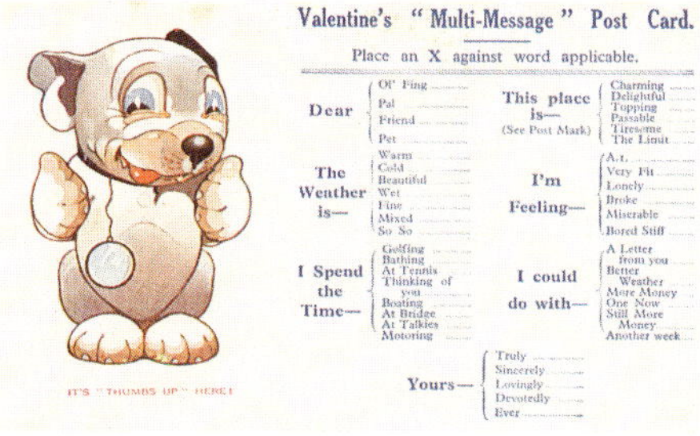

VALENTINE & SONS LTD.

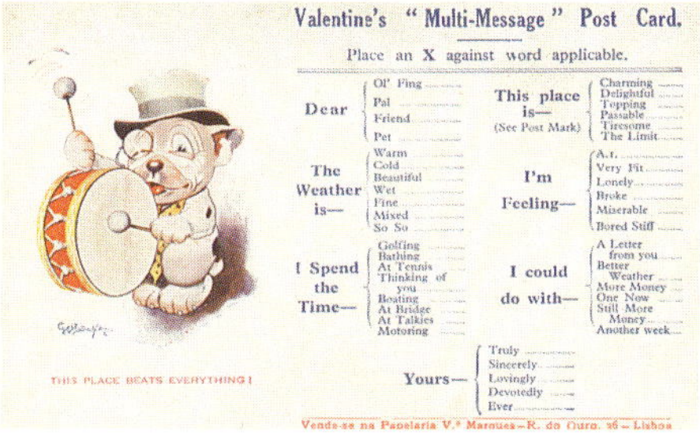

1778	1779	1780
1781	*1896 I'VE FOUND A LOVELY PLACE.	*1977 "WELL OLD COCK, I GOT YOUR 'TALE' ALRIGHT!"
*1978 "YOUR GRACES WILL BE 'AT HOME' ANY DAY!"	*1979 ANOTHER BLOOMING POW (ER) WOW CUT!	*1980 "YOU LEFT AN IMPRESSION ON ME!"
2852 HERE'S TO A CLINKING TIME.	2853 "ARE YOUR INTENTIONS STRICTLY HONOURABLE?"	2854 GIRLS ADD TO BEAUTY—BOYS GET RID OF THE ROUGH.
2855 "HURRY UP AND TAKE ME OUT."	2856 "YOU'D BREAK ANY GIRL'S HEART!"	2857 GIVE US A THOUGHT SOMETIMES.
3116 I WONDER IF BOYS MEAN ALL THEY SAY?	3117 I LOVE YOU FOR YOURSELF, DEAR, AND NOT FOR YOUR GIFTS.	3118 I'LL BE TRUE AS LONG AS YOU, BUT NOT A MOMENT AFTER.

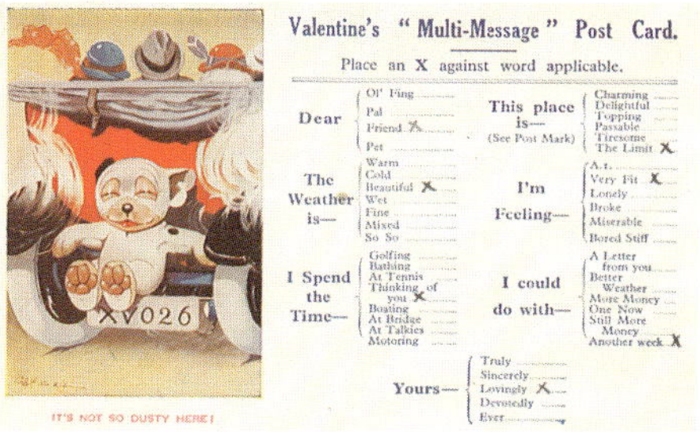

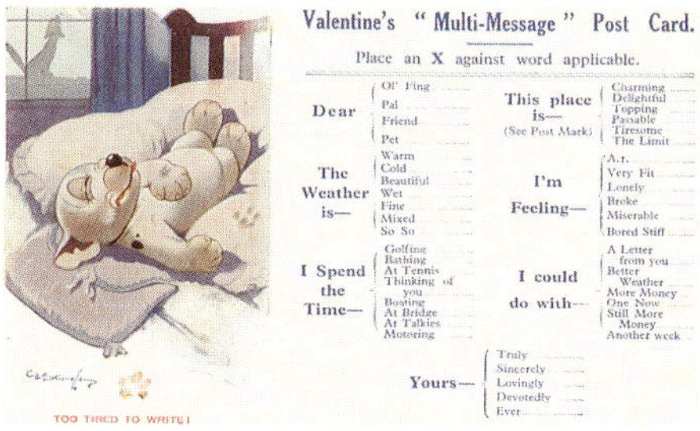

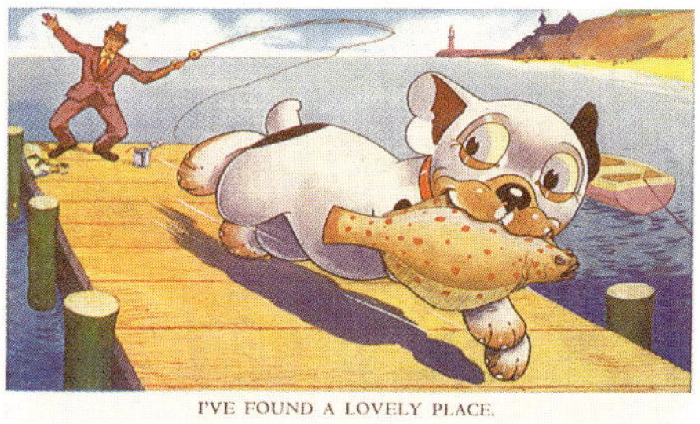

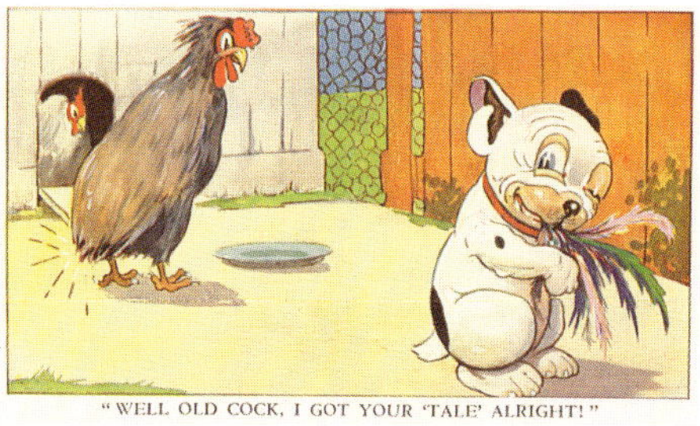

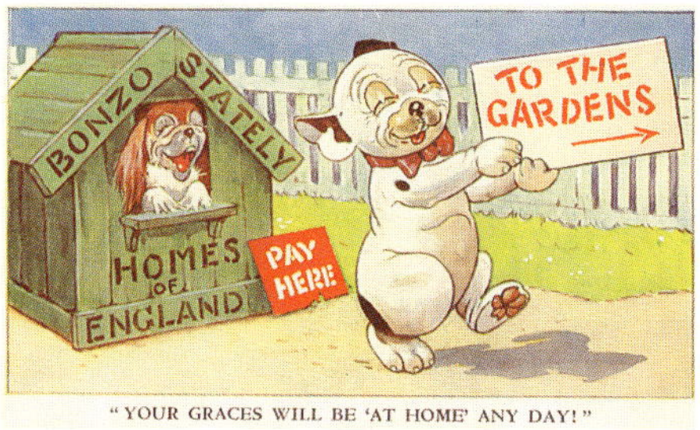

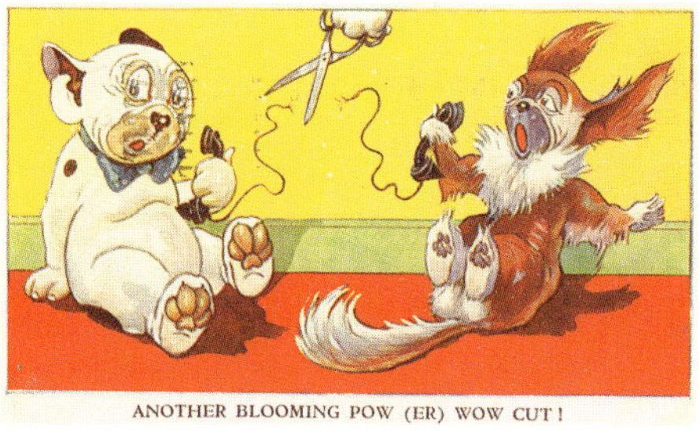

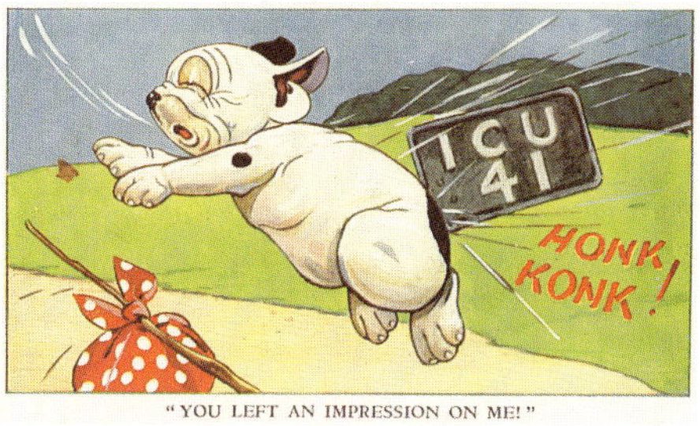

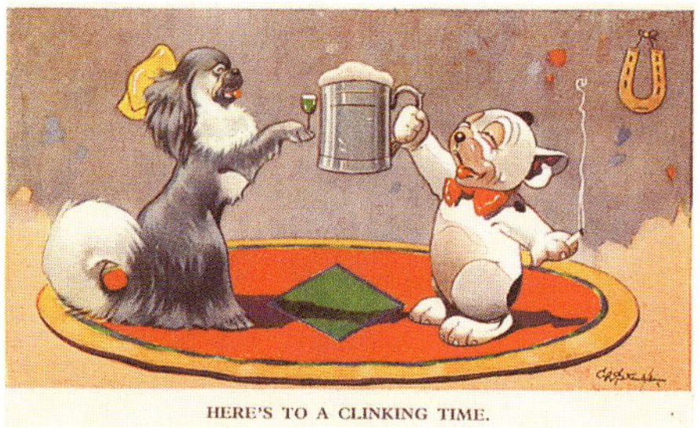

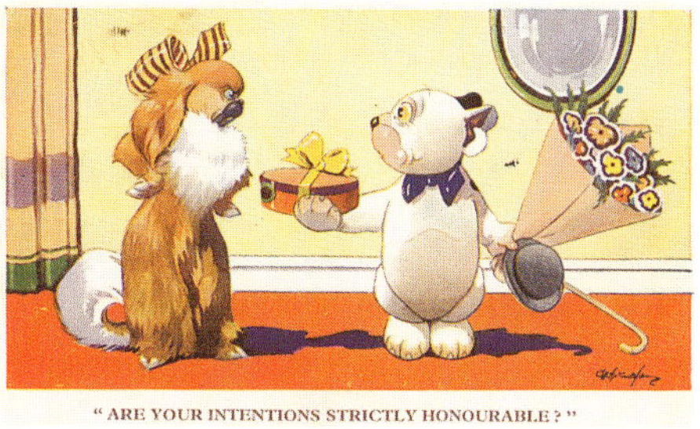

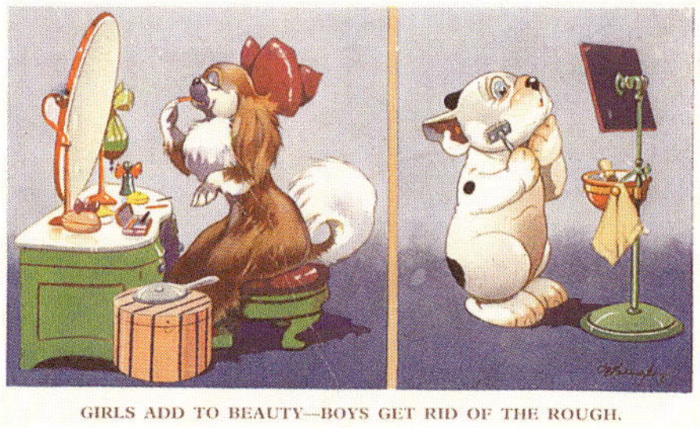

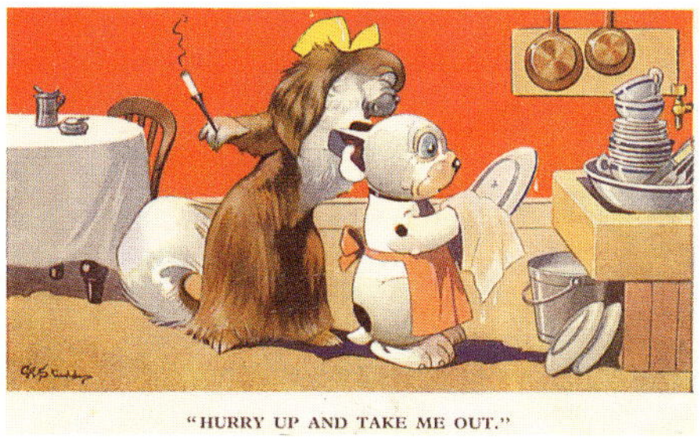

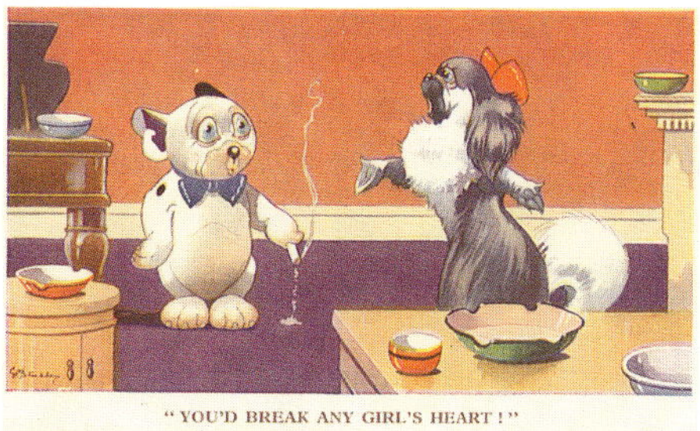

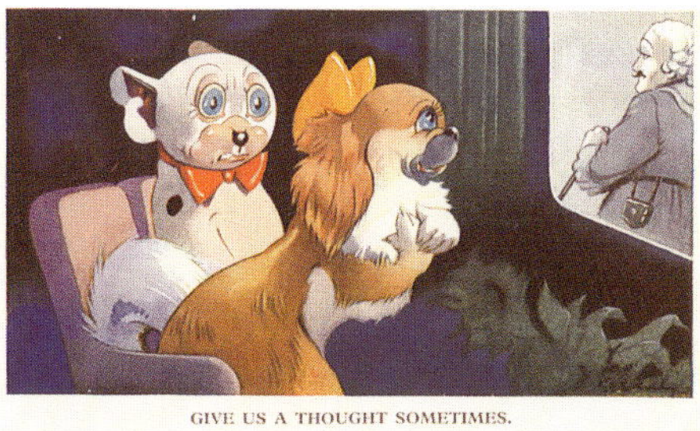

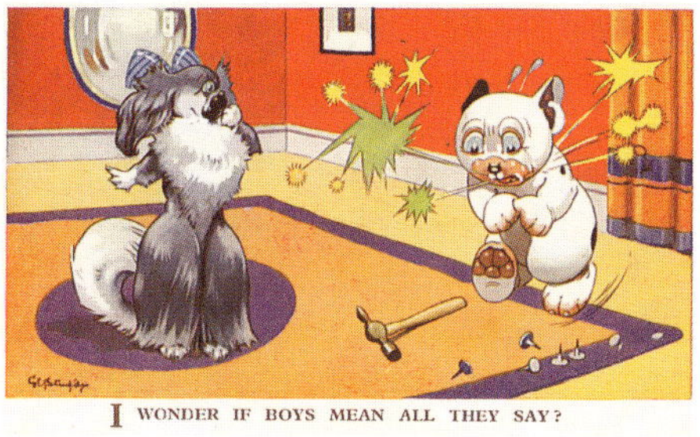

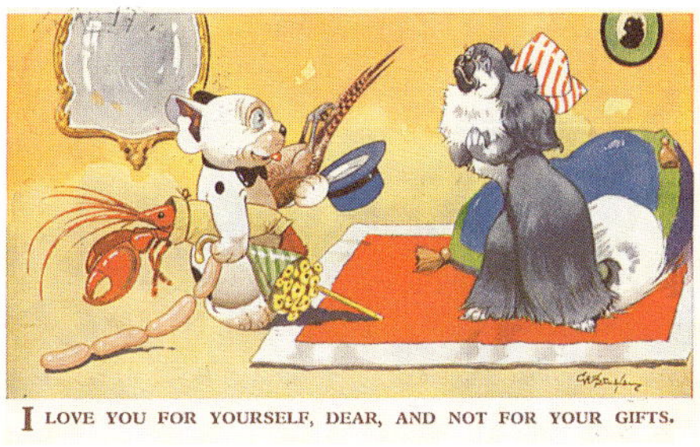

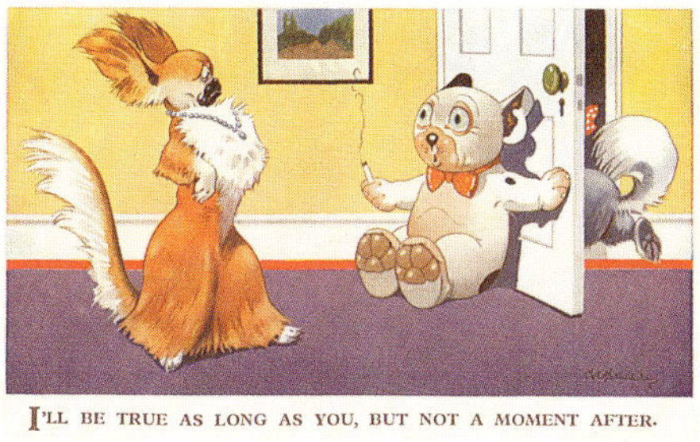

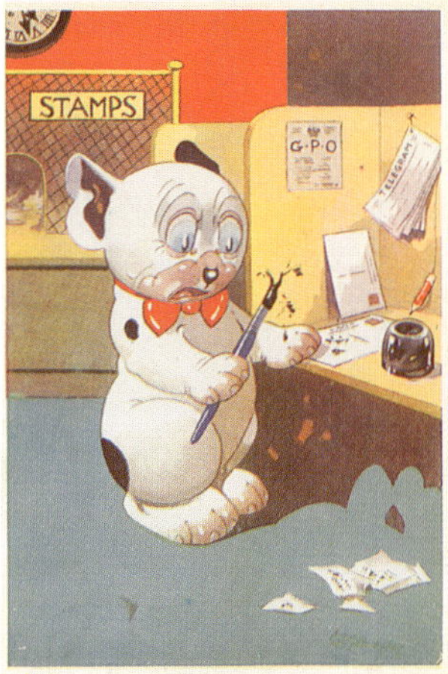
STAMPS
G·P·O

YOU'RE WONDERFUL AT NOT WRITING.

3235

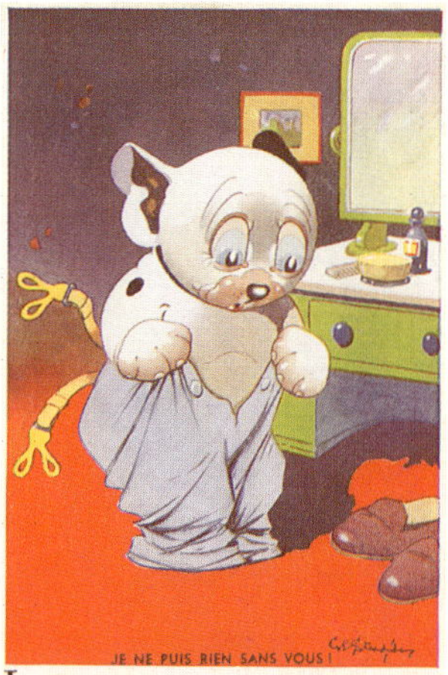
JE NE PUIS RIEN SANS VOUS!

I CAN'T FACE THE WORLD WITHOUT YOU.

3236

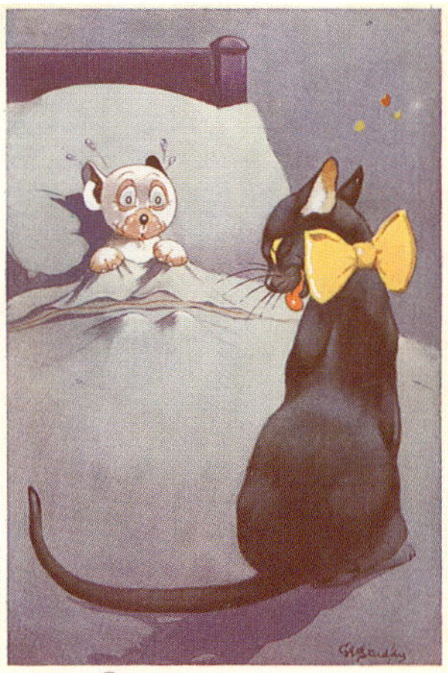

OO-ER—HERE'S LUCK.

3238

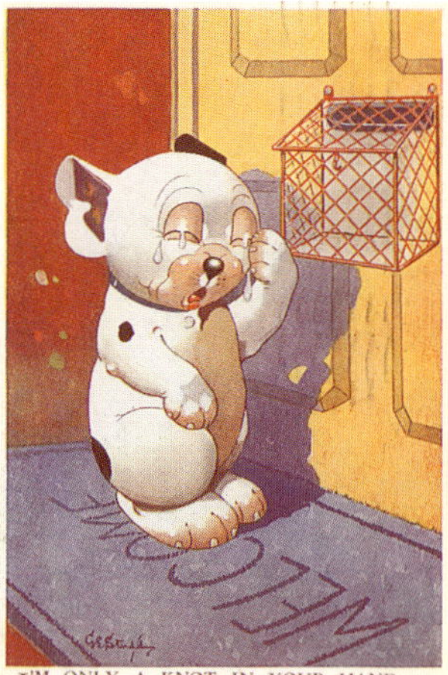

I'M ONLY A KNOT IN YOUR HANDKERCHIEF AND THAT'S COME UNDONE.

3239

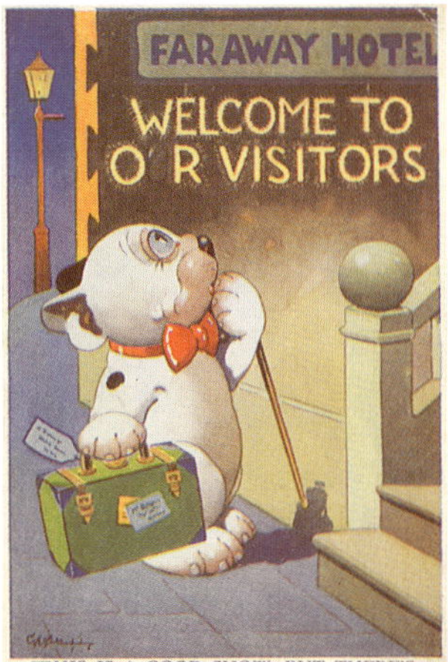
FARAWAY HOTEL
WELCOME TO
O' R VISITORS

THIS IS A GOOD SHOW, BUT THERE'S SOMETHING MISSING,—"U."

3240

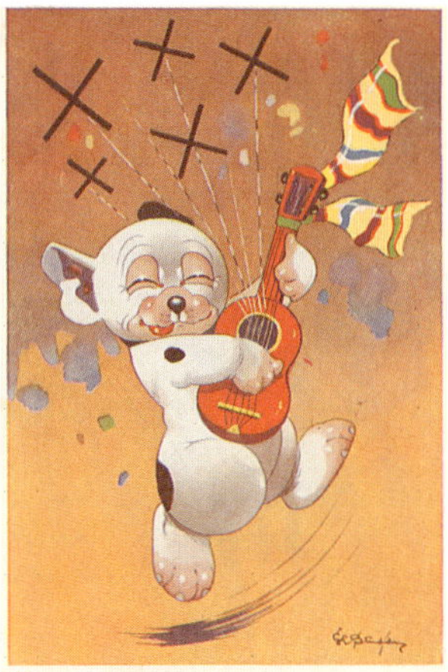

THE SAME OLD TUNE FROM ME TO YOU!

3371

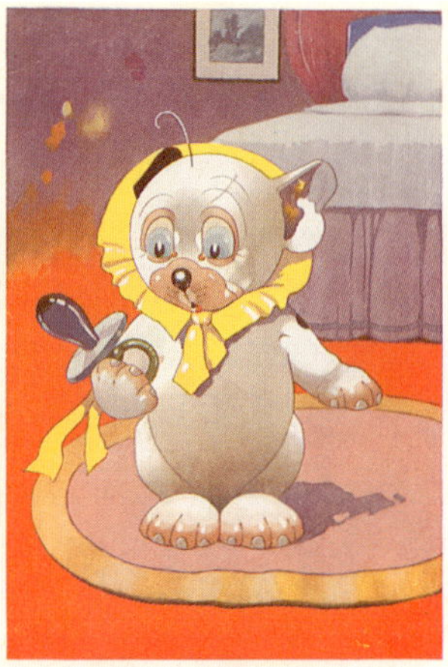

NOW FOR A SPOT OF GRUB AND SO TO BED.

3372

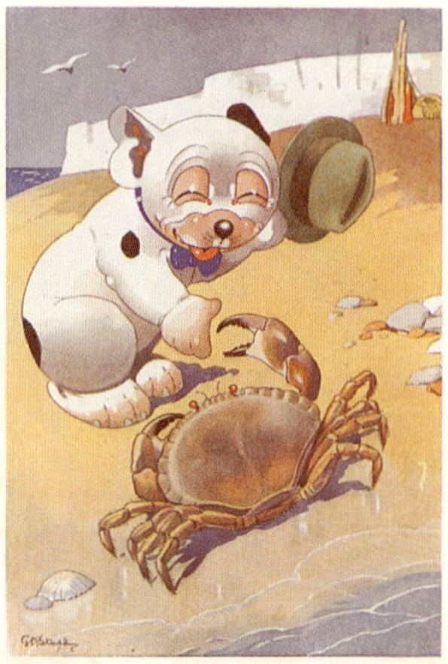

HOW ARE THE LITTLE NIPPERS?

3373

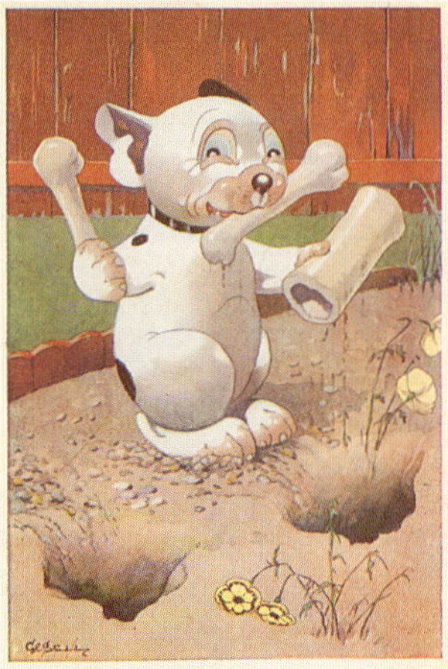

REAL GOOD DIGS HERE.

3374

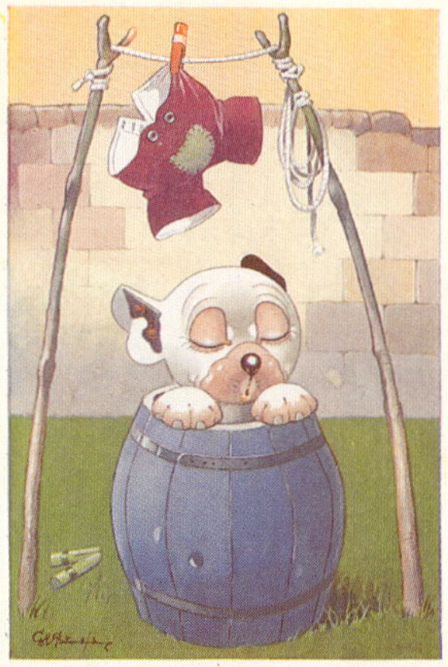

ONE SHORT LITTLE LINE.

3375

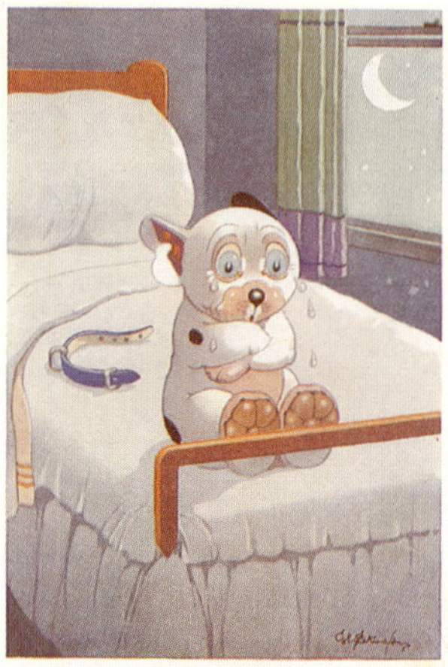

THINK OF ME THINKING OF YOU!

3376

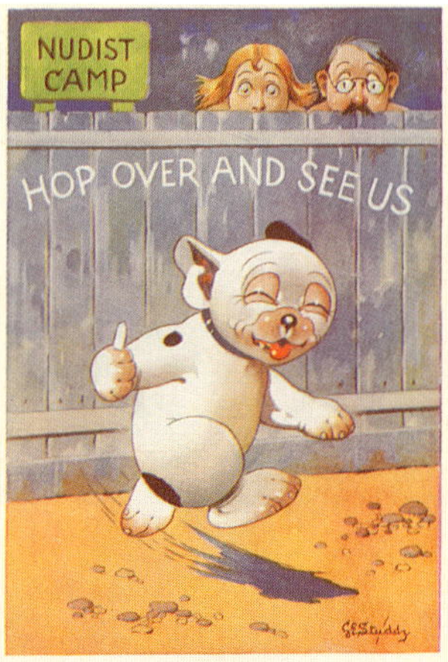
NUDIST
CAMP
HOP OVER AND SEE US

JUST A HURRIED SCRIBBLE!

3491

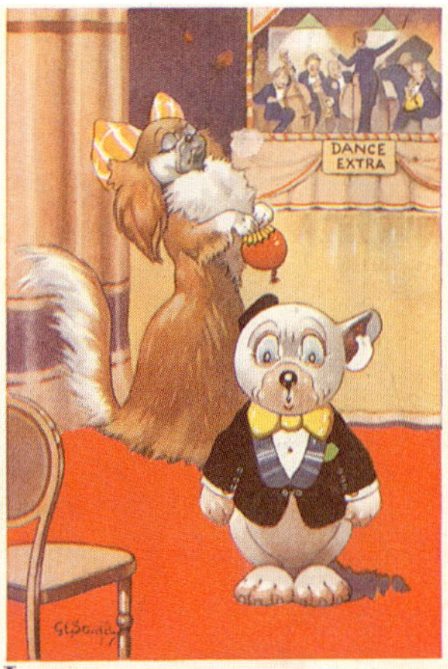
DANCE
EXTRA

I'M NOT A GIRL TO BE PICKED UP EASILY.

3492

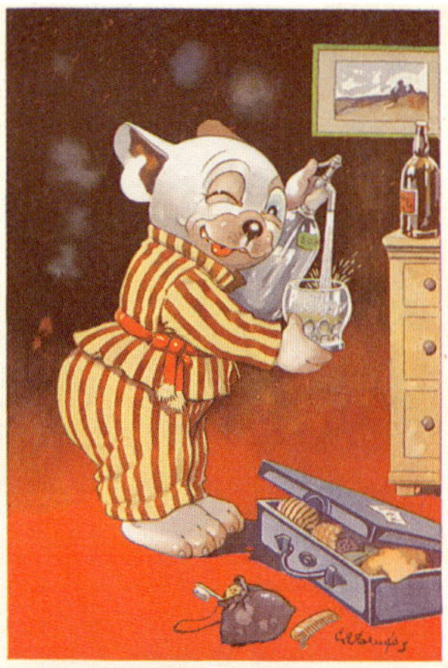

THIS IS IN PLACE OF KISSING YOU GOOD-NIGHT!

3493

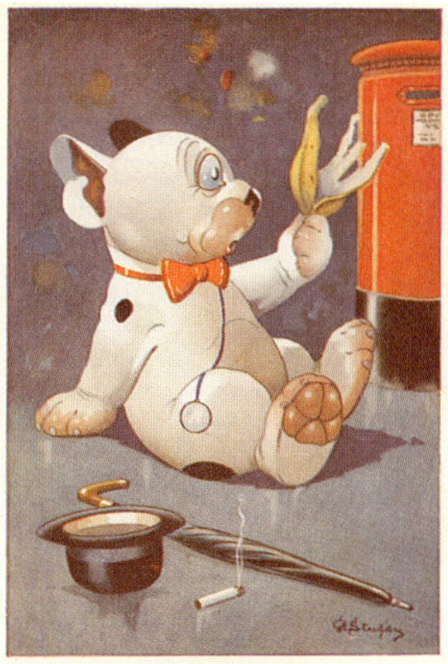

FANCY ME FALLING FOR YOU!

3494

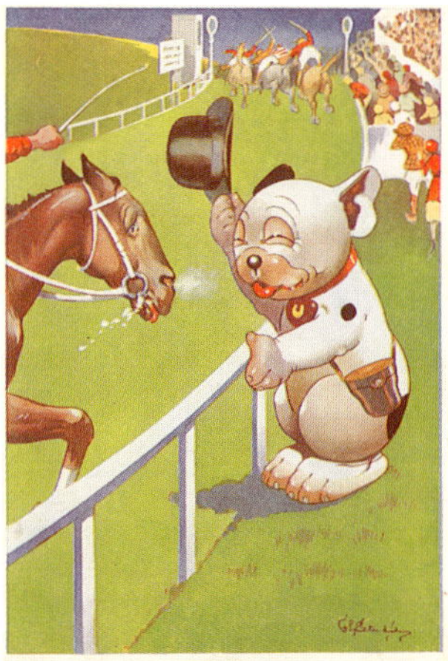

I HOPED I SHOULD SEE YOU BEFORE THIS

3495

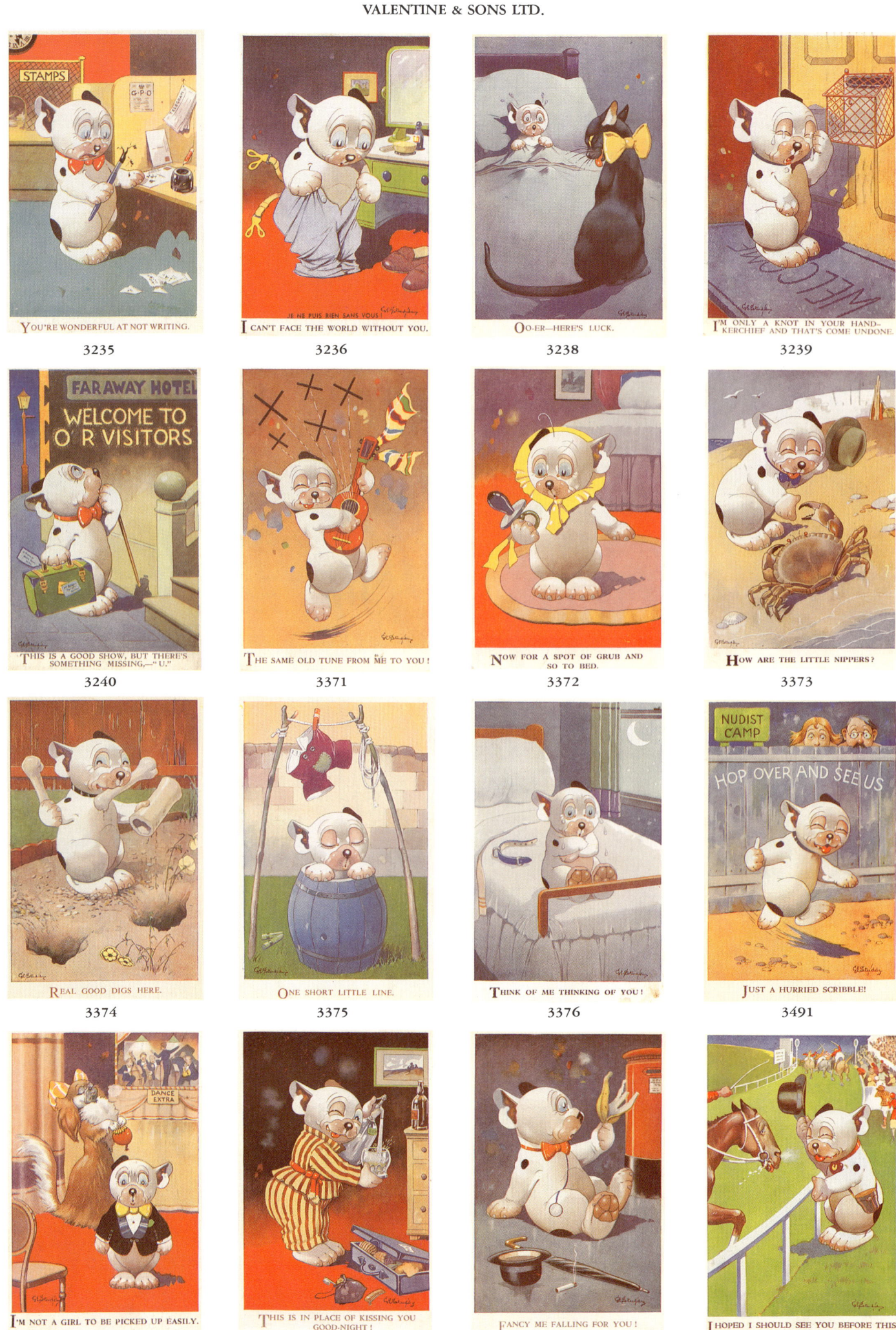

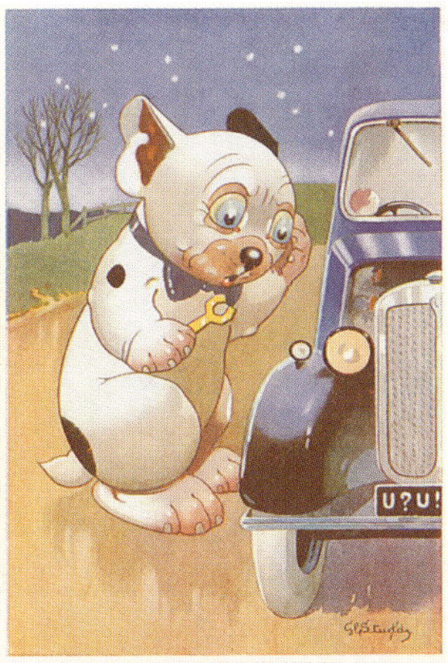
U?U!
I THOUGHT I UNDERSTOOD YOU, BUT I DON'T.

3496

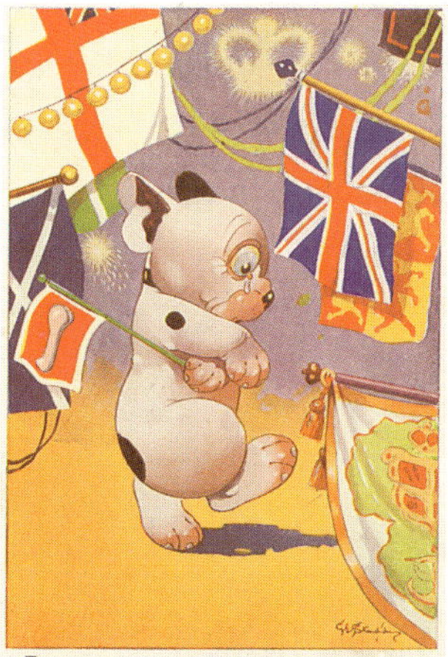
I CAN'T GO GAY WHILE YOU'RE AWAY.

3684

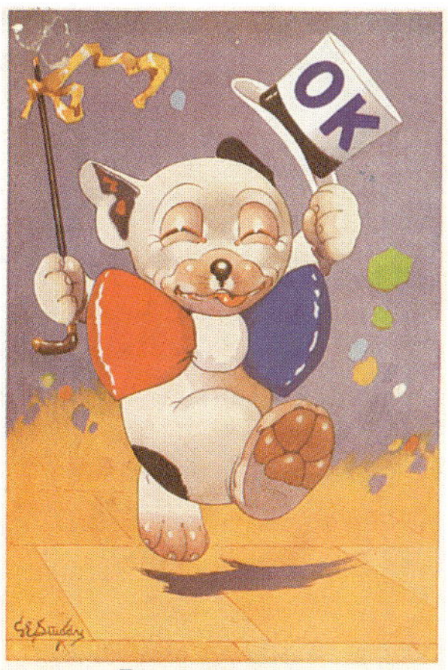
OK
IT'S O.K. WITH ME.

3685

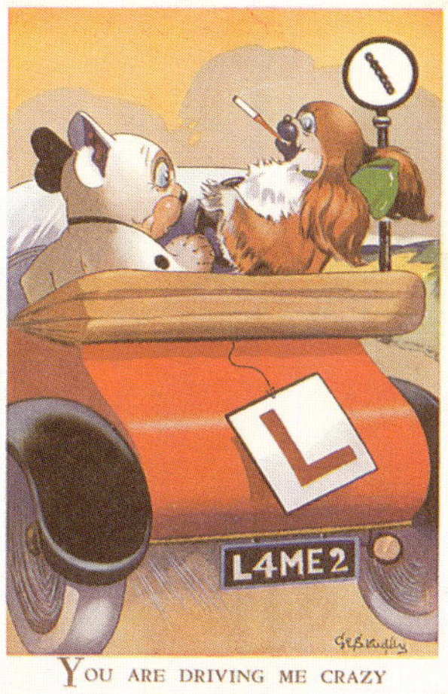
L
L4ME2
YOU ARE DRIVING ME CRAZY

3720

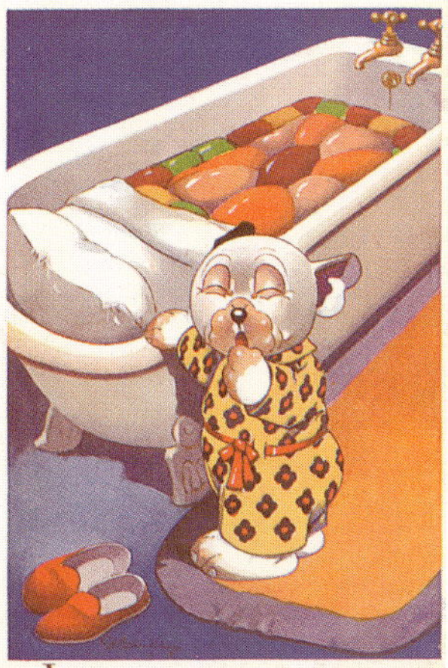
JUST MANAGED TO GET FIXED UP

3725

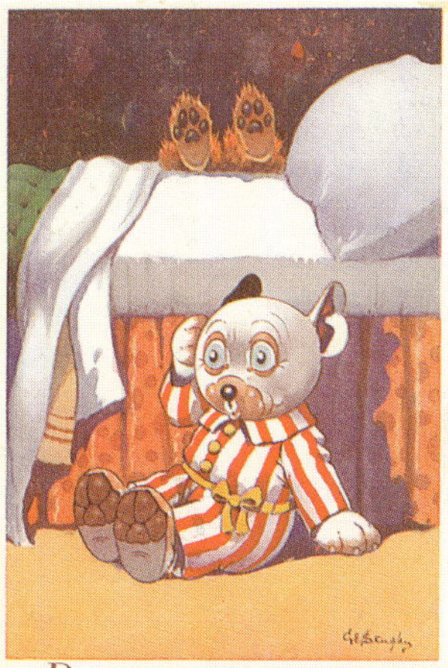
DON'T SAY WE'VE FALLEN OUT

3727

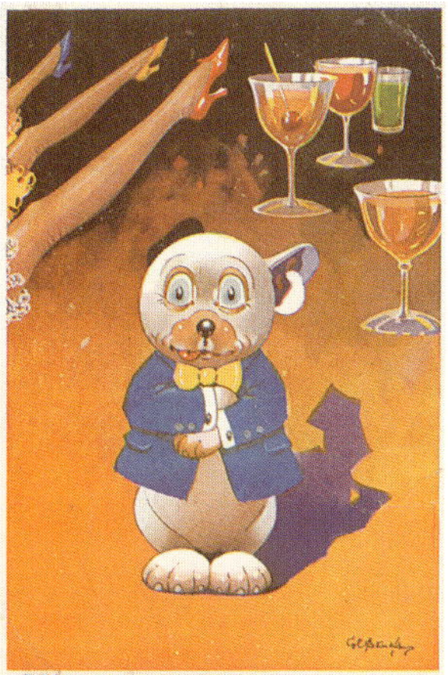
HOW CAN ONE BE GOOD IN A WORLD LIKE THIS!

3728

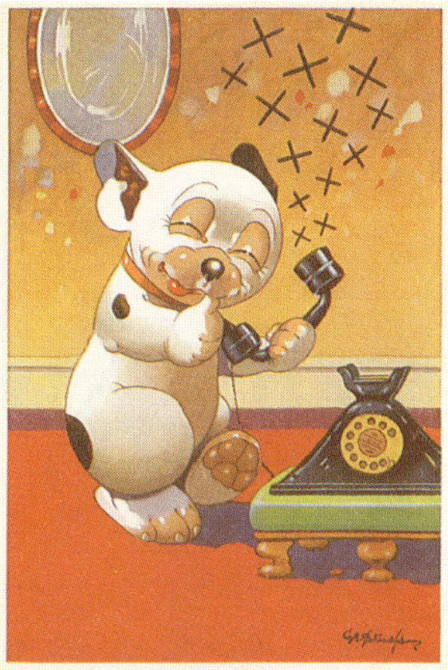
IT'S LOVELY TO HEAR FROM YOU.

3729

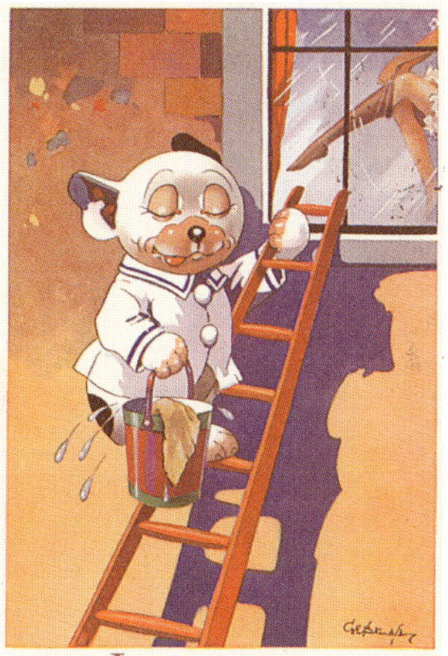
I'LL BE SEEING YOU

3730

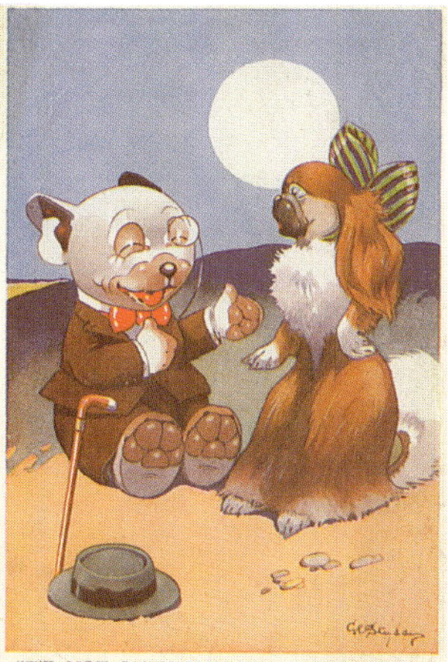
"I'D NOT ONLY SIGN THE PLEDGE, BUT I'D TURN NUDIST FOR YOU DEAR!"

3793

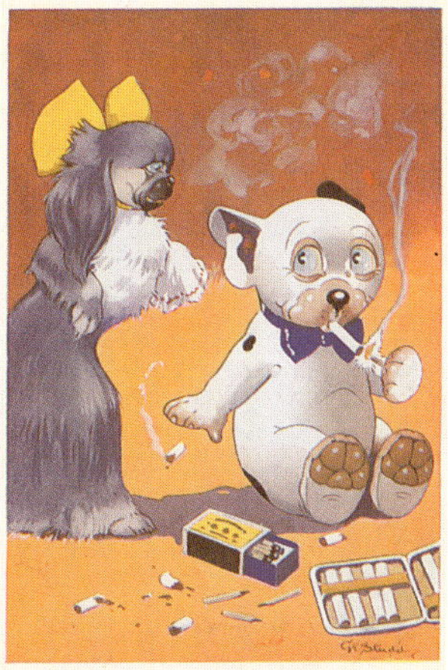
"ISN'T IT ABOUT TIME YOU WERE DECARBONIZED, DARLING?"

3794

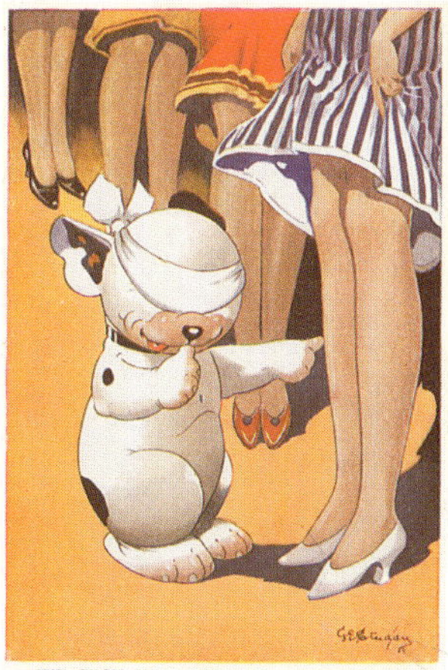
I'D PICK YOU OUT OF A THOUSAND EVERY TIME!

3795

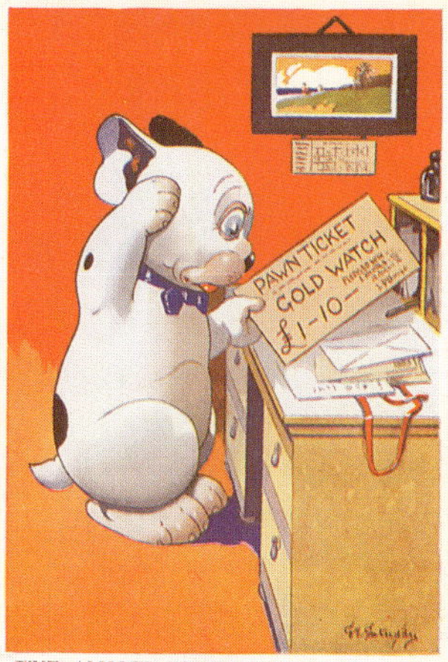
PAWN TICKET
GOLD WATCH
£1-10-
I'VE ALMOST FORGOTTEN WHAT YOU LOOK LIKE.

3796

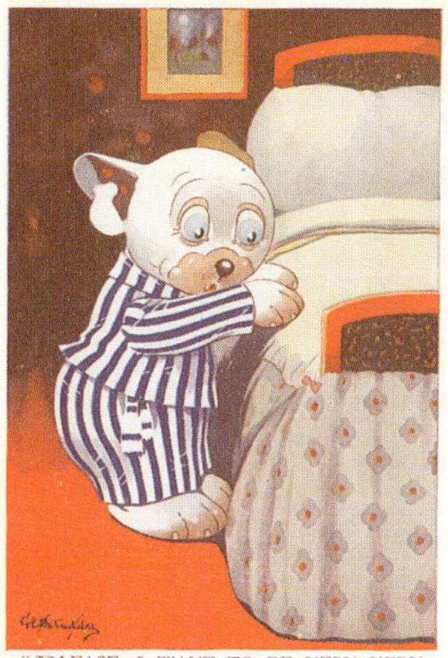
"PLEASE, I WANT TO BE VERY VERY GOOD, BUT NOT ALWAYS."

3797

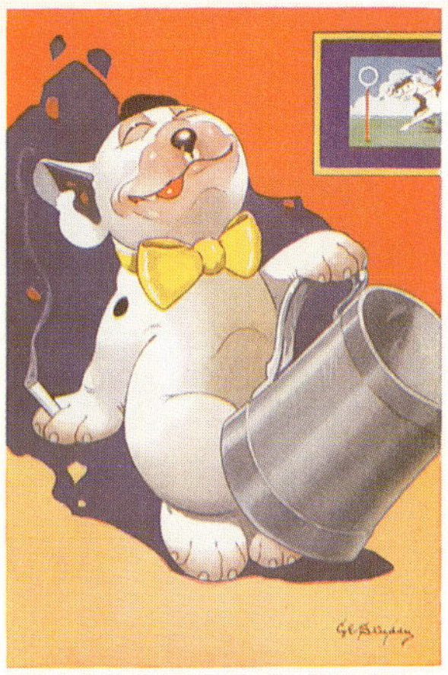
"I DIDN'T OUGHT TO TELL YOU, BUT YOU'VE GONE BANG TO MY HEAD!"

3798

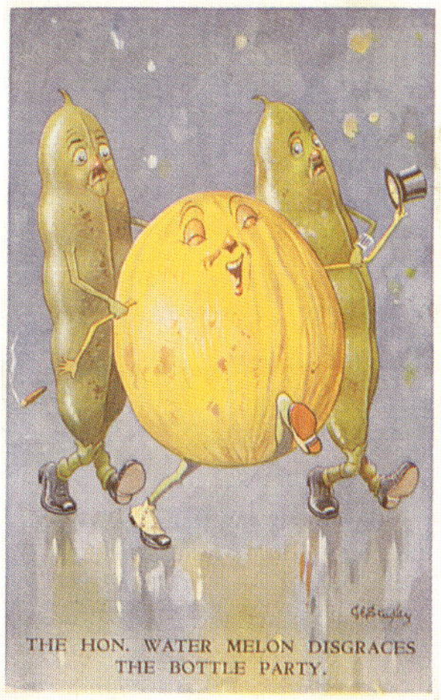
THE HON. WATER MELON DISGRACES THE BOTTLE PARTY.

3817

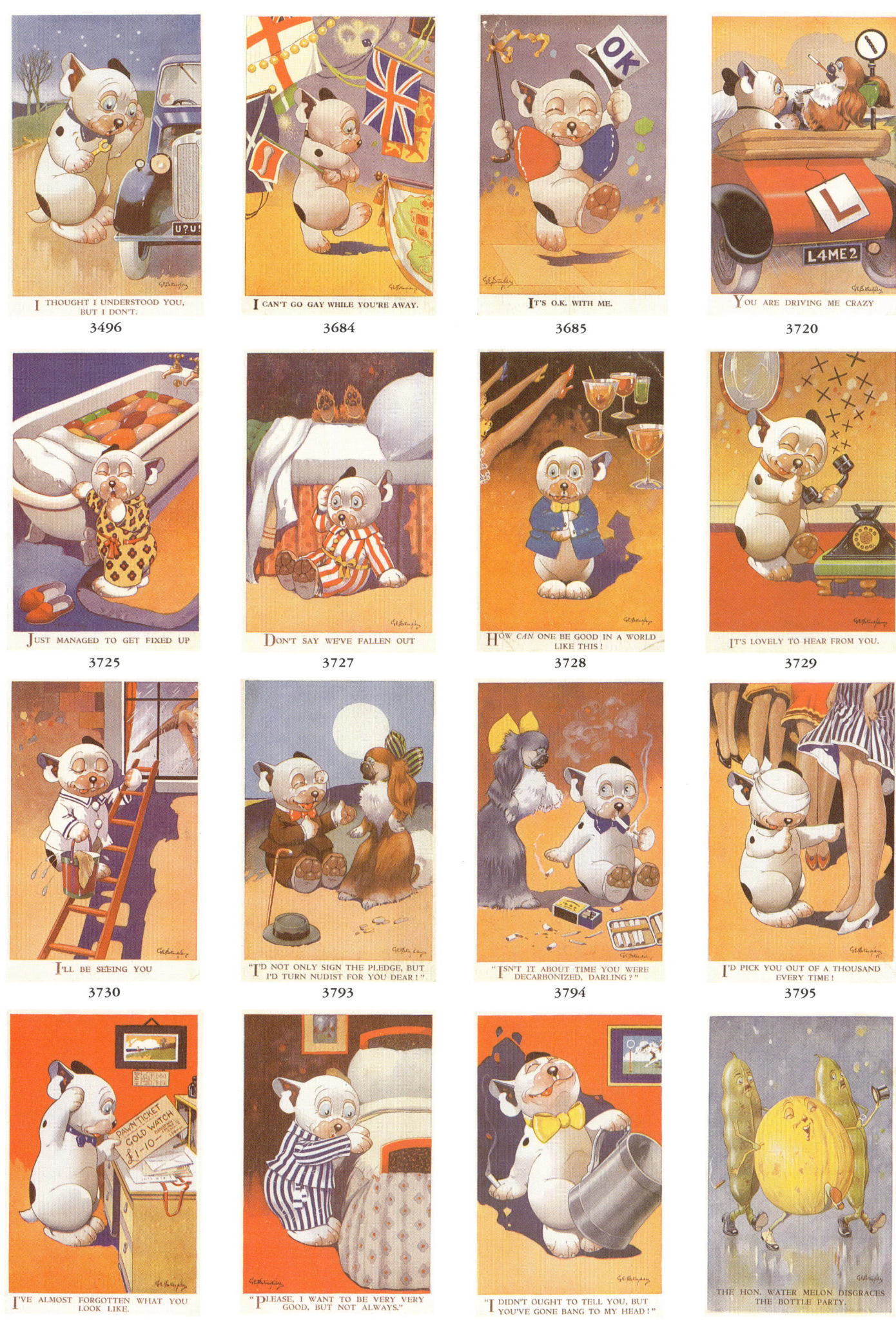

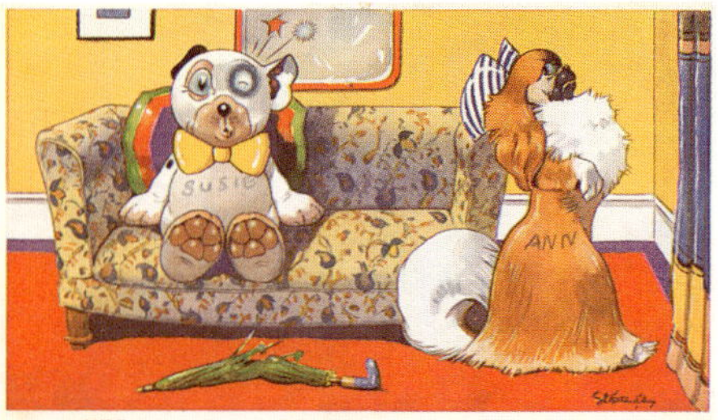
SUSIE
ANN
What's a black eye to a bleeding heart!

3119

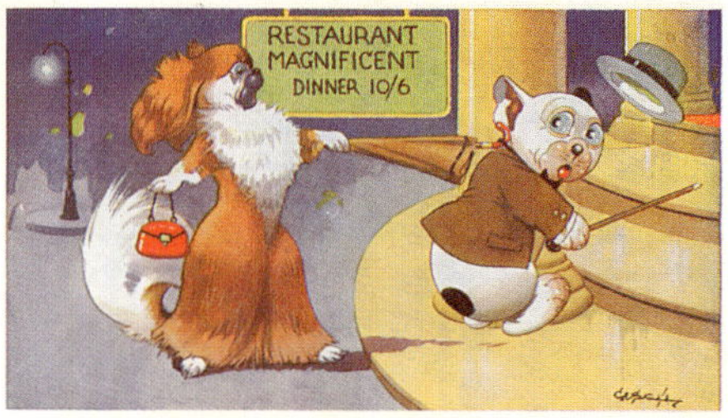
RESTAURANT
MAGNIFICENT
DINNER 10/6
We could be quite happy on poached eggs.

3120

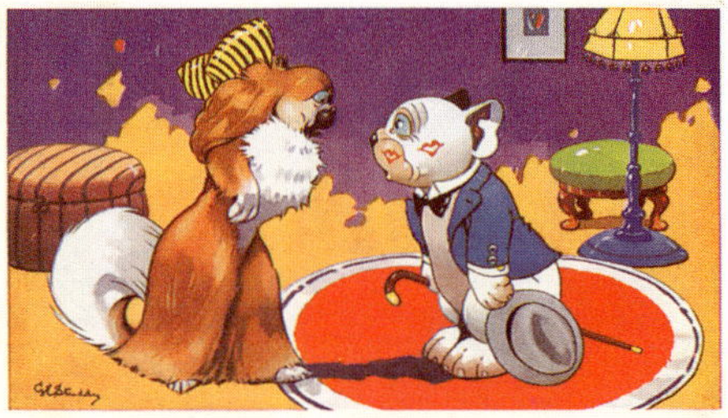
Working late at the office again?

3121

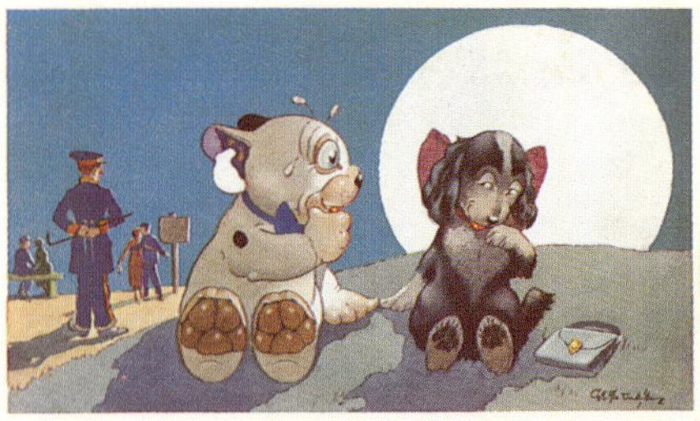
I'm much slicker when there ain't a moon.

3237

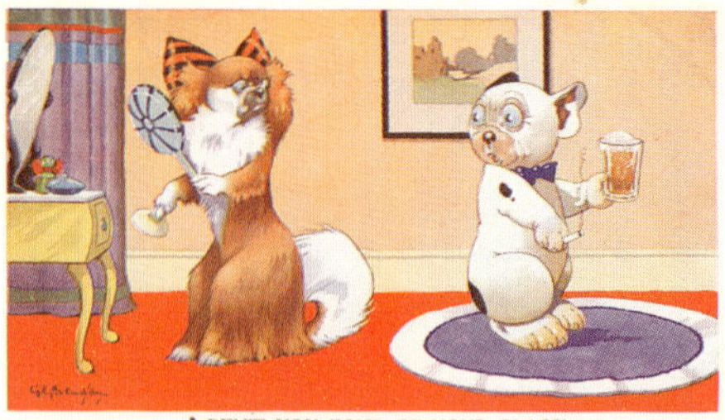
Aren't you fond of your glass!

3497

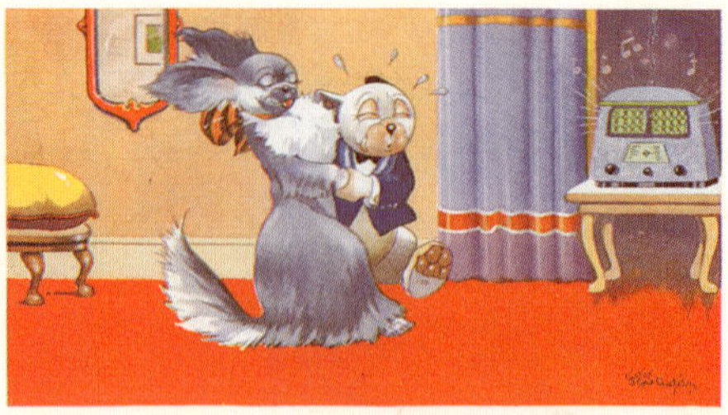
I'm crazy about dancing with you.

3498

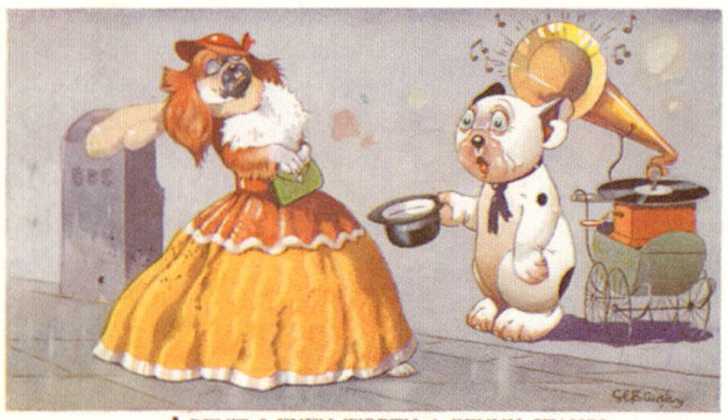
Aren't I even worth a penny stamp?

3499

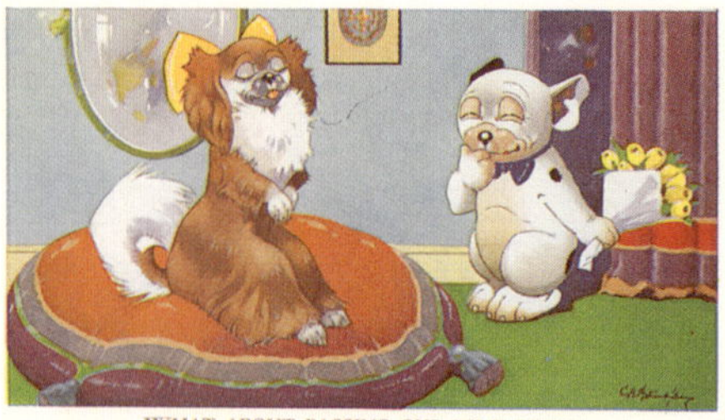
What about passing our love test?

3500

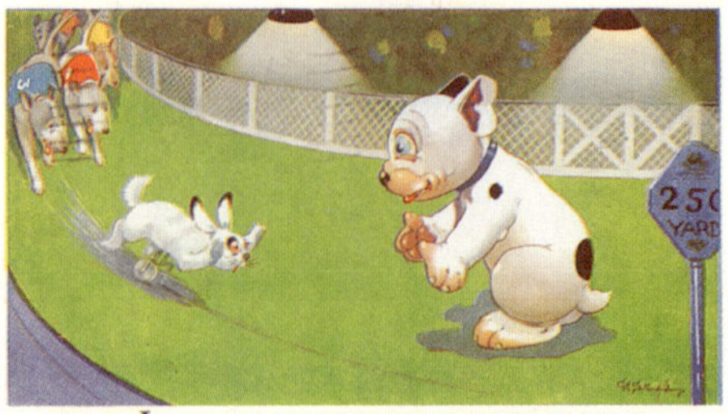
If anyone gets you, it's going to be me!

3501

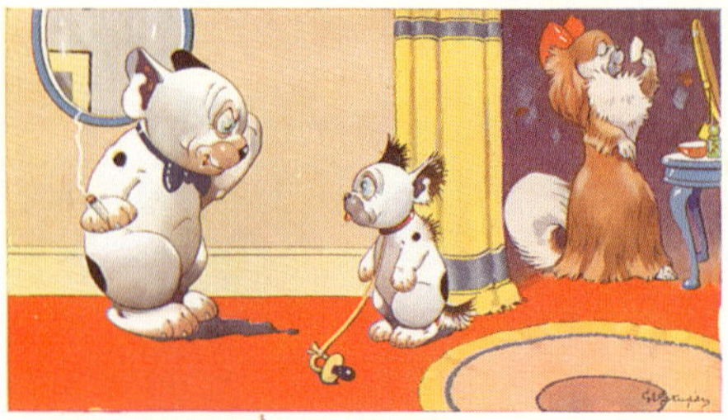
Marriage is an awful risk.

3502

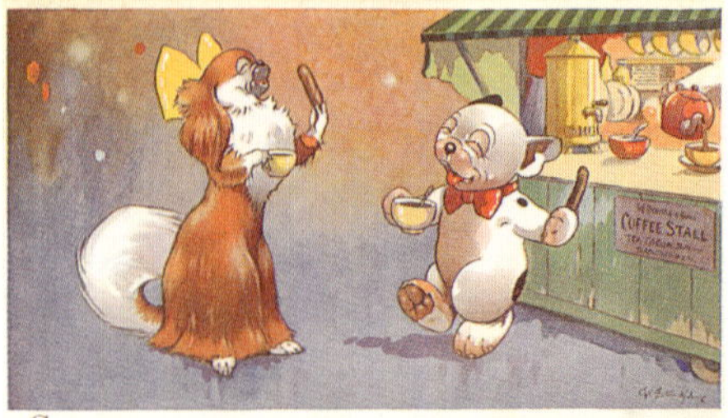
COFFEE STALL
Say kid, think of the poor blighters in the Ritz!

3719

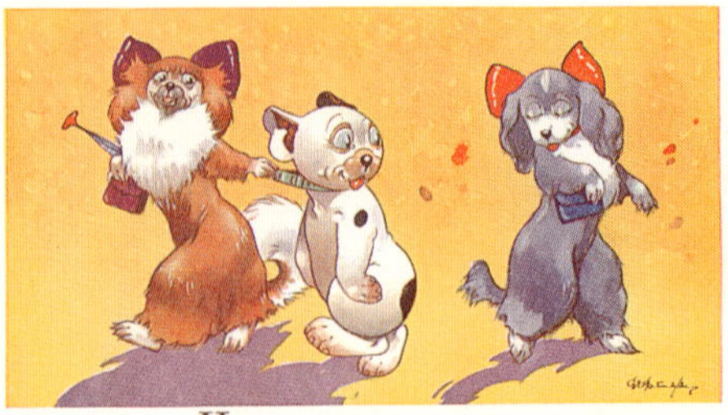
How to hold your man
QUEL DOMMAGE DE NE PAS ÊTRE SEUL !

3721

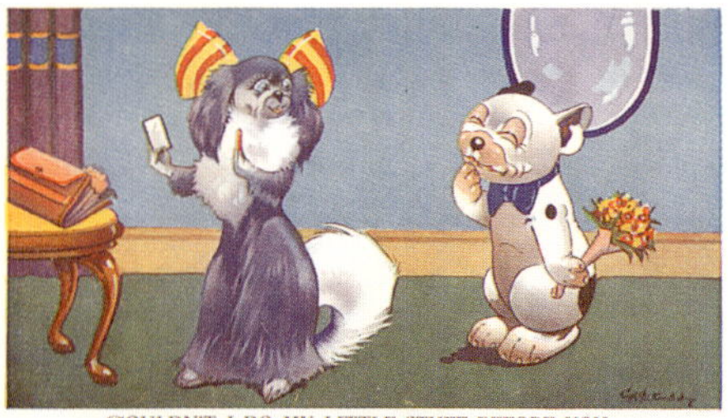
Couldn't I do my little stuff before you put on your make-up, dear?

3722

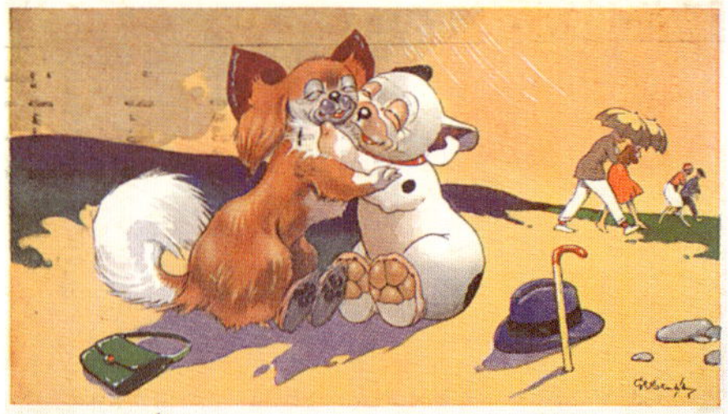
Aren't we a couple of nit-wits?

3723

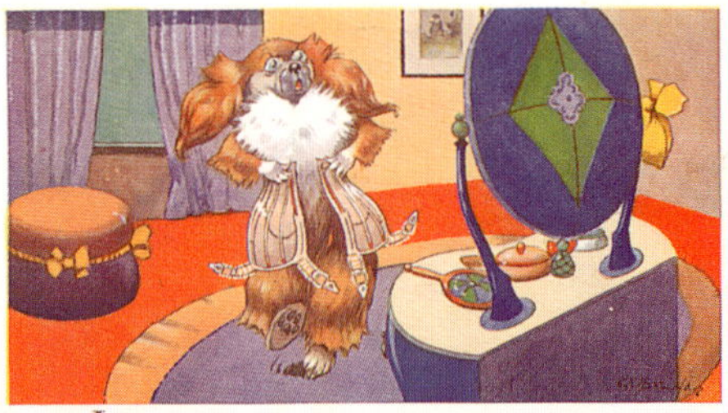
It seems such a long time since we met

3724

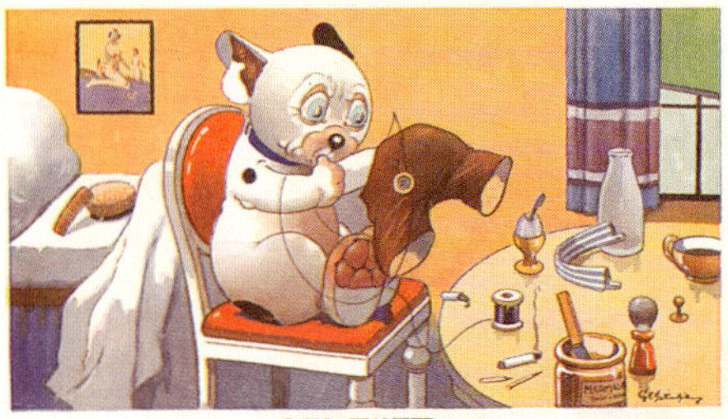
Girl wanted

3726

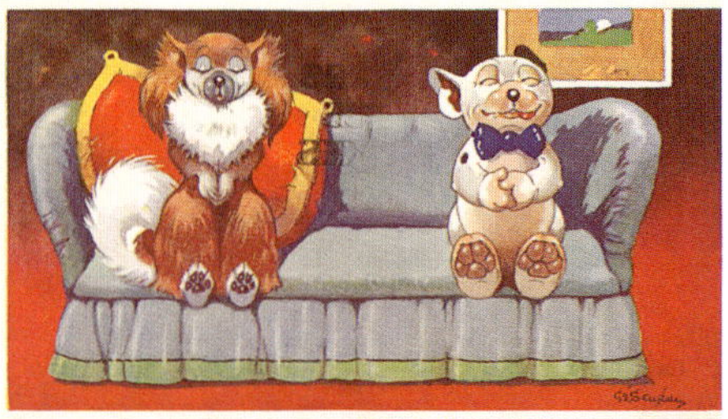
Can't we think of anything nice to do?

3864

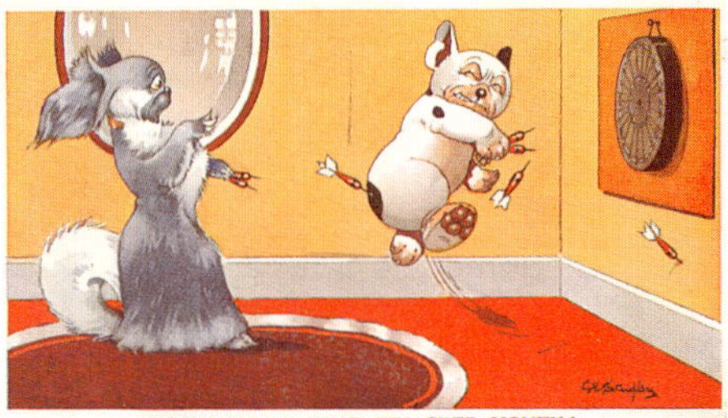
You've got Cupid whacked honey!

3865

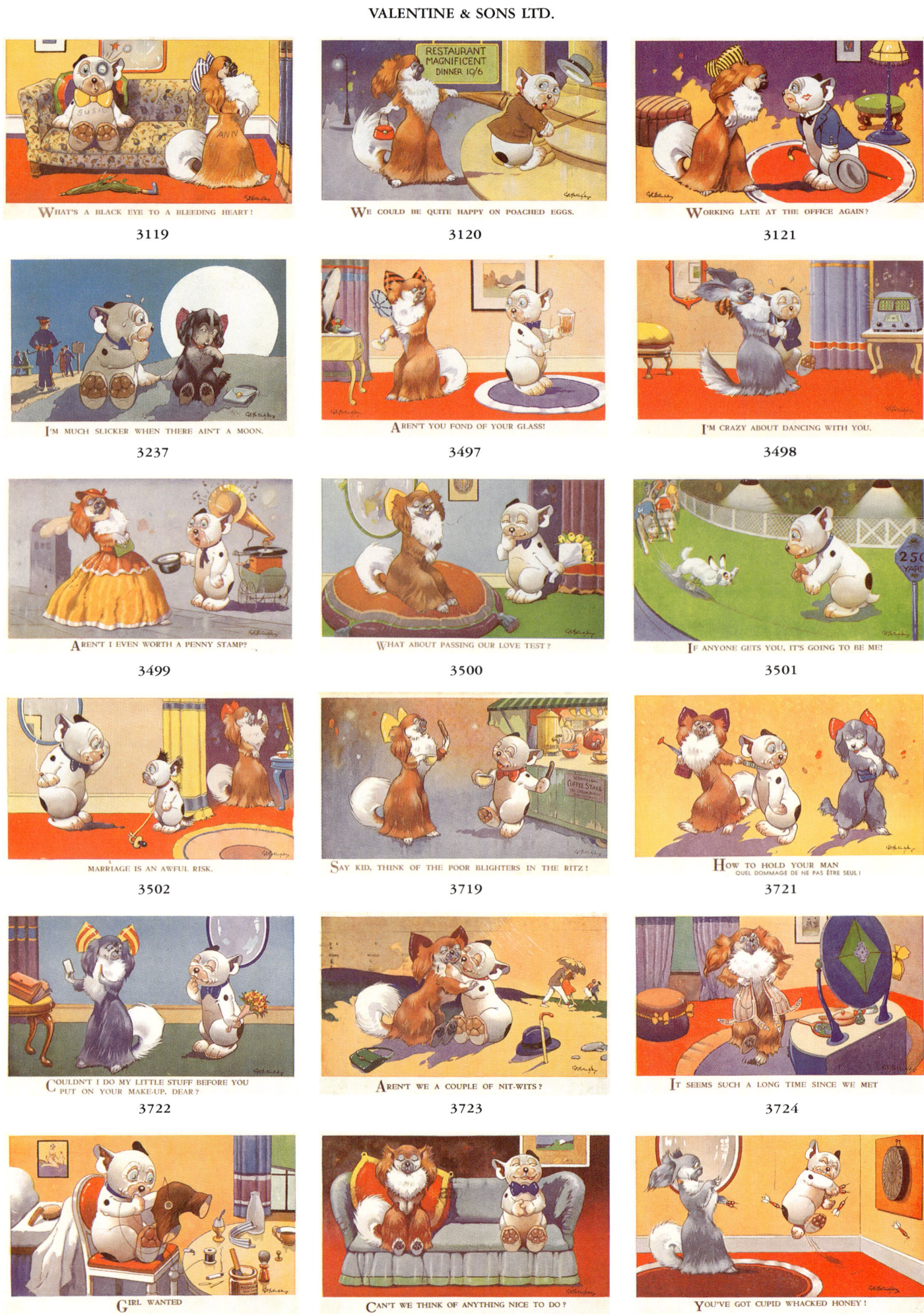

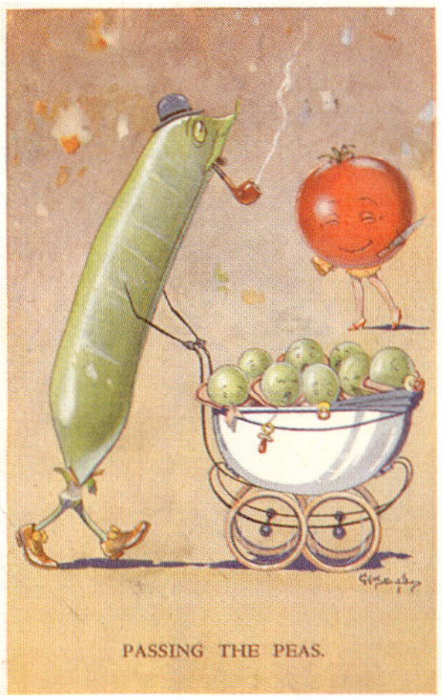
PASSING THE PEAS.

3818

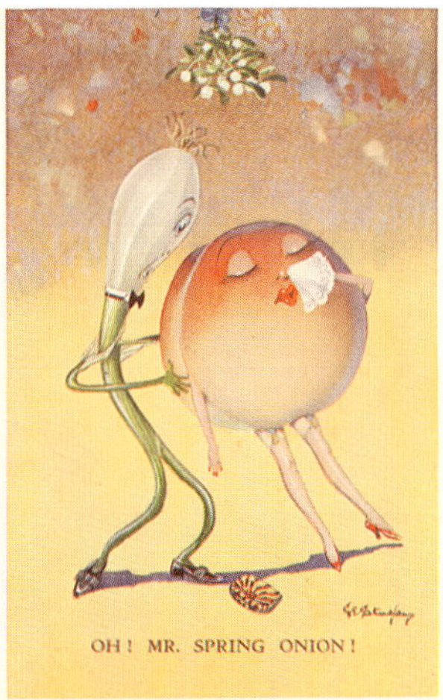
OH ! MR. SPRING ONION !

3819

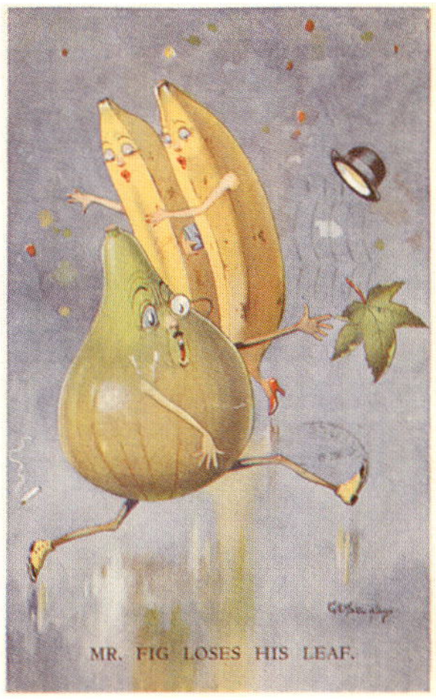
MR. FIG LOSES HIS LEAF.

3820

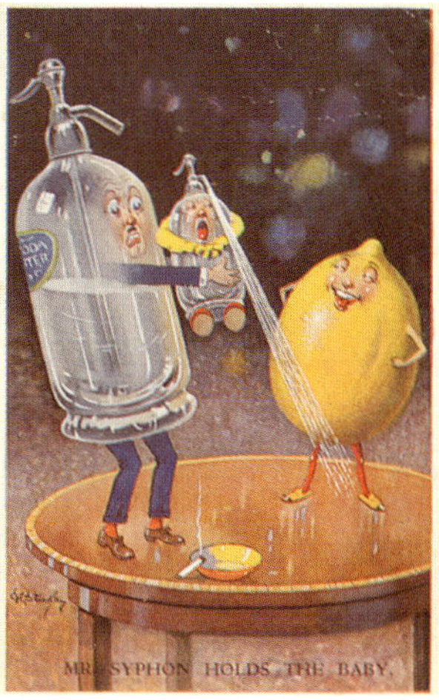
MR. SYPHON HOLDS THE BABY.

3821

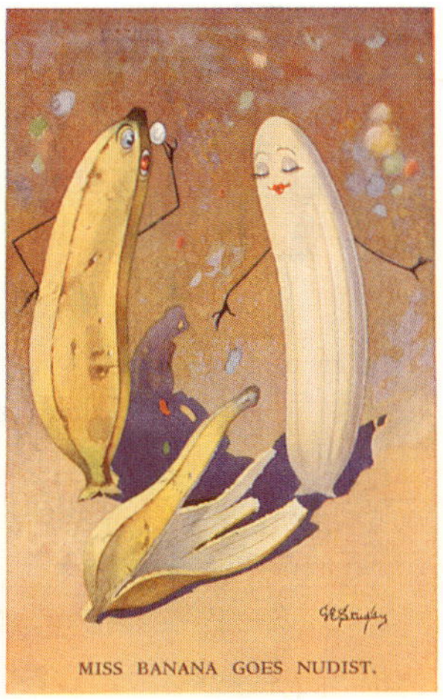
MISS BANANA GOES NUDIST.

3822

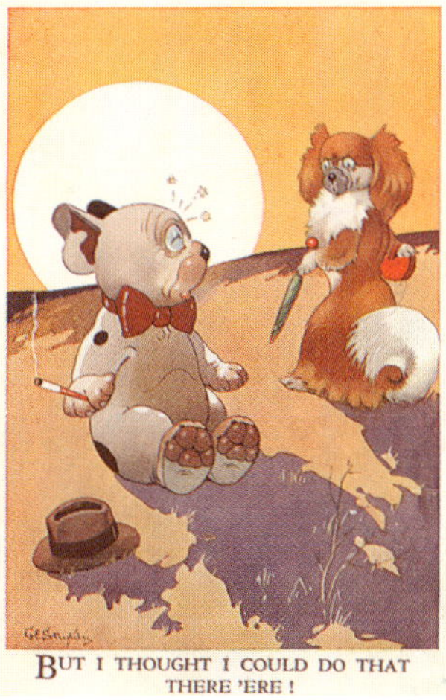
BUT I THOUGHT I COULD DO THAT THERE 'ERE !

3868

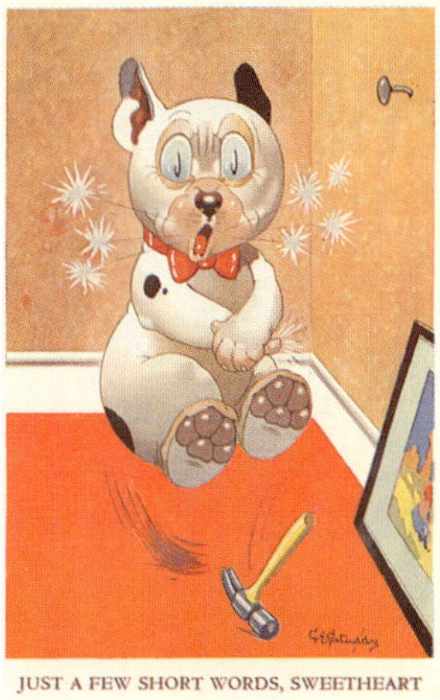
JUST A FEW SHORT WORDS, SWEETHEART

3870

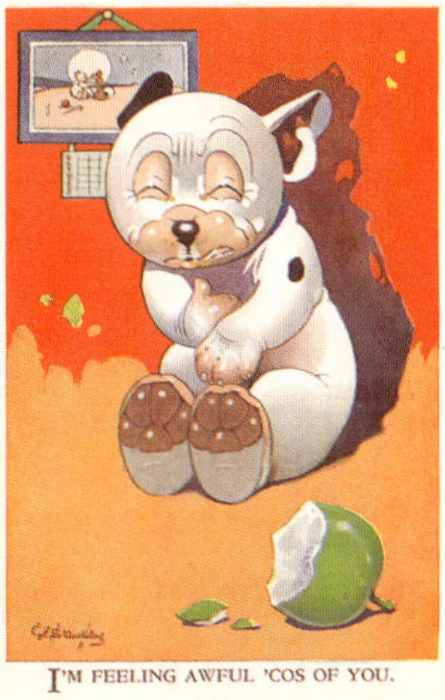
I'M FEELING AWFUL 'COS OF YOU.

3871

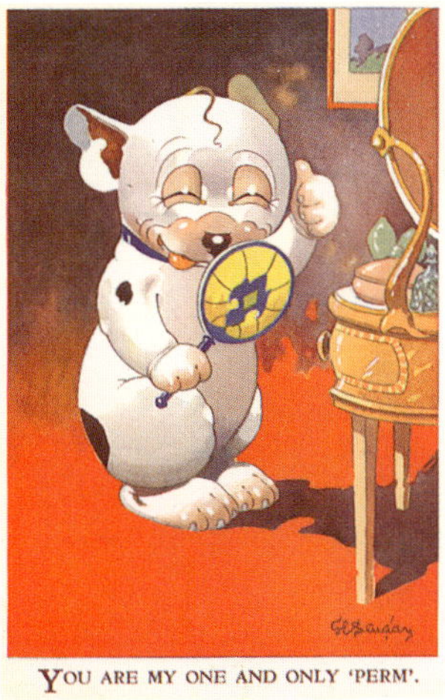
YOU ARE MY ONE AND ONLY 'PERM'.

3872

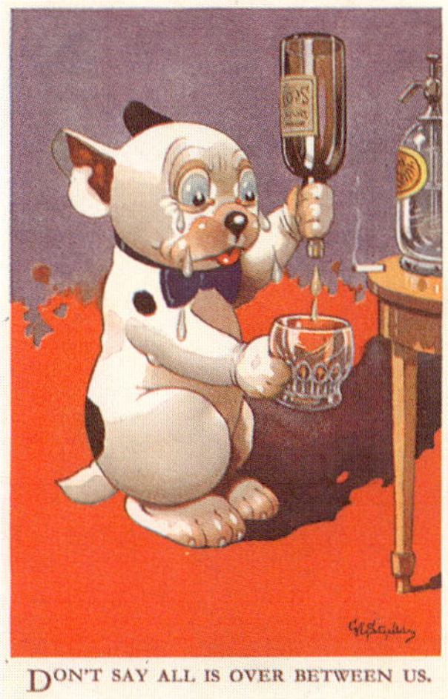
DON'T SAY ALL IS OVER BETWEEN US.

3874

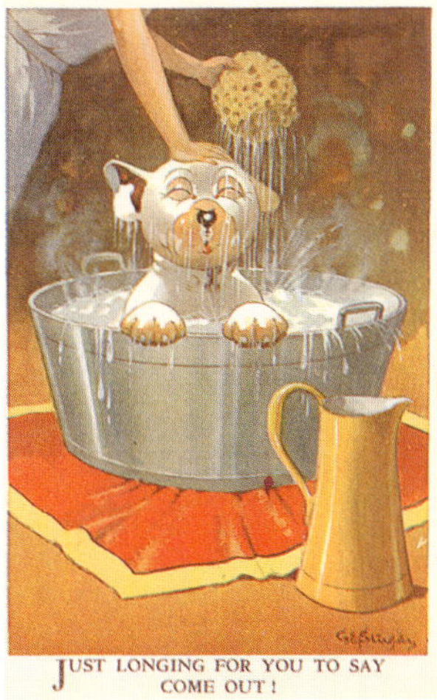
JUST LONGING FOR YOU TO SAY COME OUT !

3875

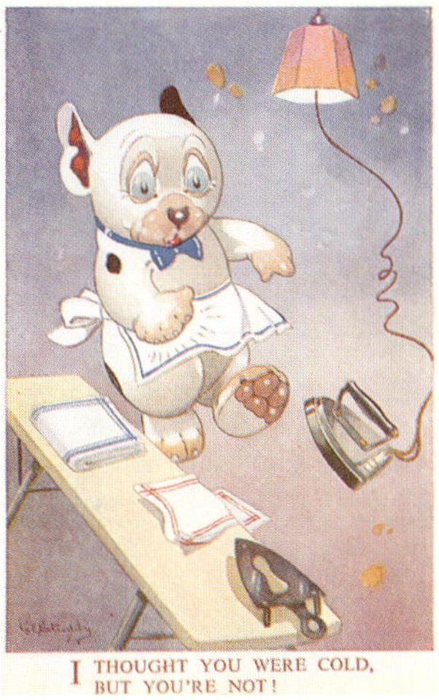
I THOUGHT YOU WERE COLD, BUT YOU'RE NOT !

4112

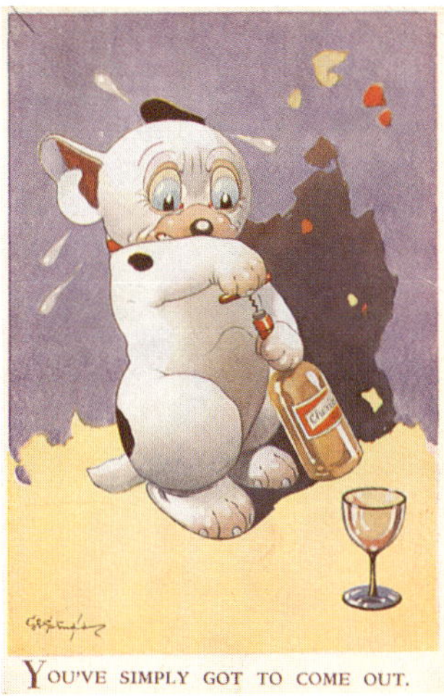
YOU'VE SIMPLY GOT TO COME OUT.

4113

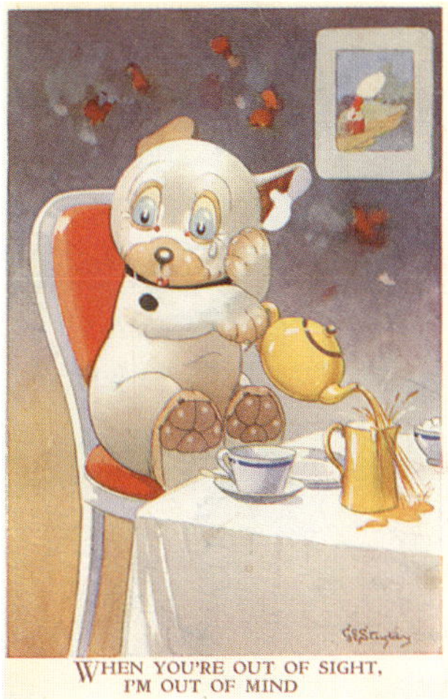
WHEN YOU'RE OUT OF SIGHT, I'M OUT OF MIND

4114

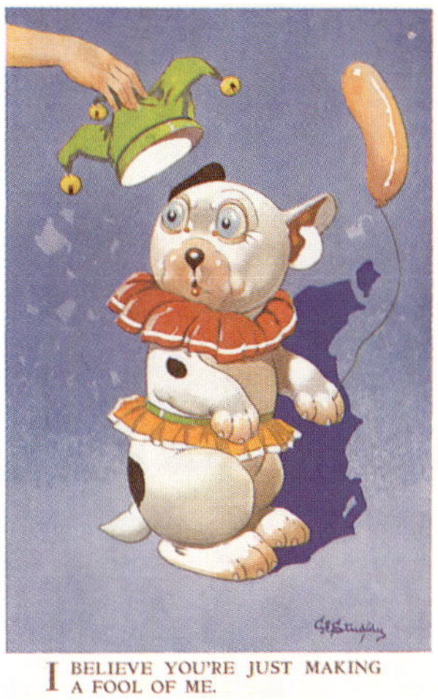
I BELIEVE YOU'RE JUST MAKING A FOOL OF ME.

4115

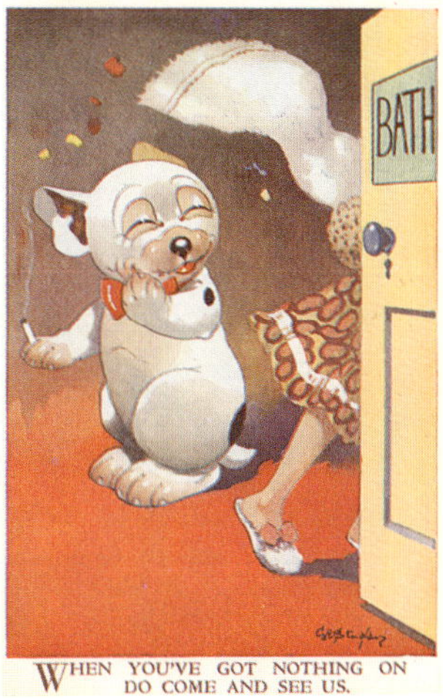
BATH
WHEN YOU'VE GOT NOTHING ON DO COME AND SEE US.

4117

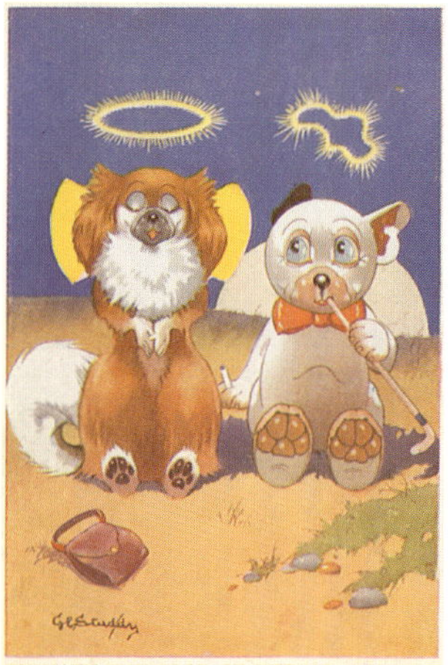

WHAT'S THE GOOD OF SITTING AROUND GROWING HALOES?

4118

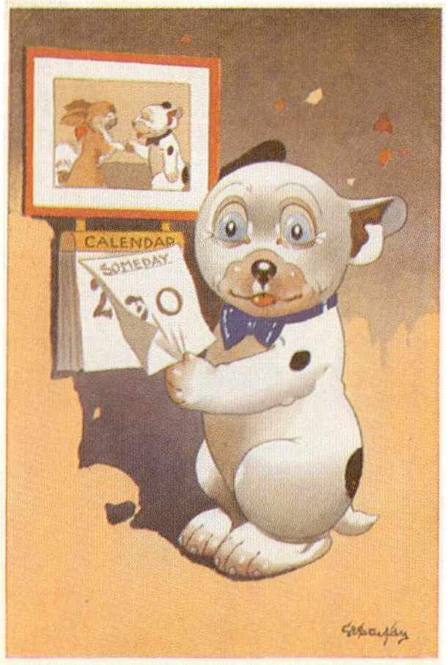
CALENDAR
SOMEDAY

HOW MANY MORE BEFORE WE MEET?

4119

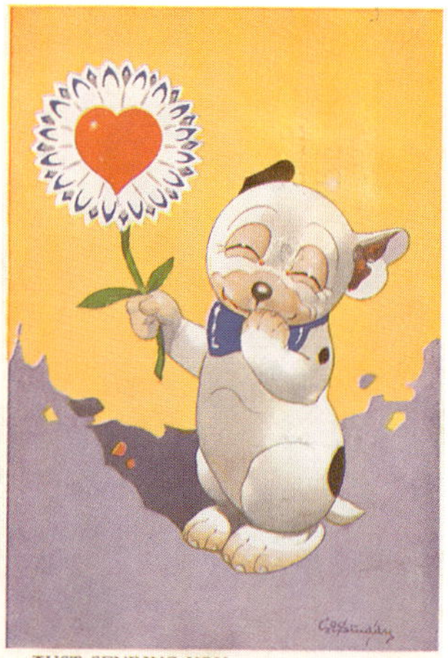

JUST SENDING YOU MY LITTLE EVERLASTING FLOWER.

4121

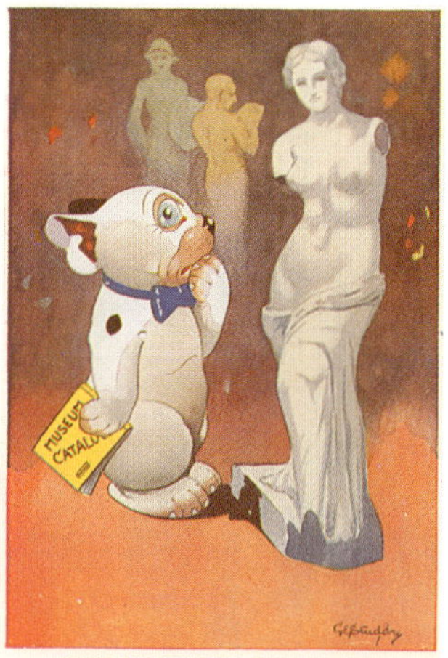

GIVE ME MY GIRL EVERY TIME!

4122

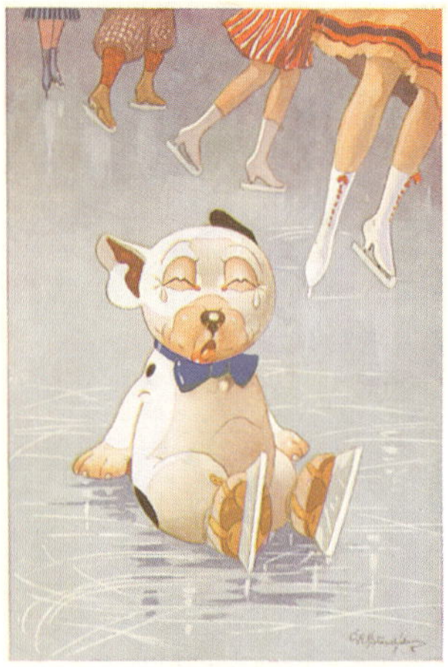

NOBODY SEEMS TO CARE WHAT HAPPENS TO ME!,

4123

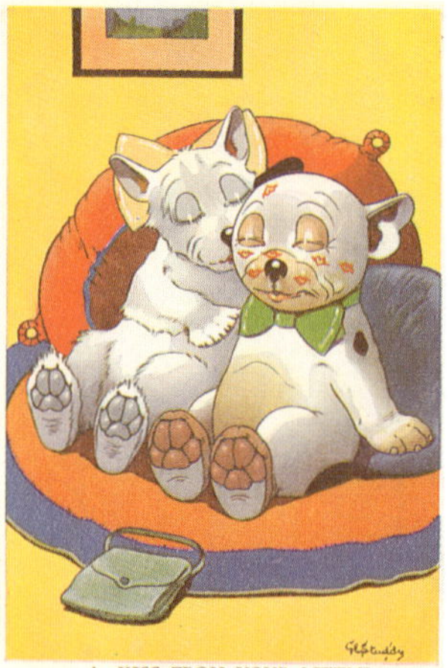

A KISS FROM YOUR LITTLE SNOW WHITE.

4245

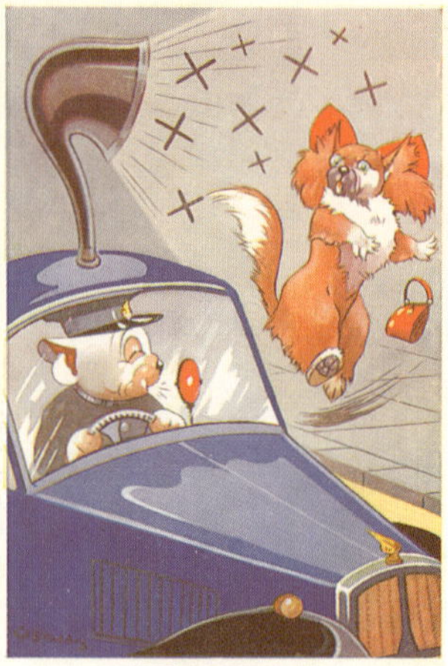

JUST A LOVING P.C.

4246

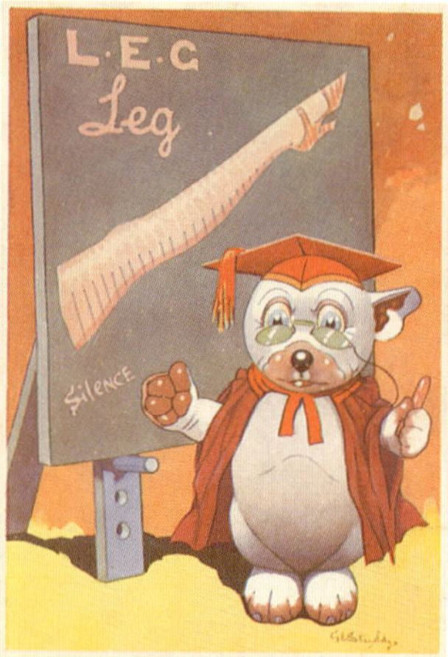
L.E.G
Leg
Silence

NOW CAN ANY BOY EXPLAIN THE WORD "APPEAL"?

4247

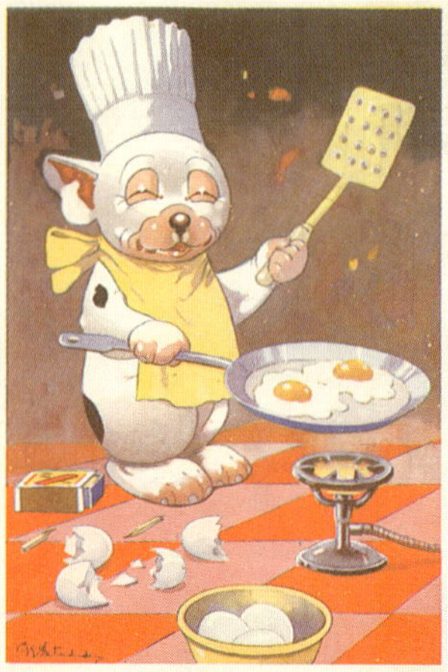

WHY NOT BLOW IN FOR A BLOW OUT?

4248

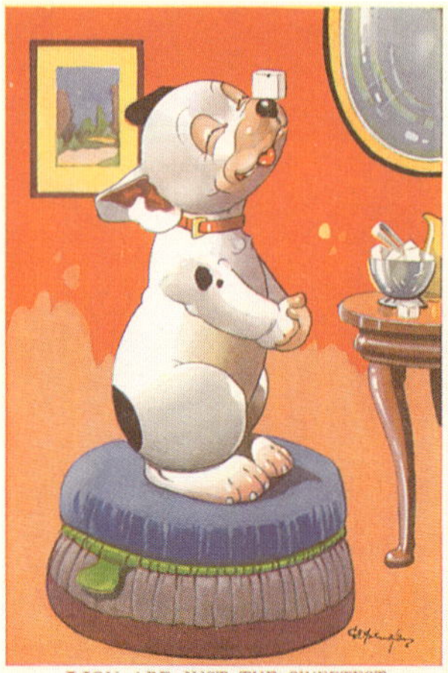

YOU ARE JUST THE SWEETEST THING IN THE WORLD!

4250

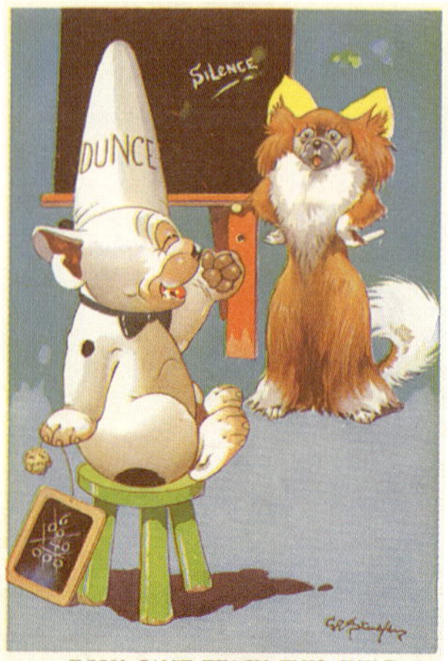
SILENCE
DUNCE

YOU CAN'T TEACH THIS CHILD ANYTHING, DEARIE!

4306

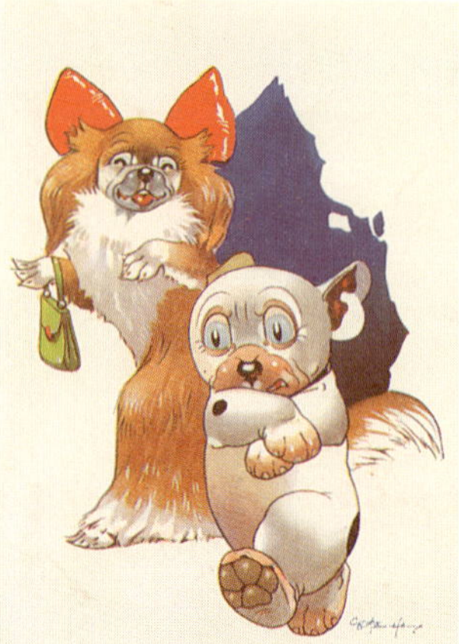

CHEER UP GRUMPY, LET'S BE HAPPY!

4308

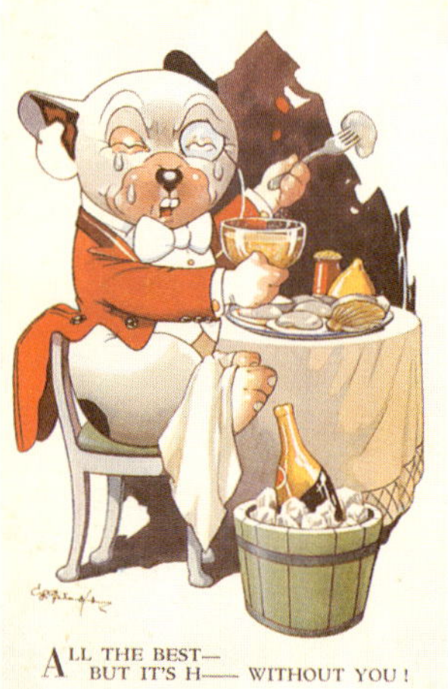

ALL THE BEST— BUT IT'S H—— WITHOUT YOU!

4309

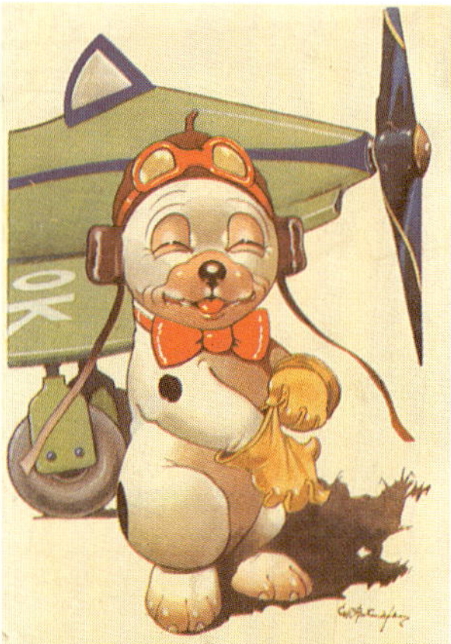
OK

WHAT ABOUT A BEER AT THE POLE, DUCKY?

4310

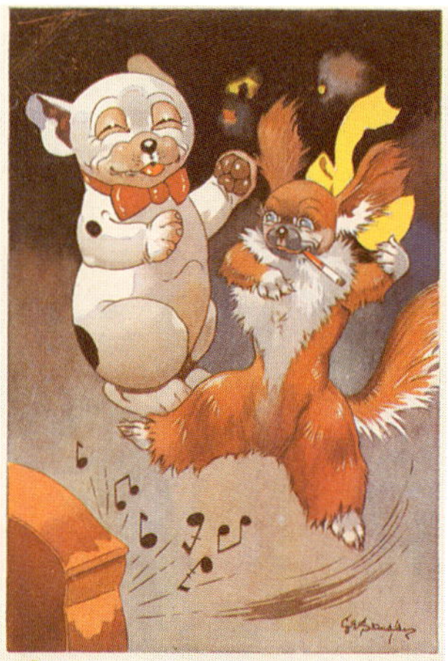

GIVE ME A GIRL WITH A SPOT OF PEP!

4312

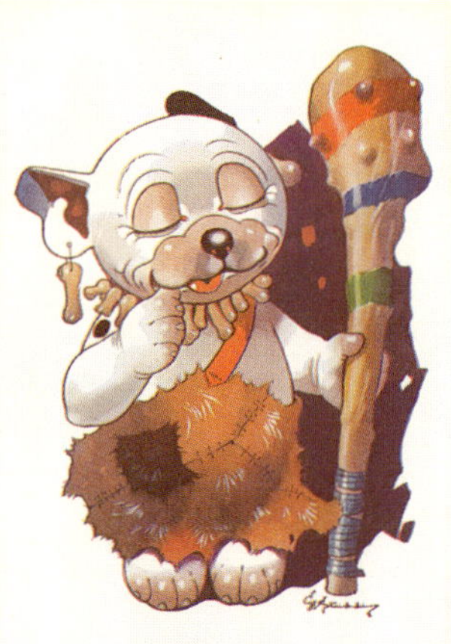

YOU ARE MY ONE AND ONLY LITTLE CAVE MAN!

4314

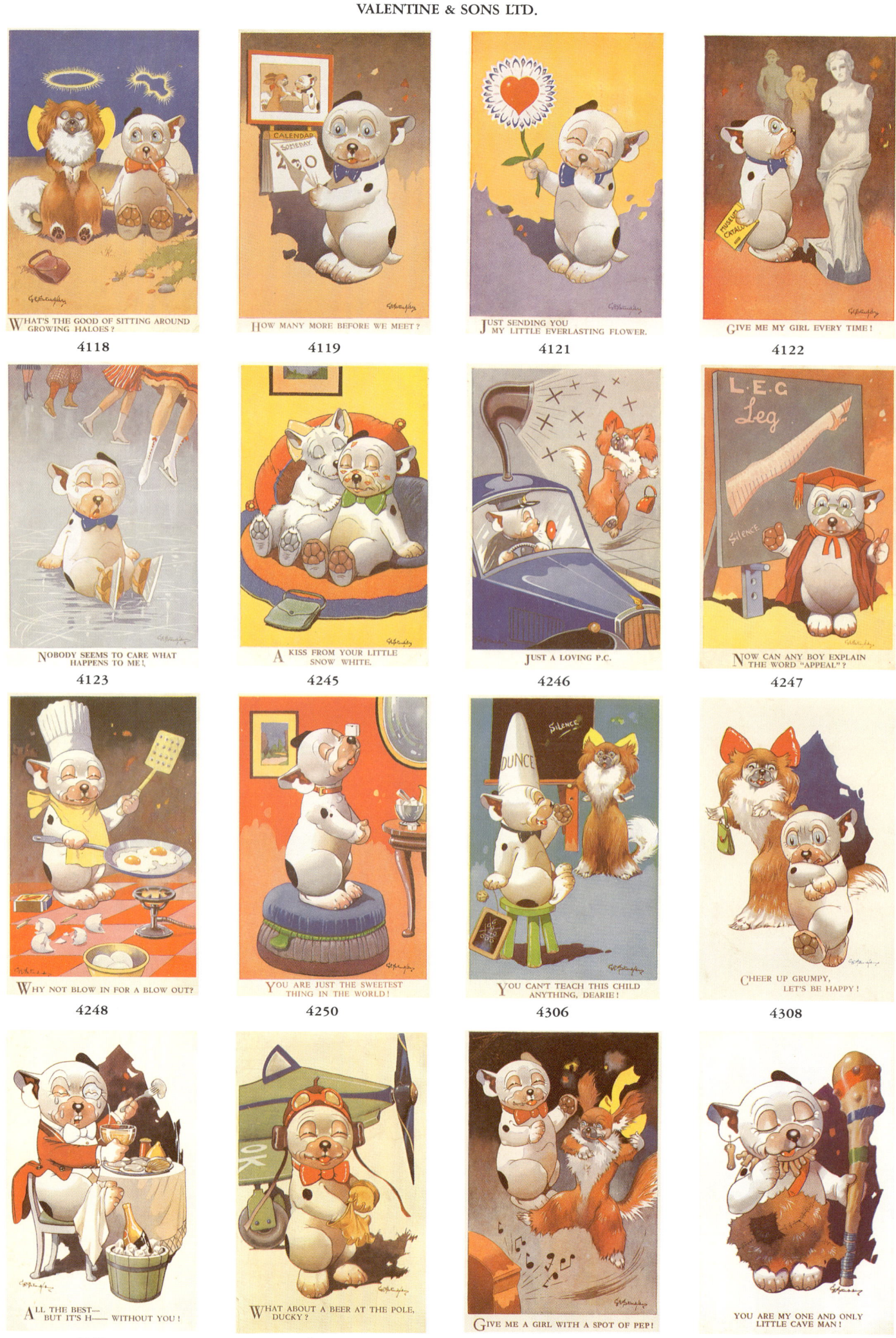

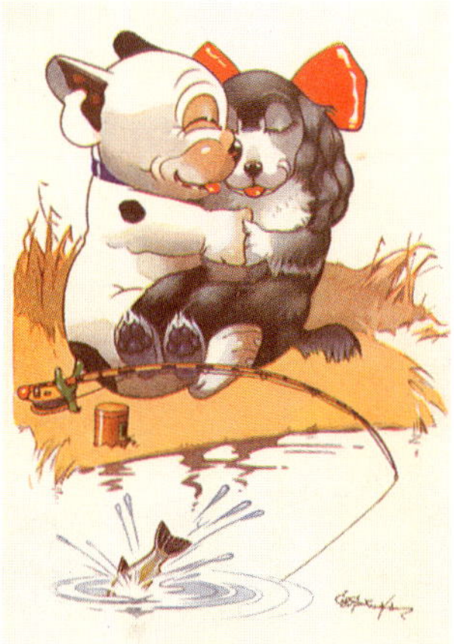

WHAT ABOUT THAT LINE?

4315

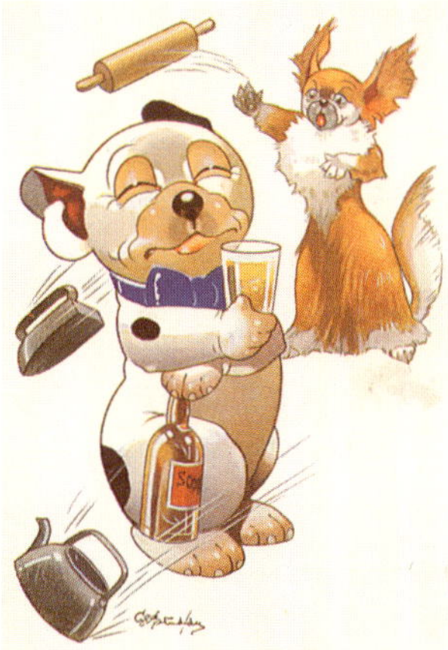

JUST KEEP ON KEEPING PLUCKY!

4316

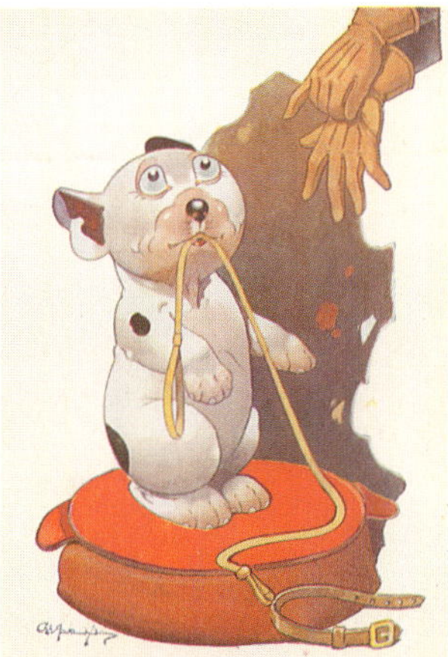

"CAN'T WE GO OUT TOGETHER?"

4594

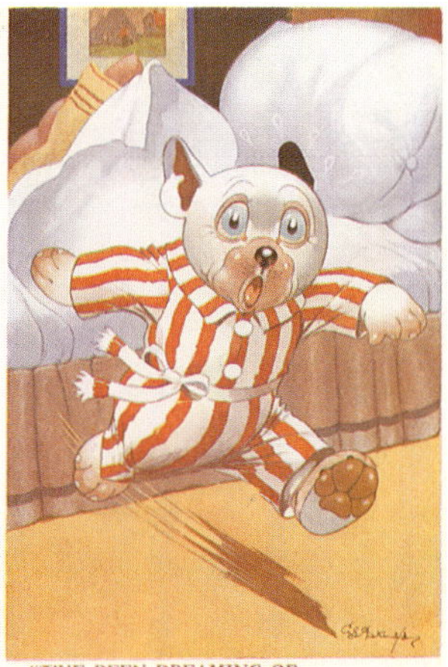

"I'VE BEEN DREAMING OF WEDDING BELLS DARLING!"

4595

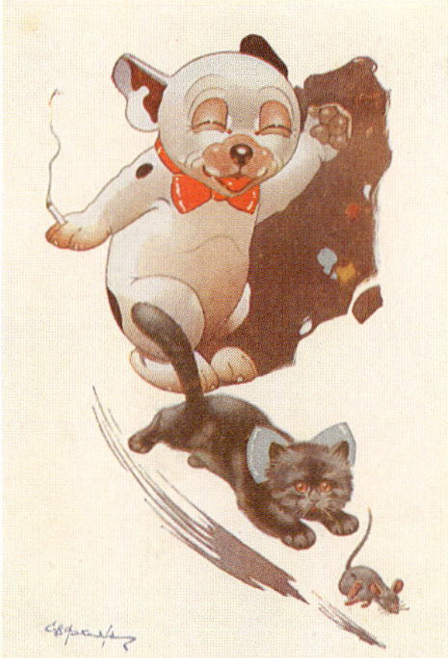

"WISHING YOU A REAL RUN OF LUCK!"

4598

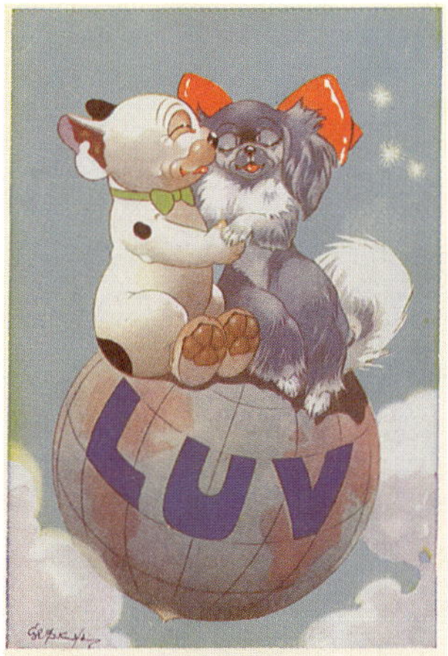
LUV

"WE LIVE IN A WORLD OF OUR OWN, BABY"

4599

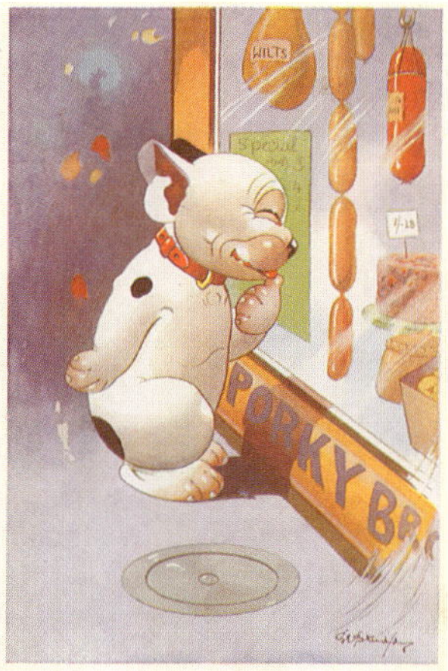
PORKY BR

"I'D LOVE TO BE ALONE WITH YOU!"

4601

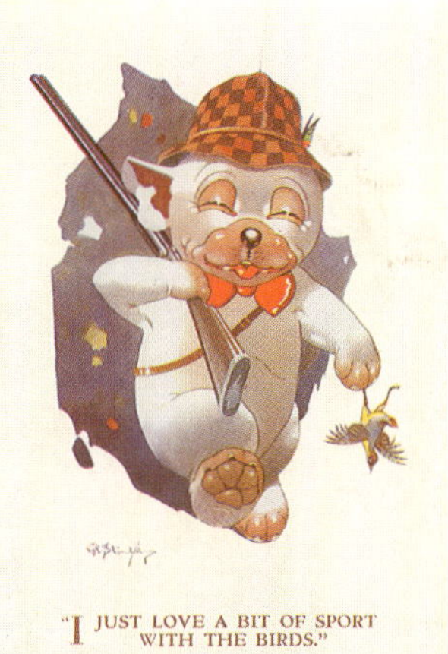

"I JUST LOVE A BIT OF SPORT WITH THE BIRDS."

4602

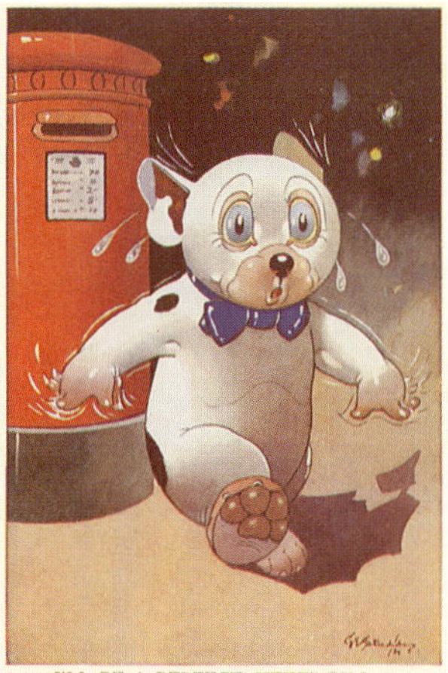

I'LL BE A PERFECT JITTER-BUG TILL I HEAR YOU'RE O.K.

4756

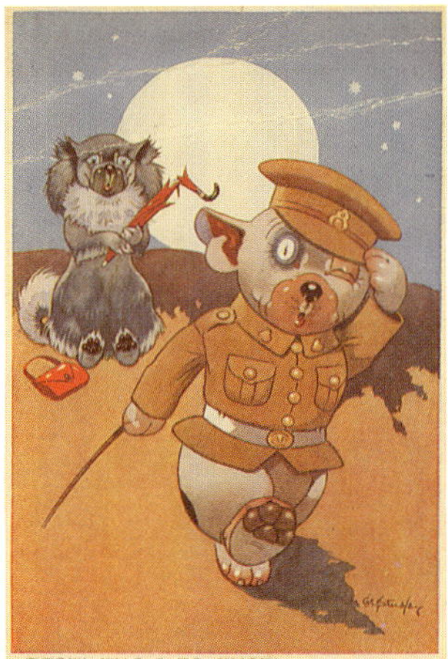

HOW WAS I TO KNOW THE GIRL WAS A CONCHIE?

4757

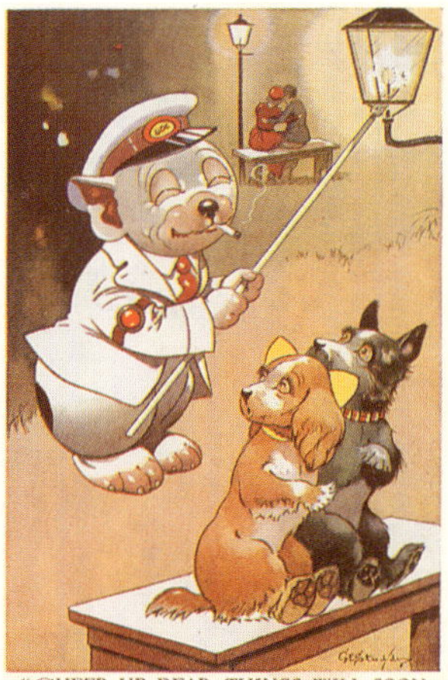

"CHEER UP DEAR, THINGS WILL SOON BE BRIGHTER ALL ROUND!"

4758

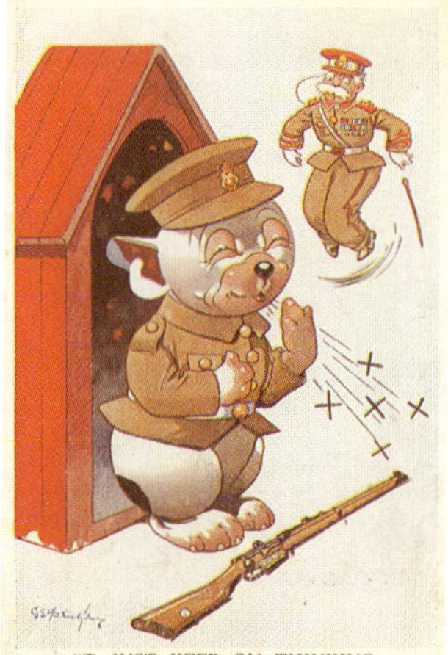

"I JUST KEEP ON THINKING OF ME GAL!"

4759

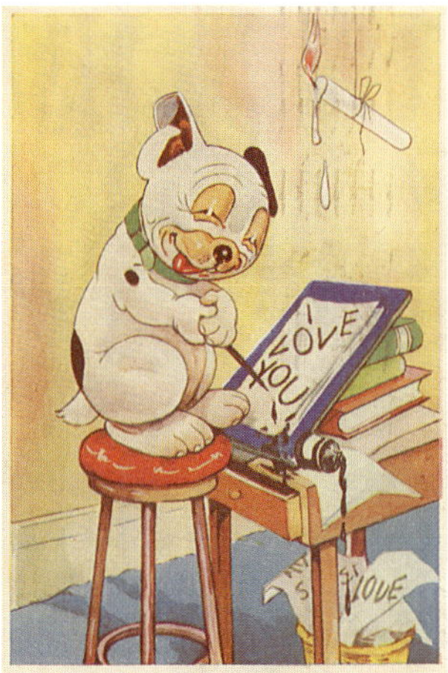
I LOVE YOU

YOU'RE A BIT OF A 'NIB' WITH THE PEN.

*5141

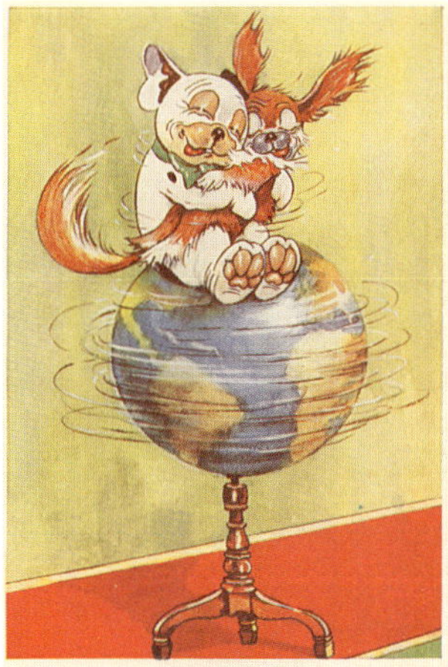

ON TOP OF THE WORLD—BUT A BIT DIZZY.

*5142

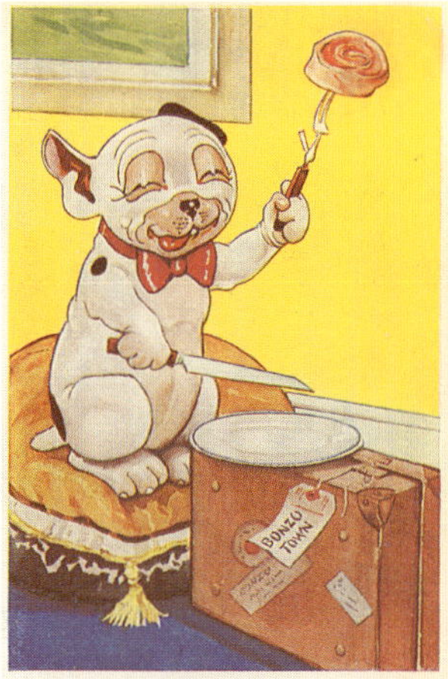

I'VE FOUND A LOVELY JOINT FOR THE WEEK.

*5143

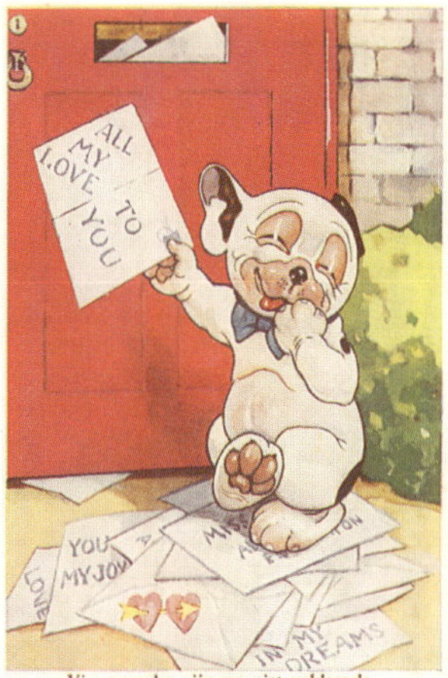
ALL MY LOVE TO YOU

Vier woorden zijn me niet voldoende,
ik dacht er véél toen ik je zoende.

*5144

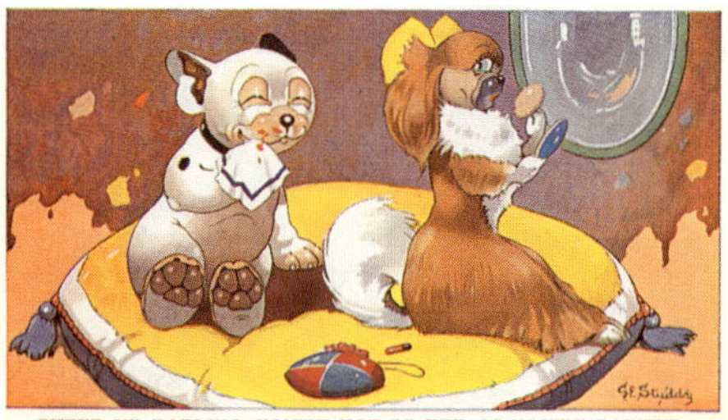
CHEER UP DARLING, YOU'RE NOT SO RED AS YOU'RE PAINTED.

3866

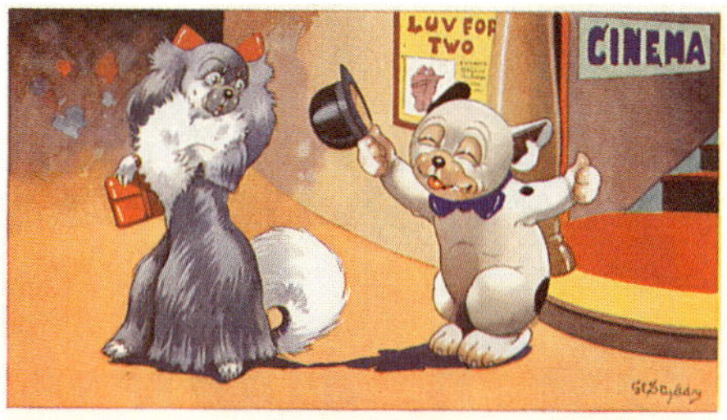
LUV FOR TWO
CINEMA
"WHAT ABOUT A LITTLE FLICK IN THE DARK ?"

3867

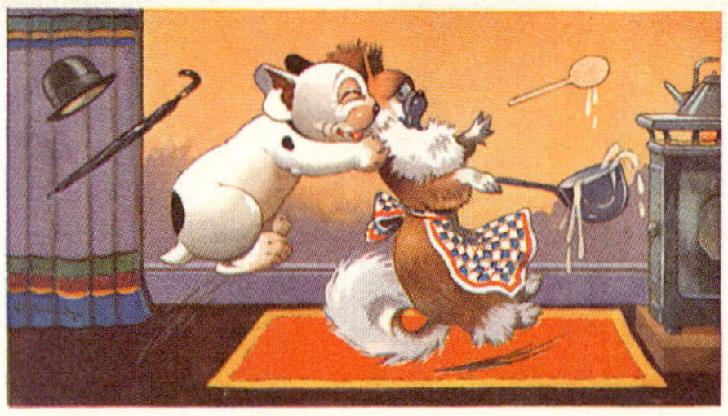
ANY TIME'S KISSING TIME FOR ME!

3869

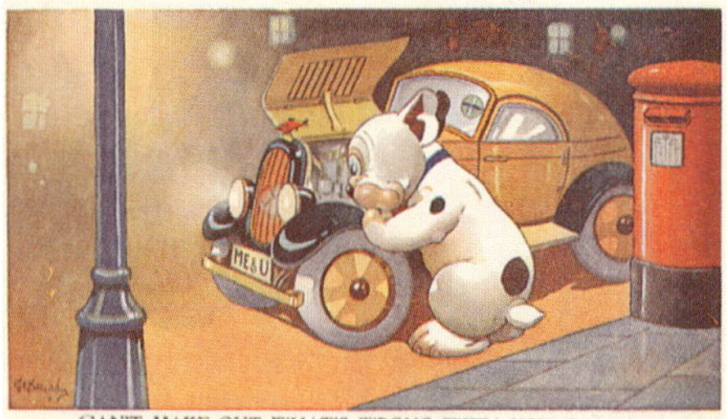
HEAD
CAN'T MAKE OUT WHAT'S WRONG WITH YOU, BABY!

3873

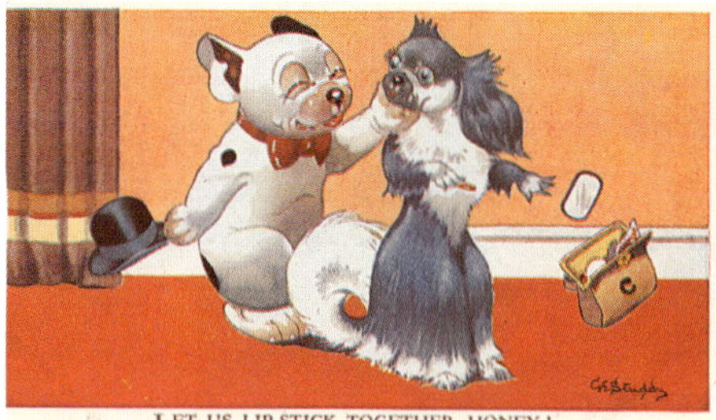
LET US LIP-STICK TOGETHER, HONEY!

4116

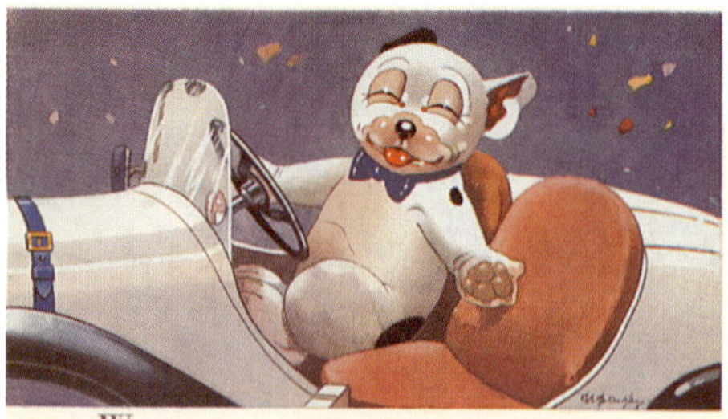
WHAT ABOUT A LITTLE SPORT IN THE SPORTS?

4120

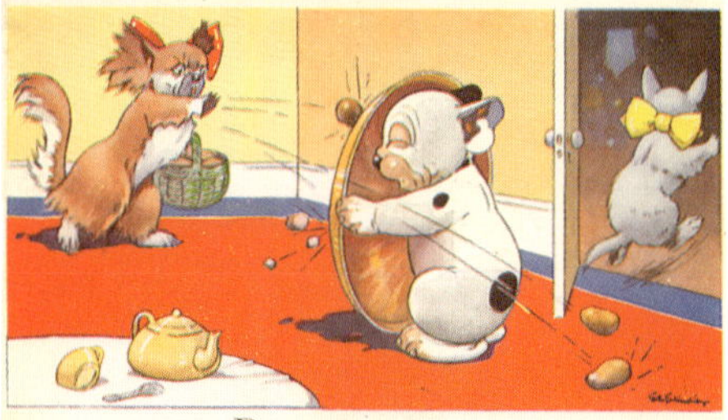
DOING A SPOT OF A.R.P.

4249

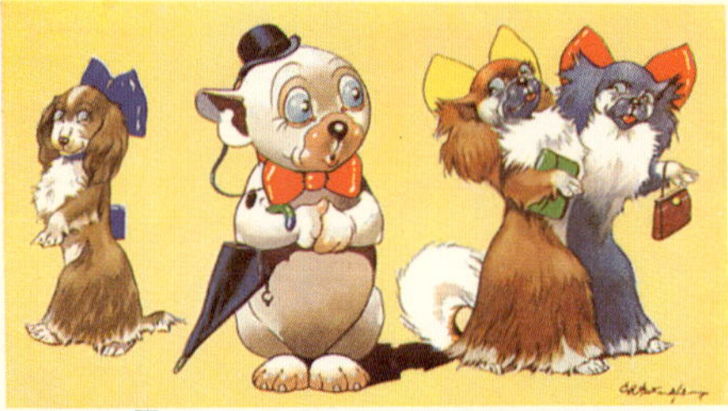
THERE'S LOTS TO DO HERE—BUT I DAREN'T.

4305

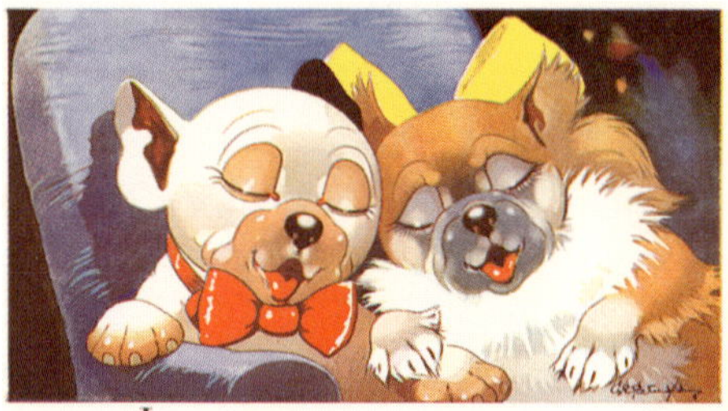
LET'S SPEND A QUIET EVENING TOGETHER.

4307

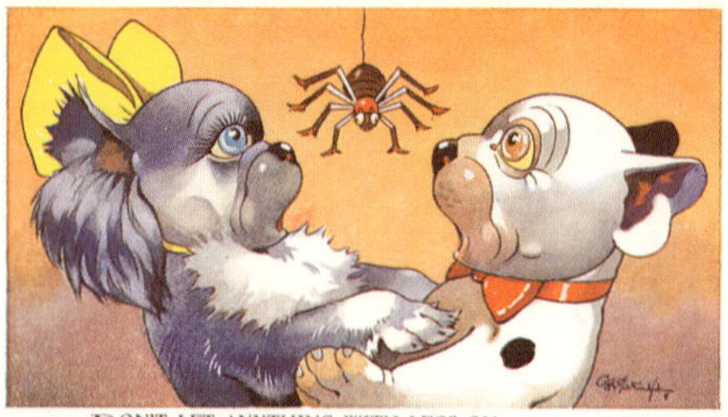
DON'T LET ANYTHING WITH LEGS ON COME BETWEEN US, DARLING

4311

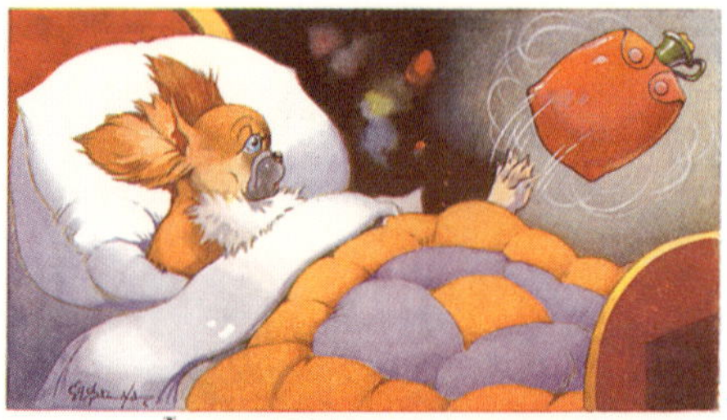
I FEEL YOU ARE COOLING OFF BABY!

4313

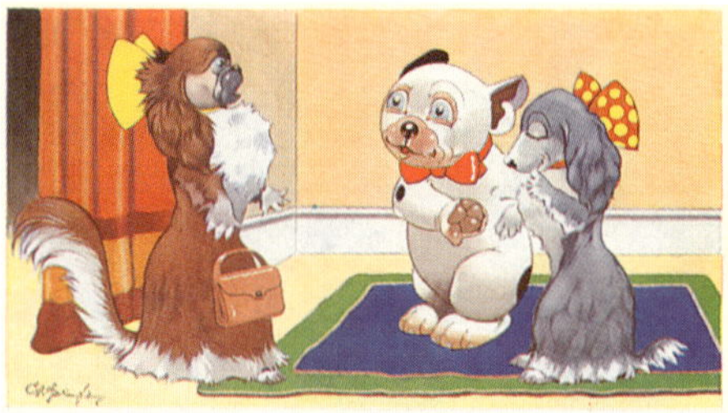
"YOU ARE MY GLAMOUR GIRL No. 1, DARLING—MEET No. 2"

4593

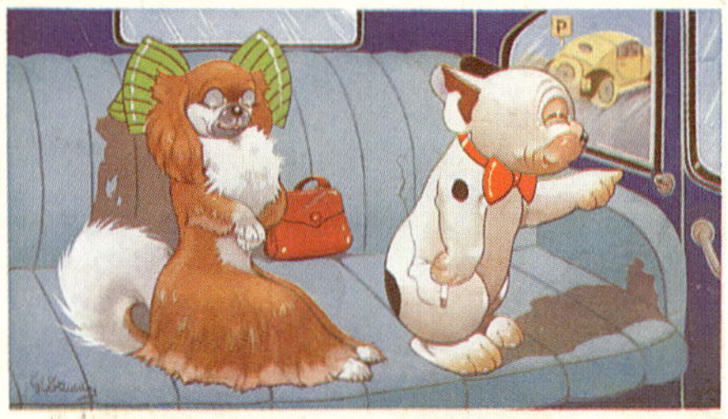
"WE NEED NO PARKING LIGHTS WHEN WE'RE TOGETHER!"

4596

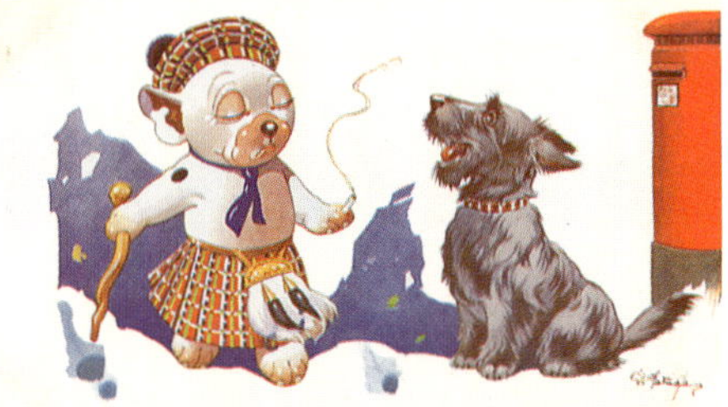
"I FEAR YOU DON'T THINK I'M GENUINE!"

4600

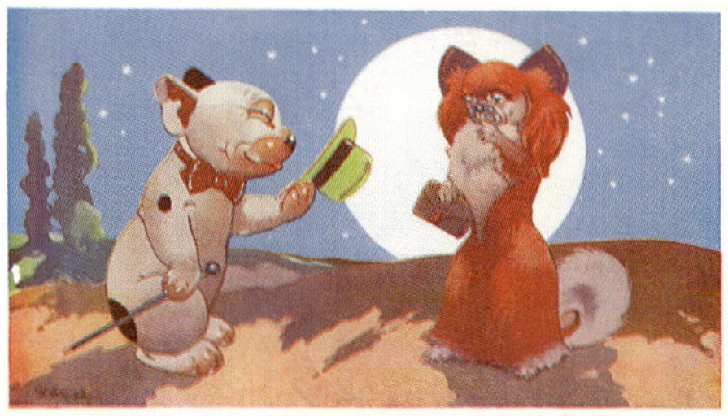
"WHAT ABOUT A SPOT OF MOON-BATHING DEARIE?"

4603

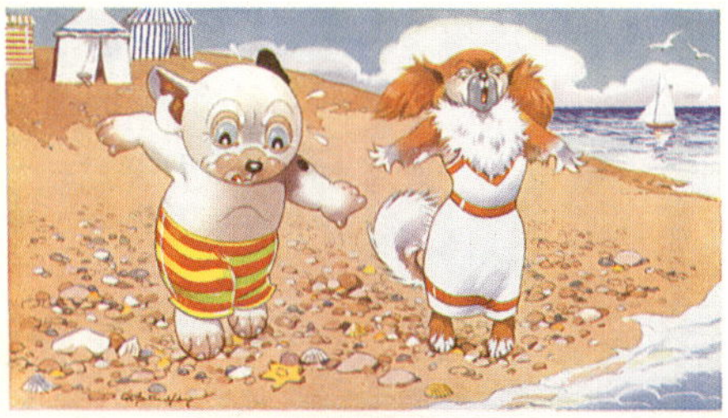
"JUST DOIN' THE SEASIDE WALK!"

4604

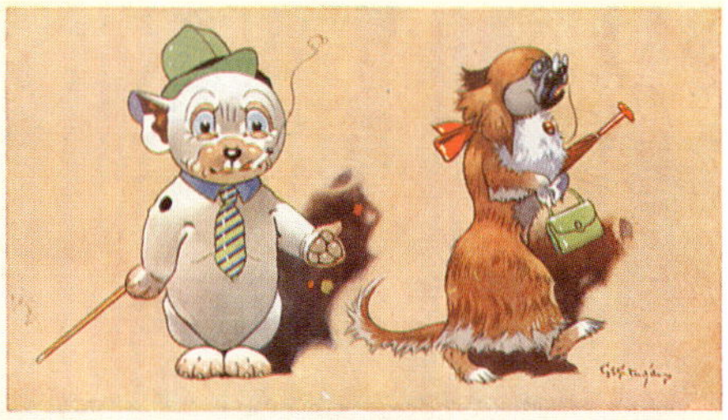
SEE WHAT COMES OF BEING GOOD ALL YOUR LIFE!

4754

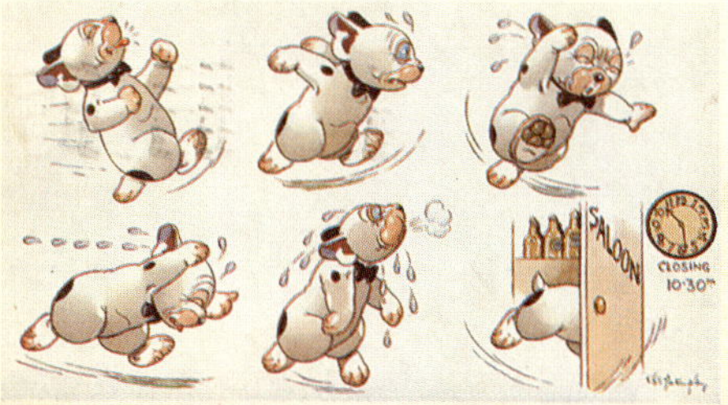
SALOON
CLOSING
10:30
JUST A FEW HINTS ON SLIMMING STUNTS DEARIE!

4755

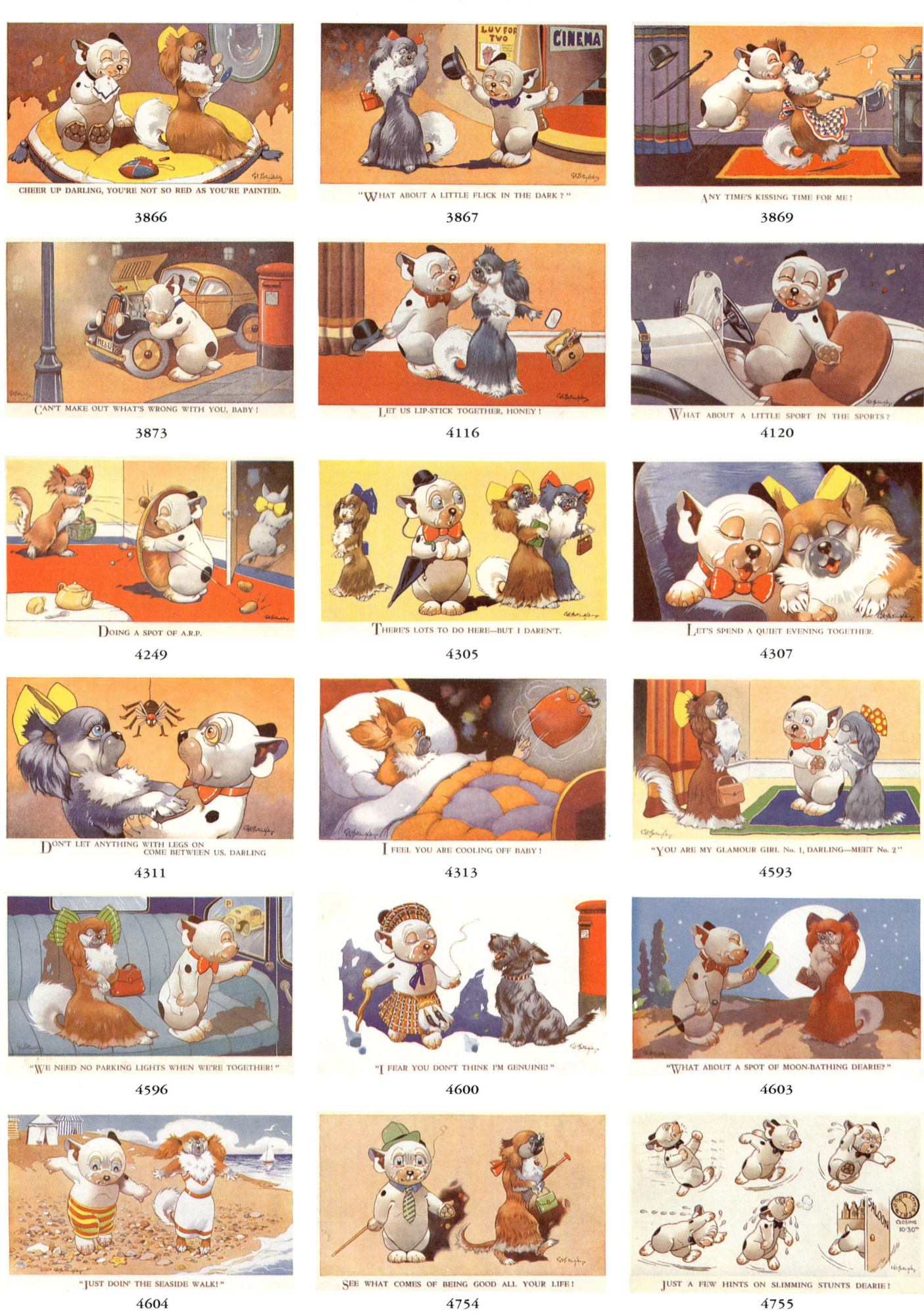

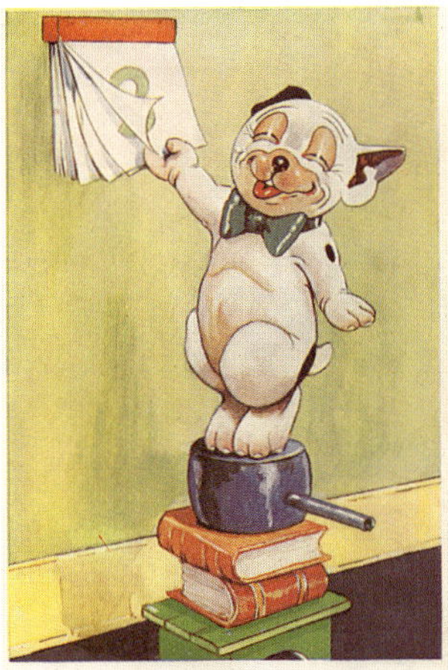

TRY TO ARRANGE A DATE WITH ME.

*5145

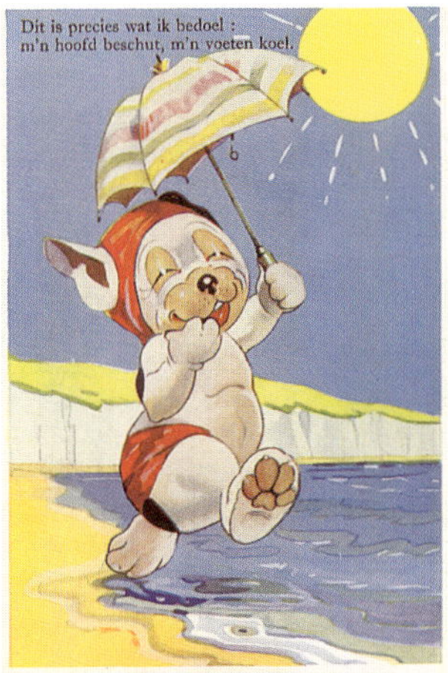
Dit is precies wat ik bedoel :
m'n hoofd beschut, m'n voeten koel.

EVEN THIS WONT COOL ME OFF !

*5263

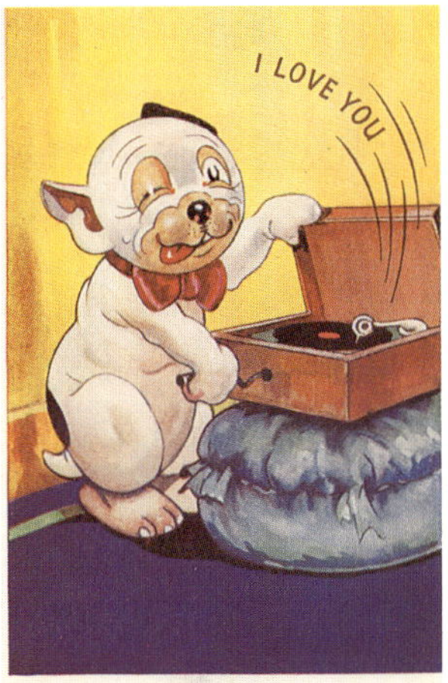
I LOVE YOU

THIS IS OFF THE RECORD !

*5264

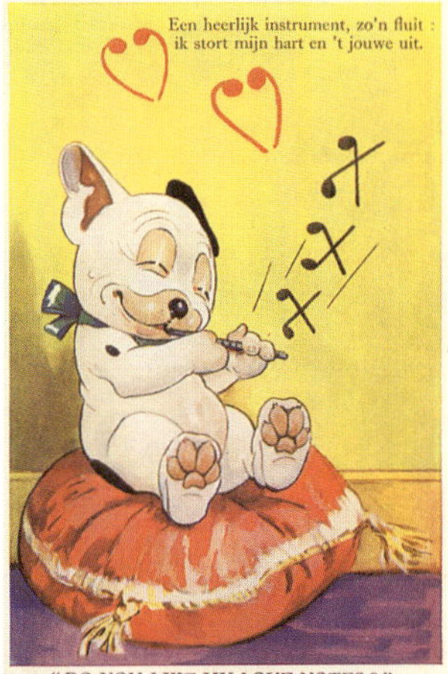
Een heerlijk instrument, zo'n fluit :
ik stort mijn hart en 't jouwe uit.

" DO YOU LIKE MY LOVE NOTES ? "

*5265

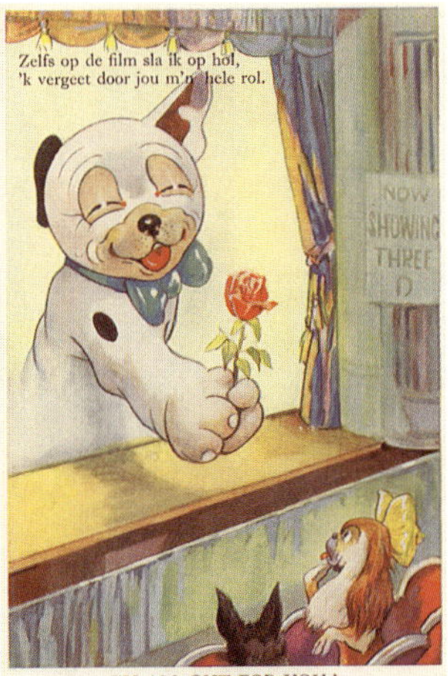
Zelfs op de film sla ik op hol,
'k vergeet door jou m'n hele rol.
NOW SHOWING

I'M ALL-OUT FOR YOU !

*5266

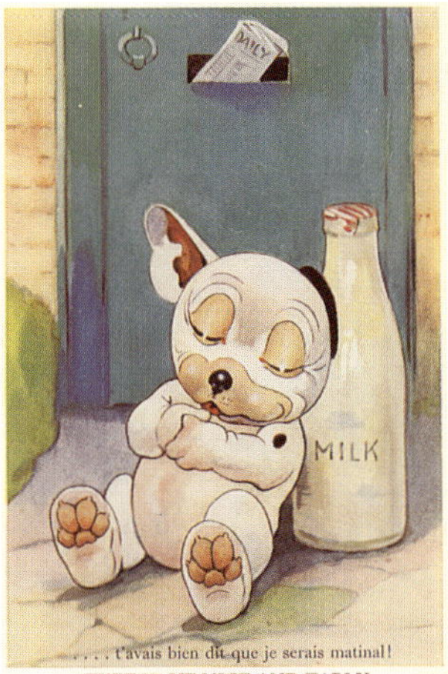
DAILY
MILK
. . . t'avais bien dit que je serais matinal!

EXPECT ME NICE AND EARLY

*5267

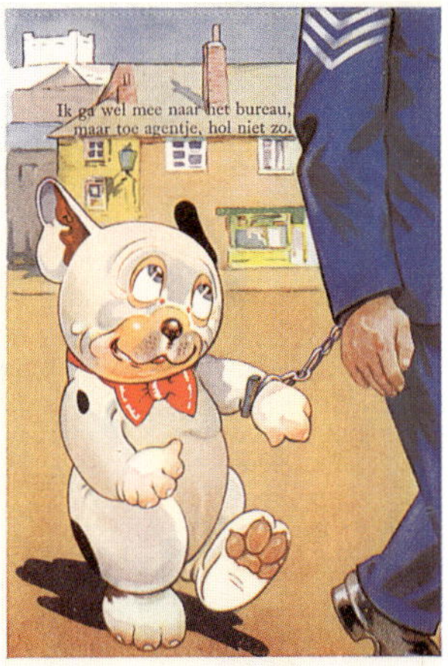
Ik ga wel mee naar het bureau,
maar toe agentje, hol niet zo.

" ENJOYING A(R)REST HERE ! "

*5446

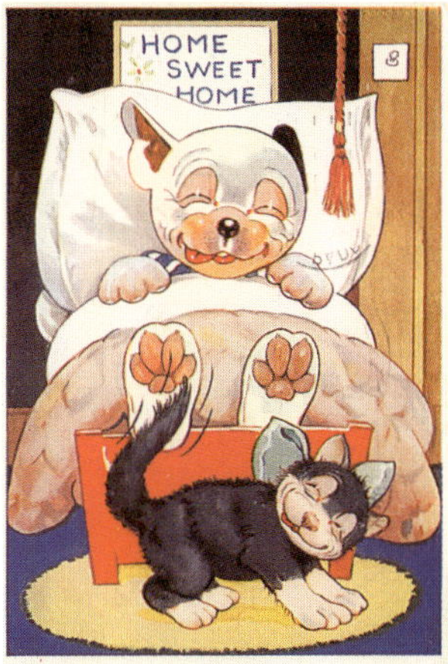
HOME SWEET HOME
8

" A TICKLISH SITUATION ! "

*5447

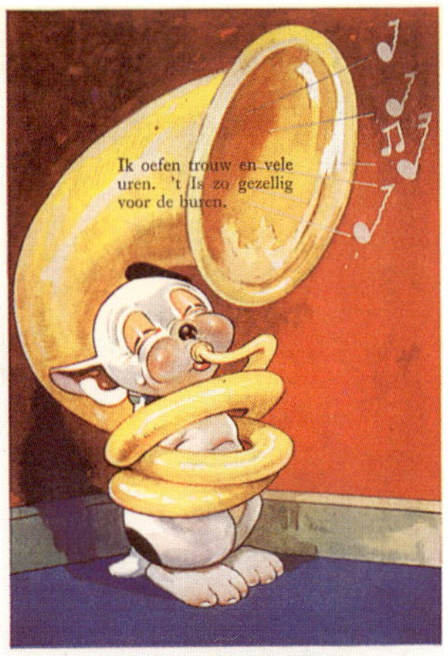
Ik oefen trouw en vele
uren. 't Is zo gezellig
voor de buren.

" NEVER A DULL MOMENT
WHEN YOU'RE AROUND ! "

*5448

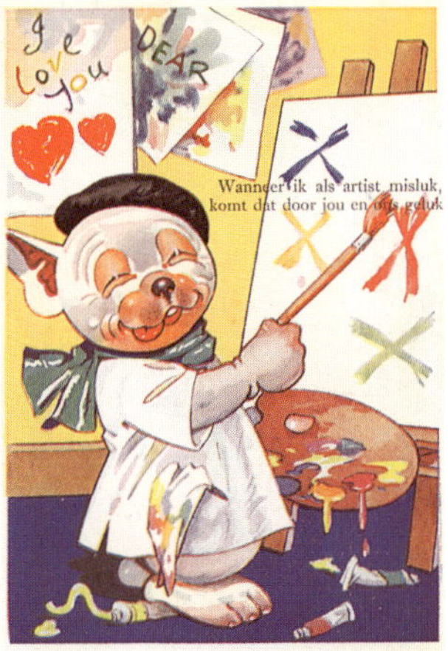
I love you
DEAR
Wanneer ik als artist misluk,
komt dit door jou en mijn geluk

" THINKING OF YOU ! "

*5449

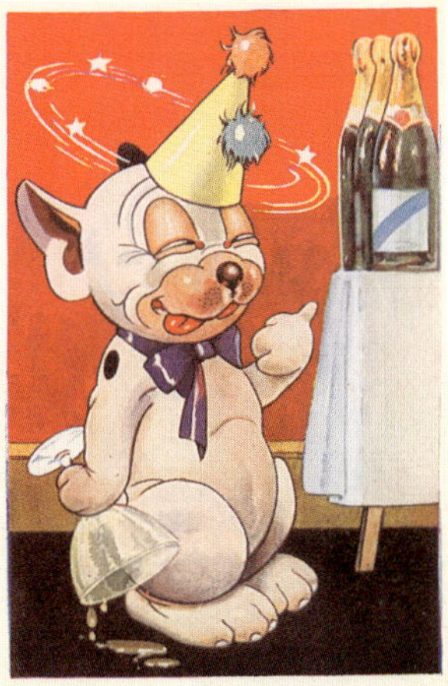

" THASH THE SPIRIT ! "

*5517

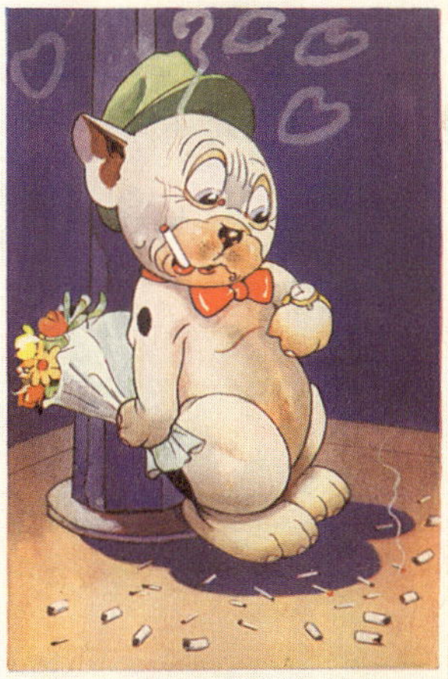

" WE'VE A DATE,
SO DON'T BE LATE ! "

*5518

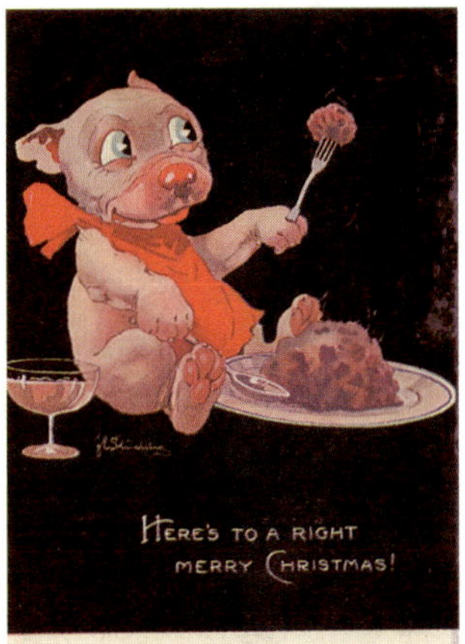
Here's to a right
merry Christmas!

With Best Wishes from

unnumbered

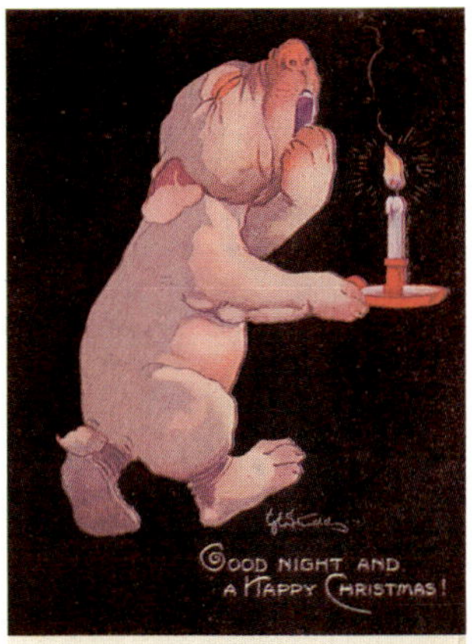
Good night and
a Happy Christmas!

With Best Wishes from

unnumbered

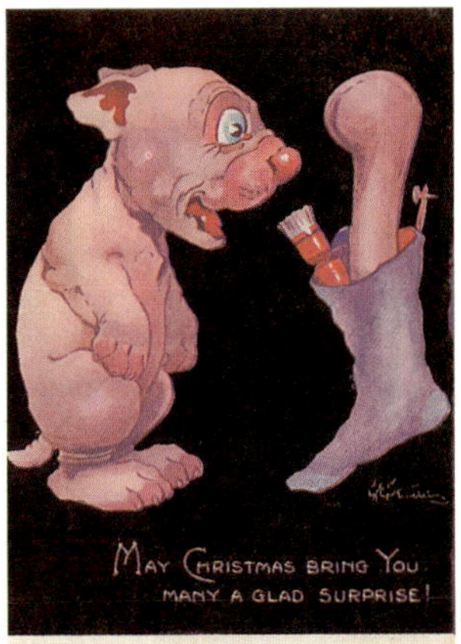
May Christmas bring You
many a glad surprise!

With Bright Hopes for You

From

unnumbered

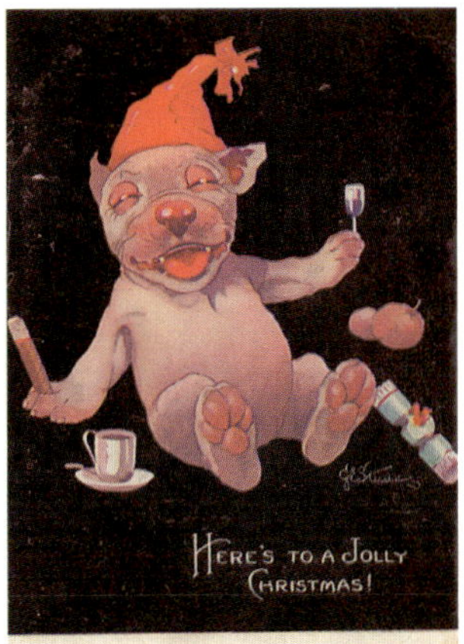
Here's to a Jolly
Christmas!

With All Good Wishes

From

unnumbered

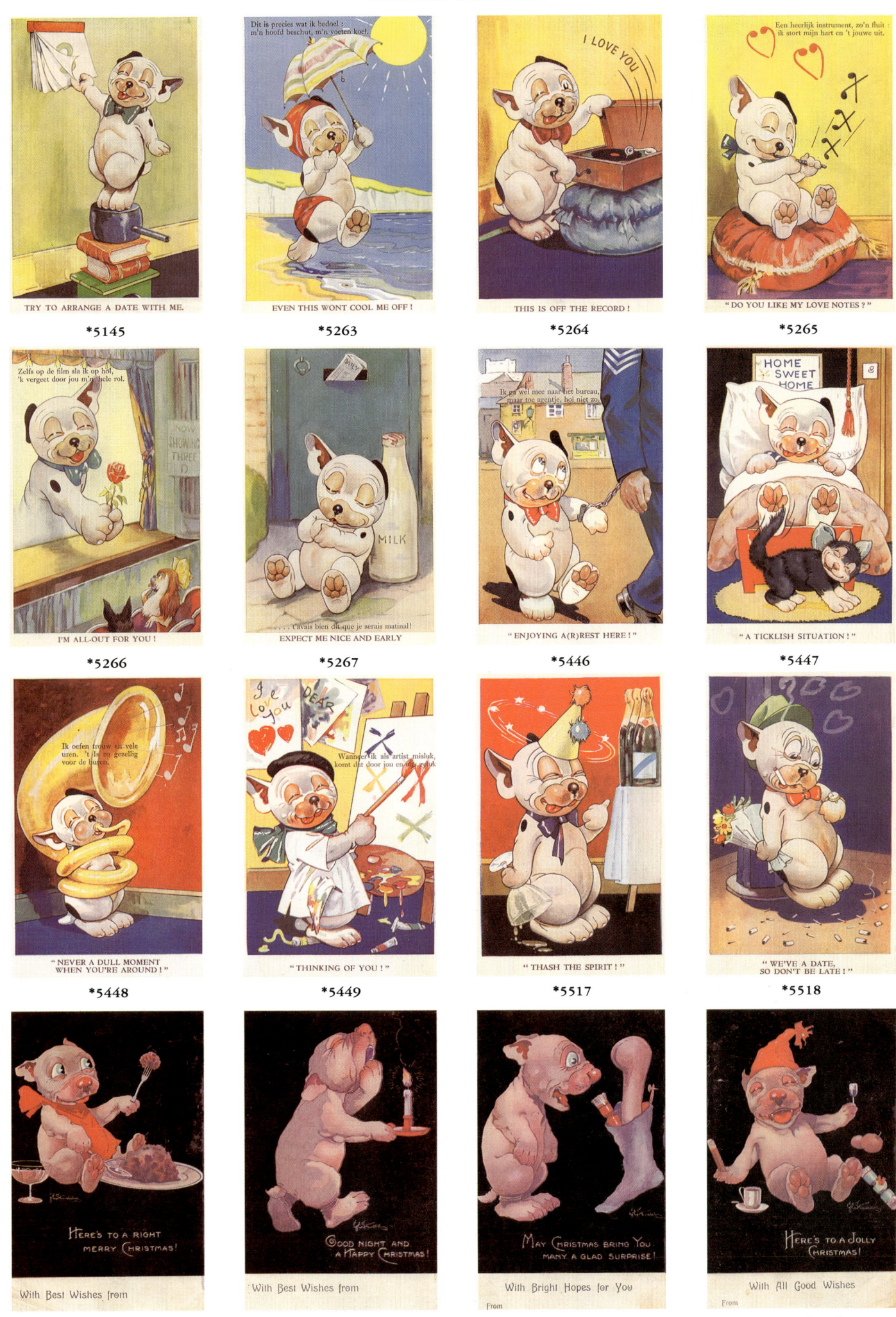

VALENTINE & SONS LTD.

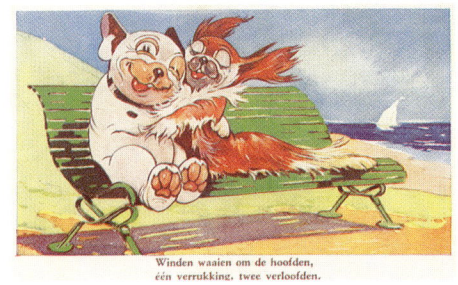
*5140

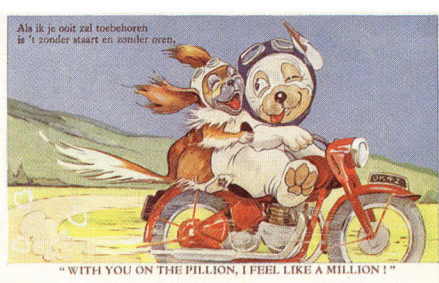
*5262

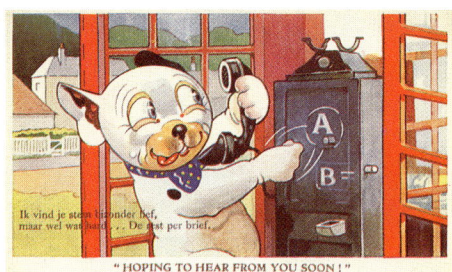
*5444

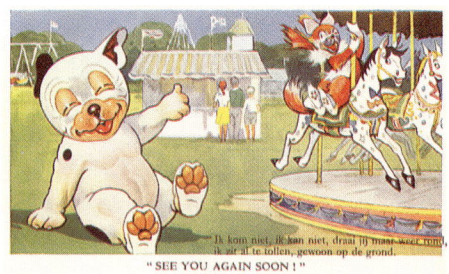
*5445

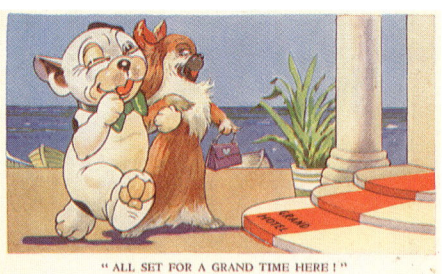
*5519

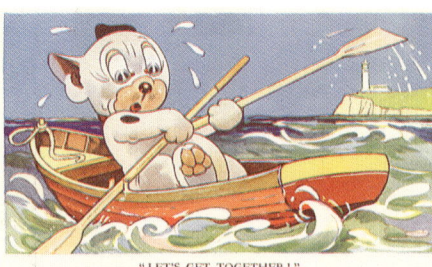
*5520

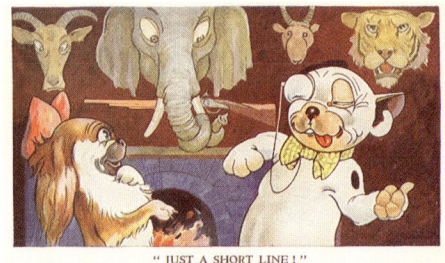
*5521

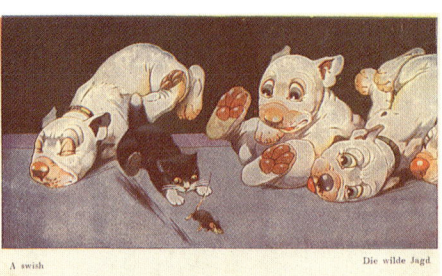
BKW1 XXIV/2

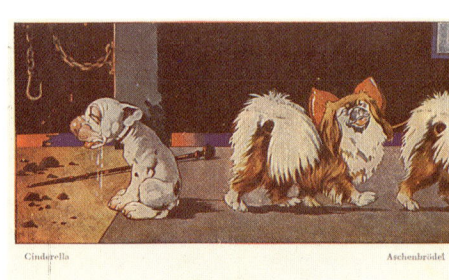
BKW1 XXIV/4

EVOLUTION OF THE MOTOR CAR

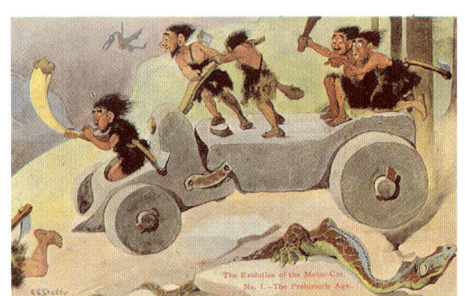
I

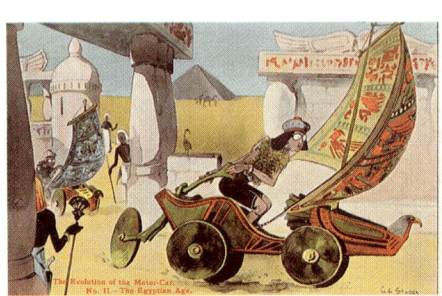
II

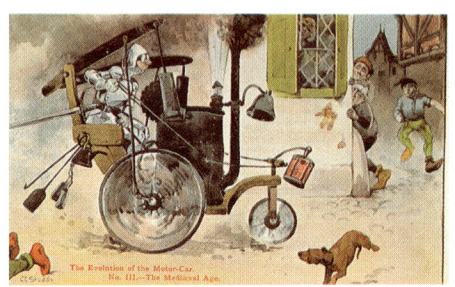
III

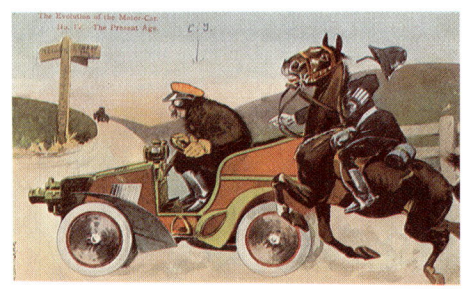
IV

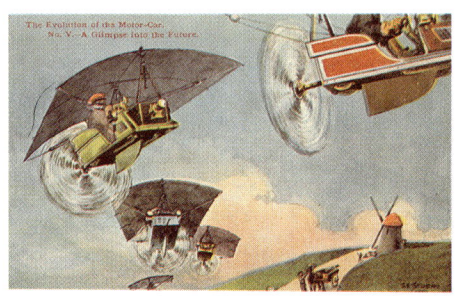
V

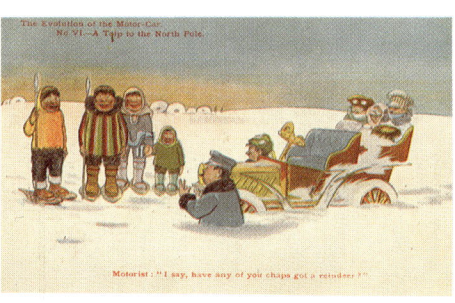
VI

106

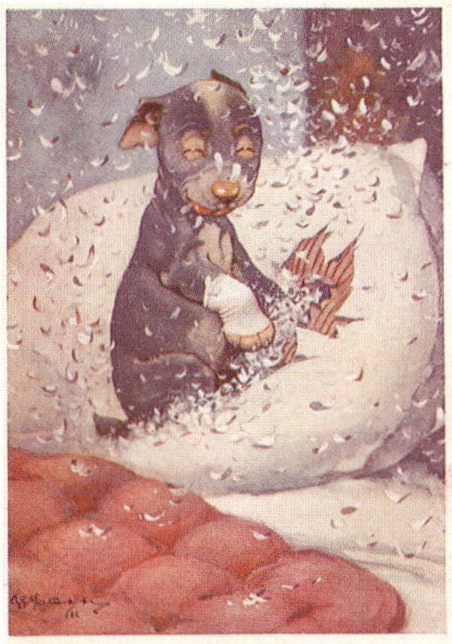
Every Day in Every Respect; I am getting Better and Better.

1000

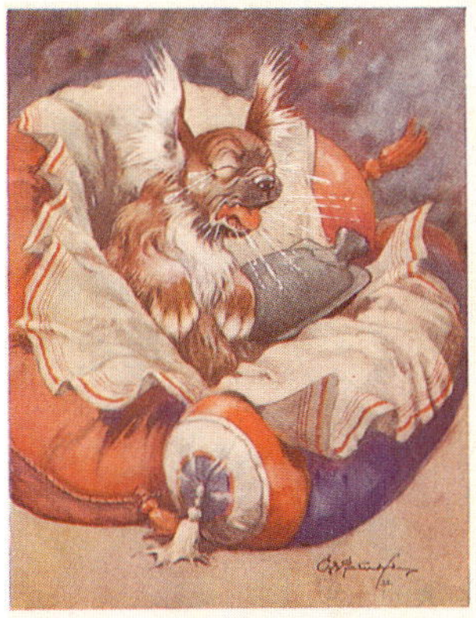
A-Tish-oo.

1001

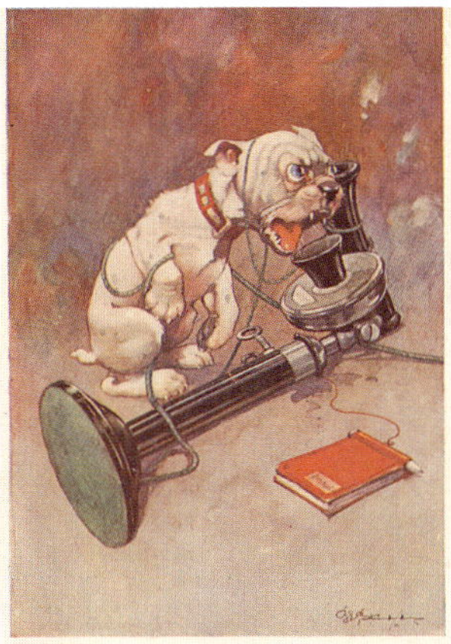
I'm not Arguing, I'm telling you!

1002

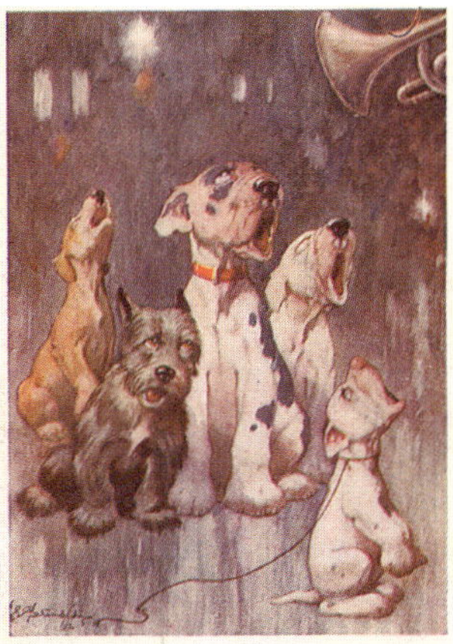
The Beggars Opera.

1003

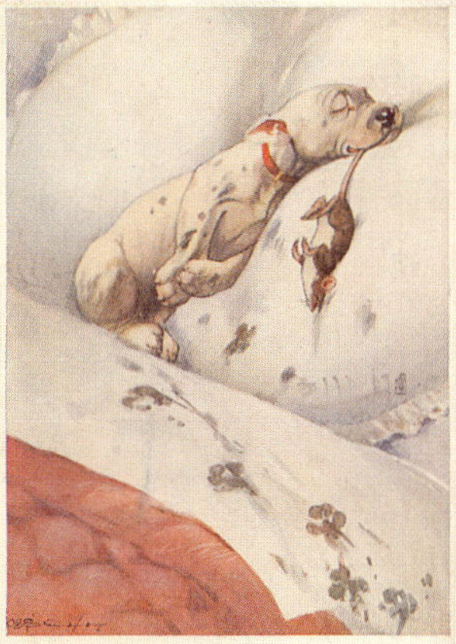
The End of a Perfect Day.

1004

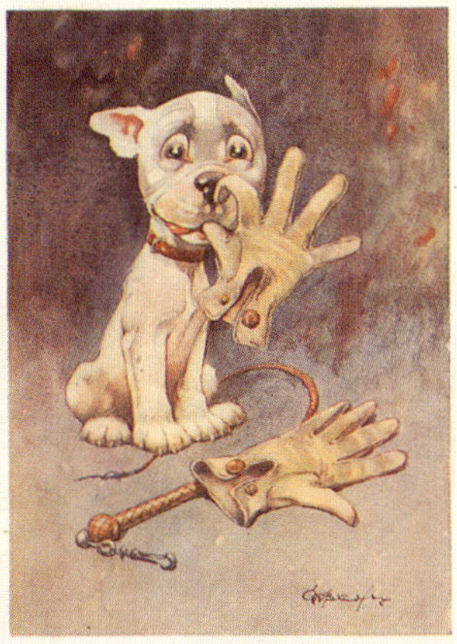
That's What I think of You.

1005

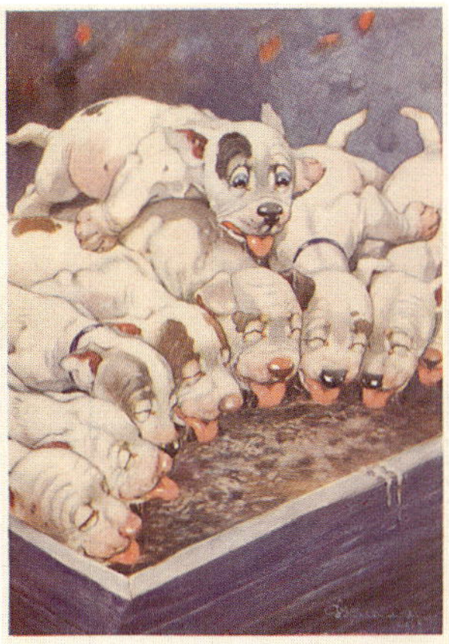
Also Ran.

1006

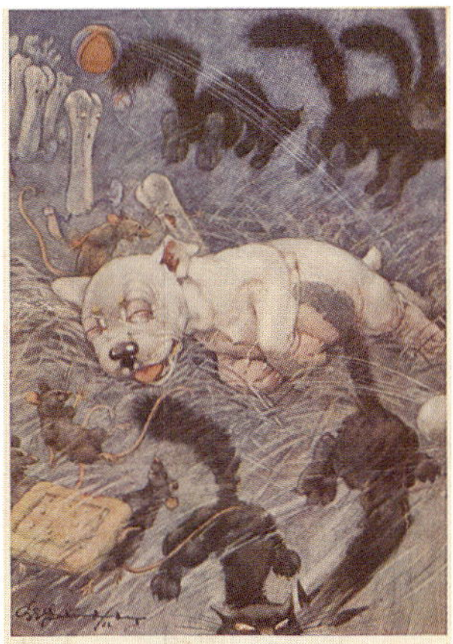
Such Stuff as Dreams are made of.

1007

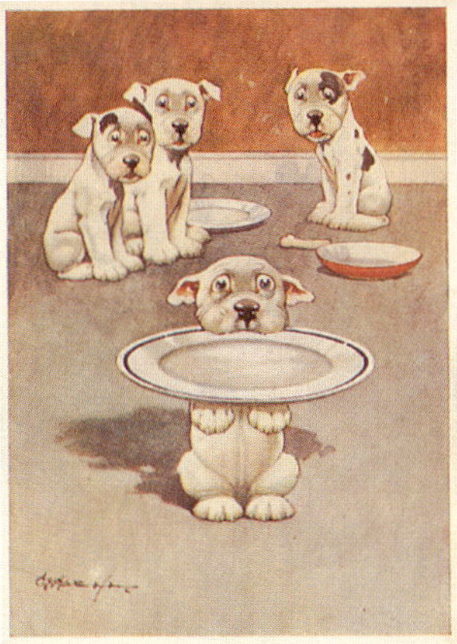
"Oliver Twist."

1008

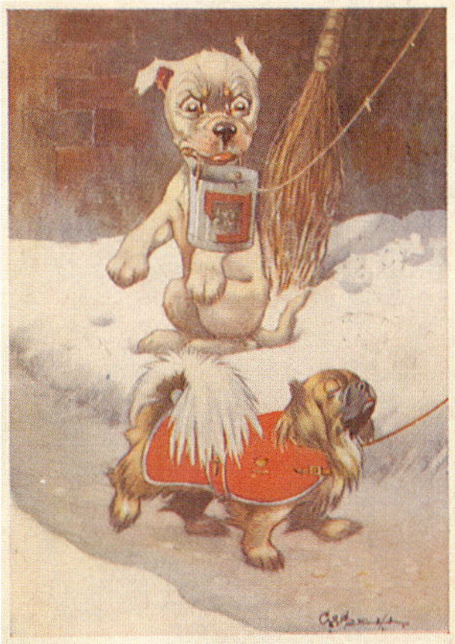
Swank.

1009

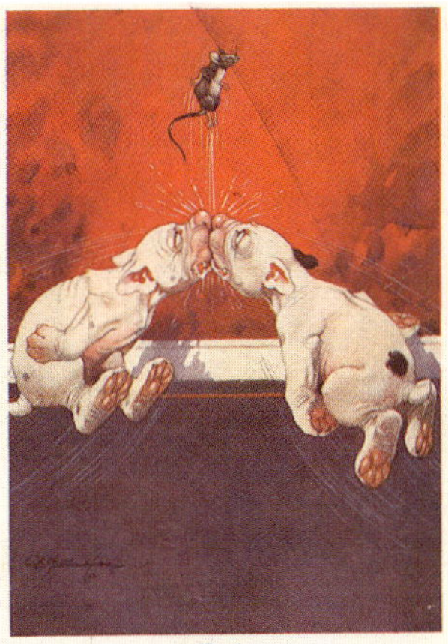
Missed.

1010

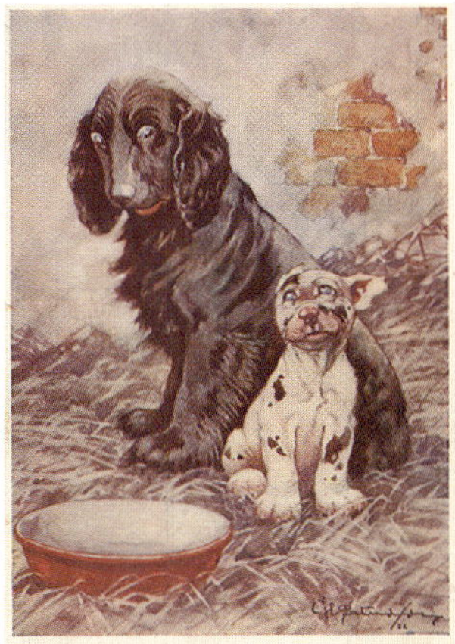
That Coal Black Mammy o' Mine.

1011

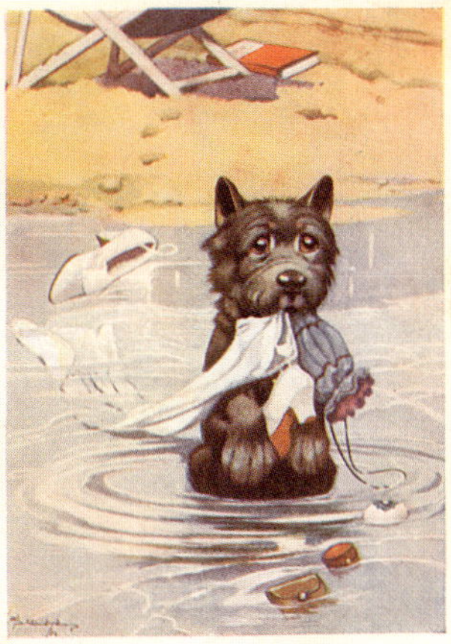
The Faithful Heart.

1012

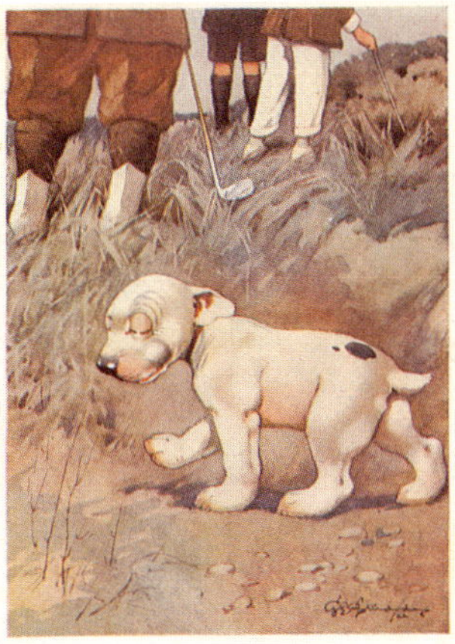
Lost Ball.

1013

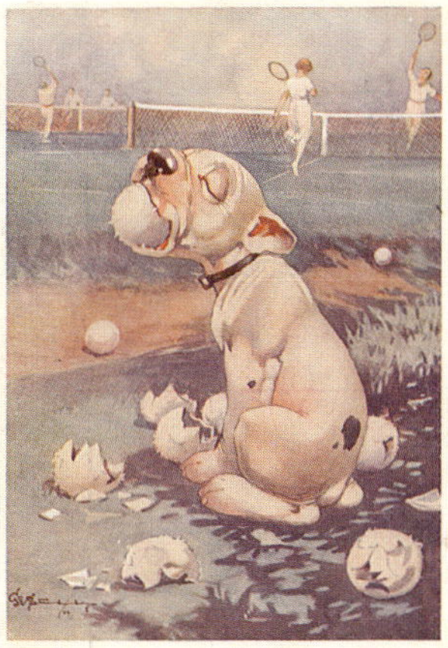
Fred the Ball Boy.

1014

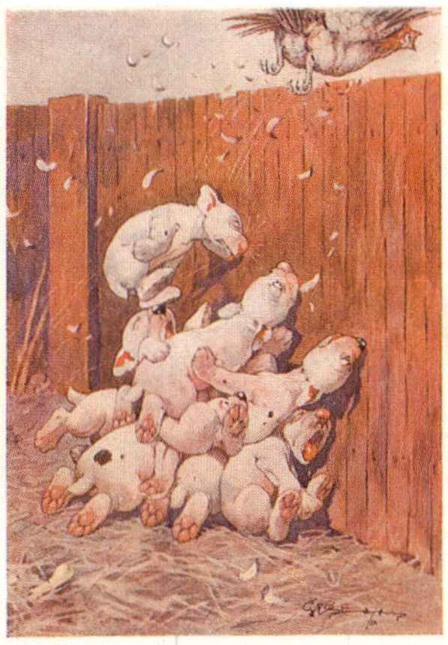
The Way of an Eagle.

1015

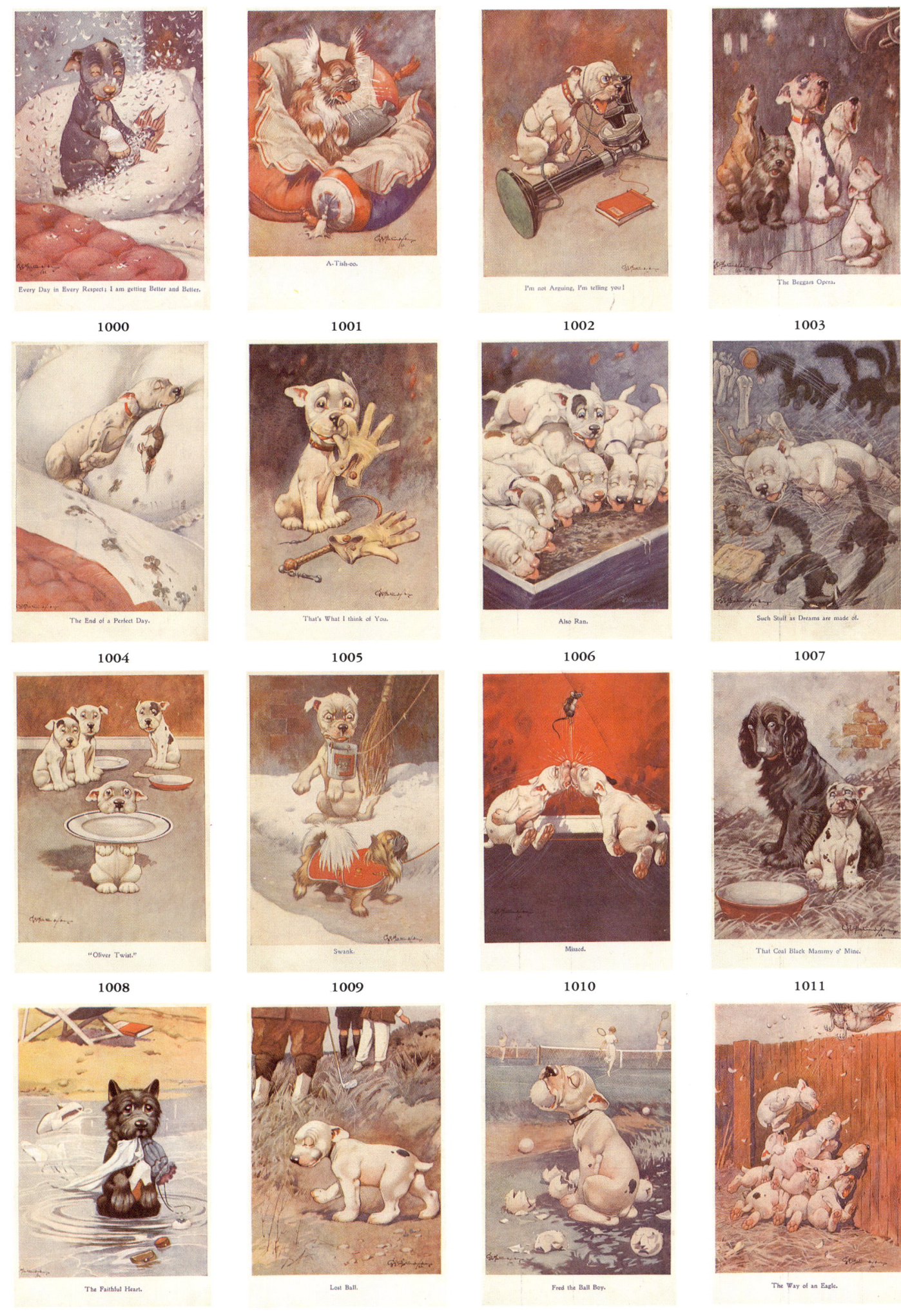

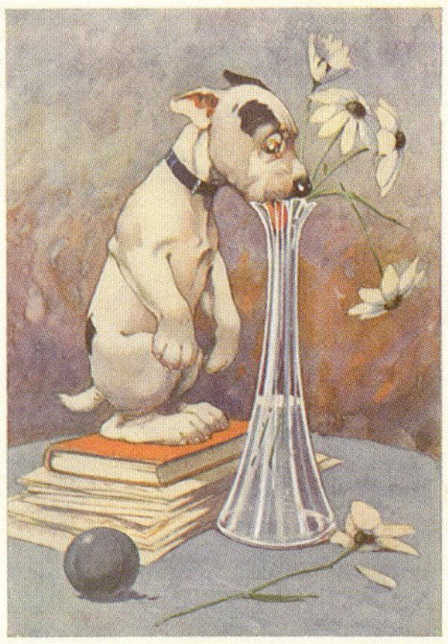

Low Tide.

1016

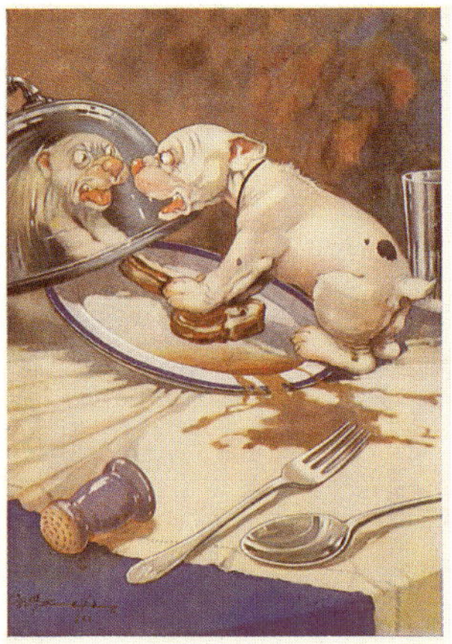

Jimmy Wild.

1017

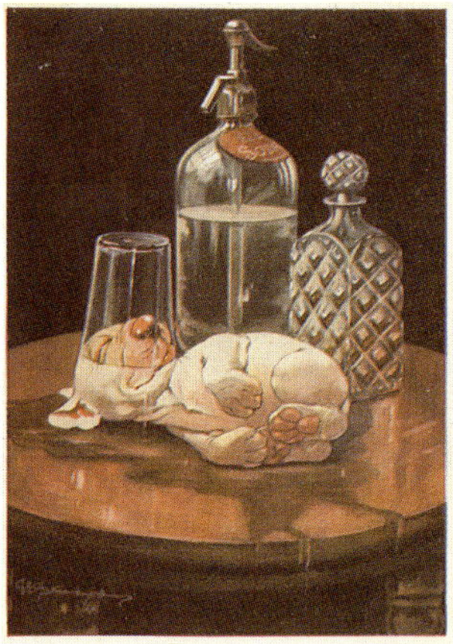

His Master's Vice.

1018

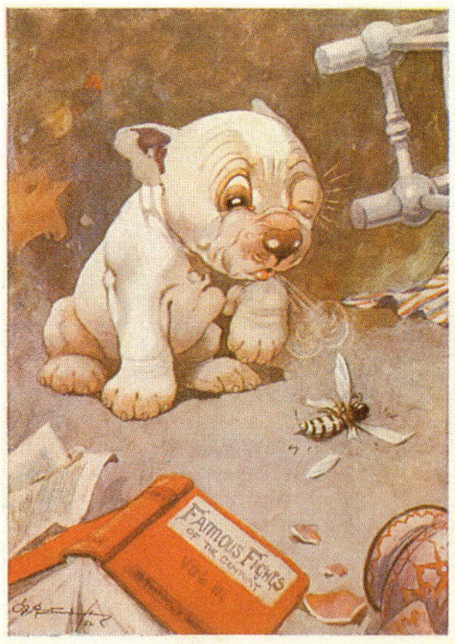
Famous Flights

Now what about it?

1019

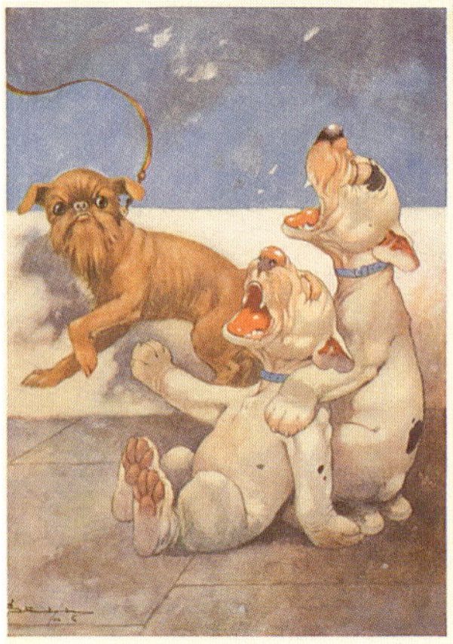

Beaver.

1020

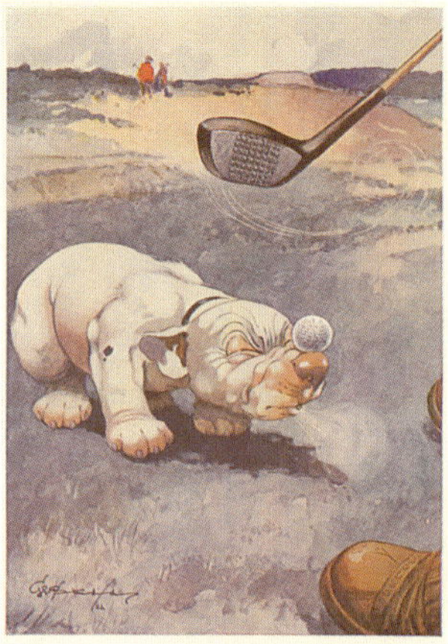

William Tell.

1021

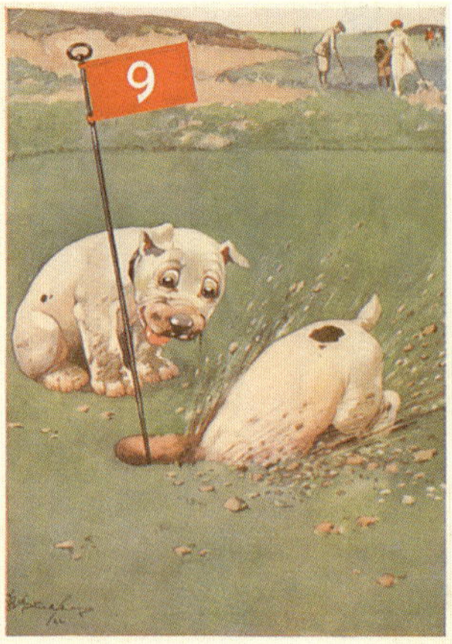
9

Rabbits, I Believe?

1023

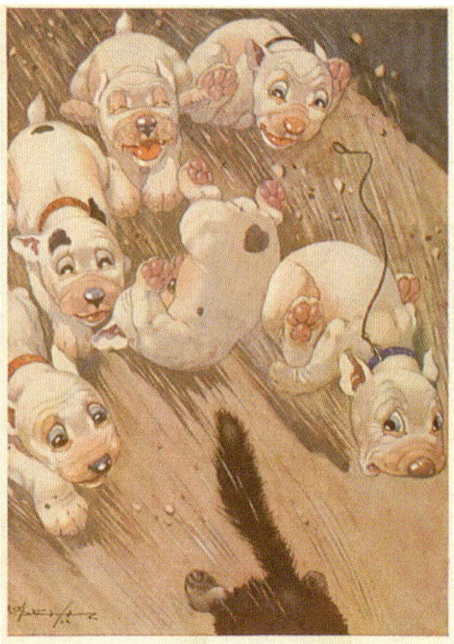

Tip and Run.

1024

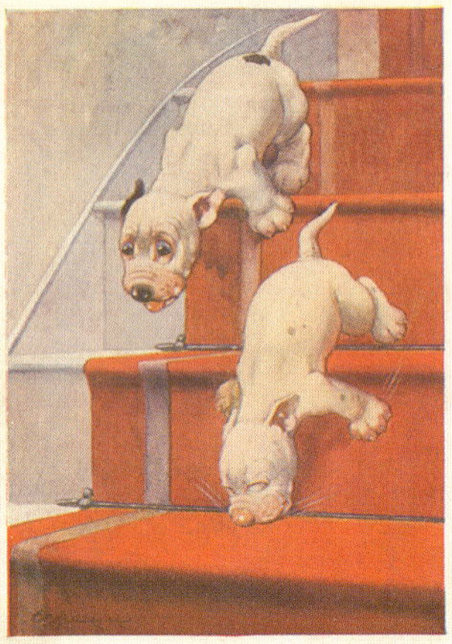

The Edge o' Beyond

1025

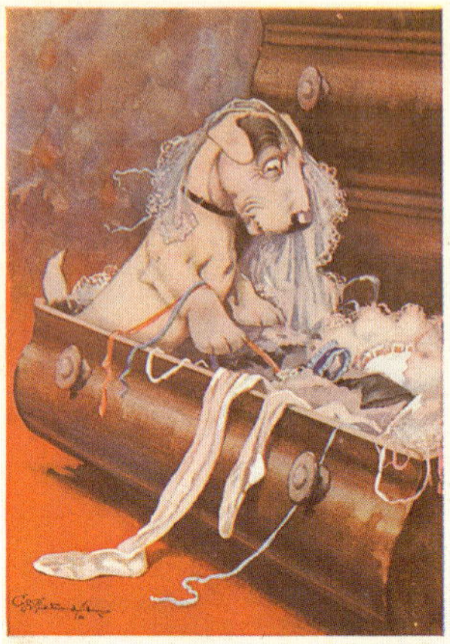

Alice in Wonderland

1026

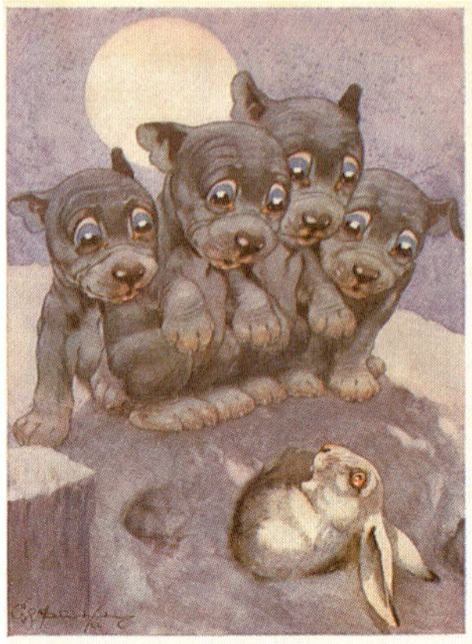

Bogey Four

1027

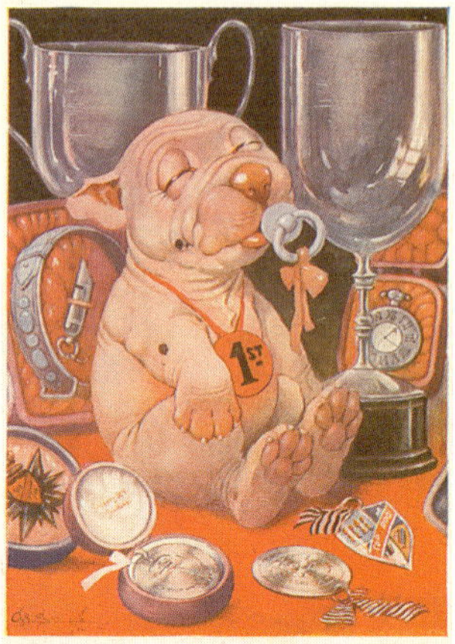
1st

Top Dog

1028

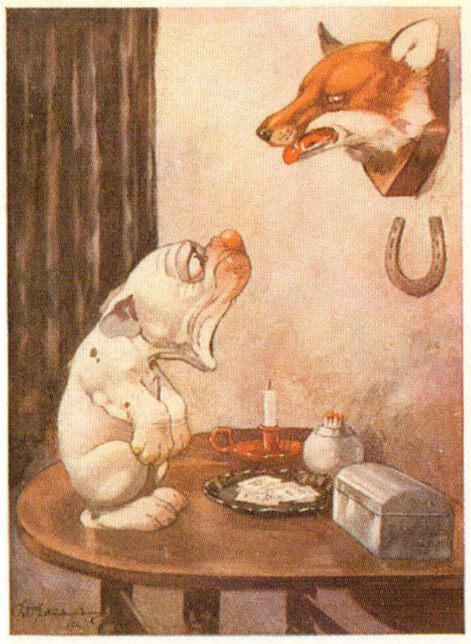

Bonzo's Hymn of Hate

1029

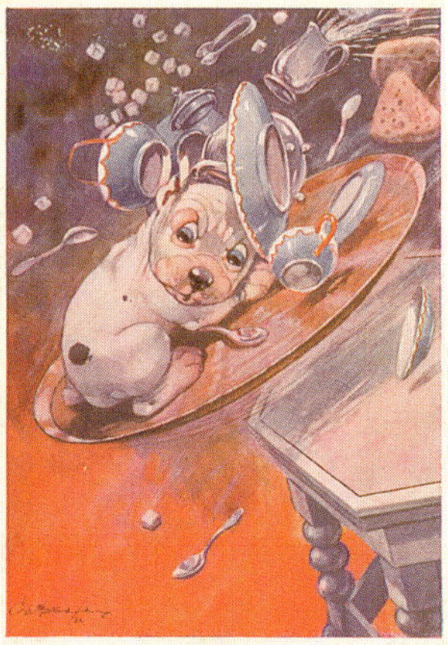

Any More for the Bus?

1030

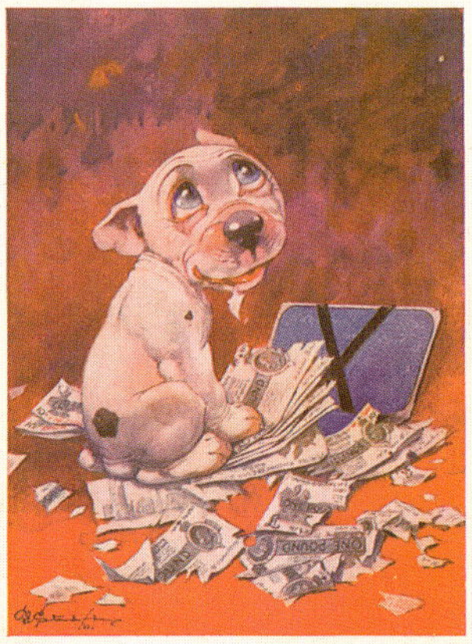

Angel Face

1031

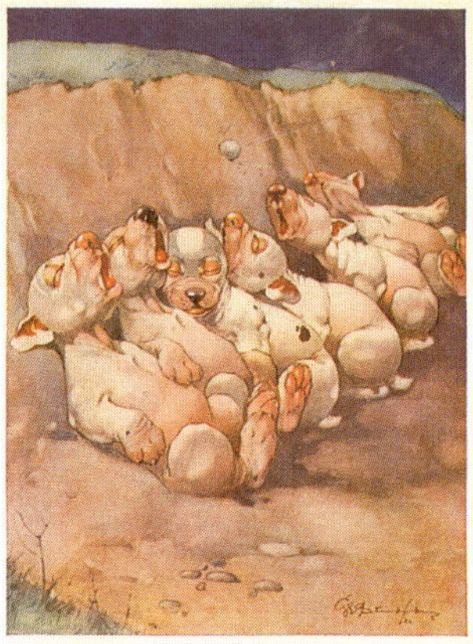

Dormy Six

1032

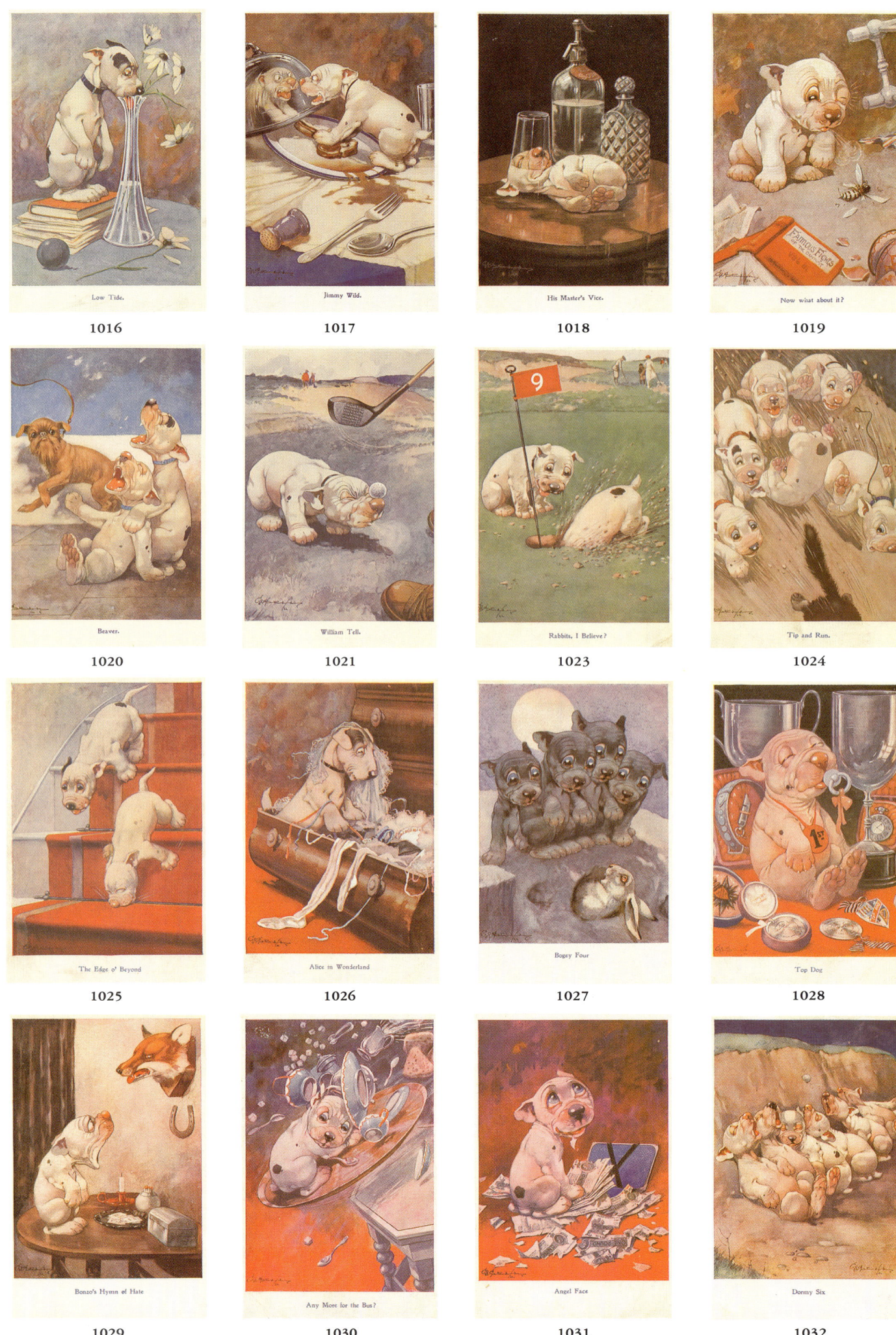

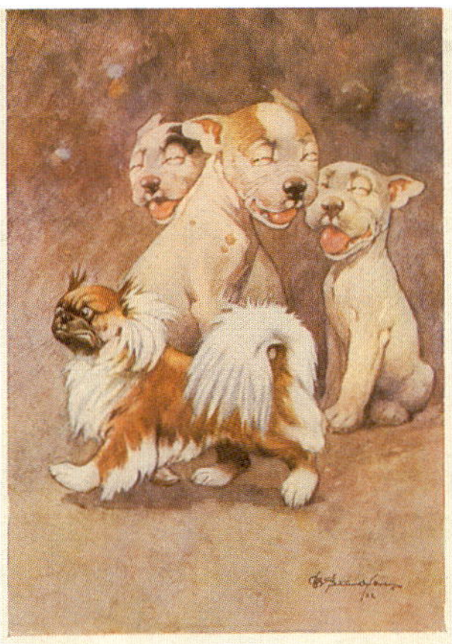

Carry Your Tail, My Lord

1033

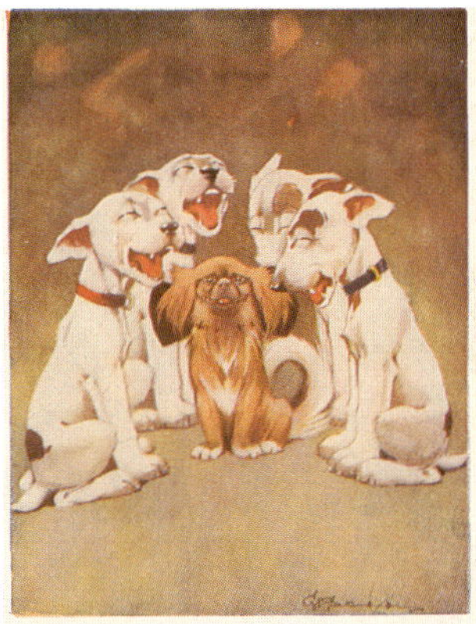

The Pekingese Tells One

1034

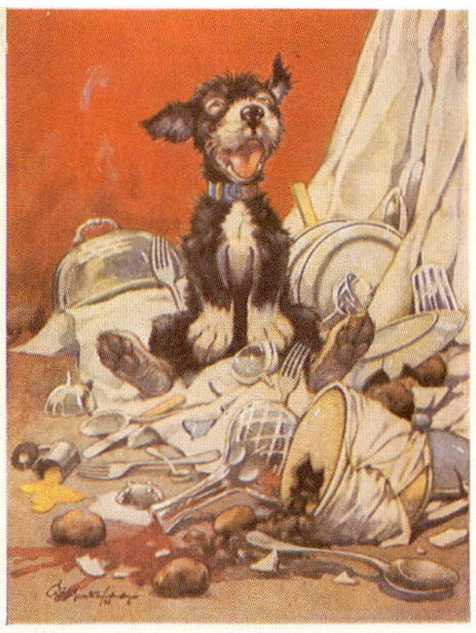

There You are Then

1035

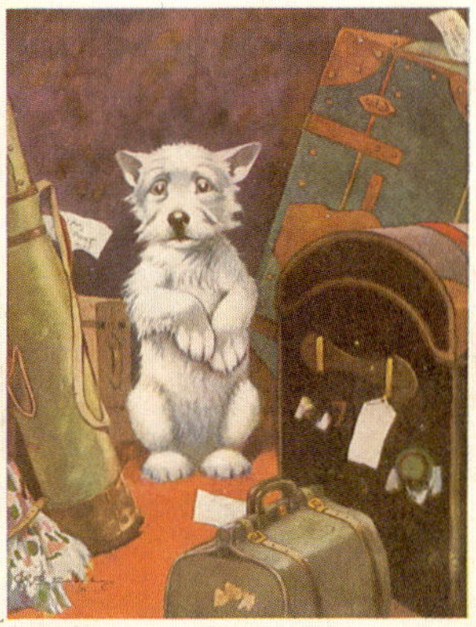

What about me?

1036

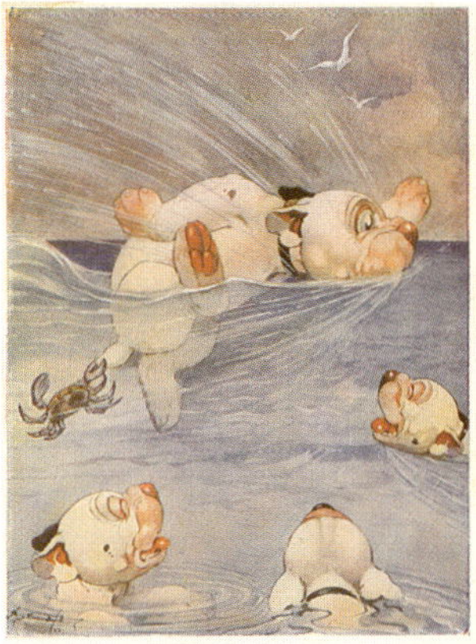

Bonzo Swims the Channel.

1037

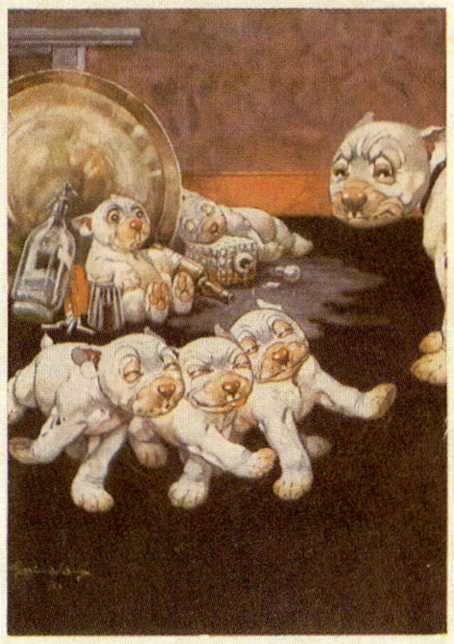

The Bonzos Have a Couple.

1038

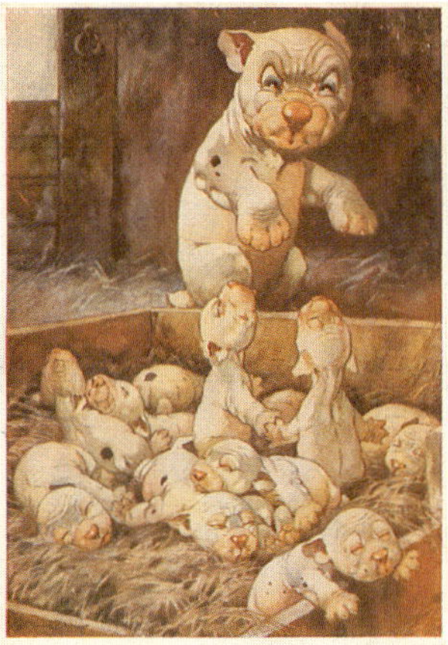

How the Deuce Did this Happen?

1039

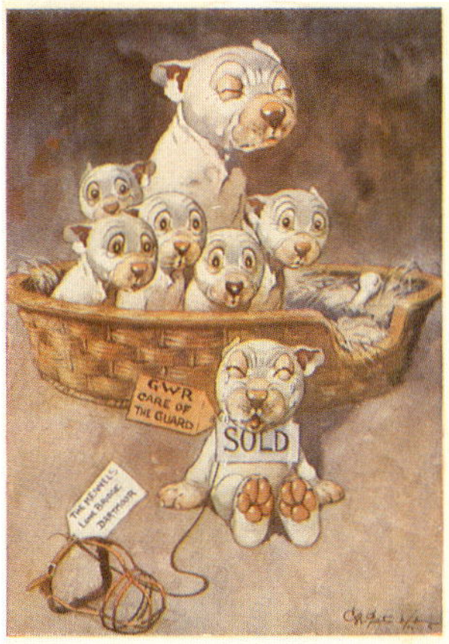
GWR
CARE OF
THE GUARD
SOLD

Bonzo Sells a Pup.

1040

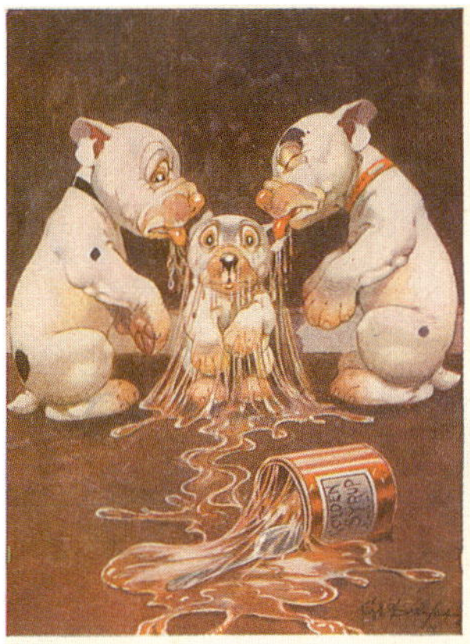

Treacle Tart.

1041

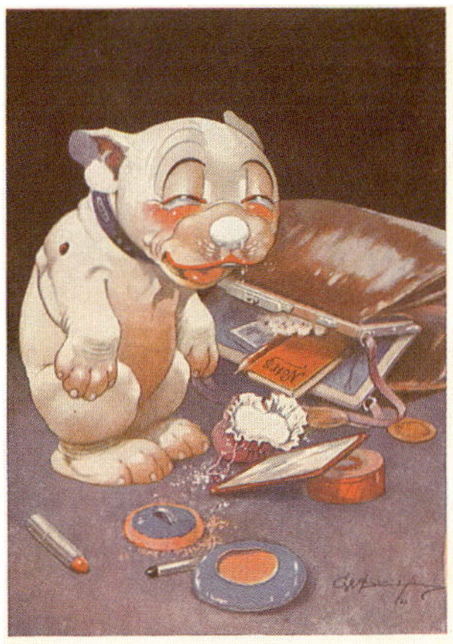

His Mistress's Vice.

1042

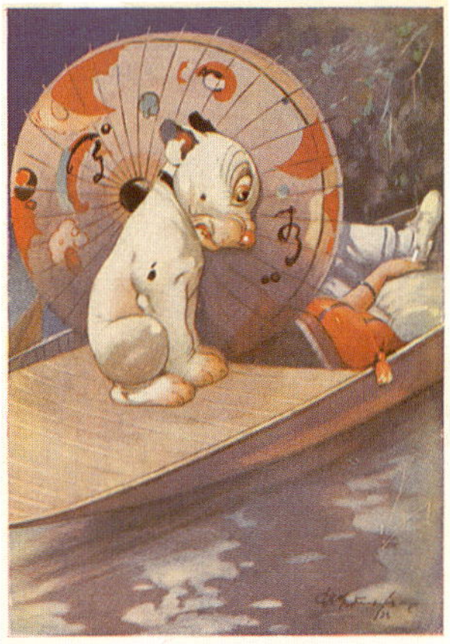

Listening In.

1043

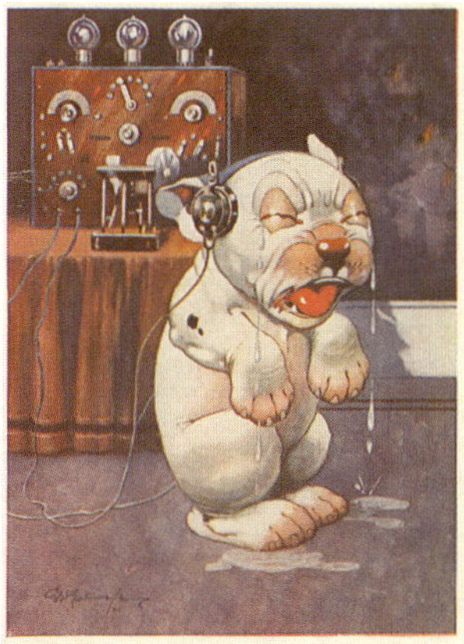

Is, what I hear of you, true?

1044

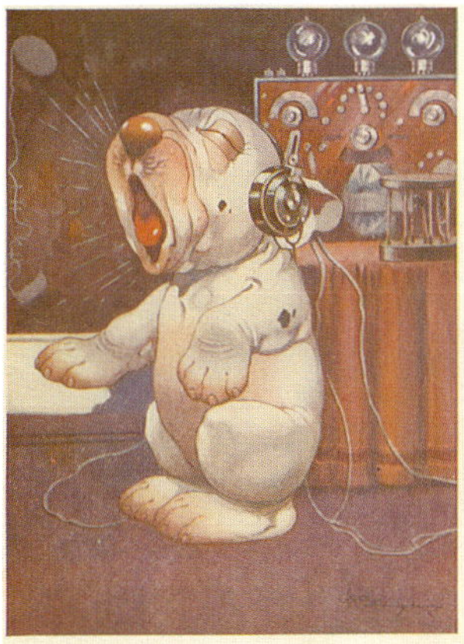

Operatic Number
(*You are Queen of My Heart to Night*).

1045

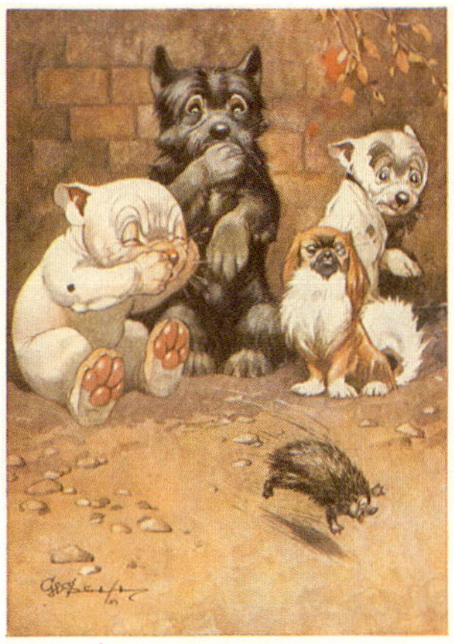

The Road Hog.

1046

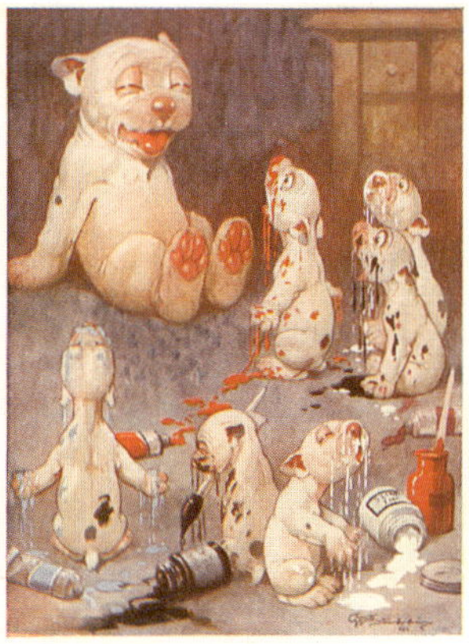

The Art School

1047

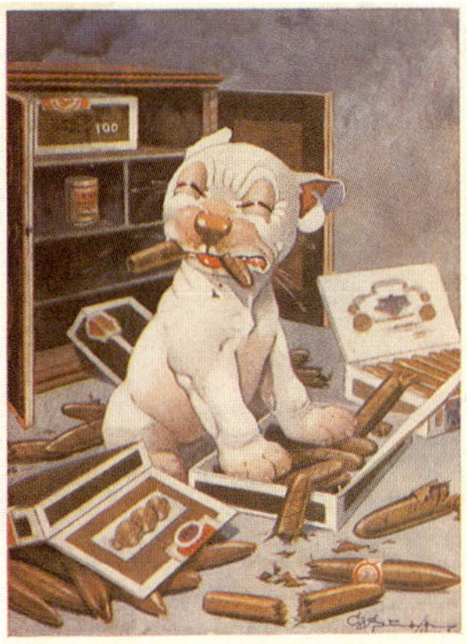

Which is it that Master Likes So Much?

1048

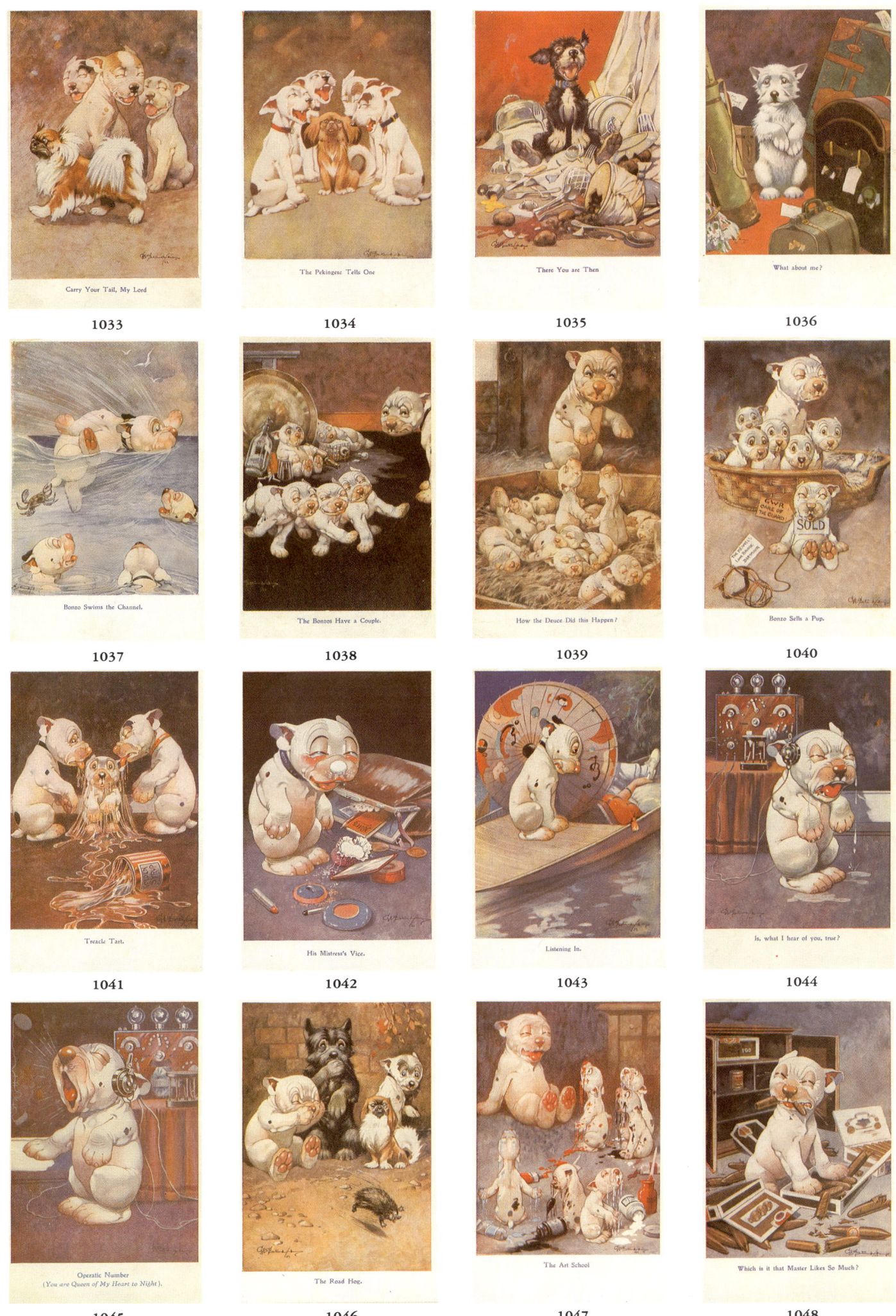

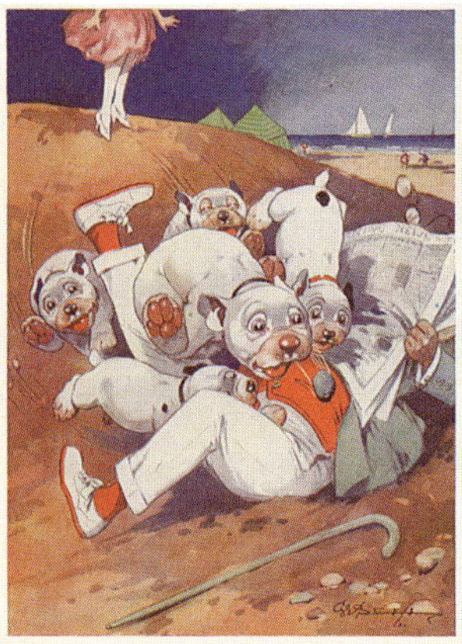
We are a Sporty Little Crowd down here.

1049

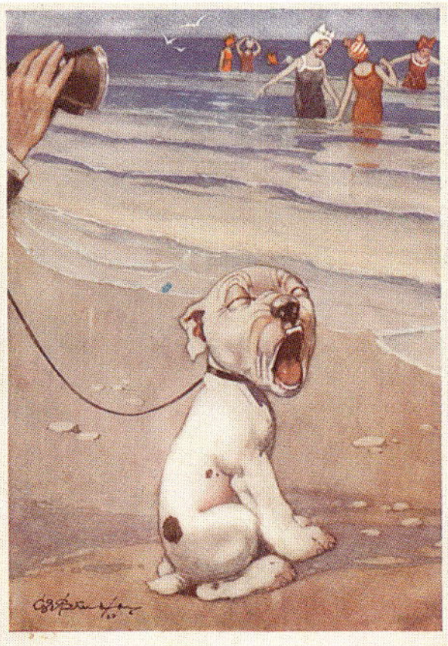
Tired Tim.

1050

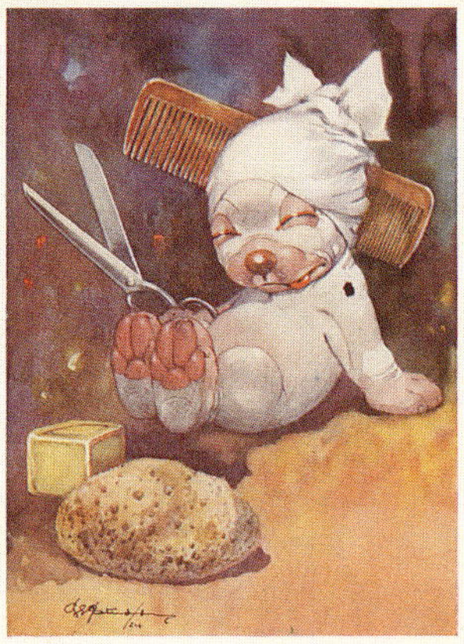
To be Shingled or not to Shingle, that is the question.

1051

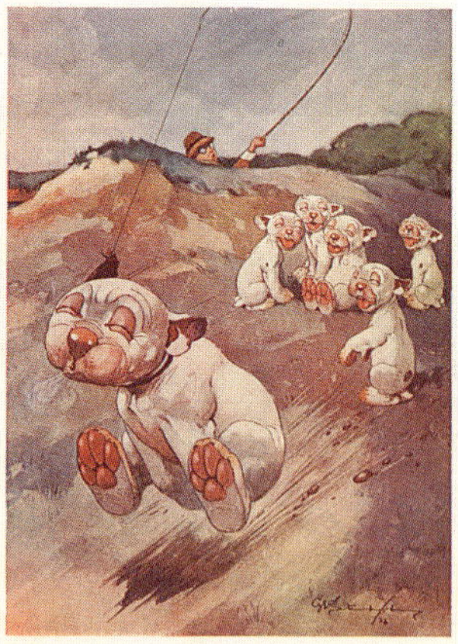
Just a Line.

1052

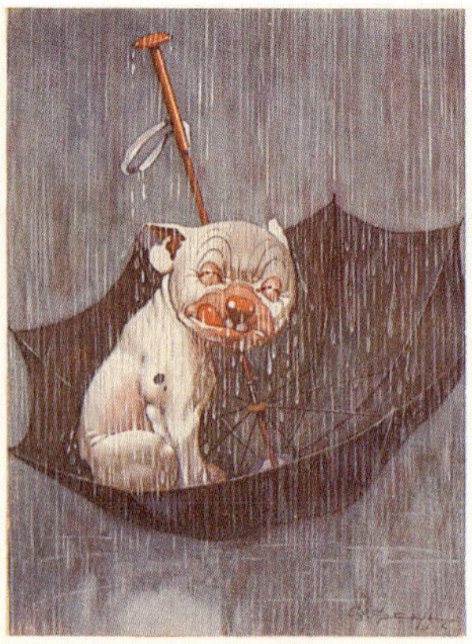
Somewhere the Sun is Shining.

1053

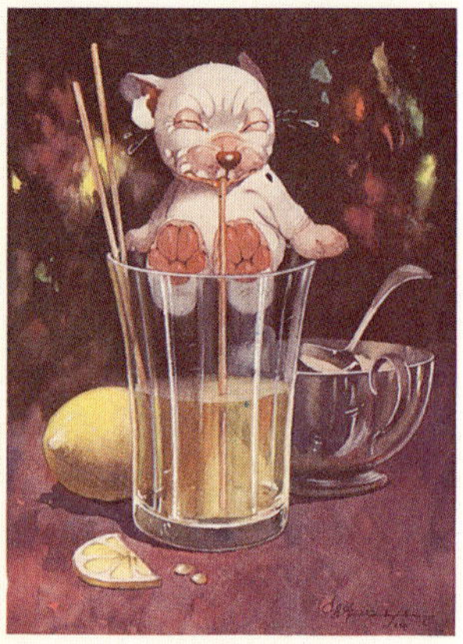
A Soft Drink.

1054

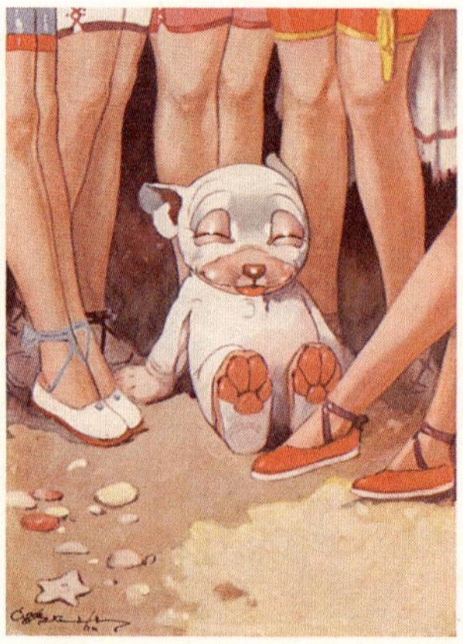
Not a Word to the Wife.

1055

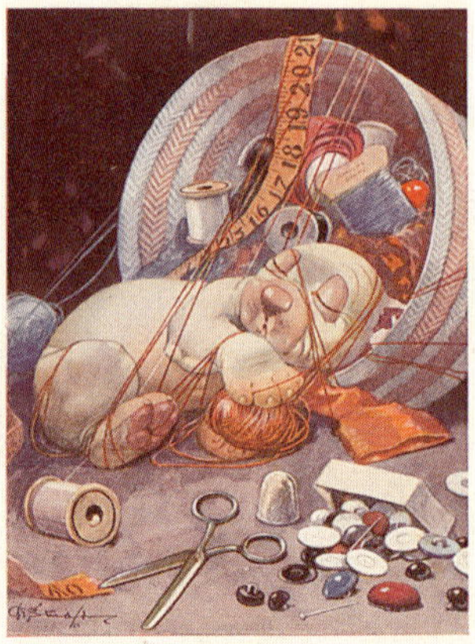
Mother's Help.

1056

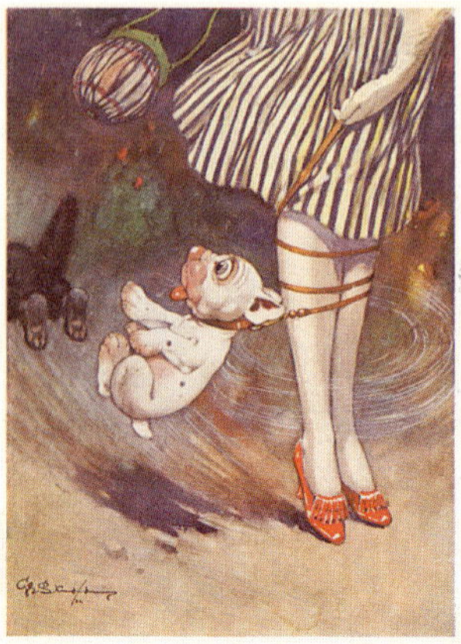
A Leg Pull.

1057

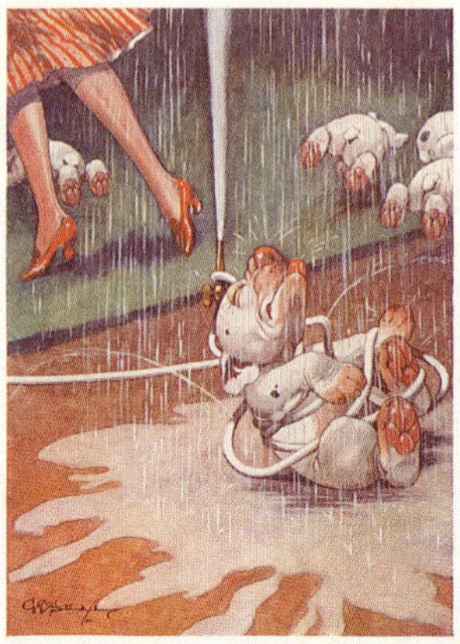
Say When.

1058

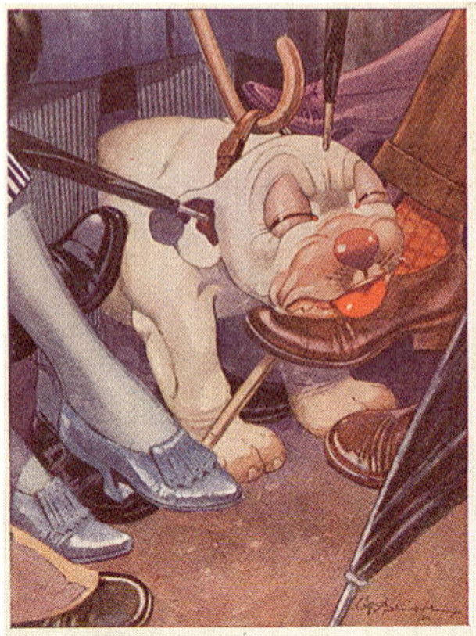
Coming Home from Wembley.

1059

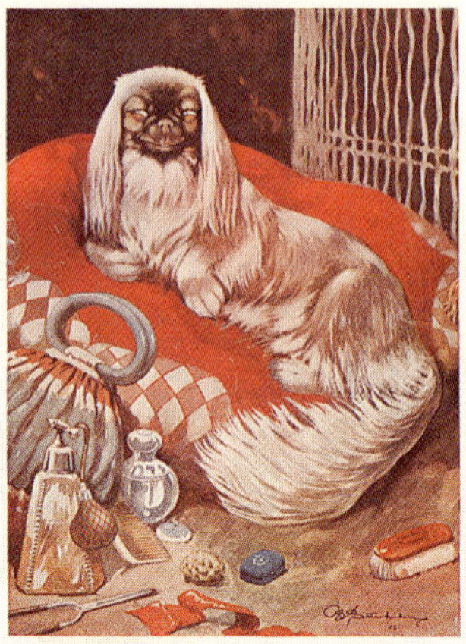
The Show Girl.

1060

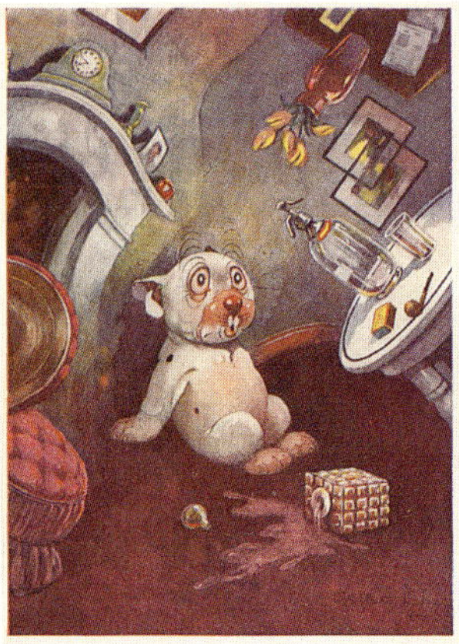
One Over the Eight.

1061

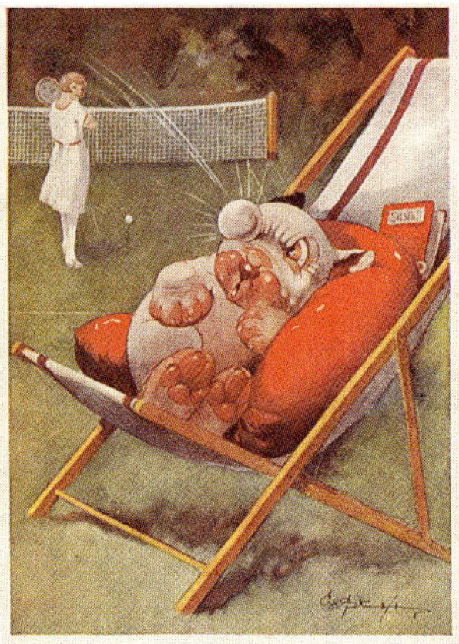
Deuce.

1062

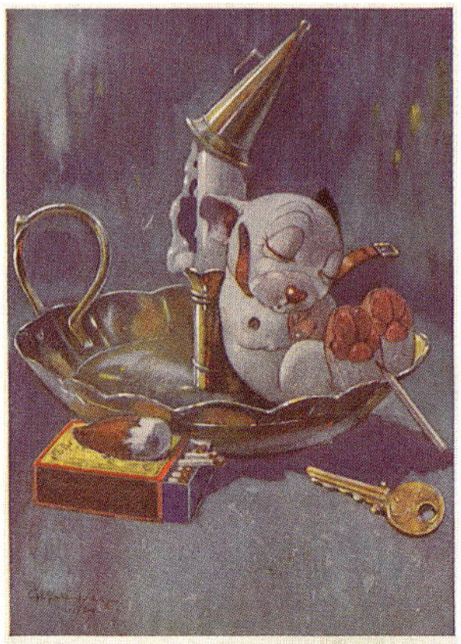
Three o'Clock in the Morning.

1063

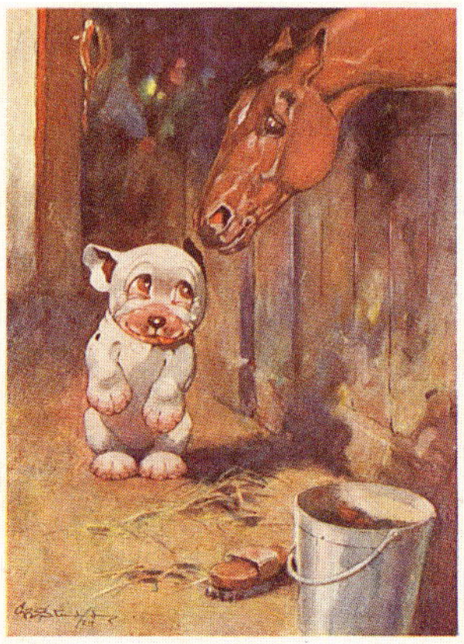
Stable Information.

1064

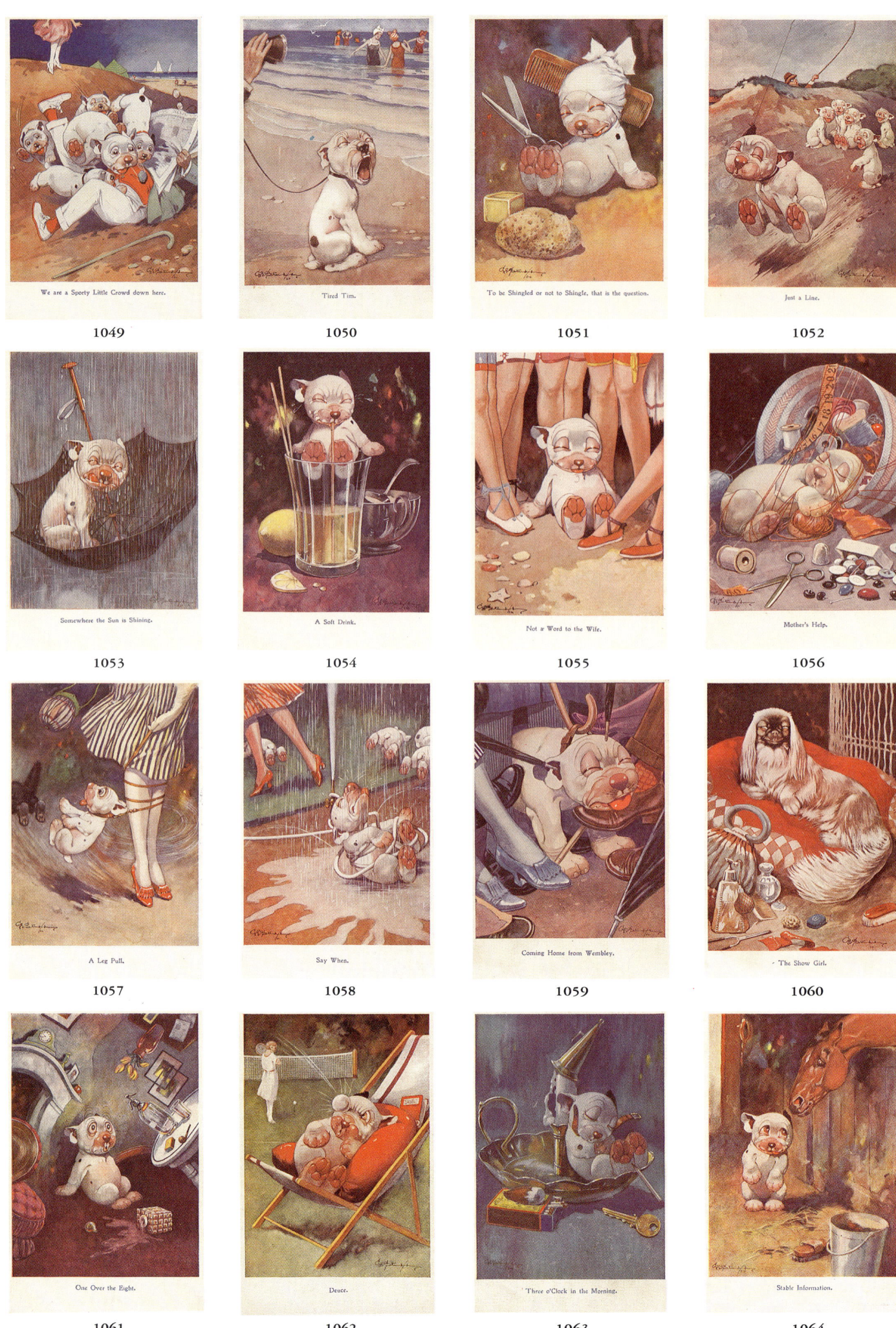

The "R.P.S." Series

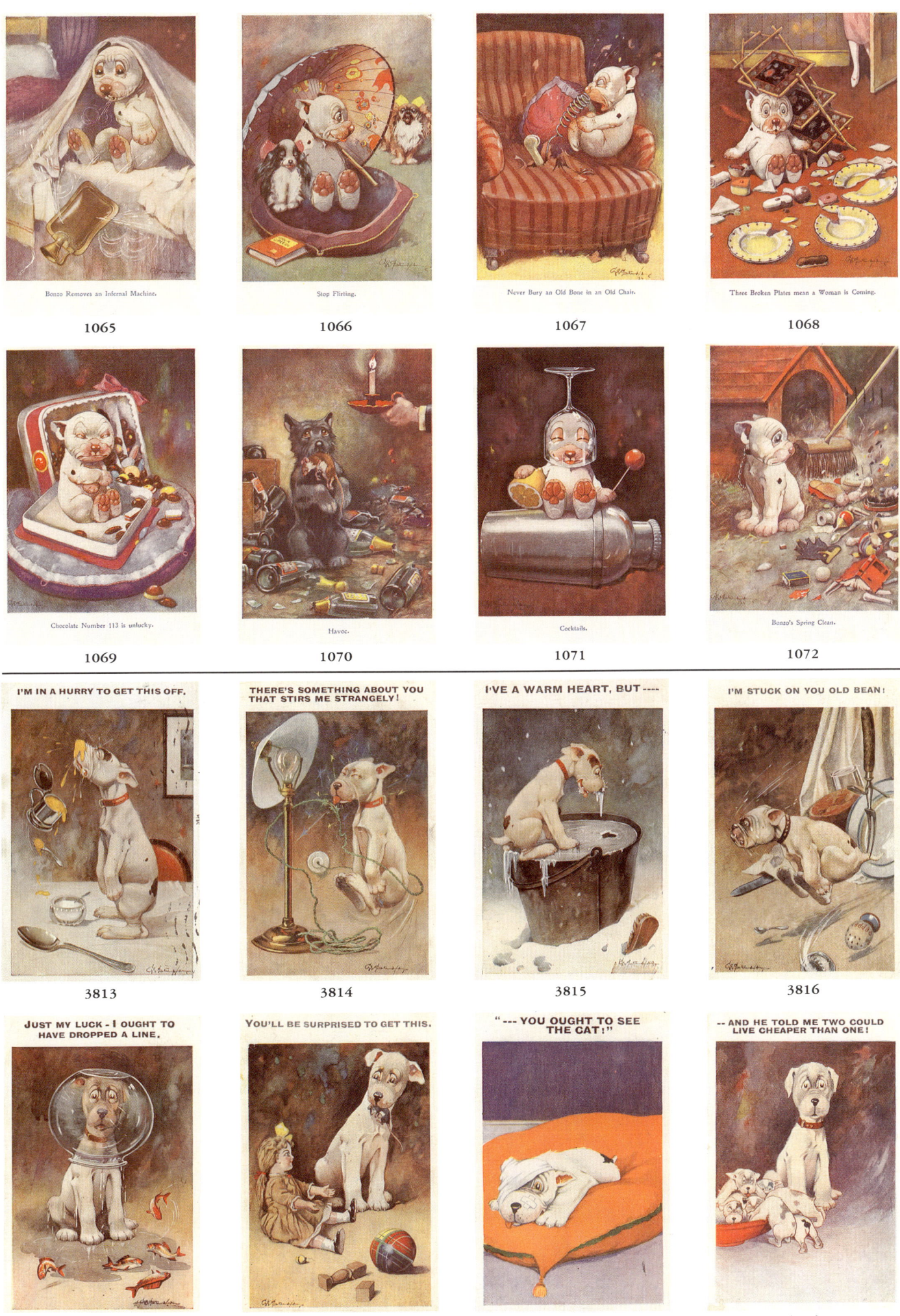

Inter-Art Co., "COMIQUE" Series

BKWI Bonzo Series

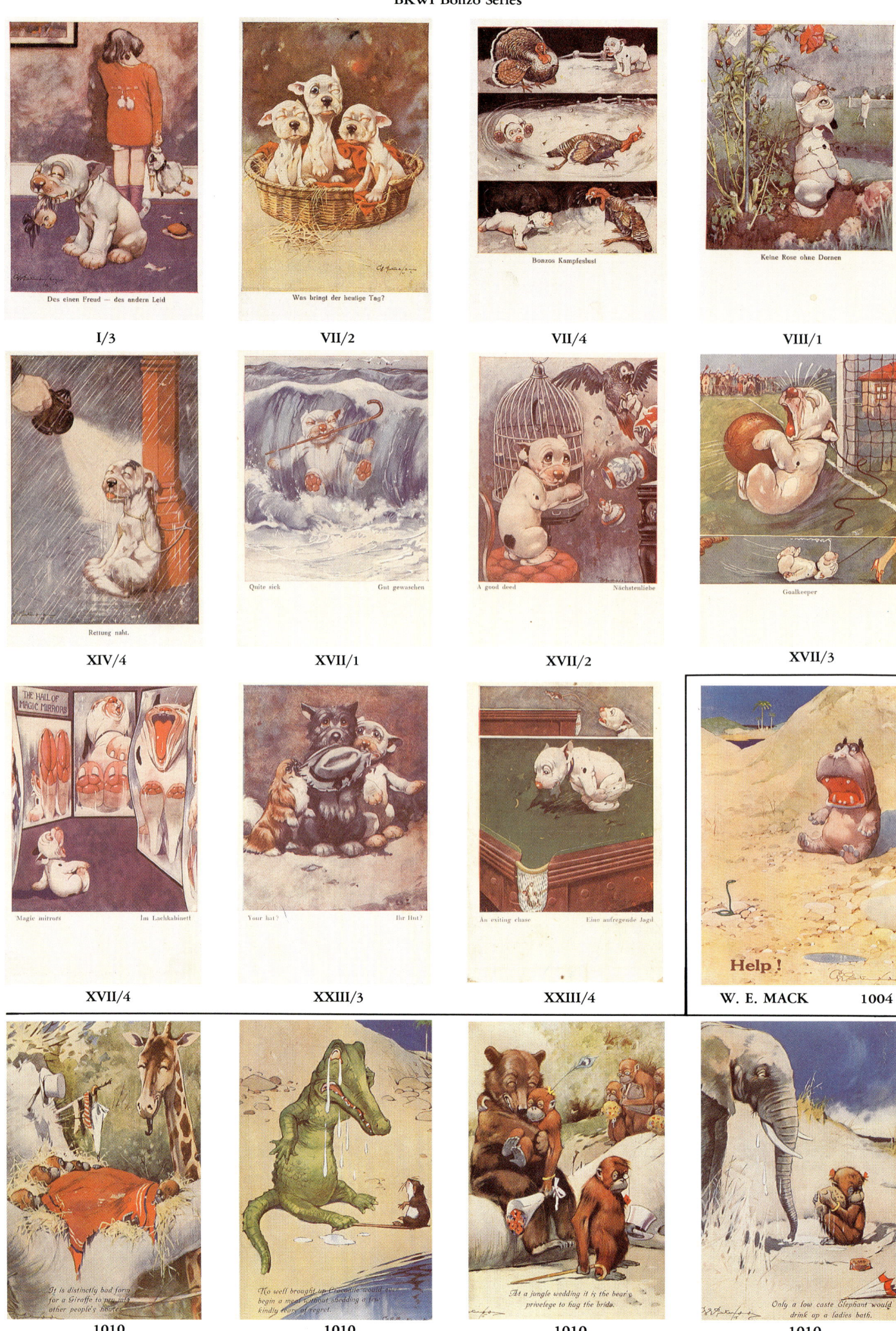

VIVIAN MANSELL & CO.

VIVIAN MANSELL & CO.

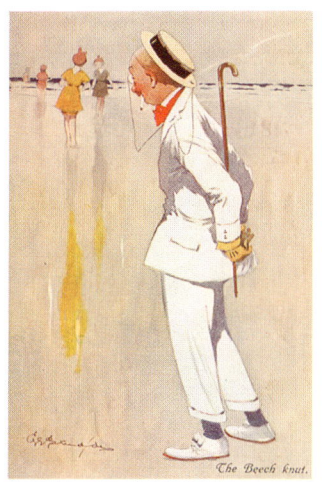
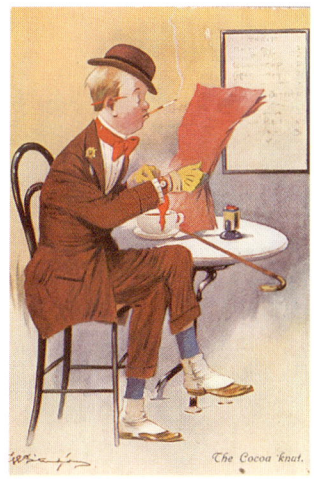
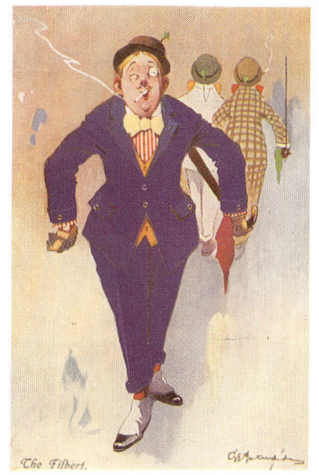
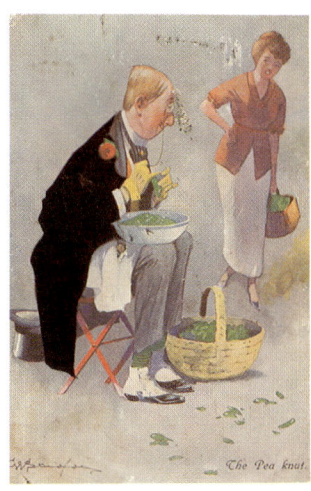

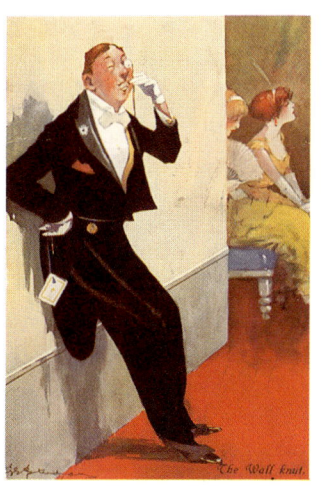
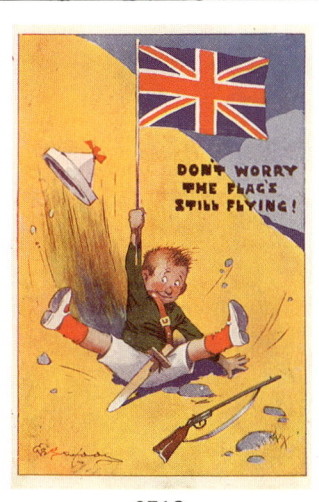
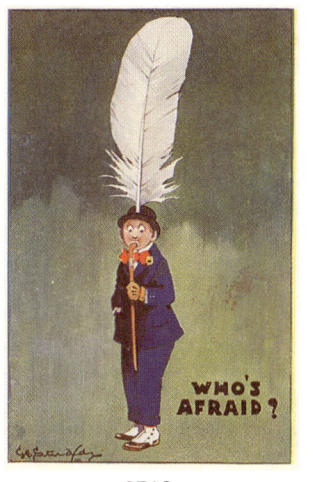
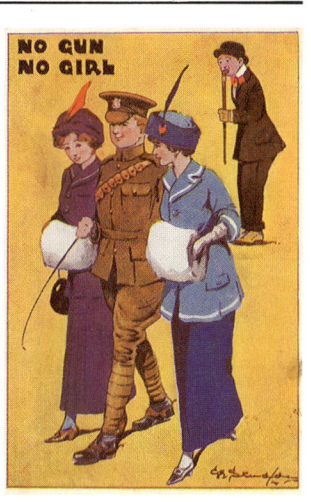

2718　　　　2719　　　　2721

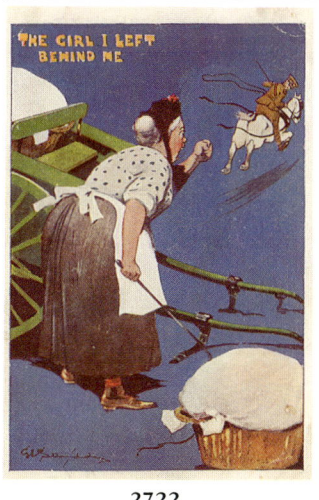
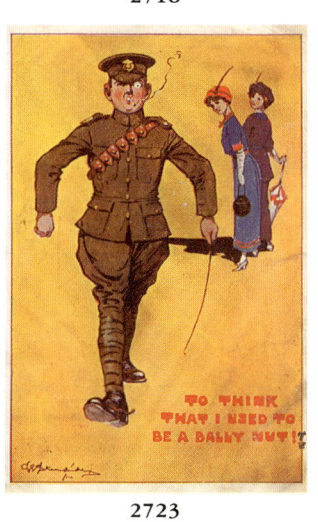
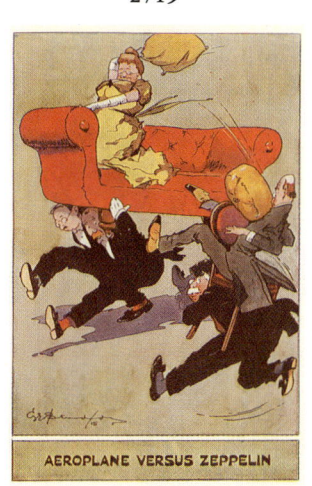
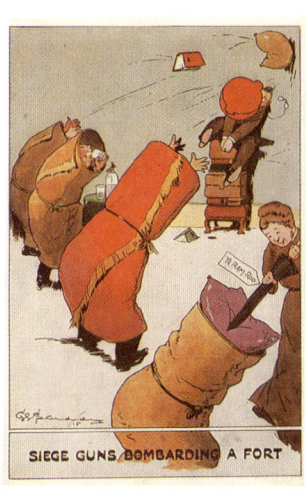

2722　　　　2723　　　　AEROPLANE VERSUS ZEPPELIN　2820　　　SIEGE GUNS BOMBARDING A FORT　2821

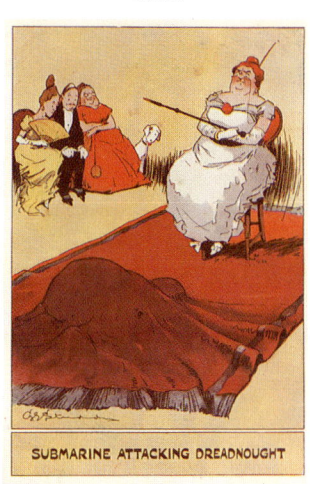
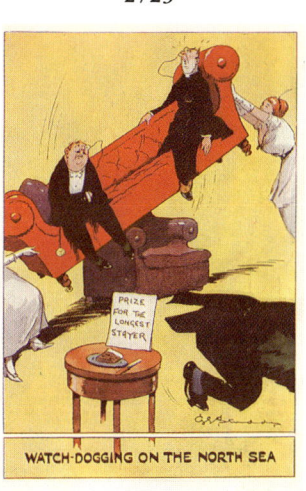
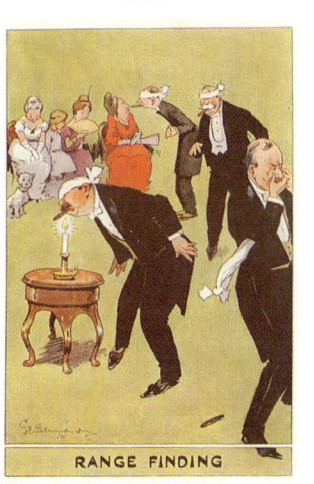
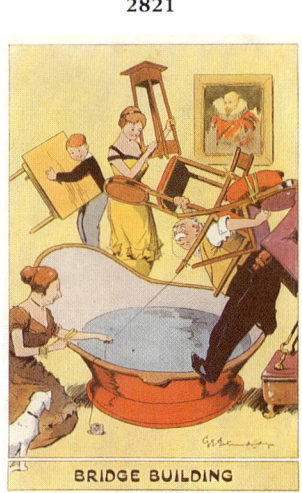

SUBMARINE ATTACKING DREADNOUGHT　2822　　　WATCH-DOGGING ON THE NORTH SEA　2823　　　RANGE FINDING　2824　　　BRIDGE BUILDING　2825

The "Henderson" Post Cards

The "Henderson" Post Cards

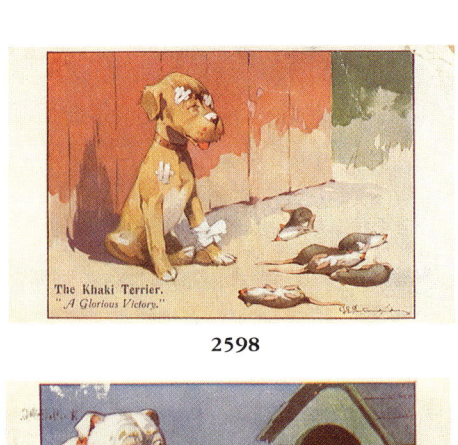
2598

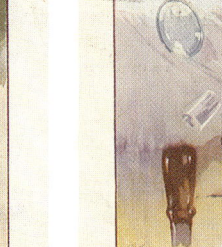
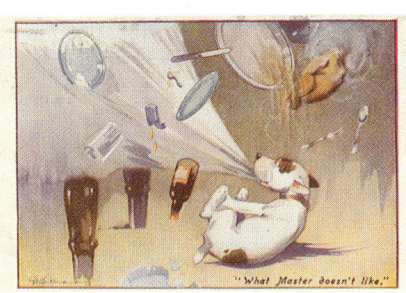
2600

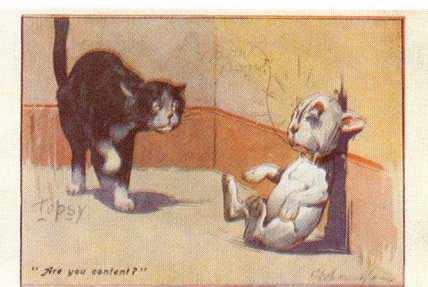
2601

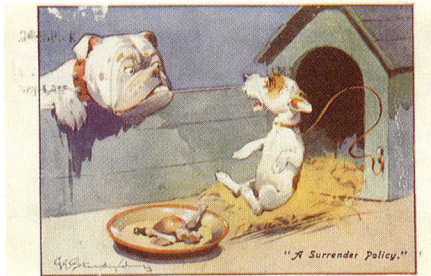
2602

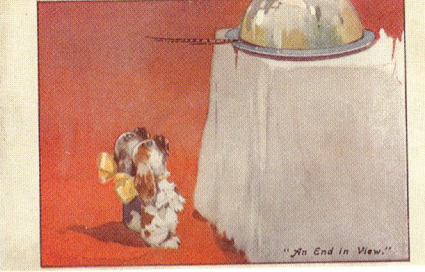
2603

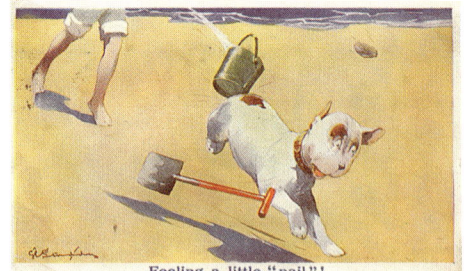
2948

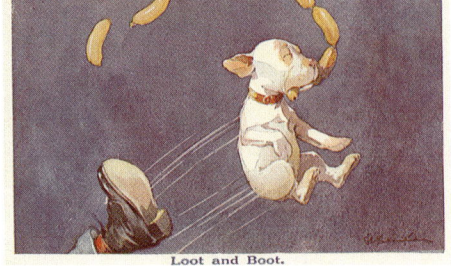
2949

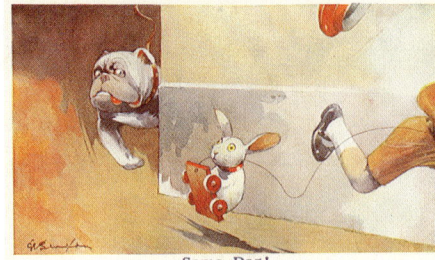
2950

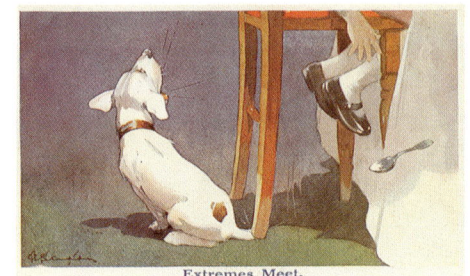
2951

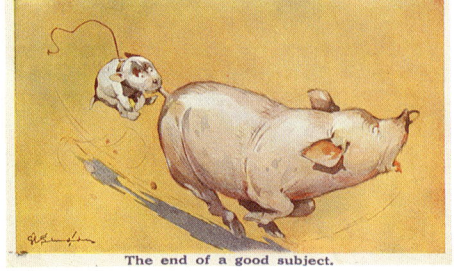
2952

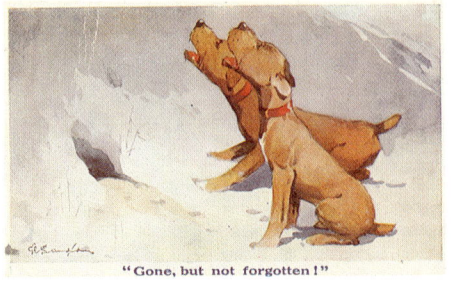
2953

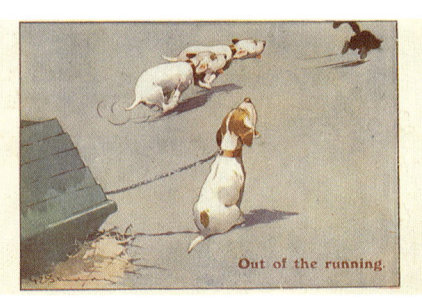
J. SALMON 2147

"ACADEMY" Picture Post Cards

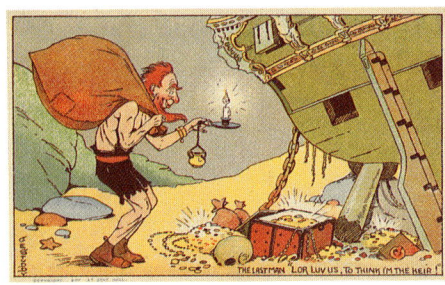
1019

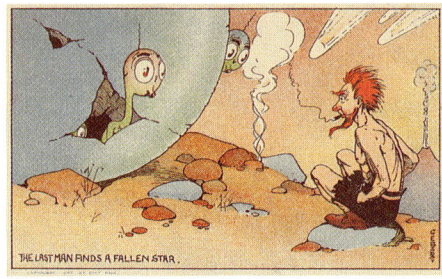
1021

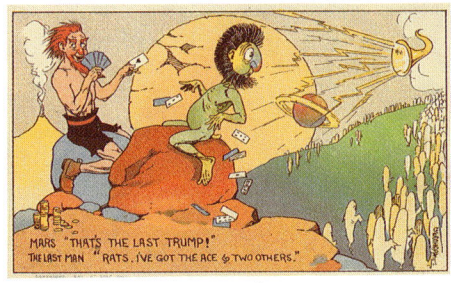
1024

HUMORESQUE

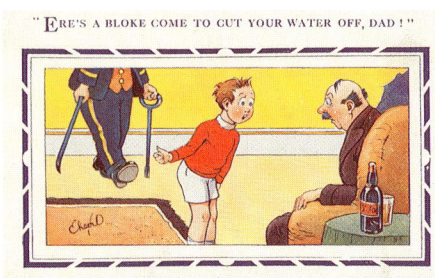
unnumbered

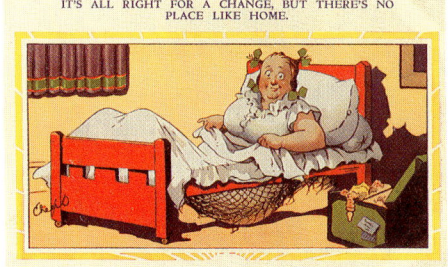
3301

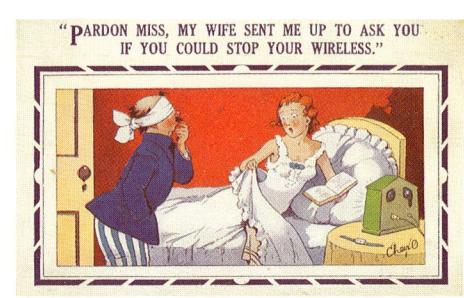
4581

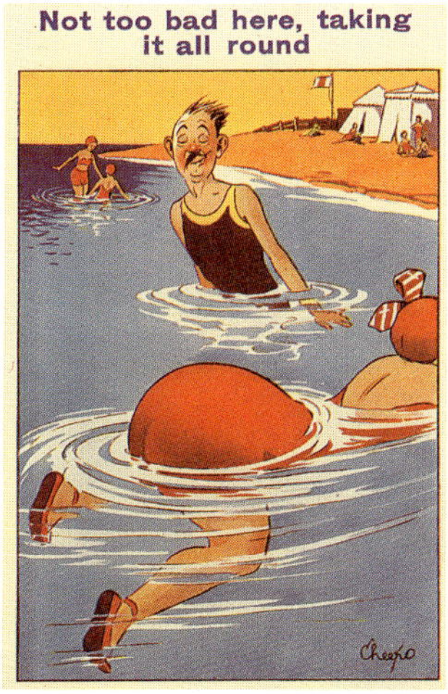
Not too bad here, taking
it all round
3068

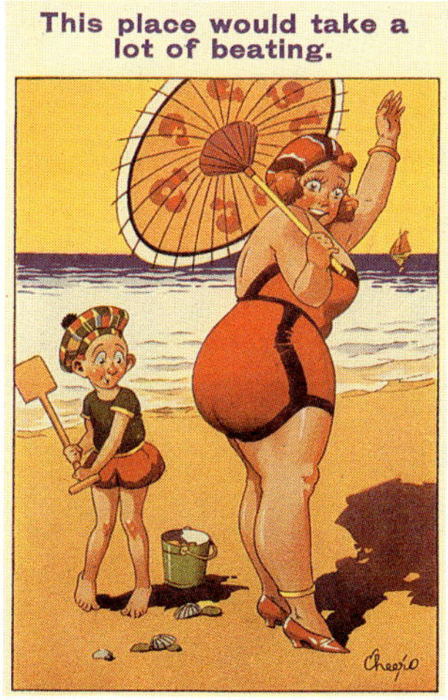
This place would take a
lot of beating.
3070

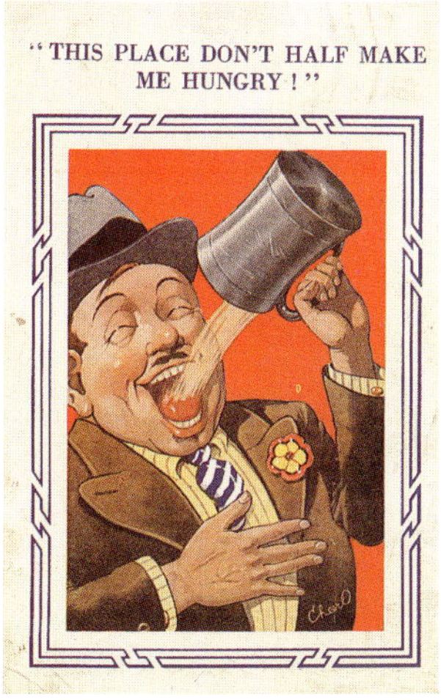
"THIS PLACE DON'T HALF MAKE
ME HUNGRY!"
3153

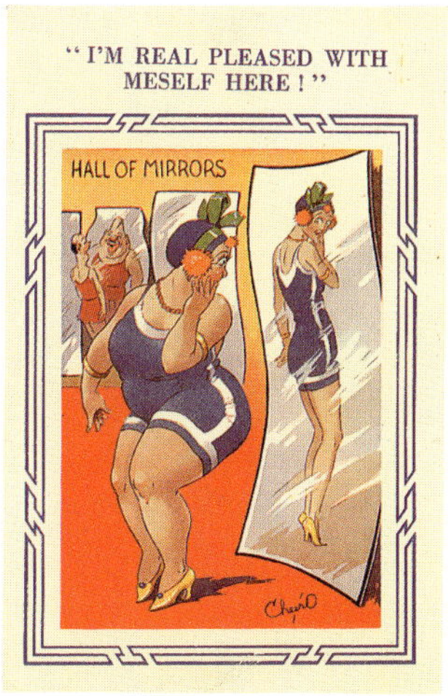
"I'M REAL PLEASED WITH
MESELF HERE!"
HALL OF MIRRORS
3154

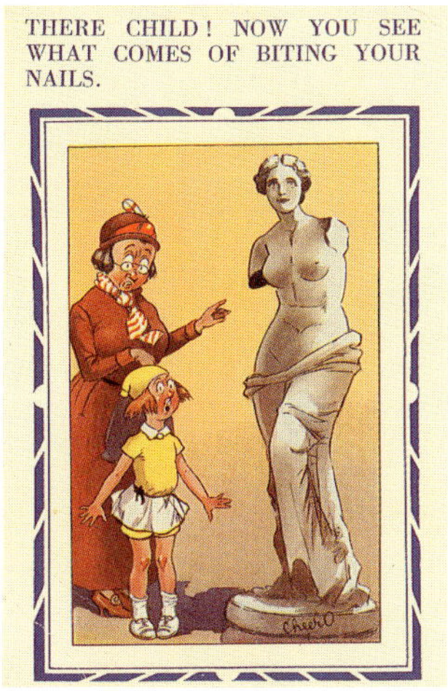
THERE CHILD! NOW YOU SEE
WHAT COMES OF BITING YOUR
NAILS.
3293

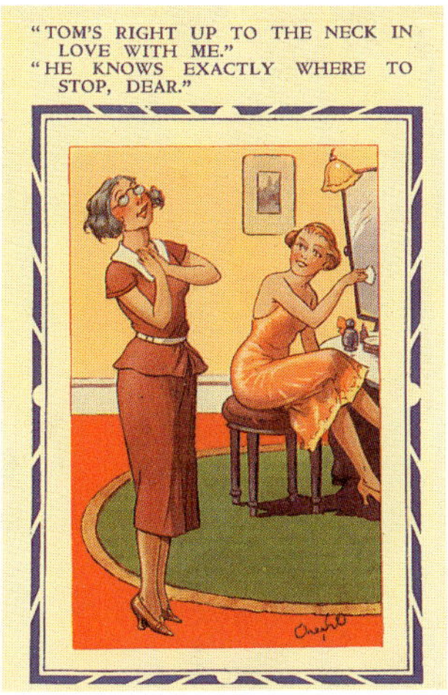
"TOM'S RIGHT UP TO THE NECK IN
LOVE WITH ME."
"HE KNOWS EXACTLY WHERE TO
STOP, DEAR."
3294

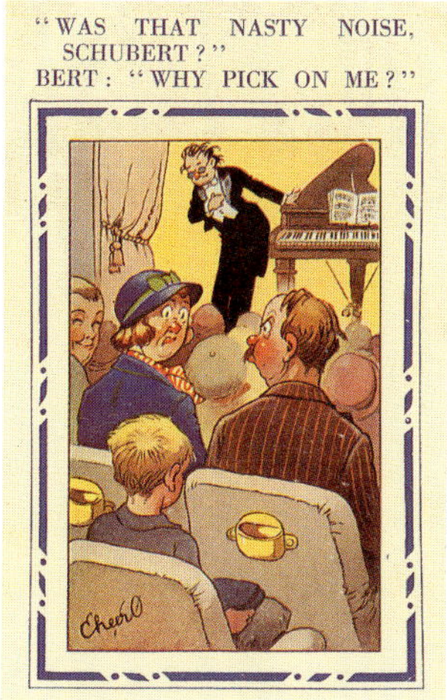
"WAS THAT NASTY NOISE,
SCHUBERT?"
BERT: "WHY PICK ON ME?"
3295

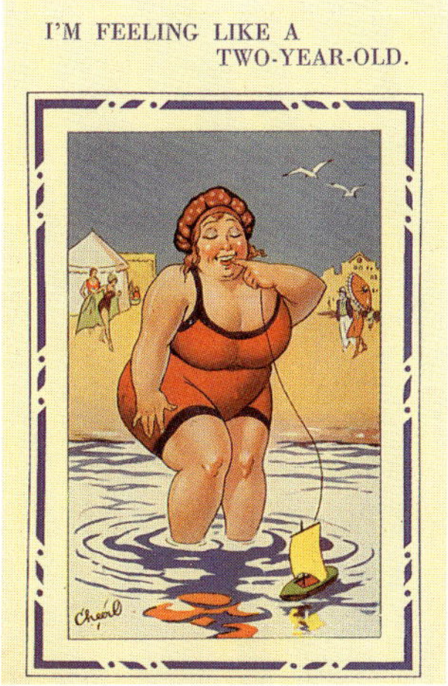
I'M FEELING LIKE A
TWO-YEAR-OLD.
3298

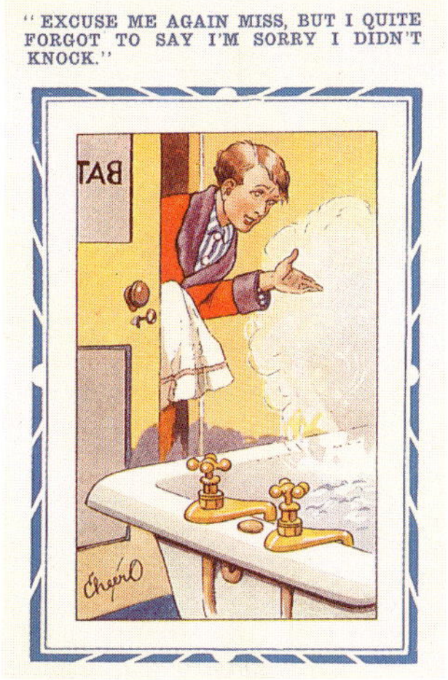
"EXCUSE ME AGAIN MISS, BUT I QUITE
FORGOT TO SAY I'M SORRY I DIDN'T
KNOCK."
3463

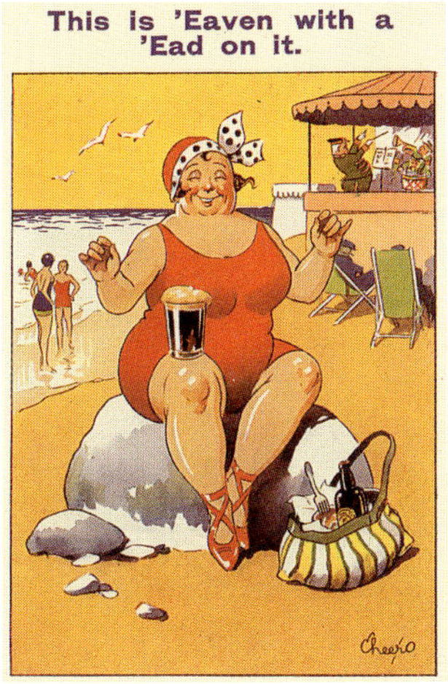
This is 'Eaven with a
'Ead on it.
3702

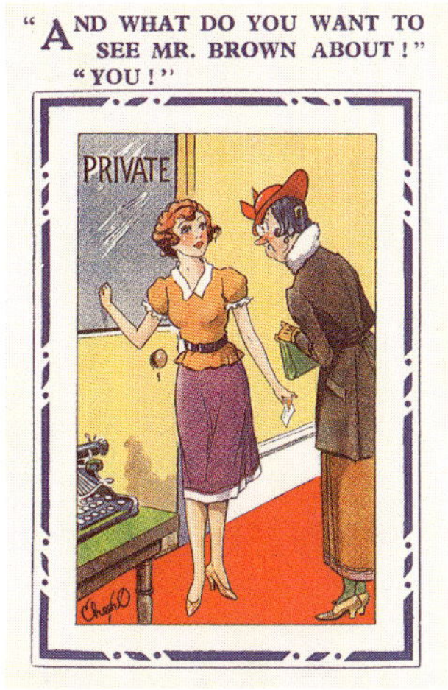
"AND WHAT DO YOU WANT TO
SEE MR. BROWN ABOUT!"
"YOU!"
PRIVATE
unnumbered

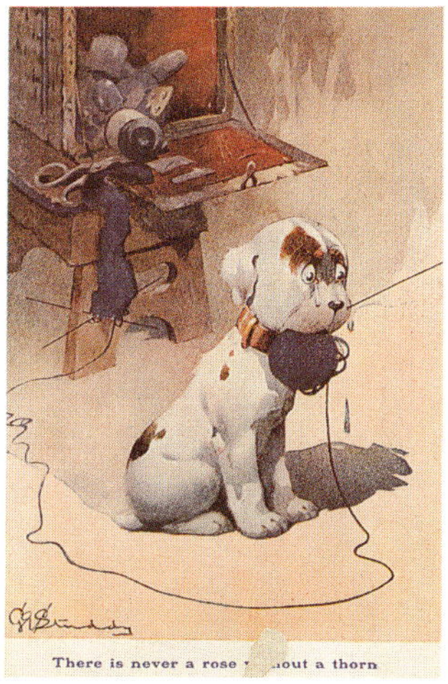
There is never a rose
out a thorn
1878

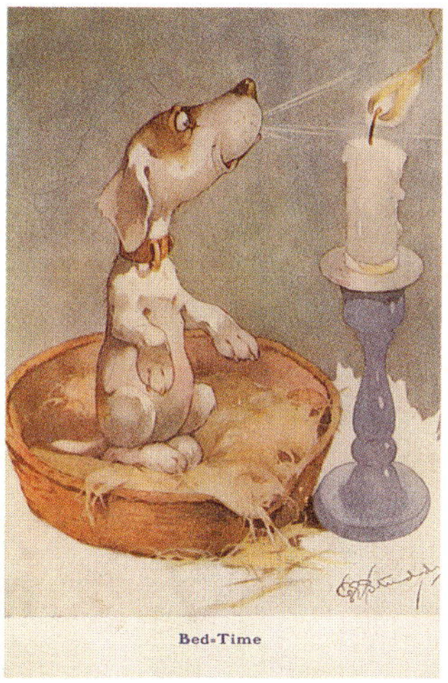
Bed-Time
1882

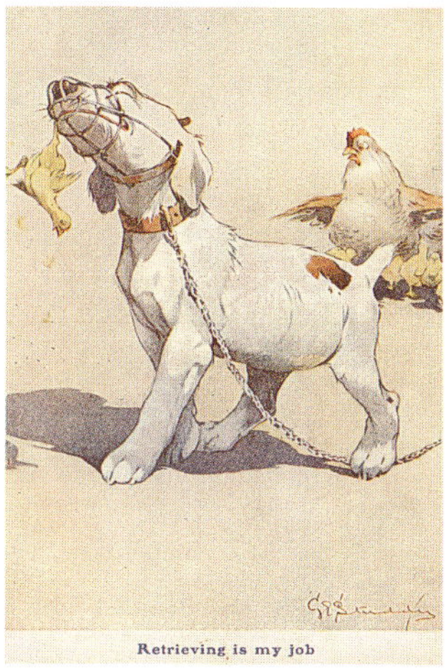
Retrieving is my job
1884

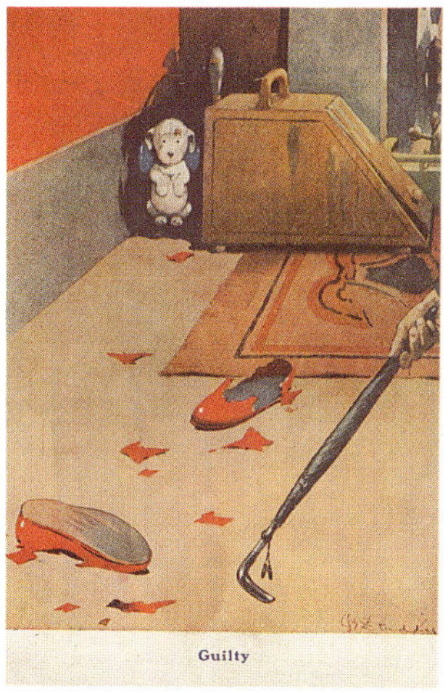
Guilty
1888

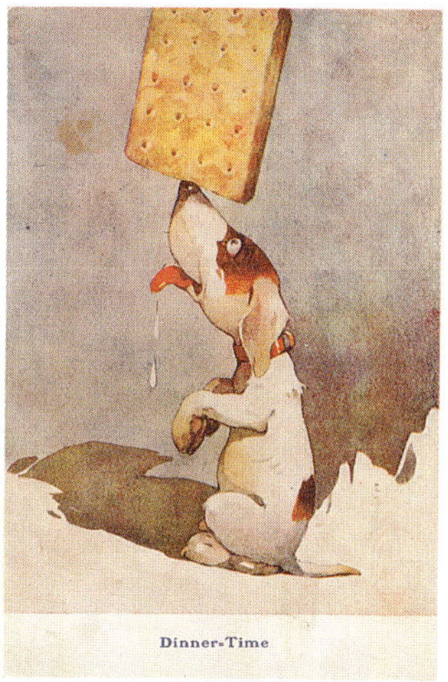
Dinner-Time
1897

VALENTINES SERIES

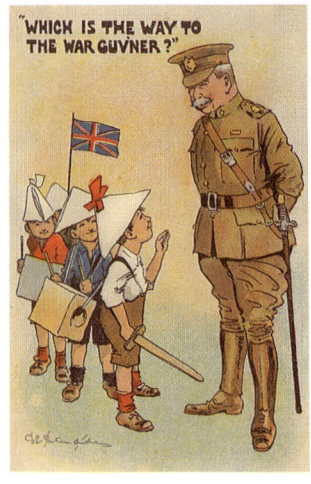
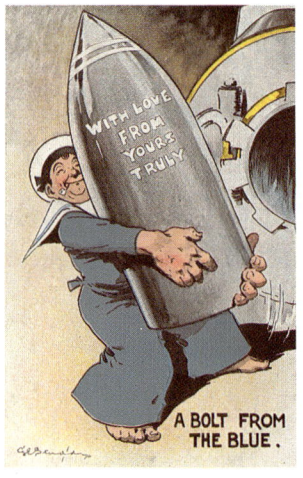
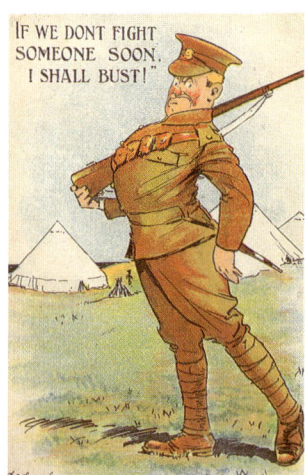
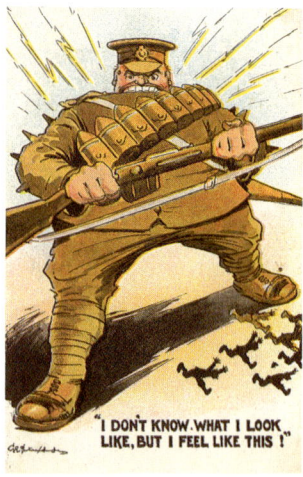

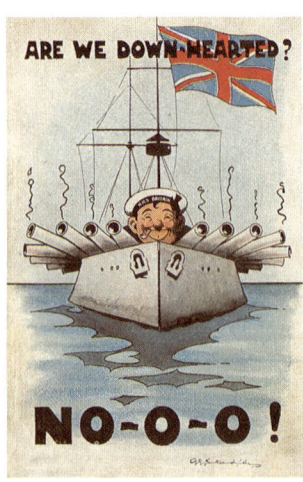
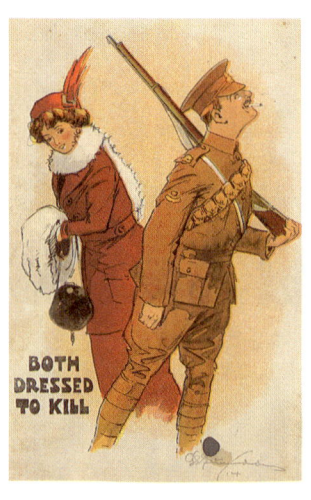
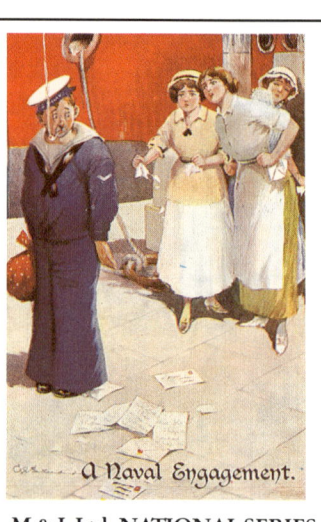
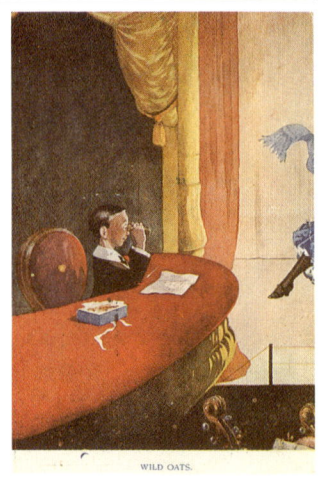

| | | M & L Ltd. NATIONAL SERIES | LAWRENCE & JELLICOE 5029 |

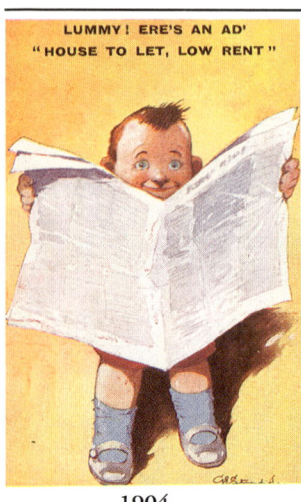
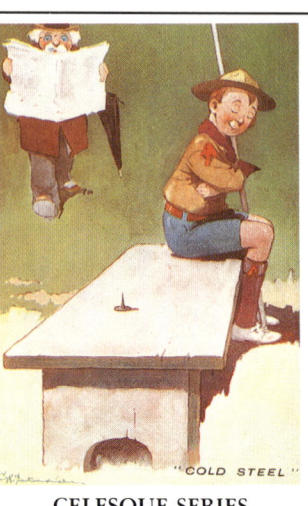
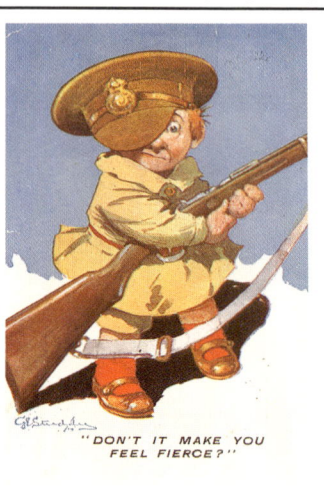
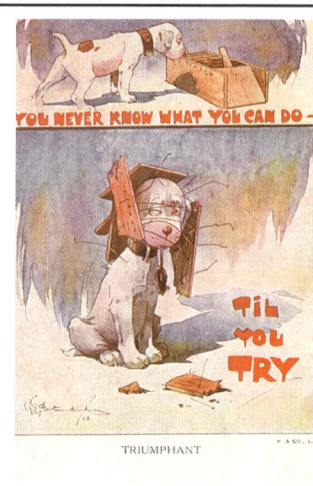

| 1904 | CELESQUE SERIES | | E. J. Hey & Co. |

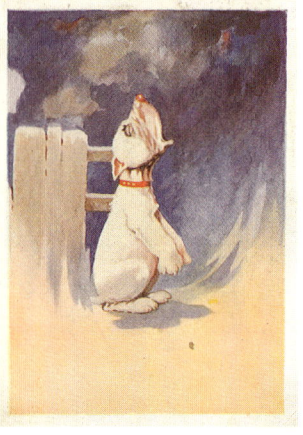
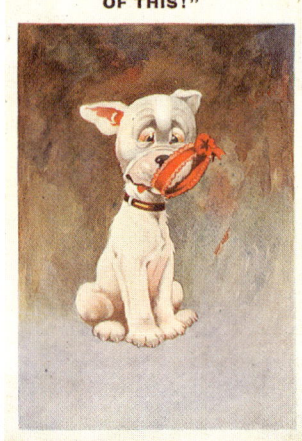
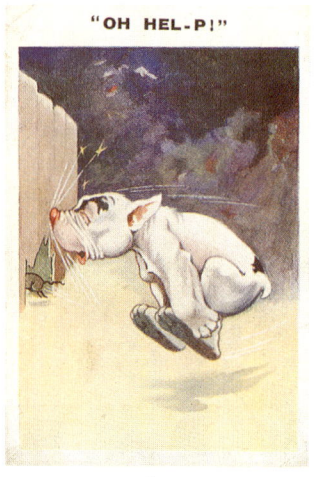
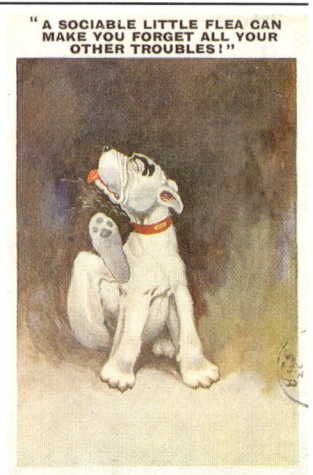

| 259 | 260 | 263 | 264 |

The Milton "Comic" Series

G. A. & Co. Ltd.

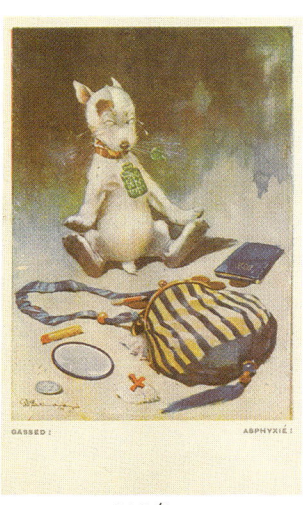 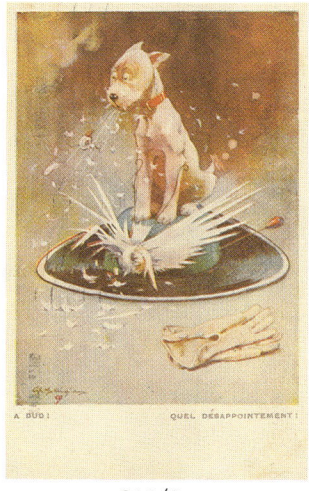 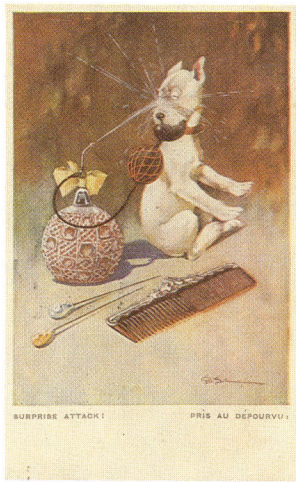 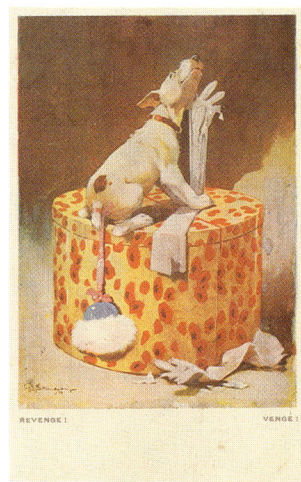

| 815/1 | 815/2 | PHOTOCHROM 2091 | Raphael Tuck & Sons 9144 |

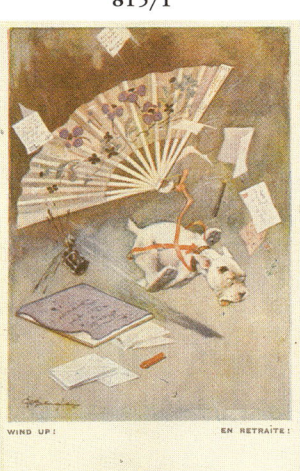 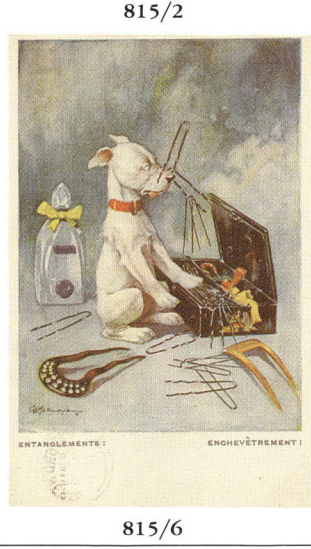 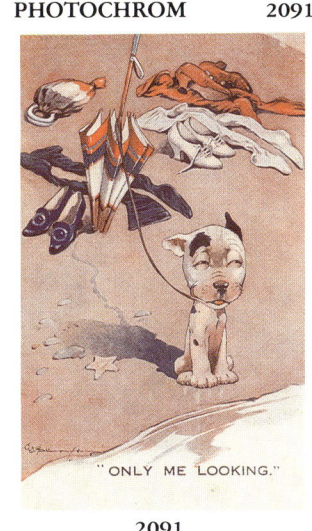 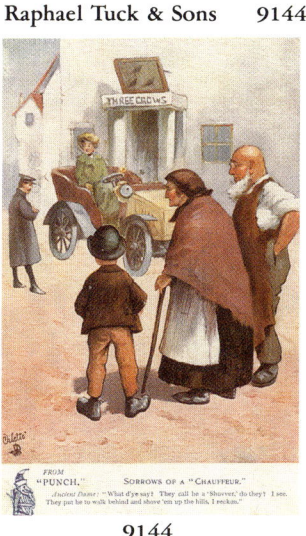

| 815/5 | 815/6 | 2091 | 9144 |

ADVERTISING CARDS

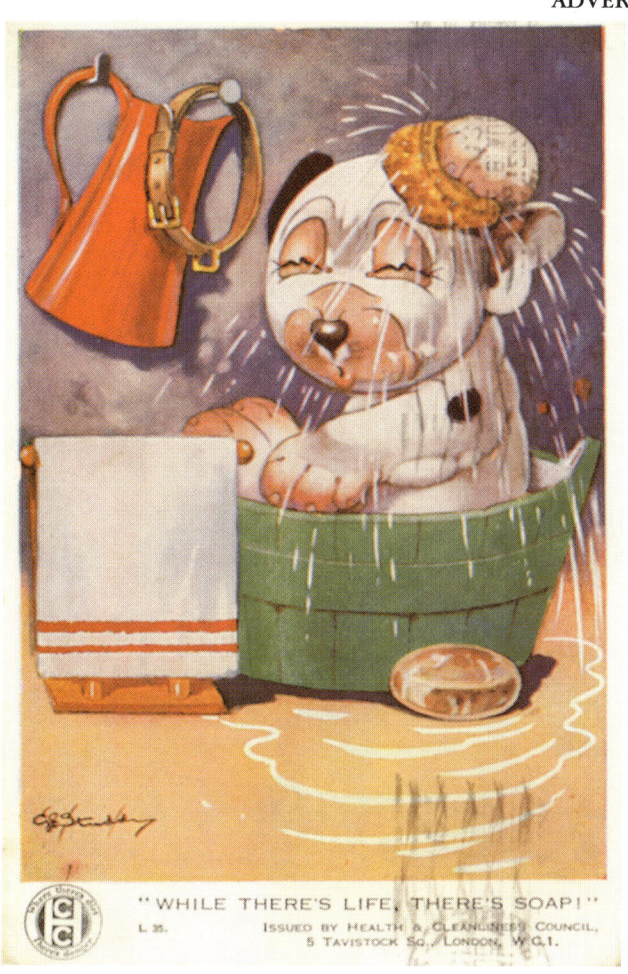

L. 35

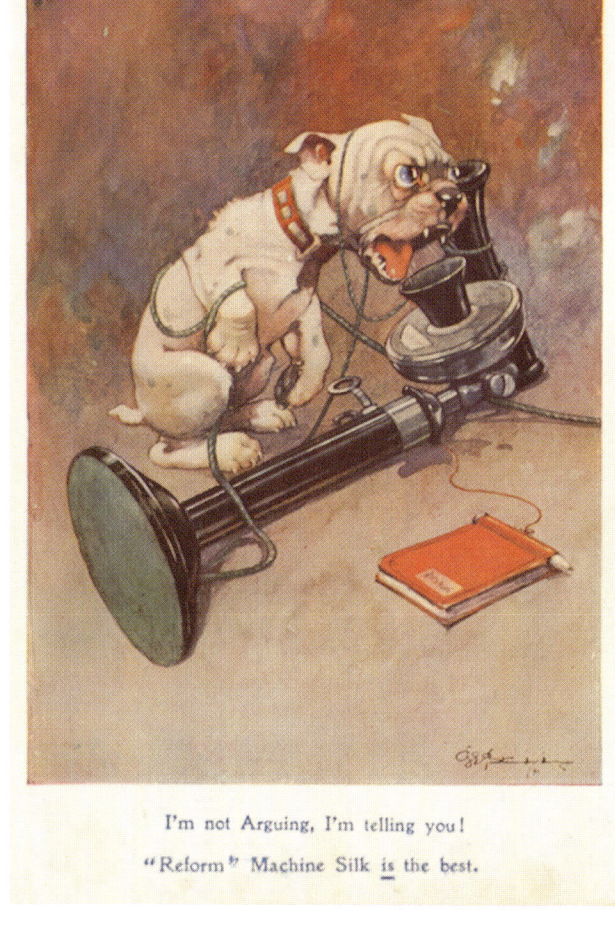

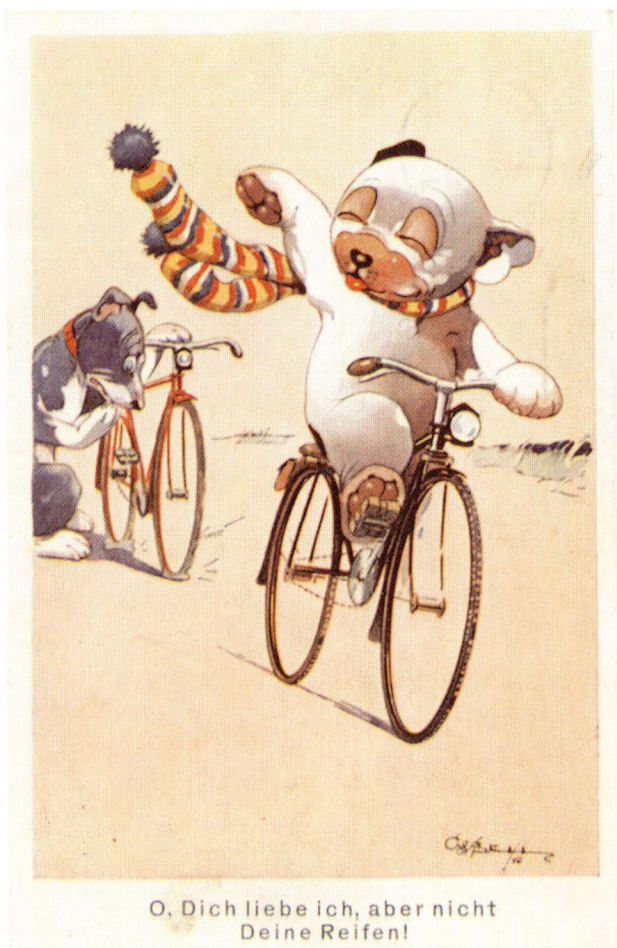

O, Dich liebe ich, aber nicht Deine Reifen!

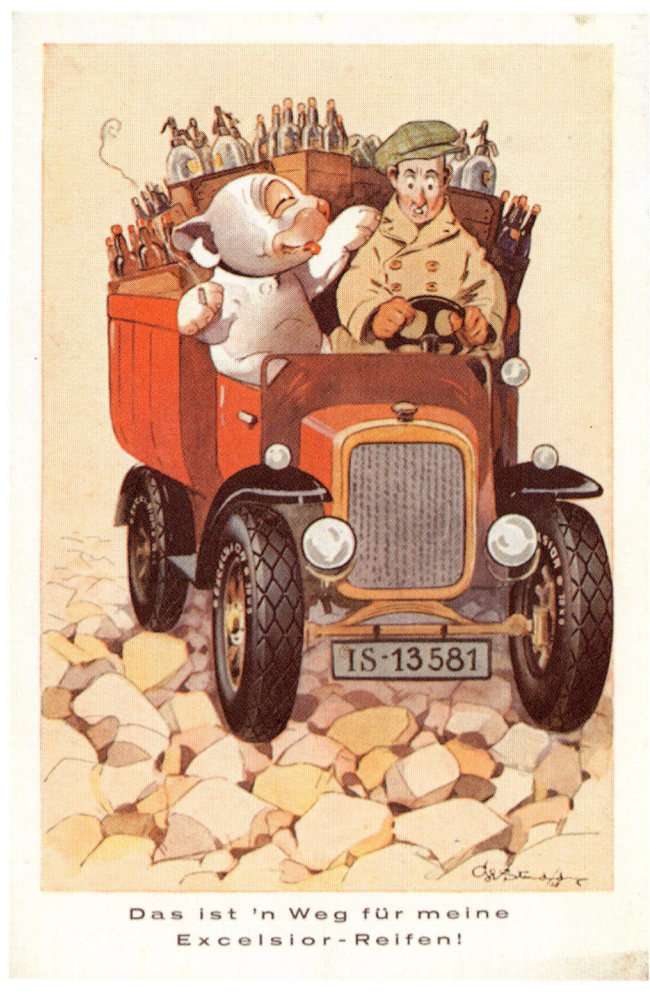

Das ist 'n Weg für meine Excelsior-Reifen!

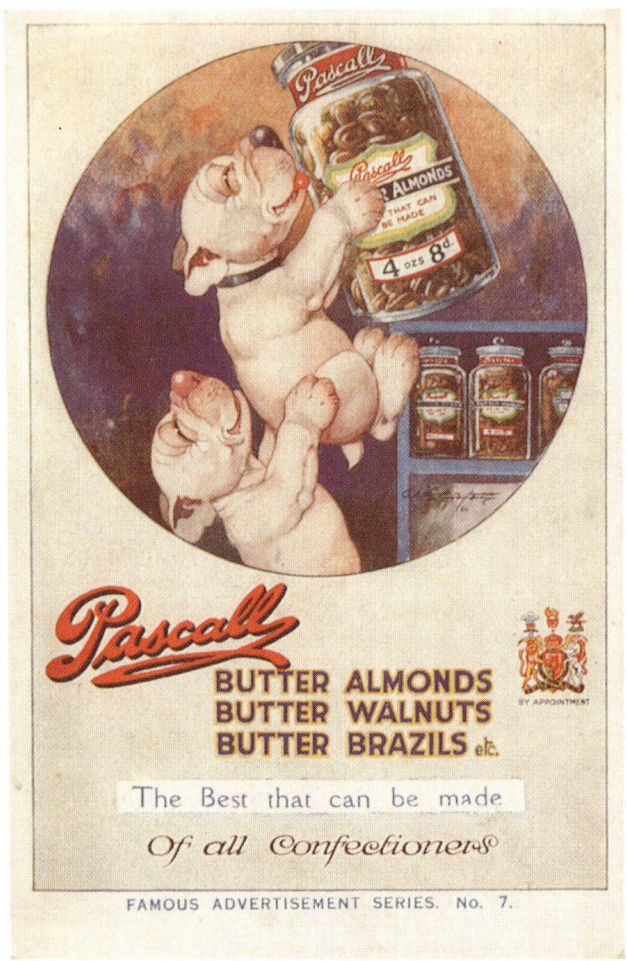

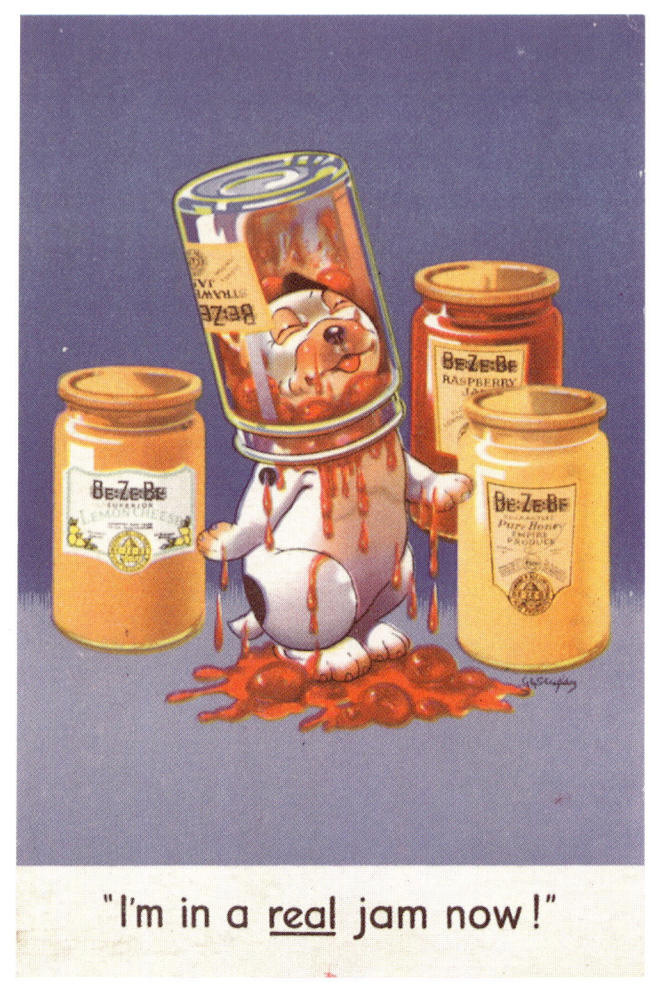

"I'm in a real jam now!"

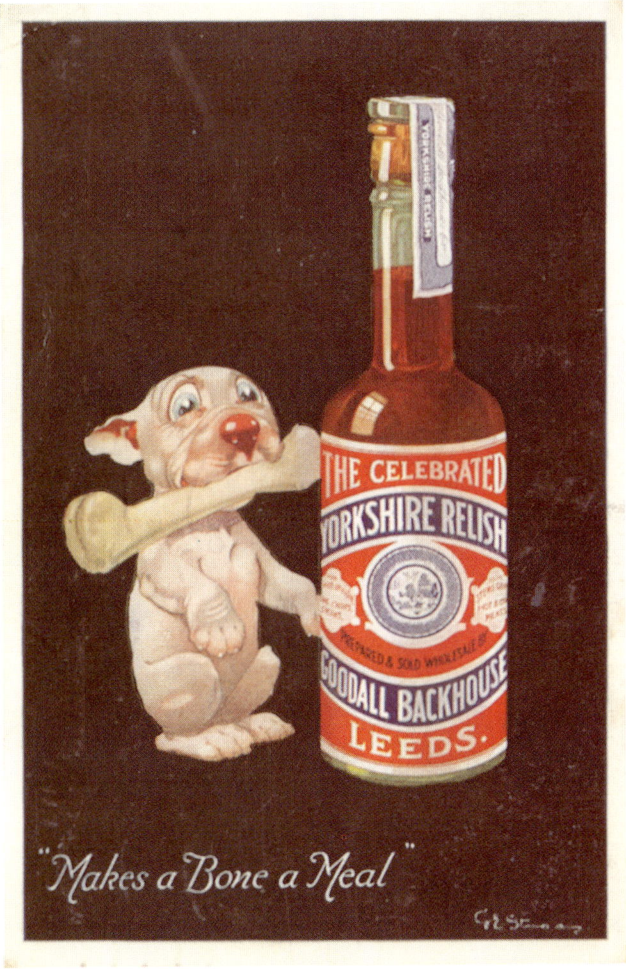
YORKSHIRE RELISH
THE CELEBRATED
YORKSHIRE RELISH
PREPARED & SOLD WHOLESALE BY
GOODALL BACKHOUSE
LEEDS.
"Makes a Bone a Meal"

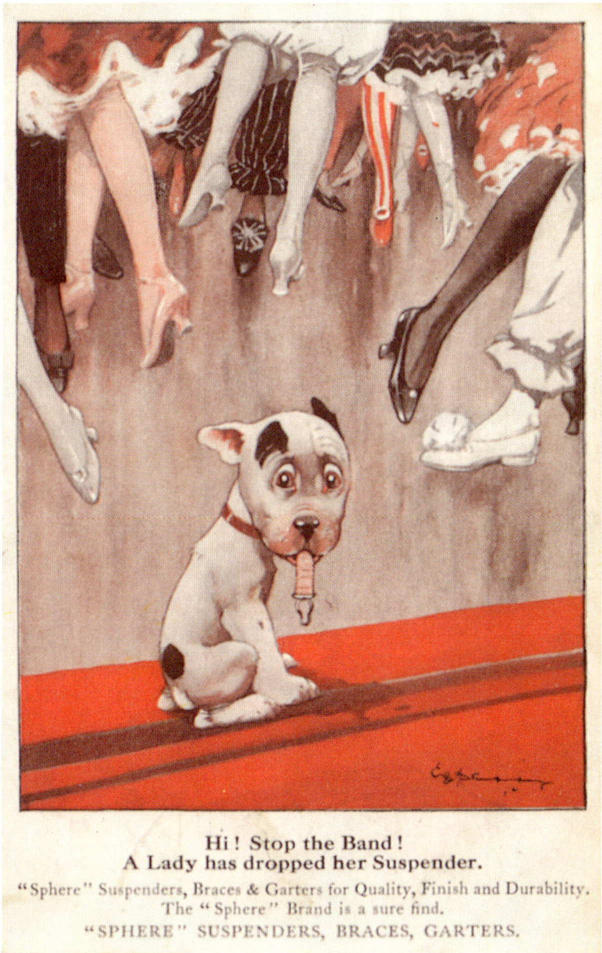
Hi! Stop the Band!
A Lady has dropped her Suspender.
"Sphere" Suspenders, Braces & Garters for Quality, Finish and Durability.
The "Sphere" Brand is a sure find.
"SPHERE" SUSPENDERS, BRACES, GARTERS.

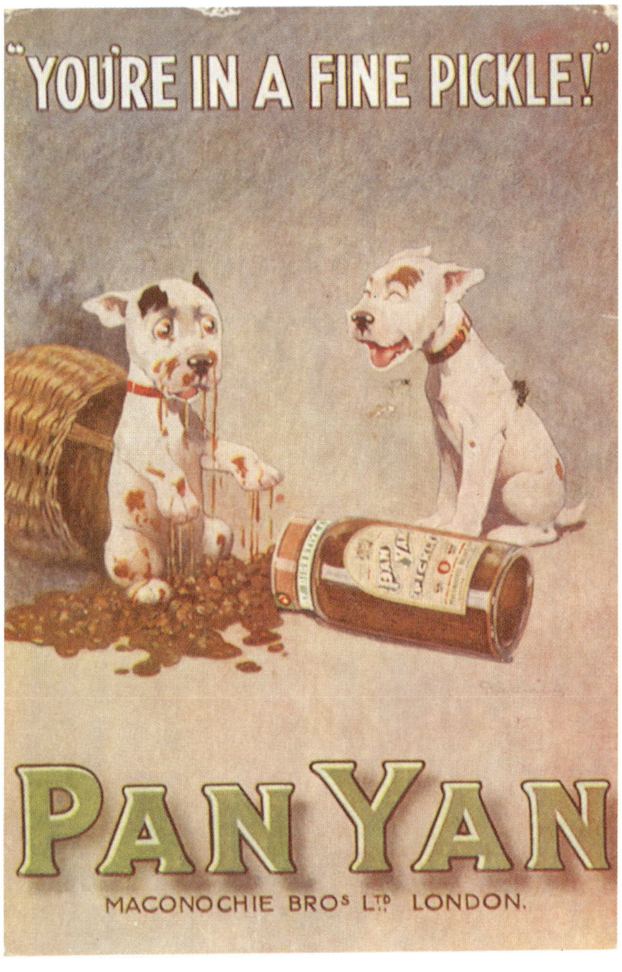
"YOU'RE IN A FINE PICKLE!"
PAN YAN
MACONOCHIE BROS LTD LONDON.

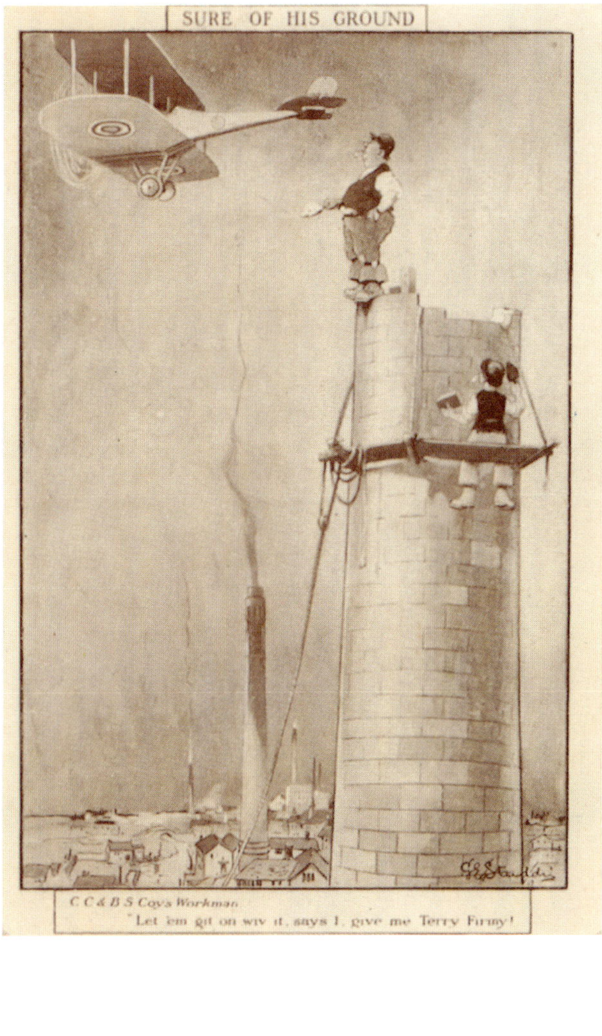
SURE OF HIS GROUND
C C & B S Coy's Workman
"Let 'em git on wiv it, says I, give me Terry Firmy!"

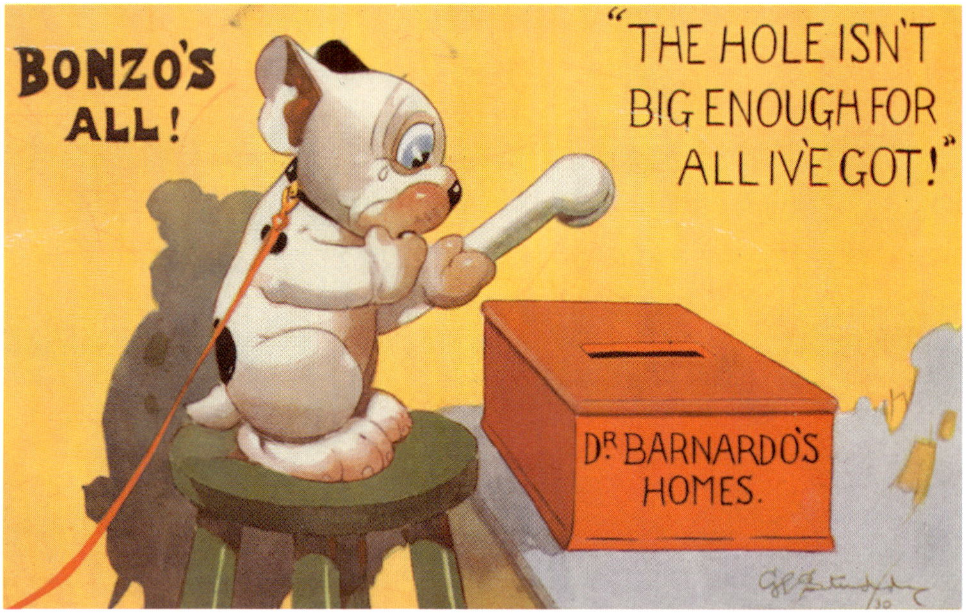
BONZO'S ALL!
"THE HOLE ISN'T BIG ENOUGH FOR ALL I'VE GOT!"
DR BARNARDO'S HOMES.

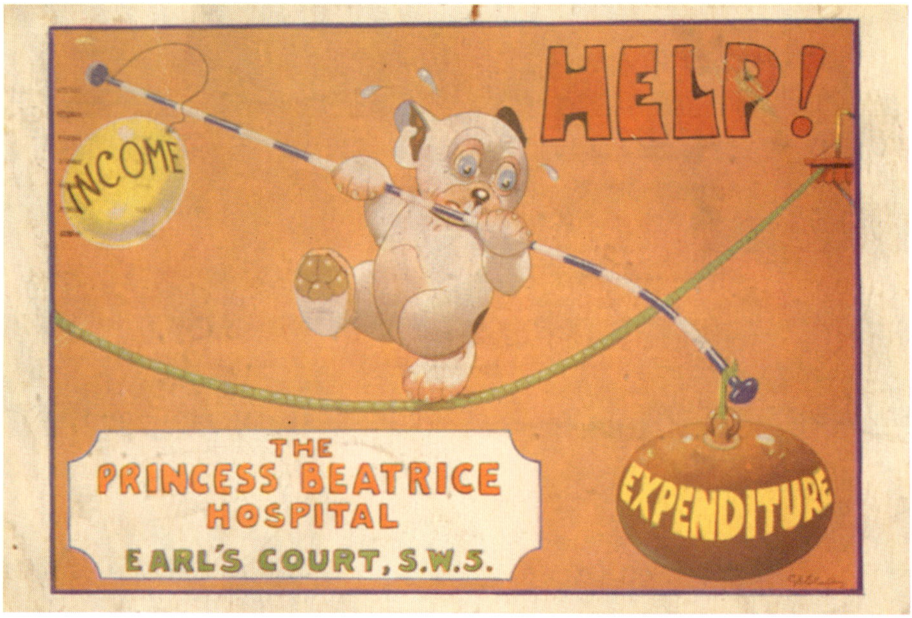
HELP!
INCOME
THE PRINCESS BEATRICE HOSPITAL
EARL'S COURT, S.W.5.
EXPENDITURE

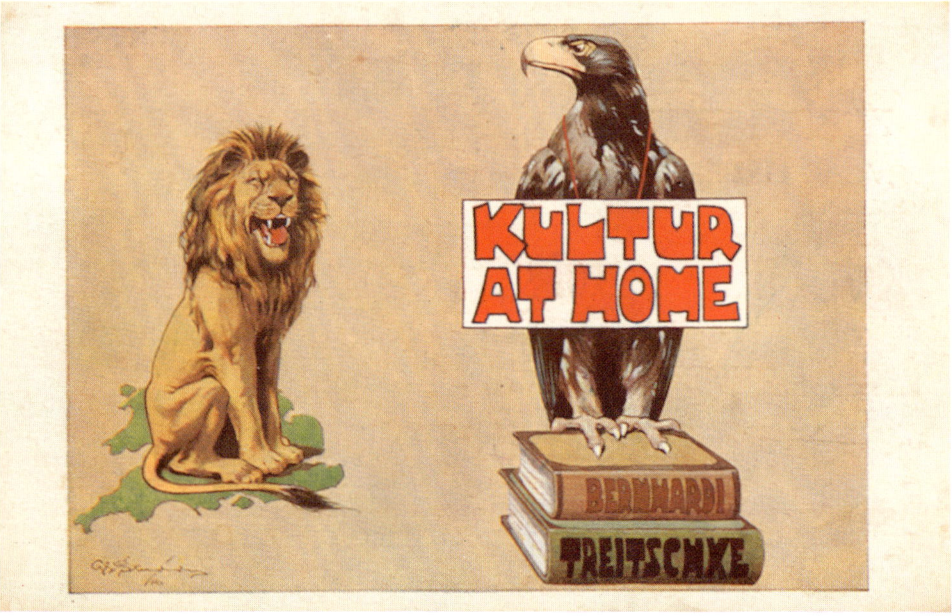
KULTUR AT HOME
BERNHARDI
TREITSCHKE

INDEX OF POSTCARDS AND PUBLISHERS

This index relates to the preceding pages of postcards. Listings are in the same order but vertical and horizontal cards have been separated – vertical cards have (V) after the number and horizontal cards (H). Numbers and captions are as they appear on cards used for compilation. Capitals, lower case letters and punctuation are all shown, although italics are not. It should be noted that some issues of the same card may differ to a small degree.

Pages 76–120 show all card designs traced up to the time of publication. Many were used more than once overprinted with a birthday greeting or made as a mailing novelty with pull-out photographic views. In most cases new numbers were issued, indicated here by a system of cross-referencing in parenthesis after the caption. Valentine's card No. 36 will be shown to be the same pictorially as Valentine's No. 1691, by the addition of (Val. 1691). Likewise card 1691 has (Val. 36) as a suffix.

The names of most publishers have been abbreviated. Thus 'Val.' = Valentine's, 'G & P' = Gale and Polden, 'J.H.' = James Henderson, 'I.A.' = Inter-Art, 'B.T.C.S.' = British Throughout Comic Series. 'W & L' = Wohlgemuth & Lissner, 'B.P.C.' = Bonzo Post Card, 'J.S.' = J. Salmon, 'M.' = Milton, 'W.E.M.' = W. E. Mack, 'G.F.' = Gallery Five and 'W &K' = Wildt and Kray. Where the publisher's name only comprises initials (as B.K.W.I.) it is entered as it appears.

Valentine's continued production of cards for a short time after Studdy's death using another artist. Although these are strictly 'not Bonzos' they have been included to show as nearly as possible the full Valentine range. In both sections they are indicated with * alongside the number. All other non-Studdy 'Bonzos' have been omitted.

Some numbers have no captions. This occurs when it is known or assumed that a card of that number was issued but research has been unable to trace either the caption or picture.

Mailing Novelty cards were designed to be printed with the names of various towns. A concertina strip of local views was inserted underneath a flap. Cards were produced with the name of any place and these are not included as variations in this index.

VALENTINE AND SONS LTD., DUNDEE AND LONDON.

VALENTINE & SONS LTD. DUNDEE AND LONDON.

No.	Orient.	Caption
Set No 1/A	(V)	"Many Happy Returns of Your Birthday." I JUST HAD TO CATCH THIS POST MY DEAR, TO SEND YOU THE GREETINGS WRITTEN HERE. (Val. 1379)
Set No 1/B	(V)	Birthday Greetings. I'D LIKE TO BE THE FIRST TO SAY "MANY HAPPY RETURNS OF THE DAY." (Val. 2514)
Set No 1/C	(V)	Best Wishes for "Record" Happiness this Birthday. HERE IS SOMETHING REALLY TRUE TO SHOW JUST WHAT I THINK OF YOU. (Val. 2279)
Set No 1/D	(V)	To Greet Your Birthday. MY PEN IS LIKE MY HEART TO-DAY – "TOO FULL" FOR ALL I'D LIKE TO SAY! (Val. 2520)
Set No 1/E	(V)	Birthday Greetings. A PICTURE POSTCARD JUST TO SAY "I WISH YOU LOTS OF FUN TO-DAY!" (Val. 1641) (Val. 2052.6)
Set No 1/F	(V)	A Line To Greet Your Birthday. CAN'T MOVE FROM HERE TILL I SEND THIS "P.C." WITH WISHES OF THE BEST FROM ME! (Val. 2285)
2/A		
2/B	(V)	Birthday Congratulations. I WISH WITH HEARTY SALUTATIONS, SUCCESS IN ALL THE CELEBRATIONS. (Val. 3115)
2/C	(V)	Birthday Greetings. A LITTLE LINE TO GREET YOU HERE WITH WISHES HEARTY AND SINCERE. (Val. 3375)
2/D	(V)	To Greet Your Birthday. I SEND THIS CARD TO LET YOU SEE THAT YOU ARE ALL THE WORLD TO ME. (Val. 2290)
2/E	(H)	Here's to a Happy Birthday. GOOD HEALTH – SUCCESS AND ALL GOOD CHEER BE YOURS FOR MANY A HAPPY YEAR! (Val. 2852)
2/F	(V)	Birthday Congratulations. I FEEL SO HAPPY, I COULD SING AND PLAY IN HONOUR OF THIS HAPPY DAY. (Val. 3032)
29	(V)	I WISH I COULD SEE YOU. (Val. 1518)
34	(V)	DON'T WORRY ABOUT ME – I'VE GOT A SPARE! (Val. 1688)
L 35	(V)	"WHILE THERE'S LIFE, THERE'S SOAP!" (Val. 1289)
36	(V)	CAN'T SAY I'M FEELING TOO GOOD. (Val. 1691)
222	(H)	"I'M EXPECTING YOU ANY TIME DEAR!"
223	(V)	IT WILL BE A FAR FAR BETTER WORLD SOON DEAR!
224	(H)	"FOR THE DURATION AND EVER AFTER!"
225	(V)	IT'S THE KILTIES THAT INTEREST THE SKIRTIES!
226	(H)	YOU CAN SEE I WISH YOU GOOD LUCK!
227	(V)	I DON'T KNOW WHERE TO THINK OF YOU – BUT I'M ALWAYS THINKING!
347M	(V)	"GOT IM!" (VALENTINE'S "FINE ART" SERIES – Cut-out Novelty) (Val. 347)
347	(V)	"GOT 'IM!" (Val.347M)
348	(V)	"I 'SHURE YOU I'M NOT!"
349	(V)	MERRY THOUGHTS
379	(H)	"FLYING IS BEST FOR YOU DARLING – IT KEEPS YOU AWAY FROM THE GIRLS."
380	(H)	"I FEEL LIKE A GENERAL WHEN I'M WITH YOU DEAR."
381	(H)	NEXT TIME I SEE YOU I'LL SINK YOU AT SIGHT.
382	(V)	"MISS MY GIRL AWFUL – I DO."
383	(V)	HEAVEN HELP HITLER NOW DEAR!
384	(V)	I COULD DO WITH A NEW PHOTOGRAPH OF YOU GIRLIE!
385	(V)	JUST DROPPING YOU A FEW LEAFLETS. (Val. 1902)
386	(H)	THEY CAN'T RATION LOVE.
387	(V)	THERE'S LOTS OF THINGS TO THINK OF BUT I ALWAYS THINK OF YOU.
388		
389	(H)	"I ALWAYS FEEL I'M IN HEAVEN WHEN I'M WITH YOU!"
390	(V)	"I'M NEVER SHORT OF SUGAR 'COS YOU'RE SO VERY SWEET."
501	(V)	THERE'LL NEVER BE A WAR ON BETWEEN YOU AND ME, DEAR! (Val. 501A)
501A	(V)	I WISH YOU WERE HERE TO JOIN ME! (Val. 501)
502	(V)	I'M BEGINNING TO THINK SOMEBODY LOVES ME!
503	(V)	"THIS IS TO SAY I'M O-KAY." (Val. 4597)
503	(V)	I'M FAR FROM THE MADDING CROWD!
504	(V)	WHY NOT A SPOT OF PEACE IN SPITE OF WAR?
505	(V)	GREETINGS FROM THE WHOLE DAM FAMILY!
506	(V)	JUST CHANGING MY "CHECK" TO TAKE YOU OUT.
638	(V)	"WHO SAYS GOWF?" (Val. 1416)
639	(V)	"SPOT THE WINNER!"
640	(V)	"TELL US ANOTHER!"
641	(V)	TWO'S COMPANY!
709	(V)	WHERE'ER WE BE IT'S V.V.V.!
710	(V)	JUST A HAPPY LITTLE LETTER TO YOU!
711	(V)	WE'VE ALWAYS LAUGHED TOGETHER, LOVE, SO LET'S SMILE WHILST WE'RE APART!
712	(V)	ALL BECAUSE I OFFERED HER A COUPON FOR A KISS!
713	(V)	"HI MISS! YOUR BLACKOUT IS NOT TOO GOOD!"
714	(V)	JUST DOING A BIT OF WISHFUL THINKING DEARIE!
840	(H)	HAPPY BIRTHDAY! The little flowers I send to-day Will tell you in their own sweet way That I – FORGET-THEE-NOT! (VALENTINE'S "STUDDY" SERIES)
841	(H)	FOR YOUR BIRTHDAY I send these flowers Posthaste to say – wish you every Joy to-day! (VALENTINE'S "STUDDY" SERIES)
842	(H)	The Three Bears are here with a bouquet of flowers, To wish You many happy hours On this Your Birthday, dear! (VALENTINE'S "STUDDY" SERIES)
843	(V)	HAPPY BIRTHDAY to You! Hullo! Hullo!! I send you here Fond wishes for Your Birthday, dear. (VALENTINE'S "STUDDY" SERIES)
844	(H)	JUST OUT! And in time to wish You – A HAPPY BIRTHDAY! (VALENTINE'S "STUDDY" SERIES)
888	(V)	"I'M COUNTING EVERY SECOND TILL WE MEET."
912	(V)	A FRIEND IN NEED.
913	(H)	YOURS IN HASTE.
914	(V)	HERE'S FOR LUCK!
915	(V)	I DID BUT SEE HER PASSING BY!
916	(V)	"DON'T GO DOWN THE MINE DADDY!" (Val. 997)
917	(V)	NOW WE UNDERSTAND EACH OTHER!
918	(V)	Birthday Greetings LIKE "BONZO" MAY YOU HAVE A BRIGHT SURPRISE TO GLADDEN AND DELIGHT YOUR EYES. (Val. 941)
918	(V)	A Happy Birthday HERE'S "BONZO" WITH WISHES SINCERE AND HEARTY FOR A JOLLY TIME AT YOUR BIRTHDAY PARTY.
918	(V)	Birthday Wishes LIKE "BONZO" MAY YOUR FRIENDS PROVE TRUE, AND THIS GLAD DAY REMEMBER YOU. (Val. 941) (Val. 1448)
918	(V)	Birthday Greetings "BONZO" HAS COME TO LET YOU SEE. YOU'RE ALWAYS KEPT IN MIND BY ME. (Val. 941) (Val. 1449)
918	(V)	To Greet Your Birthday. MAY YOU LIKE "BONZO" HAVE A FEAST OF BLISS AND EVERY BIRTHDAY HAPPEN JUST LIKE THIS.
918	(V)	A Happy Birthday "SWEETS FOR THE SWEET," AND WISHES FOND AND TRUE: I SEND PER "BONZO" THIS GLAD DAY TO YOU.
931	(H)	"MY WONDERFUL ONE!"

VALENTINE AND SONS LTD., DUNDEE AND LONDON.

932 (H) STILL BUZZING AROUND!
933 (H) "BONZO" BRINGS YOU GOOD LUCK!
934 (H) ARRIVED HOME SAFELY!
935 (H) "NICE LITTLE BIT OF FLUFF!"
936 (H) I WISH I COULD JOIN YOU!
941 (V) Christmas Greetings. LIKE "BONZO" MAY YOU HAVE A BRIGHT SURPRISE TO GLADDEN AND DELIGHT YOUR EYES. (Val. 918)
941 (V) Christmas Greetings. "BONZO" HAS COME TO LET YOU SEE, YOU'RE ALWAYS KEPT IN MIND BY ME. (Val. 918) (Val. 1449)
941 (V) Christmas Greetings. LIKE "BONZO" MAY YOUR FRIENDS PROVE TRUE, AND THIS GLAD DAY REMEMBER YOU. (Val. 918) (Val. 1448)
941
941
941
967 (V) WHAT ARE YOU UP TO NOW?
968 (V) LOVE'S LABOUR LOST. (Val. 1137)
990 (V) NEVER WAG A WHITE TAIL BEFORE A BLACK KITTEN.
991 (V) THIS PLACE "SUITS" ME ALL RIGHT!
992 (V) IT'S A GREAT LIFE! (Val. 1058)
993 (V) 'SAY IT WITH MUSIC!' (Val. 1058)
994 (V) HERESH TO YOU! (Val. 1058)
995 (V) KEEP YOUR EYE ON THE BALL. (Val. 1058)
996 (V) ANOTHER FUNNY "P.C." FOR YOU. (Val. 1058) (Val. 1467)
997 (H) WHO TOLD YOU THAT ONE? (Val. 916)
998 (V) WHAT'S THIS I'M HEARING ABOUT YOU? (Val. 1058) (A.R. I.B. 1526-1)
1016 (V) WHAT IS LOVE AT FOUR BOB A DOUBLE!
1017 (V) EVERYTHING O.K. JUST GOING TO HAVE A BATHE.
1018 (V) "THE FIRST THING I DO IS TO WRITE TO YOU." (Val. 1018)
1018 (V) FROM *CAMBRIDGE* ("MAIL NOVELTY") (Val. 1018)
1019 (V) "DELIGHTED TO HEAR FROM YOU!"
1020 (V) "I'M GOING CRACKERS ALWAYS THINKING OF YOU!"
1051 (H) "THERE'S NO PLACE LIKE HOME."
1052 (H) MY WORD! BLACK CATS ARE LUCKY!!
1053 (V) I HATE BEING PARTED FROM YOU. (Val. Series 1138) (A.R. I.B. 1522-4)
1053B (V) "Every Good Wish under the Sun I send to a wonderful Baby of ONE"
1054 (V) THE VIEWS HERE ARE LOVELY. (Val. 1486) (Val L1438) (GF. 08.23-2M339)
1054B (V) "I sing a song of love to you, And send a kiss 'cos you are TWO"
1055 (V) ONE PAYS FOR BEING NAUGHTY!
1055B (V) "Fancy you being really THREE! Here's lots and lots of love from Me"
1056B (V) "Good Wishes for a lovely Day, Lots of Presents, fun and play"
1057B (V) "Though Butterflies are bright and gay, May you be happier still to-day"
1058B (V) Six little candles all alight, May everything to-day be bright"
1058 (V) Birthday Greetings. Here's "Bonzo" wishing you a hearty And a Merry Birthday Party. (Val. 922)
1058 (V) Birthday Greetings. I could play the livliest music Till night, from early morn, Because - Well, just because - this is The day that you were born. (Val. 993)
1058 (V) Birthday Greetings. "Listen in" and you'll surely hear That I wish you a Happy Birthday, Dear. (Val. 998) (A.R. I.B. 1526-1)
1058 (V) To Greet Your Birthday. Here's wishing you the best of health, The best of joy and lots of wealth; Long years of bliss, yea, nothing less, Than perfect Peace and Happiness (Val. 994)
1058 (V) Birthday Wishes. I've stopped all the traffic That's coming your way, Just to let your friends greet you On this happy day. (Val. 996) (Val. 1467)
1058 (V) Birthday Greetings (?) Here's wishing you a "Round" of ..... (Val. 995)
1060 (V) JUST A WEE NOTE (Val. 1777) (B.P.C. 1060)
1073 (V) I'M HERE!
1074 (V) I WISH YOU WEREN'T SO COLD (Val. Series 1138)
1075 (V) I'VE GOT THE PIP!
1076 (V) I DREAM OF YOU! (Val. Series 1138) (Val. 1781)
1077 (V) THAT CRUISIN' FEELING.
1078 (V) I CAN'T SAY HOW I'VE MISSED YOU.
1079 (V) THIS SHOW ISN'T ALL BAD
1120 (V) I'VE MARKED MY HOTEL WITH A CROSS.
1121 (V) "I TOOK A BOAT OUT TO-DAY." (A.R. I.B. 1578)
1122 (V) JUST SITTING ON THE SANDS ENJOYING THE BREEZE.
1123 (V) I'VE STRUCK A MOST EXPENSIVE SPOT!
1124 (V) "IT'S NOT SO DUSTY DOWN HERE!" (Val. 1442L) (Val. 1780) (Val. Series 1138)
1125 (V) LOOKS LIKE A WASH-OUT. (Val. Series 1138) (A.R. I.B. 1581)
1126 (V) KEEP YOUR PECKER UP. (Val. Series 1138)
1127 (V) SO THIS IS LIFE. (Val. Series 1138)
1128 (V) I'M FEELING "CHAMPION".
1129 (V) HULLO! EVERYBODY!
1130 (V) I SHALL BE HERE FOR SOME TIME!
1131 (H) ALL OURS!
1132 (V) "THE FIRST MOVE IN THE GAME."
1133 (V) I'M STRUCK ON THIS PLACE!
1134 (V) I WAS SURPRISED TO HEAR FROM YOU!
1135 (V) GENTLEMEN PREFER SITTING OUT!
1136 (H) I'M LOOKING FORWARD TO A LIVELY TIME! (Val. Set 1252)
1137 (V) I'VE JUST JOINED THE MUSTARD CLUB. (Val. 968)
Series 1138 (V) Birthday Wishes MAY ALL YOUR FONDEST DREAMS COME TRUE; AND ALL THE WORLD GO WELL WITH YOU! (Val. 1076)
Series 1138 (V) To Greet your BirthdayBE JOLLY LIKE POLLY FOR, DON'T YOU SEE, SHE COMES WITH THE BEST OF WISHES FOR ME. (Val. 1126) (A.R. I.B. 1581)
Series 1138 (V) A Birthday GreetingTHOUGH ICES ARE COLD MY HEART 'TIS TRUE, IS WARM WITH LOVING THOUGHTS OF YOU. (Val. 1074)
Series 1138 (V) To Greet Your BirthdayI HATE BEING PARTED FROM YOU ON YOUR BIRTHDAY. (Val. 1053) (A.R. I.B. 1522-4)
Series 1138 (V) Birthday GreetingsI HOPE YOU'LL BE IN THE SWIM TO-DAY AND ENJOY YOURSELF IN EVERY WAY. (Val. 1125)
Series 1138 (V) Birthday Wishes.I've come to wish you'll have ever so hearty, A time with your friends at your Birthday Party. (Val. 1127)
Series 1138 (V) I've come as fast as I could to say ..... (Val. 1124) (Val. 1442L) (Val. 1780) (Full caption unknown)
1200 (V) I'M MISSING YOU DREADFULLY (Val. Set 1252) (B.P.C. 1200)
1201 (V) I'M IN GREAT SPIRITS HERE! (Val. Set 1252) (Val. 1515)
1202 (V) EVERY DOG HAS HIS DAY! (Val. Set 1252)
1203 (V) I'VE GOT MY EYE ON YOU! (Val. Set 1252)
1204 (H) THERE'S A FUNNY TALE GOING AROUND HERE! (Val. Set 1252)
1205 (V) I WISH I COULD HANG ON HERE!
1206 (V) I DON'T LOOK LIKE GETTING HOME YET!
1207 (V) I'VE JUST REMEMBERED I FORGOT TO WRITE YOU! (Val. Set 1252) (Val. 1444L) (Val. 1516)
1208 (V) IT'S PERFECTLY AWFUL WITHOUT YOU
1209 (V) BETWEEN OURSELVES (Val. Set 1252)
1210 (V) WHEN'S YOURS COMING OFF? (Val. Set 1252)
1211 (V) THE MORE WE HAVE TOGETHER THE MERRIER WE WILL BE (Val. Set 1252) (A.R. I.B. 1670/3)
1237 (V) "LOVE ON PAPER, LADY, IS BETTER THAN NO LOVE AT ALL."
1238 (V) I'VE DROPPED IN ON AN IDEAL SPOT.
1239 (V) "JUST LONGING FOR A QUIET LITTLE EVENING WITH YOU."
1240 (V) I ALWAYS FEEL LIKE THIS WHEN I'M WITH YOU.
1241 (V) EVERYTHING O.K. HOTEL GRAND.
1242 (V) I'LL SOON BE SEEING YOU AGAIN.
Set 1252 (V) Birthday Greetings.Between ourselves I wish you here A very Happy Birthday, dear! (Val. 1209)
Set 1252 (V) Birthday GreetingsJust out to wish for you this day An "egg-ceptional" time in every way.
Set 1252 (V) Birthday Remembrance.Reflected in this glass you'll see What untold bliss I wish for thee. (Val. 1203)
Set 1252 (V) To Greet Your Birthday.May the picture here my wish express, For health, and wealth, and happiness. (Val. 1202)
Set 1252 (V) Birthday Greetings.I've just remembered what date this is So I'm wishing you every joy and bliss. (Val. 1207) (Val. 1444L) (Val. 1516)
Set 1252 (V) Birthday Greetings.With wishes sincere and ever so hearty - For a real jolly time at your Birthday party. (Val. 1201) (Val. 1515)
Set 1252 (H) Birthday GreetingsI'm round again this day to greet - "May you always be able to make ends meet!"(Val. 1204)
Set 1252 (V) A Birthday Wish.Here's wishing many blithe and gay Returns of this happy day. (Val. 1211) (A.R. I.B. 1670/3)
Set 1252 (V) Birthday Greetings.To greet your Birthday in the usual way - But I wish it had been your Wedding Day! (Val. 1210)
Set 1252 (H) Birthday Wishes.Here's my wish in a humble rhyme - "May you wake up to a lively time!" (Val. 1136)
Set 1252 (V) Birthday Wishes.I come to wish you a round of bliss And a record score of joy with this. (Val. 1200) (B.P.C. 1200)
Set 1252 (?)
1254 (V) THIS MAKES ME THINK OF YOU! (G.F. 08.23-2M340)
1255 (V) JUST DROPPING YOU A CARD! (Val. 1393)
1256 (V) CAN'T SAY WHEN I'M COMING BACK.
1257 (V) IF I ONLY THOUGHT YOU'D MISS ME - BUT YOU DON'T!
1258 (V) I'M SENDING YOU THIS FOR LUCK! (Val. 1393) (Val. L1445)
1259 (V) CHEERIO! I'M STILL ALIVE!
1260 (V) DON'T WORRY ABOUT ME!
1261 (V) GIVE MY LOVE TO ALL AT HOME
1262 (V) LOOKING FORWARD TO SEEING YOU AGAIN! (Val. L1440)
1263 (V) I'M GETTING ON FINE HERE! (Val. 1393)
1264 (V) I REALLY HAVEN'T TIME TO WRITE! (Val. 1393)
1265 (V) I DIDN'T DO IT!
1288 (V) I LOVE HAVING SOMEONE TO TALK TO (Val. 1393)
1289 (V) "WHILE THERE'S LIFE, THERE'S SOAP!" (Val. L35)
1290 (V) I'VE GOT TO HUG SOMETHING TILL WE MEET AGAIN. (Val. 1393)
1291 (H) THUMBS UP! I'LL SOON BE WITH YOU!
1292 (V) JUST A LINE FOR AULD LANG SYNE. (Val. L1436)
1293 (V) I'M JUST WONDERING IF YOU'RE AS GOOD AS YOU LOOK. (Val. 1393)
1294 (V) HAD A KILLING TIME LATELY. (VALENTINE'S "OOLOO" SERIES)
1307 (V) UP TO MY EYES JUST NOW! (Val. 1443L)
1308 (V) NOTHING TO WRITE HOME ABOUT.
1309 (V) THAT REMINDS ME - SOME FOLKS ARE A BIT SLOW.
1310 (V) I'M RAISING QUITE A DUST HERE.
1311 (V) "I'LL BE ROUND AGAIN SOON!" (Val. 1393) (Val. 1439L)
1312 (V) KEEPING OFF THE BIRDS.
1368 (V) JUST TIME TO BLOW YOU A KISS
1369 (V) I'D BE VERY GLAD OF A LINE FROM YOU.
1370 (V) YOU FILL MY WAKING THOUGHTS.
1371 (V) HERE'S A GOOD ONE FOR YOU.
1372 (V) I HOPE THAT THIS WILL THROW SOME LIGHT ON REASONS WHY YOU NEVER WRITE.
1373 (V) WE'RE GOING THE PACE HERE. (Val. 1468L)
1374 (V) FORGET-ME-NOT.
1375 (V) I'M BEHIND WITH THAT LETTER HOPE THIS'LL MAKE AMENDS. (G.F. 08.23-2M335)
1376 (V) Birthday Greetings ARE YOU SURE IT'S ME YOU LOVE? (As below)
1376 (V) ARE YOU SURE IT'S ME YOU LOVE? (As above)
1377 (V) CAN'T THINK OF MUCH TO SAY.
1378 (V) I'M EXPECTING ONE FROM YOU.
1379 (V) JUST CAUGHT THE POST. (Val. 1/A)
1393 (V) Birthday Greetings MAY YOU HAVE A SKY-HIGH TIME TODAY, AND MAY EVERYTHING GO OFF "OK." Mailing Novelty (Val. 1255)
1393 (V) To Greet Your BirthdayWORDS ARE JUST WORDS BUT THE WISHES I SEND ARE THE HEART'S BEST DESIRES FOR THE GOOD OF A FRIEND. (Val. 1288)
1393 (V) Birthday GreetingsA LITTLE THING TO LET YOU SEE SOMEONE THIS DAY REMEMBERS THEE! (Val. 1293)
1393 (V) To Greet Your BirthdayAN OLD HORSE SHOE I SEND YOUR WAY FOR IT MEANS GOOD LUCK, THIS HAPPY DAY! (Val. 1258) (Val. L1445)
1393 (V) Birthday WishesHERE'S WISHING YOU FOR OLD TIME'S SAKE AN AMPLE SHARE OF YOUR BIRTHDAY CAKE! (Val. 1263)
1393 (V) Birthday GreetingsMAY YOU HAVE A JOLLY GOOD TIME TO-DAY AND THE HOURS PASS SWEETLY IN EVERY WAY! (Val. 1264)
1393 (V) Birthday GreetingsIF I WERE WITH YOU DEAR TO-DAY I'D HUG YOU IN THIS SELF SAME WAY! (Val. 1290)
1408 (V) HOW CAN I PROVE MY LOVE IF I MUSTN'T EVEN TRY!
1409 (V) PITY YOU EVER LEARNT TO FORM FOURS DEAR!
1410 (V) HERE'S A LOAD OF LUCK COMING YOUR WAY.
1416 (V) IT'S A GREAT GAME AT *OXFORD* A VIEW OR TWO INSIDE FOR YOU (MAILING NOVELTY) (Val. 638)
L1435 (V) It takes a lot to beat *LLANDUDNO* (Val. 1487) (Val. 1779)
L1436 (V) I've just remembered I forgot to write you from *CLIFTONVILLE* (Val. 1292)
L1437
L1438 (V) Come and see me at ______ any time! (Val. 1054) (Val. 1486)
1439L (V) Having all the Fun of the Fair at this Place! (Val. 1311) (Val 1393)
L1440 (V) Looking forward to seeing you again at *BOURNEMOUTH* (Val. 1262)
L1441

VALENTINE AND SONS LTD., DUNDEE AND LONDON.

1442L	(V)	It's not so dusty at _____ (Val. 1124) (Val. 1780) (Val. Series 1138)
1443L	(V)	Up to my eyes at the Seaside. (Val. 1307)
1444L	(V)	Just a line for Auld Lang Syne from an old friend. (Val. 1207) (Val. Set 1252) (Val. 1516)
L1445	(V)	I'm sending you this for Luck from CLIFTONVILLE (Val. 1393) (Val. 1258)
1448	(V)	BONZO BRINGS SOME LOVELY VIEWS FROM BOURNEMOUTH (MAILING NOVELTY) (Val. 918) (Val. 941)
1449	(V)	When You think of Retiring come to CLACTON-ON-SEA (MAILING NOVELTY) (Val. 918) (Val. 941)
1467	(V)	Held Up at CAWSAND Another funny "P.C." for you. (MAILING NOVELTY) (Val. 916) (Val. 1058)
1468L	(V)	We're going the pace at last. (Val. 1373)
1486	(V)	The views are Lovely at CLACTON-ON-SEA (MAILING NOVELTY) (Val. 1054) (Val. L1438)
1487	(V)	It takes a Lot to Beat KINGSBRIDGE (MAILING NOVELTY) (Val. L1435) (Val. 1779)
1514	(V)	YES! IT'S ONE FROM ME
1515	(V)	JUST A FUNNY P.C.!
1515	(V)	Always Merry and Bright at BEDALE (MAILING NOVELTY) (Val. 1201) (Val. Set 1252)
1516	(V)	I've just remembered I've forgotten to write You from ABERGELE So here's a Card with Views. (MAILING NOVELTY) (Val. 1207) (Val. Set 1252) (Val. 1444L)
1516	(V)	DO BLOW IN ONE EVENING! (Val. 1568)
1517	(V)	I'M STILL AT THE OLD ADDRESS!
1518	(V)	I WISH I COULD SEE YOU! (Val. 29)
1519	(V)	PACK UP AND PAY US A VISIT! (Val. 1563)
1528	(V)	I'm "on velvet" at SIDMOUTH (MAILING NOVELTY)
1562	(V)	I'VE JUST READ YOUR NOTE!
1563	(V)	HAVE YOU LOST YOUR PEN? (Val. 1569) (W&L 2545)
1563	(V)	Pack up and come to ILFRACOMBE (MAILING NOVELTY) (Val. 1519)
1564	(V)	I'M EVER SO SORRY I DIDN'T WRITE.
1565	(V)	I REALLY OUGHT TO GET AN ANSWER TO THIS! (G.F. 08.23–2M 338)
1566	(V)	JUST A LOCAL SOUVENIR. (Val. 1570)
1567	(V)	JUST A GENTLE REMINDER!
1568	(V)	There's Room for You at BRIXHAM (MAILING NOVELTY) (Val. 1516)
1568	(V)	CAN'T SAY WHEN I'LL BE LEAVING HERE. ("MOTOR EMOTION")
1569	(V)	IT'S A TIGHT SQUEEZE HERE. ("MOTOR EMOTION")
1569	(V)	Just a Scrape of the Pen from BRIXHAM (MAILING NOVELTY) (Val. 1563) (W&L 2545)
1570	(V)	All the Way from DERBY JUST A LOCAL SOUVENIR! (MAILING NOVELTY) (Val. 1566)
1570	(V)	THINGS ARE TAKING A FUNNY TURN HERE! ("MOTOR EMOTION")
1571	(V)	I DON'T SUPPOSE YOU EXPECTED TO SEE THIS "P.C."! ("MOTOR EMOTION")
1572	(V)	AREN'T YOU GLAD TO HEAR FROM ME? ("MOTOR EMOTION")
1573	(V)	THIS IS THE PLACE FOR A CHANGE! ("MOTOR EMOTION")
1585	(V)	With Best Wishes from BIDEFORD (MAILING NOVELTY) (Val. 1689)
1586	(V)	Better than Work at SANDOWN, I.W. (MAILING NOVELTY) (Val. 1690)
1587	(V)	Just One Word from BIRCHINGTON-ON-SEA (MAILING NOVELTY) (Val. 1687) (Val. 2006)
1588		
1589		
1590	(V)	Best Wishes from CLACTON-ON-SEA Here's Luck! (MAILING NOVELTY) (Val. 1636)
1635	(V)	O, My Hat! I'm gittin' as brown as a nigger at SIDMOUTH (MAILING NOVELTY) (Val. 1950)
1636	(V)	Here's one for you from FRINTON-ON-SEA (MAILING NOVELTY) (Val. 1902)
1636	(V)	Here's Luck. (Val. 1590)
1637	(H)	I'm keeping my end up here.
1638	(V)	Just a dip in the ink
1639	(H)	We'll be happy together, whatever the weather!
1640	(V)	Only just time for a scratch
1641	(V)	So glad to hear from you (Val. I/E) (Val. 2052-6)
1642	(V)	May all your troubles be little ones! ("MOTOR HUMOUR")
1643	(V)	Just passing another "P.C." to you. ("MOTOR HUMOUR")
1644	(V)	This is a nice place for a change. ("MOTOR HUMOUR")
1645	(V)	Hope this finds you up to scratch. ("MOTOR HUMOUR")
1646	(V)	A 'P.C.' always make a difference: let's hear from you. ("MOTOR HUMOUR")
1647	(V)	I'd like to settle down here. ("MOTOR HUMOUR")
1678	(V)	A Note or Two from SANDOWN, I.W. (MAILING NOVELTY) (Val. 2143) (Val. 2278F)
1683	(V)	"Pop" in and join us at SOUTHSEA. Mailing Novelty (Val. 2145)
1687	(V)	JUST ONE WORD! (Val. 1587) (Val. 2006)
1688	(V)	DON'T WORRY ABOUT ME – I'VE GOT A SPARE! (Val. 34)
1689	(V)	IF THIS DOESN'T BRING YOU LUCK – NOTHING WILL! (Val. 1585)
1690	(V)	I THINK I'M MISSING A BIT! (Val. 1586)
1691	(V)	CAN'T SAY I'M FEELING TOO GOOD (Val. 36)
1692	(V)	DON'T SAY IT'S BROKEN OFF!
1693	(V)	KEEP NICE AND BRIGHT, DEAR, TILL WE MEET AGAIN!
1694	(V)	MOVIES ARE BETTER THAN TALKIES!
1695	(V)	PLEASE DON'T MAKE LIGHT OF THIS!
1696	(V)	GO ON! SAY YOU'VE RUN OUT OF JUICE AGAIN!
1696*	(V)	LET'S MAKE UP AND BE FRIENDLY.
1697*	(V)	SORRY – UNAVOIDABLY DETAINED.
1698*	(V)	I'M DROPPING IN SOON.
1734*	(H)	JUST A FEW LINES.
1735*	(H)	WHATEVER HAPPENS I'M STICKING TO YOU.
1736*	(H)	EXPECT TO MAKE A BIG SPLASH HERE.
1752	(V)	What about "A Wee One" at SANDOWN, I.W. (MAILING NOVELTY) (Val. 2512)
1753	(V)	Feeling at Home at BRIGHTON (MAILING NOVELTY – CHEERIPUP SERIES) (Val. 2506)
1767	(V)	IT'S GRAND TO GET A SPELL OFF FROM WORK!
1768	(V)	I'M SURE I SHALL LIKE THIS SPOT. (GF 08.23–2M337)
1769	(V)	YOU AND I WERE NEVER MEANT TO PART DEAR! (Val. 1980.4)
1770	(V)	I'M DOING A BIT OF BOATING HERE.
1771	(V)	THIS IS JUST TO SAY YOU REALLY ARE A DUCK! (Val. 2052.3)
1772	(V)	A LINE TO REMIND YOU OF ME!
1776		
1777	(H)	HERE'S A NOTE FOR YOU! ("Multi-Message" Card) (Val. 1060) (B.P.C. 1060)
1778	(H)	IT'S "THUMBS UP" HERE! ("Multi-Message Card")
1779	(H)	THIS PLACE BEATS EVERYTHING! ("Multi-Message Card") (Val. 1435) (Val. 1487)
1780	(H)	IT'S NOT SO DUSTY HERE! ("Multi-Message Card") (Val. 1124) (Val. 1442L) (Val. Series 1138)
1781	(H)	TOO TIRED TO WRITE! ("Multi-Message Card") (Val. 1076) (Val. Series 1138)
1792	(V)	Shall I Never See Your Face Again at DWYGYFYLCHI (MAILING NOVELTY) (Val. 3030)
1793	(V)	Having a Busy Day at ABERGELE & PENSARN (MAILING NOVELTY) (Val. 2851)
1794	(V)	Feeling Lonely Without You at WEYMOUTH (MAILING NOVELTY) (Val. 3027) (AV No 73)
1816	(V)	I'VE LOST MY HEART PROPERLY THIS TIME!
1817	(V)	I HATE BEING AWAY FROM YOU! (Val. 1980.6)
1818	(V)	I'M LUCKY TO HAVE FOUND YOU! (Val. 1980.1)
1819	(V)	YOU'VE FAIRLY CAUGHT MY EYE!
1820	(V)	I NEVER FORGET AN OLD ACQUAINTANCE. (Val. 1980/3)
1821	(V)	I HOPE YOU ARE GOING ON ALRIGHT!
1823	(V)	I'm Learning Something at CHESTER (MAILING NOVELTY) (Val. 3720)
1894*	(V)	I HAVEN'T HEARD FROM YOU.
1895*	(V)	IF I COULD GET YOU BACK I'D NEVER LET YOU GO.
1896*	(H)	I'VE FOUND A LOVELY PLACE.
1902	(V)	Having a High Old Time at BARMOUTH (MAILING NOVELTY) (Val. 385)
1902	(V)	"HERE'S ONE FOR YOU – WHERE'S MINE?" (Val. 1636)
1903	(V)	I WISH I'D SEEN YOU BEFORE!
1904	(V)	I WISH I WAS GRIPPING YOUR HAND.
1905	(V)	WATCHING AND WAITING FOR SOMEONE!
1906	(V)	"AREN'T YOU GLAD THE SPEED LIMIT'S GONE?"
1907	(V)	I'M TOO FAR AWAY TO BE KISSED.
1949	(V)	YOU WEREN'T EXPECTING THIS.
1950	(V)	AHM GITTIN' AS BROWN AS A NIGGER. (Val. 1635)
1951	(V)	O! BABY – AIN'T YOU BIN NAUGHTY! (Val. 2052/2)
1952	(V)	'NUFF SAID' (Val. 2007) (Val. 2052.1)
1953	(V)	O.K. CHIEF!
1954	(V)	I'M THINKING OF YOU AND YOU ALONE OLD THING
1977*	(H)	"WELL OLD COCK, I GOT YOUR 'TALE' ALRIGHT!"
1978*	(H)	"YOUR GRACES WILL BE 'AT HOME' ANY DAY!"
1979*	(H)	ANOTHER BLOOMING POW(ER) CUT!
1980*	(H)	"YOU LEFT AN IMPRESSION ON ME!"
1980.1	(V)	Birthday Greetings! HOPE YOU'LL FIND EVERYTHING LUCKY TO-DAY. (Val. 1818)
1980.2		
1980.3	(V)	Birthday Greetings HOPE EVERYTHING GOES WITH A BANG ON YOUR BIRTHDAY.
1980.4	(V)	Birthday Greetings I'M WISHING HERE FOR AULD LANGS SYNE THAT HEALTH AND WEALTH BE EVER THINE! (Val. 1769)
1980.5		
1980.6	(V)	Birthday Greetings HERE'S WISHING YOU ALL YOU'VE SET YOUR HEART ON! (Val. 1817)
1981*	(V)	YOUR ONE OUT OF THE BAG!
1982*	(V)	"I'M CRACKERS OVER YOU!"
2006	(V)	ST. VALENTINE'S DAY GREETINGS. (Val. 1587) (Val. 1687)
2007	(V)	Greetings for St. Valentine's Day! MY HEART IS THINE, DEAR VALENTINE! (Val. 1952) (Val. 2052.1)
2021	(V)	I JUST CAN'T GET YOU OUT OF MY HEAD! (Val. 2278/C)
2022	(V)	I'M JUST TAKING THINGS QUIETLY. (Val. 2278/D) (GF 08.23–2M336)
2023	(V)	AT THE MOMENT I'M KEEPING UP FINE! (Val. 2278/B)
2024	(V)	THERE'S NO BAD LUCK 'CEPT WHEN I'M AWAY FROM YOU!
2025	(V)	IF I DON'T HEAR FROM YOU SOON!
2026	(V)	WHAT ABOUT A BIT OF GRUB TOGETHER?
2052.1	(V)	To Greet Your Birthday WITH ALL MY HEART I SEND THIS KINDLY GREETING A HAPPY BIRTHDAY AND AN EARLY MEETING! (Val. 1952) (Val. 2007)
2052.2	(V)	A P.C. for Your Birthday. I hope you'll get a "Fine" time to-day And be Forced to be happy in every way! (Val. 1951)
2052.3	(V)	BIRTHDAY WISHES YOUR JUST A PERFECT LITTLE DUCK, SO HERE'S TO WISH YOU LOTS OF LUCK! (Val. 1771)
2052.4		
2052.5		
2052.6		A Birthday Wish YOU'LL BE EVER SO GLAD TO GET THIS TO-DAY FOR IT'S WISHING YOU HAPPINESS ALL THE WAY. (Val. 1/E) (Val. 1641)
2143	(V)	GRAND OPERA! (Val. 1678) (Val. 2278/F)
2144	(V)	HOME JOHN!
2145	(V)	HARK HARK THE LARK! (Val. 1683)
2146	(V)	JUST DREAMING OF YOU!
2147	(V)	I WISH YOU WERE IN MY ARMS!
2148	(V)	JUST WISHING YOU LUCK AT A FILLING STATION!
2193	(V)	TRYING TO GET YOU ON THE LONG WAVE!
2194	(V)	DON'T SAY YOU'VE FORGOTTEN ME ALTOGETHER!
2195	(V)	FED-UP WITH SIGHT-SEEING HERE!
2196	(V)	"OH, HOW I MISS YOUR LILY-WHITE HAND AND LONG TO SEE YOU SMILE!"
2197	(V)	HAVING A JOB TO KEEP COOL (Val. 2278/E)
2198	(V)	"IF YOU CAN'T CRUISE – BOOZE!"
2278A		
2278B	(V)	Birthday Greetings. JUST SLIPPING ALONG TO WISH YOU MANY HAPPY RETURNS! (Val. 2023)
2278C	(V)	Birthday Greetings! I JUST CAN'T GET YOU OUT OF MY HEAD TO-DAY! (Val. 2021)
2278D	(V)	To Greet Your Birthday! MAY THE BEST OF GOOD THINGS BE EVER YOURS. (Val. 2022) (G.F. 08.23–2M336)
2278E	(V)	Birthday Greetings! WISHING YOU "A – NICE" TIME TO-DAY. (Val. 2197)
2278-F	(V)	For A Happy Birthday! MAY FORTUNE BROADCAST A HAPPY TIME FOR YOU. (Val. 1678) (Val. 2143)
2279	(V)	MY FAVOURITE! (Val. 1/C)
2280	(V)	WISH I COULD SQUEEZE YOU TOO!
2281	(V)	I'LL GET A NOTE OUT OF YOU OR BUST.
2282	(V)	WISH YOU COULD JOIN ME.
2283	(V)	"NO! I AIN'T LONELY, NO!"
2284	(V)	I CAN'T DO WITHOUT YOU FOR LONG.
2285	(V)	ONLY ONE LITTLE LINE. (Val. 1/F)
2286	(V)	I'M FEELING CHAMPION.
2287	(V)	HANG IT I MUST BE IN LOVE!
2288	(V)	NOT A CHEEP FROM YOU, YET.
2289	(V)	HAPPY DAYS AND LONELY NIGHTS.
2290	(V)	WHERE ON EARTH HAVE YOU GOT TO? (Val. 2/D)
2387	(V)	I LUV YOU MORE THAN YOU LUV ME.
2388	(V)	I CAN PLAY OTHER GAMES AS WELL.
2389	(V)	"COME OUT AND HAVE SOME GRUB."
2390	(V)	BONZO TESTS THE LEG THEORY! "THIS ONE'S FOR YOU!"
2391	(V)	"BALLYHOO OLD BEAN!"
2392	(V)	Keep a soft spot for me
2426	(V)	BOB UP AGAIN SOON DEAR!
2427	(V)	FEELING TEN YEARS YOUNGER ALREADY!
2428	(V)	JUST MANAGING TO KEEP THINGS GOING!

VALENTINE AND SONS LTD., DUNDEE AND LONDON.

2429	(V)	TRYING TO BEER UP WITHOUT YOU!
2430	(V)	FANCY YOU FALLING FOR ME!
2431	(V)	HAVING A DAZZLING TIME!
2504		
2505	(V)	ALL FOR THE LOVE OF A LADY. ("CHEERIPUP" SERIES)
2506	(V)	TWO'S COMPANY. ("CHEERIPUP" SERIES) (Val. 1753)
2507	(V)	YOU'LL NEVER FIND ANOTHER LIKE ME. ("CHEERIPUP" SERIES)
2508	(V)	THREE'S A CROWD. ("CHEERIPUP" SERIES)
2509	(V)	NICE GIRLS NEVER TELL. ("CHEERIPUP" SERIES)
2510	(V)	NOT HAVING TOO BAD A TIME!
2511	(V)	SEEING IT AIN'T LIKE DOING IT!
2512	(V)	WHAT ABOUT A WEE ONE? (Val. 1752)
2513	(V)	THINGS AREN'T WHAT THEY USED TO BE.
2514	(V)	I WISH I COULD SEE YOUR FACE. (Val. 1/B)
2515	(V)	I OFTEN DREAM OF YOU.
2516	(V)	"GOOD-NIGHT, EVERYBODY, GO - O -D- NIGHT!"
2517	(V)	"NIGHTY-NIGHT, OLD THING."
2518	(V)	JUST TO AMUSE YOU.
2519	(V)	"HOPE TO SEE YOU AGAIN SOON!"
2520	(V)	"MY PEN IS TOO FULL FOR WORDS!" (Val. 1/D)
2521	(V)	"JUST 'COS I HAVEN'T HEARD FROM YOU."
2661	(V)	I'LL BE LOOKING YOUR WAY SOON.
2662	(V)	I'M GETTING MUCH TOO FOND OF YOU.
2663	(V)	DIRECTLY WE PART I MISS YOU!
2664	(V)	I THINK YOU ARE SIMPLY GREAT.
2665	(V)	I'M NEVER TOO BUSY TO SEE YOU.
2666	(V)	YOU CAN'T HELP GETTING OFF DOWN HERE.
2691	(V)	"I'M NO ANGEL, BUT I'M NOT A NUDIST!"
2692	(V)	"HAVING A HECK OF A NAUGHTY TIME!"
2693	(V)	"BOB UP AND SEE ME SOMETIME!"
2694	(V)	"GIVE ME SHORTS FOR FREEDOM!"
2695	(V)	"CHEER UP, OLD SPORT! THAT'S NOTHING TO THE MARRIAGE KNOT!"
2696	(V)	"I'LL BE SEEIN' YE YET!"
2846	(V)	DO SAY YOU'RE STILL FOND OF ME!
2847	(V)	"GOLLY! WHERE'S MY HEART?"
2848	(V)	"HOW'S LIFE?"
2849	(V)	"THIS OUGHT TO WAKE YOU UP!"
2850	(V)	"PUT A WORD ON A P.C."
2851	(V)	"DOING A SPOT OF SUN-BATHING." (Val. 1793)
2852	(H)	HERE'S TO A CLINKING TIME. (Val. 2/E)
2853	(H)	"ARE YOUR INTENTIONS STRICTLY HONOURABLE?"
2854	(H)	GIRLS ADD TO BEAUTY - BOYS GET RID OF THE ROUGH.
2855	(H)	"HURRY UP AND TAKE ME OUT."
2856	(H)	"YOU'D BREAK ANY GIRLS HEART!"
2857	(H)	GIVE US A THOUGHT SOMETIMES.
2982	(V)	I'M A POOR FISH, BUT I LOVE YOU
2983	(V)	LIFE IS SO DIFFERENT SINCE I MET YOU
2984	(V)	HOW MUCH LONGER BEFORE I SEE YOU
2985	(V)	JUST A FEW WORDS
2986	(V)	AND HOW'S THINGS AT YOUR END?
2987	(V)	THAT'S QUEER, THERE WASN'T ONE IN THE OTHER BOTTLE
3027	(V)	WITHOUT YOU, THE WHOLE WORLD'S BLUE! (Val. 1794) (AV No 73)
3028	(V)	HERE'S LUCK IN THE DIRTY THIRTIES!
3029	(V)	I THINK IT'S TIME YOU HEARD FROM ME!
3030	(V)	SHALL I NEVER SEE YOUR FACE AGAIN? (Val. 1792)
3031	(V)	BEEN FRIGHTFULLY TIED UP LATELY.
3032	(V)	OH! HOW I WISH THIS WERE YOU! (Val. 2/F)
3110	(V)	ALAS, YOU WERE NOT MADE FOR ME!
3111	(V)	DON'T SAY I'VE GOT NO LEG APPEAL
3112	(V)	TRY TO KEEP SMILING.
3113	(V)	HOW I WISH YOU WERE HERE TO KISS ME GOOD-NIGHT!
3114	(V)	DOING MY BEST TO BE JOLLY WITHOUT YOU.
3115	(V)	WHY BE MARRIED? (Val. 2/B)
3116	(H)	I WONDER IF BOYS MEAN ALL THEY SAY?
3117	(H)	I LOVE YOU FOR YOURSELF, DEAR, AND NOT FOR YOUR GIFTS.
3118	(H)	I'LL BE TRUE AS LONG AS YOU, BUT NOT A MOMENT AFTER.
3119	(H)	WHAT'S A BLACK EYE TO A BLEEDING HEART!
3120	(H)	WE COULD BE QUITE HAPPY ON POACHED EGGS.
3121	(H)	WORKING LATE AT THE OFFICE AGAIN?
3235	(V)	YOU'RE WONDERFUL AT NOT WRITING.
3236	(V)	I CAN'T FACE THE WORLD WITHOUT YOU.
3237	(H)	I'M MUCH SLICKER WHEN THERE AIN'T A MOON.
3238	(V)	OO-ER – HERE'S LUCK.
3239	(V)	I'M ONLY A KNOT IN YOUR HAND-KERCHIEF AND THAT'S COME UNDONE.
3240	(V)	THIS IS A GOOD SHOW, BUT THERE'S SOMETHING MISSING, - "U."
3371	(V)	THE SAME OLD TUNE FROM ME TO YOU!
3372	(V)	NOW FOR A SPOT OF GRUB AND SO TO BED.
3373	(V)	HOW ARE THE LITTLE NIPPERS?
3374	(V)	REAL GOOD DIGS HERE.
3375	(V)	ONE SHORT LITTLE LINE. (Val. 2/C)
3376	(V)	THINK OF ME THINKING OF YOU!
3377		
3378		
3379	(?)	THE FIRST MOVE IN THE GAME.
3491	(V)	JUST A HURRIED SCRIBBLE!
3492	(V)	I'M NOT A GIRL TO BE PICKED UP EASILY.
3493	(V)	THIS IS IN PLACE OF KISSING YOU GOOD-NIGHT!
3494	(V)	FANCY ME FALLING FOR YOU!
3495	(V)	I HOPED I SHOULD SEE YOU BEFORE THIS
3496	(V)	I THOUGHT I UNDERSTOOD YOU, BUT I DON'T.
3497	(H)	AREN'T YOU FOND OF YOUR GLASS!
3498	(V)	I'M CRAZY ABOUT DANCING WITH YOU.
3499	(H)	AREN'T I EVEN WORTH A PENNY STAMP?
3500	(H)	WHAT ABOUT PASSING OUR LOVE TEST?
3501	(H)	IF ANYONE GETS YOU, IT'S GOING TO BE ME!
3502	(H)	MARRIAGE IS AN AWFUL RISK.
3684	(V)	I CAN'T GO GAY WHILE YOU'RE AWAY.
3685	(V)	IT'S O.K. WITH ME.
3719	(V)	SAY KID, THINK OF THE POOR BLIGHTERS IN THE RITZ!
3720	(V)	YOU ARE DRIVING ME CRAZY (Val. 1823)
3721	(V)	HOW TO HOLD YOUR MAN
3722	(V)	COULDN'T I DO MY LITTLE STUFF BEFORE YOU PUT ON YOUR MAKE-UP, DEAR?
3723	(H)	AREN'T WE A COUPLE OF NIT-WITS?
3724	(V)	IT SEEMS SUCH A LONG TIME SINCE WE MET
3725	(V)	JUST MANAGED TO GET FIXED UP
3726	(V)	GIRL WANTED
3727	(V)	DON'T SAY WE'VE FALLEN OUT
3728	(V)	HOW CAN ONE BE GOOD IN A WORLD LIKE THIS!
3729	(V)	IT'S LOVELY TO HEAR FROM YOU.
3730	(V)	I'LL BE SEEING YOU
3793	(V)	"I'D NOT ONLY SIGN THE PLEDGE, BUT I'D TURN NUDIST FOR YOU DEAR!"
3794	(V)	"ISN'T IT ABOUT TIME YOU WERE DECARBONIZED DARLING?"
3795	(V)	I'D PICK YOU OUT OF A THOUSAND EVERY TIME!
3976	(V)	I'VE ALMOST FORGOTTEN WHAT YOU LOOK LIKE.
3797	(V)	"PLEASE, I WANT TO BE VERY, VERY GOOD, BUT NOT ALWAYS."
3798	(V)	"I DIDN'T OUGHT TO TELL YOU, BUT YOU'VE GONE BANG TO MY HEAD!"
3817	(V)	THE HON. WATER MELON DISGRACES THE BOTTLE PARTY. (Fruity Fables)
3818	(V)	PASSING THE PEAS. (Fruity Fables)
3819	(V)	OH! MR. SPRING ONION! (Fruity Fables)
3820	(V)	MR. FIG LOSES HIS LEAF. (Fruity Fables)
3821	(V)	MR. SYPHON HOLDS THE BABY. (Fruity Fables)
3822	(V)	MISS BANANA GOES NUDIST. (Fruity Fables)
3864	(H)	CAN'T WE THINK OF ANYTHING NICE TO DO?
3865	(H)	YOU'VE GOT CUPID WHACKED HONEY!
3866	(H)	CHEER UP DARLING, YOU'RE NOT SO RED AS YOU'RE PAINTED.
3867	(H)	"WHAT ABOUT A LITTLE FLICK IN THE DARK?"
3868	(V)	BUT I THOUGHT I COULD DO THAT THERE 'ERE!
3869	(H)	ANY TIME'S KISSING TIME FOR ME!
3870	(V)	JUST A FEW SHORT WORDS, SWEETHEART
3871	(V)	I'M FEELING AWFUL 'COS OF YOU.
3872	(V)	YOU ARE MY ONE AND ONLY 'PERM'.
3873	(H)	CAN'T MAKE OUT WHAT'S WRONG WITH YOU, BABY!
3874	(V)	DON'T SAY ALL IS OVER BETWEEN US.
3875	(V)	JUST LONGING FOR YOU TO SAY COME OUT!
4112	(V)	I THOUGHT YOU WERE COLD, BUT YOU'RE NOT!
4113	(V)	YOU'VE SIMPLY GOT TO COME OUT.
4114	(V)	WHEN YOU'RE OUT OF SIGHT, I'M OUT OF MIND
4115	(V)	I BELIEVE YOU'RE JUST MAKING A FOOL OF ME.
4116	(H)	LET US LIP-STICK TOGETHER HONEY!
4117	(V)	WHEN YOU'VE GOT NOTHING ON DO COME AND SEE US.
4118	(V)	WHAT'S THE GOOD OF SITTING AROUND GROWING HALOES?
4119	(V)	HOW MANY MORE BEFORE WE MEET?
4120	(H)	WHAT ABOUT A LITTLE SPORT IN THE SPORTS?
4121	(V)	JUST SENDING YOU MY LITTLE EVERLASTING FLOWER.
4122	(V)	GIVE ME MY GIRL EVERY TIME!
4123	(V)	NOBODY SEEMS TO CARE WHAT HAPPENS TO ME!
4245	(V)	A KISS FROM YOUR LITTLE SNOW WHITE.
4246	(V)	JUST A LOVING P.C.
4247	(V)	NOW CAN ANY BOY EXPLAIN THE WORD "APPEAL"?
4248	(V)	WHY NOT BLOW IN FOR A BLOW OUT?
4249	(H)	DOING A SPOT OF A.R.P.
4250	(V)	YOU ARE JUST THE SWEETEST THING IN THE WORLD!
4305	(H)	THERE'S LOTS TO DO HERE - BUT I DAREN'T.
4306	(V)	YOU CAN'T TEACH THIS CHILD ANYTHING, DEARIE!
4307	(H)	LET'S SPEND A QUIET EVENING TOGETHER.
4308	(V)	CHEER UP GRUMPY, LET'S BE HAPPY!
4309	(V)	ALL THE BEST - BUT IT'S H_____ WITHOUT YOU!
4310	(V)	WHAT ABOUT A BEER AT THE POLE, DUCKY?
4311	(V)	DON'T LET ANYTHING WITH LEGS ON COME BETWEEN US, DARLING
4312	(V)	GIVE ME A GIRL WITH A SPOT OF PEP!
4313	(H)	I FEEL YOU ARE COOLING OFF BABY!
4314	(V)	YOU ARE MY ONE AND ONLY LITTLE CAVE MAN!
4315	(V)	WHAT ABOUT THAT LINE?
4316	(V)	JUST KEEP ON KEEPING PLUCKY!
4593	(H)	"YOU ARE MY GLAMOUR GIRL No. 1, DARLING – MEET No. 2"
4594	(V)	"CAN'T WE GO OUT TOGETHER?"
4595	(V)	"I'VE BEEN DREAMING OF WEDDING BELLS DARLING!"
4596	(H)	"WE NEED NO PARKING LIGHTS WHEN WE'RE TOGETHER!"
4597	(V)	"THIS IS TO SAY THAT I'M O-KAY." (Val. 503)
4598	(V)	"WISHING YOU A REAL RUN OF LUCK!"
4599	(V)	"WE LIVE IN A WORLD OF OUR OWN, BABY"
4600	(H)	"I FEAR YOU DON'T THINK I'M GENUINE!"
4601	(V)	"I'D LOVE TO BE ALONE WITH YOU!"
4602	(V)	"I JUST LOVE A BIT OF SPORT WITH THE BIRDS."
4603	(H)	"WHAT ABOUT A SPOT OF MOON-BATHING DEARIE?"
4604	(H)	"JUST DOIN' THE SEASIDE WALK!"
4754	(H)	SEE WHAT COMES OF BEING GOOD ALL YOUR LIFE!
4755	(H)	JUST A FEW HINTS ON SLIMMING STUNTS DEARIE!
4756	(V)	I'LL BE A PERFECT JITTER-BUG TILL I HEAR YOU'RE O.K.
4757	(V)	HOW WAS I TO KNOW THE GIRL WAS A CONCHIE?
4758	(V)	"CHEER UP DEAR, THINGS WILL SOON BE BRIGHTER ALL ROUND!"
4759	(V)	"I JUST KEEP ON THINKING OF ME GAL!"
5140*		Winden waaien om de hoofden, een verrukking, twee verloofden. (Dutch caption)
5141*	(V)	YOU'RE A BIT OF A 'NIB' WITH THE PEN.
5142*	(V)	ON TOP OF THE WORLD - BUT A BIT DIZZY.
5143*	(V)	I'VE FOUND A LOVELY JOINT FOR THE WEEK.
5144*		Vier woorden zijn me niet voldoende, ik dacht er veel toen ik je zoende. (Dutch caption)
5145*	(V)	TRY TO ARRANGE A DATE WITH ME.
5262*	(H)	"WITH YOU ON THE PILLION, I FEEL LIKE A MILLION!"
5263*	(V)	EVEN THIS WON'T COOL ME OFF!
5264*	(V)	THIS IS OFF THE RECORD!
5265*	(V)	"DO YOU LIKE MY LOVE NOTES?"
5266*	(V)	I'M ALL-OUT FOR YOU!
5267*	(V)	EXPECT ME NICE AND EARLY
5444*	(V)	"HOPING TO HEAR FROM YOU SOON!"
5445*	(H)	"SEE YOU AGAIN SOON!"
5446*	(V)	"ENJOYING A(R)REST HERE!"
5447*	(V)	"A TICKLISH SITUATION!"
5448*	(V)	"NEVER A DULL MOMENT WHEN YOU'RE AROUND!"
5449*	(V)	"THINKING OF YOU!"
5516	(V)	"I'M HERE TO STAY."

VALENTINE & SONS LTD., DUNDEE AND LONDON

5517*	(V)	"THASH THE SPIRIT!"
5518*	(V)	"WE'VE A DATE, SO DON'T BE LATE!"
5519*	(H)	"ALL SET FOR A GRAND TIME HERE!"
5520*	(H)	"LET'S GET TOGETHER!"
5521*	(H)	"JUST A SHORT LINE!"

VALENTINE'S SERIES.
The Evolution of the Motor-Car.

No. I.	The Prehistoric Age.
No. II.	The Egyptian Age.
No. III.	The Mediaeval Age.
No. IV.	The Present Age.
No. V.	A Glimpse into the Future.
No. VI.	A Trip to the North Pole. Motorist: "I say, have any of you chaps got a reindeer?"

The "R.P.S." Series Post Cards

1000	Every Day in Every Respect; I am getting Better and Better. (BKWI V/2)
1001	A-Tish-oo.
1002	I'm not Arguing, I'm telling you!
1003	The Beggars Opera
1004	The End of a Perfect Day.
1005	That's What I think of You.
1006	Also Ran.
1007	Such Stuff as Dreams are made of. (BKWI XV/4)
1008	"Oliver Twist."
1009	Swank.
1010	Missed.
1011	That Coal Black Mammy o' Mine. (BKWI X/3)
1012	The Faithful Heart.
1013	Lost Ball. (BKWI 1/4)
1014	Fred the Ball Boy. (BKWI XV/3)
1015	The Way of an Eagle.
1016	Low Tide.
1017	Jimmy Wild.
1018	His Master's Vice.
1019	Now what about it?
1020	Beaver.
1021	William Tell.
1023	Rabits, I Believe? (BKWI XIV/3)
1024	Tip and Run. (BKWI 111/1)
1025	The Edge o' Beyond
1026	Alice in Wonderland
1027	Bogey Four
1028	Top Dog
1029	Bonzo's Hymn of Hate
1030	Any More for the Bus?
1031	Angel Face
1032	Dormy Six
1033	Carry Your Tail, My Lord
1034	The Pekingese Tells One
1035	There You are Then
1036	What about me?
1037	Bonzo Swims the Channel. (R.P.S. 1037)
1037	Going on Swimmingly; How are you? (R.P.S. 1037)
1038	The Bonzos Have a Couple.
1039	How the Deuce Did this Happen?
1040	Bonzo Sells a Pup.
1041	Treacle Tart. (R.P.S. 1041)
1041	I am stuck here but I've got some good Pals (R.P.S. 1041)
1042	I hope you have given up this bad habit. (R.P.S. 1042)
1042	His Mistress's Vice. (R.P.S. 1042)
1043	Listening In.
1044	Is, what I hear of you, true? (R.P.S. 1044)
1044	Sentimental Song. (Alas the Poor Dog had None). (R.P.S. 1044)
1045	Operatic Number (You are Queen of My Heart to Night).
1046	The Road Hog. (BKWI X/4)
1047	The Art School (BKWI XX/2)
1048	Which is it that Master Likes So Much? (BKWI XX/2)
1049	We are a Sporty Little Crowd down here.
1050	Tired Tim.
1051	To be Shingled or not to Shingle, that is the question.
1052	Just a Line.
1053	Somewhere the Sun is Shining.
1054	A Soft Drink.
1055	Not a Word to the Wife.
1056	Mother's Help. (BKWI XIII/1)
1057	A Leg Pull.
1058	Say When.
1059	Coming Home from Wembley.
1060	The Show Girl.
1061	One Over the Eight.
1062	Deuce.
1063	Three o'Clock in the Morning.
1064	Stable Information.
1065	Bonzo Removes an Infernal Machine. (BKWI IX/1)
1066	Stop Flirting.
1067	Never Bury an Old Bone in an Old Chair.
1068	Three Broken Plates mean a Woman is Coming.
1069	Chocolate Number 113 is unlucky.
1070	Havoc.
1071	Cocktails.
1072	Bonzo's Spring Clean.

(N.B. Card no. 1022 was never issued)

Inter-Art Co., Florence House, Barnes, London S.W.
"COMIQUE" Series

No. 3813	I'M IN A HURRY TO GET THIS OFF.
No. 3814	THERE'S SOMETHING ABOUT YOU THAT STIRS ME STRANGELY! (B.T.C.S.)
No. 3815	I'VE A WARM HEART, BUT _____ (B.T.C.S.)
No. 3815	"I've broken the ice!" (same picture as 3815 above)
No. 3816	I'M STUCK ON YOU OLD BEAN!
No. 3817	JUST MY LUCK - - I OUGHT TO HAVE DROPPED A LINE. (AR 1603/2)
No. 3818	YOU'LL BE SURPRISED TO GET THIS. (AR 1603/3)
No. 4323	"Hang the people next door, I'm going to have a good yell!" (M 259)
No. 4324	
No. 4325	"_____ YOU OUGHT TO SEE THE CAT!"
No. 4326	- AND HE TOLD ME TWO COULD LIVE CHEAPER THAN ONE!
Un-numbered	"AND WHAT DO YOU WANT TO SEE MR BROWN ABOUT!" "YOU!"

B.K.W.I. Bonzo Serie

I/3	Des einen Freud – des andern Leid
I/4	Schlecht placiert (RPS 1013)
III/1	Die wilde Jagd (RPS 1024)
V/2	Das Leben ist doch schön (RPS 1000)
VII/2	Was bringt der heutige Tag?
VII/4	Bonzos Kampfeslust
VIII/1	Keine rose ohne Dornen
IX/1	Eine Höllenmaschine! (RPS 1065)
X/3	Klein aber rein. (RPS 1011)
X/4	Ein stachliche Geschichte! (RPS 1046)
XIII/1	Nach getaner Arbeit! (RPS 1056)
XIV/3	Wo steckt er denn? (RPS 1023)
XIV/4	Rettung naht.
XV/3	Bonzo als Balljunge! (RPS 1014)
XVI/4	Bonzo's Träume (RPS 1007)
XVII/1	Quite sick Gut Gewaschen
XVII/2	A good deed Nachstenliebe
XVII/3	Goalkeeper
XVII/4	Magic mirrors Im Lachkabinett
XX/2	Not my taste Nicht mein Geschmack (RPS 1048)
XXI/2	The Art School Die Malschule (RPS 1047)
XXIII/3	Your hat? Ihr Hut?
XXIII/4	An exciting chase Eine aufregende Jagd
XXIV/2	A swish Die wilde Jagd
XXIV/4	Cinderella Aschenbrödel

W.E. MACK, HAMPSTEAD N.W.3.

1004	Help! (J.S. 1004)

VIVIAN MANSELL & CO Fine Art Publishers, London

Un-numbered	The Beech knut.
	The Cocoa knut.
	The Filbert.
	The Pea knut.
	The Wall knut.
No. 1010	Only a low caste Elephant would drink up a ladies bath.
No. 1010	At a jungle wedding it is the bear's privelege to hug the bride.
No. 1010	No well brought up Crocodile would ever begin a meal without shedding a few kindly tears of regret.
No. 1010	It is distinctly bad form for a Giraffe to pry into other people's houses.

The "Henderson" Post Cards.
(James Henderson & Sons Ltd., London.)

Series B10 "Studdy's Dogs"

2598	The Khaki Terrier. "A Glorious Victory."
2599	
2600	"What Master doesn't like."
2601	"Are you content?"
2602	"A Surrender Policy."
2603	"An End in View." (J.S. 2144)

Series B14

2718	DON'T WORRY THE FLAG'S STILL FLYING!
2719	WHO'S AFRAID?
2720	
2721	NO GUN NO GIRL
2722	THE GIRL I LEFT BEHIND ME
2723	TO THINK THAT I USED TO BE A BALLY NUT!

Series B17

2820	AEROPLANE VERSUS ZEPPELIN
2821	SIEGE GUNS BOMBARDING A FORT
2822	SUBMARINE ATTACKING DREADNOUGHT
2823	WATCH-DOGGING ON THE NORTH SEA
2824	RANGE FINDING
2825	BRIDGE BUILDING

Series B21 "Some Dogs."

2948	Feeling a little "pail"!
2949	Loot and Boot.
2950	Some Dog!
2951	Extremes Meet.
2952	The end of a good subject.
2953	"Gone, but not forgotten!"

J. SALMON (SEVENOAKS, ENGLAND)

1004	Help! (E. Mack, King Henry's Road, Hampstead, London.) (WEM 1004)
2130	I hear you calling me.
2131	When on a good thing, stick to it at BAKEWELL.
2132	
2133	This is the place for a good Blow.
2134	
2135	Ever been had?
2143	"But Things like that you know must be After a Famous Victory"
2144	This place makes you long for lots of things you've never had. (J.H. 2603)
2145	I was surprised by the beauty of this place.
2146	I'm having a "stunning" time
2147	Out of the running.

"ACADEMY" Picture Post Cards Humourous Series

"LAST MAN" by G.E. Studdy.

No. 1019	THE LAST MAN "LOR LUV US, TO THINK I'M THE HEIR."
No. 1020	
No. 1021	THE LAST MAN FINDS A FALLEN STAR.
No. 1022	
No. 1023	THE LAST MAN "AHOY MARS!" GENTLE STRANGER "MARS BE BLOWED, I'M VENUS."
No. 1024	MARS "THAT'S THE LAST TRUMP!" THE LAST MAN "RATS, I'VE GOT THE ACE & TWO OTHERS."

HUMORESQUE
(signed with pseudonym Cheero)

3068	Not too bad here, taking it all round
3069	
3070	This place would take a lot of beating.
3153	"THIS PLACE DON'T HALF MAKE ME HUNGRY!"
3154	"I'M REAL PLEASED WITH MESELF HERE!"
3293	THERE CHILD! NOW YOU SEE WHAT COMES OF BITING YOUR NAILS.
3294	"TOM'S RIGHT UP TO THE NECK IN LOVE WITH ME." "HE KNOWS EXACTLY WHERE TO STOP, DEAR."
3295	"WAS THAT NASTY NOISE, SCHUBERT?" BERT: "WHY PICK ON ME?"
3296	
3297	
3298	I'M FEELING LIKE A TWO-YEAR-OLD.
3301	IT'S ALL RIGHT FOR A CHANGE, BUT THERE'S NO PLACE LIKE HOME.
3463	"EXCUSE ME AGAIN MISS, BUT I QUITE FORGOT TO SAY I'M SORRY I DIDN'T KNOCK."
3702	This is 'Eaven with a 'Ead on it.
4581	"PARDON MISS, MY WIFE SENT ME UP TO ASK YOU IF YOU COULD STOP YOUR WIRELESS."
Un-numbered	"AND WHAT DO YOU WANT TO SEE MR. BROWN ABOUT!" "YOU!"

NOT MARKED (Either Humoresque or number) printed in Eire.
"ERE'S A BLOKE COME TO CUT YOU WATER OFF, DAD!"

GALE & POLDEN LTD., London, Aldershot, and Portsmouth.

1878	There is never a rose without a thorn
1882	Bed=Time
1883	
1884	Retrieving is my job
1888	Guilty (W&K 2939)
1897	Dinner=Time

VALENTINES SERIES

Un-numbered	"WHICH IS THE WAY TO THE WAR GUV'NER?"
	A BOLT FROM THE BLUE.
	"IF WE DON'T FIGHT SOMEONE SOON, I SHALL BUST!"
	"I DON'T KNOW WHAT I LOOK LIKE, BUT I FEEL LIKE THIS!"
	ARE WE DOWN-HEARTED? NO-O-O!
	BOTH DRESSED TO KILL

M. & L., Ltd. NATIONAL SERIES

1325	A Naval Engagement.

THE LAWRENCE & JELLICOE SERIES POST CARDS

5029	WILD OATS.

CELESQUE SERIES
PUBLISHED BY THE PHOTOCHROM CO. LTD., LONDON AND TUNBRIDGE WELLS

1904	LUMMY! ERE'S AN AD' "HOUSE TO LET, LOW RENT"
1904	Lummy! Ere's an ad' "House to let, low rent." at *Great Missenden*
1904	"LUMME! HERE'S AN AD. 'HOUSE TO LET. LOW RENT'!"
1904	"AIN'T KITCHENER A MARVEL." (All No. 1904 cards have the same image)
Un-numbered	"COLD STEEL"
Un-numbered	"DON'T IT MAKE YOU FEEL FIERCE?"

E.J. Hey & Co. London E.C.

Un-numbered	TRIUMPHANT

The Milton "Comic" Series.
Woolstone Bros., London, E.C.

259	"HANG THE PEOPLE NEXT DOOR I'M GOING TO HAVE A GOOD YELL!" (I.A. 4323)
260	"I'D LIKE TO FIND THE OWNER OF THIS!"
261	
262	
263	"OH HEL-P!"
264	"A SOCIABLE LITTLE FLEA CAN MAKE YOU FORGET ALL YOUR OTHER TROUBLES!"

G.A. & Co. Ltd., 13, GRAY'S INN ROAD, LONDON W.C.1.

Serie No. 815/1	GASSED! ASPHYXIE!
Serie No. 815/2	A DUD! QUEL DÉSAPPOINTEMENT!
Serie No. 815/3	SURPRISE ATTACK! PRIS AU DÉPOURVU!
Serie No. 815/4	REVENGE! VENGÉ!
Serie No. 815/5	WIND UP! EN RETRAITE!
Serie No. 815/6	ENTANGLEMENTS! ENCHEVÊTREMENT!

THE PHOTOCHROM CO. LTD., LONDON AND TUNBRIDGE WELLS

Design No. 2091   "ONLY ME LOOKING."

Raphael Tuck & Sons' "OILETTE" MOTORING JOKES from "PUNCH."

9144	SORROWS OF A "CHAUFFEUR." Ancient Dame: "What d'ye say? They call he a 'Shuvver,' do they? I see. They put he to walk behind and shove 'em up the hills, I reckon."

GALLERY FIVE (Published 1981)

08.23–2M335	I'M BEHIND WITH THAT LETTER. HOPE THIS'LL MAKE AMENDS. (Val. 1375)
08.23–2M336	I'M JUST TAKING THINGS QUIETLY. (Val. 2022)
08.23–2M337	I'M SURE I SHALL LIKE THIS SPOT. (Val. 1768)
08.23–2M338	I REALLY OUGHT TO GET AN ANSWER TO THIS! (Val. 1565)
08.23–2M339	THE VIEWS HERE ARE LOVELY. (Val. 1054)
08.23–2M340	THIS MAKES ME THINK OF YOU! (Val. 1254)

A.R. & CO.

1.B. 1526-1	WHAT'S THIS I'M HEARING ABOUT YOU? (Val. 998) (Val. 1058)
1603/1	
1603/2	Jetz sitz' ich im Glashaus. (IA 3817)
1603/3	Wenn Du' nicht bist, dann ist's das Mäus' chen. (IA 3818)
1.B. 1670/3	ES IST ALLES NUR SCHAUM. (Val. 1211) (Val. Set 1252)
1.B. 1522-4	"Ich kann nicht allein sein." (Val. 1053) (Val. Series 1138)
1.B. 1578	Seeräuber. (Val. 1121)
1.B. 1581	Mach', das Du wegkommst! (Val. 1126) (Val. Series 1138) Wildt & Kray, London E.C.
Series No. 2939	GUILTY. (G&P 1888)

BRITISH THROUGHOUT. COMIC SERIES.

Un-numbered	"Oh! I'm shocked!" (I.A. 3814)
Un-numbered	"I've broken the ice!" (I.A. 3815)

"Bonzo" POST CARD

1060	JUST A WEE NOTE. (Val. 1060) (Val. 1777) (with moving plastic Eyes and Squeaker. Printed in Great Britain for U.S.A.)
1200	"KEEP YOUR EYE ON THE BALL!" (Val. 1200) (Val. Set 1252) (with moving plastic eyes. Printed in Great Britain for U.S.A.)

EYRE & SPOTTISWOODE

6439	"He who would the daughter win, Must with the mother first begin."

Wohlgemuth & Lissner. Berlin. Primus – Postkarte

No 2545	Falls Dir die Feder eingerostet ist. (Val. 1563) (Val. 1569)

A V Lda, LISBOA. (Portugal)

No 73	O mundo sem si é uma noite escura! (Val. 1794) (Val. 3027)

A LIST OF BOOKS, KNOWN TO THE AUTHORS, WRITTEN AND ILLUSTRATED BY G. E. STUDDY

FISHING A DIAGNOSIS .... With symptoms by G. E. Studdy, by Hugh Tempest Sheringham. Pub. Field & Queen. 1914.
THE STUDDY DOG PORTFOLIOS.
Pub. The Sketch from 1922 (6 issues).
THE BONZO PAINTING BOOK.
Pub. John Swain & Sons Ltd. c. 1924.
UNCLE'S ANIMAL BOOK. Drawn and written in verse by G. E. Studdy.
Pub. F. Warne & Co. London & New York. 1923.
**FISHING, IT'S CAUSE, TREATMENT AND CURE .....
Symptoms** by G. E. Studdy, by Hugh Tempest Sheringham. Pub. P. Allen & Co. London. 1925.
THE BONZO BOOK.
Pub. Partridge, London. 1925.
MR. BONZO COMES TO TOWN.
by G. E. Studdy and George Jellicoe.
Pub. Thos. Allen, Toronto. c. 1923–1927.
(Also in this series: BAD BOY BONZO, BONZO'S SEASIDE HOLIDAY, BONZO'S COUNTRY HOLIDAY, THE GOOD DEEDS OF BONZO and THE ADVENTURES OF BONZO.)
THE NEW BONZO BOOK.
Pub. Partridge, London. 1927.
THE BONZOOLOO BOOK.
Pub. Partridge, London. 1927.
BONZO COLOURING BOOK.
Pub. Deane & Son. 1934.
BONZO AND US.
Pub. Partridge, London. 1931.
BONZO. THE GREAT BIG MIDGET BOOK.
Pub. Dean's Great Big Midget Books. 1934. (2 different issues with same title.)
BONZO LAUGHTER ANNUAL.
Pub. Dean & Son, London. 1935.
BONZO'S ANNUAL.
Pub. Dean & Son, London. 1936.
(Annuals also published in 1937, 1938, 1947, 1948, 1949, 1950, 1951 and 1952.)
BUSY BONZO AND HIS PALS.
Pub. Bendix Publishing Co. Ltd. London. no date.
BONZO'S BOOK OF STORIES.
Pub. Dean & Son. London. no date.
DOPEY & DOTTY.
by Florence Royle.
Pub. John Crowther Ltd. no date.
A DAY WITH DOPEY.
by Florence Royle.
Pub. John Crowther Ltd. no date.
BONZO'S STORY BOOK.
Pub. Dean & Son Ltd. no date.
BONZO'S HAPPY DAY.
Pub. Dunlop Press, London. no date.
(Also in this series: BONZO'S LEAP YEAR, BONZO'S HAPPY FAMILY, BONZO'S LITTLE HOLIDAY, BACHELOR BONZO and BONZO'S BRAN PIE.)
A BOX OF TRICKS.
by G. E. Studdy.
Pub. John Swain & Son Ltd. London. no date.
(Also in this series: A LUCKY DIP and PUPPY TAILS.)
BONZO.
Pub. Hachette (France). 1932.
BONZO II LE FARCEUR.
Pub. Hachette (France). 1933.
BONZO ET LES SAUCISSES.
Pub. Hachette (France). 1935.
JEEK .... Illustrated by the Author.
by G. E. Studdy.
Pub. Hamish Hamilton. London. 1940.

ANIMATED CARTOON FILMS BY G. E. STUDDY

STUDDY'S WAR STUDIES No. 1. Produced by Gaumont. 450 ft. Released 28.12.14.
"The series is of a topical character, and a number of humorous aspects of the Great War are presented on the screen. The rapid building-up of the sketch, which speedily takes definite shape before our eyes, is distinctly fascinating." (Review from 'Kine Monthly Film Record', January 1915.)
STUDDY'S WAR STUDIES No. 2. Produced by Gaumont. 450 ft. Released 15.1.15.
"Perhaps the favourite of the series will be the evolution of the German sausage into the perfected Super-Hun, an admirable portrait of the Kaiser, in which, with subtle sarcasm, he is depicted with his sword carried on the wrong side. The other subjects treated include an allusion to the Scarborough Raid, the Kaiser choosing a new suit and complaining that the Spring fashions offer nothing but 'checks', and a very amusing study of the man in the street struggling with the pronunciation of Russian names." (Review from 'Bioscope' 28th January 1915.)
STUDDY'S WAR STUDIES No. 3. Produced by Gaumont. 450 ft. Released 25.2.15.
Not reviewed.
HIS WINNING WAYS. (Studdy's War Studies No. 4.) Produced by Gaumont. 65 ft. Released 26.4.15.
The cartoonist's hand draws a German U-Boat named "The U-Limit", and gives it the Kaiser Bill moustache. Exclaiming, "Gawd I'm great at knocking down girls!" he punches Miss Trawler, Miss Collier, Miss Falaba and Miss Neutral.
BONZO. Produced by New Era. 687 ft. Released 20.1.25.
"A cartoon subject which will rival Felix the Cat and provide excellent items for all programmes. Bonzo is by no means a slavish copy of his predecessors. He is, in fact, a very doggy dog, whom it is a delight to watch. The producer, W. A. Ward, has collaborated admirably with the artist, and we look forward to seeing more of their work. The first example is most amusing and shows Bonzo's acrobatic efforts to capture some sausages out of his reach on a shelf, incidentally allowing for a scrap with a kitten. The conception is

extremely simple, but also it is typically doggy, and there is no need for explanations to point the working of the dog's mind." (Review from 'Kinematograph Weekly' 23rd October 1924.)

BONZO (No. 2.) Produced by New Era. 500 ft. Released 23.2.25.
"Bonzo is depicted making a pie of wierd ingredients which include whisky, a dead mouse, a cheese and other comestibles. Having made it, he puts it in the oven and is eventually blown through the wall when the pie explodes." (Review from 'Kinematograph Weekly' 5th February 1925.)

BONZO (No. 3.) Produced by New Era. 500 ft. Released 9.3.25.
"Studdy has made Bonzo steal a goose, get chased by a policeman, put in the dock, and finally escape with his spoil, which looks like compounding a felony! Topicality is introduced when Bonzo climbs a pipe-stack in brilliant cat burglar style." (Review from 'Kinematograph Weekly' 12th March 1925.)

BONZO (No. 4.) Produced by New Era. 500 ft. Released 23.3.25.
Not reviewed.

BONZO (No. 5.) Produced by New Era. 521 ft. Released 6.4.25.
Bonzo dreams he is chased by cats and turned into sausages.

CHEE-KEE THE VAMP. Produced by New Era. 500 ft. Released 20.4.25.
Bonzo has trouble with Chee-Kee his Pekingese sweetheart.

BONZO (No. 7.) Produced by New Era. 459 ft. Released 4.5.25.
Now reviewed. Title unknown.

PLAYING THE DICKENS IN AN OLD CURIOSITY SHOP. Produced by New Era. 459 ft. Released 18.5.25.
Bonzo, working in an antique shop, has trouble with the clocks.

BONZO (No. 9.) Produced by New Era. 500 ft. Released 1.6.25.
Not reviewed. Title unknown.

BONZOI INO ON BONZO BROADCASTED. Produced by New Era. 465 ft. Released 15.6.25.
When Bonzo is rejected by his Pekingese sweetheart, he transmits himself to Hollywood by radio waves and becomes the film star 'Bun Chaney'.

BONZO (No. 11.) Produced by New Era. 500 ft. Released 29.6.25.
Not reviewed. Title unknown.

BONZO (No. 12.) Produced by New Era. 500 ft. Released 13.7.25.
Not reviewed. Title unknown.

DETECTIVE BONZO AND THE BLACK HAND GANG. Produced by New Era. 505 ft. Released 27.7.25.
Bonzo foils the Black Hand Gang in their plot to kidnap a jockey.

BONZO (No. 14.) Produced by New Era. 500 ft. Released 10.8.25.
Not reviewed. Title unknown.

POLAR BONZO. Produced by New Era. 500 ft. Released 24.8.25.
Bonzo's adventures at the North Pole.

BONZO (No. 16.) Produced by New Era. Released 7.9.25.
Not reviewed. Title unknown.

THE TOPICAL BONZETTE. Produced by New Era. 463 ft. Released 21.9.25.
Burlesque on the *Topical Gazette* type of newsreel: a new horse trough in Piccadilly Circus; Jack Bonzobbs the cricketer; Professor Bonzo the fancy diver; Joe Bonzo the boxer in training.

SANDY MacBONZO OR BONZO GOES TO SCOTLAND. Produced by New Era. 500 ft. Released 5.10.25.
Bonzo visits Scotland.

BOOSTER BONZO OR BONZO IN GAY PAREE. Produced by New Era. 500 ft. Released 19.10.25.
Bonzo visits Paris.

BONZO THE TRAVELLER. Produced by New Era. 500 ft. Released 2.11.25. (Reissued on 9.5mm film for the home market in 1935.)
"Here is Bonzo's first picture (on 9.5mm) which depicts him in Gay Paris, and later, having tired himself out swimming the channel, in a cinema and dreaming that he finds the actual North Pole. Then he wakes up!" Review from 'Pathéscope Monthly' April 1935.

TALLY HO BONZO. Produced by New Era. 500 ft. Released 16.11.25. (Reissued on 9.5mm in 1935.)
"Bonzo covets some aniseed balls, steals a bagful, and gets his deserts in the form of one of the sweets in a tin can securely tied to his tail. Pack of hounds! Bonzo does not see why he should let them capture Master Reynard (the Fox). With the aid of the aniseed ball he lays a false scent and succeeds in hoodwinking all but one of the persuing pack." Review from 'Pathéscope Monthly' June 1935.

BONZOBY. Produced by New Era. 500 ft. Released 30.11.25.
Bonzo replaces Dog Toby in a street Punch and Judy show.

BONZO (No. 23.) Produced by New Era. 500 ft. Released 14.12.25.
Not reviewed. Title unknown.

BONZO (No. 24.) Produced by New Era. 500 ft. Released 28.12.25.
Not reviewed. Title unknown.

The above listings are reproduced by kind permission of Denis Gifford and are taken from his book 'British Animated Films, 1895-1985 ©Denis Gifford 1987

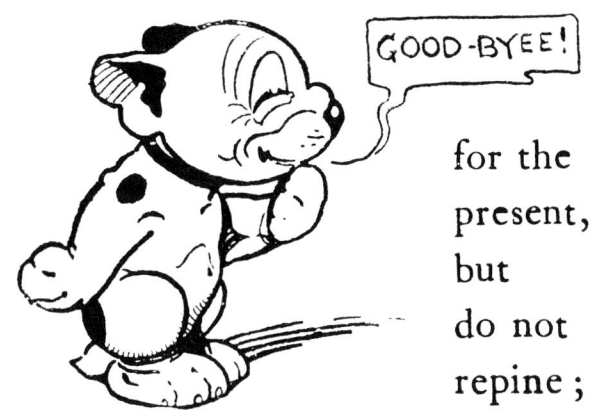

for the
present,
but
do not
repine;
We'll meet again later, in shadow or shine,
And that being so, with a shake of the pawr,
Let's say, as the French : "O-ravwar ! O-ravwar !"

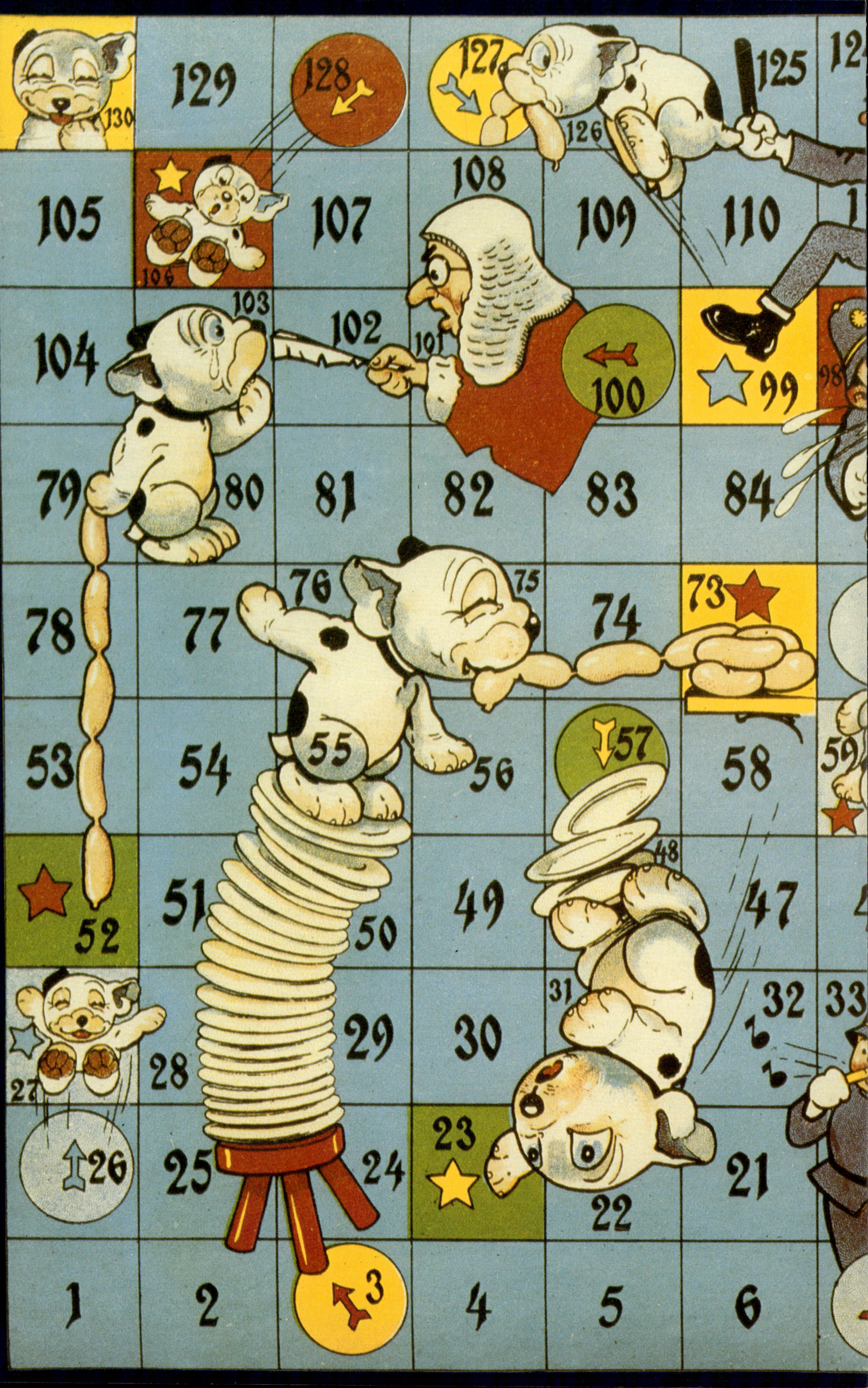
130
129
128
127
126
125
105
106
107
108
109
110
104
103
102
101
100
99
98
79
80
81
82
83
84
78
77
76
75
74
73
53
54
55
56
57
58
52
51
50
49
48
47
27
28
29
30
31
32
33
26
25
24
23
22
21
1
2
3
4
5
6